True Believer

True
Believer

HUBERT HUMPHREY'S
QUEST FOR
A MORE JUST AMERICA

James Traub

BASIC BOOKS

New York

Basic Books
Hachette Book Group
1290 Avenue of the Americas, New York, NY 10104
www.basicbooks.com

Printed in the United States of America

First Edition: February 2024

Published by Basic Books, an imprint of Hachette Book Group, Inc. The Basic Books name and logo is a registered trademark of the Hachette Book Group.

The Hachette Speakers Bureau provides a wide range of authors for speaking events. To find out more, go to hachettespeakersbureau.com or email HachetteSpeakers@hbgusa.com.

Basic Books copies may be purchased in bulk for business, educational, or promotional use. For more information, please contact your local bookseller or the Hachette Book Group Special Markets Department at special.markets@ hbgusa.com.

The publisher is not responsible for websites (or their content) that are not owned by the publisher.

Print book interior design by Bart Dawson.

Library of Congress Cataloging-in-Publication Data
Names: Traub, James, author.
Title: True believer : Hubert Humphrey's quest for a more just America / James Traub.
Description: First edition. | New York : Basic Books, 2024. | Includes bibliographical references and index.
Identifiers: LCCN 2023019504 | ISBN 9781541619579 (hardcover) | ISBN 9781541619562 (ebook)
Subjects: LCSH: Humphrey, Hubert H. (Hubert Horatio), 1911–1978. | Vice-presidents—United States—Biography. | United States. Congress. Senate—Biography. | Legislators—United States—Biography. | United States—Politics and government—1945–1989. | Minneapolis (Minn.)—Biography
Classification: LCC E748.H945 T73 2024 | DDC 973.923092 [B]—dc23/eng/20230907
LC record available at https://lccn.loc.gov/2023019504

ISBNs: 9781541619579 (hardcover), 9781541619562 (ebook)

LSC-C

Printing 1, 2023

To my team—E.W.E. and A.E.T.

Contents

Part 3: White House Ordeal

Part 4: Rebirth

Introduction

A T 10:30 P.M. ON AUGUST 29, 1968, VICE PRESIDENT HUBERT Humphrey advanced to the podium of the International Amphitheater in Chicago to deliver his acceptance speech for the Democratic nomination for president—a moment that represented the fulfillment of a lifelong dream. At virtually that same moment, a contingent of National Guardsmen riding in armored personnel carriers and jeeps with barbed-wire barriers mounted on their hoods began firing tear gas to keep three thousand demonstrators, opposed to the Vietnam War and to the political liberalism that Humphrey embodied, from marching on the convention center. As Humphrey recited what he hoped would be healing verses from St. Francis—"Where there is hate, let me sow love"—the guardsmen were shoving journalists as well as activists into waiting paddy wagons to be deposited in jail. As Lou Breese and His Orchestra, situated underneath the podium, launched into a double-time rendition of "Happy Days Are Here Again," policemen beat back another crowd of protesters massed in Grant Park across from the Hilton Hotel, where Humphrey and the senior figures of the Democratic Party were staying. "The whole world is watching," the kids chanted—and, alas for Humphrey, it was true.[1]

As the boy mayor of Minneapolis in the years after World War II and then as the foremost champion of civil rights and racial justice in the US Senate from 1949 to 1965, Humphrey had always been with the activists. "I was raising Cain with the system before you were born!" he shouted at a clutch of students protesting one of his speeches. But no longer; now he was Lyndon Johnson's vice president. The men who surrounded him, and deafened him with their

1

cheers inside the amphitheater, were the labor leaders, the political professionals, the big-city bosses with rubbery jowls and smoldering cigars. The protesters, the idealists, and the hippies and yippies clamoring outside called him a war criminal. "Dump the Hump!" they yelled. "All that I had ever been as a liberal spokesman seemed lost," Humphrey would bitterly recall. "All that I had accomplished in significant progress was ignored."[2]

Humphrey would emerge from the shipwreck of Chicago 17 points behind his Republican challenger, Richard Nixon. Though in the last weeks of the 1968 election he almost pulled out a miraculous victory, Humphrey would suffer a loss that devastated the generation of Democrats who had grown up with him through the Depression, the New Deal, World War II, the Cold War, and the great liberal resurgence of the early 1960s. The election marked the end of something large. One could not say that liberalism died in 1968, for Nixon did not dismantle the activist state that he inherited. But the optimism and idealism that had sustained the Democratic Party and the nation since 1932 had run its course.

Yet Humphrey's own optimism and idealism remained miraculously intact. In 1970 he would return to the Senate, the institution he loved and in which he felt deeply at home. There he continued rousing liberals to battle. That fight was elemental to Humphrey; he really had been raising Cain before the campus hecklers were born. They despised his compromises, but Humphrey had always treated compromise as the very essence of politics, and of political change. So, too, ambition: Humphrey was ambitious enough to have made compromises he could not excuse, yet he hungered for office in order to do great things. And he had; Humphrey had lived long enough to see what pragmatism, ambition, and patience could accomplish—civil rights, Medicare, foreign aid, nuclear nonproliferation. In those last years of his life, in fact, the tireless, hectoring senator from Minnesota had sought to blaze a path for liberalism that would put the New Deal coalition back together. Only his death in 1978, at age sixty-six, put an end to Humphrey's struggle for a more perfect union.

IN AN EARLIER BOOK, *WHAT WAS LIBERALISM?*, I DESCRIBED HUBERT Humphrey as the incarnation of mid-twentieth-century American liberalism. For Humphrey, as for such writers and thinkers as Arthur Schlesinger Jr., Reinhold Niebuhr, and Lionel Trilling, liberalism meant a faith in the individual, openness to debate, optimism about man's prospects, and a pragmatic skepticism toward all absolutes, doctrinal or theological. They were in this regard the heirs of the great nineteenth-century liberal thinkers—John Stuart Mill, Benjamin Constant, Alexis de Tocqueville. But by Humphrey's time, American liberals had also adopted a political viewpoint that would have been alien to those founding figures. Inspired by the example of President Franklin D. Roosevelt, they understood the state not as a leviathan threatening personal liberty but as an active agent guaranteeing to the ordinary citizen "the right to his economic and political life and liberty, and the pursuit of happiness," as FDR had put it. Liberals were social democrats.[3]

In the generation after World War II, liberals sought to extend the New Deal, above all by fully including Black people in the rights and privileges of citizenship. Liberalism came to be associated with a commitment to civil rights; this was the great cause of Hubert Humphrey's life, both as mayor of Minneapolis and as a US senator. The liberal project was global as well as domestic, since the rise and reach of the Soviet Union posed a threat to liberal democracy and to the "liberal world order" that the United States had established after the war. A new generation of "Cold War liberals" regarded the Soviets as an existential threat that had to be contained and ultimately defeated. So, too, of course, did conservatives; what distinguished Humphrey and the other Cold War liberals was the belief that the United States could win this war by showing people around the world that democracy could bring peace and prosperity to the poor and the marginalized more effectively than communism did. That meant foreign aid and disarmament abroad, and civil rights and social justice at home.

After 1968—after riots and violence at home and the calamity of Vietnam abroad—the word "liberal" fell out of fashion. President Ronald Reagan succeeded in reducing the term to an epithet for hapless idealists who thought more government was the answer to everything—and it never recovered. The liberal consensus of 1960 is now ancient history. In 2016 the United States elected its first avowedly illiberal president; Donald Trump treated tolerance, compassion for our fellow citizens, and faith in an active government and the liberal world order as laughable. Despite his loss in 2020, Trump left behind a poisonous contempt for all those who do not share his views.

Yet liberalism is not dead. President Joe Biden, who overlapped for a term in the Senate with Humphrey, shares the liberal temperament as well as much of the liberal agenda both at home and abroad. Liberals are regaining their nerve. The political philosopher Michael Walzer has written a book defending what he calls "liberal as an adjective"—one describing a set of values and habits that shape commitments to economic justice or sexual equality and check their tendency to rigidity and sectarianism. In *A Thousand Small Sanities*, the *New Yorker* writer Adam Gopnik has defended liberalism from those who regard it as heedless, spiritually hollow individualism. The Substack "Liberal Patriotism" seeks to redefine a liberalism that can attract the middle class as well as the disadvantaged and coastal elites. What all these authors have in common is a fear that liberalism is threatened as much from the left, with its demands for purity and preoccupation with matters of identity, as from the populist, openly illiberal right. We find ourselves once again in Hubert Humphrey's world, for in 1968 Humphrey would be abandoned by white working-class voters angry over the rise of crime, violence, and "permissiveness" as much as by the antiwar left. Liberalism always finds itself beleaguered at a moment of radical polarization.

I RETURN TO HUMPHREY IN ORDER TO EXPLAIN WHAT LIBERALISM was at its ascendant moment, why it mattered so much to so many people, why it abruptly lost its appeal to the majority of Americans—and, perhaps, how it might rejuvenate itself. But I did not aim to write an allegory. Humphrey's own astonishing vitality, his generosity and compassion, his idealism and pragmatism, his endless search for solutions to every last problem that plagued Americans and just about everyone else, bursts through the confines of any formulaic account. Humphrey was an extraordinary person, a florid and abundantly gifted figure. So, too, of course, are many of the people who climb the greasy pole of political power. But Hubert Humphrey was also profoundly *good*. He was kind to people who could never help him in his climb—to them especially. He loved people, and people—ordinary citizens, aides, Senate colleagues, even reporters—loved him. Bill Moyers, who was a young Senate aide when he met Humphrey, once said, "He made it legitimate to be an idealist in politics."[4]

Bill Connell, Humphrey's most trusted political aide, once explained his attraction to the man by saying, "When you were involved with Humphrey it really made you feel good—you were caught up in something that made you feel good. And so he made people feel good about themselves and what they were doing." That, Connell said, "was the source of his strength."[5] Humphrey never lost his faith in politics, in compromise, and, above all, in the fundamental goodness of America. In the very last days of the 1968 campaign, when both he and the nation had endured so much pain, he said, "I have always believed that the basic decency within this nation would one day enable us to lift the veil from our eyes and see each other for what we are as people—not black or white, not rich or poor, not attending one church or another, but as people, standing equally together free of hate or suspicion."[6]

Humphrey had a "story," as political marketers today would call it, that verged on myth. He was born in a small town in South Dakota, almost exactly in the middle of the continent. His father, a druggist, seemed illuminated from within by the bright currents of the prairie—the eagerness, the optimism, the democratic individualism. An agnostic in matters of faith, he worshiped at the populist altar of William Jennings Bryan. Young Hubert was the acorn that did not fall far from the paternal tree. Where his father had Bryan and Woodrow Wilson, young Hubert revered FDR. He had the charisma of the passionate believer without the stridency of the ideologue. He worked harder than anyone, made more friends than anyone, talked faster and more ardently than anyone. A Humphrey speech could no more be resisted than a prairie cyclone. He could have been mayor-for-life of Minneapolis, but his ambitions lay much higher.

Humphrey achieved glory—every kind, moral, political, and psychological—at an early age. At the 1948 Democratic National Convention, the thirty-seven-year-old mayor and senatorial candidate agreed to lead a quixotic effort to place in the party platform a ringing endorsement of civil rights—in the teeth of the southern segregationists who controlled much of the party machinery. He would be antagonizing not only the forces of Jim Crow but President Harry Truman, who feared that a split in the party would doom his electoral campaign. Humphrey quailed; he did not have the martyr in him. But he resolved, as he put it later, that "the time had come to suffer whatever the consequences." This man of too many words then delivered before the party, and the nation, a ten-minute address that changed the world. "The time has arrived in America," he cried, "for the Democratic Party to get out of the shadow of states' rights and walk forthrightly into the bright sunshine of human rights." Not since Bryan had railed at "the cross of gold" in 1892 had a candidate so electrified a convention. To the outrage and astonishment of the South, the motion to incorporate the language carried. The NAACP called the vote "the greatest turning point for the South and for America which has occurred since the Civil War."[7]

Such moments of glory are vouchsafed to the prophets, like Bryan, who are quick to choose truth over power. Humphrey no more wanted to be a soothsayer than a martyr; he wanted truth *and* power. He had the pragmatist's belief that compromise today could bring victory tomorrow; in the depths of the conservative 1950s, he told civil rights activists that they should accept, not just half a loaf, but "a crumb," confident that someday soon they would get the whole loaf. Humphrey didn't disdain politics; he *loved* politics. An inveterate patter of forearms and squeezer of shoulders, he was equally happy campaigning in the hustings and dickering on the floor of the Senate. Early in his tenure he came under the tutelage of Lyndon Johnson, the wiliest of all the creatures in Washington's jungle. Johnson taught him how to count votes and how to read the hearts of his colleagues. Humphrey's friends in the civil rights movement looked on in dismay as he made bargains with a figure they regarded as a crafty defender of Jim Crow. Don't sell him short, Humphrey always said. Once Johnson became president, Humphrey deployed both his passionate commitment to justice and the guile he had learned from his mentor to navigate the 1964 Civil Rights Act through the shoals of a southern filibuster—the supreme achievement of his legislative career.

I WAS NINE YEARS OLD WHEN THE CIVIL RIGHTS ACT PASSED—TOO young to know Humphrey's role or even his name. He only swam into my ken, so far as I can recall, a year later; and already he had become a figure of mockery. In 1964 Johnson chose his protégé as his running mate. After a smashing victory, Humphrey was poised to become the most consequential vice president in history, with portfolios stretching from legislative management to the coordination of civil rights enforcement. But Johnson changed his mind; he wanted a servant, not a copilot. Humphrey's humiliation was legendary. And so I first encountered his name in the spring of 1965, when the satirist Tom Lehrer sang, "Whatever became of you, Hubert / We miss you, so tell us, please / Are you sad, are you cross / Are you gathering moss / While you wait for the boss / To sneeze?"

To people of my parents' generation, Humphrey really was "a fiery liberal hero"; to my generation, he was a punch line. But to people slightly older than me—the generation that was being sent off to fight in Vietnam—he was Johnson's partner in prosecuting an evil war. When Johnson chose not to run in 1968 and Humphrey filled the vacuum, he was on the wrong side of the only line that mattered. A combination of loyalty and fear kept him from breaking with Johnson on the war; old friends abandoned him and young people despised him. Every day he had to paste a grin on his face and head out to endure new trials, an effort that drained his reserves of élan. Had he been a different kind of man—a purist, like some of the people he most admired—Humphrey would never have been in this position and thus could have spared himself a great deal of suffering; yet he would have accomplished so much less. Humphrey's career clarifies the moral and psychological calculus of political compromise.

And it clarifies something else that lives with us today. Humphrey did not lose in 1968 because of the war; the liberals ultimately came back. He lost because the working-class white voters who had constituted the core of FDR's coalition abandoned him for either Richard Nixon or George Wallace, the latter a proto-Trump figure. Here are the roots of the populist anger that defines so much of our own political culture. Humphrey spent the last decade of his life trying to find a way out of this conundrum. Addicted to political life, he returned to the Senate in 1970. After yet another unsuccessful bid for the nomination in 1972, Humphrey devoted himself to rethinking the policy prescriptions of the 1960s. He tried to fashion a foreign policy that would satisfy the growing clamor for economic justice in the developing world. At home, he sought to move away from the divisive language of group rights in order to formulate a new doctrine of "economic justice" for all, including a universal right to a decent job with fair compensation. It is no coincidence that Joe Biden has also attempted to broaden the appeal of the Democratic Party—and to restore faith in the efficacy of democracy—by rejuvenating the fortunes of a postindustrial working class, white as well as Black. The Democrats have been trying to fuse the interests of working-class whites and disadvantaged Blacks since the Populist era in the late nineteenth century; they haven't yet found the key.

Hubert Humphrey did not regard his own life as a tragedy. Quite the contrary: he was irrepressible and optimistic to the very last. In our own time, in so many ways darker than his, we need to hear his voice.

PART 1

The Rise of a Liberal Hero

1

Home

"Everything in my memory is about
Doland, South Dakota."

HUBERT HUMPHREY WAS BORN ON MAY 27, 1911, ABOVE THE
family drugstore in Wallace, South Dakota, a tiny hamlet
very close to the east-west midpoint of the United States.
When he was two, the family moved to Doland, a lonely whistle-stop
on the Chicago and Northwestern line running straight across the
great flat prairie stretching west from Minnesota. Doland was a town
of 600 souls. The broad dirt boulevard of Main Street, which ended
at the train depot, was lined with crenelated brick buildings quickly
and resolutely erected after a fire had decimated most of the town in
1913: the C. W. Morland General Store; the farm implement store and
the harness store; the creameries, which took in the milk that farmers brought in on horse-drawn wagons; two barber shops; the large
and stately City Hotel; and, the town's pride, the two-story Doland
Opera House, whose upper floor held a 450-seat theater, equipped
with dressing rooms and drops and four changes of scenery, while

11

on the ground floor stood the Underwood Bowling Alley and Reed Auto Sales. The Doland Public School, only a few hundred yards from the train depot, housed all students grades K through 12. The tallest structures in town were the two grain elevators and the spire atop the Methodist church. Doland had a pool hall; but you couldn't get in much trouble there, since in 1909 the county had voted to go dry.

Very little distinguished Doland from Prairie Center or Belle Plain or any of the other stops on the Chicago & NW. Not much, in fact, distinguished it from a thousand other such places at a time when the majority of Americans still lived on or near the land. It was a homogeneous, close-knit, proud little town where all doors were open, everyone knew almost everything about everyone else, and people took care of one another as a matter of course. The townsfolk strongly resembled one another in matters of politics, class, religion, and race. Almost everyone was a churchgoing Republican. Doland had a Catholic church, but so few Catholics that it could be served only by a traveling priest. The one Jewish family ran the grocery store. There were no Black people in Doland or anywhere nearby.[1]

Many people born into places like Doland find them claustrophobic; the literature of the prairie is full of characters gazing longingly at trains as they pull out of town in a great cloud of dust and steam. Others come to regard such cloistered spots with benevolent irony. Humphrey's friend Julian Hartt, who moved to Doland from the slightly more cosmopolitan city of Groton, later said, "I thought it was the sorriest excuse for a town I ever saw."[2]

Hubert Humphrey felt little irony, and no regret, about Doland. All his life, he thought of his boyhood home as an inner compass keeping him to a true path. Humphrey returned to Doland to deliver speeches in 1952, and 1964, and 1968 and 1976. That last time, the ex-vice president, once again senator from Minnesota, stood on a platform erected at the end of Main Street, looked out at the crowd of teachers and classmates from fifty years earlier, and fell into a reverie. "To me," he said, "Doland was my dad and my mom, my sisters and my brother." It was the school right behind him, and the little park nearby, and it was Gordon Twiss, the banker, and Les Coats, and Walt Hoffer and Tip Miles, who ran the *Doland Times-Record*. "Everything in my memory is about Doland, South Dakota," Humphrey said. When he returned in thought to his boyhood, he went on, he recalled "a sense of being, and a sense of belonging, and a sense of caring." As he stood there, with the nation's bicentennial only a few weeks away, he wanted his old neighbors to know that Doland was not a remnant of a vanished America but its essence. "What is America?" Humphrey cried. "America is another word for humanity. How do you define it? You define it by the word 'freedom' and 'people.'"[3]

That was the kind of high patriotic corn that had been making Humphrey's more urbane friends wince ever since he had left South Dakota. Humphrey had trained as a political scientist; he knew that it was absurd to flatten an entire country into a moral signifier. And in 1976 the Vietnam War and Watergate had just begun receding into the national rearview mirror; most liberal Democrats practiced a rueful form of patriotism. Yet Humphrey's sentimentality was not a posture; it was Doland, speaking in and through him. For Humphrey, Doland *was* America; he idealized the one as he idealized the other. "I consider my childhood," he once said, "to be just about as American as apple pie."[4] Perhaps, objectively, it was so. The newscaster Eric Sevareid was born one year after Humphrey in Velva, a hamlet in North Dakota that sounds very much like Doland. "We were," Sevareid wrote in his memoirs, "a true democracy in that huddled community of painted boards. . . . No doubt there was envy at times and small bitternesses here and there. But not many lived in fear of another." For all the rarefied talk of the classless society, Sevareid reflected, "what men wanted was Velva, on a national, on a world scale."[5]

The actual, historical Doland had been laid out in 1882 as the railroad came through, building new towns every ten miles. (The town was named after the local landowner who had filed homestead rights around the train depot.) Eastern South Dakota boomed in the eighties as settlers who had come too late to Minnesota, Wisconsin, and Iowa moved west, and as immigrants arrived, chiefly from Scandinavia. Most of the men of Doland worked farms outside of town or delivered oil or water to farmers or hauled produce for them or sold or serviced farm equipment. Nobody in the region got rich from farming; the soil in the prairie was too thin to produce the bumper crops of wheat or support the giant dairy farms of Minnesota or Wisconsin. Since the farmers scraped by, so, too, did the men in town who sold them cars or tractors or groceries, or put up their field hands during harvest season. Doland had some poverty but no real wealth. The people were inured to hardship; they, or their parents, had arrived in Doland with all their goods loaded in a wagon, and then had scratched a farm out of the soil and built their homes, often at first out of sod.

As the owners of the town's pharmacy, the Humphreys occupied an upper rung of this very modest hierarchy. They lived in a two-story square gray clapboard house with a steeply pitched roof in the residential neighborhood south of Main Street. In the front yard were cottonwood trees for Hubert and his older brother, Ralph, to climb. Behind the house was a coop for the chickens that grandfather Sannes—his mother, Christine's, father—had given Hubert to tend, as well as currant bushes from which Christine made jam; deeper into the backyard was a little orchard with apple, plum, and cherry trees. What is known of the inside of the house comes mostly from Humphrey himself. In the unpublished transcript of an interview for a 1964 television show, Humphrey said that he still dreamed about the house, and described, as if entranced, the hardwood floors, the wallpaper, the marble-topped dressers.[6] The family housekeeper's name, he volunteered, was Happy.

Hubert himself might well have been called Happy; in fact he was called Pinky, though there is some dispute as to the origin of the nickname.[7] Humphrey did not shed this slightly infantilizing nickname as he grew older. He was still known as Pinky in his mid-twenties; correspondents from South Dakota continued to head letters sent to Humphrey as mayor of Minneapolis with "Pinky" or "Pink." A man who had loved his boyhood as Humphrey had was not disposed to molt those boyish feathers.

The rhythms of Pinky's life were the rhythms of Doland life. In the summer he and his friends swam in the swimming hole just outside town and played baseball on a team he had organized; his father brought gallons of root beer from the soda fountain. In the winter he skated on a frozen creek and went sledding on the very gentle hills to the east of town. When the evening freight train pulled in, the boys would run down the platform barefoot and hop up into the train while the crew was unloading lumber and jump off into a sandpit below. Or they would stand quietly and stare off to the east, where the tracks disappeared into the endless prairie. Not until he was thirteen years old would Humphrey take the overnight train to Minneapolis with his father, a trip that required them first to drive their Model A fifty miles east to Watertown.

Like most boys in Doland, Pinky began working early—in his case, at age six. The train carried his stock of newspapers—the *Minneapolis Tribune*, the *Saint-Paul Pioneer Press*, the *Chicago Herald Examiner*, the *Toledo Blade*, the *Saturday Evening Post*. Too little to carry the papers, he would haul them in a wagon, shouting out his wares at the top of his lungs. He picked up old tires and tin scraps around Doland for a dollar. He dug up neighbors' gardens and put away vegetables in their root cellars. He cut and stacked wood. When he got older, Pinky simonized cars. "I never had a day I didn't work," Humphrey would recall. "I never heard about a vacation."[8] Work, in turn, meant self-sufficiency. Pinky maintained two bank accounts and bought all his own clothes from the age of twelve.

Exactly how it was that Pinky could appear to spend all day working, all day racing around town, and all day talking was a mystery to those around him. A high school English teacher once said of him, "If you called on him first, that was the end of it for the other students."[9] A perpetual motion machine, young Hubert wasn't so much domineering as irrepressibly exuberant. Julian Hartt recalled attending a football game against Doland High while he was still a middle-school student at Groton; an infuriating little squirt ran up and down the sidelines screaming what were presumably extremely mild imprecations at the Groton side. A few years later, when the Hartts moved to Doland, that former runt, now revealed to be Hubert Humphrey Jr., was the first to doff his cap, extend his hand, and befriend the newcomer.[10]

Pinky was an inveterate organizer, an instigator of harmless pranks, a boon companion, and an all-around model young person. He was the kind of boy who would always run an errand for a neighbor or a shut-in. He mooned after girls but did not go out with them.

His strongest public oath was "gosh" or "golly." Pinky went out for everything: he starred in the theatricals, played all sports, volunteered at church, joined the Scouts. He honed his modest boxing skills with a punching bag and jump rope. He played halfback and offensive guard in football—though he topped out at 120 pounds as a senior—and forward in basketball, while running middle distance in track. (Humphrey later claimed to have run a very creditable 2:07 half mile.[11]) He specialized in school spirit, teamwork, and the highest of all goods—fair play. "He was," Hartt writes, "the joy of every sound coach's desiring: a born and dedicated morale officer." As a sophomore, Pinky broke his ankle on a running play—and kept playing. (Forty years later, he remembered the guy who tackled him—"Jim Lovelace, he runs a café in Doland, South Dakota to this day.")[12]

Above all, Pinky talked. He and Hartt helmed the Doland debate squad, which in 1928, Pinky's junior year, won the district championship and competed in the state tourney. Upon graduation Pinky was offered a debate scholarship to a small teacher's college. He also wrote editorials for "Hiscopep," the *Doland Times-Record*'s high school column, on such suitably grave topics as "The Problems of Youth."[13]

IN HIS MEMOIRS, AND IN COMMENTS THROUGHOUT HIS LIFE, HUBERT Humphrey had far less to say about his mother, Christine, than about her father, Andrew Sannes, a Norwegian immigrant who had sailed the world as a merchant marine, married, and then, in 1885, at age thirty-eight, moved to America with his wife and two-year-old Christine. Five years later Andrew built a sod house in the middle of the great blank prairie of South Dakota, moved his family and all their belongings in an ox-drawn cart, and took up the grindingly hard and lonely life of a farmer. He was a slender man with a pointed chin, sharp features, and piercing eyes. Pinky loved hearing his stories about Russia, China, and Cuba, but he also revered him as a model of granite rectitude. Despite his life at sea, Andrew Sannes was a model farmer, an early practitioner of crop rotation, a frugal, prudent, tireless cultivator whose sheds always wore a fresh coat of paint and whose tractors still ran smoothly after forty years. The farm, as Humphrey later put it, looked as clean and orderly as a garden: "He fought weeds as if they were the plague." Grandpa Sannes put Pinky to work raking up stray grains of wheat; every year he gave the boy a calf, for which he would be responsible on his regular visits to the farm. The Humphreys weren't farmers; it was from his grandfather, with whom he spent most of his summers as a boy, that Humphrey learned the virtues of husbandry. "The care of soil," he later said, "has something to do with the molding of character."[14] Humphrey was a townsman who would always regard the farmer as the salt of the earth.

Andrew Sannes so prospered that he was able to send his daughter to a local state college. After two years, Christine returned home to the village of Lily to become a teacher. She was, like her father, a stern and fervent Lutheran, Republican in her politics and conservative in her values, shy and quiet in manner. At a church social she met a charming and freethinking young pharmacist. Hubert Humphrey must have seemed quite exotic to Christine, but he was a native, a Yankee, and a fine young man, and Andrew granted his consent. The two married in 1906.[15]

Born in 1882, the first Hubert Humphrey was raised on the family farm in Elk River on the banks of the Mississippi thirty miles north of Minneapolis. His father, John, was barely educated, but his mother, Adeline, said to be of "pronounced intellectual tastes," would read aloud to the family in the evening from the works of Hugo, Dickens, Scott, Twain, Thackeray, and Hawthorne. The Humphrey boys grew up with expectations quite unusual in Elk Grove; all three became remarkably erudite. Hubert's older brothers, John and Harry, attended the University of Minnesota. Harry studied German, French, Italian, and botany, and received a PhD in plant science from Stanford. He would go on to become a prominent official in the US Department of Agriculture and a prodigious writer of letters to his nephew Hubert on politics and history, as well as the fine points of language. ("Don't say sure when you mean surely.") John would ultimately make a living as a certified public accountant in California and then Kentucky, but in 1904, when he would have been about twenty-five, he published a little volume of poetry consisting of, among other things, a wilderness epic titled "The Recompense," and "Spenseriana," an homage to *The Faerie Queen* ("In land of faery, Gloriana's home, / Where courteous knights and lovely ladies roam . . .").[16]

Hubert did not follow his brothers' path, though it's not clear whether the family could no longer afford his education or his nature was too itinerant for college. After graduating from high school he peddled an elixir that, like many of the patent medicines of the day, consisted largely of alcohol. Hubert then moved to Lily and opened an unlicensed drugstore. Unable to make a go of it, he moved Christine back to Minnesota, where he worked in a pharmacy and then returned to his old life as a peddler, selling candy door-to-door.[17] In 1909, when he was already twenty-seven, Hubert returned to South Dakota, opening up a proper pharmacy of his own in Wallace, another one-horse town scarcely bigger than Lily. Hubert uprooted the family yet again in 1913 for Doland, a town big enough to support a proper pharmacy and elevate the Humphreys to the dignified, middle-class standing in which Hubert Jr. was raised.

Hubert Humphrey Sr. was a knockabout, a stubbornly self-made man. His vagrant life had made him a gentle eccentric who did not think or even live as most men around him did, but who spoke with a wisdom, a fixity of belief, that more conventional people admired. The lack of a university education seemed to have widened rather than narrowed his mind. Hubert Sr. subscribed to the *Christian Science Monitor* and the *New York Herald* as well as local and regional papers. He read widely in religion and politics. When, later in life, conservative family members paid a visit, he would instruct his daughter Frances to hide his copy of Voltaire and Darwin's *Origin of Species* under the sofa. He knew to be careful even of his wife, who discovered that she had married the kind of man who cared more about his books than his income. Christine worried constantly; and Hubert gave her grounds for her fears. One day she sent him off to buy supplies and he came back instead with an armload of books, which she promptly dumped in the nearby river.[18] Christine was the practical one in the family. Yet she made up little poems to amuse the children and read them Dickens novels. Frances later said that Hubert got his puckish sense of humor from his mother.[19]

The elder Humphrey was an avowed atheist who regarded religion as a branch of philosophy and found Buddhism no less interesting than Christianity. At dinner one evening he turned to Hubert's best friend and said, "Julian, what can you tell us about Confucius?"[20] In fact, the arrival of Julian's father, the Reverend Hartt, put an end to the elder Humphrey's free-thinking heterodoxy. Hubert Sr. either experienced a religious conversion or found Christian doctrine as explicated by his erudite friend more interesting than atheism. In 1924 he agreed to be baptized alongside his boys and became the town's most voluble Sunday school teacher.

Christine came from stern Lutheran stock; she and the children never missed a Sunday service. Young Hubert was raised in what we would today call an evangelical culture. Itinerant preachers roamed the prairie and often held weeklong revival meetings in Doland, where townsfolk heard lurid tales of God's mercy and vengeance, professed their sins, and accepted their salvation through Jesus. Religion at Doland's Methodist Episcopal church was a simple and strict affair. The white walls were bare save for a framed copy of the Ten Commandments and a record of Sunday school attendance. Congregants sang traditional Protestant hymns, such as "What a Friend I Have in Jesus." The Reverend Hartt, though a worldly figure by Doland's standards, laid down a severe doctrine. (He was also Doland's scoutmaster.) Julian Hartt, who later became a Yale professor of theology, later recalled that his father was more inclined to preach about the evils of liquor and the temptations of the flesh than the earthly ministry of Jesus. The minister's, and the town's, idea of holiness lay, Hartt recalled, in "the pursuit of perfection in outward-looking Christian character and conduct as well as unremitting struggle to stifle unclean and uncharitable thoughts."[21] Yet underneath, or alongside, the fixation with sin and salvation lay Doland's own deep ethos of neighborliness, decency, and compassion. Even the town's most ardent supporters of Republican free-market principles, Hartt observed, accepted that "among the poor there were many admirable people, victims of circumstances rather than defects of character."[22]

Hubert Humphrey sat through these services and sermons every Sunday of his young life; yet the fear and trembling before the Lord never entered his soul. His belief in the fundamental goodness of mankind, which he absorbed both from his father and from his own experience of Doland, was ineradicable. Some of his aides would tell a biographer that they regarded him as a secular humanist.[23] They had some reason to think so, for Humphrey would become only an intermittent, if a thoroughly comfortable, churchgoer. He did not thumb through the Bible for inspiration, did not reflect on matters of the spirit, and showed little interest in the doctrinal questions that separated one Protestant sect from another. He attended both Methodist and Congregational churches.

Yet the regular churchgoing of Humphrey's boyhood laid down a deep deposit of moral precepts and scriptural commandments that he would draw on, often unconsciously, all his life. Religion was more a felt experience than a source of doctrine; he stitched his Christianity with the ethos of Doland, the wisdom of his father, and the ringing language of the Declaration of Independence to form a seamless garment. According to his friend Arthur Naftalin, who met him in 1942, Humphrey would often say, "How do I know there is a God? Because all men are brothers. And if all men are brothers, then there's got to be a common father."[24] Humphrey's God, in short, was a liberal. He later said, "My early church experience really conditioned my attitude to civil rights and human rights. When the New Testament tells us that we are all one human family, I can't see how there is room for segregation, bigotry, or intolerance."[25]

HUBERT HUMPHREY SR. WAS A TALL MAN WITH BLUE EYES AND DARK hair; in later years he wore rimless spectacles that gave him a professorial mien. His loving son recalled him as a "broad-shouldered man" with "big, strong hands" and "a jutting chin"—"much better-looking than either of his sons."[26] In temperament he was not just an optimist but a true romantic, in love with the land and its people. He was of the generation of Willa Cather and Carl Sandburg, Midwesterners who looked upon the great prairie as almost a new beginning for mankind. "Just think of it, boys," he would say—or so his son would later recall—"here we are in the middle of this great big continent, here in South Dakota, with the land stretching out for hundreds of miles, with people who can vote and govern their own lives, with riches enough for all if we will take care to do justice."[27] The younger Hubert would be a second-generation sentimentalist.

The family's pharmacy, H. H. Humphrey's, thrived as farm prices rose in World War I, when agriculture collapsed in much of Europe. Farmers could be counted on to buy Vicks VapoRub and Lydia Pinkham's Compound (for menstrual cramps) and toothpaste and notepads and baseball mitts.[28] The store also served as Doland's de facto salon. By 1919, Hubert Sr. had joined the city council for the first of four two-year terms and thus counted as one of Doland's leading men. Many evenings, and almost all Saturdays, the other town fathers—Doc Sherwood; the two bankers, Paul Brown and Fred Gross; the postmaster, Al Payne; and later the Reverend Hartt—would gather in the soda fountain at the back of the store and talk. The conversation ranged across local, national, and global affairs. The pharmacist did much of the talking; he was known as not only one of the most bookish men in town but one of the most opinionated. Some of his views were regarded as beyond the pale and were tolerated only because he was considered profoundly decent and thoroughly reliable. Only once did Hubert Sr. commit what was regarded as an unpardonable offense against acceptable opinion: after attending the 1928 Democratic National Convention as a South Dakota delegate, he came back raving about the nominee, Al Smith. The candidate was not only a Democrat but an Irish Catholic who opposed Prohibition, a red line in God-fearing Doland. The Reverend Hartt considered Smith a "boozer" who would be taking orders straight from the pope. Doland's chief divine was so deeply scandalized that he and his dear friend stopped speaking for several years.[29]

Hubert Sr. was a restless man who took every opportunity to venture out into the great world, and occasionally dragged it back to Doland. He so fell in love with classical music that at times he would drive three hundred miles to Minneapolis to hear a concert. In 1920 he began stocking the new Edison phonograph and RCA Victor records. A store circular lists recordings of "Yes, We Have No Bananas," classical art songs, and even Yiddish folk tunes.[30]

Ads for the new paraphernalia appeared regularly in the *Doland Times-Record*. H. H. Humphrey invited readers to "hear the phonograph that baffled James Montgomery Flagg." The Edison people had challenged the famed artist and illustrator to go to Carnegie Hall and listen to the great soprano Anna Case, and then to an Edison record, and to tell which one was real. He couldn't. Hubert Sr. duplicated the experiment, booking an opera performer touring the Midwest into the Doland Opera House, where she sang behind a curtain either before or after the town pharmacist had played a recording of her voice. It is doubtful whether the druggist made a profit on his phonographs—or even that he expected to. He could afford his extravagances as long as times were good; the reckoning would come soon enough.

The elder Humphrey was a born pedagogue. He would often close the drugstore late at night, come home, roust the children from bed, and read to them from one of the treasured volumes in his library—a biography of Thomas Jefferson or Abraham Lincoln or Edward Gibbon's *Decline and Fall of the Roman Empire*. Frances would sit in his lap while Pinky sat raptly by his side.[31] Pinky was his father's prize student, the receptacle of the ideals and passions he could barely disclose to his stolid wife. Increasingly, the father kept his younger son close by. The pharmacy opened up at 7:00 a.m. and stayed open until 10 or 11 or even midnight. By age eight Pinky was working in the store before school, when the men from Montgomery Ward's and the First National Security Bank and Newberry's and Gamble's would drift in for coffee, rolls, and talk. By the time he was ten, his father would have him working the soda fountain, perched on a little platform to get his head above the counter. Rather than running off to see his friends, Hubert would often stay late listening to the worldly talk in the ice cream parlor, which he regarded, even later in life, as a setting little short of the Athenian agora. Only rarely did any of the men get hot under the collar. "Dialogue and conversation," Humphrey later wrote, "meant having something to say but drawing out others; being passionately concerned with the people and the issues but tempering that passion with respect for those who thought differently."[32]

It was the elder Humphrey who thought differently: he was a Democrat in a sea of Republicans. Hubert Sr. said that he pledged himself to the party the first time he heard William Jennings Bryan speak, perhaps during the 1896 presidential campaign, when he would have been fourteen. At least twice a year, Hubert recalled, his father would recite to the family Bryan's "Cross of Gold" speech, the thunderous oration on monetary policy and the gold standard that the Nebraska crusader delivered at the party convention that year.[33] Today that speech has come down to us for its stupefying peroration: "You shall not crucify mankind upon a cross of gold!" But the address was much more than its concluding line; the journalist William Allen White, otherwise a Bryan critic, recalled the event as "the first time in my life and in the life of a generation in which any man large enough to lead a national party had made his cause that of the poor and the oppressed."[34] Bryan defied the business interests that then dominated both the Democratic and Republican Parties. "My friends," he cried, "it is simply a question that we shall decide upon which side shall the Democratic Party fight. Upon the side of the idle holders of idle capital, or upon the side of the struggling masses?"[35] That was the essence of Hubert Sr.'s worldview.

The elder Humphrey was a compassionate man who automatically sided with the underdog. "In our home," he once wrote to an inquiring journalist, "high-hatting anyone was strictly taboo."[36] If anything, the poor were to be treated with greater deference than the privileged. In his autobiography, Hubert Humphrey wrote that he once walked into the pharmacy with a friend from the shantytown at the edge of Doland and said, "Dad, Jonathan here doesn't have any shoes, and his feet are so cold they're blue."[37] His father immediately took some money from the cash register and led the boy down the street to buy him socks and boots. The only Black people young Hubert ever encountered in Doland were the ones in the work crews that came to grade the county road that ran through town. Hubert adopted them as playmates and they happily reciprocated, letting him ride around in their mule-driven dump trucks and buying his newspapers, lest Hubert return home with unsold copies. Christine was appalled;

Humphrey doesn't recount his father's reaction, but he surely would have approved this unthinking egalitarianism.[38]

Hubert Sr. was a serious thinker who embraced the precepts of populism. Populists like Bryan regarded farmers and small business-men as America's real producers of wealth, and finance—which for them meant above all the Chicago Board of Trade, which set com-modity prices—as the chief predator of a free-market jungle. They favored cheap credit—thus the silver standard; the breakup of "trusts" and combines; the establishment of an income tax; and the direct election of senators (then appointed by state legislatures). Populism appealed to men and women who felt crushed by the system. For that very reason, the upstanding citizens of Main Street regarded it as an abomination. Hubert Humphrey Sr. was one of the exceptions. "My father was a total populist," Hubert would say in 1942. "He wanted to break everything up."[39]

Radicalism flourished in the Upper Midwest in the period from the 1890s to the outbreak of World War I. The Non-Partisan League (NPL), which had been born out of the North Dakota Socialist Party, deeply shaped politics in the Dakotas and Minnesota into the 1920s, forging alliances with Democrats and Republicans and electing many candidates to statewide office. Hostile to Wall Street like the Populists but fundamentally socialist in outlook, the NPL advocated state own-ership of grain elevators and flour mills and state regulation of rail-roads.[40] As a young man in Wallace, Hubert Sr. had tried to organize a branch of the league. That must have particularly horrified Christine.

Populism effectively subsumed the Democratic Party during the generation in which Bryan served as the party standard-bearer. But for all his appeal to the little man, Bryan was a back-looking figure who never found a language in which to speak to the nation's rap-idly growing population of urban workers. In 1912 Bryan was finally elbowed aside as the Democratic nominee by the scholarly and gen-teel Woodrow Wilson, an unapologetic member of the national elite who did not preach class warfare, as Bryan had. Yet Wilson's idealism, his deep belief in the goodness of man, and above all of Americans, held a romantic appeal equal in its own way to Bryan's. Real radicals regarded Wilson as a servant of the ruling class; but Hubert Sr., while open to radical ideas, idolized the courtly academic. *The New Freedom*, Wilson's collection of speeches from the 1912 campaign, served as the Humphrey family's political bible; Hubert Sr. would read passages to the children as he did with Bryan. "The laws of this country do not prevent the strong from crushing the weak," the Princeton political scientist declared. The old Jeffersonian dictum that the government that governs least governs best no longer applied to a world of giant institutions. "The law has to step in and create new conditions under which we may live."[41]

Hubert Sr.'s politics were a compound of Bryan's scorn for Wall Street and big business, Wilson's faith in a benevolent but limited state, and his very own sense of decency. Only once did Doland divide sharply enough to allow, or compel, the elder Humphrey to take a stand according to these principles. In 1927 or 1928, when he was serving as mayor, a private firm in Huron sought to buy the town's electric plant, promising to lower rates and expand service. At a raucous meeting in the opera house, Mayor Humphrey reminded his fellow citizens that the electric plant had always provided good service and warned them against the blandishments of this new suitor. His friends and neighbors thought he was throwing money away, and the vote went against him. Young Hubert had been away on a Boy Scout camping trip. When he came back and paid a visit to Thompson's butcher shop—to buy some wieners, he recalled—Mr. Thompson said, "Your dad almost got beaten up last night."[42] Perhaps that was hyperbole—but not in Hubert Humphrey's memory.

THE YOUNG HUBERT HAD NOT KNOWN HIS FATHER WHEN HE WAS scrambling to survive and dragging his young wife back and forth across the Midwest. He did not regard his father's exotic interests as unaffordable extravagances, as his mother did. He worshiped the father he knew—wise, generous, principled, and loving. Idealization was in young Hubert's nature; he loved his father as uncritically as he loved Doland. Yet he was hardly alone in feeling that way about either the town or the man. Neighbors old enough to have known the elder Humphrey confirm the son's portrait of a small-town philosopher with a questing mind and a kindly nature.[43] What *is* remarkable is that the reverence Hubert felt toward his father scarcely waned as he grew older and learned to compare him to other men. "Dad set high standards for me," he would write at age fifty-five. "The one fear I've had all my life was that I would disappoint him."[44]

Humphrey's love of his fellow man, his habit of idealization, his faith in what was good, guarded him all his life from the cynicism that is the occupational hazard of the politician. But it also made him vulnerable. He was inclined to put more faith in promises than he should have, and then to suffer bitter disappointment when his hopes were dashed. He was often taken aback by the toughness of politics and could not muster toughness on his own behalf. He was, so to speak, deficient in cruelty. Not all fathers return love for love. The great mentor of his adult life, Lyndon Johnson, learned how to turn Humphrey's generosity and deference to his own advantage. Johnson did not suffer from father-love: *his* father had let him down, and he never forgave or forgot. That gave Johnson the capacity for cruelty that Humphrey so conspicuously lacked.

2

Loss

"I thought it was the end of the world."

T O GROW UP IN PARADISE IS TO RISK EXPULSION. HUBERT HUM-
phrey had been raised in a world that had the beauty and sim-
plicity of folklore; and then the forces of history intruded. The
Depression came much earlier to farm country than it did to Wall
Street, and when it did, the Humphreys came very close to sharing
in the general ruin. That peculiar pattern, of harmonious small-town
life upended by immense and impersonal forces, would shape Humphrey's politics for the rest of his life. Humphrey would later write
that while his father incarnated the Puritan ethic and the twenties'
gospel of success, "these myths could not stand up against the reality
of failure everywhere."[1]

The second decade of the twentieth century had been a boom
time for American farmers; the wheat farmers of the Upper Midwest
had plowed up land previously considered marginal and had taken
out large loans to buy new equipment. And then, very quickly, European agriculture had recovered from the wreckage of war. American crop prices collapsed; the gross income of American farmers

dropped 70 percent between 1919 and 1921. After a decade of rising fortune in Doland, the Humphreys faced desperate times. Since farmers no longer had the cash to buy cold remedies or paint or school supplies, Hubert Sr. took a course in veterinary medicine to learn how to vaccinate hogs and cattle. The pharmacy began to specialize in products such as Humphrey's Get-'Em-Quick Louse Exterminator, to delouse poultry and livestock (active ingredients: naphthalene, nicotine, tobacco powder, and sulfur).[2] Hubert often accompanied his father into the countryside to distribute the anti-cholera serum and vaccines farmers wanted for their cattle, hogs, and poultry. Sometimes he went on his own, which meant helping a farmer flip over a two-hundred-pound hog to insert the needle.

One day young Hubert came home from school and found his parents standing with a stranger under the big cottonwood tree on their front lawn. His mother was crying. She told him they were surrendering the house, on which they had stopped making payments months before. In his memoirs, Humphrey writes, "My father talked to the man for a short time, signed a paper, and then the man went away. Afterward, Dad wept."[3] Hubert had to leave the house in which he had grown up, whose every detail was etched in his mind. The Humphreys moved across town to a humble prefabricated house with an oddly unfinished look; the porch didn't even have a roof.[4] Other Dolandites must have suffered similar losses of status during this terrible time; but to Hubert the episode felt cataclysmic. At that moment, he later wrote, "for all practical purposes the joys of childhood came to an end." He learned for the first time that his father, whom he had never known to cry, was not omnipotent and could be overborne by forces larger than himself, and that life was far more fragile than he had ever imagined. The title of this chapter in Humphrey's memoirs is "The Loss of Home"—not "a" home or house, but "home."

Writing more than forty years later, Humphrey recalled the date of this terrible event as 1927, when he was fifteen or sixteen. In fact, according to a recent biographer, the transaction occurred in October 1922, when Hubert would have been only eleven.[5] The idyll of boyhood was in fact much shorter than Humphrey recalled. The shock of loss hit him at a time when he would have been much more vulnerable.

He discovered at an earlier age the bitter feeling of humiliation. The older Humphrey was not, of course, dissembling. Our memories exist in the form of a story we tell ourselves. The shattering of Humphrey's pastorale so early did not fit with his inner narrative of Doland and of his life; so, presumably, he preserved his idealization by moving the catastrophe to a later period.

Soon enough, almost everyone in Midwestern farm country had a story like the Humphreys—or much worse. By 1925, 175 banks across South Dakota had closed their doors.[6] In 1926, the State Bank of Doland, which had seemed as firmly fixed in the town landscape as the grain elevators or the water tower, went under. That was where Hubert Sr. had kept the proceeds from the pharmacy, and where Hubert Jr. had kept all the money he had earned from his jobs. As one bank after another went under, farmers lost their life savings. Farmers who had taken out mortgages to expand production found that they could no longer meet their monthly payments. Over the course of the 1920s about a third of South Dakota farmers would lose their farms to the banks. Out on his rounds, the teenaged Humphrey saw abandoned plots, collapsing barns, broken-down equipment. He saw the fear, the sense of helplessness, etched on the faces of his neighbors, men and women who had always seemed to him indomitable. The bottom had suddenly dropped out on everyone.[7]

Hubert graduated from high school as class valedictorian in 1929. The obvious next step was to join his older brother, Ralph, at Dakota Wesleyan, a Methodist college in Mitchell, South Dakota. Alternatively, Hubert could have gone to Brookings State in nearby Brookings. His father, however, wanted him to go to the University of Minnesota. He never said why, but Hubert intuited that his father regretted that he had not been able to follow his own brothers there. Perhaps Hubert Sr. could not bear the idea that his namesake and alter ego would wind up behind a pharmacy counter as he had. That fall the two men drove the three hundred miles to Minneapolis in the family's new green Model A—a profligate purchase at a moment of economic collapse.

The eighteen-year-old Hubert Humphrey was a shade under six feet, reed-thin, pale, with a hairline already receding slightly above a high forehead. He was terribly polite, awkward, self-conscious, eager to please—a hick from small-town South Dakota in one of the nation's great public universities. He goggled at the massive campus buildings. Hubert enrolled in classes without any clear plan—French, chemistry, sociology—and did well enough. He joined the debate team but didn't make the school paper. He learned how to dance and met a girl at a dance who became his first girlfriend. He often hitchhiked home on weekends, and seems not to have made any lasting friends, which was not like him. After the fall semester his father told him he could no longer afford the $10-a-week allowance he had been sending, so Hubert got a job washing dishes for 20 cents an hour at the campus drugstore, where he also cadged enough food to keep from starving.

In June Hubert returned to Doland and went back to work in the drugstore. By this time business was so bad that both Hubert and Ralph agreed to leave school to help their father out. But Hubert Sr. was not the only family member looking out for the young man's future. Hubert had begun writing regularly to Uncle Harry, who had taken a shine to the young man. At Christmastime, Harry sent a $50 check with a note: "This is something to start you back to school."[8] His father still needed him in the store; but after five years of Depression, small-town South Dakota now felt to him like a terrible dead end. Hubert Sr. gave his son permission to return to Minnesota with an uncharacteristic expression of despair. "There's only one thing to do here," Humphrey later recalled his father saying, "and that's just fade away and go broke." Hubert promptly hitchhiked back to Minneapolis.[9]

Hubert Sr. had been keeping the business going by taking out loans that he could no longer repay. In the summer of 1930 he received a dunning letter from a law firm demanding the $66.80 that remained on a loan of $350 he had taken out five years earlier. He sent a $10 check along with a plaintive note: "It has been necessary for me to carry my customers for a long time owing to the crop failures." He added an appeal to the creditor's better angels: "There is only one thing that will bring us through and that is an appreciation of our own difficulties and indulgence in the other fellow's."[10] That was a fine sentiment; but the plain fact was that Hubert Sr. was facing ruin. Later that fall he showed up unannounced in the drugstore where Hubert worked to tell him that the family was leaving for the much bigger city of Huron, forty miles to the south and west, where he had already rented a house. The Humphrey family had slipped another notch down the social order. At the end of March, after he had finished his exams, Hubert rushed home to Huron, where his father had opened a new drugstore. He and Ralph moved into the basement and went to work. Another $50 check from Uncle Harry was not going to return him to college this time; the business could not survive without the boys. Hubert's future looked very dark: it was not at all clear when the Depression would lift sufficiently for the drugstore to survive without him.

A city of ten thousand, Huron had vastly more to offer than Doland had. The drugstore was located on Dakota Avenue, the main shopping street, a proper paved boulevard lined with shops and cafés and banks and even hotels and movie theaters. A four-story office building stood across the street from the pharmacy. But the Huron of 1931 was spiraling downward along with virtually all of rural America. Wheat that had fetched $2.76 a bushel in the palmy days of World War I now sold for 25 cents a bushel. And then, starting in 1930, something much worse than oversupply hit the American farmer, above all in the Upper Midwest and West—drought. Soon there was virtually no wheat crop at all, and thus no farm income. Per capita income in South Dakota dropped to $129 per annum by 1933—about $2.50 a week. Starving cattle wandered over barren fields, feeding on the thistle that blew over the stubble. Farm families piled into wagons and left for the West. Small towns went bankrupt; schools closed. Farm foreclosures averaged twenty thousand a month in the fall of 1931.[11]

Nineteen thirty-two was a very hard year for Huron, and for the Humphreys. The family drugstore barely hung on. Farmers had no money to pay, so the Humphreys accepted a chunk of beef or a few dozen eggs. Humphrey writes, "We swapped drugs for chickens, plucked and cooked them, made chicken salad, and sold it in sandwiches." The pharmacy went into the patent medicine business, distributing "Humphrey's Chest Oil" and "Humphrey's Sniffles," as well as a special compound for hogs known as "Humphrey's BTV," which stood for "body tone veterinary." The Humphreys felt that, at worst, these nostrums did more good than harm.[12]

Hubert gave up his dreams for the future, throwing himself into whatever activities could keep him occupied. He became head of the Beadle County Young Democrats, which must have been a very modest organization. He took over as scoutmaster of the Boy Scout troop at Huron's Methodist church, holding basketball games in the church basement and bringing the boys to the drugstore to give them something to do. Hubert's combination of zeal, industry, and leadership would have made him an ideal scoutmaster. In the "Record Book of Troop #6, Huron, South Dakota," he kept exacting records of every merit badge earned by every member of the troop, listed all their accomplishments, and recorded the names of the teams into which he organized the boys—Panthers, Flying Eagles, Rattlesnakes, Bears. Pinky—for he was still known that way—dated several girls, but he barely had enough money to take them to a movie. He struck one of them as terribly nervous—constantly fidgeting. He gave her a ring, but he didn't feel ready to marry, and she ended the relationship and married someone else.[13]

Hubert's work habits, intelligence, enthusiasm, and personal warmth made him a very good pharmacist. In 1932 Hubert Sr. decided that he would keep Ralph with him and send Hubert to the Capitol College of Pharmacy in Denver—the same training he himself had received in lieu of college. The younger Humphrey must have been very lonely there, for in one of his letters Hubert Sr. thanks him for writing every day. "Your letters to me, Hubert, are regular love letters," his father wrote. "Well, Hubert, I return to you all the love and affection a father can bestow upon a son." He offered shrewd pointers on the men who would examine his son. ("Vila is susceptible to flattery.")[14] Hubert applied almost superhuman zeal to the task of committing the vast lexicon of pharmaceutical names and dosages to memory. Incredibly, he completed a two-year program in six months. But he did so at a real cost to himself. He told his sister Frances that right before the exam he almost fainted out of nervous tension. "Some of the emotional and spiritual things he went through that year to spiritually and physically survive changed him," Frances later said.

Something essential drained out of him. Her brother, who not long before had looked upon the world with irrepressible good cheer, now had what she called "a nervous stomach."[15]

In late 1932 Hubert came back from Denver and assumed his place behind the counter. The wind howled, the dust blew, the farms withered. The young men and women Hubert had met in Minneapolis advanced another year in school. Only one good thing happened: he met Muriel Buck at a dance at Huron College, where she was a student. Muriel was not put off by Hubert's nervousness, his poverty, his high seriousness. She and a friend started dropping by the drugstore, and Hubert worked up the courage to ask her for a date. This posed logistical problems, since Hubert worked all day and all night, save when he was running Troop #6 or directing the fortunes of the Young Democrats. But they found opportunities to go dancing. Soon they were writing one another love letters when Muriel went off to the family cabin in the summer.

The Bucks were Huron gentry. Muriel's father, Andrew, was a banker who had invested in land and founded a wholesale business in butter, eggs, and poultry. He, too, had faced desperate straits when the banks went under, but he had managed to pay off his debts and sell the firm to a larger company. Andrew sat on the board of a local bank, served as a deacon of the Presbyterian church, and adhered to the small-town Republican creed against which Hubert's father had waged a lonely struggle. Economic conditions would never improve, he wrote his business partner, "so long as we are burdening ourselves with new taxes, and giving away and spending recklessly millions of Federal money."

Muriel was a refined young woman, demure and polite, pretty without being particularly striking. She played piano extremely well, but she could also sew and cook and keep house. She was levelheaded, unlike Hubert, who could soar up into the stars and then sink down into the dumps. While almost anything could move Hubert to tears, Muriel was dry-eyed. Earthbound though she was, however, Muriel may also have responded to the ambitions simmering in her young swain, because she had hopes for herself that made her look beyond the confines of their small town. Beneath her photo in the Huron High

School yearbook of 1930, she wrote, "I'll do something bye and bye, and I'll be famous before I die." She and Hubert adored one another. They missed each other terribly when they were apart and peppered their letters with endearments. "I just want to tell you again," Hubert wrote in one—because he had already told her so many times—"that I am so deliciously in love with you."[16] If he was going to be stuck in Huron for the rest of his life, at least he would have a partner he loved.

ANDREW BUCK'S DOCTRINE OF SMALL GOVERNMENT AND SELF-reliance held sway in Washington as it did in South Dakota. President Herbert Hoover, though not the heartless servant of the plutocracy that he is now often seen to be, was in thrall to a Republican ideology that exalted free markets and "rugged individualism" even as the Depression felled even the most rugged of individuals. He rejected proposals to prop up the rural economy. As farm income cratered, Hoover finally agreed to authorize a $500 million fund to purchase surplus grain at well above market prices; but that sum was so inadequate that the funds were depleted without making a dent in farm prices. (By late 1932 South Dakota farmers had received a grand total of $368,000 in subsidy payments.) The farm radicalism of an earlier generation now roared back to life. In May 1932, Midwestern farmers convened in Des Moines to establish the Farmers' Holiday Association, calling on farmers to withhold sales—a "holiday"—until they received a "fair valuation" based on pre–World War I prices. In August, farmers across the Midwest vowed to begin withholding produce from the market. The movement in South Dakota was based in Huron, and in August the Humphreys, father and son, watched an angry crowd of five thousand farmers march to a meeting in the city's main square. If a revolution or even mob violence broke out, Hubert Sr. warned, they and their little store would not be spared—"not because we had ever been well-to-do, but simply because, when people lose everything they have, they turn on those who have a little and are visible."[17]

That summer, when the Democratic Party met to nominate the governor of New York, Franklin D. Roosevelt, the party adopted a farm plank that promised "enactment of every constitutional measure that will aid the farmer to receive for basic farm commodities prices in excess of cost." In 1928 Hubert Sr. had seen Roosevelt place Al Smith's name in nomination, and he had come home a passionate FDR man. Now the Humphreys had a new household hero. Hoover had won 58 percent of the vote in 1928, but FDR administered such a drubbing that the incumbent was able to carry only six states, all in the Northeast, the Republican heartland. Even South Dakota gave FDR 63.6 percent of its vote.

Within days of taking office, on March 4, 1933, Roosevelt introduced the Farm Relief Act; it passed on May 12. The bill established an Agricultural Adjustment Administration that was authorized to do exactly what farmers had been demanding since 1923: purchase surplus produce and pay farmers to keep it out of the marketplace. Milo Reno, the rafter-raising head of the Farmers' Holiday Association, had planned to call for another boycott May 13; when FDR signed the new law, Reno called off the strike. Despite the terrible hardship in rural America, the movement fizzled out in 1933. As one historian notes, "A growing conviction that the administration had concern for the farmers' welfare and the slow improvement of farm prices had driven pickets from the highway—they would never return."[18]

The new mechanisms of active government were being assembled just as a cataclysm of biblical proportions struck the prairie. On the morning of November 12, 1933, the skies over eastern South Dakota began, unaccountably, to darken. A great black cloud appeared on the horizon. A "darkness more intense than that of night" blotted out the sun, as the *Evening Huronite* would poetically observe the following day.[19] Then came a high-pitched whine, the sound of a great mass whirling through the sky. And then—the apocalypse. The worst dust storm in the history of the nation swept over farms and cities, burying plows and covering storefronts in a dense sand that consisted of the aerosolized, desiccated soil of the Great Plains, by then three years into its catastrophic drought. Roofs blew off homes; cars, blind in the darkness, slammed into one another on the roads.

Hubert Humphrey watched the storm approach from the pharmacy. "It looked like a terrible smoke cloud," he would say years later. "Debris—thistles and tumbleweeds—came before the storm. I thought it was the end of the world." The "black blizzard" was not the first to hit eastern South Dakota, but it was by far the worst. Farmers in the region felt that they had been afflicted by a series of Old Testament plagues: first the collapse of prices, then the Depression, drought, and swarms of grasshoppers, which, as Humphrey recalled, "ate the paint off the buildings" when there was nothing else left to consume.[20] In the aftermath of this latest cataclysm, not only had farming become impossible but great masses of cattle, their stomachs lined with dirt, died within weeks. The rural economy had been obliterated. What Humphrey would recall, decades later, was the sense of helplessness and futility that the dust storm left in its wake. "That dust got all the way inside you," he told the Doland High School graduating class of 1968—"into your eyes and throat and lungs . . . and then into your thoughts and hopes. I remember that it didn't seem worth holding your head up."[21]

There wasn't any help to speak of. A relief program run by the state and partly funded by the federal government was then providing a few hours of employment a week for 17,000 South Dakotans. This had been plainly inadequate even before the dust storm hit. Over the summer, Governor Tom Berry had shocked FDR with pictures of the drought and the grasshopper plague; the president had authorized $60 million in drought relief, with $23 million to go to South Dakota.[22] A yet greater mass of funds from the National Industrial Recovery Act, which had in turn established the Civil Works Administration (CWA) with an initial budget of $3.3 billion, had not yet reached the Upper Midwest. Yet the catastrophe provoked an astonishingly rapid response. On November 18, six days after the storm, state authorities notified the relief recipients that they would be transferred, effective immediately, to Civil Works. They would be paid 50 cents an hour, double the federal minimum wage that the government had just established, for thirty hours a week.

In the ensuing days, the number of beneficiaries was increased to 22,500, then 36,000, then 47,000—all the unemployed men (and a very few women) who could be found in the state. On the 24th, a check for $9,031 arrived in Huron to pay the workers of Beadle County for the week. These payments would continue through much of the 1930s. Harry Hopkins, administrator of the CWA, insisted that local authorities find meaningful public projects to replace the make-work that had previously been the lot of the poor. Those projects still live in the collective memory of rural South Dakota. Don Mendel, a retired farmer outside of Doland, recalls his grandfather telling him about his work for the Works Progress Administration (WPA), which, along with the Public Works Administration, would ultimately take over the job-creating role of the CWA. "The farmers around here graveled that road with horses and wagons," he says, pointing out a window. Harvey Woolman, who still lives on the family farm outside of Huron, says that his father worked on a WPA project to build the Spink County dam.[23]

That wasn't the end of the federal largesse. On December 8, Huron received $107,000 for street improvements. On the 9th, 1,600 wheat farmers in the county sent applications to Washington for payment for 42,894 bushels of wheat sequestered from the market. By the middle of December, Washington was paying $630,000 a week to keep South Dakotans—almost all of them farmers—fully employed, and had transferred to the state $3,229,000 in agricultural payments. Business in town was up 70 percent over the year before. On the 23rd, the *Huronite* was able to write, "Huronians today looked forward to one of the merriest Christmases the community has experienced for several years."[24]

The people of South Dakota, like farmers all over the country, and especially in the West, would continue to suffer, for the drought would last through 1934 and drive tens of thousands from their farms, and indeed from the state itself. But they would not starve; and in the ensuing years farm prices would inch upward. Something new had happened. Farmers had suffered immemorially from vast forces they could not control; and immemorially they had been left to their own devices. Herbert Hoover had made an ineffectual gesture at assistance. FDR had shown that the federal government could act, effectively and quickly, to keep the wolf from the door. He had exposed the hollowness of Republican reaction while blunting the force of radicalism. In January 1949, in the first interview he gave after he had become the freshman senator from Minnesota, Hubert Humphrey would say, "I learned more about economics from one dust storm in South Dakota than I did in all my years at college."[25]

HUBERT KEPT EXCHANGING LETTERS WITH UNCLE HARRY, THE most soigné figure in his life. Harry always wrote on the stationery of Washington's very tony Cosmos Club, to which he belonged. Harry was a high-minded, moralizing Christian Scientist but also an arch and knowing Washingtonian. In 1934 he wrote to say that he had just returned from a trip to Quebec and Montreal—"a city that feels like a real city and has the feel of a metropolis"—and was soon to leave for a conference in Amsterdam. Then he planned to visit France, Switzerland, Italy, and England. These letters must have materialized like a shimmering oasis in the desert of eastern South Dakota. In the summer of 1935, Hubert was looking forward to the first visit of his life to the nation's capital, where the Boy Scouts would be holding their annual jamboree. At the last minute, the jamboree was canceled owing to a polio outbreak. Uncle Harry, his guardian angel, then intervened once again, sending Hubert a check for the bus fare.[26]

This twenty-four-year-old unsalaried druggist from the sticks dreamed of Washington the way other children of the Midwest—the ones who read *Variety* for gossip about the Broadway shows—carried a torch for Manhattan. By a stroke of good fortune that must have felt like predestination, Hubert had arrived at the acme of the second stage of the New Deal. In May Congress had passed legislation that led to the establishment of the WPA; in July, the National Labor Relations Act, guaranteeing workers the right to organize, bargain, and strike; and in August, the epochal Social Security Act, protecting Americans from poverty in old age. Hubert saw the machinery of the New Deal at work. He sat in the Senate gallery and heard Louisiana's Huey Long, a fantastic figure in white shoes, cream-colored suit, and orange tie, hold forth at splendid length; he visited the monuments and walked in the footsteps of the great men he had only read about in books or heard about from his father. And he was moved as he had never been before. In a letter to Muriel, he wrote, "Washington D.C. thrills me to my very fingertips. I simply revel and beam with delight in this realm of politics and government." Washington had shown Hubert Humphrey his destiny. "I intend to set my aim at Congress," he wrote. "Don't laugh at me, Muriel." The ambition would have been laughable, if touching, for any other star-struck yokel. But a Humphrey was always prepared to do the hard work. "I need to do more reading, more writing, more thinking, if I ever want to fulfill my dream of being someone in the world." He needed to read and think "always as a liberal," like his hero. "Roosevelt," he wrote, "is a super-man."[27]

Humphrey had glimpsed the heavens; now the stony ground of South Dakota felt insufferable. His stomachaches, which had disappeared in Washington, resumed; he was thin as a wraith. For all that he adored Muriel, he kept postponing the wedding day, showing an unaccustomed irresolution. He finally agreed that they would marry September 3, 1936. A signal event occurred only a week beforehand: the FDR campaign bandwagon rolled through Huron. Hubert Sr., who had become a figure in state politics, wangled an invitation for himself and his namesake to FDR's private railcar. Perhaps they shook the great man's hand; at any rate, they stood near him and basked in his radiance. The wedding was not quite so dramatic. Hubert and Muriel married at the Presbyterian church at 8:00 a.m. on a weekday, so that Hubert Sr. could hurry back to the drugstore. They began their five-day honeymoon by driving Frances, who needed to catch a train back to George Washington University, from Huron to Minneapolis. They ate in cafeterias as they drove across Minnesota in Hubert Sr.'s car. Hubert hit a cow twelve miles out of Huron and had to have the car pushed all the way home.

The new couple moved into a tiny rented house and began to talk about their future. Muriel later said, "Hubert hated the wind, it really bothered him. And the dust! It would depress us terribly. You couldn't live in that country, you couldn't exist almost, if you didn't have some kind of imagination, and ideals that would keep you going."[28] Humphrey had both imagination and ideals. But how to begin the path?

He and Muriel concluded that he had to return to the University of Minnesota. Now a new obstacle appeared, one uniquely difficult for Hubert Humphrey to surmount. He was not the only family member with dreams; not, in fact, the only one with dreams of a political career. Hubert Sr. had decided in early 1936 to indulge the great passion of his life by running for the state assembly. In early May, Hubert wrote to Muriel to say that in the Democratic primary his father had carried every precinct in Huron and the surrounding area. That fall he would win the general election. In the very modest world of South Dakota Democratic politics, the fifty-four-year-old novice was a rising star. There was talk in party circles that he might have a shot at the nomination for governor (though no Democrat could actually win). But the plan hinged on Hubert accepting the role behind the drugstore counter that his father would finally forsake. Loyal as he was, how could he refuse? But how could he accept? The father's life would mean the son's death. At this time in his life, Humphrey later told a friend, he found himself thinking, "Gosh, I'll live and die out here and nobody's ever going to know that I ever was." He *had* to get out.[29]

Yet Hubert could not bring himself to act; another year crawled by. Hubert Sr. began serving in Pierre, for the first time tasting the joys of active politics. How long would it be before his talents had made him a force in the state? Muriel urged Hubert to overcome his scruples and speak directly to his father. One night in August 1937, the twenty-six-year-old Humphrey finally summoned the courage to do so. In order to have some privacy, they sat in the Model A outside the house at midnight, after they had closed the store. "I told him how depressed I was," Humphrey later wrote, "almost physically ill from the work, the dust storms, the conflict between my desire to do something and my loyalty to him." His father listened silently, compelled to recognize that he could fulfill his own ambitions only at the cost of his son's. That was, for a man constituted like Hubert Humphrey Sr., an intolerable proposition. Finally he said, "Hubert, if you aren't happy, then you ought to do something about it."[30]

And he did. In September 1937, Hubert and his parents and Muriel piled into the Model A and drove the ten hours to the University of

Minnesota. Hubert would never again live in South Dakota and never again work at the store. His father would serve only one term in the statehouse. Twelve years later, when his son had been elected to Congress, Hubert Sr. would say in an interview, "I think he's doing just exactly what I'd like to have done if I had the ability. I can see in him the desires I had."[31]

3

Books

---

*"[The New Deal philosophy] is not afraid of the new. . . .
It is adventurous, willing to take risks, . . . everlastingly
desirous of going forward and doing something about an
unsatisfactory situation."*

T HE HUBERT HUMPHREY WHO RETURNED TO THE UNIVERSITY
of Minnesota campus in September 1937 was a very different
man from the one who had first arrived there eight years earlier. He was a married man of twenty-six. He had spent the previous
six years languishing on the prairie. Inside himself, he believed that
he could be somebody; now, finally, he had the chance to show the
world who he was. Humphrey had an extraordinary mind, though
still largely untrained; fierce ambition and bottomless energy; and a
winning personality that brought others to his side. He still had no
idea what he wanted to study; he just knew *that* he wanted to study.
He signed up for an implausible twenty-one credits; he had, after all,
bored his way through a two-year pharmacy program in six months.
But since he and Muriel were virtually penniless, they also had to

work. Humphrey found a job as a pharmacist and Muriel as a book-keeper. They took a one-room apartment with a shared bathroom—a "third-floor garret," Humphrey wrote—and lived off hamburger. For fun they would go dancing or make popcorn and play Monopoly.

In the spring, Humphrey took American Constitutional Development with Evron Kirkpatrick, a scholar fresh from his Yale PhD. The class's extremely demanding syllabus included foundational texts such as *The Federalist Papers* and Alexis de Tocqueville's *Democracy in America* as well as many of the great works of history and government of the era, including Charles Beard's *Economic Interpretation of the Constitution*, and Samuel Eliot Morison and Henry Steele Commager's *Growth of the American Republic*. The class read dozens of seminal Supreme Court cases and law review articles.[1] Though he had received a grounding in history and government at Doland High School and had continued reading under his father's tutelage, Humphrey would have been encountering most of these texts for the first time. He was dazzled, and utterly enthralled. Humphrey already felt that he knew what he believed; but he barely knew *why* he believed it, or how others had come to believe it, or to believe something very different. Not every student in class would have cared; but he did, very much. Humphrey devoured everything and talked constantly in class, every bit as irrepressible a force as he had been at Doland.

The class proved to be the catapult that launched Humphrey on his life path. Over the next two years, he would complete three years' worth of classwork, taking virtually everything the Political Science Department had to offer. The value-neutral social sciences had by now gained firm purchase in American universities, and political science, under the longtime chairmanship of William Anderson, offered a deep immersion in political process. By the mid-thirties, however, the department had diversified. Owing to the burgeoning interest in the practical work of government fostered by the relentless experimentation of FDR's New Dealers, the department had established the Public Administration Center to train future civil servants.

Anderson had also hired bright young men like Kirkpatrick, and even an avowed Socialist, Benjamin Lippincott, who had studied under Harold Laski at the London School of Economics.[2] In 1938, the Minnesota University Press would publish *On the Economic Theory of Socialism*, which Lippincott coauthored with two colleagues. Lippincott argued that a socialist economy would be not only more just but more efficient than a capitalist one.[3] He may have been the first Socialist Humphrey had encountered. But the second-generation pharmacist was not to be shaken from his faith in free enterprise; he was, Lippincott recalled, a thoroughgoing moderate at a moment when it was not only permissible but intellectually fashionable to adopt a radical critique.

Humphrey quickly made friends everywhere. One day in Kirkpatrick's class he got into an argument with Orville Freeman, the starting fullback on the football team. After Humphrey had buried Freeman under a blizzard of quotations from William Jennings Bryan and Woodrow Wilson, the two continued talking after class, with the spindly older man badgering the younger one with questions and comments about Golden Gopher football, which he followed fanatically. Humphrey invited Freeman to join him on the debate team, which, unlike the football team, went through the season undefeated.[4] Freeman and Kirkpatrick, who was a year younger than Humphrey, often joined Hubert and Muriel for popcorn and talked long into the night—frequently about Minnesota politics, a subject that intrigued all of them. For all that he was taking a backbreaking course load and working on the side, Humphrey appeared to spend all his time talking. And he was the kind of talker to whom people listened. One day William Anderson asked Kirkpatrick who the young man was who seemed to be just outside his office window every day surrounded by a knot of listeners. "That's Hubert Humphrey," said Kirkpatrick. A different group, Kirkpatrick later recalled, typically surrounded Humphrey in the drugstore.[5]

The Humphreys had a hard life in Minneapolis. They moved half a dozen times, trying to find a place they could afford with enough room for their first child, Nancy, born in 1938. At one apartment Humphrey earned reduced rent by acting as janitor and handyman. "I swabbed toilets, I repaired the roof, fixed the plumbing, cleaned the sewers, shoveled the snow, and besides that, worked six hours a day in the drugstore for twenty cents an hour," Humphrey recalled.[6] But hard work was second nature for him. He still found time to travel the Midwest on the debate team; to run Delta Sigma Rho, the public speaking fraternity; and to serve on the Labor Committee, which sponsored a conference on labor problems. Humphrey was inexhaustible and omnipresent. And he was, of course, an A student.

Humphrey graduated Phi Beta Kappa and summa cum laude. He had fallen in love with scholarship; now he thought of teaching, not politics, as his vocation. Humphrey dreamed of going to Princeton, Woodrow Wilson's alma mater, but he didn't have the money. Kirkpatrick wrote to his friend Charles Hyneman, an older and more established scholar at Louisiana State University, calling Humphrey "the best student I have had to date at Minnesota." Hyneman wrote back to say he might be able to offer Humphrey a job as a teaching assistant, for $50 a month, while he pursued his graduate studies. That was a paltry sum, even by Depression standards, for a married man with a child; but it was the best offer available. Humphrey sent in an application. He tried to explain his unusual career arc, writing that he had attended pharmacy school only because "I really doubted that I would ever be able to complete my university education."

Humphrey was on good terms with the whole department, and five of his professors wrote recommendations for him. All of them remarked on his intelligence, on his kindly and gregarious nature, and on his fascination with practical politics. Kirkpatrick stressed his maturity, his sound judgment, his "real qualities of leadership." The others found a gentle way of warning Hyneman that this young scholar could be a handful. "Perhaps a bit enthusiastic," wrote Oliver P. Field. "While he is of the aggressive type," wrote Joseph R. Starr, "he does not offend in this respect."[7] Humphrey plainly had the makings of something, though perhaps not an academic.

THE SOUTH WAS A PLACE HUBERT HUMPHREY HAD ENCOUNTERED only in books. In August 1939, temporarily leaving Muriel and Nancy behind, he took a train to central Louisiana and then a bus west to Baton Rouge and the LSU campus. The sultry climate, the dense clumps of Spanish moss, the rickety wooden shacks along the road made him feel as if he had left the known world for the tropics. Humphrey had only met a few Black people in his life; in Baton Rouge they were everywhere, but as if behind a screen, for Jim Crow laws enforced a rigid hierarchy. On one side of every streetcar was a sign that read "For Colored Patrons Only." Every doctor's office had a "colored" entrance, every bus and train depot had separate waiting rooms. The tiny apartment he took on Highland Avenue near campus was close enough to a Black neighborhood that he saw the open sewage ditches that ran along the streets.

Since Blacks could not enroll and certainly could not teach at LSU, the only person of color Humphrey got to know in Baton Rouge was the baby's nanny, Maggie. He learned from her the bone-deep suspicion that Black people had for policemen or bill collectors or any other figure of white authority. Of course Humphrey had known about Jim Crow; but he was still appalled to encounter it in person. "No one, I thought, could view black life in Louisiana without shock and outrage," he later wrote.[8] Yet scarcely anyone did. He learned, rather, that the feudal racial arrangements of the South allowed whites to feel that they lived with Black people in far greater intimacy than did northern liberals like him—which, he reflected ruefully, was true. Baton Rouge opened Humphrey's eyes to the reality of racism not only in the South but in the North.

Yet LSU was itself a monument to big-government liberalism, though not the kind Humphrey was accustomed to. The campus had been the pet project of Governor Huey Long. Humphrey already knew about Long: he had seen him campaign for FDR in 1932, and he had heard him speak in Washington in 1935. Long was a populist who had become governor in 1928 running under the slogan, "Every man a king, but no one wears a crown." In a state long ruled, and kept in subjection, by the petrochemical industry, Long imposed oil and natural resources taxes to help pay for an ambitious agenda that included asphalted roads and bridges and a new port in New Orleans, free textbooks, public hospitals, and night school to end illiteracy (including among Blacks). And he built a beautiful new university campus in open fields several miles from the state capital.

In 1928 LSU had been a backwater with a "C" rating from accreditors. By the time Humphrey arrived, it had a new medical school and grand brick buildings built around a greensward, and, of course, a giant football stadium.[9]

Long had been elected to the Senate in 1930 (though he continued to serve as governor until 1932). He was almost certainly preparing to run against Roosevelt—from the left—when he was assassinated in Baton Rouge in 1935. Thanks to his lurid ending, the scandals that surrounded his tenure, and the iron control he exercised over state politics, Long was dismissed, at least in the progressive circles Humphrey moved in, as a tin-pot dictator and even a fascist. But Humphrey recognized in Long the kind of Midwestern figure of his childhood who had stood with "the people" against "the interests." As he would later put it, "Long had the tongue of a demagogue, but he had the heart of a compassionate man."[10] Then and later, the openhearted populism of a Huey Long or a William Jennings Bryan exerted a far stronger pull on Humphrey than did the Fabian socialism he had found at the University of Minnesota.

For a man fascinated by politics, as Humphrey was, Louisiana had the appeal of the truly baroque. The corruption that had smoldered mostly underground in Long's time exploded in glorious fireworks under the tenure of Richard Leche, an acolyte. When Humphrey arrived on campus, the student newspaper, *The Reveille*, was purple with details of a scandal that had engulfed the university itself. President James Smith had been arrested by federal agents that summer after evidence emerged that he had spent sums far in excess of his salary; the university had been featherbedding contracts and kicking back several hundred thousand dollars to Smith and his confederates as well as to the governor and his circle. Smith was convicted and imprisoned that November, and Leche two years later.[11] If, like Humphrey, you believed devoutly in a government of laws rather than men, the downfall of Longism offered a sharp reminder of the dangers of populism—though also a highly entertaining spectacle.

Life for the Humphreys was even harder in Baton Rouge than it had been in Minneapolis. The drab apartment Humphrey had found consumed $35 of his $50 monthly stipend. When Muriel came down with Nancy, she at once began supporting him, as she had from the time they had married. She found a job as a typist for students and professors in the department, and made ham salad sandwiches that Hubert sold to students for a dime each. Charles Hyneman, who became as close to Humphrey as Evron Kirkpatrick had been, helped him out by asking him to speak at a women's club event in New Orleans that paid $50. The subject was Louisiana state taxes, about which Humphrey knew absolutely nothing when Hyneman approached him. The host later called Hyneman to say that Humphrey had given the best speech the group had ever heard. She didn't know that her speaker was so poor that he had spent the night of the talk in the bus station rather than a hotel.

Humphrey spent most of his time in Baton Rouge reading, thinking, and writing; intellectually, it would be the most focused period of his life. He decided to write his master's thesis on "The Political Philosophy of the New Deal." Though at this time Humphrey expected to pursue his doctorate, he did not write the thesis as an intellectual exercise designed to put him one step further on the academic ladder. Though he was careful to allude to the most up-to-date theories about, for example, the role of pressure groups in the forging of legislation, the text read like a declaration of principle written in a state of heightened urgency. By late 1939 Hitler had annexed Czechoslovakia, neutralized the Soviet Union, and conquered Poland. Democratic America was soon to enter a war with fascist Germany with the future of the world in the balance. Never before had democracy faced such a trial by fire. In his introduction, Humphrey noted that Hitler and FDR had both been raised to power by popular grievance in the face of economic failure. Yet the two nations had responded very differently. The American people had chosen a democratic path dictated both by their political history and by the character and beliefs of the president they had elected.[12] FDR was a liberal, as Humphrey understood the word; he had put liberalism to the supreme test, and it had passed. The subject of this study was Hubert Humphrey as much as it was FDR, for in it Humphrey attempted, for the one time in his life, to plumb the historical and intellectual depths of his own political principles.

The philosophy of the New Deal rested on an analysis of the world economic crisis that was different from that of both the acolytes of laissez-faire on the right and socialists on the left. Capitalism had failed, Humphrey wrote, but not in its very nature so much as in its operation. The energies of industrial expansion had waned and given way to "the exploitation of investors and the consuming public by stock market manipulation and monopoly price maintenance." Here was an echo of the populist anger at Wall Street that Humphrey had absorbed from his father and learned from the hardship of farm life in South Dakota. The New Dealers recognized, Humphrey went on, that "the mechanism had run down temporarily and the solution was to wind it up again, after certain repairs had been made and new parts substituted."[13] (This homely metaphor would have been very winning had Humphrey not lifted it from one of his sources, Louis Hacker's *American Problems of Today*, which had appeared a year earlier.[14]) FDR and his team did not deny the existence of class antagonism, as businessmen did, but neither did they seek, like the Communists, to "enthrone the proletariat" at the acme of an inverted class system; instead they sought to abolish class antagonism by lifting the proletariat into "a different state" through a combination of revitalized growth and a careful plan of national redistribution. They believed that capitalism, guided by government, could solve the problems that capitalism had created.

The New Deal had a philosophy, Humphrey argued, but not an ideology. Its spirit was pragmatic, experimental—the attitude FDR had summed up by saying that novel problems required novel solutions. Here, of all places, the author soared into a rhapsody scarcely consistent with academic neutrality. The New Deal philosophy, he declared, "is not afraid of the new. Neither does it cling to the old. It is adventurous, willing to take risks. It is scientific in temper, everlastingly desirous of going forward and doing something about an unsatisfactory situation, even if one experiment must be abandoned and a new one tried."[15] Hoover's watchword had been "wait." FDR's had been "act." The reader could hardly mistake the author's deep sense of identification with the latter.

Though this experimental, incremental temper did not constitute an ideology, neither could it be reduced to that tepid word "reform." The cumulative effect of the New Deal had been to uproot the older liberalism of the free market in favor of a new "democratic collectivism" that ushered in what Humphrey called "the service state." That change was revolutionary in American terms, for until that time the grip on the American mind of what New Dealer and author Harold Ickes had called "rugged individualism" had elevated the dog-eat-dog ethos of the marketplace into a governing principle.[16] That ethos belonged to a nineteenth-century world of small farmers and shopkeepers. The service state, though brought into being by the exigency of the Depression, was ultimately an adaptation to the new reality of the industrial society that tied farmers and workers to the national economy. Social democracy was a response to the conditions of modern life.

But at what cost? If a "democratic collectivist" accepted the need for a welfare state, was he not also surrendering at least some part of the faith in individual liberty that had always constituted the core of liberalism? The progressives, who sought a government of experts, had been prepared to make that sacrifice; others regarded it as ominous. In *The Good Society*, published in 1937, Walter Lippmann had written that it was all too easy "to let oneself become enchanted with the notion that the promises of the Providential State can be reconciled with the blessings of liberty."[17] Lippmann warned of the dangers of the new social democracy. But FDR *did* believe that justice could be reconciled with liberty; and so did the author. Humphrey quoted extensively from the speech that FDR had given in 1932 at the Commonwealth Club of San Francisco, where he had made the case that in a modern, industrial world only an active, though carefully circumscribed, state could protect the liberty of powerless individuals.[18]

Humphrey devoted a chapter of his thesis to this question. He asked whether it was the case that New Deal programs had limited personal freedom and thus implied an unavoidable trade-off between liberty and well-being. His answer was no: as the New Dealers understood, it was not the state that endangered liberty, but "poverty and ignorance, insecurity and fear."[19] Democracy, with its promise of liberty, could not survive mass immiseration. Roosevelt had rescued American democracy. He had made democracy something real and warm-blooded by bringing government "down to the people" through his programs of public works and farm supports. And he had done so with no sacrifice of personal freedom. Humphrey used the language of "negative" and "positive" liberty later made famous in Isaiah Berlin's 1958 lecture "Two Concepts of Liberty." The democratic state had a profound obligation not to impinge upon personal freedom; FDR had respected that obligation. But the modern state also had to facilitate the positive liberty that helps individuals realize their own aspirations for a good life (which was precisely how Berlin would define positive liberty). FDR had done that, too. The modern liberal state, in short, reconciled liberty and justice rather than pitting them against one another.

Humphrey's thesis adviser, Alexander Daspit, criticized the essay as a work of advocacy rather than neutral analysis and asked for an extensive rewrite. Charles Hyneman told Humphrey that Daspit was leaving for Harvard and could largely be ignored. But you could see his point. Humphrey, like his hero, FDR, was a man of action; he had written his own manifesto. Though his views would evolve over the years as America moved rightward, he would never really depart from the faith in the welfare state—and in capitalism—that he expressed in his thesis.

Humphrey hoped to continue his education at Harvard, and Hyneman wrote a lavish recommendation to Harvard's dean of graduate studies. He praised Humphrey's wide reading in the social sciences. "He is unusually quick, imaginative, capable of sharp analysis," Hyneman observed. "I find him unusually free of dogma; not overly burdened by unverified assumptions. He works hard, persistently, apparently with eagerness." Humphrey had never kicked the reputation that trailed him to Baton Rouge, and Hyneman conceded that "Humphrey has been criticized as over-inclined to talkativeness." It was true, Hyneman wrote, that Humphrey "spends a great amount of time in conversation." Nevertheless, he added, "I consider this quality definitely an advantage rather than a handicap. Talking is an important part of Humphrey's method of educating himself." In any case, Hyneman concluded, the passage of time was bound to "subordinate his natural inclination to conversation." That prediction proved unduly optimistic.

4

Fusion

"We want Humphrey!"

A S HE RETURNED TO MINNEAPOLIS IN THE SUMMER OF 1940, Humphrey felt that he had found the answer to his destiny: he would serve American democracy as a teacher and scholar of political science. Others who knew him, including Charles Hyneman and Evron Kirkpatrick, believed that his gifts lay elsewhere. Hyneman later told the story of one of the academics at Baton Rouge who conducted Humphrey's oral exam. I'm afraid, he had said, we're going to have to fail you. As the candidate looked at him in shock, the scholar added, "We want to get you out of this servile profession, and get you into politics where you belong."[1] Humphrey had dreamed of a life in politics at least since his 1935 trip to Washington. Already he was trying, in a small way, to make a name for himself in public debate. In February 1940, while he was still at LSU, Humphrey had written a 3,500-word letter to the editor of the *Daily Plainsman*, Huron's chief newspaper, accusing Republican senator Karl Mundt of leveling "defiling, infamous, cheap and unfair criticism" of FDR's Reciprocal Trade Agreement Program, part of his policy to liberalize trade policy under the Reciprocal Trade Agreements Act of 1934. The letter, which covered almost an entire page of the paper, would have left Huron in no doubt that its native son had become a formidable scholar and polemicist. ("Cuban lard imports from the U.S. increased from $500,000 in 1933 to $4 million in 1936 . . . ")[2]

But Humphrey was in no position to indulge idle dreams. He was a twenty-nine-year-old graduate student with a wife, an eighteen-month-old baby, no savings, and no real prospects. Before classes resumed, Kirkpatrick found him an entry-level New Deal job training adult-education teachers for the WPA in Duluth, and then loaned him $250 to buy a car. In order to save money, Muriel and Nancy stayed with the Buck family in South Dakota. That fall the WPA offered to make Humphrey Twin Cities director of the program. Humphrey had planned to teach at the university while pursuing his graduate studies, but he couldn't afford to pass on the $150 a month he would get from the federal government. He and Muriel made a down payment on a small house in southeast Minneapolis.

Humphrey quickly impressed his superiors. Many of the teachers he inherited had come to regard their WPA stipend as a license for paid retirement. Humphrey vowed to fire any of them who failed to sign up the ten students needed for a class. When he made good his threat, the shocked employees "raised unshirted hell," Humphrey wrote in his memoirs, alerting bureaucrats in Washington to the injustice they had suffered. But Humphrey's boss defended him, saying, "I never thought I'd find anyone with the guts to fire anyone on WPA for not working."[3] Humphrey also encountered Minnesota's distinctively radical politics. Quite a few of these ex–public school teachers were either Stalinists or Trotskyites. They treated one another with a smoldering hatred, sitting on opposite sides of the room when Humphrey addressed them. Kirkpatrick, the head of the Minnesota Federation of Teachers, regarded the Trotskyists as benign ideologues but the Stalinists as hard-line party members, and had enlisted Humphrey in his effort to drive them out of the profession.

Humphrey's combination of brilliance, amiability, and zeal propelled him rapidly up the ladder to state director of the worker education program. He had never gotten to know Minnesota as a student; now he crisscrossed the state, speaking in practically every union hall in every town and city. "Worker education" was designed not only to give union men new skills, but also to relax the class antagonism between labor and management by exposing the workingman to a wider world, a congenial idea to a man who did not believe that class interests were unalterably opposed. Humphrey taught classes in parliamentary procedure and public speaking; one evening a week, on his own, he held a class in current events. He enlisted virtually the entire Political Science Department of the university, including Kirkpatrick and Lippincott, to teach as well. At one of them Humphrey persuaded two scholars to debate American entry into the war then building in Europe. Herb McCloskey, studying for his doctorate under Kirkpatrick, took the standard left-wing view that because the British, like the Germans, were servants of international capital, the United States should stay out. Humphrey, in theory the moderator, intervened and very calmly and politely demolished McCloskey's fine graduate student edifice. Then he walked over and the two men hugged. McCloskey was now a friend for life.[4]

Humphrey was working all day and most nights; but that still left some free time. He began earning extra money giving speeches, usually for $10 apiece. The head of the Minnesota Democratic Party asked him to deliver talks for FDR in the 1940 campaign. He wrote to good-government groups such as the Committee to Defend America by Aiding the Allies, offering to help in case they were short of speakers. By early 1942, Humphrey was being deluged with requests—and he only said no if he had a conflict. He spoke to the Fifth District American Legion of Minneapolis, the First Lutheran Church, the Women's Auxiliary of the Oak Park Home (an orphanage), the electrical workers local, Navy-Marine Post No. 472, the Knights of Columbus, the Minneapolis Businessmen's Association, and at the Lily High School commencement. Though he almost never used a prepared text, Humphrey had a menu of subjects: "Total War and Total Peace," "The Price of Indifference," "Wake Up America," and so on.

Occasionally the local paper dispatched someone to cover these events. A reporter for the *St. Cloud Times* attended the annual lunch of the Minnesota League of Poets in the ballroom of the Curtis Hotel in Minneapolis, where Humphrey had been booked as keynoter. After Miss Eda Flagg of Winona received an award for her patriotic poem "This Freedom," the "brilliant and inspiring" young speaker was introduced. Humphrey launched into "Total War and Total Peace," possibly at a velocity that kept the reporter from transcribing an entirely coherent version of his address. "It is better to light a candle than to curse the darkness," the young WPA official cried. "Christianity is the essence of true democracy and the Atlantic Charter. Our American people must know what the Four Freedoms are. They must be trained in American citizenship. We must value our rich heritage, and be willing to fight to keep it, before it is too late."[5]

This fusion of the Sermon on the Mount and the Declaration of Independence, texts he had been taught to worship in church and at home, was a leitmotif of Humphrey's speeches. The Christian flock and the democratic citizenry were one: "We, the common people, just as Peter, are the rock on which the faith must rest." Yet Humphrey infused these Sunday school bromides with a sense of fierce urgency. Together, they could defeat fascism but only with the total effort required to win a total war. Humphrey told a conference of librarians that they must regard themselves as soldiers; at a time when the Nazis were burning books, he scolded, "librarians and educators have been too soft and apathetic in their explanation and denunciation of this streamlined twentieth century tyranny."[6]

Now, finally, at thirty-one, the furious energies that beat inside Humphrey burst forth in a kind of frenzy, a fervent mixture of patriotic ardor, personal ambition, and sheer metabolism. In March, he wrote to his father in a tone that almost violated the unspoken family ban on vanity. He had, he said, opened over fifty new worker education programs for the WPA. His speaking schedule was booked through July. He was about to be promoted to one of the four top WPA jobs in the state. He would be coming in regular contact with mayors, city councilmen, the governor. He was, he said, disgusted with the way big business complained about FDR and then slacked off when they were called to join the war effort. "I don't care whether I'm liked or disliked," he wrote. "I'm going to be heard and recognized." That was a new note of pugilism; Humphrey was itching for a fight. And he knew where he wanted to wage it: he told his father that he was planning to run for Congress.[7]

Humphrey had certain gifts to a marked degree. He had more hours in a day than other people did; he needed only a few hours of sleep, and his mechanism never seemed to wind down. He would work all day and then deliver a speech or even two. Muriel would wait up for him at home or with his friends from the university—Evron Kirkpatrick, Orville Freeman, Herb McCloskey, and Art Naftalin, another graduate student. Humphrey would burst in the door close to midnight with a dozen anecdotes about who he had talked to and how he had spoken and what he had learned. They would drink Cokes and play gin rummy and talk about politics. (Their wives, in the manner of the day, would sit separately and talk about family and babies.) Every one of them thought their friend was destined for a career in public office.[8]

Humphrey was restless for a change of work and even of setting. He worried about moving his family, which grew to four when Hubert III, known as Skip, was born that June; but he also yearned to live in Washington, home of the great experiment in government activism that he had written about. Charles Hyneman, then working in Washington, recommended Humphrey to the federal Office of Civilian Defense. Humphrey applied there as well as at the State Department Office of Foreign Relief and Rehabilitation Operations and the Minneapolis branch of the National Labor Relations Board. None of them offered him a job. In the end he accepted a promotion to run the WPA's War Manpower Commission in Minnesota. There his role was to set up vocational programs so that WPA workers could leave the federal dole for permanent jobs in industries serving the war effort.

No civil service job could contain Humphrey's energies; he wanted to run for office, but he couldn't find a way in. An FDR Democrat like Humphrey couldn't win anything so long as the vote on the left was divided between the Democrats and the state's Farmer-Labor Party, which for the past quarter-century had controlled the votes of the left, including socialists and even Communists. The one exception to this rule was the mayoralty of Minneapolis, a nonpartisan office.

By now Humphrey had come to the attention of the leading political figures in the Twin Cities; he was the kind of eager, idealistic young man whom older men wanted to recruit. Late one night in December 1942, he called Naftalin to say that he had been encouraged to run for mayor. Naftalin, who had been working as a newspaperman, had told him lurid tales of the city's gangland life. "Do you think I'll get shot?" Humphrey asked.[9] The prospect apparently didn't deter him. In March 1943, Walter Judd, a Republican who had just won the Minneapolis congressional seat, introduced Humphrey to his key backers, Republicans all, including prominent businessmen and, most importantly, Gideon Seymour, executive editor of the *Minneapolis Star-Journal*. At the same time, Judge Vincent Day, a leader of progressive forces in the state, put Humphrey in contact with Farmer-Labor officials. All of these men urged Humphrey to run for mayor.

Years earlier, a few distinguished men had served as mayor of Minneapolis. Since then, most had been timeservers and crooks. The mayoralty had virtually no power, though it did offer opportunities for graft, chiefly by looking the other way while local racketeers controlled liquor and gambling in the city. The incumbent, Marvin Kline, was a lackluster veteran of local politics whose career would come to an abrupt end twenty years later, when he would be convicted of grand larceny, and sentenced to ten years in prison, for bilking what a federal judge described as an "unconscionable" sum from the polio foundation he directed. Running for mayor was not an obvious career choice for a political scientist and a New Deal man. But Humphrey was already thirty-two, the same age at which Harold Stassen, known as the Boy Wonder, had become governor of Minnesota five years earlier. He was impatient to satisfy the hunger for a life in politics that had been burning in him since he was a young man. Once he was assured of receiving the endorsement of the Central Labor Union of the American Federation of Labor (AFL), and thus of the modest financial support that would come with it, Humphrey agreed to run. He and Kirkpatrick and Naftalin went down to the courthouse to file. The primary was only nineteen days away, and he was a complete unknown. What's more, Judd's Republican backers had lost interest in Humphrey's candidacy as soon as he had accepted labor support.

Hubert Humphrey now unleashed himself on an unsuspecting citizenry. He spoke at union halls and high school gyms and Kiwanis luncheons and churches and synagogues and anywhere else where half a dozen people would gather. Humphrey's circle of friends, who drove him to events—the Humphreys had no car—now got to see his magic up close. Kirkpatrick recalled coaching Humphrey between performances. "I might have twenty minutes or half an hour, or whatever it would be," he recalled, "to tell him what I'd dug up and found out about the subject he was going to speak on. And then he'd stand up for an hour and a half, really laying the thing out, relating it to everything he knew, getting in the humor that he got in and that sort of thing."[10] Humphrey appeared not to be speaking but talking; because he paid almost no attention to whatever prepared text he had, he could improvise as he felt the mood of his listeners and read their reactions. People who knew nothing about this skinny young political scientist with the high, piping voice and the machine-gun delivery would soon be clapping and cheering, bound to the speaker by an almost electric current.

What made Humphrey so extraordinary was that he cared so much both about the subject he was talking about—whatever it was—*and* about the people he was talking to. Many years later, he said,

> You have to give to people. I don't just *make* a speech. I *give* a speech. . . . And when the speech is over, I get mad when these guys keep tugging at me and saying, 'Gotta get to your next appointment,' as though the next appointment were the Second Coming. I know that at many of these political meetings there are always a lot of families who have taken the trouble to pack the kids into the car and drive into town to hear me and maybe meet me. So I give them a speech, and I want it to be a good one.

And then he would stop and talk to mom and dad and the kids. "Spending five minutes with a kid," Humphrey said, "is like going to the beach."[11]

Humphrey brought his evangelical force to the high-minded propositions of a political scientist. He chose government reform as the subject of his inaugural campaign speech. The following week he reminded businessmen that unionism constituted the very heart of democracy, while admonishing workers that "the day of knock-down and drag-out fighting in labor organizations is over." He proposed to reform police training and the operation of social service agencies, and to keep schools open late to deal with the problem of juvenile delinquency, a bugbear of mid-century America. He had a ten-point program to make Minneapolis "the city of the future." But Humphrey did not only tread the clouds. In a May 7 speech on radio station WLOL he charged Mayor Kline with practicing "a do-nothing philosophy . . . based on straddling the fence and evasion of responsibility." The novice candidate wisely deleted a passage he had drafted comparing weak presidents—"Tyler, Fillmore, Polk, Harrison, Van Buren, Harding"— to strong ones like Jefferson, Jackson, and others in Humphrey's own pantheon of heroes. Instead, he sought to demonstrate that Mayor Kline had kept none of the campaign promises he had made in 1941.[12]

Humphrey had almost no money, no name recognition, and no newspaper endorsements, save that of the *Spokesman*, the city's Black-owned newspaper. Yet he still managed to finish second to Kline in an eight-man race, qualifying him for the two-man runoff. Humphrey now managed to raise $12,000, primarily from the city's unions, allowing him to conduct a better-financed version of his manic three-week primary sprint. He sent a cheeky cable to Kline saying, "I hereby extend to you an invitation to meet me in open debate before the citizens of Minnesota"—a duel that Kline wisely declined to wage.[13] On May 25, Humphrey read in the morning newspaper that Kline would be alleging in a speech that evening that the Humphrey campaign was infested with "racketeers," a term understood to refer to labor-based crime, such as illegal strikes. Never before had Hubert Humphrey been accused of anything graver than prolixity. An outraged and very canny Humphrey marched to the mayor's office, where, before the City Hall press corps, he loudly demanded that Kline substantiate the charge. After first demurring, Kline absurdly claimed that Humphrey planned to appoint George Murk, the head of the musicians' union, as police chief. Humphrey shouted that he "never had dreamed of such a thing." And then, shaking with fury, he vowed, "If you make these untrue charges involving me, Kline, you'll be sorry before you get through with me." After a series of harsh exchanges, the two were persuaded to shake hands and pose for a picture, which ran in the next day's *Morning Tribune*. But that night Kline gave the speech with the accusation.[14]

On June 14 the incumbent defeated his upstart challenger by a bare five thousand votes. It was a remarkable showing, but Humphrey, who had left his government job to run for mayor, was left with a $1,300 debt—a sum that almost equaled his 1943 income of $1,777.80. He had a wife and two children to support. He was still slowly paying down a $400 loan that Uncle Harry had given him three years earlier. And he had no source of income save for his speeches. At that moment Humphrey received an offer that came very close to turning his head. Several weeks after the election, Gideon Seymour, the local editor, invited him to his office for a private chat. Seymour told Humphrey something he already knew—that no one could win high office in Minnesota as a Democrat—and then added that a man with Humphrey's skills could be elected governor or even senator so long as he switched to the Republican Party. Muriel later recalled that Seymour also offered Humphrey a lake house valued at $35,000 or maybe $39,000—"in those days, a fortune." Humphrey talked the offer over with his wife and Herb McCloskey until four in the morning. This dark night of the soul—"almost a Faustian struggle," McCloskey said—only ended when Humphrey concluded that he could not, even for all the treasures of the earth, abandon the faith of his father.[15]

It was true, as Seymour also reminded Humphrey, that in Minnesota a Republican could be a liberal. Governor Stassen was not only a progressive but a "one-worlder," like Wendell Wilkie, who advocated a postwar world government. A Democrat couldn't win at all; the party had never been a force in Minnesota, and in the 1940s it consisted largely of urban Catholic factory workers and the local bosses who called the shots. The Farmer-Labor Party, on the other hand, brought together an uncomfortable mix of moderate farmers and small-town folk and militant ex-Populists and industrial workers in the Twin Cities and the iron mines of Duluth. Fierce unionization battles in the 1930s had radicalized many of the members, who belonged to the strongly pro-Communist Congress of Industrial

Organizations (CIO). The state's immensely popular and charismatic Farmer-Labor governor, Floyd Olson, had tied the party to FDR and driven the Communists into the wilderness. But in 1936 Olson died in office; the new governor, Elmer Benson, an agrarian Populist of the old school, fondly looked forward to the demise of capitalism and welcomed the Communists back into the party.[16] When Harold Stassen crushed Benson in the ensuing election, Farmer-Labor collapsed into a brawl among mainstreamers, Stalinists, and Trotskyists. The Trots were prepared to seek fusion with the equally enervated Democrats in order to create a Rooseveltian party in Minnesota, but both conservative Democrats and radical Farmer-Laborites blocked the effort. At its 1943 convention, the Hennepin County Farmer-Labor Party, the largest and among the most intractable in the state, adopted an explicitly Marxist platform.

This was the bleak political landscape that Hubert Humphrey surveyed as he contemplated his political future. It was in his nature to act rather than to brood. In July, barely a month after the loss to Kline, he wrote a twelve-page letter to Frank Walker, the US postmaster general and chairman of the Democratic National Committee, urging the party to press for fusion in Minnesota. When a perfunctory response arrived, Humphrey got on a bus to beard the chairman in his den. This was an extremely rash, possibly deluded, act for a young man who knew no one in Washington and barely had the money for bus fare. Yet this odyssey was to take its place in the Humphrey mythos as an episode of gumption, persistence, and sheer good luck. In his memoirs Humphrey describes showing up at Walker's office in the Mayflower Hotel every day for five days without getting to see the great man. He appears, from his description, to have been so fixated on seeing Walker that he made no effort to see anyone or anything else while he was in the nation's capital, a city that he regarded as the most fascinating place in the world. Finally Humphrey returned to Uncle Harry's Maryland home, where he had been staying, picked up his suitcase, and trudged back to the bus depot. Before climbing on the bus, he drowned, or at least moistened, his sorrow in a cocktail at the Hotel Willard. As a last-ditch measure, Humphrey called an old Huron friend of his father, a former postal official named W. W. Howes. Howes, in turn, called Walker and told him that he needed to meet this son of an old friend. Walker promptly dispatched a giant black limo to the hotel. Whisked into his presence, Humphrey delivered his narrative, presumably in his usual headlong fashion. Walker, Humphrey writes, "promised to be in touch." And the young pilgrim floated on to the bus.[17]

Humphrey had taken his destiny in his own hands; and now fate began to repay him. First, Macalester College in Minneapolis offered to pay him $500 to teach political science in the coming school year—a pittance but at least a beginning. Then Frank Walker, true to his word, dispatched a senior lieutenant, Oscar Ewing, to work out the terms of fusion between the Democrats and the Farmer-Laborites. The Soviets were committed to helping reelect Roosevelt; for the Bensonite wing of Farmer-Labor, fusion with the Democrats now constituted not an intolerable compromise of principle but a political imperative. Each side established its own fusion committee; Evron Kirkpatrick chaired the group for the Democrats.

The two party conventions met in the Radisson Hotel in Minneapolis April 14 and 15. Humphrey was made "temporary chairman," which would allow him to ride herd on the fusion process, and chosen to deliver the keynote address. In his speech, as Humphrey crowed in a letter to Hyneman, he "really laid it to 'em." He took as his subject the history of the party, which, for all that it lived in the shadows of Minnesota politics, he had inherited almost as a birthright from his father. Founded by Thomas Jefferson with the credo of "equal rights to all and special privileges to none," the Democratic Party had passed into the hands of Andrew Jackson, who stood with the common man against the "financial aristocracy." Then—skipping over the elemental facts of slavery and white supremacy, to which the party was devoted for virtually its entire history—Humphrey came to the era of William Jennings Bryan. "To him, more than any other Democrat, must be ascribed the awakening of the average man to his stake in his government and the revival in dynamic form of the principles of Jefferson and Jackson." Those seeds, in turn, "blossomed in the idealism of Wilson," and finally, in the nation's darkest hour, flourished gloriously under FDR.[18] Here, for the first time, Humphrey deployed his years of reading and writing in political science and political history to inspire a partisan crowd.

Then came the work of fusion. Humphrey pressured a still reluctant Farmer-Labor group to join a "fusion committee" of both parties, which met all night and finally reached an agreement at 6:30 the next morning. The two parties then met as one to adopt resolutions and choose candidates for statewide office. Who should run for governor if not the new party chairman who had laid it to 'em the night before? A party member took the floor and nominated Humphrey. Instantly the eight hundred delegates joined a chant: "We want Humphrey! We want Humphrey!" They stomped and shouted and whistled. The demonstration lasted an hour; Humphrey was drafted by acclaim. But there were two serious problems: neither Humphrey nor his friends thought that he could beat the popular Republican incumbent, Luther Youngdahl, and Humphrey had already informed party leaders that he planned to go into the military. What should he do? Humphrey left the hall and walked the streets around the Radisson. He had applied to the Naval Reserve and had passed the physical. How could he run for office at a time when every available young man was going to Europe to fight fascism? Yet that tumultuous applause—would he ever hear it again? "Never in my life did I feel quite so emotionally upset," he wrote to Hyneman. He knew, as a matter both of morality and sober political calculation, that he had to decline. He returned to the convention floor. "I want to go into the armed forces if I am acceptable," he told the delegates. "I want to be with those other young men and women in the armed forces, and you can't deny me that privilege."[19] That gallant appeal, of course, only enhanced Humphrey's status.

Hubert Humphrey had catapulted himself into a new realm. As chairman of the Democratic-Farmer-Labor (DFL) Party's State Central Committee, he had a paying job. In 1944 he would earn $5,027.78, almost triple his income the year before; almost half came from the DFL. (The rest came from Macalester, speeches, and the weekly radio addresses he now delivered for the Minnesota Broadcasting Corporation.) And he was a power broker. When a lawyer in Duluth approached him about a federal judgeship that had just become available, Humphrey explained that two other candidates—including Vincent Day—had already made the same request. He wrote to Frank Walker on behalf of the acting postmaster in Huron, who wanted a full-time appointment. He visited Washington for the annual meeting of the American Political Science Association and made the rounds of party officials. Uncle Harry was so moved by his example of "moral rectitude and decency," he wrote in a letter, that he canceled the last $100 of Hubert's debt.[20]

Humphrey was not only a local but, at least in a modest way, a national player. In February 1944, when Vice President Henry Wallace had come to Minneapolis to address the as-yet-unfused partisans of the two parties, it was Humphrey who had introduced him to the crowd—a great honor for this young college professor. Humphrey regarded Wallace, a Midwestern populist and visionary like the great Bryan, as the one figure capable of succeeding FDR. Afterward, Wallace's secretary, Edward Young, wrote to thank Humphrey for his help, adding, "We shall watch your progress with interest and hope."[21] Humphrey had included Young's office among his visits on his trip to Washington. In July, Humphrey went to Chicago as part of the Minnesota delegation to the Democratic National Convention. When Wallace's name was placed in nomination, Humphrey seized the state banner and led a tumultuous parade through the hall on behalf of his hero. He delivered a seconding speech in which he compared Wallace to Jefferson, Jackson, Bryan, and Wilson—"a living symbol of the Declaration of Independence and the Four Freedoms."[22]

Humphrey had been dismayed when FDR's own allies had maneuvered to dump Wallace in favor of Harry Truman, widely regarded as a tool of the St. Louis Democratic machine. But he threw himself into the campaign against Republican Tom Dewey. Tom Hughes, chairman of the FDR campaign at Carleton College in southern Minnesota, invited the party leader to address the student body and drove him for an interview with the local daily, the *Mankato Free Press*. The passage of almost eighty years had not dimmed Hughes's memory of this political phenomenon. "He was a kind of tornado," Hughes recalled. "He burst into the editorial rooms and they barely came up breathing. They said he was the greatest thing since Floyd B. Olson."[23] He was that, and more.

5

Mayor

"He has a powerful urge to right wrongs and plenty of streamlined ideas on how to do it."

IN THE FIRST HALF OF THE 1940S, HUMPHREY HAD LEARNED HOW to talk about politics; he had learned how to inspire and how to teach. He was ready for state or national office; instead, he became a mayor of a large industrial city. The job forced Humphrey to learn something new: how to work with other people, including people who didn't share his views, in order to get things done. He learned how to rally public opinion to overcome resistance. He learned how to use power—not secretly or cynically, but openly, harnessing voters' ideals rather than their fears. Humphrey's three and a half years as mayor of Minneapolis would not only make him a national figure among liberals, but would also teach him the skills he needed to become the nation's most effective liberal legislator.

By the end of 1944, two paths lay before Humphrey: military service or elective office. Everything else was either unavailable or undesirable. Service came first. Earlier that year the navy had turned

Humphrey down because of an old hernia and his color blindness. He had then applied to the army and was deferred on the grounds that he had a family. In December, at a time when virtually all eligible men were being called up, he was ordered to take another physical. Humphrey felt that his moment had finally come. He told the commanding officer at Fort Snell in Minneapolis, "I'm labeled political and if I don't go into the service it will haunt me the rest of my days." The officer rejected him anyway. On February 13, 1945, he was declared fit only for "limited service," and thus not subject to call-up.

No one could say that Humphrey hadn't tried to serve his country—though, as he feared, the time would come when they would say just that. Now the other path lay open. He had almost beaten Mayor Kline when he was a nobody; now he was far better known and he had access to money and important figures in the city. He had won the support of John Cowles, the all-powerful publisher of the *Minneapolis Star-Journal*. Humphrey recruited as campaign manager his college friend Orville Freeman, who had since gone on to serve in the Marines and had been gravely wounded in the jaw, neck, and shoulder on Guadalcanal—a shield against allegations of draft-dodging. He also enlisted Arthur Naftalin, the tough-minded ex-newspaperman. By the time the campaign was up and running in April, five hundred Humphrey volunteers were putting up posters, knocking on doors, evangelizing in their churches and Rotary Clubs. Perhaps most important of all, he had gained widespread support from both business and labor. World War II was finally drawing to a close—American forces would enter Berlin in May—and both sides were more prepared to accept the cooperative, managerial relationship Humphrey had advocated in 1943.

A new country, and a new city, were taking shape in the aftermath of the terrible war; hopes for a peaceful and prosperous future required new thinking about housing, employment, public works, slum clearance, and the like. Humphrey, of course, had plans for absolutely everything. One day he stopped off at his old campus to talk to the editors of the University of Minnesota's daily newspaper about housing for returning veterans. One of the editors, Geri Joseph, later recalled that Humphrey began by sitting on a table and just talking to a few of them, but word soon got around about the unknown young man speaking about public policy with such easy mastery and deep feeling; students began squeezing into the newspaper's offices and the hallways to hear him. "The atmosphere in the room was really electric," recalled Joseph, who would become one of the great friends and political allies of Humphrey's life.[2] That was how Humphrey recruited both friends and voters—by showing them his inner light. Kline could barely emerge from his own shadow. When the incumbent accused his foremost challenger of promising a "Utopia" he could not deliver, since the city charter placed budgeting and legislative authority in the city council, Humphrey shot back that a mayor could get things done if he really wanted to. In the primary election, Humphrey fell just short of winning an outright majority against thirteen candidates, including Mayor Kline, whom he beat almost two to one.

Minneapolis in the mid-1940s was an increasingly prosperous city with a terrible reputation as one of the "poison spots of American crime," in the gaudy phrase of a 1944 Senate criminal investigation committee.[3] During Prohibition, the city's proximity to Canada had made it a regional distribution hub for illegal alcohol. A gang known as "the Combination" ran bootlegging operations, and a network called "the Syndicate" controlled gambling. Minneapolis bookies set the football line—the point spread—for much of the country. The city government was widely believed to have an understanding with organized crime. This seedy alliance was brought into garish relief on January 15, 1945, when Arthur Kasherman, publisher of a scandal sheet that feasted on news of corruption in the Twin Cities, was gunned down late at night while parked in his car with a female companion (who was unscathed). Kid Cann, head of the Combination, was arrested and then released. The killer was never found. In March, the Social Club, one of the city's most notorious gambling joints, was finally closed down when federal immigration officers—not local cops—busted the place, finding one hundred men and women playing blackjack, faro, dice, and roulette.[4]

The citizens of Minneapolis were sick of being a national laughingstock. In the general election, facing Kline, Humphrey took off the gloves. Though he had no intention of running "a campaign of rumor or slander," as he put it, he had no scruple about reminding voters of the most sensational allegations against the incumbent. The week before the election, Humphrey delivered a speech on crime. In what had already become a pattern, the initial draft was terribly high-minded, opening with an explanation of the root causes of juvenile delinquency, before Humphrey thought better of it and decided to hammer Kline on corruption and vice. How was it, he asked, that the slots and the brothels dimmed their lights whenever a new grand jury was impaneled and then reopened when the heat was off? "What power waves the magic wand over the city?" he asked provocatively. "Is there an invisible government in Minneapolis—responsible to no one—that dictates what certain law enforcement policies should be?"[5] At times the challenger was even more explicit, charging that Kline was financing his campaign through "pay-off money from illegal gambling establishments."[6] Perhaps that was the influence of Humphrey's new friend and supporter Freddy Gates, a Runyonesque character who ran a penny arcade on Hennepin Avenue and knew everyone in the city's underworld; but Humphrey showed that he was not averse to going for the jugular.

Kline, increasingly desperate, responded with a public letter asserting the "known fact" that Humphrey had Communist support, and strongly implying that Humphrey himself was a closet Communist. In case that didn't stick, Kline also claimed that Humphrey had rigged his draft classification to allow him to run for office. Humphrey responded with a radio address. "I speak to you as a Scoutmaster," he huffed, before systematically taking the air out of Kline's allegations. The old wheelhorse never had a chance. On June 11, 1945, Humphrey became the youngest person ever elected as mayor of Minneapolis. He won by the largest margin in decades, taking twelve of the city's thirteen wards.

Freddy Gates, who looked to Humphrey to clean up the town, had offered him a tutorial in the tight links between organized crime, the police, and politicians. Humphrey got a taste of this unholy alliance even before he took office. A few days after the election he received a visit from Chickie Berman. Chickie's brother Dave ran the Syndicate in collaboration with Frank Costello, the famed New York mobster. "Whaddaya want?" Chickie bluntly asked the mayor-elect. "What's your proposition?" Humphrey responded. Berman suggested a 25 percent rake-off from the Syndicate's gambling operation—the standard split. "I don't think that's a good deal for me," Humphrey coolly rejoined. "Let's make it 75–25, my 75 and your 25." Berman cried, "My God, that would break us." "That's exactly right," said Humphrey—"and that's exactly what's going to happen to you." It is worth noting that this melodramatic and self-serving account comes not from Humphrey himself but from his aide William Simms, whom Humphrey had asked to sit in on the meeting.[7]

Humphrey saw that he would have to break a deeply entrenched culture. He found himself writing to the police chief, Elmer F. Hillner, to demand that he raid a brothel, or an illegal saloon, that he had previously brought to the chief's attention. "I insist that the night captain be reminded of his duty and that immediate action be taken," said a frustrated mayor.[8] The city charter empowered the mayor to appoint one, and only one, official—the police chief—though even that was subject to the approval of the city council. Humphrey needed to appoint a new chief who would not only take decisive action but signal to citizens that action was the new order of the day.

The new mayor found an ideal partner. A few years earlier, while at the WPA, Humphrey had worked with Ed Ryan, the head of the police department's internal security division. Ryan was a G-man who had trained with J. Edgar Hoover's FBI, then regarded as the gold standard of law enforcement. At six foot four and 225 pounds, Ryan looked the part. But he had lived in France before the war, spoke excellent French, and loved classical music. And he was, like his boss-to-be, a righteous man. Ryan had been bucked down to street cop after defending the right of fascist orator Gerald L. K. Smith—whose views he abhorred—to speak at the Minnesota Auditorium. Ryan was a dedicated anti-Communist who had arrested alleged subversives. Rather than make the appointment on his own, Humphrey set up a Law Enforcement Committee to recommend a chief, perhaps hoping that a consensus candidate might overcome the inevitable resistance in the city council to a police chief whom aldermen couldn't control.

The committee settled on Ryan. Humphrey used speeches and radio addresses to warn the council against tying his hands on law enforcement. After balking for a week, on July 11 the council confirmed the choice.

Ryan acted fast. On his first day in office he suspended an autocratic precinct chief. Ten days later, Detective Eugene Bernath, head of the morals squad, raided Jack's, a well-known gambling house. "The honeymoon is over," Ryan told reporters, lest the message had not yet gotten through. "The guillotine is now being readied. And we're not going to be too particular about whose head lands in the basket."[9] Through the summer and early fall, Ryan and Bernath shut down brothels, gambling houses, and illegal saloons. Bernath sent undercover investigators into burlesque shows. Humphrey had promised that he wouldn't turn Minneapolis into a "9:00 town," and police files show that citizens were not denied their constitutional right to a good time. An officer reported that after sitting through *Maid in the Ozarks*, a three-act play rife with "indecent gestures suggestive of strong sexual desire," he simply warned the producer to prohibit underage attendance and asked him to remove "some offensive portions."[10] The real goal was to drive organized crime out of town. On November 15, Chief Ryan declared that he had smashed the rackets that controlled illegal liquor distribution and nightclubs. That boast may have been premature. But by the time Humphrey left office, *The New Republic* was able to quote an FBI finding that there was "no organized vice in Minneapolis."[11]

No less important, at least politically, Humphrey had taken command of the city in a way mayors were not supposed to be able to do. He made crime control a personal crusade. At the end of his twelve-hour days, he sometimes rode in squad cars on the night shift, seeing for the first time the city's seedy nightlife and the squalor of its slums. He concluded that most of the cops were good men who took petty bribes because they were drastically underpaid. Humphrey's friend and aide Max Kampelman once saw him in a conference room outside his office speaking earnestly to bar owners and their wives. He knew, Humphrey said, that the police shook them down; if they would agree to pay more for their liquor licenses he could afford to raise the cops' salaries. The tavern owners fell silent, possibly, Kampelman thought, because they knew very well that it was the aldermen, not Humphrey, who controlled police salaries. Then Humphrey turned to the wives. "Don't you want your husbands involved in a legitimate business," he asked, "where policemen aren't bribed and you and your children don't have to fear being shamed by dishonor and dishonesty?" The appeal to better angels was pure Humphrey. "He had an instinct," Kampelman wrote, "for making change unthreatening and compromise tolerable."[12] The liquor licenses went from $1,000 to $1,200.

Everywhere he turned Humphrey ran into the limits of his authority. When he tried to revoke the liquor license of the Casablanca, scene of a gangland murder, the city attorney said the mayor had no power to do so. In order to get two new deputy inspectors appointed, he had to go through the city council's committees on Ways and Means, Personnel, Payrolls and Classifications, and Police. He pleaded with the head of Ways and Means to raise the ceiling of police personnel from 510, a very low number for a city of 500,000, and almost 100 fewer than the headcount of 1928, when the city had 68,000 fewer people. It would take the mayor two years of time-consuming struggle to increase the size of the force, modestly raise salaries, and institute a forty-hour week.

Kline may have protested too much, but it was true that Minneapolis was ungovernable by design. Even the aldermen didn't really control city affairs; much of the real budgeting and administrative authority lay with a series of commissions, pension funds, and boards—the Board of Education, the Board of Estimate, the boards of Parks, of Welfare, of Libraries. The various parts of the system seemed to have been assembled with the goal of diffusing authority and ensuring that no one would take responsibility for anything. And the aldermen, in league with both underworld figures and organized labor, had blocked all efforts to repair this creaky contraption. The city government was a self-perpetuating stalemate machine.

A different kind of politician would have cultivated the aldermen and probed the system's pressure points. Humphrey was neither that canny nor that cynical. Instead he formed a parallel government of his own. As a political scientist and a student of the New Deal, he believed in the application of expertise to government. He often said that planning was not a euphemism for "regimentation" but a recognition that complex problems required complex solutions. In his first year in office he formed mayor's committees on Health, Law Enforcement, Traffic Safety, Tax and Finance, Housing, and Civil Rights. These groups constituted a kind of mirror version of the municipal boards, with none of their actual power, but all the energy and the creativity they lacked. Committee members included academics, activists, professional practitioners, and leaders of influential groups, including labor and churches. Humphrey made a point of including all segments of society, including those thought to be antagonistic to one another. He believed that all could be coaxed into working for the common good—and that there was, in fact, a common good.

The most prominent of the committees was the Mayor's Council on Human Relations. Humphrey had suggested the idea in his inaugural speech before the city council, along with a pointed reminder about the war effort just concluded: "Let us not fail to remember that wherever dictatorship has gained control its first attack was on a racial or religious minority."[13] The reference to religion was not accidental. Minneapolis was a notoriously antisemitic town. In a 1946 article, journalist Carey McWilliams would describe the city as "the capital of anti-Semitism in the United States," a place where Jews not only could not join social clubs but were not accepted into civic groups such as the Rotary Club or the Elks, and were confined by real estate agents to all-Jewish neighborhoods.[14] Antisemitic incidents were common. On two separate occasions in the spring of 1945, groups of teenage boys had attacked Jews, in one case yelling, "Let's get the damn Jews!" The chief of the police department's Juvenile Division, insisting that no fight had taken place, released the suspects. Jewish residents of Minneapolis regarded both the beating and the official indifference as par for the course.[15]

Humphrey had spoken at every synagogue in Minneapolis multiple times. He understood the problems of the city's Jews, and he was determined to root out antisemitism. What was more remarkable was his equal concern for the plight of Black people. While

Minneapolis had a relatively large Jewish population of about twenty-five thousand, Black residents numbered only five or six thousand. Humphrey had nothing to gain by courting the Black vote. Race had never registered as an issue in municipal politics; the treatment of Blacks in Minneapolis was not significantly more disgraceful than it was elsewhere in the North, not to mention the South. Blacks were excluded from most unions, from most solid blue-collar jobs, and from virtually all white-collar professions. As late as 1939, 60 percent of the city's Black population was on welfare, though employment numbers improved significantly when white men went off to war.[16]

Yet Mayor Humphrey took on racism even more forcefully than he did antisemitism, and he did so through deeds as well as words. He paired Black and white officers on patrol. When he heard about a local café that refused to serve Black people, he invited William Seabron, head of the local Urban League, a civil rights organization, to join him there for lunch. Black people saw that the new mayor didn't behave toward them the way other white people did, and certainly the way city officials had in the past. In August 1945, officer Bernath of the morals squad raided the Dreamland, a Black-owned café, in the course of a murder investigation, hauled off two Black women who had no connection to the crime, and threw them in jail. Alerted by a call from Cecil Newman, founder and editor of the *Spokesman*, Humphrey hopped into a squad car, raced to the jail, and ordered Bernath, his right arm against vice, to release the women. The mayor then made sure he was seen taking Newman and the two women to an all-night café.[17] Newman later recalled that Humphrey never said "you people" when talking about Blacks. In fact, said Newman, Humphrey rarely singled out Blacks: "He talked about what we human beings, what we Americans, have to do." The two men had first met when Humphrey was working at the WPA, where Blacks had typically been denied access to white-collar jobs. "And he, very quietly, very effectively, saw that was straightened out," said Newman.[18] That was why the *Spokesman* had endorsed Humphrey in 1943.

Humphrey felt that he was simply applying the lessons he had learned from his father and from the scriptures. Yet he was also an avid consumer of the literature of civil rights. The collection of articles and pamphlets he would consult before writing a speech constitutes an informal record of enlightened mid-century attitudes. The file included pieces on the Jewish right to a homeland and the moral obligation to accept displaced persons, as well as speeches by Henry Wallace and Helen Gahagan Douglas, the outspoken anti-fascist congresswoman from California. Most involved issues of race. In "The Negro Wants Full Equality," Roy Wilkins, then the assistant secretary of the NAACP, wrote, "The Negro is here. He is thoroughly American. He thinks and lives in the American tradition." Humphrey also kept a copy of "The Bigot in Our Midst," by the psychologist Gordon Allport. A bigot, explained Allport, was one who "under the tyranny of his own frustrations, tabloid thinking and projection" finds a scapegoat to blame for his own sense of failure.[19] Racism was a form of irrational thinking that served a psychological need; unlike a brute calculation of self-interest, paranoia could be addressed, if painfully, by bringing the truth to the surface. Allport would later become renowned in the social sciences for his "contact hypothesis," which argued that bringing people into contact with disfavored groups could reduce prejudice.

Americans were just beginning to recognize the full horror of racism. Gunnar Myrdal's great work, *An American Dilemma*, was published in 1944. Myrdal was unsparing in his scrutiny of the "pathological" economic condition of Black Americans, as well as the consequences of paltry spending on their education, housing, and health care. ("The majority of the Negro population," Myrdal revealed to shocked readers, "suffers from severe malnutrition.")[20] Yet Myrdal did not despair of progress. Because even the most racist southerner believed in "the American Creed" of equality and individual liberty, he argued, he had had to convince himself of the racial inferiority of Blacks to justify the caste system within which he lived. The paradox—the dilemma—could not last. "The racial beliefs," Myrdal concluded, "have begun to be slowly rectified in the whole nation."[21] Humphrey appears not to have read *An American Dilemma* before 1948, yet he thought about American racism just as Myrdal and Allport did. In a 1947 speech he would talk about how we seek to rationalize our prejudice because we are troubled by our "American conscience."[22] For that very reason, Humphrey believed that exposing the reality of racism could go a long way toward erasing it.

Humphrey impaneled the Mayor's Council on Human Relations in February 1946. The group included businessmen, educators, union officials, left-wing activists, and one Black and one Jewish member. Humphrey cannily appointed as chairman the Reverend Reuben Youngdahl, brother of the state's Republican governor, Luther Young-dahl. The council produced theater pieces with titles such as "Tolerance Can Be Taught," as well as radio documentaries illustrating real-life cases of discrimination in housing and employment. It also took up a subject dear to the mayor's heart: the training of police in racial and religious sensitivity. Using a curriculum developed by the American Council on Race Relations, police officers were taught to examine what we would today call "unconscious bias," and to try to gain an understanding of the concerns of minority communities. They were also given specific guidance in preventing localized disturbances from escalating into race riots.[23]

In its most ambitious initiative, the council hired Black sociologist Charles Johnson to lead a "community self-survey" designed to disclose the ground truth of race relations in Minneapolis. Johnson and his colleagues at Fisk University enlisted and trained ordinary citizens to gather information, exposing volunteers to a reality few had known before. In the dead of winter in early 1947, five hundred people went out to interview white businessmen, doctors, ministers, and real estate agents, asking about what job or membership opportunities, if any, they offered to nonwhite and non-Christian citizens. They interviewed five hundred minority families about living conditions, police treatment, and the like. The self-survey demonstrated what was no surprise, that discrimination against Blacks was systematic, and intolerance toward Jews widespread. Nevertheless, the actual results mattered less than the experience of gathering them. The project brought whites into contact with Blacks, Christians with Jews, the well-off with the poor.

That said, these were strictly voluntary activities that suffered from the intrinsic shortcomings of such programs. The Human Relations Council rarely made progress when it met with local businessmen accused of discriminatory practices. And it made little headway when it sought to enlist the legal powers vested in the city council, which declined a proposal to deny permits to builders who insisted on restrictive housing covenants. The city council also refused to make the Human Relations Council an official body eligible for public funding. Humphrey always preferred the appeal to better angels to acts of coercion; but he learned that entrenched racial attitudes could not be dislodged through acts of enlightenment.

Indeed, he learned this lesson firsthand. In late 1946 Humphrey began receiving threatening letters, some from a neo-Nazi organization called the Democratic Nationalist Party. One vowed that he would "meet [his] just retribution" on "judgment day" if he did not stop promoting "Jewish Communist interests." Humphrey shrugged off the hate mail, but police officials insisted on parking a squad car manned by an armed officer outside his home. On February 6, 1947, as Humphrey returned home late at night and Muriel let him inside, a shot clanged off the house just above his head. Two more shots followed. Humphrey said nothing in public and remained nonchalant; an FBI investigation implicated a white supremacist in Minneapolis, but the suspect was never charged.[24] Humphrey's half-serious question to Art Naftalin five years earlier had proved to be not at all far-fetched.

Humphrey believed that tolerance could be taught, but he also believed that it needed to be legally mandated. In 1941 FDR had established a Fair Employment Practices Commission (FEPC) to outlaw job discrimination. Many civil rights leaders regarded it as the most progressive action taken at the federal level since the end of Reconstruction. But the FEPC had lapsed with the end of the war. A very few cities and states had created FEPCs of their own. Humphrey, determined to do so in Minneapolis, broached the idea in his inaugural address, and he and his aides worked out the language of a proposed ordinance to be submitted to the city council in the fall of 1945. The council debated the plan the following February, but it refused to adopt a version of the FEPC that prohibited private firms as well as government agencies from practicing job discrimination. Humphrey hammered away on the issue in public. According to an adulatory article by the trailblazing Black journalist Carl Rowan, a prominent Black leader told the mayor that since he had "all the colored vote," he could go easy on the FEPC, which wasn't going to gain approval in any case. (The unnamed figure was Cecil Newman.) Instead, Humphrey delivered a fifteen-minute radio address on the subject.[25] Finally, in January 1947, the council passed a strong version of the FEPC. Minneapolis became the first city or state in the country to establish a commission with the power to investigate complaints. Those found in violation of the ordinance could be fined $100 or sentenced to ninety days in jail.[26]

The city council, as always, did its best to hobble the new Commission on Fair Employment Practices, declining to approve its members until May, or to appropriate any funds at all until December. The commission's files show that by May 1948 it had received a grand total of twenty-one complaints of discriminatory practice. By the end of 1949, it had handled seventy-five complaints, though only in six cases did it resolve a complaint by securing employment or promotion. Humphrey tried to make the system work through suasion. He sent letters to local firms asking them to hire Black employees; he implored Donald Dayton, head of the local retail association, as well as of the department store that bore the family name, to urge his members to hire Black salesclerks. He personally thanked businessmen who had hired a single Black employee. Yet only seven had been hired by the time Humphrey left office.[27]

Nevertheless, Humphrey had changed the civil rights climate of Minneapolis, as he had changed the city's law and order climate. He had made it plain that discrimination was intolerable to a person of conscience. Of course he hadn't eliminated prejudice, but he had made it seem ignoble. Local civil rights organizations, including the Urban League, regarded Humphrey as the greatest champion they had ever had. And Humphrey had, in turn, placed Minneapolis in the front ranks of progressive cities. Cities around the country—though not in the South—wrote to city hall asking for a copy of the ordinance and requesting a visit from the mayor. Humphrey traveled to Washington to deliver testimony before the Senate Subcommittee on Labor and Public Welfare. He had elevated himself into the ranks of men such as New York's Fiorello La Guardia—big-city mayors in the New Deal mold.

Humphrey also made good on his promise to serve as an honest broker between management and labor. Minneapolis had a spectacular history of labor violence. In the first years of the twentieth century local businessmen had formed an organization called the "Citizens Alliance," whose purpose was to eradicate union sentiment and to smash strikes. As late as the 1920s the city had only about twenty-five thousand unionized employees. The rise of labor radicalism in the thirties hit Minneapolis hard. The Communist hard core was led by the five Dunne brothers, variously organizers, theoreticians, publicists, and muscle. In 1934 the Dunnes gained control of the Teamsters local and declared a strike that, in turn, provoked a series of bloody street battles with police officers and the private militia of the Citizens Alliance.[28] Employers were forced to recognize the union; Victor Dunne, the Twin Cities' leading Trotskyist, went on to recruit two hundred thousand members across the state. World War II produced a temporary truce, in Minneapolis and elsewhere, but labor unrest became endemic once wartime wage and price controls came to an end.

Humphrey, a union man, told Chief Ryan that he would not allow the police to be used against strikers without his express permission. But he also sympathized with employers; he was, as he often said, a small businessman himself. In 1947 Humphrey played a central role in settling a telephone workers strike and a truckers strike, earning respect from both sides. His most dramatic intervention came the following year, when the city's teachers walked off the job. The background to the strike had an only-in-Minneapolis quality. The city council had authorized a school budget of $13 million in 1948, but the board of education only had revenue of $11 million. The board had just agreed to grant teachers a sizable raise, but in December 1947 the board announced that instead it would reduce expenses by cutting one month from the school year, thus reducing teachers' salaries by almost 10 percent.

As soon as the teachers struck, in February 1948, Humphrey persuaded the city council to add another $2 million to the school budget; but the school board refused to accept the additional funds. Humphrey then wrote a furious letter accusing the board president, the Reverend Morris C. Robinson, of bad faith. Sending a copy of the letter to the head of one of the two teachers unions, Humphrey privately said that he had reason to believe that the board was open to reversing its decision and granting teachers a raise, though a more modest one than it had originally offered. Humphrey then sent a cable to both parties and the school superintendent proposing a five-person mediating team; he would, he threatened, appoint all five members himself if any of the parties refused. He acknowledged the obvious: he had "no legal authority to compel acceptance of this proposal." Nevertheless, no one else was stepping forward; and Humphrey knew that, three weeks into the strike, the pressure from enraged parents was growing intolerable. On March 22, the day he had set as his deadline, both parties agreed to a raise of $40 a month, near the upper limit of what Humphrey had predicted the teachers could get.[29] It had been a remarkable demonstration of fair-mindedness, persistence, and almost reckless brinksmanship.

The mayor was a one-man beehive. He worked sixteen-hour days, sometimes sleeping in the office. To one correspondent this father of three admitted—or rather, bragged—"I haven't been home for supper five times in three months."[30] Muriel not only raised the kids on her own, as many women of her generation did, but had to be ready when Humphrey called just before midnight to say he was coming back to their home in southeast Minneapolis for a late-night snack and palaver with Naftalin and Freeman and Kampelman. Humphrey resembled La Guardia, not only in his politics, but also in his ubiquity, for he seemed to see every sparrow that fell in Minneapolis, and to catch it before it hit the ground. He spent countless hours finding sublet apartments and Quonset huts and any other available dwelling for returning veterans who couldn't find a place to live. When Humphrey's milkman told him one morning about a single mother who was about to be evicted for nonpayment of rent, Humphrey raced across town and found the woman crying on the sidewalk. She explained that her husband was still in the service and her relief check hadn't arrived. Humphrey found the landlord and said, "I'm the

Mayor of Minneapolis. I'll guarantee the woman's rent payment."[31] Humphrey often said, "I love this city," and he seemed to include each of its citizens in his affections.

But Humphrey was never just a municipal fix-it man with a tool-kit on his belt; his vision was national. He fired off telegrams to Minnesota congressmen berating them for letting national price controls lapse when ten thousand veterans in the state were, he said, trying to get through college on a fixed income of $90 a month. Minnesota was one of only eight states that had no law authorizing public housing agencies, thus preventing municipalities from accessing federal housing funds. Humphrey wrote to state legislators begging them to pass such a law—which they finally did in July 1947. He dashed off telegrams to President Harry Truman and his cabinet members. During his time in office, he gave four hundred radio addresses and made about two thousand speeches. Humphrey didn't give speeches to win elections; he gave them because he could.

By the time he ran for reelection in the spring of 1947, Humphrey had become a human incarnation of postwar Minneapolis—progressive, optimistic, hardworking, clean-living, and relentlessly cheerful. He was voted Outstanding Young Man by the Junior Chamber of Commerce, and Man of the Year by the city's press. Humphrey's reelection committee included not only union leaders but also the head of the Minneapolis Chamber of Commerce and leading industrialists. He was endorsed by all the city's leading dailies. In the primary election, where winning an outright majority was almost unheard of, Humphrey took 62 percent of the vote. In the general election against Frank F. Collins, a sacrificial lamb chosen when no one more prominent would run, he took two-thirds of the vote and all thirteen of the city's wards. The editors of the *Minneapolis Star Tribune* wrote, "His vigor and persuasiveness have invested the office of mayor with a kind of civic leadership that it does not possess, under our archaic charter, except in the hands of a very able incumbent."[32]

That archaic charter became Humphrey's great white whale. Not only did the powerlessness of the mayoralty frustrate him at every turn, but his own background as a political scientist had given him insight into the importance of systems of governance. In November

1945 he had appeared before the Citizens Charter Commission, a clearinghouse for reform ideas, to advocate wholesale change in the charter. He proposed abolishing all boards save the board of education, reducing the city council in size, transferring the council's executive authority to the mayor while leaving it with legislative powers, and establishing a budgetary authority that would report to the mayor. He called his plan a "strong mayor–strong council" system. And he immediately ran into resistance, not only from aldermen and board officials, but from organized labor. The head of the Teamsters local told Humphrey bluntly that he never would have won labor support had he admitted his ambition to rewrite the rules of government—which he had not done.

Humphrey put his aide Arthur Naftalin in control of the Citizens Charter Commission. In February 1947 the commission published a draft charter incorporating most of Humphrey's earlier proposals. Under its terms, the mayor would serve for four years with a higher salary, enjoy veto power over council legislation, appoint all heads of departments and members of boards, and oversee the city's budgeting process. City government would have the authority to levy an income tax, which it did not then have. Outraged citizens wrote in complaining that the mayor would bleed them white; Humphrey (or an aide) wrote a personal response to each letter, a practice he would keep up for the rest of his career. He distributed a highly disingenuous memo to city employees insisting that he had had nothing to do with the proposal. And he laid down the law to critics who accused him of fomenting a coup d'état. To the head of the board of estimate, Humphrey wrote, "What in the dickens are you talking about when you say that the proposal of the Citizens Charter Commission for a central finance office means dictatorship and a political machine for the mayor? . . . That is a falsehood, and you are well enough informed about our city government to know it."[33] It was an early sign of just how tough Humphrey could be when he felt that he stood on the side of the angels (as he almost always did).

Nevertheless, Humphrey needed to placate organized labor—and he did. After George Phillips, head of the Central Labor Union, told the mayor that labor would not support the reform if the council was reduced in size, that proposal was eliminated from the final draft. At labor's behest, Humphrey postponed a referendum planned for early 1948. Despite his claim of an arm's-length relationship with the Citizens Commission, Humphrey wrote to the head of the group suggesting it take out a full-page ad rebutting the leading criticisms of the reform. But he never won over labor, and he never won over many liberals who feared a legislatively sanctioned "bossism." The referendum was not held until December 1948, by which time Humphrey's attention had turned elsewhere. The reform proposal was defeated.

Despite that failure, Humphrey had proved the claim that he had thrown in Mayor Kline's teeth in 1945: a mayor could get a lot done in Minneapolis if he wanted to. By acting as if he had powers that he did not in fact have, by forging his parallel government of experts and ordinary citizens, by seizing the bully pulpit, by working harder than any normal human being could, by believing in people perhaps more than they deserved, Humphrey had changed Minneapolis. He broke the grip of the rackets, reduced labor conflict, built public housing. He produced a new consensus behind his own progressive ideals and his commitment to civil rights. He left behind a generation of talented young men who had joined his campaigns or his government, and who would henceforth turn the city and the state into bastions of liberalism—Walter Mondale, the future senator; Orville Freeman, future governor and Kennedy cabinet member; Arthur Naftalin and Donald Fraser, both future mayors. They would perpetuate the progressive Minneapolis and Minnesota that Humphrey had done so much to bring into being.

Humphrey himself became a national figure. *The Nation* titled a profile "The Amazing Mr. Humphrey."[34] *The New Republic* tallied his impressive achievements before noting that critics accused the mayor of glibness. "But Humphrey is not shallow," the author concluded. "He has a well-knit liberal philosophy and an enormous affection for people. He has a powerful urge to right wrongs and plenty of streamlined ideas on how to do it."[35] As early as 1946, a Humphrey boomlet—probably set off by Arthur Naftalin—had the mayor replacing Henry Wallace as Truman's secretary of commerce. By the following year, his supporters were urging him to run for governor against the popular Luther Youngdahl. In June 1947 he wrote to his sister Frances to say that he had too much respect for Youngdahl to run against him, and had instead set his sights on the Senate seat occupied by Joseph Ball, a conventional Republican. The one man who believed in him most deeply imagined him scaling giddy heights. "I haven't given up thinking that something higher than Governor or Senator is in store for you," Hubert Sr. wrote in July. "Be prepared. You will be called to high office & duty."[36]

6

Fighting the Commies

"We are not prepared to see the century of the common
man become the century of the Comintern."

HUBERT HUMPHREY HAD RUN FOR MAYOR IN PART BECAUSE IT was a nonpartisan position: being a Democrat was not an impediment, as it would have been in any partisan election. He had then secured at least a potential political future by fusing the Democrats and Farmer-Labor. But he hadn't actually solved the underlying problem; his own path upward was still blocked so long as the Democratic-Farmer-Labor Party remained a Popular Front group sympathetic to communism. If he couldn't break the left's grip, Humphrey would have to resign himself to being Minneapolis's mayor-for-life.

While the undisputed master of Minneapolis, he remained a virtual pariah in the DFL. In March 1946, the Bensonite wing of the party had executed a coup by electing 120 of 160 delegates at the DFL convention for Hennepin County, which included Minneapolis and was thus by far the largest in the state. Humphrey lost his seat and attended the state convention in June at the St. Paul Hotel as an at-large delegate. There he discovered just how deep the schism between the liberals and the hard core of the left had grown. Though he was the keynote speaker, the mayor had to be escorted into the hall by his driver; he was greeted by jeers and cries of "fascist" and "war-monger." A sergeant-at-arms shouted at him, "Sit down, you son of a bitch, or I'll knock you down." Humphrey never got the chance to deliver the speech.[1] He did, however, persuade the forces on the left to make what must have seemed like a harmless concession, accepting his aide Orville Freeman as party secretary, and Eugenie Anderson, a delegate from the Mississippi River town of Red Wing and a new Humphrey ally, as second vice chair.

The Communists in Minnesota had followed the lead of the national party. The war years had forged virtually all elements of American society, including Communists once Hitler had invaded the Soviet Union, into a single fighting mass. In May 1944 the Communist Party of the United States—or CPUSA—had announced that it had ceased domestic political activities in order to support the Allied effort. That sense of solidarity could not survive the victory. For the Communists, struggle was perpetual and endemic; but what had provoked the crisis was, first, the replacement of FDR, Stalin's great partner, by Harry Truman, regarded on the left as a cat's paw of the forces of reaction, and then the collapse of the postwar spirit of comity, once Stalin had installed a puppet government in Poland. On March 5, 1946, British prime minister Winston Churchill declared that an "iron curtain" was falling across Europe. Only a year before, Communist front organizations such as the National Citizens Political Action Committee, as well as the Communist-influenced unions within the CIO, had celebrated Truman as a hero of the fight against fascism; now they damned the United States as the center of world reaction.[2]

In the summer of 1946, Eugenie Anderson invited Humphrey, Art Naftalin, and Evron Kirkpatrick to Red Wing to meet James Loeb, a prominent Washington figure. Loeb was president of the Union for Democratic Action (UDA), a liberal anti-Communist group. In May,

Loeb had written a letter to *The New Republic* calling on progressives to leave Popular Front coalitions that welcomed Communists, who, he said, could not be trusted to accept the rules of democratic politics, and thus would eventually engulf their rule-abiding coalition partners.[3] He might as well have been talking about the DFL. When she learned that Loeb was vacationing nearby, Anderson invited him over to meet Minnesota's leading liberal anti-Communists. Loeb expounded his views to an audience already primed to agree.

Humphrey had always thought of himself as both a "liberal" and a "progressive"; so, too, had Loeb, along with such founding figures of the UDA as theologian Reinhold Niebuhr. In their lexicon, liberals descended from a Jeffersonian tradition that prized individual political rights, while progressives, whose more recent lineage ran back to Lincoln and then to Teddy Roosevelt, used the language of economic and social rights. FDR had proved that you could be both—that was the premise of Humphrey's master's thesis. But figures on the left increasingly questioned the Rooseveltian synthesis. And the most important figure driving a wedge between the two sides was, shockingly, Henry Wallace. This new-generation prairie populist had become the spokesman of the small farmer—the Jeffersonian yeoman—as editor of his family's publication, *Wallace's Farmer*. Wallace was gaunt, austere, strangely withdrawn, intellectually fierce, a voice distilled as if by fire—just the kind of figure to appeal to both generations of Humphreys. As FDR's secretary of agriculture, Wallace had drawn up the Agricultural Adjustment Act, making him a hero to farmers second only to FDR himself. He had stuck by Roosevelt as other cabinet members had decamped, and in 1940 the president chose him as running mate.

In an interview many years later, Humphrey said that he had regarded Wallace as "a very good friend." He had invited Wallace to his home on his swings through Minneapolis.[4] "No man," Humphrey wrote, "seemed more closely aligned with the Midwest, with the Populist liberals, Farmer-Laborites, Nonpartisan Leaguers, and ardent New Dealers than Wallace."[5] In February 1944 Humphrey had had the great honor of introducing Vice President Wallace to a crowd of eight thousand at the Minneapolis Armory, where Wallace had congratulated him and his allies on the DFL fusion.[6] But, unlike FDR, and unlike Humphrey, Wallace believed that Soviet totalitarianism posed far less of a threat to the United States than did American anti-communism. Throughout 1943 and 1944 he delivered fiery speeches warning that the forces of capital were plotting to wreck the New Deal. He predicted that World War III would break out if "fascist interests motivated largely by anti-Russian bias get control of our government."[7] Whatever his differences with businessmen, the president did not consider them a fascist fifth column; he came to regard Wallace as a liability and a dangerously loose cannon. Thus he had made sure that Truman, rather than Wallace, would serve as his running mate in 1944. Humphrey was bitterly disappointed; he wrote Wallace to express dismay over the eclipse of the "one world" vision they shared, and to reassure him that "We"—the progressive forces in Minnesota—"are looking forward to having you as our presidential standard-bearer in 1948."[8]

Progressives prevailed on FDR to make Wallace his secretary of commerce. When the president died in April 1945, many looked to Wallace as their new leader. Wallace viewed himself in the same light. And with the war over, and the breach between Washington and Moscow growing, he made a concerted, and completely unsuccessful, effort to persuade Truman that Moscow was not to blame for the Cold War. Wallace finally brought his private beliefs to the public in a speech sponsored by leading Popular Front groups at Madison Square Garden September 12, 1946. Explaining that he was "neither anti-Russian nor pro-Russian," just as he was "neither anti-British nor pro-British"—placing adversary and ally on the same moral plane—Wallace called on the United States to concede Eastern Europe to Russia as its own legitimate sphere of influence.[9] Wallace had, in fact, cleared the speech in advance with Truman, who must have given it a very cursory read. What's more, Wallace had left out some significant criticisms of the Soviets at the urging of his left-wing hosts. Nevertheless, Truman promptly fired him.

Wallace was no Communist, but he had defined himself as anti-anti-Communist, just as many nonparty members on the left did. Humphrey recalled being "shocked" to hear from Wallace the kind of pro-Soviet apologetics that had become common currency on the DFL left. Though he received a number of letters from progressives imploring him to protest the sacking, Humphrey instead wrote to President Truman congratulating him on the appointment of New York's Averill Harriman to replace Wallace.[10] Six weeks after the Madison Square Garden speech, Wallace came to Minneapolis on a speaking tour. Humphrey, who had not yet given up on his champion, pulled him aside for an hour-long conversation about the rising Communist influence inside the DFL. Wallace, he recalled, was "incredulous," and "said that we must not tolerate it." In fact, Wallace's scorn for anti-communism had made him captious in the face of such claims. At a luncheon speech that day he defined a Communist as "a Democrat seeking a job that a Republican wants." The next morning Humphrey found the former vice president at breakfast soaking up adulation from the very party members he had warned him about.[11] "Anyone who works for peace is okay with me," he said.

Wallace's attack on America's world standing, as well as his defense of Soviet control of Eastern Europe, was profoundly orienting for Humphrey, and indeed for a whole generation of liberals who had emerged from World War II with deep feelings of reverence for the United States and the democratic values it embodied. In a series of articles in *Politics*, the essayist Dwight Macdonald lampooned Wallace as a "corn-fed mystic" who "thinks of himself as . . . an instrument through which God will guide America onward and upward."[12] Humphrey denounced Wallace's implicit acceptance of "spheres of influence." In a letter, he compared Wallace's concession of Eastern Europe to the Soviets to Neville Chamberlain's surrender of Czechoslovakia to Hitler.[13] The comparison of the Soviets to the Nazis would have been profoundly odious to the DFL's left wing, which regarded American capitalism as an evil almost equal to Nazism. But as news of Stalin's show trials and mass liquidations began to appear in the West, liberals increasingly spoke of a totalitarianism of the left as well as the right. (Hannah Arendt would publish *The Origins of Totalitarianism*, which makes this argument, in 1951.)

This was precisely the issue that Jim Loeb had broached with Humphrey and his circle that summer. Loeb was one of those invaluable people who combine intellectual depth with organizational skills and sound instincts for people. Humphrey had impressed him; by that time, after all, the young mayor of Minneapolis had earned a national reputation as a fearless urban reformer and advocate of civil rights. In mid-November, Loeb wrote to Humphrey to say that he and a group of colleagues, including historian Arthur Schlesinger Jr., labor leader Walter Reuther, and *New York Post* editor James Wechsler, had begun working out the details of a "thoroughly liberal and non-Communist program." They would be meeting in Washington in January, and were "extremely anxious for you to join us." Loeb was, in fact, so ardent about Humphrey that he wrote separately to Arthur Naftalin to ask him to urge Humphrey to come. "My own opinion," wrote this preeminent talent spotter of political activism, "is that Mayor Humphrey is one of the most promising political figures in the country."[14]

Loeb and his crowd feared that liberals would be swallowed up by Popular Front leftism unless they explicitly stood against it. That worry became all too plausible in the last days of 1946 when the nation's leading Popular Front groups merged to form the Progressive Citizens of America (PCA), a political party in embryo. The anti-Communist liberals convened in Washington just a week later, on January 4, 1947. Humphrey never made it: the Minneapolis airport was snowed in, and he contented himself with sending a cable listing the domestic issues he hoped the meeting would take up—a permanent Fair Employment Practices Commission at the federal level, new programs in public health, education, research, and so on. Among the 150 figures who gathered that day were most of America's leading thinkers and actors on the center-left: in addition to Loeb, Niebuhr, Wechsler, Reuther, and Schlesinger, they included the labor leader David Dubinsky, the journalists (and brothers) Stewart and Joseph Alsop, the economist John Kenneth Galbraith, and, most important of all, former First Lady Eleanor Roosevelt, perhaps the most admired person in the country at that moment. They agreed to dissolve the UDA in favor of a new organization, Americans for Democratic Action (ADA), which would actively promote a liberal anti-Communist program, though without seeking to organize a third political party. Henry Wallace, now the editor of *The New Republic* and a fervent supporter of the PCA, felt sufficiently threatened by the new alignment that he foolishly wrote that "Eleanor Roosevelt, to the best of my knowledge, is not a member or an officer of the ADA." Loeb gleefully responded that she was both.[15] The struggle between these two factions would determine the future of left-of-center politics in America.

At the end of March, the ADA convened to draw up a plan of action and elect officers. Humphrey was chosen as one of six vice chairmen. The mayor attended along with Art Naftalin and Eugenie Anderson. In its official statement, the ADA organizing committee asserted that peace and prosperity "could be achieved by economic planning, the enlargement of fundamental liberties and international cooperation." That was a blunt message to free-market conservatives who did not consider economic planning to be consistent with fundamental liberties—a claim that economist Friedrich Hayek had famously advanced in his 1944 polemic, *The Road to Serfdom*. The group's constitution also included an explicit statement to the left-wingers who had joined the PCA: "No person who is a member of or a follower of any totalitarian organization or who subscribes to totalitarian beliefs may become a member of Americans for Democratic Action."[16]

Was that Cold War paranoia, or perhaps hyperbole? Membership in the CPUSA certainly never exceeded one hundred thousand or so; few adherents of the PCA were party members. Yet Communists had gained control over key institutions in unions, on magazine staffs, and in left-wing lobbying groups; and party members, in the United States and elsewhere, were answerable to Moscow. Philip Murray, head of the CIO and a founding member of the ADA, concluded that the increasingly strident and anti-American Communist line left him no choice but direct confrontation. "If Communism is an issue in any of your unions," Murray told the CIO executive board in July 1947, "throw it to hell out."[17] The DFL may have had no more than three hundred party members in its ranks, yet by late 1946 they had gained effective control over the party—an extraordinary situation in postwar America. Eugenie Anderson would later observe that while the number of independent radicals vastly outnumbered party members, the ability of Communists to control the DFL "was a very good demonstration of how a minority can control a majority, if the minority knows what it wants and is willing to use almost any tactics."[18]

How, then, to drive the totalitarians from the party? At first Humphrey turned to the Democratic National Committee. He began writing to DNC chairman and Postmaster General Robert Hannegan in February 1947 but heard nothing back. In June he wrote to Gael Sullivan, the party's executive secretary, stating flatly that no Democrat was going to get elected until the Bensonites had been sent packing. "We need organizers," Humphrey desperately wrote in September. "We need money." But the party had no wish to wade into the state's internecine warfare. "I have something to contribute in politics," a furious Humphrey wrote back to Sullivan. "I believe that I have made sufficient contacts throughout the country so that my presence within the Democrat party is of some little importance."[19] Humphrey would continue sending these letters throughout 1947; at times Sullivan wrote or cabled back promising action, but the DNC never lifted a finger on Humphrey's behalf.

But if Humphrey couldn't make use of his own party, he could turn to the ADA. Minnesota had formed one of the first, best-organized, and best-funded chapters of the organization. It was a Humphrey operation, led by Anderson, Naftalin, and Freeman. The first state treasurer was Eugene McCarthy, then a young professor at St. John's College. From the outset, Humphrey and his allies regarded the ADA as a kind of disciplined cadre that could infiltrate and then conquer the DFL. On January 20, days after the chapter had been organized, Walter C. Lundberg, the chairman of the state ADA political committee, wrote to Freeman deprecating the obvious path of "education and lobbying" as hopelessly ineffective in the face of an entrenched adversary. Instead he suggested an effort to "completely displace the present leadership of the DFL," and then openly disavow the Communists. It won't take many people, Lundberg wrote in the tones of a devout Leninist, but they must be highly disciplined and completely loyal.[20] The ADA cadre would do to the Communists what the Communist cadre had done to the DFL.

Humphrey was still a nobody in the Democratic Party, but he was increasingly becoming the public face of the ADA. In July, Loeb wrote to ask if he would work his magic on the hustings. "Our chapters are extremely anxious to know you, to hear you and to exploit you," Loeb asserted. He promised that the exploitation would be mutual: "The attendant public relations would be helpful all the way around." That summer Humphrey went out to San Francisco and spoke to the faithful. The ADA couldn't offer Humphrey money, but it could help in other ways. In September Humphrey sent a cable to Leon Henderson, the ADA founding chairman, asking for material for an upcoming speech on price controls. Henderson sent back a draft of a speech along with a note that he had persuaded a columnist in *The Nation* to write a piece about the address.[21] The ADA also offered Humphrey a kind of postgraduate education on the fly. At the September meeting of the national board, Arthur Schlesinger outlined the main conclusions of the foreign policy report he was then drawing up. When Humphrey returned to Minneapolis, he sent Schlesinger a mash note in the usual effusive Humphrey style, recalling how he had read and reread a piece the Harvard scholar had written the year before in *Life* magazine making the case for a liberal postwar foreign policy.[22]

It was foreign rather than domestic policy that separated ADA liberals from PCA progressives; and 1947 was the year in which Harry Truman determined American Cold War policy for the next generation. In April, deeply concerned about Soviet advances in southern Europe and the Balkans as British forces withdrew, he asked Congress to provide $400 million in economic and military assistance to Greece and Turkey. Although the president declared that the United States would support "free peoples who are resisting attempted subjugation by armed minorities or by outside pressures," neither the Greeks nor the Turks could seriously be described as free.[23] Many liberals recoiled at what came to be known as the Truman Doctrine, but two months later, Secretary of State George Marshall announced a massive, multiyear effort to rebuild the shattered states of Europe through an unprecedented program of economic assistance. This was the Marshall Plan, which over the next four years would provide more than $15 billion to the former Allies in Western Europe. The program was liberal foreign policy writ large, and retrospectively cast the Truman Doctrine as the hard edge of a broad program of democratic revival. Schlesinger's foreign policy report concluded that the Truman Doctrine conformed to the principles of "containment" laid down the year before by diplomat George Kennan, but added that the commitment must not become a blank check for anti-Communist regimes. The report celebrated the Marshall Plan and urged the Truman administration to spend whatever it took to rebuild Europe.

Hubert Humphrey had no doubt where he stood: communism was fascism in left-wing clothing. "The police state is the police state," he said when the ADA national board debated its position on Truman's foreign policy. Too many people "are not clear in their own mind that the Communist state is of the menacing proportions of the fascist state."[24] Henry Wallace, by contrast, erupted in prophetic fury. In Truman's America, he forecast, "liberties will be restricted; standards of living will be forced down; families will be divided against each other; none of the values that we held worth fighting for will be secure."[25] The Marshall Plan did not mollify him. Because the Soviet Union and the Eastern bloc states were not included, Wallace blasted the program as "the Martial Plan."

The battle lines were now sharply drawn both nationally and locally. The PCA was sending professional organizers into Minnesota with the expectation that Wallace would run on a party ticket. Humphrey would have no chance of beating Joe Ball, the Republican Senate incumbent up for reelection in 1948, if he couldn't first break the left-wing stranglehold on the DFL. In October, mayoral aide George Demetriou sent letters to the editors of *The World Telegram* and *The New Leader* in New York asking for dirt on Sam K. Davis, editor of the pro-Communist CIO paper, *Minnesota Labor*. Davis had run for governor of Minnesota on the Communist Party line in 1934. However, said Demetriou, "We lack further damaging evidence as to his party affiliations."[26] (This may have been an oblique reference to information in FBI files that Humphrey had access to as mayor.) Demetriou was not a man given to subtlety: the following March he would write to James Wechsler requesting "a brief bibliography of what a man who wants to smear Henry Wallace ought to read."[27]

Humphrey had never fought this way—not on the football field, and not against Marvin Kline. But then he had been fighting for himself; now he was waging a holy war against what he considered a supreme evil. He had been raised to regard such a battle as the greatest good of a man's life. His father had never fought an adversary more dangerous than an out-of-town power company; but perhaps he wished he had. Humphrey had found a dragon worth slaying. The fact that his own political future hung in the balance only intensified his sense of self-righteousness.

Throughout the spring and summer, Orville Freeman had used his position inside the DFL to establish a Young DFL chapter at the University of Minnesota and to recruit hundreds of young people, including Macalester undergraduates Walter Mondale and Donald Fraser. At the Young DFL state convention in November, the anti-Communist Freemanites outshouted a rival slate and gained control of the youth wing of the party. Humphrey delivered one of his rafter-raising speeches. Asked whether he believed that the left faction were Communist Party members, he cracked, "Well, if they're not members, they are cheating it out of dues money."[28]

Freeman was precisely the kind of disciplined and driven figure Walter Lundberg had in mind for his coup d'état. Hardened by his service in the Pacific, this bespectacled young lawyer had the decisiveness of a natural leader. Unlike Humphrey, who would bring out the knife only with his back to the wall, Freeman had the kind of hot temper that sought confrontation. In 1946 he had called a DFL candidate for Congress a secret Communist. Himself ambitious for office, Freeman recruited allies by promising a fight to the death against the Commies.[29] No less important, as DFL secretary he had access to the party's records and the activities of local branches. He, Naftalin, and Anderson, often joined by Humphrey himself, drove across the state to attend meetings of party committees, many of them in the grip of the Communist hard-liners. There they would call on their local supporters. The liberals would call for a vote and then use their superior numbers to oust the officeholders. "The Communists fought back hard," Humphrey fondly recalled years later. "But if they stayed up until midnight, we stayed up until 3 A.M. If they issued five press releases, we put out ten. . . . It was tough, and sometimes the fight got dirty. But we were just as tough as the Communists were—and sometimes just as mean."[30]

On December 7, the DFL's executive committee struck back, adopting a resolution directly addressing the divisions. The resolution asserted that in order to win the party's nomination for Senate, Humphrey had begun organizing "disgruntled and discredited forces," and "injecting factional strife where agreement on principles prevailed." A later statement accused the mayor of cozying up to industrialists, which was certainly true, and of favoring a "dictatorship charter," which was just as clearly false.[31] Humphrey saw that, for once, he had no reasonable middle ground to occupy. Throughout this period, he had been getting anguished letters from non-Communist leftists imploring him to heal the breach between the two sides. Now, when he received yet another two days after the December 7 blast, Humphrey responded with a snarl. "I think it's about time that I count my friends," he shot back, adding, "either people are for me or they're against me." Referring to a congressman sympathetic to the left, he wrote, "If Blatnik's supporters are going to knife me, I'm going to let my supporters do as they see fit in retaliation."[32]

By now the gentlemanly mayor was wielding a stiletto of his own. Senator Howard McGrath of Rhode Island had now become DNC chairman, and in the first days of the new year Humphrey sent him a furious five-page letter accusing state party officials of standing aside while calumnies were hurled at him. Humphrey really was a rising star in the party, and it's not clear why neither Steven Harrington, the state finance head, nor Harold Barker, state party chair, had lifted a finger in his behalf. Either Harrington "gets right by Humphrey," the mayor fumed, "or I am going to do everything I can to play a lone game of complete independence with no obligations whatsoever to either the Administration or the National Committee." Sullivan once again promised to iron out the problem but to no avail. Humphrey thus found himself fighting both the left-wing ideologies and the party professionals.[33]

Victory or defeat in the party civil war would be determined by an otherwise inconsequential event: the DFL precinct caucuses, which were to be held April 30, 1948. The delegates chosen there would meet at county conventions, where they would in turn choose the delegates to the state convention as well as to ones held in each of Minnesota's eight congressional districts. The district conventions would choose candidates for congressional races while at the state level candidates for state offices, as well as delegates to the national party convention, would be selected. In short, whoever won the battle at the precinct level would control the party—the one and only party in the country that would pit the Popular Front forces against the anti-Communist ones. Throughout late 1947 and early 1948, Eugenie Anderson and Orville Freeman had been using their position inside the DFL to recruit local leaders to their side. On February 20 they sprang a trap from the leftists' own playbook, calling a meeting of the normally moribund Central Committee. The meeting allowed the Humphrey-ites to gain control of the party structure, and thus to determine the calendar and shape the process for the selection of delegates.[34] The DFL apparatus had now fallen into the grasp of the ADA: all but one committee member belonged to the state body.

It is hard to fathom just how many levels Humphrey was now operating on simultaneously. As the mayor of a city of five hundred thousand souls he carried out his tasks with a zeal that consumed most of his waking hours. At the state level, he was fighting a do-or-die battle for the soul of his party. And as the vice chairman of the ADA and a leading voice of liberalism, he was playing an increasingly prominent role in national politics. In January 1948, Max Lerner, editor of *PM*, wrote to congratulate Humphrey on "being boomed for the Vice-Presidency." But the liberals increasingly regarded Truman as dead weight. The disaffection was in part ideological: the president had never been able to overcome his reputation as a machine pol despite his genuine commitment to the New Deal agenda. The FDR men who had at first surrounded him had dropped off one by one. But the real problem was political, for by the spring of 1948 Truman's approval rating had fallen to 36 percent. In a letter to Jim Loeb March 24, Humphrey wrote of "the subject everyone is talking about": "How can we peacefully and effectively get rid of our present incumbent. There is no enthusiasm for Truman out here." He posed the same question to ADA chair Leon Henderson and to Chester Bowles, a Truman economic official and leading liberal thinker.[35]

Politicians always panic when their president's ratings go south in advance of an election. But the presence of a powerful third-party candidate—and one who had bolted the Democratic Party—vastly increased the anxiety level. On December 29, 1947, in a fiery denunciation of Truman's Cold War policy, Henry Wallace had declared that he would run for president at the head of the New Party, sponsored by the PCA. No well-informed person believed that Wallace could be elected president; a poll the previous fall found that 62 percent of Americans thought Truman had been "too soft" on the Soviets while only 6 percent shared Wallace's claim that he had been "too tough."[36] But even a 6 percent shift could both elect a Republican and, what was yet more disturbing, reduce liberalism to a splinter of a fragmented left. It was the imperative to shore up the president's left flank that produced the Humphrey vice presidential boomlet. In late 1947, Leon Henderson had sent Humphrey a letter reporting that Ed Flynn, the Tammany boss who controlled much of New York's Democratic Party, insisted that Truman could only be reelected with a real liberal as his running mate. "This," Henderson wryly noted, "offered an opportunity to speak about the Mayor of Minneapolis about whom Ed has heard and about whom he wanted to hear more."[37] Humphrey was the bright young star everyone wanted to know. In late January, when Humphrey made a trip to Washington, the ADA arranged a lunch for him at the Mayflower Hotel with the journalists who shaped opinion in the nation's capital: Stewart Alsop, Fred Friendly, James Wechsler, Richard Strout of the *Christian Science Monitor,* and Ernest Lindley of *Newsweek,* the author of an FDR biography Humphrey knew well.

In the first days of spring, Humphrey and the ADA tried to lay the groundwork to dump Truman. The two leading candidates for a draft were former general Dwight D. Eisenhower and Supreme Court Justice William O. Douglas. Eisenhower's views and even party affiliation were unknown, while Douglas was a crusading liberal; neither had expressed any interest in running for office. Humphrey focused his attention on Douglas, who had been born in Minnesota. He wrote to him on April 1 to invite him to address the state ADA. Douglas declined, but said he was eager to meet the ADA vice chair. The following week Humphrey sent a cable to Leon Henderson urging the ADA not to endorse Truman but instead to issue a call to "leading progressives" to declare their candidacy. In mid-April the organization formally resolved to back no candidate for the Democratic nomination, and soon issued buttons saying, "Draft Eisenhower Douglas."[38]

The battle raging inside the left would have its first test in the DFL caucuses. Henry Wallace signified the state's importance by naming Elmer Benson himself as his national campaign chairman. In the middle of April, Senator Glen Taylor of Idaho, Wallace's running mate, paid a three-day visit to the state to rally supporters in advance of the caucuses. Humphrey responded by raising the pressure on fence-sitters, writing a series of letters to local officials who had allowed their names to be listed as members of a Wallace front group. He offered to help them draft a letter of resignation. In a message to "DFL Liberals," he declared that if the left carried the caucuses, "the Communist Party will have in Minnesota and the nation a 'front' organization that will command a wide hearing because it will bear the name of a major party." Humphrey practically begged Steven Harrington, the state party finance head, to fund a countereffort, but by now Humphrey was seen as a leading anti-Truman schismatic. He wrote yet again to Gael Sullivan denying the allegation while conceding that he did believe the Democratic convention should be allowed to nominate whomever it preferred.[39]

On April 23 Humphrey took to the airwaves to announce what everyone in Minnesota politics already knew—that he was challenging Joseph Ball for the Senate seat. After attacking Ball as an isolationist, he immediately turned to Ball's "new and strange ally," a third party on the far left. "We, too, believe in the century of the common man," said Humphrey, alluding to the title of Henry Wallace's most famous speech. "But we are not prepared to see the century of the common man become the century of the Comintern." That was a kidney punch to a man who not long before had been Humphrey's hero. The caucuses would be held in seven days, and Humphrey used the speech to once again mobilize his forces inside the party. "Our people," he cried, "believe in a militant and vigorous democratic program of the middle—a program of political freedom for ourselves and other people and economic opportunity for mankind everywhere." He advocated a program of decisive action on civil rights, economic growth, defense spending, and health and welfare.[40] A few days later Humphrey wrote to Jim Loeb to ask him to persuade James Wechsler or syndicated columnist Drew Pearson to write about his campaign. Loeb, in turn, agreed to lend him an ADA political operative and to put him together with potential financial backers in New York.[41]

By this time Humphrey and his lieutenants had built what was in effect an undeclared statewide political party in the form of the ADA. The Hennepin County branch—the heart of the organization—circulated a set of instructions to all members. "Determine immediately what ward and precinct you live in," members were instructed. Then they should contact their ward chairmen, who would in turn put them in contact with their precinct captains. "Have your friends in for coffee or for an evening. Talk politics with them; find out where they stand." Once they had recruited a critical mass of sympathizers for their precincts, they were to elect officers. Each group would hold pre-caucus preparations on April 23. At 7:00 p.m. on the 30th, the groups were to meet prior to going en masse to the caucus. Once the meeting began, members were instructed, they had to insist on a fair election and then see that correct forms were filled out immediately. They should prepare to stay until midnight, "because *delay* is a typical Communist tactic."[42]

Humphrey's team of young idealists proved to have more passion, and more staying power, than the forces on the left. The liberals won smashing victories in St. Paul and Duluth. In Minneapolis, the Bensonites contested the legitimacy of the liberal gathering, holding caucuses of their own. But Humphrey's confederates vastly outnumbered them; the *Star Tribune* reported that in the second ward alone, four hundred supporters jammed the Labor Temple, where they were greeted by the mayor himself.[43] The following week, state ADA secretary Doris Tuller sent an exuberant report to Leon Henderson outlining the magnitude of the victory. ADA activists had captured virtually every county organization; since the left-wingers had all been pledged to Wallace, the DFL delegation at the national convention would be

almost unanimously pledged to support a Democrat. The Humphrey-
ite victory had vindicated liberalism itself, just as Humphrey had said
it would.[44]

The county organizations met May 14, and Mayor Humphrey
delivered a rousing keynote address to the Hennepin County DFL
(minus the leftists, who held a separate caucus). "We have not been
willing for the sake of what some people would call unity," he cried,
"to sell our principles and our belief in the fundamental principles of
democracy." When the state convention met a month later in Brain-
erd, Humphrey had to wait until the Credentials Committee, controlled by his loyalists, approved his Hennepin County delegation.
Then the convention, and the party, were his. He got Orville Freeman
approved as the new party chairman, prevailed on delegates not to
endorse Truman for president, and then, face flushed and tie askew,
delivered his acceptance speech after the party nominated him for the
Senate. He offered one of his history lessons on the development of
progressivism in Minnesota, urged his listeners to reject the politics
of revolution and of reaction, and then turned to his own upcoming
Senate campaign. In the one passage that made the papers the next
day, Humphrey shouted, "It'll be a campaign long to be remembered.
Win lose or draw, I guarantee the opposition they'll know they've
been someplace and been in a fight. Let's not spare the horses."[45] He
went on so long that he was forced to say, "Well, folks, just as I get
warmed up, what do they do to me? They tell me two more minutes,
and I have so much to tell these delegates . . ."

Hubert Humphrey had now been launched into orbit. He had
reached the upper atmosphere thanks to the efforts of a new generation of well-educated and deeply dedicated young liberals. They had
proved that idealists didn't have to be patsies, that they could beat the
leftists at their own game, that the place in between revolution and
reaction was not a sterile middle ground but, in a phrase Humphrey
had begun to use, a "vital center." They had replaced both the doc-
trinaire leftists of Farmer-Labor and the ward heelers of the Democratic Party. Minnesota became liberal in 1948; so it would remain
thereafter.

7

The Bright Sunshine of Human Rights

"For me personally, and for the party, the time had come to suffer whatever the consequences."

THE DEMOCRATIC PARTY IN 1948 HAD DOMINATED NATIONAL politics for almost sixteen years, the longest tenure by either party since the Republicans in the second half of the nineteenth century. But Truman's dismal poll numbers had convinced both liberal activists and party professionals that the string was about to be snapped. While many of them hoped to find a replacement for Truman in the upcoming campaign, they expected a Republican sweep. This dire prospect raised a fundamental question for Hubert Humphrey and his colleagues at Americans for Democratic Action: What was the future of liberalism in a post-FDR world? How could liberalism survive in a Democratic Party pulled to the right by its southern base and to the left by the forces around Henry Wallace? On March 2, Humphrey wrote to Chester Bowles with a desperate plea: "The ADA must do something to gain a reputation for being a spearhead of progressive thought." Three weeks later, he wrote to Leon Henderson, the ADA's chair, suggesting that that something was civil rights. A "bold stand," he said, just might "liberalize the Southern Democratic party." Even if it didn't, he added, "perhaps defeat in 1948 is not too big a price to pay for that."[1]

Humphrey's friends had been thinking along the same lines. On April 14, Jim Loeb wrote him to say, "Whether or not HST is the Democratic candidate, it seems to us absolutely essential that the civil rights issue be defended at the National Convention." Would Humphrey be willing to send out a letter cosigned by two or three other senior figures asking party leaders to pledge themselves to a forceful civil rights plank in the party platform?[2] The request itself shows the extraordinary place in the liberal firmament this big-city mayor had reached. Humphrey's willingness to lead this effort would make his reputation as a crusader for justice.

Civil rights were the great unfinished business of the Democratic Party, as well as its decisive fault line. For reasons both moral and political, Democrats could no longer put off an issue they had ignored even as they had become the party of the common man. The modern Democratic Party had, of course, evolved from the party of slavery and of violent resistance to Reconstruction. It long remained in thrall to the South. Forty percent of the votes for Grover Cleveland in 1892 and for Woodrow Wilson in 1912 had come from the South. Since Blacks in the South were prevented from voting, those votes were virtually all white. Despite FDR's smashing victory in 1932, Southern Democrats controlled the key legislative committees and refused to endorse legislation that would weaken the economic dependence of Blacks on whites that underpinned the Jim Crow system. In private, the president didn't bother to sugarcoat the harsh reality. He told Walter White of the NAACP, "If I come out for the anti-lynching bill, they will block every bill that I ask Congress to pass to keep America from collapsing. I just can't take that risk."[3]

Civil rights was a peripheral issue even for dedicated liberals in the 1930s; Humphrey did not mention the question in "The Political Philosophy of the New Deal." Liberals thought about issues of class rather than race. Yet by the 1940s demographic change had begun to produce political change. Between the beginning of World War I and the end of World War II, 3 million Black people moved from the South to the North—from a place where they couldn't vote to a place where they could. They moved chiefly to a group of highly industrialized states: New York, Pennsylvania, Ohio, Michigan, Illinois, and California. Suddenly Black voters exercised real power in many of the states with the largest electoral votes. What's more, 1.2 million Black men had served in a war that pitted democracy against a monstrous racist ideology. When they came home, many of these veterans were no longer prepared to look down at their feet in the company of a white man. That, in turn, spurred civil rights activity. The NAACP had established its Legal Defense Fund in 1939; the organization began filing lawsuits in the hopes of overturning the "separate but equal" doctrine that the Supreme Court had protected in the 1896 *Plessy v. Ferguson* decision. Black activism and pride frightened and enraged many in the South: an outburst of lynchings accompanied the return of Black servicemen.[4]

Liberals had extremely low expectations of Truman, a Missourian whose conversation was littered with racial epithets; yet in fact he was far more enlightened than FDR. (The relation between the two in this regard bears comparison to that between the not-quite-southern Lyndon Johnson and the northern patrician John Kennedy.) In September 1946, Walter White, who had been rebuffed by FDR a decade earlier, joined a group of civil rights activists at a White House meeting where they told President Truman about the racial violence spreading across the South. "Mr. Truman's face became pale with horror," White later wrote. "His voice trembled with deep emotion as he assured us that steps must be taken immediately to stop this wave of terrorism before it got out of hand."[5]

That November, the beating the Democrats took in the by-election included a substantial hemorrhage of the Black vote that had gravitated to the party thanks to the New Deal. The following month, impelled by his very real moral anger as well as his political instincts, Truman impaneled the President's Commission on Civil Rights, with a mandate to recommend legal changes to end the systematic subjugation of Black people. One year later, the panel submitted a 178-page report, "To Secure These Rights," which proposed denying federal funds to any program that required segregation, and thus imposing a crushing penalty on Jim Crow laws; the establishment of a permanent Fair Employment Practices Commission, which FDR had (reluctantly) established by executive order; the passage of laws prohibiting the poll tax and making lynching a federal crime; and the creation of a Civil Rights Commission and a Civil Rights Division in the Justice Department. No federal document remotely as ambitious had been issued since the end of Reconstruction seventy years before.

Once Truman agreed, in February 1948, to endorse the report, southern leaders realized that this president could not be trusted to preserve their social order. At a convening of the nascent States' Rights Party in Jackson, Mississippi, in May, delegates pledged that no southern state would endorse a candidate committed to a civil rights platform. Moreover, members promised to reassemble in Birmingham immediately after the Democratic National Convention should the party defy their wishes. At the annual Jefferson-Jackson Dinner in Arkansas, more than half the 850 participants staged a walkout when Truman's voice came over a loudspeaker. The Ku Klux Klan held rallies across the South, and hate-filled letters swearing violence poured into the White House and to members of the Civil Rights Commission.[6] Truman, who had mistakenly believed he could count on southern loyalty, stopped talking about civil rights.

This, then, was the vise in which liberals found themselves caught in the early spring of 1948. Henry Wallace had conducted an almost reckless tour of the South addressing large Black crowds, committing himself heart and soul to the cause of civil rights. Wallace might be able to steal enough of the Black vote to prevent any Democrat from winning. But the South had made it all too clear that any real commitment to civil rights could destroy the coalition FDR had built. The politics of the issue thus cut both ways. Yet for a nation that had just emerged victorious from a war against an ideology of race hatred, civil rights felt like a moral imperative rather than a political calculation. And the very fact that liberals had given up on Truman, and thus on winning the 1948 election, was liberating. At the same moment that Humphrey was telling Chester Bowles that ADA liberals had to seize the ideological initiative, Leon Henderson was writing to Howard McGrath, chairman of the Democratic National Committee, to insist that the DNC "initiate a convincing campaign" on civil rights. "The great body of independent progressives is less concerned with the political fortunes of any party than with the grave challenge to the fundamental rights of the people," Henderson admonished. The ADA would endorse only those candidates who supported the recommendations of Truman's commission.[7]

Humphrey had political calculations of his own. Henry Wallace's entry into the race had further dimmed his prospects for a victory over Joe Ball in Minnesota, for many of his most passionate supporters would be attracted by Wallace's stance on civil rights and the New Deal, if not by his sympathies for Moscow. Humphrey needed to make the Democratic Party safe for liberalism. Idealist though he was, he saw, more clearly than many another self-proclaimed pragmatist, that the party needed to move on civil rights in order to win the growing Black vote and to hold on to the party's left wing. Humphrey was the rare mayor with a truly national vision. That helps explain why he promptly informed Jim Loeb that he would issue the letter committing party leaders to the cause of civil rights.

In a note to colleagues, Loeb explained that he hoped to enlist James Roosevelt and Jacob Arvey, the party boss in Chicago, as cosignatories. The ADA, he said, would organize the whole campaign but remain in the background, only emerging to lobby once the letter had been published. During this period, Humphrey was consumed with his fight to break the left-wing hold on the Democratic-Farmer-Labor Party, to overcome resistance to his proposed reform of the city council, and to organize his campaign to unseat Ball and become the first Democrat Minnesota had sent to the Senate since the state had been founded. Loeb did the work of rounding up Roosevelt and Arvey and contacting other party figures.[8]

On June 10, under his own name and not as ADA vice chair, Humphrey began sending out dozens of copies of the letter to leading liberals. Until now, he noted, only the southern opponents of civil rights had raised their voices about the upcoming convention. "It is essential," he wrote, "both for the moral position of our party and for reasons of political realism, that those of us in the North and West make our position abundantly clear and with equal vigor." Humphrey asked recipients to sign a pledge on civil rights, stating, "We hereby declare that we shall actively seek, at Philadelphia, to make the accomplishment of the program a part of our party's platform for 1948." On July 5 he held a press conference to publicize the letter; the signatories included New York City mayor William O'Dwyer, former New York governor Herbert Lehman, Senator Robert Wagner of New York, former US treasury secretary Henry Morgenthau, FDR Jr. and James Roosevelt, former congressman Will Rogers Jr. of California, Congresswoman Helen Gahagan Douglas of California, and dozens of other prominent figures. Hubert Humphrey occupied the center of this great liberal wheel.[9]

In the weeks before the convention the attention of Democrats was focused not on their platform but on the effort to draft Eisenhower or Douglas. Humphrey's name was still being bandied about as a possible vice president. There was talk that Eleanor Roosevelt herself would endorse Humphrey on the floor. Humphrey's brash aide George Demetriou wrote to Jim Loeb to note that the mayor's own father would be joining the South Dakota delegation and to suggest that "it will be a dramatic gimmick" to have the elder Humphrey nominate the younger. Hubert Sr. promptly wrote to his son promising to do so if asked. Rather than gushing over the prospect, he offered thoughtful advice, suggesting that, since Truman was likely to win the nomination, "it will be wise politically not to show your hand for any other candidate, but to vote for Truman and keep yourself in the good graces of the Administration."[10] That turned out to be sage advice. On July 6, Eisenhower announced that he would not "identify myself with any party" and thus would not be a candidate for office. Douglas declined as well. The party was stuck with Truman. Nevertheless, liberals continued to hope that Truman would choose one of their own as running mate rather than the odds-on favorite, the seventy-one-year-old senator Alben Barkley of Kentucky.

In late June DNC chairman McGrath had appointed Humphrey—despite his apostasy—to the platform's seventeen-member Preliminary

Drafting Committee as well as the civil rights subcommittee. Liberals would depend on him and on Andrew Biemiller, an ADA founder and former Wisconsin congressman, to carry their banner. The convention was to begin Monday, July 12, but the platform committee and subcommittees began meeting the prior Thursday. Humphrey distinguished himself right away, if only by sheer volubility. Liberal columnist Doris Fleeson wrote that "Hubert Humphrey, an experienced spellbinder with a durable larynx, is questioning every witness with a campaign speech in miniature—and not a very small miniature at that." The Minneapolis mayor, Fleeson explained to her readers, was hoping to "project his personality" as a potential vice president.[11] But Truman was not about to pick the leader of the dump-Truman movement as his running mate.

Despite the president's endorsement of the findings of his own commission, administration officials had made it plain that they did not want the civil rights language to significantly deviate from the 1944 plank, which had blandly stated, "We believe that racial and religious minorities have the right to live, develop and vote equally with all citizens, and share the rights that are guaranteed by our Constitution. Congress should exert its full constitutional powers to protect those rights." In his testimony before the civil rights subcommittee, Walter White described the 1944 plank as completely unacceptable to Black Americans. Another witness warned that Black voters were prepared to go for Wallace. Others might abandon the party for the GOP, whose platform had virtually endorsed the report of the Truman commission.[12]

The platform debate only began on Monday, when the White House presented its preferred language—a literal restatement of the 1944 plank preceded by the words "We again state our belief that . . ." and "We again call upon Congress to exert . . ." A furious argument broke out, with Humphrey and Biemiller on one side and senior Democrats on the other. The two liberals denounced the draft as "a sellout to states' rights over human rights." An angry and possibly inebriated Scott Lucas, Senate minority leader from Illinois, pointed a scornful finger at Humphrey and asked, "Who is this pipsqueak who wants to redo Franklin D. Roosevelt's work and deny the wishes of the present

President of the United States?"[13] Humphrey would not have endeared himself to Lucas any more than to Truman by his and the ADA's very public campaign to find a new presidential candidate.

Over the weekend Senator Francis Myers of Pennsylvania, chairman of the drafting committee, had appointed a five-member group, which included none of the liberals, to come up with a compromise solution. At 3:30 a.m. on Tuesday, Myers emerged to announce the new wording, which was virtually identical to the old. Humphrey had been waiting for the announcement; immediately he convened a caucus of liberals, who rejected the new language and insisted on the inclusion of at least the main points of the Truman commission. Humphrey may have slept for a few hours before the platform committee reconvened; the members then spent eleven hours fighting anew over the civil rights language. Humphrey offered a compromise proposal only demanding an end to desegregation in the military, but even this modest resolution went down to defeat, 70–30. That having failed, Humphrey said that liberals would not accept a text that did not commit the party on a permanent Fair Employment Practices Commission, anti-lynching legislation, voting rights, and the desegregation of the armed forces—not the whole agenda of "To Secure These Rights," but its core principles. Humphrey spoke passionately and lengthily, as was his wont. In fact, he speechified: "No one in this room has a deeper and more sincere belief in the democratic institutions of this country than I have."[14] Every few hours he emerged from the steam bath of the crowded conference room to brief the press on the latest developments. For all his rhetorical bravura, he wasn't quite sure where he stood: at one point he told reporters that he regarded the compromise plank as "broad and conclusive."[15]

A sweaty, exhausted Humphrey now retreated to his fourth-floor suite at the Bellevue-Stratford Hotel to decide on the next move. The suite had become liberal HQ, and it was jammed with members of the Minnesota delegation, civil rights activists, labor leaders, ADA officials, and Humphrey's own trusted circle of advisers, including Orville Freeman and Eugenie Anderson. There was beer in the sink and the bedlam of shouted conversation. The moment of truth had arrived. Though the ADA risked losing its precious relationship with the Democratic Party, the group's officials had agreed to submit a minority report to the convention and demand a vote on the floor. But the final decision, Joe Rauh Jr. of the ADA later said, depended on one man. "That was Hubert Humphrey."[16]

No one stood to lose as much as Humphrey. He had built a reputation not as a prophetic voice but as a pragmatic political leader; he risked destroying it in a single stroke. He would need the support of the Democratic Party to defeat Joseph Ball; he could lose that, too. And he was hearing from professionals who knew what they were talking about that the split over civil rights could doom Truman's election. Who was he to provoke such a cataclysm? Yet Humphrey's commitment to the Democratic Party was not pragmatic but moral; the party had stood for his own deepest convictions since he was a boy. How could he, situated as he now was, abet an act of moral surrender? And what if the pros were wrong, and the real key to Democratic success lay in taking the Black vote away from Henry Wallace? Never in his life had Humphrey endured such crushing pressure. He talked and talked and talked, trying to see his way clear to a solution. The Minnesota delegation wanted him to stand firm; the labor leaders were prepared to sacrifice civil rights for labor rights.

Finally, Humphrey spoke to the one man whose opinion meant the most to him: his father, who was sitting there—serenely, one imagines—amid the noise and confusion. Hubert Sr. had been writing to his son regularly—about the new drugstore he was opening in Huron, about Hubert's younger sister, Fern, who had returned home after her husband had been killed in a plane crash, about Muriel when she came down with the flu. But he never failed to include a fatherly homily. "You are," he had written on New Year's Day of 1947, "as gracious to the poorest mortal as you are to the richest and most powerful. That attitude will make you more powerful than your most bitter adversary." The father's dreams for the son were boundless; a year earlier he had written with a prophesy that the 1948 convention would be deadlocked, that in a spellbinding speech Hubert would "give them the works from both barrels," just like Bryan in '96—and that the party would turn to him as its savior.[17]

Hubert Sr. was a prudent small businessman as well as a prairie idealist. He did not want his son to sacrifice himself on the altar of principle, and at first he said as much. But Hubert Jr. kept explaining why he felt the moment had come to act. Then his father said, "This may tear the party apart, but if you feel strongly, then you've got to go with it. You can't run away from your conscience, son. You've got to go with it." He expected the worst. "But," he said, "you'll at least have the eight votes of the South Dakota delegation." Hubert then talked to Muriel, laying out the stakes for his own career. Muriel told him, less equivocally than his father had, to stand his ground. He felt that he knew what he had to do.[18]

The debate in the hotel suite raged on until 5:00 Wednesday morning. Humphrey had been working with Rauh on the language of a resolution, but he was desperate to find a formulation that would not seem to repudiate Truman, for whom he had never lost respect. Finally Eugenie Anderson cut the Gordian knot by proposing that they prefix a single sentence to the demand for the four key civil rights commitments: "We highly commend President Truman for his courageous stand on the issue of civil rights." That was what Humphrey needed; now he was prepared to present the minority report on the floor of the convention.[19] "For me personally, and for the party, the time had come to suffer whatever the consequences," Humphrey later wrote.[20] That was what his father had said to him; the obligation to choose conscience over self-interest was precisely what his father had drummed into him since boyhood.

That morning, Andrew Biemiller secured a promise from House Speaker Sam Rayburn, the convention chairman, that the liberals would get a roll-call vote from the convention. So, too, Rayburn said, would southern forces, who opposed the compromise language from the opposite direction; they wanted a reaffirmation of states' rights. Each side would get an hour. ADA lobbyists fanned out to hotel suites across Philadelphia seeking support for their position and trying to firm up the vote count. At first it seemed they could count on no more than 150 out of 1,200 votes. But they kept buttonholing; and they began to win over the bosses. Ed Flynn, the Tammany sachem who had pressed Leon Henderson to introduce him to the Minneapolis phenom, and Jacob Arvey of Illinois, who had cosigned the civil rights letter, and David Lawrence of Pennsylvania, and Frank Hague of New Jersey, and John Bailey of Connecticut vowed that they and their delegations would vote for civil rights. These men may not have known the fine points of the poll tax, but they represented states with large Black populations and they knew very well how to add. "Look, you kids are right," Flynn told Biemiller and Humphrey as they prepared to go before the convention. "We've got to stir up the interests of the minority group in this election; otherwise we're dead."[21] The Truman people became more and more agitated as the FDR coalition seemed to be unraveling before their eyes. On the convention floor, David Niles, Truman's administrative assistant and his point man on civil rights, told Rauh that he "had ruined the chances of the best liberal product to come down the pike in years, and we wouldn't get fifty votes."[22]

The floor fight was scheduled for the afternoon. The southerners went first. Dan Moody, the former governor of Texas, submitted a resolution to amend the platform by stipulating that "the reserved power of the states" included "the power to control and regulate local affairs and act in the exercise of police power." That careful language was too indirect for the hard-liners. A Tennessee delegate proposed language reaffirming the Democratic Party's commitment to "the fundamental principle of States Rights" while a Mississippian proposed to explicitly affirm state jurisdiction over the conduct of elections, employment practices, and "segregation within the states." Andrew Biemiller then presented the liberals' minority report, noting as he did so that the platform had not given "due recognition to the courageous fight of President Harry Truman for civil rights."[23]

The southerners then made their case. They were followed by Maurice Tobin, the former governor of Massachusetts, who argued for leaving the civil rights plank just as it was. All this time Humphrey had been sitting in the back of the hall, scribbling over his typescript. That morning, while dressing, he had dictated his thoughts to Milton Stewart of the New York ADA. Stewart had worked it into a short speech typed in capital letters. As Humphrey sat in the convention center, new thoughts and new words came to him, and he wrote them out by hand at the bottom of his text. It was late afternoon by the time he walked to the podium. Though rain had slightly cooled the room, Truman's Secret Service detail had sealed the doors in the expectation that the president would arrive, driving the temperature indoors into the nineties. Convention Hall was jammed with 15,000 people—of whom 1,200 were delegates—and they stood shoulder to shoulder. Cigarette smoke drifted through the stale air.

Humphrey wore a big yellow Truman pin and a dark suit because he would be on television (though no video record of the speech remains). This would be, he knew, the most important speech he had ever given in his life. He was still slim, his chin still firm, his hairline already receding. He made a point of speaking slowly and forcefully. He knew he had only ten minutes; every word would count. Humphrey began with conciliation. Civil rights was "a hard issue," he said. He acknowledged the many colleagues who felt as strongly as he did on the subject, "yet are in complete disagreement with me." His "admiration" for them had only grown after several days of difficult debate. The minority report that he had come to endorse was directed to no one region, he went on. All parts of the country had "infringed freedoms"; all groups had suffered "vicious discrimination." Humphrey praised Truman for courageously issuing "the new emancipation proclamation." And then he pivoted. "Every citizen has a stake in the emergence of the United States as the leader of the free world," Humphrey shouted—for by now his durable larynx was filling the hall. "That world is being challenged by the world of slavery. For us to play our part effectively, we must be in a morally sound position." Here was Humphrey's first public statement of the philosophy that would come to be known as "Cold War liberalism," one of whose central tenets was that the United States could win the ideological battle with Soviet communism by demonstrating at home the moral superiority of democracy.

In spite of his own wish for unanimity, Humphrey went on, "there are some matters which I think must be stated clearly and without qualification." That sentence was in the typescript. Then Humphrey began reading the words he had written out himself. "There can be no hedging—no watering down," he cried. "My friends, to those who say that we are rushing this issue of civil rights, I say that we are 172 years late!" Humphrey now entered on his peroration, the most stirring of the millions of words he would utter over the ensuing three decades. All were written in pencil in his clean, A-student script.[24] "To those who say that this civil rights program is an infringement of states' rights, I say this"—and here, his high voice shaking with emotion, Humphrey paused briefly, for effect—"that the time has arrived in America for the Democratic Party to get out of the shadow of states' rights and walk forthrightly into the bright sunshine of human rights. People—people—human beings, this is the issue of the twentieth century, people of all kinds, and these people are looking to America for leadership and they are looking to America for precepts and example." If the sentence didn't scan, the passion and the patriotism struck deep chords with the men and women in the hall.

Humphrey was inclined to speak at great length about the historical background and the policy details of whatever proposal he happened to be descanting on. Now he did neither: his language was rhetorical and inspirational. He ended on a note both ringing and calculated: "We proudly hail and we courageously support our President and leader, Harry Truman, in his great fight for civil rights in America."[25] Humphrey had finished in slightly under his allotted ten minutes—yet he had said everything that needed to be said. Paul Douglas, an economist and intellectual who would be elected to the Senate from Illinois that fall, called it "the greatest political oration in the history of the country," save perhaps for Bryan's "Cross of Gold" speech. Humphrey, he said, "was on fire, just like the Bible speaks of Moses."[26] As Humphrey spoke, the murmurs in the hall had swelled into bursts of clapping and cheering. When he finished, delegates from a dozen northern states grabbed their standards and paraded up and down the center aisles—just as Humphrey had done for Henry Wallace four years earlier. Watching on television, a furious Truman called Humphrey and his fellow enthusiasts "crackpots."[27]

Once calm was restored, the delegates easily voted down several southern resolutions. Then came time for the vote on the liberal report. All the big northern states with large Black populations—Michigan, then New York, then Pennsylvania—voted for the minority report.

Wisconsin put the resolution over the top, and Humphrey leaped up and clenched his fists. The final tally was 651½ to 582½. The Democratic Party, the party of secession and of racial violence, had committed itself for the first time to the cause of civil rights. To many it felt like a moment of refounding. The NAACP called the vote "the greatest turning point for the South and for America which has occurred since the Civil War."

The Jim Crow faction of the party had threatened to bolt if the platform embraced the Truman commission report. In fact, once Sam Rayburn gaveled the convention back into order to nominate Truman, only the Mississippi delegation and half the Alabama delegation, led by a beefy Birmingham sheriff named Bull Connor, walked out. Political reporters writing the next day took the view that the South had blinked.[28] Two days later, six thousand delegates gathered in Birmingham to declare the advent of the States' Rights Party and chose Strom Thurmond of South Carolina as their presidential candidate. The revolt of the Dixiecrats, as the party came to be known, would peter out in 1948. But it was a shot across the bow of the Democratic Party. Hubert Humphrey had said to himself that he would do the right thing "whatever the price." That price would only be fully tallied many years later.

In those days the whole country followed the political conventions; sixty million Americans had heard Humphrey on the radio and ten million more had watched him on TV. A few days before he had been prepared to surrender his career on the altar of principle; now, in the manner that every passionate idealist dreams of but few live to see, he had become a hero to millions simply by virtue of doing the right thing. When Mayor Humphrey got off the train in Minneapolis on Sunday, July 18, two thousand jubilant citizens were waiting to greet him. He was carried on their shoulders amid a forest of signs, many of them reading, "Humphrey, Champion of Human Rights." As cars honked wildly and the Police Band, the Elks Band, and the Working Boys and Girls Band belted out tunes, Hubert and Muriel were driven in an open car to a reception at the Nicollet Hotel. Hubert Humphrey was the pride of Minnesota; the time had come to move to a national stage.[29]

PART 2

A Force in the Senate

A Harsh Welcome to America's No. 1 Liberal

"Can you imagine the people of Minnesota sending that damn fool down here to represent them?"

I F TRUTH, AS IT WAS UNDERSTOOD IN AMERICANS FOR DEMO-cratic Action and the Democratic-Farmer-Labor Party and in Philadelphia the evening of July 14, 1948, were also the undisputed truth of Washington DC, in the years after World War II, then Hubert Humphrey, the darling of the liberals, would have occupied a commanding position once he got there. But it wasn't so. The national politics of the day was governed by truths almost entirely at variance with the ones that had put Humphrey's name in the newspapers. Humphrey knew that, of course; he was a politician. But he could not, at first, accept the reality before him. He would flap inside the Washington cage until he almost broke his wings. Then he would learn how to fly in his own way.

First Humphrey had to defeat Joe Ball. For all the formidable advantages he now had, no mayor of Minneapolis had ever gone on to much of anything, save jail. No Democrat had ever been elected to the Senate in Minnesota. The DFL was itself untested. And Humphrey would be facing an incumbent who enjoyed the support of the state's business community and virtually all its newspapers. Ball was a former newspaperman, a friend of Harold Stassen, whom Stassen had appointed in 1940 to replace a Republican who had died in office. He was a dependable voice of business but also a confirmed internationalist, who had shocked his own party by endorsing FDR over Thomas Dewey in 1944. A forward-looking Chamber of Commerce Republican like Michigan's Arthur Vandenberg might have been almost unbeatable, but Ball had turned isolationist under Truman, even voting against the immensely popular Marshall Plan. He had also been one of the main sponsors of Taft-Hartley, legislation sharply curtailing the ability of unions to organize and strike, which Truman had vetoed, and which the Senate had passed over his veto. Ball was the number one target for organized labor in the 1948 elections. In August, Stassen issued an endorsement that sounded more like a critique, openly expressing his disagreement with Ball on Taft-Hartley and the Marshall Plan.[1]

The ADA focused on two candidates in 1948—Paul Douglas in Illinois and Humphrey. And the organization delivered handsomely for its vice chairman, lining up support from Philip Murray and William Green, heads of the CIO and the AFL, respectively; Hollywood director Melvyn Douglas; and Eleanor Roosevelt, who released a statement saying, "People have learned to believe and trust in this vigorous young Mayor and I want to join in sending him my best wishes and appreciation for a very good citizen of the United States."[2] A poll taken August 22 showed Humphrey leading Ball by 10 points—and the campaign had barely begun. Once it did, after Labor Day, Humphrey typically spoke to more voters in a day than the phlegmatic Ball did in a week. He campaigned from morning to night, delivering seven hundred speeches and hitting every one of the state's eighty-seven counties at least twice. As one of his biographers notes, Humphrey glad-handed his way through "the Sauerkraut Festival at

Springfield, Watermelon Day at Sanborn, Turkey Day at Worthington, the Bohemian Dance at Owatunna, and the Finnish Society at Duluth."[3]

The Progressive Party had planned to run a candidate against this hated pawn of the Truman wing of the party. Elmer Benson had at one time planned to run himself—because, as a political reporter for the *Minneapolis Star Tribune* explained, "he disliked Humphrey more than he disliked Ball." Humphrey also worried that the progressives would field a candidate in the primary. In June he wrote an angry letter to John Blatnik, a left-wing DFL congressman from Duluth who had pointedly refused to endorse him. While Blatnik himself counted on running unopposed, Humphrey threatened, "I have my friends in Duluth and the Iron Range who are becomingly increasingly alarmed over the way things are going." The primary challenge never materialized, and on September 30 PCA head Beanie Baldwin announced that the party, while not endorsing Humphrey, would not run a candidate against him. Humphrey managed to stifle the intense sense of vindication he must have felt, saying only, "They know my program and I am grateful they will support it." (On October 10, in Minneapolis, Wallace was able to bring himself to say, "I do most earnestly hope that Ball does not win.")[4]

In a radio speech October 5, Humphrey laid out his philosophy of government. He remained the FDR man he had long been. "There are those who talk about government as the 'dead hand,'" he said, referring plainly to Dewey. "I say to them that government is not the 'dead hand.' It is, it must be, the warm heart of our nation." Humphrey's liberalism always felt less like an ideology than a distillation of the message of the Gospels and the wisdom of the Founders. What was new in his thinking was the recognition that in the face of the threat of totalitarianism, from the left as well as the right, liberalism had to be a world vision as well as a domestic one. The Marshall Plan, Humphrey said, constituted liberalism in foreign policy. "Anyone, my opponent or the Communist Party, who voted against or fought against the Marshall Plan, sought inhumanly to deny the right of people to live," he proclaimed. Humphrey was an idealist who believed in "one world." By that he and others meant not world government but global disarmament, the international control of atomic energy, and a strengthened United Nations commanding an international police force.[5]

In mid-October, Harry Truman arrived in Minnesota. By now "give-'em-hell Harry" had replaced the equivocal Truman of the summer. Truman was campaigning as a full-throated heir to the New Deal and a champion of civil rights. Right after the convention he had issued an executive order establishing a Fair Employment Board. The civil rights victory at the convention had energized liberals and even Truman himself. Both the ADA and the CIO had endorsed him. A candidate who had been dismissed and derided was now closing the gap with Dewey. In a speech in St. Paul, where he sported a big "Humphrey for Senator" button, the president laid into Ball as "a champion of reaction" who had abandoned his sensible principles as soon as he had reached Washington.[6]

On October 18 an increasingly desperate Ball claimed to have discovered a "startling similarity" between Humphrey's platform and that of the CIO, the progressives, and the Communist Party. "Could it be," he asked, that the leaders of the DFL and the national Democratic Party, like the Communists, aspired "to wreck our capitalist system"? Humphrey had already played and won this game against Marvin Kline; now he reminded voters that it was he who had driven the leftists out of the DFL.[7] Ball wisely refused to debate Humphrey unless the latter agreed to restrict the topics to Taft-Hartley and the Marshall Plan, which Humphrey had refused to do. It had been tabulated that Humphrey spoke three words in the time it took Ball to produce one. And what words! A Ball aide later explained, "If we'd let Hubert at Ball with no holds barred, the carnage would have been awful. . . . He would have covered the waterfront. He brings in the flag, the landing of the Pilgrims, the Battle of Gettysburg, 'Lafayette, we are here,' the fall of the Alamo, 'Don't give up the ship,' the Bible and everything else when he gets rolling. He's really wonderful."[8]

Humphrey enjoyed virtually universal support from the Black community and, thanks to his passionate advocacy of the new state of Israel, the Jewish community. His secret weapon, however, was labor. Walter Reuther had paid for another campaign aide. Both the AFL and the CIO sent operatives from mill to mill touting Humphrey. The Minnesota Central Labor Union staffed phone lines and hired operators to badger union members to register and vote. Four hundred electrical workers got a holiday on Election Day to do door-to-door canvassing. The support of organized labor would remain central to Humphrey's political fortunes for the remainder of his career—a boon when unions enjoyed broad public support, a mixed blessing when they came to be seen as the working-class branch of the Establishment.

Incredibly, Humphrey won all but two of the state's counties. Thanks in part to that strong showing, Truman won Minnesota's eleven electoral votes—and, of course, in one of the great political miracles of American history, the presidency itself. Hubert Humphrey would be heading to Washington at what appeared to be a moment of liberal renewal. His own brave stand in Philadelphia had not cost him his political future; it had been the making of him.

HUMPHREY ARRIVED IN WASHINGTON IN JANUARY 1949 AS NOT ONLY the most famous of the crop of freshmen—which included his Louisiana friend Russell Long, Paul Douglas of Illinois, and a tall and gangly Texan named Lyndon Johnson—but possibly the poorest. As mayor he had earned only $6,000 a year; saving money had been impossible. He had sold his house in southeast Minneapolis for $9,500; the cheapest house he could find near Washington, on Coquelin Terrace in the suburb of Chevy Chase, had cost $12,000. When the mover arrived with a bill for over $1,200, Humphrey didn't have the money; the family's belongings stayed in the truck until a check from his father arrived. He and Muriel now had four children to feed and clothe: Nancy, ten; Skip, seven; Robert, five; and Douglas, two. Their house had to be furnished beyond what the Humphreys had brought from home, and the raw dirt yard had to be landscaped. Humphrey's Senate salary was $12,500 (a figure that had increased a grand total of $2,500 over the previous quarter-century). He was paying off loans he had taken out from Joe Rauh and Freddy Gates. Humphrey made ends meet, as he had in the past, by accepting virtually every invitation to give a paid speech that came his way; that year he would earn $8,933 in speaking fees. Then, and for years to come, Humphrey would have to work furiously just to keep his head above water.[9]

Yet he *was* famous. On the second Sunday following the election, Humphrey received the ultimate tribute to celebrity when he was booked on *Meet the Press*. Thrown into the lion's den, the senator-elect emerged almost unscathed. He was confronted with an ADA pamphlet from that spring demanding that Truman step aside to give the Democrats a shot at winning. "Do you still think you and the rest of the ADA were right in wishing to ditch Truman?" he was asked. "I think we were dead wrong," Humphrey shot back. "And I think that confession is good for the soul." A startled reporter for the *Washington Post* blurted out, "I think that's magnificent." Humphrey flawlessly fielded several tough chances on price controls and Taft-Hartley. And he reassured the graybeards that he knew his place: "I'm the junior Senator from Minnesota and I have an awful lot to learn and I know it."

That humble pose could not survive contact with reality. On January 5 the ADA chose Humphrey to replace Leon Henderson as chairman. Humphrey was now the nation's leading voice of liberalism. He had hundreds of speaking invitations sitting on his desk when he first arrived at work. *Time* magazine introduced him to America as "a hard-working, fast-talking fireball from the Midwest," a survivor of the Dust Bowl raised on Jefferson and Paine, a dynamo who got through his punishing days popping Life Savers and smoking Lucky Strikes.[10] His modest biography was already taking on mythic dimensions.

Official Washington, however, was not America; and there Humphrey would not be forgiven for breaking ranks with the president—even if doing so had ultimately served the president's own interests. In the Senate and around the White House, Humphrey was regarded as a bumptious arriviste who had to be put down—and hard. Because a special session of the previous Congress was held in the first three weeks of January, newcomers had to find temporary quarters; only Humphrey received no accommodation and had to borrow a friend's office downtown. When veteran senators formally introduced the freshmen to their colleagues, neither of Minnesota's Republicans performed the courtesy, and Humphrey had to watch the proceedings by himself from the Senate Gallery.[11] He had hoped for a place on the Education and Public Welfare Committee, through which most social legislation passed, and Foreign Relations or Banking. Majority Leader Scott Lucas, the party solon who had called him a pip-squeak in Philadelphia, gave Humphrey the first one, but then assigned him to Government Operations and the Post Office, the bottom rung of the status ladder. Thus did the powers that be exact their petty revenge on America's number one liberal, who had not only championed civil rights but led the campaign to get rid of the incumbent president.

Despite his protestations of humility, Humphrey was seen as a showboat before he so much as opened his mouth in the Senate. His northern colleagues barely deigned to speak to him while southerners treated him less as a fellow member of the chamber than a pamphlet-brandishing abolitionist. Humphrey was not without blame. In mid-January, at his first press conference as chairman (still interim) of the ADA, he had declared that there were enough votes in Congress to pass civil rights legislation "if members are honest and sincere." Then he made matters much worse by adding, with what must have seemed like ludicrous swagger, "I warn them that if they are not honest and sincere there may be trouble for them in the future."[12] Yet at bottom, Humphrey insulted the South simply by being who he was. Several days after taking office, he brought Cyril King, a Black aide, to lunch in the Senate dining room. The Black steward, no doubt mortified, told Humphrey that only whites were permitted there; Washington itself was very much part of the Jim Crow South. Humphrey would not budge, and King was finally seated to avoid a fuss.[13] That simple, gentlemanly act turned Humphrey into a civil rights extremist.

Soon after, Humphrey heard the courtly Richard Russell of Georgia say to a group of southern colleagues—loud enough that Humphrey knew he was intended to hear—"Can you imagine the people of Minnesota sending that damn fool down here to represent them?"[14] Humphrey was devastated. "Never in my life have I felt so unwanted as I did during those first few months in Washington," he would later say. "I was unhappy in the Senate, uncomfortable, awkward, unable to find a place."[15] Another man might have withdrawn into a proud solitude, but Humphrey was only fully himself in company: he needed to talk, to befriend, to put his arm around others and feel theirs around him. A measure of the pain he experienced was the intensity of the gratitude he felt toward the few men who showed a human side—Lister Hill of Alabama, who escorted him to the Senate floor after he had been shunned, or Millard Tydings of Maryland, who defended him in debate after he had made the unpardonable error of publicly criticizing Senator Harry F. Byrd, a leader of the Southern Bourbons. "Senator Tydings' words were like the tender loving care of a mother when you're sick," as Humphrey tellingly put it many years later.[16] Nevertheless, in the dozens of letters he wrote to friends in those years, Humphrey never breathed a word of his suffering, for doing so would have felt like a devastating admission of failure. Only Muriel knew how terrible that first year was for him.

Humphrey could have relieved his suffering by trimming his sails to the prevailing wind, but he refused to do so. On March 2, having waited a prudent and no doubt excruciating six weeks, he delivered his maiden speech in the Senate. It was on the proposed Missouri Valley Authority (MVA), which would supply low-cost power, irrigation, and flood control in the Midwest, as the Tennessee Valley Authority had in the Southeast. Perhaps he intended this in part as an homage to his father, who, in a letter written immediately after the election, had said he had "struggled so many years against the forces of nature" that an MVA had become his "hope and dream." Holding the floor for a good half hour, Humphrey called the measure "a symbol of liberalism to the great majority of Americans who voted liberal last November and in other Novembers."[17] (The measure ultimately failed.)

Work was Humphrey's salvation at this low point in his life. Truman had, after much hesitation, run a frankly progressive campaign. Wallace's support had collapsed in the fall as liberals defected to Truman. Strom Thurmond and the Dixiecrats had taken only four states. Now, in the view of Humphrey and other liberals, it fell to Congress and the Truman administration to implement the will of the people. That meant, above all, the civil rights plank to which the party had committed itself in Philadelphia. But the southern forces that had lost the battle in Philadelphia were not about to lose the war in Washington. They had blocked Truman's early efforts to promote civil rights with the filibuster. When Truman had proposed a permanent Fair Employment Practices Commission in 1946, lawmakers had delivered endless speeches over the routine vote to accept the previous day's *Congressional Journal*, the body's official record, claiming that the prayer opening the session had not properly invoked the Supreme Being.[18]

Truman's attempt to pass civil rights legislation in a 1948 special session had provoked a full-scale fight over the rules governing cloture, the procedure whereby the Senate limited debate. Senate rules stipulated that debate could be ended only by two-thirds of members present. During the special session, the presiding senator, Arthur Vandenberg, had ruled that a motion to change the cloture rules did not itself constitute the kind of "pending measure" to which cloture applied. In other words, you couldn't end debate on a motion to change the rules on how to end debate—which meant, as Vandenberg himself conceded, that, "in the final analysis, the Senate has no effective cloture rule at all."[19] The rules would have to be changed in order for civil rights legislation to have any chance of passing.

Even the Senate's few liberals showed surprisingly little interest in rewriting those rules. The best thing on offer was a proposed compromise by Democrat Carl Hayden of Arizona and Republican Kenneth Wherry of Nebraska that would stipulate that debate over "motions" as well as "measures" could be ended by cloture. Humphrey was prepared to support Hayden-Wherry for lack of a better idea. He had made his own position clear before the debate began. Invited to appear on *Meet the Press* once again in February, he had virtually invited southerners to bolt over civil rights, airily saying, "If anyone wants to leave on account of that platform, that's their privilege."[20] In a letter to the *New York Times* that was rash even by his own standards, Humphrey had warned that "the Truman Administration must come quickly to the decision that it cannot refuse the inevitable split over civil rights that exists in the Democratic party."[21]

The debate on Hayden-Wherry began in early March. Two fresh-men, Russell Long and Lyndon Johnson, made their maiden appear-ances on the floor defending the filibuster as currently structured. In a message simultaneously of personal moderation and of obe-dience to the South, Johnson said that he favored anti-lynching laws and opposed the poll tax; but he claimed to believe that "the Negro . . . has more to lose by the adoption of any resolution outlawing free debate in the Senate than he stands to gain by the enactment of the civil rights bills as they are now written."[22] Though Vice President Alben Barkley reversed Vandenberg's ruling on current Senate rules, the Senate voted to overturn him, ensuring that southerners could fil-ibuster even the modest Hayden-Wherry measure to death. Richard Russell, leader of the southern forces, now fashioned a compromise of the compromise, allowing cloture on motions but requiring a vote of two-thirds of all members rather than just of those present, thus rais-ing, rather than lowering, the barrier to ending the filibuster. Only twenty-three members voted against the Russell motion, showing how few senators were prepared to take on the South. A week or so later, Majority Leader Lucas, fearful of holding up the entire Fair Deal agenda, threw in the towel on civil rights, effectively putting the entire subject aside until the next Congress. Humphrey wanted to propose a resolution demanding that the Congress stay in session until it had debated civil rights but found few takers.

The debacle exposed several unpleasant truths that Humphrey was reluctant to acknowledge. First, in voting for Truman, the Amer-ican people had not delivered a mandate for civil rights. One poll had found that two-thirds of respondents opposed a permanent FEPC.[23] The ADA liberals had persuaded themselves that America had become a left-of-center country in which the great danger to liberalism lay in the far left. Truman's miraculous last-minute victory demonstrated that the country was more conservative than they thought. Second, and in part for that reason, far more senators regarded civil rights as politically harmful to them than helpful. That was, they would have said, an "honest and sincere" conviction. William S. White, a *New York Times* Washington reporter and leading anthropologist of Sen-ate folkways, would later write that "the true majority" on the 1949 civil rights legislation "was made up of those openly opposed and those secretly opposed and filled with secret hope that the issue could somehow be put aside."[24] The filibuster solved that problem for members of both parties outside the South and the liberal Northeast.

Humphrey continued to believe, as Gunnar Myrdal had, that Americans suffered from a profound conflict of values that could be resolved only by granting full equality to Black people. In a speech at Howard University in early March, he said, "Americans realized that discrimination clashed with our credo, that it was wrong— dead wrong!" The "hypocrisy" of calling for democracy abroad while denying it at home had provoked a deep sense of "moral guilt."[25] But whatever might be true of the Rotarians in Minnesota who had come around in the face of Humphrey's "Community Self-Survey" could not be said of the knights-errant of the Lost Cause who controlled the Senate. In early February, Humphrey had been booked on NBC Radio along with Allen Ellender, the senior senator from Louisiana. At first Ellender claimed to oppose the civil rights agenda for purely constitutional reasons. But when the host asked about the role of "white supremacy," Ellender dropped the pretense. "White supremacy?" he asked. "Well, white leadership. Now that you bring up the subject, I would say that the Negro himself cannot make progress unless he has white leadership. If you call that 'supremacy,' why, suit yourself. But I say that the Negro race as a whole, if permitted to go to itself, will invariably go back to barbaric lunacy." A startled Humphrey took "sharp exception," and ticked off a list of great Black figures. Ellender ignored him.[26]

Some of these men, such as Russell Long, were progressives who supported Truman's Fair Deal programs. All of them, however, stood atop a feudal order that had not been disturbed since federal troops had been withdrawn from the South after the 1876 election. They had lost the Civil War, but they had won the peace; and few of them felt even the smallest twinge of guilt about that victory. In mid-March, as the filibuster was winding down, Willis Robertson of Virginia took to the floor specifically to ridicule Humphrey as a romantic crusader "for the Holy Grail, which is civil rights." Warming to his subject, Robertson observed that "the war between the States" could have been avoided by "a peaceful compromise and settlement." Only the other day, he went on, he and Senator James Eastland of Mississippi had paid a visit to Gettysburg. There they had gazed out from Cemetery Ridge, site of Pickett's Charge, where brave men had "laid down their lives in defense of a principle of government, namely, States' rights, human rights, and personal liberty."[27] The Senate, as William White wrote all too aptly, "was the South's unending revenge upon the North for Gettysburg."[28]

HUMPHREY'S FIRST YEAR IN OFFICE PROVED TO BE TERRIBLY GRUELing, both for him and for Muriel. She was a resourceful woman who sewed her own clothes, entertained Hubert's friends or aides when they arrived with him late at night, and bucked up her husband when he came home, as he sometimes did, in tears from a fresh humiliation or setback. Muriel was raising four children almost entirely on her own in a strange city where she knew few people. She felt worn down—she never would have used the word "depressed"—and in June she checked into a hospital. The doctor said that she was not ill. "I feel that your difficulty is purely on a basis of fatigue associated with some emotional tension," he wrote. He recommended a vacation. No doubt embarrassed by her frailty, Muriel piled the kids into the family Buick the moment school let out and drove them 1,200 miles to a summer cabin in Minnesota. The first session of the Eighty-First Congress, one of the longest on record, would last until October 29. Humphrey stayed in Washington and returned home only briefly. Feeling contrite, he promised to take Muriel to Europe on vacation once the session ended. In early November they went to Union Station to board a train to New York. But it was not to be. At the station Humphrey was paged and called to a telephone, where he learned that his father had suffered a massive stroke while writing a sermon. He immediately canceled the trip and found a flight home. Hubert Sr. died several days later.[29]

Very few men—certainly very few men who are extraordinarily successful—preserve into adulthood the worshipful feelings they had about their fathers as boys. Hubert Humphrey did. At that moment he lost his best friend, his mentor, his inner voice. He told Max Kampelman, who had come to Washington as his chief legislative aide, that he had always felt that he could never go wrong because if he did, his father would pick up the phone and give him hell. What now? When Kampelman reminded him of that comment a year later, Humphrey said, "Dad is still looking over my shoulder."[30] Humphrey would never entirely fill the void left by his father's death.

During his first year Humphrey had introduced legislation to extend Social Security payments to government employees, to provide health insurance to the poor, and to subsidize school construction. He was the living incarnation of the political faith in government activism, and thus a perfect target for conservatives who regarded big government as the royal route to socialism. In August 1949 a right-wing Minnesota newspaper calculated the total cost of all the bills Humphrey had supported at a whopping $30 billion. His adversaries in the Senate now discovered a new line of attack. Republicans had introduced legislation requiring President Truman to slash 10 percent of expenditures in all departments, and Humphrey had filed an objection in his role as member of the Government Operations Committee. Senator Wherry of Nebraska rose to ask unanimous consent to have the $30 billion list placed in *The Congressional Record* "to show the inconsistency of the Senator from Minnesota."[31] Humphrey shot to his feet to defend himself, demonstrating the absurdity of the alleged figure. But whether the number was right or wrong, the charge stuck, because Humphrey really was a free-spending liberal.

Humphrey now handed his enemies the shovel with which to bury him. Convinced that the $30 billion allegation had been leaked by a Senate body called the Joint Committee on Reduction of Non-Essential Federal Expenditures, in February 1950 he rose in the Senate to call for the committee's abolition. This body offered a perfect example of the playground rules that governed the august US Senate. Harry Byrd, the reactionary kingpin from Virginia, had established the committee in 1936 as a platform from which to launch missiles, mostly harmless, at New Deal spending. It had survived to 1950 because no one would take away a perk from Byrd, who staffed the committee with cronies. Humphrey, all too susceptible to the romantic faith that truth conquers all, convinced himself that he could slay this venerable dragon. He introduced evidence he had gleaned from the American Political Science Association of the "distorted picture" of the federal expenditures Byrd's committee had publicized. He observed that Dr. George Galloway, "an outstanding authority on legislative reorganization," had found that the committee's role overlapped with that of an executive agency and had no reason for being. "It is my firm conviction," he declared, "that this committee serves no useful purpose and is merely used as a publicity medium." After several more choice observations, the junior senator from Minnesota sat down, no doubt feeling very pleased with himself.[32]

Knowing, perhaps, that revenge is a dish best served cold, Byrd waited six days before mounting his counterattack. The performance was so heavily advertised that Supreme Court Justices Herman Minton and Harold Burton, both former colleagues of Byrd's, were in attendance. Humphrey had spoken before a near-empty chamber, as he often did; now, as columnist Drew Pearson—who took Humphrey's side—observed, "more Republicans and Dixiecrats turned out to defend Byrd than listened to the debate on the Marshall Plan and Atlantic Pact."[33] Byrd began by noting that Humphrey's onslaught had come when he was absent—a serious violation of senatorial etiquette, though Humphrey himself had had no idea of Byrd's whereabouts. Byrd said he had been visiting his ailing mother. Having thus gained the moral high ground, he enumerated what he claimed were nine misstatements that Humphrey had made, though his defense of the committee was at least as tendentious as Humphrey's critique. As for the charge about publicity, Byrd said sardonically of his accuser, "I am not aware that he is of the shrinking-violet type." Perhaps, he added, he should take such an allegation from a "publicity expert" as praise. Little of substance that Byrd said hit home; what stung was the parade of senators, Democrat and Republican, northern and southern, who used the moment to declare their high regard both for Senator Harry Byrd and for the work of his committee. The fourteen colleagues who so testified included the gentlemanly Walter George, whom Humphrey had once regarded as a protector. And then, the spanking fully administered, the senators, like so many ducklings, filed out of the chamber behind Byrd.

Humphrey did not back down. "The shrinking violet," he cried, "has not been clipped." His response was every bit as detailed as Byrd's, and quite a bit longer. A week later Humphrey returned to the lists, reading into the record a *Washington Post* editorial endorsing his view. He fed yet more fuel into the fire by accusing Byrd of plagiarizing a contemporaneous report by the Committee on Expenditures of the Executive Department, which Humphrey held up as an actually useful alternative to the Byrd committee. He unearthed statements by federal agency heads directly contradicting Byrd's claims of featherbedding. He ridiculed the senator's "pride" in savings for which he was not responsible.

It was, taken all in all, a performance more brave than wise. Humphrey had absurdly claimed that the joint committee's $127,000 annual appropriation constituted "the no. 1 example of waste and extravagance" by the federal government. While the committee did, in fact, compel government agencies to waste a great deal of time and manpower complying with demands for data, the federal government squandered far more elsewhere. Humphrey was not the right combatant; nor had he found a citadel worth besieging. He had reinforced the image of him inside the Senate as a feckless crusader and thus deepened his own isolation. After a year in office, Humphrey bid fair to be the Don Quixote of the United States Senate.

9

Cold War Liberal

---

*"So long as men and women and children of color
are discriminated against in the United States,
the colored people of the world have the right
to suspect our privileged friendship with them."*

IN APRIL 1949, HUBERT HUMPHREY WAS ATTACKED IN THE SEN-
ate as a stooge for the Communists. Wasn't it true, asked Senator
William Jenner of Indiana, later to become Joe McCarthy's wingman, that Americans for Democratic Action was part of a coalition
of "eighteen Communist-front organizations"? Jenner said he had
been shocked to discover that the ADA was sponsoring a program to
send young Americans to study government in England, a socialist
country by his reckoning. Wasn't that a scheme of indoctrination?
Humphrey leapt to the defense of the ADA, an organization "unalterably opposed to totalitarianism, whether from the left or from the
right." Soon he was in full flight, defending European social democrats, the dignity of labor, and the democratic neutrality of India's
Jawaharlal Nehru. He assailed imperialism, saying, "We cannot be

for freedom in Europe and colonialism and enslavement in Asia. This is one world. It requires one foreign policy." He lavished praise on the Marshall Plan. One thing about the freshman senator: attack him and you'd unleash a swarm of bees.[1]

Virulent anti-communism was hardly new in America; the House Un-American Activities Committee, impaneled in 1938, had riveted the nation with its investigation of Hollywood in 1947 and of State Department official Alger Hiss the following year. But events both at home and abroad kindled this flame into a forest fire. On September 22, 1949, the Truman administration announced that the Soviets had exploded a nuclear bomb, suddenly achieving parity with the United States, at a time when the Red Army fielded ten times as many soldiers as the United States. A week later the nationalist government of China fled to Formosa, leaving the world with not one but two Communist regimes at the helm of continental empires. Americans who had grown complacent in their new global dominance were shocked. How had this been allowed to happen? A young congressman named John F. Kennedy echoed the rhetoric of the "China lobby" when he told a crowd in Boston that "the pinks" in the upper circles of government—code for Secretary of State Dean Acheson and his circle—had betrayed the nation. "What our young men had saved," Kennedy alleged, "our diplomats and our President frittered away."[2]

The fury continued to mount. On January 21, 1950, Hiss was found guilty of espionage. On the 27th, Klaus Fuchs, an atomic scientist, was arrested for spying—the first break in the case that would lead to the arrest, and ultimately the execution, of Julius and Ethel Rosenberg. Two weeks after that, Joseph McCarthy, Republican senator from Wisconsin, delivered a speech in Wheeling, West Virginia, in which he claimed to have in his hand a list of 205 State Department officials "that were made known to the Secretary of State as being members of the Communist Party and who nevertheless are still working and shaping policy in the State Department."[3] By the time McCarthy delivered a speech in the Senate ten days later, the number had dwindled to 81. But he had learned, as later demagogues would, that even the most reckless allegations can catapult a man to fame so long as they're delivered with an air of self-righteous certainty. Soon McCarthy would appear on the cover of both *Time* and *Newsweek*—and the Red-baiting genie was all the way out of the bottle.

Indeed, the same day that McCarthy lobbed his hand grenade in Wheeling, Homer Capehart, a fulminating Indiana Republican, unleashed a war cry on the Senate floor: "How much more are we going to have to take? Fuchs and Acheson and Hiss and hydrogen bombs threatening outside and New Dealism eating away at the vitals of the nation!"[4] And behind the McCarthys and the Capeharts stood the Daughters of the American Revolution and the American Legion and the Chamber of Commerce, and media magnates such as Colonel Robert McCormick of the *Chicago Tribune*, and of course J. Edgar Hoover and the FBI. That thunderous voice threatened to drown out not just the left but the vital center. Unlike the old and self-serving American ideology of laissez-faire that FDR had confronted, the Red-baiters spoke of liberalism as a form of treason.

Humphrey had, of course, made his national reputation as a fervent liberal who was not afraid to speak out bluntly about the menace of internal subversion. The rise of anti-Communist hysteria led him to acknowledge the danger to civil liberties that others on the left had been warning of throughout this period. The "Communist menace," he told the 1949 graduating class of Bennington College, was "relatively insignificant," especially compared to the danger the bellicose new mood posed to "critical, nonconformist, creative thinking."[5] He joined others in denouncing McCarthy's speech in Wheeling, stating that "to destroy the name of a man is to perform the most immoral, un-Christian, indecent act which possibly could be done."[6] In advance of the most egregious speech McCarthy ever delivered on the Senate floor, the June 1951 rant in which he placed Secretary of State George Marshall at the center of "a conspiracy so immense and an infamy so black as to dwarf any previous venture in the history of man," Humphrey tried to organize his fellow Democratic senators into a mass walkout. (Instead, they simply declined to attend.)[7]

Humphrey and other liberals opposed the single most dangerous piece of anti-Communist legislation to appear before Congress, a bill introduced by Senator Pat McCarran of Nevada that would require

Communist and affiliated organizations to register with the attorney general and provide a list of members. It would also establish a Subversive Activities Control Board with the power to determine whether or not an organization fell into that category.

Already, however, liberals had come to recognize the political costs of anti-anti-communism, and most, including Humphrey, agreed to support a "compromise" measure that empowered the president to detain anyone suspected of espionage or sabotage—to imprison them, that is, in a peacetime concentration camp. The debate took place in September 1950, and one liberal after another rose to denounce the McCarran bill. Humphrey was as fervent as any. "If hysteria ever grips America," he said, "if this proposal ever becomes a vehicle for the passions of dissension and disunity and bigotry and intolerance, may God help America, for a bill such as this makes it legal for the executive branch to strike down opposition."[8] And then Humphrey voted for the bill, as did most of his friends (though some, like Estes Kefauver of Illinois, did not). The compromise legislation, itself quite pernicious, having been voted down, Humphrey was unwilling to oppose the McCarran bill. He later admitted to a sense of shame over the initial vote; he had, he said, "never been more unhappy in my life."[9]

President Truman, who privately called the bill the greatest threat to American civil liberties since the Alien and Sedition Act of 1798, had the courage to veto it. This led to a peculiar, and painfully instructive, spectacle. Humphrey, Paul Douglas, William Langer of North Dakota, and several others decided to stage a southern-style filibuster to prevent the inevitable vote to override Truman's veto for as long as possible. Conservatives left the chamber while the small band of liberals handed off speaking assignments; others slept on army cots in the corridors, or in their offices, in order to be ready for a quorum call. Langer, a sixty-four-year-old populist known at home as "Wild Bill," began speaking at midnight, growing more and more hoarse until, at 5:13 a.m., he staggered, turned toward Humphrey, and said, "I yield to—," and then collapsed. Humphrey caught him on the way down and laid him out on the Senate floor. Capitol guards removed the senator and took him to the hospital.[10] The Senate then proceeded to vote 57–10 to overturn the veto. The fiasco taught Humphrey how much discipline was required to play the filibuster game.

It is easy, in retrospect, to see Humphrey's flirtation with anti-Communist legislation as an act of political cowardice. Yet he was typically standing alongside figures such as Douglas and the seigneurial Herbert Lehman of New York, lawmakers whose courage and independence were beyond question. Like them, he felt that domestic communism was weakened but by no means defeated; he continued to worry about Communist penetration of some American institutions, above all unions. He may have been influenced in this regard by his chief legislative aide, Max Kampelman, who had postponed his teaching career in order to follow Humphrey to Washington. Kampelman was both more of an intellectual than Humphrey and more of an ideologue. He had been a conscientious objector in World War II, and had left New York for Minnesota as a volunteer for a "starvation experiment" designed to test the physiological effects of food deprivation. But Kampelman was also a fervent anti-Communist who knew and feared the Trotskyite left. In the late forties he had written a doctoral dissertation on the struggle between the Communists and the CIO.[11] Kampelman would later become a leading "neoconservative," along with many others who, like him, were Jewish ex-leftists who migrated into the Reaganite camp. As his aide, he may have persuaded Humphrey that the CIO had not fully purged itself of Communist influence, for in late 1951 Humphrey announced that he would hold hearings on the subject. Humphrey told an interviewer that the Communist Party was using unions to infiltrate key industries, including electricity generation, communication, transportation, and docks, and said that he might propose legislation prohibiting Communist-dominated unions from engaging in collective bargaining.[12] But the hearings turned up no new evidence, and Humphrey, perhaps embarrassed, or even relieved, abandoned the issue.

Yet liberal anti-communism was not a contradiction in terms, as the Red-baiters insisted, but a coherent worldview that came to be known as "Cold War liberalism." The anti-totalitarian liberalism of the late thirties and forties had regarded the left, not the right, as its chief threat, and had positioned itself accordingly. In his master's thesis, Humphrey had argued that FDR had used the instrument of limited government to deal with the great problems of social and economic justice that the totalitarians insisted could be solved only by unlimited government. The same was conspicuously true of the text widely seen as the bible of the Cold War liberals: Arthur Schlesinger's *The Vital Center*, published in 1949.[13] Schlesinger was savage on "the fellow traveler" whose "sentimentality" had "softened up the progressive for Communist permeation and conquest," yet he had nothing to say about right-wing anti-communism, which did not then feel like a grave threat to democracy.[14] Liberals had won that battle: they had purged the big unions of their Communist factions, and they had cured mainstream organizations of their infatuation with Popular Front politics. Liberal pressure had pushed Truman to the left, and he had become a fit instrument for liberal aspirations. Now liberals had to respond to a very different threat from the right.

Humphrey became the leading political spokesman for Cold War liberalism. He had long taken the view that the fight against totalitarianism, whether in the form of fascism or communism, operated above all at the level of ideas, even of faith, and could be permanently won only by demonstrating that democratic capitalism delivered prosperity and justice for the average citizen more effectively than communism did. The anti-Communist attack on Humphrey, on the ADA, and on liberalism broadly led him not to pull in his horns but to carry the battle of ideas to the public and to the Senate floor. Along with the ADA's leading intellectuals, including Schlesinger, Reinhold Niebuhr, and John Kenneth Galbraith, Humphrey would make the case for Cold War liberalism.

In early 1950, arguing for a comprehensive federal law criminalizing lynching, Humphrey said, "I can think of no measure which will do more to raise the moral stature of Americans in the eyes of the world than the passage of the bill which we have before us."[15] In mid-May, he said much the same of a bill to establish a permanent Fair Employment Practices Commission: "So long as men and women and children of color are discriminated against in the United States, the colored people of the world have the right to suspect our privileged friendship with them."[16] (When Senator Spessard Holland of Florida declared the legislation a piece of Communist propaganda, Humphrey wildly accused him of "blasphemy," at which point he was instructed to sit down, having violated Senate rules of decorum.) The following month, when he and Paul Douglas, Herbert Lehman, Wayne Morse of Oregon, and five others reintroduced the whole package of civil rights bills, Humphrey quoted from a Soviet broadcast to India to the effect that while Blacks couldn't vote in America, all citizens in the Soviet Union enjoyed equal rights of participation. Friends from Indonesia and Nigeria, Humphrey said, had separately told him that 486 Blacks had been lynched in America the year before—when the true number was three. We are winning the military battle, Humphrey said, but "we are losing ground on the ideological front."[17]

Humphrey's conviction that civil rights were a matter not only of simple justice but also of national security kept him from losing heart despite the hopeless political odds. At the very beginning of the Eighty-Second Congress, in January 1951, he sent a letter to President Truman asking him to establish an FEPC by executive order, as FDR had done in 1941. (The civil rights leaders A. Philip Randolph and Walter White had sent the same proposal to Truman the month before.) Humphrey observed that the Korean War, which had begun the previous June, had produced a manpower shortage, as World War II had; the nation could not afford bigotry. He tried to persuade the president that the failure of civil rights legislation to date had not "in any way dimmed the determination of the American people to be guided by the Golden Rule." Truman, an extremely shrewd judge of the wishes of the American public, did not agree, and instead issued a vague statement reiterating the legal prohibition against discrimination in war plants.

Humphrey was prepared to keep fighting and losing battles over civil rights, but he could not accept the venom that was regularly directed at him in the southern press. He felt misunderstood; more to the point, he recognized that he could never be elected president so long as the South regarded him as an inveterate foe. In November 1951 Humphrey sent a letter to the editors of twenty-two newspapers across the South explaining why he supported civil rights. He began, as he had in his speech at the Democratic National Convention, with strenuous efforts to disarm his wary audience, noting the "close bond" between Minnesota and the South, which were both dependent on the export of raw material. National economic development, he said, would bring benefits to both regions. He then commended the progress made in the South on education, health, and housing. "It is wrong and unjust," he observed, "to single out any area of the country as the worst offender" on civil rights. Then, rather than making a moral case he knew he couldn't win, he offered the Cold War logic that he now routinely used in the Senate and on the stump. In the face of the Communist challenge, he wrote, it had become more important than ever that America stand as "one nation indivisible." Nonwhite people everywhere were demanding their rights. "The day of white supremacy is over," Humphrey wrote. "It is always immoral and is today impossible."[18] The fact that Humphrey appears to have believed that his readers might be persuaded by this logic implies an almost touching faith in the powers of reason.

Humphrey's letter was widely distributed. Many southern liberals wrote back to him saying they had tried—and usually failed—to get the editors of their local papers to publish it. But racial liberals were thin on the ground in the South; and Humphrey's appeal to the higher good of the fight against communism seems not to have prompted any fresh reflections among the partisans of Jim Crow. The *Tampa Tribune* ran an article under the heading "Boos for a Blatherskite" that called the appeal "irrational and intemperate." Humphrey exchanged a number of letters with William B. Ruggles, the editor of the *Dallas Morning News*. Each professed his respect for the other's candid opinion without in any way changing it. The letter was probably a harebrained idea. But Humphrey would never surrender his belief in mankind's better angels.[19]

HUMPHREY WAS HARDLY ALONE IN ARGUING THAT "THE PRESTIGE OF democracy" hung in the balance of the civil rights debate. The authors of Truman's civil rights report had written in 1947 that "the United States is not so strong, the final triumph of the democratic ideal is not so inevitable that we can ignore what the world thinks of us or

our record." During the FEPC debate, William Benton, a Connecticut Democrat and former delegate to the United Nations Educational,
Scientific and Cultural Organization (UNESCO), had recalled how
"Communist propaganda twisted and distorted our civil rights problem in the channels of world communication."[20] The urgent need to
wage and win the war of ideas against communism didn't change
the liberals' idea of what was just, but it did impart a new urgency to
the struggle for justice. That struggle was not just domestic but also
global. The outlook of the Cold War liberals was marked by a striking mixture of idealism and bellicosity: precisely because they saw the
contest between the United States and the Soviet Union in profoundly
moral and civilizational terms, they were not prepared to yield an
inch to the Soviets. They could not fully accept the passive metaphor
of "containment," coined by diplomat George Kennan in his famous
1946 "Long Telegram." Humphrey used the word pejoratively, to sig-
nify a passive defense of American territory and assets rather than
the affirmative struggle for freedom that he favored. He regarded the
Korean War as the necessary military component of that campaign;
he supported President Truman's request for a drastically increased
defense budget and for universal military training. He favored offering help to both insurgent leaders and democratic activists behind the
Iron Curtain.[21] At a time when Republicans advocated shrinking the
army to reduce spending, Humphrey wanted not only to keep troops
in Europe but to post them in Asia to prevent Chinese expansion.

Neither, however, did Humphrey and the Cold War liberals join
conservatives, such as the political theorist James Burnham, in calling
for a military "rollback" of Soviet gains in Eastern Europe. Humphrey
thought of the Cold War less as a military contest than as a struggle to win the loyalty of the hundreds of millions of people in Asia,
Africa, and Latin America who would no longer accept the suffering and injustice that had been their immemorial lot and had begun
to critically examine the two rival world systems. The great instruments that America brought to this battle were its democratic way of
life, which people intrinsically preferred to "the slave system," and
the generous aid made possible by its great prosperity—what today
we would call "soft power." In 1950 Humphrey called for spending

$500 million to expand the Voice of America from Europe to Asia. He called for "a Marshall Plan in the realm of ideas."[22] The Marshall Plan was Humphrey's master metaphor for American foreign policy (and often for domestic policy as well, since over the years he would call for "a Marshall Plan for the cities" and for all sorts of other targets). The Marshall Plan had demonstrated that America was a new kind of great power that wielded its strength not to coerce but to assist, and that advanced its own interest by improving the lot of its allies. This unprecedented investment had not only helped put Europe back on its feet but blunted the rising popularity of Communist parties in France, Italy, and elsewhere. The "penny-pinchers" of the "Taft-McCarthy school," Humphrey said, complained bitterly about the billions Washington had sent to Europe; but they seemed to believe that "the flames of communism . . . can be blown out by the breath of blowhards."[23]

What had worked in Europe would surely work in Asia and elsewhere. In his 1949 State of the Union address, Truman had called for "making the benefits of our scientific progress and industrial advancement available for the improvement and growth of underdeveloped areas." The idea of providing technical assistance to poor countries, known as Point Four, because it was the fourth point of the foreign policy section of Truman's otherwise forgettable speech, became a cornerstone of the foreign aid program. The early advocates of foreign aid blithely assumed that economic development would lead to political reform, and thus to democracy.[24] In retrospect, Humphrey was plainly guilty of this all-American optimism; foreign aid was too vital a weapon in the Cold War for him to seriously consider its shortcomings. Nevertheless, he had the foresight to call for assistance to be explicitly targeted to social and economic change—to land reform, universal public education, the encouragement of trade unions, rural electrification, social security, and decent housing. Recipients, he said, must be encouraged to safeguard human rights, above all the rights of women.[25] Only in recent decades have American and international aid organizations embraced this gospel of democratic development.

Humphrey was India's greatest champion in Congress. He was in regular contact with his friend Chester Bowles, now the ambassador to India, and he met with visiting Indian officials, including Madame

Pandit, the sister of Prime Minister Jawaharlal Nehru. Conservatives regarded India as all too close both to Moscow and Peking, and considered its planned economy a facsimile of the Communist system. For the Cold War liberals, however, India was the largest nation in the world that stood between the two camps, and thus the greatest prize in the ideological struggle. (Only in 1955 would India formalize its neutral position by joining, and leading, the Non-Aligned Movement.) The Mutual Security Act of 1951 promised assistance only to "friendly countries"; in the midst of a famine that year, a $190 million grant of wheat was batted back and forth while a debate raged over India's neutrality. Humphrey noted that Russia had given India fifty thousand tons of wheat, and had scattered hundreds of "information centers"—propaganda kiosks—across the country. The Voice of America had no presence at all. Were we, Humphrey asked, prepared to "lose" India? Indochina could go next, then Burma, Ceylon, and Thailand—an early expression of the "domino theory."[26] (The bill ultimately passed with a rider, which Humphrey opposed, requiring India to repay the grant in the form of rare-earth minerals.)

India wasn't a hard case for Humphrey; the problem lay with autocratic allies such as Pakistan or South Korea or Taiwan. This issue would vex the United States throughout the Cold War. In his 1947 ADA report, Schlesinger had argued that supporting authoritarian governments—Francisco Franco's Spain or Chiang Kai-shek's Taiwan, for example—was a tactical error, because it allowed Stalin to claim that only the Communists could be counted on to oppose the fascists.[27] Humphrey shared that view. In October 1950, he complained on a radio show that the United States continued to support the emperor Bao Dai, France's puppet in Vietnam, though "he had been on the banks of the Riviera during the past months" while the Communist leader Ho Chi Minh had been "leading the fight" against the colonizers. Washington should instead be seeking out "native, liberal, positive leaders from their own people." Humphrey did not identify any such figures.[28]

Humphrey's distaste for autocratic allies led to a celebrated donnybrook on *Meet Your Congressman*, a TV news show, in April 1951. When the arch Red-baiter Homer Capehart, senator from Indiana, suggested arming Chiang to invade the mainland, Senator Herbert Lehman of New York shot back that doing so offered a virtual invitation to start World War III. When Capehart accused Lehman of being "sympathetic with Communist China," Humphrey shouted back, "That is absolute vilification." Capehart repeated the charge. Humphrey called him a "prevaricator." Capehart, according to news accounts, called his colleague "an SOB without the initials." Humphrey jumped out of his seat, and the two engaged in "pushing, shoving, grappling and arm-flailing." Afterward, the former Boy Scout troop leader wryly recalled, "I didn't even say gosh darn."[29] Nobody could say he wasn't prepared to stand up for his convictions.

Two years after arriving in Washington, this most gregarious of politicians remained lonely. In Minneapolis he had formed a circle of like-minded men and women that he moved with almost all the time. Now he had no circle; and of course he no longer had a father. He barely had a staff: his former mayoral aide William Simms attended to constituent issues in Minnesota, while virtually everything else fell to Max Kampelman. Humphrey was staggering under his workload. In the summer of 1951, Art Naftalin came out from Minnesota to help with staff work; he was shocked to find his exuberant friend dragging around like "a beaten man." Humphrey's neighbor and old friend Russell Long felt similarly pained to see him thrashing around in the Senate and making enemies among his fellow Democrats. One day in the fall of 1951, Long said to him, "You know, Hubert, you've been going into that public Senate dining room, but if you really want to get acquainted, you should go into that little private dining room in the back where the senators eat."[30] Long offered to escort him into this inner sanctum, where Republicans sat at one long table and Democrats at another. Humphrey eagerly agreed.

Humphrey was as alien a creature to the southern barons as they were to him. All they had seen was a self-righteous ideologue and pedant who didn't know when to sit down and shut up. They had never seen or felt Humphrey's warmth, his self-deprecating humor, his simple and sincere fondness for others. Humphrey, for his part, had plunged into Senate life without making an effort to understand the institution's culture. He had quickly come to see himself as little David fighting a reactionary Goliath, a posture that came naturally to him. But as he got to know these pillars of the Senate, he began to recognize that they were far less ideological than he thought—save on the one, existential issue of civil rights. Otherwise, whether you were a liberal or a conservative, sided with business or labor—"all of those things were considered to be your personal prerogative," Humphrey discovered.[31]

The men of the inner dining room were creatures of the institution that many of them had inhabited for decades; they had set its codes and mastered its rules. They put great stock by forms: they wore three-piece suits and practiced an archaic form of high-flown oratory. They were inclined to be tolerant and even gallant, though, as William S. White would later put it, they were "intolerant towards any who would in any real way change the Senate, its customs or its way of life," as Humphrey himself had done by launching an attack on Harry Byrd's fiefdom.[32] That very conservatism and pompous self-regard drove away most of the liberals; neither Paul Douglas nor Herbert Lehman, for example, ever penetrated the inner sanctum or felt any wish to do so. Humphrey, however, wanted to be a member of the club and wanted the esteem of the members, and he found himself liking some of them, and even being liked in return.

Humphrey began to come in from the cold when he waged the kind of fight that the fellowship of the inner sanctum respected. The Korean War had begun in June 1950, when North Korean forces crossed the 38th parallel into the south. Amid growing Cold War tensions, President Truman called for an additional $4.5 billion in defense spending. The Senate Finance Committee was tasked with drawing up supplemental tax legislation. That committee, like all important committees, was controlled by a Southern Democrat, Walter George; the senior Republican was Eugene Milliken of Colorado. Both were deeply versed in the arcana of tax law and had used their superior knowledge to write bills that favored the business lobbies, which in return contributed to their campaigns and paid them to take cushy trips to resorts in order to address their members. The supplemental tax bill the committee reported out was larded with measures that lowered tax exposure for corporations and the wealthy at the cost of increasing tax rates on ordinary earners.

Humphrey was shocked; and he was unwilling to simply wave this gross injustice through the legislative gates, as others were. But he stood at the edge of a wilderness: tax law was not only intrinsically difficult but *terra incognita* for him. Along with Senators Paul Douglas, Herbert Lehman, and William Langer, he spent ten days poring over the legislation with officials from the Truman administration. One of them, Joseph Pechman, a young tax analyst in the Treasury Department who would later become the dean of American tax scholars, later described Humphrey as "the quickest study I ever met."[33] Humphrey worked closely with Douglas, a highly regarded economist at the University of Chicago before joining the Senate, to write a statement targeting a dozen of the more egregious loopholes in the legislation. As an added precaution, he went first to Senator George to tell him what he intended to do. Humphrey would later write that his colleague said, "Go right ahead. That's what a senator is supposed to do."[34]

On September 20, 1951, Humphrey rose in the Senate. For once, he spoke not from rough notes but from a prepared text. He began, as was his wont, by disclaiming expertise and insisting that he wished to learn rather than to instruct. And then he proceeded to instruct. According to the tax tables included in the supplemental legislation, he argued, a "$3,000-a-year married man" would need to earn another thousand dollars to have the after-tax income he would have had in 1944. Immediately Senator John Williams of Delaware, a businessman and avowed foe of government spending, asked Humphrey to yield. That was slightly early for such an interruption to be fully consistent with senatorial courtesy, and an irate Humphrey snapped, "The Senator from Minnesota does not yield. I have worked a long time to prepare my statement, and I think it needs to be said." Because he was not a member of the Finance Committee, Humphrey was considered an amateur and was not being taken seriously. He had to ask Senator Douglas, sitting in the chair, to admonish his colleagues to stop talking to each other.[35]

Humphrey now embarked on a long and remarkably detailed discussion of the loopholes in question; he started at noon and ended at 6:00. The use of family partnerships, he explained, allowed high-income and thus high-tax individuals to "split" their income with spouses and children who would pay at a lower rate—even though no one pretended that "one-year-old Charlie" was helping run the enterprise in question. This prompted a response from Robert Kerr of Oklahoma, possibly the most feared and disliked man in the Senate. Surely, said Kerr, the senator from Minnesota did not dispute the tax-free treatment of a family gift; a family partnership constituted just such a gift. Not at all, Humphrey shot back—the gift no longer belongs to the giver, while the senior partner continues to control the partnership, which is why the courts had disallowed the tax treatment in question. And so it went, a vast fencing match with Humphrey, and occasionally Paul Douglas, on one side, and Kerr, Williams, Milliken, and George on the other. Humphrey was enjoying himself immensely, at one point observing, "I do not think there is any better way in the world to find out what goes in framing a tax bill than to get into a little scrap about the facts." The experts he had consulted were sitting in the gallery, and Max Kampelman, sitting next to him, had arranged to signal them to come downstairs for a conference in case Humphrey got stuck. Kampelman later said that almost never happened.[36]

It was strange that Humphrey was taking the lead rather than Douglas, who could have stood on a more than equal footing with Milliken and George. Douglas was considered by almost everyone save himself as one of the finest minds in the Senate. But he didn't relish a little scrap as much as Humphrey did. Douglas was fifty-eight years old; at age fifty he had left his sinecure at Chicago to become the oldest volunteer in the history of the Marines. Shipped off to Asia, he had insisted on going to the front lines, and at Okinawa he had been gravely wounded while carrying another soldier to safety. Douglas lost the use of his left arm. A member of the ADA, he had joined the Senate the year before, as Humphrey had, and was expected to lead the charge for the Fair Deal on the economic front. But Douglas, though utterly fearless, had done his fighting. He was an intellectual who spent his evenings reading Aristotle, Tocqueville, and Burke. Across from his desk he had placed copies of Holbein's portraits of Erasmus and Thomas More, reminders of the humanist foundations of the liberal tradition. In personal matters Douglas was as unbending as More himself, refusing to accept gifts valued at more than $2.50 and returning his monthly disability check on the grounds that he didn't need it.[37]

Humphrey regarded Douglas as a Nestor. "I was his student," he later said.[38] He could never be self-sufficient, as Douglas was; but neither did he value purity as Douglas did. He was perfectly happy to work with the Walter Georges of the Senate when he could, and to fight them when he had to. Douglas was delighted to hand the younger man ammunition, especially if he could do so in a way that amused himself. He quoted Gilbert and Sullivan and an unidentified quatrain of nineteenth-century English verse. Humphrey kept loading and firing, taking on the tax treatment of stock options and then the oil depletion allowance—a sacred issue for oilmen and their congressional defenders, such as Senator Kerr, as Humphrey well knew. Each detail of the tax code, by itself, felt like higher math. But Humphrey never lost sight of the meaning of the whole. "I want to remind the Senate of the United States," he said, echoing the language of Jefferson, "that this bill is giving special privileges to the few and raising the tax rates of the many."

The Humphrey/Douglas position was foredoomed by the politics of tax policy, which is to say the power of the few over the many. Humphrey and Douglas lost on almost everything, though it is important to bear in mind that postwar tax rates were fantastically confiscatory by contemporary standards, reaching 50 percent for married filers with $32,000 in income and topping out at 91 percent. (The corporate rate was 42 percent on profits over $50,000.) Nevertheless, Humphrey had made tax fairness a national issue in a way that it had not been before. He gained the respectful attention of the nation's leading columnists: Marquis Childs wrote that while most senators happily left tax policy to their few expert colleagues, Humphrey had mastered the subject, and zeroed in on the worst inequities, "after two months of concentrated study."[39] No less important, Humphrey had proved to his colleagues that he was a workhorse, not a show horse. Afterward, George and Milliken came over to Humphrey to congratulate him on his performance. After eighteen months in the Senate, Humphrey was far from the inner sanctum but no longer in outer darkness.

10

Lyndon Johnson and the Instruments of Power

"I want to work with you and only you
from the bomb throwers."

HUBERT HUMPHREY WAS TOO GIFTED AND AMBITIOUS A POLI-
tician to flounder for long. After several years in office he
had become the acknowledged leader of the modest liberal
faction in the Senate, a man with a national standing to protect and
advance. In March 1952, he reluctantly agreed to stand as a favorite
son in Minnesota's Democratic primary with the understanding that
the delegation would go with Truman should the president choose to
run for reelection. On March 29, Truman announced that he would
not do so. Humphrey had already so established his standing as a
leader of liberal forces in the Senate that his Connecticut colleague
Brien McMahon and John Bailey, the state's Democratic boss, came
to his office to ask him to run for president. Humphrey, understanding that the time was not yet ripe, declined.[1] Nevertheless, on

April 6 he confirmed to the *New York Times* that he would accept a vice presidential berth were it offered. It was reported that Humphrey was Truman's choice to deliver the keynote address at the Democratic National Convention.[2]

With Truman out of the picture, the Democratic Party's identity was an open question for the first time in twenty years. The party was split into irreconcilable factions, North and South, with a few progressive southerners and moderate figures from the West and Midwest standing in between. Who would gain the upper hand? The fight for the nomination would help determine the answer. The first out of the gate was Estes Kefauver, a border-state politician from eastern Tennessee, a populist progressive who had run for office in a coonskin cap, a big, fiercely ambitious, self-dramatizing figure who had gained instant national fame by chairing hearings into organized crime. Southerners regarded him as a renegade because he opposed the poll tax and was no worse than lukewarm on the Fair Employment Practices Commission. Standing against him was Richard Russell, the vizier of the southern forces, who had apparently forgotten his own dictum that the nation would never elect a president from the old Confederacy.

Waiting diffidently in the wings was Adlai Stevenson, the governor of Illinois and a political aristocrat. His grandfather had been Grover Cleveland's vice president, and his father had been secretary of state for Illinois. Like many another aristocrat—like the young FDR, in fact—Stevenson was witty, charming, gracious, eloquent, and not altogether serious about politics. He had the views of a moderate Republican: under close questioning from worried liberals, Stevenson revealed that he was opposed to public housing and to federal aid to education, favored cuts in government spending, and regarded civil rights as a matter to be decided at the state level. Nevertheless, he had won liberal acclaim by desegregating the Illinois National Guard and sending it into the city of Cairo to calm a race riot. He had testified on behalf of Alger Hiss at a time when doing so took real courage. Stevenson *sounded* liberal; he spoke in wonderful rolling periods, invoked the nation's founding ideals, and, though no intellectual himself, sought their company. Truman saw Stevenson as the Democrat with the best chance of winning in 1952 and tried to recruit him; but in April the governor withdrew from a race that he had never entered.

Humphrey very much preferred Kefauver, whom he considered a true liberal. In any case, he hoped to play a prominent role at the convention. He was sure to be in the thick of the most important platform debate, on civil rights. During the spring, he was asked to join discussions with two relatively progressive southerners, Congressman Brooks Hays of Arkansas and Senator John Sparkman of Alabama, in the hopes of finding compromise language. He demurred when Herbert Lehman demanded a plank explicitly committed to an FEPC with enforcement powers, but he also declined to sign off on language acceptable to the South.[3] As he had demonstrated with his olive-branch letter of the previous fall, Humphrey was no longer eager to defy the Jim Crow South—but neither would he surrender his principles. In July, when Massachusetts governor Paul Dever insisted at a meeting of the National Governors Conference that any civil rights plank be acceptable to the South as well as the North, Humphrey, addressing the NAACP National Convention, cried, "I will not be any part of any deal to any compromise, any shenanigans, or any sellout on the fundamental principle of democracy, equality or human dignity."[4] He vowed to do what he could to commit the party to ending the filibuster.

By the time the Democratic convention opened in Chicago in mid-July, with the outcome still very much in doubt, the delegates faced not one but two issues of civil rights. The first question was whether southern delegations, some of whom had walked out in 1948, should be seated if they refused to promise that they would put the nominee's name on the ballot. The issue came down to Mississippi and Texas. Frank McKinney, chairman of the Democratic National Committee, proposed language that would have allowed them to be seated so long as they were in compliance with state law—which in their case did not require accepting the convention's choice. This provoked an outburst from Humphrey, who called McKinney a "political traitor."[5] Kefauver and New York's Averill Harriman, who had also declared his candidacy, demanded the seating of the rival delegations pledged to support the nominee. Party professionals, including

McKinney, concluded that the two liberal candidates hoped to prompt the South to walk out of the convention, and thus improve either of their chances of beating Stevenson. The Illinois governor, who, to no one's surprise, had not resisted a "draft Stevenson" movement, agreed to the compromise language as the price of winning southern support. The Mississippi and Texas delegations were seated.

The civil rights subcommittee of the platform committee heard testimony from the nation's major civil rights groups, which demanded improvements on the 1948 plank in the form of an explicit endorsement of a strong FEPC and a call to end the filibuster. Americans for Democratic Action joined the call. But this time, unlike 1948, there was no major figure prepared to risk a breach in the name of high principle. Humphrey agreed not to insist on the FEPC language; the platform would call for an "equal employment opportunity commission"—itself a sop to the South—with "effective" rather than "enforceable" powers. The plank on filibusters was removed to a separate passage on "democratic governance."[6] Nevertheless, Humphrey could feel that he had honored the spirit, if not the letter, of his promises to the civil rights community. The platform committee adopted the language of 1948; if there had been no progress, neither had there been retreat. Southern delegates had not, in fact, walked out; arch-segregationist Spessard Holland even called the plank "moderate."[7] Perhaps Dixie felt reassured by Stevenson's notable lack of passion on the subject. Though the party leadership was not about to let Humphrey give the keynote, as the president had wished, he did have the satisfaction of hearing Gene McCarthy, now a member of the House, deliver a short and handsome speech placing Humphrey's name in nomination as Minnesota's favorite son. McCarthy spoke of the senator as "a liberal Democrat by birth, rearing and conviction," not omitting a sweet reference to the late Hubert Sr. McCarthy's speech set off a twenty-one-minute parade by a dozen state delegations.[8]

The liberal faction at the convention, led by Humphrey, favored Harriman or Kefauver. But with Stevenson coming on strong, Humphrey and Governor G. Mennen Williams of Michigan met with the candidate, who said he would be open to Kefauver as a running mate.

Humphrey and his group met with Kefauver and then with Harriman. Out on the convention floor, they could feel the mood shifting toward Stevenson. At 3:30 in the morning on July 25, Humphrey convened five hundred liberal delegates in a hotel ballroom. Most of them, he later told the *New York Times*, regarded Stevenson as a Dixiecrat and a spokesman for the big-city machines—the Democratic Party pre-FDR. Drawing on his conversations, Humphrey reassured the crowd that Stevenson was "certainly liberal enough for us to back." By 6:00 a.m., when the meeting finally ended, most of the delegates had agreed to switch their votes to Stevenson.[9] Humphrey was quoted as saying, "Stevenson is all right, just so long as another liberal is on the ticket."[10]

By virtue of his willingness to compromise in the face of an intransigent reality, Humphrey had made himself a power broker, at least within his own limited realm—a very different role from the one he had played four years earlier. He had not, it is true, won many concessions. Stevenson did not choose "another liberal" as running mate; he selected John Sparkman, a dependable disciple of Russell's on civil rights if not on labor or social spending. This was not the Democratic Party that Humphrey had so passionately embraced as a young man. *The New Republic* called Stevenson the most conservative Democratic candidate for president since John Davis in 1920. The *Times* summed up the ticket by observing that "the FDR-Truman philosophy of government is nearing the end of an era."[11] Stevenson seemed only marginally less conservative than his Republican rival, Dwight D. Eisenhower, though Ike's views remained a secret. That did not, however, stop Eisenhower's running mate, the notorious Red-baiter Richard Nixon, from accusing Stevenson of holding "a Ph.D. from Dean Acheson's cowardly college of Communist Containment."[12]

Humphrey was now a Stevenson man, come what may. He threw himself into the campaign with his usual frenetic enthusiasm, electioneering across eighteen states. But the combination of liberal fatigue after two decades of Democratic rule, Stevenson's air of cool disengagement, and the national reverence for Ike, the most beloved general since Ulysses S. Grant, made the outcome a foregone conclusion. Stevenson carried most of the old Confederacy as well as

Kentucky and West Virginia—nine states and eighty-nine electoral votes in all. He lost the big industrial states that had been the core of FDR's electoral coalition by 10 to 15 points. That coalition now lay in tatters. Stevenson had not been able to provide the answer to the question of what the Democratic Party stood for in the new era of prosperity, and in the face of vicious attacks that cast the party as "soft on communism."

THE GOP HAD CARRIED NOT ONLY THE PRESIDENCY BUT THE HOUSE and the Senate, which now had forty-eight Republicans, forty-seven Democrats, and an independent, Wayne Morse of Oregon, who caucused with the Republicans. With the former majority leader, Ernest McFarland, having lost his Arizona seat to Barry Goldwater, the new role of minority leader was available. This was not a hotly contested position, but one senator, Lyndon Johnson, the Texas freshman, wanted it very much. As Johnson began buttonholing colleagues, the liberal ranks stiffened against him. Like Sparkman, Johnson was an economic progressive but a member in perfect standing of the anti-civil rights bloc. Like most other southern leaders, Johnson had not lifted a finger for Stevenson during the campaign. Liberals such as Paul Douglas and Herbert Lehman had never fraternized with Johnson; nor had he issued any invitations to them. Johnson was widely known as a young intimate of the inner dining room, a protégé of Richard Russell and of House Speaker Sam Rayburn, another Texan. But Johnson had reached out to Humphrey. He had, in fact, according to a former Johnson aide, George Reedy, delivered the full Johnson treatment. As they rode together on the Senate's underground subway in the spring of 1951, Johnson had troweled on the flattery as only he could do, praising Humphrey for his eloquence and knowledge. But then he had turned in an instant, barking, "But goddamn it, Hubert, why can't you be something but a gramophone for the NAACP? . . . You're spending so much time making speeches that there is no time left to get anything done."[13]

Humphrey was not accustomed to being spontaneously addressed by a member of the inner sanctum, and he warmed to Johnson immediately. Soon he was coming over to Johnson's office for drinks after work. In his magisterial account of Johnson's life, Robert Caro argues that the supremely intuitive Johnson sensed Humphrey's loneliness and knew that he could bind this vulnerable figure to him with the offer of friendship.[14] Humphrey had not yet begun frequenting the inner dining room. Certainly it was Johnson—as Caro notes—who vouched for Humphrey with southerners such as Walter George and even Richard Russell. "It's fair to say," Humphrey would later observe, "that Lyndon Johnson did more to bring me into those more social relationships with the conservative members of the Democratic Party than any other person in the Congress."[15] It was to no small extent thanks to Johnson that Humphrey came to understand that "social relationships," rather than ideological conviction, were the coin of the realm in the US Senate. This was precious wisdom for a man as fundamentally likable—and as desperately eager to be liked—as Humphrey.

After the 1952 election, Humphrey, Douglas, Lehman, and the other liberals tried to find a standard-bearer to run what was sure to be a futile campaign against Johnson for minority leader. Humphrey was, as always, open about his feelings. Asked by reporters if he supported Johnson's bid, he said, "It would be better to have someone who wasn't clearly identified with a sectional group."[16] Even that wasn't quite true, for the liberals approached Lister Hill of Alabama—who turned out already to be committed to Johnson. They finally had to settle on the seventy-six-year-old James Murray of Montana, a faithful New Dealer who had served without much distinction since 1935. This constituted almost laughable amateurism from the point of view of a consummate professional like Johnson, who had come to expect no better from the liberals. But he wanted to separate Humphrey from the pack. Johnson asked for his vote, but Humphrey said he was already committed to Murray. That's too bad, the Texan said; I was thinking about making you minority whip. Not a man to be won over with a bribe, Humphrey declined. However, when the liberals recognized that Johnson might agree to offer them the kind of choice committee assignments they had long been denied in exchange for support, Humphrey agreed to lead a delegation to Johnson's office.

There ensued a sequence of exchanges that Humphrey would describe again and again, always in the same words, even though they made him look like a babe in the woods. He *was*, he learned, a babe in the woods that Lyndon Johnson inhabited. He was telling the story of an apprenticeship—a word he used—that would shape the remainder of his career in the Senate. Johnson, as Humphrey later wrote in his memoirs, told the group that he already had all the votes he needed and thus had no need to bargain with them. With that, they were dismissed. By the time Humphrey had returned to his office, Johnson had called him and summoned him to return. "Let me tell you something, Hubert," Johnson then said in the tone of blunt command that was second nature to him. "You're depending on votes you don't have. How many votes do you think you have?"

"Well I think we have anywhere from thirteen to seventeen."

"First of all, you ought to be sure of your count. That's too much of a spread. But you don't have them anyway." Humphrey went down his list and Johnson told that him that he already had personal commitments from many of them—including Lester Hunt of Wyoming, who had accompanied Humphrey to Johnson's office. A master angler of men, Johnson was now reeling in America's number one liberal. "You could have been minority whip," he said, "and you'll regret your decision, but at least you didn't talk out of both sides of your mouth." Once Johnson had been elected leader, he said, "I want to work with you and only you from the bomb throwers"—Johnson's word for outspoken liberals.

Johnson's prediction about the vote count was dead accurate, as it almost always was. Humphrey found that he was one of the few men who had pledged their votes to Murray to have actually kept his promise. That was another revelation. Leader Johnson summoned Humphrey once again and asked for the wish list that he hadn't bothered to hear the first time around. This time Johnson would be bestowing favors, not accepting a deal. Humphrey said the liberals wanted to have Murray on the Policy Committee, which Johnson controlled. Lehman wanted Judiciary. Done, said Johnson. Why is it, Johnson asked, that none of the liberals ever asked to be on Finance? Didn't they understand that was where the real power lay—not to mention opportunities for fund-raising? They agreed that Paul Douglas would go on Finance. "Now you go back and tell your liberal friends that you're the one to talk to me and that if they'll talk through you as their leader we can get some things done."[17]

There was a gift for Humphrey as well: Johnson asked him to move to the Foreign Relations Committee, granting him a role on the one policy area that Humphrey cared about as much as civil rights—and that, unlike civil rights, would actually matter in an Eisenhower administration. The Senate GOP caucus was dominated by Midwestern isolationists, very much including their leader, Robert Taft of Ohio, who was himself moving to Foreign Relations. Johnson understood that Eisenhower was far more comfortable with Truman's internationalism, and saw that the Democrats could give Ike crucial support that could be traded for concessions on domestic policy. Johnson was prepared to elevate Humphrey and another freshman, Mike Mansfield of Montana, a scholar of foreign affairs, over more senior figures in the party who also coveted the slot. "Mansfield out-knows Taft, and Humphrey can out-talk him," as Johnson put it.[18] In order to take the position, however, Humphrey would have to leave both Agriculture and Education and Labor. Humphrey bridled; as a Minnesota senator, he needed to stay on Ag to fight for his constituents. When Johnson flatly refused, Humphrey asked if he could be first in line when a vacancy appeared. Johnson agreed, and a year later Humphrey was back on the Agriculture Committee.

Lyndon Johnson was to become the most important man in Hubert Humphrey's life after his father. Hubert and Hubert Sr. were bound by love. The ligatures that bound Humphrey to Johnson were of course much weaker, not to mention less symmetrical; yet each found in the other something he did not have, and needed. Both were plain men who felt an intuitive bond with the ordinary citizen. They shared the primal experience of having grown up at the edge of the prairie and living through the catastrophe of the Dust Bowl.[19] Both saw in the benevolent state fostered by FDR a means of addressing human suffering. But the larger misery hadn't entered Humphrey's soul; he was the lucky man who had been at one with his town, his family, his friends. Life had taught him to trust people long before he learned reasons for distrust. The Johnson family, by contrast, had lost the family ranch, their social standing, and their money when Lyndon was twelve. And they lost it thanks to feckless investments by his father, Sam. At sixteen, Lyndon had had to work behind a mule on a road gang in the blazing West Texas summers. His own world, and his surrounding world, were much harsher than Humphrey's; only thanks to his superhuman will did he rise out of the dust. He learned to trust no one save himself, to use others, to climb over them lest they climbed over him.[20]

While Hubert Humphrey was an intellectual who had at one time planned to become a political scientist, Lyndon Johnson had gone no farther than Southwest Texas State Teachers College, where he had devoted far more energy to running school politics than he had to reading books. Johnson never had time to read books; his life was consumed by the exhausting business of getting ahead. He may actually have meant what he said to Humphrey on the Senate underground, for Johnson was acutely self-conscious about his lack of formal education; though stupendously persuasive in front of one person or a knot of voters at a county courthouse, Johnson utterly lacked Humphrey's gift for pouring his convictions into a speech. He could sound insincere even when he wasn't—though he often was. He knew how to get a man to vote his way far better than he knew how to advance the abstract merits of a political proposition. That skill, Johnson would have said, was for "the Harvards," not for politicians.

Johnson and Humphrey had radically different ideas of what politics *was*—that is, what means it offered to achieve their goals. Johnson neatly encapsulated the difference many years later, in 1964, in a recorded phone conversation with Minnesota governor Karl Rolvaag. Liberals, he said, don't understand that in order to change things "we need to get the instruments of power in our hands." Those instruments included the House Ways and Means Committee and the Rules Committee—not "the newspapers." Johnson went on to illustrate his point. "The great mistake Hubert did when he came here is that the first thing he did he tried to roll up his sleeves and re-make America. And it took me about five years to get his feet on the ground and get him back where he could have a little influence." He recalled how Harry Byrd "ground him up like sausage meat." As Johnson explained, "We have to take 'em on, but when we take 'em on *we* have to win. And we have to do it through organization."[21]

Democratic politics not only permits but requires both Johnson's inside-out approach and the outside-in approach that he accused Humphrey of practicing. Humphrey had gotten where he was by using institutions that lay outside politics, very much including the newspapers. He had imposed real change on Minneapolis without ever gaining control of the levers of power. He had purged the Communists from the Democratic-Farmer-Labor Party with a combination of ruthlessness and guile that LBJ would have admired, but he also placed civil rights at the center of the Democratic Party's agenda by sheer force of eloquence, idealism, and passion. Yet while Humphrey was eager to absorb Johnson's wisdom, it did not occur to Johnson that Humphrey had anything to teach him. Though only three years older than his Minnesota colleague, Johnson had spent a decade in the House before reaching the Senate. By that time he was fully formed as a political animal. His way of thinking and acting had gotten him to where he was, and he was not a man to doubt his own instincts. The relationship between the two could never have been fully equal, and not only because Johnson was the party leader. Johnson brooked equal or subordinate relationships only so long as he had to; his need to dominate amounted to an insatiable hunger. Humphrey never sought that kind of power over others, which violated everything he had learned from his father and from Doland. And so from the outset Lyndon Johnson would dominate Hubert Humphrey.

BEFORE THE BEGINNING OF THE NEW SESSION, A COALITION OF groups known as the Leadership Conference on Civil Rights called on liberal legislators to stage a new push to break the filibuster. The effort seemed hopeless, but activists believed that they had hit on an ingenious new approach. Unlike the House, the Senate had always conducted itself as a "continuing body," since two-thirds of its members remained from the previous session; its rules, including cloture, thus automatically carried over from the previous session. The solution to this problem lay in moving, as the first order of business of a new session, that the Senate was *not* a continuing body and needed to adopt new rules as the House did. On January 3, while the Democrats remained in power, Herbert Lehman and Clinton Anderson of New Mexico asked Vice President Barkley, presiding over the Senate, to so rule. But before Barkley could act, Robert Taft, acting after prior agreement with Lyndon Johnson, moved to table the motion. When the tabling motion passed 70–21, liberals knew that Hubert Humphrey's new friend would remain every bit the enemy of civil rights he had been in the past.[22]

Humphrey never publicly criticized Johnson, though neither did he still his own voice. Early in the new session he and seven cosponsors presented the familiar package of civil rights bills—anti-lynching, poll tax, prohibition on desegregation in interstate transport, and so on. Three days later he put into the hopper a bill to establish a Civil Rights Commission with a purely educational role. "In all frankness," he wrote to a friendly journalist, "I don't think we have the votes for anything more than such a limited objective. My purpose is to move civil rights off dead center and make some progress on this important subject."[23] But the bill never made it out of committee. With Stevenson now the Democratic Party's standard-bearer and Johnson as the Senate leader, civil rights seemed to have reached a dead end. The ADA no longer demanded action on the subject, though of course civil rights activists did; even the redoubtable Eleanor Roosevelt said that white people in the South deserved "understanding and sympathy" as much as Black people did.[24]

For Humphrey, foreign policy began to fill the vacuum left by civil rights and by domestic policy more broadly. Republican foreign policy was torn between two hopelessly incompatible impulses. The party platform had condemned containment as "negative, futile and immoral, a cynical abandonment of countless human beings to a despotism and godless tyranny."[25] The GOP identified itself, by contrast, with the goal of regaining the "captive nations" of Eastern Europe, strongly implying that a Republican government would not rest while the Soviets controlled Eastern Europe. But on the domestic front the party had vowed to end the era of big government, to cut taxes and state spending. That goal could not be reached without making significant cuts in defense spending, which inevitably signaled to the Soviets that the saber-rattling was just rhetoric. Ike was a prudent commander-in-chief who had no intention of contesting Russian control over the Eastern bloc, as he would demonstrate by conspicuous inaction when Soviet tanks crushed a rebellion in Hungary in 1956. His national security policy depended on America's immense, if rapidly diminishing, advantage in nuclear weapons to deter further Soviet meddling.

Humphrey opposed Eisenhower both from the left and the right. This could be said of many of the Cold War liberals, yet Humphrey seemed simultaneously further to the left and further to the right. The death of Stalin, announced March 6, 1953, ushered in a brief and tumultuous period in which interim Soviet leaders, including Lavrenty Beria, the feared head of the security services, announced what appeared to be a serious loosening of Stalin's airless tyranny. Humphrey worried that Americans eager for peace would be taken in, as they had been by their wartime gratitude to "Uncle Joe." In April Humphrey began warning of Soviet peace feelers. "If we relax for a moment in the building of our defense forces," he said in a Minnesota radio broadcast, "we are playing right into the Soviets' hands."[26] In his keynote speech to the ADA national convention in May, Humphrey first recognized that domestic communism was nothing like the menace it had been five years earlier, but then admonished his listeners not to shy away from the language of anti-communism at a time when Soviet authorities were "enticing us into a position of weakness." He even warned against Communist infiltration of the ADA itself—a new note, at least publicly.[27]

Humphrey was the complete Cold War liberal. He was both more "Wilsonian"—more passionate about the United Nations and multilateralism—*and* more fervently anti-Communist than many of his more hardheaded and pragmatic colleagues at the ADA. In June 1953 Humphrey began what became a regular tradition of rising in the Senate to pay tribute to peoples trapped behind the Iron Curtain. He saluted the people of East Germany on their brief and futile rebellion, and in succeeding days reminded his colleagues of the plight of

Czechs, Bulgarians, and Ukrainians. He called for a vast increase in aid to West Germany, as well as an expansion of trade to ensure that both Germany and Japan felt the benefits of alliance with the West. He darkly warned the Senate of the consequence of cuts in defense spending, saying, "We cannot crawl along on our stomachs before these monsters, hoping to get some crumbs from their table. Our security is in strength."[28]

Ike must have found it rich to hear Humphrey and other Democratic hawks, such as John F. Kennedy, or Stuart Symington of Missouri, accuse him of "crawling" before an adversary. He stole a page from their own liberal hymnal by saying, in April, "Every gun that is made, every warship launched, every rocket fired signifies, in the final sense, a theft from those who hunger and are not fed, those who are cold and are not clothed."[29] Yet Humphrey would not have acknowledged the irony, because he did not accept the implied zero-sum solution; he advocated a low-interest rate, high-growth economy that would produce enough revenue for guns *and* butter. What stood in the way, he asserted, were the "financial barons" in Eisenhower's "cabinet of millionaires," who, he said, worried too much about inflation and too little about broad national prosperity—a claim to which he was to return toward the end of his career.[30] Then, as later, Humphrey's critics said that he was, in effect, calling for a free lunch—expansion without inflation.

Humphrey's perch on the Foreign Relations Committee allowed him to advance one of his favorite causes, foreign aid. In early 1954 he submitted a bill that would send surplus farm products to needy foreign countries, who would pay in local currencies that the United States would use for local investments. Congress passed the bill, which was seen as an ingenious way of helping both American farmers and impoverished nations. In the ensuing decades, PL 480, widely known as the Food for Peace program, would send billions of dollars' worth of American surplus abroad, becoming perhaps the best-known face of the foreign aid program.

It was not Europe but Asia that seemed to pose the gravest threat to American national security. Soviet actions had become predictable, but Red China was a new force in the world. Humphrey wanted to spread the Marshall Plan to Asia because the battle for hearts and minds was being waged there. In April 1954 Eisenhower asked Congress to authorize American military support for the French fight against a Communist insurgency in Vietnam. Though Ike was loath to support French colonial control, he feared Chinese expansionism; he used the homely metaphor of a row of toppling dominoes to describe the dreadful possibility of the insurgency spreading across Southeast Asia. Containment, which had worked in Europe, seemed to be failing in Asia. Two weeks later Vice President Nixon declared that America must be prepared to put "our boys" into the fight against Communist expansion in Asia.

Humphrey favored economic assistance to Vietnam but balked at the demand for troops (which Ike himself was careful not to repeat). He observed that American soldiers would do nothing to solve the two great questions posed there: First, "What is the objective for which the native population would fight?" The answer was "freedom"; but the French had refused to promise Vietnam its independence. Second, "What is our objective?" The answer was "democracy," for that was the only permanent bulwark against Communist aggression. Humphrey saw little prospect of democracy under the rule of Emperor Bao Dai. As with Chiang Kai-shek three years earlier, Humphrey recognized the danger posed by America's autocratic allies.

Yet Humphrey also wanted a strong military response; he did not question the logic of the domino theory. "Losing Southeast Asia is unthinkable," Humphrey said. "It cannot happen. It will not happen."[31] If Vietnam fell, he told the Senate, then the rest of Indochina would go Communist, then all Southeast Asia, then even India and Ceylon (today's Sri Lanka). The Communists could choke off supply routes for vital resources, such as rubber.[32] Only freedom and democracy could stop Communist expansion; but if that was so, then the United States simply did not have the instruments to succeed in Asia as it had in Europe. Vietnam could not be lost but also could not be won. Neither Humphrey nor Johnson or Kennedy, who both broadly shared his views, could find their way out of this dilemma.

IN 1954 HUMPHREY WAS UP FOR REELECTION. HE WORRIED, AS always, about his right flank. His office received a steady stream of letters complaining that, unlike Senator Joe McCarthy from next-door Wisconsin, he was lukewarm in the fight against communism. Humphrey always responded with the same formula. "You may be sure that I share your concerns about subversion and Communist infiltration," he would write, and then remind the correspondent of his sterling record fighting Communists in the DFL and standing up to the Reds abroad.[33] To those who complained of "Fifth Amendment Communists," who invoked the Fifth Amendment protection against self-incrimination rather than testifying in the investigations of alleged communism, he would issue a gentle reminder of the need to abide by the Constitution. When one St. Paul resident demanded that Congress criminalize Communist Party membership, Humphrey wrote, "As you probably know, J. Edgar Hoover has always taken the position that outlawing the Communist Party would drive it further underground." We should trust the FBI, he added. "It would be a tragic effort to impede its activities in this way."[34]

Humphrey had taken on McCarthy frontally a few years earlier, when the stakes were lower. Now, with the Wisconsin senator standing at the head of a vast anti-Communist crusade, Humphrey kept a lower profile. He may have allowed himself to be guided by Johnson, who resisted calls to expel or censure McCarthy, though his behavior had grown increasingly reckless. In July 1953 Humphrey was standing next to Johnson as the latter read an item off the United Press International ticker in the Senate cloakroom. McCarthy had accused a group of prominent Protestant clergymen, including G. Bromley Oxnam, the Methodist bishop of Washington DC, of Communist sympathies. Johnson knew that Oxnam was a close friend of Harry Byrd's. He told Humphrey, "As long as McCarthy was eating up you ADA bomb throwers, as long as he was just on the generals and the State Department, that was raw meat for him. . . . But with all these bishops, especially Bishop Oxnam, he picked the wrong guy."

Yet Johnson still wasn't ready to act. Only a year later, after McCarthy had destroyed his own reputation in nationally televised hearings convened over wild allegations he had lodged against the US

Army, did Johnson convene the Democratic Policy Committee and call for a bipartisan commission to consider a resolution to censure McCarthy—not for destroying innocent lives, but for bringing the Senate into disrepute. Humphrey sat with Johnson as he weighed each of the three Democrats he would appoint—a conservative, a liberal, a former judge. McCarthy then made the further mistake of denouncing the committee. "I had always said that McCarthy would destroy himself when he went after the Senate itself," Johnson told Humphrey. He was right, of course: the committee endorsed the resolution, and the Senate voted for censure, 67 to 22. An earlier Humphrey would have been appalled at the dilatory and indirect tactics, the insistence on institutional prerogative. But Humphrey later told this story to illustrate Johnson's acute sense of timing and his deep understanding of his own colleagues—his ability to get things done.[35]

Humphrey had no trouble understanding Johnson's reluctance to cast the Democrats as the anti-anti-Communist party; he shared it himself. Max Kampelman, whose dissertation on the CIO would appear in book form in 1957—with an introduction by Humphrey—may have continued to press his boss to take on the Communist-inspired union locals. In May 1954, Humphrey and Paul Douglas cosponsored a bill that would have allowed the National Labor Relations Board to invalidate a "non-Communist affidavit" filed by a labor leader if he had refused to testify under oath that he had personally signed the affidavit and that it was true.[36] In July, Maryland Republican John Marshall Butler introduced a bill to include "Communist-infiltrated" bodies among those required under the terms of the McCarran Act to register with the attorney general. (His real goal was to ban unions with Communist affiliation.) On August 12, after quietly winning the agreement of both liberals and conservatives in the Democratic Party, Humphrey unveiled an alternative to Butler's bill. The Communist Control Act would have essentially outlawed the Communist Party. Because the First Amendment plainly protects political speech by a political party, the act stipulated that the CPUSA should be understood not as a political entity but rather as "an instrument of a conspiracy to overthrow the Government of the United States of America."[37]

The bill constituted an ingenious piece of political positioning. After having censured McCarthy, Democrats were eager to reaffirm their loathing of communism. Paul Douglas cosponsored the bill. Wayne Morse, a former law school dean, signed on. After Humphrey spoke, Senators Kennedy, Morse, and John Pastore of Rhode Island competed in anti-Communist rodomontade. Republicans, including outright McCarthyites such as Pat McCarran, furious at seeing their thunder stolen, then took turns denouncing the measure as unconstitutional and in any case futile, since yesterday's "card-carrying Communists" had gone underground—precisely the argument that Humphrey had made to his Minnesota correspondent. Ike's attorney general, Herbert Brownell Jr., seeing a weapon he hadn't asked for and didn't want, opposed the measure. But Republicans swallowed their fury and voted for the bill, though the House eliminated the provision making party membership a crime. Humphrey had, at a stroke, neutralized the shibboleth that his party was "soft on communism." The professionals were deeply impressed: columnists Joseph and Stewart Alsop called the move "cleverly conceived, ruthlessly executed and politically adroit."[38]

It was also deeply cynical. One furious constituent asked Humphrey, "Are you really that worried about being re-elected?"[39] Arthur Schlesinger, now ADA cochair, wrote an editorial in the *New York Post* arguing that had the bill passed, "the Department of Justice would have been committed to a program of mass round-ups and prosecution unprecedented in American history."[40] A furious Humphrey sent a note to Kampelman complaining bitterly about his friends at the ADA: "I have just about had a bellyful of their intellectual paternalism as it related to their acceptance of me."[41] In later years he offered all manner of justification for the bill: he wanted to substitute a straightforward criminal process for congressional investigations, or he hoped to blunt McCarthy's assault on liberals—even though McCarthy was a spent force by August. He conceded, however, that "I've never been all that happy about that myself."[42] In fact, he really was that worried about being reelected. Many years later, Margaret Chase Smith, who as a Republican senator from Maine had courageously led the fight against McCarthy, would render a biting judgment of Humphrey: "He was given more credit for political courage than he deserved." Amid the anti-Communist hysteria, "Hubert was mute and did not speak out lest it risk his political survival."[43]

That was all too true. While the first article in the politician's credo is that you must live to fight another day, Humphrey had allowed his fears to get the better of his principles. In fact, he could have afforded to show more courage. Such was his popularity at home that the state's most senior Republican officeholders and celebrities—first Congressman Walter Judd, then Governor C. Elmer Anderson, then Charles Mayo of the famed Mayo Clinic—took soundings on a Senate race and then declined to run. The Republicans ultimately nominated state treasurer Val Bjornson. Humphrey reaped the benefits of his new standing in the Senate. Lyndon Johnson campaigned for him. Walter George, vastly admired in the business community for his role on the Finance Committee, chipped in a warm letter to the *Minneapolis Star*. Joseph Alsop, writing a few weeks before the election, observed that Humphrey not only had conducted a campaign "that would kill most senatorial candidates in about a fortnight" but had spent the past six years delivering favors impartially to Republicans as well as Democrats. Alsop pronounced the incumbent "practically bomb-proof."[44]

Humphrey took 55 percent of the vote against Bjornson's 42. Orville Freeman, Humphrey's friend and former aide, won the race for governor against a Republican who had defeated him two years earlier; a DFL candidate also won as Minnesota attorney general. The party sweep was widely attributed to Humphrey's organization and popularity. "The state is his," wrote the *Minneapolis Star Tribune*, "much as it was Harold Stassen's back in the days when Stassen's bids for the Presidency were news."[45] Humphrey had locked down his base at home; at the age of forty-three, he could now focus all his energies on the great ambitions he had for himself and his country.

11

A Man with Southern Connections

"The vehement heretic of yesterday
had now embraced . . .
the Doctrine According to the Senate."

THE DEMOCRATS HAD WON BACK THEIR CONGRESSIONAL
majority in the 1954 election; Lyndon Johnson was now
majority leader. He had given Humphrey, his bridge to the
liberals, a seat on the Steering Committee, which he used to direct
party affairs and, crucially, to hand out committee assignments.
Within weeks of the election Humphrey was fielding letters from
colleagues seeking plum assignments. Herbert Lehman wanted Judiciary. Estes Kefauver wanted Foreign Relations; so did Russell Long
and John F. Kennedy (though Kennedy had his aide Ted Sorensen
submit the request). Hubert Humphrey was now, as he had always
yearned to be, a force in the Senate. How would he exercise that
influence in order to advance the causes he believed in?[1]

Nineteen fifty-four had been a banner year for civil rights in America. In *Brown v. Board of Education*, the Supreme Court had ruled unanimously that racially separate schools violated the equal protection clause of the Fourteenth Amendment—the most staggering blow Jim Crow law had ever suffered. The November election had brought to both House and Senate a new group of liberals dedicated to breaking the legislative deadlock on civil rights. Working closely with the NAACP, they geared up to renew the assault on cloture on January 3, 1955, the first day of the new term. Lyndon Johnson remained an implacable obstacle to any such change. Humphrey sought to mediate between his leader and his flock by imploring the liberals to work through the Rules Committee to reform the filibuster—to use what was known as "regular order" rather than a direct assault. As Paul Douglas would later recall, Humphrey insisted that Johnson was not the southern racist the liberals imagined; he asked them to "give him a chance to see what he could do with the South." Douglas and other key figures reluctantly agreed.[2] The promised floor fight never materialized; a month later, Humphrey dropped into the Senate hopper the usual clutch of civil rights bills, now with a growing list of cosponsors.

Until this moment, civil rights leaders had regarded Humphrey as their most steadfast friend in Congress. Now they began to wonder. On January 12, Walter White, head of the NAACP, sent Humphrey a very polite letter asking him to explain why he held out any hope for the Rules Committee. White pointedly wrote that he would like to "more intelligently answer some of the inquiries that have been flooding us." At the same time he released a much harsher statement to the press complaining of the inaction of "certain senators who call themselves liberal" and pointing as a possible explanation to rumors that "some shrewd horse trading over committee memberships went on behind the scenes."

Humphrey responded that he knew the frontal assault would have failed—which was surely true—and that the confrontation might have knit back together the coalition of Republicans and Southern Democrats, thus dooming all liberal legislation—which was highly conjectural. Humphrey pointed out that, thanks in part to his own efforts, liberals held some power on Rules and other important committees. In closing, Humphrey wrote, with the asperity of one who feels accused, "I am no quitter and I don't want any of our friends spreading unfounded rumors that Hubert Humphrey is compromising or backtracking." And he sent a copy of the letter to Johnson, attaching a note that read, "Got any room in Texas for a displaced liberal?"[3] The dustup may have harmed his credibility with the NAACP, but it helped his credibility with the majority leader.

White wrote back to say that he understood Humphrey's point but would like to know what assurances, if any, he had received from Johnson. Humphrey conceded, "Lyndon Johnson did not give us any assurances on civil rights legislation." He had, however, spoken to the majority leader about passing "two or three of the less controversial measures." Humphrey then went on to say, as delicately as he could manage, "I'm sure you and I would agree that a liberal program includes more than civil rights." Of all the recent leaders, he added, Johnson had been "the most cooperative with the so-called liberal wing of the party." Yet privately, Humphrey was ashamed of his party's intransigence on civil rights. In mid-February, he wrote to Johnson with a rare note of accusation. Republicans were protesting the exclusion of Blacks from a Lincoln Day Dinner in Florida, while Southern Democrats were loudly defending Jim Crow. The Democratic Party, Humphrey warned, "is fast undermining its strength with our Negro people."[4]

In the midst of the exchange of letters, the sixty-one-year-old White, who had led the NAACP for twenty-five years, fell seriously ill; he would die of a heart attack March 21. The correspondence resumed when Roy Wilkins, White's longtime aide, wrote to Humphrey March 7. Now the tone turned more threatening. Black voters, Wilkins observed, found Ike's record on civil rights good enough to vote for him in 1956 "in the absence of any meaningful . . . legislation in the civil rights field by a Congress in the control of the Democratic party." He also criticized Humphrey and other liberals for opposing an amendment the NAACP had proposed to a massive school construction bill that would deny funding to districts that practiced segregation. Republicans had gleefully taken up the matter, hoping to force the liberals to choose between siding with the NAACP—and seeing the school construction bill go down to defeat at the hands of the South—and saving the bill by implicitly endorsing segregation. Humphrey wrote right back. "I have been working steadfastly to encourage the Democratic leadership to take some action in this field," he assured Wilkins. "I think I am making progress; in fact, I know I am." But Johnson felt no need to endorse even the cosmetic measures Humphrey had suggested. "There was no change in Johnson's opposition to civil rights," Paul Douglas was later to reflect. The only benefit went to Humphrey himself, since "his role in this matter sealed his alliance with Johnson."

Humphrey could not gain access to the inner sanctum of the Senate without losing his privileged status in the advocate community. By mid-1955 activists had realized that Johnson was going to work within the confines of Eisenhower's domestic agenda rather than seeking the fulfillment of Truman's Fair Deal. In June Americans for Democratic Action issued a report denouncing Johnson as a handmaiden of the Republicans. As it happened, the report was published at the same moment that Johnson was muscling a larger increase in the minimum wage through the Senate, as well as greater funding for public housing than Eisenhower wanted, thus demonstrating that he could accept the limits of the possible and still make real gains. Humphrey promptly took to the floor to lavish praise on Johnson as "a genius in the art of the legislative program." That was a clear rebuke to his friends at the ADA. Humphrey was soon followed by Douglas, Lehman, and Morse.[5]

Many liberals accepted Humphrey's claim that he could be far more effective from the inside than the outside. In late 1955 *The New Republic* asked whether Humphrey had been "seduced" by Johnson and other southern leaders, and concluded that he hadn't: "Humphrey has bored from within to give liberals a means of presenting their demands to the leadership." Indeed, for all his anger and disappointment over civil rights, Paul Douglas, the purest of the pure, did not come to conclude that his friend had compromised his principles. "While Hubert cooperated frequently with Johnson on parliamentary tactics," he wrote, "he never sold us out on substantive issues and continued to be a leader of the liberal ranks." If anything, Douglas thought, Humphrey pulled Johnson a little bit in his own direction. A genuine admirer of this man very different from himself, Douglas described Humphrey as "the best rough and tumble debater in our whole political arena."[6]

Had Humphrey, in fact, changed? Had he compromised his principles in exchange for power and status? Journalist William White thought that he had, though he meant it as praise. "The vehement heretic of yesterday had now embraced performance and, indeed, happily, as his understanding grew, the Doctrine According to the Senate."[7] It's true that Humphrey had been raised in the populist politics of the heroic gesture and the doomed crusade. But that wasn't the kind of political leader he had become. Humphrey had *never* been a vehement heretic, though he had come across as one when he first reached the Senate. His excitability, his bottle-rocket metabolism, made him seem like a radical when he was, by nature, a pragmatist who preferred a modest win to a noble loss. He would later explain his connection to Johnson by saying, "My kind of politics met with Johnson's in this sense—that while I was a man of liberal persuasion, I knew that you often couldn't get as much as you wanted, and therefore I was willing to settle for less. . . . And Johnson maybe convinced me more than anyone else that we could make steady progress if we just didn't bite off too much."[8]

The *Washington Post* ascribed some part of Humphrey's apparent move to the center to the influence of his increasingly conservative chief counsel, Max Kampelman.[9] But Humphrey's own ambition drove him in the direction of pragmatism: neither Herbert Lehman nor Paul Douglas expected to be elected president, and so kept clear of the Senate's inner circle. Yet even leaving self-interest aside, Humphrey was quite right in recognizing that the cloture fight had become a ritual that substituted psychic satisfactions for real achievements. He was right that Johnson could be trusted to wring out of Congress whatever modest gains were possible for the liberal side. Perhaps he was right, too, to have adopted William White's ethos of "performance." Liberals, he complained to *Time* magazine, were "too concerned with protecting procedural rights" and "proper constitutional methods."[10]

But Humphrey's growing professionalism looked to the faithful very much like compromise. Many of his own aides felt this way. In 1955 Kampelman had left to make money as a practicing attorney, and Tom Hughes, who had met Humphrey in the FDR campaign of 1944, and had come to Capitol Hill after winning a Rhodes Scholarship, took over as Humphrey's counselor. Hughes estimates that between half and three-quarters of the staff objected to the boss's alliance with Johnson. Several quit, and others remained but made their unhappiness well known. At his birthday party in 1956, staffers gave Humphrey a Confederate cap with the sardonic tribute, "For a Man with Southern Connections"—the headline of the laudatory *New Republic* piece.

A staff position with the Minnesota senator had always occupied a space between job and calling. Staffers were poorly paid, both because Humphrey didn't have the money to pay more and because he expected people to scrape by in order to do the work of the Lord, as he always had. But his aides also worked longer hours than virtually anyone else on Capitol Hill—because their boss did, too. "Humphrey would think nothing of asking for volunteers to drive him to the airport at 10:30 at night," says Hughes. "He didn't notice." Or Humphrey would close up late at night and invite his aides for a drink at the Carroll Arms, where in 1955 the disgraced Senator Joe McCarthy could be seen in a corner quietly drinking himself to death. Staff morale, says Hughes, was low. Yet most aides stayed, because they admired and even loved Humphrey, because they knew he actually cared about their welfare, and above all because they believed in the causes he stood for. He liked to tell staffers, "Always take me beyond where I am; don't just give me what I want." They wanted to join this idealistic man on his great adventure.[11]

IF HUMPHREY HADN'T SACRIFICED HIS PRINCIPLES, HE HAD, AT AGE forty-five, undergone a change of temperament. He had become a creature of the institution in which he worked. William White acutely noted that Humphrey had always been "latently" senatorial. He loved his work and was unhappy only that he could not do more to advance the causes he believed in. Humphrey spent his time with his Senate colleagues, very much including figures such as John Sparkman and John Stennis, whom he had come to see not as racists but as figures hemmed in by the South's political climate. To a Minnesota friend, he wrote, in May 1955, "I think I can honestly say that I have as many, or more, friends among the Southern Democrats here in the Senate as I have among the Northerners."[12] Humphrey liked friendly people; ideologues and theoreticians made him uncomfortable.

Humphrey wasn't less liberal than he appeared to be, but he was less adversarial than his liberal friends wanted him to be. If all men were brothers, as he deeply believed, then antagonism, whether between races or classes, was a sign of misunderstanding rather than intrinsic conflict. In Minneapolis Humphrey had been both pro-labor and pro-business; each, he insisted, needed the other. In the Senate, too, he remained the great champion of organized labor, but regarded himself as equally the friend of the businessman. He had become a great friend of Dwayne Andreas, a food-processing magnate in Minneapolis. Andreas later said that Humphrey often let him fiddle with speeches that he worried struck too antibusiness a note. He saw Humphrey as the rare liberal who fully understood the problems of businessmen. "He could go right from the most liberal labor crowd and turn around and make a conservative speech to businessmen," Andreas recalled.[13] Humphrey may have been ideologically incoherent, but he wasn't insincere.

Pragmatist that he was, Humphrey made himself the star pupil in the Lyndon Johnson Academy. During the minimum wage debate he was standing by Johnson's side when the majority leader turned to him and said, "I think we'll pass that minimum wage bill now." Johnson had waited until Spessard Holland, who had been leading the opposition, left the floor. He instantly issued a quorum call, which was required for a vote, and then just as rapidly called for a vote before Holland had had a chance to return and rally his troops.[14] On the housing bill, Humphrey's vote was crucial, but his flight from Minnesota, due to land at 2:30 in the afternoon, was delayed. In a tour de force even by his own standards, Johnson used every parliamentary tactic in his bag of tricks to put off the vote while simultaneously bullying air control officers to get Humphrey's flight on the ground. The plane landed at 4:45, Humphrey was whisked to the Senate, and he cast the deciding vote to build one hundred thousand units of public housing rather than the thirty-five thousand Ike had called for.[15]

Humphrey had always assumed that Johnson's great gift was for browbeating—for yanking a man up by his lapels and arguing him into submission. That was not a method that a man like Humphrey could put into practice. But standing by his side over the years, he came to understand that Johnson had a vastly greater range. He would later observe:

> Many people look upon Johnson as the heavy-handed man. That's not really true. He was sort of like a cowboy making love. He wasn't one of these Fifth Avenue, Madison Avenue penthouse lovers. He was from the ranch. But what I mean is he knew how to massage the senators. He knew which ones he could just push aside, he knew which ones he could threaten, and above all he knew which ones he'd have to spend time with and nourish along, to bring along, to make sure that they were coming along.

THE REAL LESSON WAS THAT JOHNSON UNDERSTOOD HUMAN MOTIVAtions with an almost novelistic subtlety—save that, unlike a novelist, he used that knowledge in order to manipulate others. "You've got to study every member of this body to know how they're really ultimately going to act," he told Humphrey. "Everything about them, their family, their backgrounds, their attitudes, even watch their moods before you even ask them to vote."[16]

But Humphrey also learned that Lyndon Johnson was a jealous lover. In the summer of 1955, Johnson suffered a serious heart attack that kept him confined to his Texas ranch. Humphrey flew down to see him as soon as he was permitted to do so. Soon afterward Johnson issued a thirteen-point manifesto, a Democratic domestic agenda he had compiled himself. In a press conference, Humphrey endorsed the agenda save for the first point: natural gas deregulation, a sop to Texas oilmen. The convalescing Johnson instantly called to shout at Humphrey for failing to toe the line. Humphrey responded with a humble apology. "I really hope, Lyndon," he wrote, "what I said did not upset you. I praised Lyndon Johnson, I praised the program. A very fine batting average, 12 hits in 13 times at bat. But you've got to leave me a little room on the gas bill."[17] This pattern of attack and rather desperate effort at mollification was to last for many years.

HUMPHREY'S SMASHING REELECTION IN 1954, HIS STATUS AS THE leading liberal in the Senate, and his demonstrated loyalty to Adlai Stevenson, the odds-on favorite to serve as the Democratic presidential nominee in 1956, had put him in a strong position to serve as Stevenson's running mate. Publicly putting yourself forward for the job almost disqualified you from getting it, but Humphrey and his staff began conducting a quiet campaign in the summer of 1955. The old gang reassembled: Orville Freeman, Max Kampelman, Art Naftalin, Evron Kirkpatrick, Gene McCarthy, and Richard Scammon, another University of Minnesota political scientist and the founder of a political research firm. In July, Herb Waters, Humphrey's chief of staff, sent friendly journalists a long memo laying out the rationale for Humphrey's candidacy, soft-pedaling his record on civil rights but playing up his deep ties to southern legislators. In September, Freeman paid a visit to Stevenson armed with talking points that Waters had drawn up.[18] The campaign seemed to be working: in October, Stevenson told Arthur Schlesinger that Lyndon Johnson wanted him to make Humphrey his running mate—and that he, Stevenson, agreed.[19]

The Humphrey plan ran through Minnesota. The state would be holding an early primary, and Humphrey argued that Stevenson could stake a preemptive claim to the nomination by entering and winning. In November, Humphrey wrote to William Blair, one of Stevenson's senior advisers, laying out plans for the campaign. He suggested that the diffident Stevenson needed a little more Humphrey in him. The candidate should meet with state and local officials. He should be prepared to show passion, even to "slam his fist down" every once in a while.[20] In fact, Stevenson had to be persuaded even to come to Minnesota to file for the primary and then to campaign. He had no more Hubert Humphrey in him now than he had had four years before. Newton Minow, a Chicago power broker and Stevenson intimate, recalled accompanying Stevenson on a visit to the LBJ ranch in late 1955. Both Johnson and Sam Rayburn told him that he had to be prepared to fight hard for the nomination. On the way back, Stevenson told Minow, "I'm not going to do that. I'm not going to run around like I'm campaigning for sheriff."[21]

In January 1956, Estes Kefauver threw a spanner in the works by announcing that he, too, would enter the primary. Kefauver had support both in farm and labor circles in the state, and he was an ardent and colorful figure on the stump. By early February, a month before the primary, Humphrey's calculation was looking shaky. Visitors to his Washington office were running strong for Kefauver. Humphrey fired off a letter to James Finnegan, Stevenson's other main confidant, imploring the candidate once again to step off his rhetorical high horse, and even to "overdramatize" the issues he cared about. Humphrey listed the issues Minnesotans wanted to hear about, including civil rights, support for Israel, and farm prices.[22] Orville Freeman, who never shied away from confrontation, as Humphrey did, wrote directly to Stevenson to suggest he find an approach that was "not based upon quips and clever statements, but rather upon human understanding and reaching people on a personal basis."[23]

The admonitions failed. Kefauver easily defeated Stevenson, in part because of a large and probably mischievous crossover vote from Republicans, who were permitted to vote in the Democratic primary. Humphrey was almost sick with humiliation. He finally brought himself to write to Stevenson, apologizing for the delay by moaning that "the shock and bloodshed was [sic] overwhelming for a few days."[24] The failure belonged far more to Stevenson than to Humphrey, but it was the kind of thing that never would have happened to Lyndon Johnson.

The setback had very little effect on the Stevenson bandwagon, though it put a temporary dent in Humphrey's vice presidential go-cart.

The campaign didn't slacken. Kampelman and Kirkpatrick began doing opposition research on their chief rival, John Kennedy. Richard Scammon found someone who could serve as press officer on the cheap. The effort may have been less than fully professional, since budget records show that the campaign raised a grand total of $1,980.[25] But it reached the most important target. At a Democratic event held in the Mayflower Hotel in Washington in July, Stevenson asked Humphrey to join him in his suite upstairs for dinner. Humphrey and Kampelman found Stevenson in his pajamas. They talked about possible running mates. Humphrey gallantly ran through the list of names, excluding his own. Stevenson said that he disliked Kefauver and considered John F. Kennedy too young. Then he said the magic words: "You know, Hubert, there's only one man left. That's you." But he would have to demonstrate support in the South. Stevenson turned to his two chief fixers, Blair and Finnegan, and said, "You sit down and work things out."[26]

This was the moment Hubert Humphrey had been dreaming of and struggling toward since he had arrived in the Senate. Recent history suggested to him that a man could only become president if he was wellborn and wealthy, like FDR, or immensely famous, like Eisenhower—unless, like Truman, he was vice president first. Humphrey had no illusions about Stevenson's prospects against a popular and revered incumbent, but he felt that the national exposure he would gain as running mate would vault him above his rivals (though it had not done that for Sparkman after 1952). Humphrey now reaped the fruits of his labors in the inner dining room, winning promises of support from Lister Hill, Sam Rayburn, Richard Russell, Walter George, and Lyndon Johnson—the political leadership of the South.

The campaign kicked into full gear several weeks before the National Democratic Convention, when Humphrey wrote a public letter to Gene McCarthy, cochairman of the Humphrey for Vice President Committee, announcing his candidacy. McCarthy traveled around the country talking to delegates. Herb Waters held discussions with key labor leaders. Kampelman wrote to newspaper editors and contacted delegates, and Dick Scammon drew up statistics making a case for Humphrey's candidacy. Humphrey himself talked to Johnson, Rayburn, and other party leaders.[27] All the vice presidential candidates had to prove their acceptability to the South, where fury over the *Brown* decision had not cooled. Kefauver was a native son who had stood with the South on cloture and had not endorsed *Brown*. Kennedy had played virtually no role in the Senate's civil rights debates and had urged the platform committee to avoid any mention of *Brown*. Only Humphrey had a lifetime of commitments to overcome. He had continued to tamp down liberal wrath at the South; in March, he had prevailed on Wayne Morse not to issue a public statement when James Eastland of Mississippi had succeeded to the chairmanship of the all-important Judiciary Committee.[28]

The convention posed a whole new series of obstacles. Joe Rauh of the ADA was playing a version of the role Humphrey had played eight years earlier, preparing for a floor fight to win a plank endorsing the court decision. Humphrey, caught in between, said on *Meet the Press* that the platform should call for the "observance" rather than the "enforcement" of *Brown*, which he felt the South could live with.[29] Privately he told Rauh that he would take an open breach on civil rights as a personal insult. The fight never happened: a torturously phrased plank took note of Supreme Court decisions "relating to segregation in publicly supported schools and elsewhere" and rejected "all proposals for the use of force to interfere with the orderly determination of these matters by the courts."[30]

Humphrey was blithely confident of his prospects, though experience should have taught him that presidential candidates deploy the running-mate offer as a glittering bauble to be dangled before the ambitious. Humphrey's supporters feared that Stevenson might declare an "open convention" in which delegates would make the choice for running mate; this would tilt the choice to Kefauver, who had amassed the most delegates.[31] Nevertheless, Bill Blair had told Humphrey to get to work on an acceptance speech. A group called Citizens for Stevenson and Humphrey was distributing literature in the convention hall. Humphrey later recalled that Kennedy, recognizing the inevitable, said, "Hubert, I'm for you."[32] On August 15, William Fulbright of Arkansas nominated him, with seconding speeches by McCarthy and Stuart Symington. Humphrey spoke to Stevenson, who remained noncommittal. Stevenson was nominated the following day.

That night, Humphrey was listening to the radio with his aides and supporters in his suite at the Blackstone Hotel when Stevenson addressed the delegates. On the question of vice president, Stevenson said, "I leave the choice to you." Humphrey sat there in a state of shock. When Stevenson called to say that he was sorry, but had come under "great pressure," the nature of which he did not specify, Humphrey was "virtually monosyllabic," Kampelman recalled. A cynical man might have said, "That's politics," but Humphrey was no cynic. He would not, or could not, accept that even a gentleman like Stevenson would so cruelly betray him. Muriel later said, "That was the worst, the bitterest defeat. He felt he had been made a fool of."[33]

Stevenson was an opaque figure. Nobody was able to fully account for the decision. According to Newton Minow, Stevenson genuinely preferred Humphrey, but "he decided at the very last minute to open it up because he thought it would bring some excitement to the convention."[34] Alternatively, the candidate may have concluded that he couldn't win the South with Humphrey as a running mate. The effect, in any case, was to destroy Humphrey's hopes; he hadn't bothered to win commitments from delegates because he felt he didn't need to. Nevertheless, his torment was not quite over. The contest now pitted Kefauver against Kennedy. Kefauver had won the Minnesota primary, but Humphrey strongly preferred Kennedy, whom he had befriended and worked with. The convention was so evenly split between them that Minnesota could determine the outcome—and the state would follow the lead of its favorite son. Humphrey could almost choose the man who would have the position that he had been sure was his only the day before. Humphrey felt that it would be wrong to countermand Minnesota's expressed preference. He was sitting with Sam Rayburn when Kefauver burst into the suite, begging for Humphrey's support with tears in his eyes. Humphrey asked Fulbright to tell the delegation that he was supporting Kefauver.

A burning sense of shame now competed with Humphrey's feeling of self-pity. He retired to his summer home in Waverly to lick his wounds while Herb Waters wrote to Kennedy explaining that his boss had faced "perhaps the most difficult decision of his political career," an appraisal that might have struck the hardheaded recipient as more than a little hyperbolic. Only on September 8 could Humphrey bring himself to write to his colleague with an extraordinary admission: "I had dreamed about you two or three nights in a row—and not a very pleasant dream either. It seems you were very disappointed in me. I guess that was my guilty conscience plaguing me throughout the night." In truth, Humphrey had made the kind of tough decision that politics forces on those at the top; Stevenson had acted far more cruelly to him. It's impossible to imagine Kennedy himself suffering such dreams—much less admitting to them. Humphrey could neither accept cruelty nor knowingly perpetrate it.

Lyndon Johnson had already concluded that Humphrey was just too nice to make it to the top; perhaps he was right. It was left to Johnson, that master Humphrey-whisperer, to console the Minnesota senator in his anguish. A few weeks after the election, Johnson wrote a letter to his friend. He did not confirm Humphrey's belief that he had been swindled—the majority leader put no such store by promises, real or alleged—but he wrote something designed to divert his friend's attention from the past to the future: "In my mind you are the Northern leader in the Senate." Humphrey wrote back admitting that he felt "very low" after listening to everybody save himself address the convention. Johnson responded almost immediately: "You certainly have had a rough year, and my heart goes out to you. There is only one consolation. I long ago realized that you were one of those bold spirits that is tempered rather than weakened by adversity." With his unerring gift for expressing just what a man wanted to hear about himself, Johnson added, "I know what this has cost you in terms of some of your personal relations with others. But it has also given you a unique status in the life of our Country." That was the cowboy lover at work. Several months later, Humphrey wrote that he had just reread Johnson's letter. That, by itself, registered the depth of Humphrey's need for emotional support. "The thoughts that you express in those three paragraphs," he wrote, "will be with me until the end of my days."[35]

THE HUMPHREYS LIVED IN THE SAME MODEST, OVERCROWDED HOUSE
on Coquelin Terrace in Chevy Chase that Hubert had gone into debt
to buy in 1949. A family vacation still meant that all six Humphreys
would pile into the car and visit Yellowstone, or that Muriel would
drive the four kids out to a rented cabin in Minnesota, with Hubert
joining them on weekends and at the end of the Senate session. Muriel
had grown up with a summer cabin, and Hubert loved nothing more
than puttering around in a boat and catching the occasional fish.
They had started scouting for lakeside property in 1950, but only in
1956 had they finally bought a two-acre property on the shore of Lake
Waverly, forty miles west of Minneapolis. At first they had planned
to build a little cottage, but both had been taken with the Johnson
guest quarters at his Pedernales ranch; Lady Bird had sent them the
blueprints. The Humphreys built a four-bedroom house with paneled
walls, a fireplace, and a living room with a beamed ceiling.

The Humphreys would come to Waverly to escape Washington
for the rest of their lives. Muriel always lit out for Minnesota as soon
as the kids were out of school. Hubert pursued his frenetic version of
relaxation. A visiting reporter later described his routine: "Hubert
Humphrey whips around the lake in a speedboat or skims it in a sail-
boat, fishes for bluegill, jumps on a trampoline, picnics with his family in the woods, water skis, swims, cleans out the swimming pool,
sweeps the garage, fights an everlasting battle with the dandelions,
and drives over to see the neighbors in his Model A Ford."[36]

Humphrey had to depend on rich friends to provide even such
modest pleasures. In order to buy and furnish the house he took out
loans from his friend Freddy Gates and from Morris Ebin, a Minneapolis businessman.[37] The same was true of schooling for his children.
None of the Humphrey kids were troublemakers, but neither were
any of them academic standouts like their father. His oldest son, Skip,
was—by his own admission—languishing at his large public high
school in Chevy Chase.[38] Muriel and Hubert wanted to send him to
private school but couldn't afford to do so. In 1957 Humphrey's friend
William Benton, who had been born in Minneapolis and gone on to
found the ad agency Benton & Bowles, and served as senator from
Connecticut from 1949 to 1953, offered to get Skip into his own alma

mater, the Shattuck School, a military academy in Faribault, Minnesota. Benton created a scholarship of which Skip was the beneficiary. In 1960, when Skip graduated, Humphrey's friend Dwayne Andreas began paying for his son Robert's tuition.

Both men would continue doing favors for their impecunious but powerful friend. Benton would write to say that he was sending Humphrey plane tickets to join him in Paris or London. He made large campaign contributions. When Humphrey was nominated as vice president in 1964, Benton wrote to Muriel to say that he was giving each of them a $3,000 check—the limit for nontaxable gifts—so they could each buy a new wardrobe. Humphrey, in turn, used his influence with Secretary of State Dean Rusk to get Benton one thing that he dearly wanted but couldn't buy—the ambassadorship to the Court of St. James. He had tried once before, with John Kennedy. He did not succeed either time.[39]

Humphrey would have a more fraught relationship with Andreas, both because the two were much closer and because Andreas, an agribusiness entrepreneur who would ultimately run the giant food-processing firm Archer-Daniels-Midland, had a great deal of business before Congress. Humphrey was godfather to Andreas's son; the Humphreys often stayed—for free—in a Miami hotel that Andreas owned. Andreas introduced Humphrey to friends in the business world and vouched for him as a friend to private enterprise. He was a major funder of all Humphrey's campaigns. Eager to promote sales of Midwestern grain, Humphrey regularly invited Andreas to join him on his foreign travels, and introduced him to senior government officials who could facilitate business deals. Food for Peace and similar programs offered immense business opportunities for grain dealers.[40] Today such a relationship would invite serious journalistic scrutiny; at the time, however, even Lyndon Johnson's genuinely unsavory ties to the giant engineering firm Brown & Root largely escaped notice.

THE BROWN DECISION, AS WELL AS LOWER-COURT RULINGS STRIKING down mandatory segregation laws, had moved the struggle over civil rights from Washington DC to the Jim Crow South. The nascent civil rights movement, starting with the Montgomery bus boycott in December 1955, demonstrated the latent political power of organized Black protest, but it also provoked a terrifying backlash. The lynching of Emmett Till in August 1955 was only the most spectacular of a spate of murders of Black men in Alabama. White Citizens' Councils brought together leading citizens in cities and towns across the Deep South; most of them left the lynching and bombing to the Klan, instead using economic power to ensure that no Black person who had the temerity to call for desegregation, or even to register to vote, could get a job or a mortgage or bank credit.[41] Not since the last years of Reconstruction had the South seen the combination of racial terror and outright resistance to federal rule that arose during this period.

The Democrats' quandary on civil rights had intensified. In the 1952 election, Stevenson had won 75 percent of the Black vote; in 1956, the number dropped to 61 percent. Once again Stevenson had carried most of the South—and almost nothing else. (Ike had won the electoral vote 457–73.) Yet southerners were prepared to lose national elections in order to preserve their way of life. In early 1956, Strom Thurmond circulated a statement claiming that *Brown* was "destroying the amicable relations between white and Negro races" that had obtained since the end of the Civil War; the statement commended those states that had refused to desegregate "by any lawful means." Nineteen of the twenty-two southern senators signed what came to be known as "the Southern Manifesto"—though Lyndon Johnson, delicately preserving his bona fides with both sides, declined to do so.

Having straddled on civil rights in the name of his own ambition, Humphrey had lost some of his standing with liberals without gaining anything for himself. In December 1956, he agreed to join the Democratic Advisory Council, a group founded by leading ADA liberals with the goal of pushing the party's domestic agenda to the left. The group issued a sixteen-point manifesto seeking "a new liberal agenda." Both the organization and the manifesto were designed to yank the party back from Lyndon Johnson, who was outraged by Humphrey's involvement. "You broke faith with me," he told Humphrey in a phone call. That note of menace produced the already-typical effect. "You are a great, great leader, Lyndon," Humphrey responded. "I was simply trying to make you an even better leader."[42] Yet Humphrey did not retreat, backing a renewed effort to reform the filibuster by seeking a declaration that the Senate was not a continuing body.

The Republicans were now prepared to compete for the Black vote. In a campaign appearance in Harlem, Richard Nixon had vowed, "If you support [Eisenhower] and elect a Republican Senate, you will get action, not filibusters."[43] Now, presiding over the Senate, Nixon not only sided with the liberals but suggested that the 1949 rule eliminating cloture from votes on the rules violated the Constitution. Johnson succeeded once again in tabling the motion, but this time the opponents won thirty-eight votes, including seventeen Republicans. In 1956 Eisenhower had submitted a civil rights bill that the House had passed; he promised to send another to Congress were he reelected. And he was as good as his word.

In 1957 Attorney General Herbert Brownell submitted a bill with four parts. The first two, the establishment of a Civil Rights Commission and a Civil Rights Division in the Department of Justice, had been proposed for years and constituted the kind of anodyne measures that Humphrey had thought, wrongly, he could get Johnson to endorse. Title III authorized the attorney general to seek injunctions for a wide range of civil rights violations, while Title IV had similar provisions that applied specifically to violations of voting rights. The bill was not everything Humphrey had wanted, but far more than he had expected to get. For Johnson, on the other hand, the bill went too far—he knew the South wouldn't accept parts III and IV as written—but it offered a vehicle to win political credit for the Democrats, prove to liberals that he was no racist, and perhaps even end the isolation of the Deep South.

Humphrey wanted a meaningful bill; Johnson just wanted a bill. Once the House passed the legislation, in June 1957, Johnson got to work making it palatable, which he felt he could do by deleting Title III and making a crucial change in Title IV. That section of the bill would have permitted trials without a jury. Since Blacks could not vote in the South, they could not serve on juries; ergo, no southerner need fear conviction from a jury for denying Black people the vote. The South would not accept the no-jury provision. Civil rights leaders, on the other hand, would not accept its elimination. At the same time, Humphrey was trying to preserve Title III through an act of strategic dilution. Brownell had included in the language of the bill a reference to the Reconstruction-era "Force Acts," which had authorized the president to use the military to enforce compliance. Southerners had cited this language to warn of dark plots to supersede state governments. On July 17 Humphrey proposed eliminating the reference. "We can have meaningful law without rubbing salt into old wounds," he said emolliently.[44] Several days later he returned to the floor to argue disingenuously that Title III conferred no new rights but simply offered citizens a new means of enforcing existing ones. Humphrey's amendment passed, but the effort at compromise failed. The Senate voted to delete Title III; nothing substantive was left save the last part.

Again, stalemate seemed to loom. Johnson worked furiously to persuade Richard Russell to hold off on a filibuster while he sought a compromise acceptable to both sides; nothing he had done or would ever do in the Senate would involve such minute and ingenious orchestration. Here Humphrey made his one meaningful contribution to the bill. Carl Auerbach, a law professor at the University of Wisconsin and a friend of Max Kampelman's, had written an article pointing out that while criminal contempt proceedings, which could send a person to jail, typically required a jury, civil proceedings, which the defendant could remedy simply by addressing the underlying complaint, often dispensed with a jury. Why not make that distinction in the voting rights law? Of course, that would mean you could safely defy the law with no fear of jail; but for that very reason the distinction might win over the South.

Humphrey brought Auerbach to Washington to meet with senators and to work with legislative draftsmen on new language. At the same time, he delivered by far his longest and most carefully reasoned speech on the bill, opposing the compromise he was then helping to broker. The Founders, he argued, had not intended the right of a jury trial to extend to trials for contempt, civil or criminal. Indeed, he went on, only the certainty of punishment at the hands of a federal judge would prevent a local official from abridging voting rights.[45] Perhaps Humphrey was salving his conscience or placating his friends in the civil rights community; but he was also stating a proposition that he believed in deeply.

Johnson ultimately persuaded Russell not to mount a filibuster in exchange for the compromise language on Title IV. On August 2 the amendment guaranteeing a jury trial for criminal, but not for civil, violations passed, 51–42. No one knew better than Humphrey how paltry the legislation was; but he also knew that nothing like it had passed before. To Roy Wilkins, who had once accused him of selling out the civil rights movement, he said, "Roy, if there's one thing I've learned in politics, it's never to turn your back on a crumb"—not half a loaf, not a slice, but a crumb. Many of Wilkins's troops were disgusted by the bill; so, too, were leading figures such as Joe Rauh. Wilkins himself was torn. He later wrote, "If I had spurned it, we might have been waiting outside the bakery for a very long time."[46] Once the NAACP voted to endorse the legislation, Humphrey was able to tell Senate liberals that it was safe to vote yes. On August 8, the Senate passed the bill 72–18. Ten days later, when he was relaxing at Waverly, Humphrey read that the House was balking at passing the Senate bill. He booked a flight to Washington and went straight to Room 1402 of the Congress Hotel, where sixteen civil rights groups had set up a war room. Humphrey managed to persuade them to issue a statement supporting the bill, though many of them opposed it.[47]

Humphrey had been a minor player; the Civil Rights Act of 1957 was Lyndon Johnson's legislative masterpiece. Yet Humphrey had played a complicated role that befit his complicated status. He had eloquently fought for the bill in its strongest form. He had helped broker a compromise that let it pass in a weak form. He had passionately opposed the compromise, celebrated the feeble outcome, and used his credibility to bring the leading civil rights groups on board. He was activist, parliamentarian, legitimator. Idealism, for Humphrey, was not only consistent with compromise but demanded it; through just such means did politics deliver a better life for the people. Politics was incremental: a crumb today could lead to a slice tomorrow, and perhaps someday the whole loaf.

How much did the law matter? Johnson biographer Robert Caro concludes that, though the measure did virtually nothing to advance

Black voting rights, "the sharp point of a wedge had now been hammered into" the southern wall, and "the rest of the wedge" would follow.[48] It's a beguiling metaphor, but the truth is that the wall of resistance would remain largely intact for seven more years, far longer than liberals or civil rights activists imagined. The politics of civil rights did not change; nor did the situation of Black people. If anything, Johnson's legerdemain illustrated the limitations of the insider, "performance" view of politics; there was something almost shocking about the discrepancy between the energy and ingenuity required to pass the Civil Rights Act and the meagre results of doing so. Real change, when it would finally come, would once again call on legislative genius—on the part of Hubert Humphrey as well as then president Johnson—but it would happen only because of the public spectacle of Black courage and white brutality in the South, and the change that confrontation wrought in public opinion.

12

Caviar with Khrushchev

---

*"The launching of the first American presidential
campaign from the steps of the Kremlin."*

B Y THE SECOND HALF OF THE 1950S, AMERICA'S HOME FRONT
was calmer than it had been in decades. The economy was
growing at around 5 percent per year while inflation aver-
aged less than 2 percent. America was becoming the first society in
history to have achieved mass prosperity—at least for white people.
This prospect had largely reduced the domestic policy debate to the
question of how best to twiddle dials. It was the threat abroad that
darkened American horizons—the Communist menace, real and
imagined. In March 1955, Secretary of State John Foster Dulles had
publicly threatened to drop atomic bombs on China if the regime
continued to bombard the islands of Quemoy and Matsu, occupied
by the forces of Nationalist China. Though the crisis receded, largely
owing to diplomacy initiated by President Eisenhower, Dulles came
to regard nuclear weapons as a trump card to be brandished by
an artful player. In a fawning article in *Life* magazine in January

1956, Dulles disclosed—or perhaps boasted—that he had threatened to use nuclear weapons "on a selective basis" against China, not only in the Taiwan crisis but also in Vietnam. "Some say we were brought to the verge of war," Dulles blandly said. "Of course we were brought to the verge of war. The ability to get to the verge without getting into the war is the necessary art."[1]

Humphrey knew a gift when he saw one. His staff notified every major Washington correspondent that he would be responding to Dulles in a major address that day. Humphrey concentrated his fire on Dulles's self-congratulatory metaphor of "the verge"—what soon came to be known as "brinksmanship." "No other responsible American statesman in our lifetime has so described an American diplomatic objective," he thundered. Moreover, since the nuclear threat Dulles said he had delivered over Vietnam was "unalterably opposed" to what he had told the Senate Foreign Relations Committee in secret testimony, he had, Humphrey claimed, been lying either then or now. The speech was covered on all the networks that night. In a front-page article, the New York Times described Humphrey's speech as "the most vehement ever made upon the Secretary of State within the internationalist wing of the Senate."[2]

Humphrey may have been engaging in some election-year hyperbole; in fact, he was among the strongest backers in the Democratic Party of Eisenhower's prudent, if unimaginative, foreign policy. (Eisenhower himself never endorsed brinksmanship as a policy.) The threat of nuclear war had receded since a summit meeting between Eisenhower and Nikolai Bulganin, the Soviet no. 2, in July 1955. Yet Dulles's swaggering talk had triggered Humphrey's deepest fears about national security in the nuclear age. At an annual meeting of the Democratic National Committee, Humphrey called on the Eisenhower administration to abandon what he called "H-bomb diplomacy"—gunboat diplomacy with nuclear weapons at the ready. The administration, he complained more broadly, had been "creating an artificial language of America as a land of power, of money, of H-bombs, but not a land of compassion, of mercy, of understanding, of sharing in the aspirations of others."[3]

Humphrey had long been a leading advocate of an "affirmative" foreign policy of aid and trade and technical assistance, of cultural exchange and global diplomatic engagement. The Eisenhower administration, he had observed in the midst of the 1954 crisis over Vietnam, had no tools with which to face Communist aggression save "massive retaliation" with atomic bombs. The United States was thus in danger of retreating into "Fortress America isolationism" behind its nuclear wall.[4] The terrible recklessness of "H-bomb diplomacy" accelerated Humphrey's search for an alternative model. He remained a staunch supporter of the United Nations even as Cold War divisions virtually paralyzed the UN Security Council. In July 1955 he attended the tenth anniversary of the United Nations' founding, in San Francisco. In a letter to Eugenie Anderson, he complained that the administration had given the event short shrift at a time when Washington could be using the United Nations to advance its goals on disarmament and development assistance. A growing number of developing nations had joined the "Non-Aligned Movement," yet Dulles had virtually ignored their initial meeting in Bandung, Indonesia, earlier that year.[5] Humphrey had long since broken with the Cold War fixation on taking sides; he felt that the United States could win over major countries such as India and Indonesia if only it was prepared to try.

In 1956 Eisenhower appointed Humphrey as a delegate to the United Nations, and Humphrey regularly took the train from Washington to New York to roam the hallways of the General Assembly. Few things made Humphrey happier. In a letter to a Minnesota friend, James Markham, he spoke of how much he had learned from listening to developing-world members, above all from delegates representing the twenty-one states, most of them former colonies, that had been admitted in recent years. He ticked off a few recent meetings: Morocco, Tunisia, Sudan, Cambodia, Laos, Thailand.[6] Humphrey came to see the United Nations as a place where the small nations had a voice and the major nations could act with them in matters of mutual interest. He advocated expanding the permanent membership of the Security Council to include seats for Germany and India. (He opposed seating Communist China.) No other major American statesmen wrestled so seriously with what the United Nations could be if the United States truly committed itself to the organization's future.

Humphrey took the lead in formulating a Democratic response to the single-minded anti-communism of the Eisenhower administration. In the aftermath of the Suez Crisis in the fall of 1956, President Gamal Abdel Nasser had turned away from Washington to forge closer relations with the Soviet Union, which until that time had been a strong supporter of secular, socialist Israel. In January 1957, Eisenhower had responded by issuing what came to be known as the "Eisenhower Doctrine," a Middle East version of Harry Truman's pledge to come to the aid of countries menaced by Communist subversion. Ike proposed to funnel money authorized for foreign assistance into military support for some of the region's autocratic leaders. Humphrey described the new doctrine as a "predated declaration of war," and criticized the president for throwing America's might behind the "most feudal and reactionary regimes" in the Middle East. Those Arab and Gulf states were, Humphrey pointed out, sworn to destroy Israel, the only democracy in the area. The administration, he said on several occasions, had done far too little to protect Israel against Arab aggression.[7]

Humphrey traveled regularly as a member of the Senate Foreign Relations Committee. In April 1957, he spent twenty-five days in the Middle East and southern Europe. He held a long meeting with Nasser, whom he found intransigent, back-looking, obsessed with real and perceived slights from the West, and unwilling to face economic and social problems that he did not know how to solve. But he recognized that marginalizing Nasser would only inflame his intense nationalism. He told reporters that the United States had no choice but to deal with the Egyptian leader, who was the legitimate representative of his people.

Humphrey never quite got over his amazement that he, a druggist's son from South Dakota, could speak on equal terms to men who shaped the destiny of nations. Though a notorious talker, Humphrey could be a very careful and empathetic listener, and when he spoke to these figures he paid as much attention to their character, their gestures and quirks, as to their policies. He was deeply struck by the differences between Nasser and Prime Minister David Ben-Gurion of Israel, a country that he had always admired and defended, but never visited. In an article he wrote for the *New York Post* after he returned home, Humphrey compared Nasser, "a military product . . . handicapped both by his lack of travel and knowledge of the world," to the Israeli leader, "a student of history—a scholar in his own right," who "typified his own country—he is rugged, courageous, imaginative." And, Humphrey pointedly added, humble. In a series of articles that he was invited to write for the Jewish Telegraph Agency, Humphrey raved about the Israeli innovations in water conservation and terracing that had made the desert bloom, and about the country's great institutions, such as Hadassah Hospital and Hebrew University. He compared Israel's pioneering spirit to that of the American West.[8] Israel was not a treaty ally of Washington, he noted, but "the unwritten alliance" between them was "based upon mutual understanding and respect."

This was an era of genuine bipartisanship in foreign policy. Upon his return, Humphrey told reporters what he had said to Nasser: Eisenhower was a man of peace, and "if he couldn't get along with Mr. Eisenhower, he couldn't get along with anybody."[9] He submitted an extensive report to the Foreign Relations Committee. "The masses of the Middle East are in revolt" not against the West, he wrote, but "poverty, serfdom, ignorance and disease." Yet the United States was blamed both for choking off aid to Egypt and for failing to press Israel to reach peace. Humphrey proposed the establishment of a Middle East Development Agency to work on regional solutions to poverty as well as to undertake serious efforts to end hostilities with Israel and to find a permanent home for the Palestinian refugees who had been expelled in the 1948 war. He also argued for a major new aid package to help Israel settle its own immigrant population. Humphrey would remain a passionate advocate for Israel who would not turn his back on the suffering of Arab peoples.

FOR HUMPHREY, THE ONLY LASTING SOLUTION TO THE MADNESS OF H-bomb diplomacy was to put a lid on the H-bombs. He mastered the intricacies of disarmament and became the key figure on the subject on Capitol Hill. The idea that states must surrender their arms to international control had been a staple of progressive international thinking since Woodrow Wilson had included such a stipulation in the Covenant of the League of Nations. In the period between the two world wars, peace and disarmament advocates held a series of conferences with the goal of limiting the arms under state control. The fine pronouncements that emerged from these meetings had crumbled to dust with the advent of World War II. But the rise of nuclear weapons gave added urgency to the peace movement, while the creation of the United Nations offered what seemed like a plausible institution in which to vest control.

In a 1950 speech at Washington Cathedral titled "God, Man and the H-Bomb," Humphrey had called for international agreements to abolish war and to mandate universal disarmament; all stockpiles would be turned over to the United Nations.[10] In 1953, along with thirty-three other senators, he signed a resolution proposing to empower the United Nations to hold talks leading to "enforceable universal disarmament."[11] Humphrey never fully squared his fear of Communist aggression with his Wilsonian faith in a world governed by law rather than force. How could the West disarm itself if the Soviets and the Chinese, whom he deeply distrusted, refused? Yet Humphrey's overwhelming wish to get things done always pulled him back from the ideal to the possible. Over the ensuing years he would become a leading figure in promoting enforceable nuclear agreements with the Soviet Union.

In January 1955, the Soviets had proposed a reduction in armed forces and the complete elimination of nuclear weapons. Though the idea represented a not-very-subtle attempt to tilt the balance of power toward Russia, which had a vast advantage in troop strength but trailed far behind the United States in nukes, the Soviets had thus seized the initiative with public opinion. Ike had responded by appointing Harold Stassen, Minnesota's former progressive Republican governor, as his special assistant for disarmament. Eager both to push the administration and assert a leading role for Congress, Humphrey persuaded Lyndon Johnson to form a disarmament subcommittee of the Foreign

Relations Committee and to make him chairman. He began holding hearings in early 1956.

The prospect of reducing the salience and the stock of nuclear weapons thrilled idealists like Humphrey and Stassen and appalled the hardened Cold Warriors around Eisenhower. Dulles managed to undermine Stassen at the ongoing UN disarmament talks in London. But the issue only grew sharper in 1956, when the United States carried out aboveground nuclear tests for the first time, in the Bikini Atoll in the South Pacific. Amid a growing public outcry against the atomic bomb, Nikita Khrushchev, the new, reform-minded Soviet premier, announced a unilateral reduction in troops and again pressed for nuclear cuts. The following year, when Stassen seemed to be making progress in the London talks, Dulles called him home and took over the negotiations himself. Along with Lewis Strauss, chairman of the Atomic Energy Commission (AEC), Dulles was convinced that verifying Soviet compliance with a test ban was technically impossible. In London he presented the Soviets with a package proposal that would have tied arms reductions to an inspection program so extensive and intrusive—with no reciprocal promise on the American side—that it guaranteed Soviet rejection. That, of course, was the goal.

This time the Soviets responded not with a "peace offensive," as they had the year before, but with a show of power. In September, Russia launched its first intercontinental ballistic missile (ICBM), followed a month later by Sputnik, the first earth satellite. Suddenly the Soviet Union seemed to be winning the arms race. The imperative was to catch up, not to call a halt. By early 1958, Dulles had persuaded Eisenhower to send Stassen packing.[12] Yet Humphrey had learned from American diplomats that the Soviets remained eager to sign a nuclear test ban. He also had reason to believe that seismic technology had become sensitive enough to detect nuclear tests thousands of miles away. And so, at this deeply unpropitious moment, he entered the nuclear debate. On February 4, 1958, Humphrey delivered a four-hour speech in the Senate, a speech so gigantic that it came equipped with its very own table of contents. Humphrey began by acknowledging the obvious: the challenge of Sputnik compelled the

United States to increase defense spending and to "regain our strength in missiles, rockets and other weapons." Yet that wasn't enough. "The nuclear age can be an inferno of death and destruction or a garden of peace and plenty," Humphrey went on, in language that John Kennedy would echo in his 1961 inaugural address.

Humphrey then launched into a lengthy critique of Dulles's proposal in London. If Russia agreed to open up the entire country for inspections, he asked, would we? Why not instead figure out what kind of inspection regime the Soviets could live with, and then see if that offered us sufficient confidence? Humphrey also proposed that Washington seek agreements on individual issues, such as the production of fissile material, rather than insisting on an all-or-nothing solution. All this was technocratic material; but underneath Humphrey's proposal was a genuine change in his thinking. In order to foster the atmosphere of trust that would make such an agreement possible, the United States needed to reduce tensions with the Soviet Union, and indeed throughout the world. Humphrey urged a new diplomacy in the Middle East and a new willingness to use the United Nations for the settlement of disputes and for economic development. He proposed a mutual reduction of American and Russian troops in Europe, and even an effort to engage China—something he had never suggested before.[13] Taken all in all, the speech constituted a comprehensive statement of a new liberal foreign policy, still firmly anti-Communist but no longer driven by fear of communism, as Democrats had been since the immediate postwar period.

The speech was panned in the mainstream press. A *New York Times* editorial said that with his plea for flexibility on disarmament, Humphrey "walks right into the Russian trap" while Europe was scarcely ready to stand on its own two feet after a withdrawal of American troops.[14] Humphrey was undaunted. On April 1, after the Soviets had announced a unilateral cessation of nuclear tests, he returned to the Senate floor to condemn "the unbelievable defeat that has befallen the American people and the people of the free world" from this propaganda coup. "What is the disarmament policy of the United States government?" he cried. "Does anybody know? How long will we have to wait to find out?"[15] Rather than wait, Humphrey forced the issue.

On April 14 he held marquee hearings of his disarmament committee in which Lewis Strauss and the atomic scientist Edward Teller maintained that the United States could not detect an underground test in the Soviet Union. Hans Bethe, the Nobel laureate in physics then heading the executive branch committee on detecting Soviet tests, said he believed it could. A month earlier, in fact, Humphrey had ridiculed the AEC for claiming that an American test could be sensed no more than 250 miles away when the nation's own survey stations recorded the effects 2,300 miles away—"leaving the impression that scientific facts are being used by someone to make a political point."[16]

Humphrey had a secret ally in the president, who considered the arms race madness. Overruling his own hawks, in late May Eisenhower sent a message to Soviet premier Nikita Khrushchev asking for a meeting of nuclear scientists to discuss the feasibility of a test ban treaty. The two leaders agreed to convene an eighteen-nation Disarmament Conference in Geneva at the end of October. Humphrey was widely seen as the congressional impresario of this breakthrough for peace. He scored an appearance on *Meet the Press* June 1. Humphrey had done his homework, as always, and he argued that advances in seismography had made it possible to detect an underground test 6,800 miles away. Teller was wrong and Bethe was right.[17] Humphrey had put the issue of disarmament on the national agenda and forced, or helped guide, the administration's hand through an extraordinary combination of public oratory, congressional dramaturgy, and the mastery of technical detail. Another five years would pass before the two sides would sign the disarmament treaty of which Humphrey dreamed. But as with civil rights, Humphrey's fundamental faith in politics and in the American people gave him the confidence to assiduously plow and seed and furrow the ground, knowing that finally it would yield a flourishing crop.

By now Humphrey had long since mastered the elaborate maneuvers required on *Meet the Press* and the other news shows. He effortlessly turned aside questions about civil rights that only would have alienated southern senators, as well as a new question that suddenly many were asking: Are you running for president? "I'm not running for president," he said.

That was true—but only in the Washington sense of plausible deniability. Humphrey had begun, very tentatively, talking to his close friends and aides about a run in 1960. In June, his friend Dick Schifter sent a memo to Max Kampelman outlining the kind of capabilities needed in a campaign director. The following month someone close to Humphrey—probably Kampelman—reached out to James Rowe, a Washington lawyer and political mastermind, to see if he might be available should Humphrey run.[18] Whatever Humphrey did, then, he did with one eye on the race. He was positioning himself as the Democratic Party's "pace-setter" on foreign affairs, in the words of *The New Republic*.[19] He called for a "dynamic new Marshall Plan" for India rather than the modest package of loans Eisenhower had proposed. He advanced a "four-point plan for peace"—food aid, health, loans, disarmament.[20] In speeches before the Senate, Humphrey lambasted Eisenhower's foreign policy for falling behind on missiles, chiseling on foreign aid, and backing autocrats. "A total challenge from a totalitarian society," he cried, as if reprising one of his speeches from 1944, "demands a total response from, and a total commitment by, our own free society."[21] Humphrey does not seem to have been bothered by the contradiction between calling for disarmament and lacerating the Republicans for allowing a "missile gap" with the Soviets to develop. Ike, who knew very well that the missile gap was partisan nonsense, prudently resisted the Cold War liberals' call for increased defense spending.

In the election that fall a raft of liberals was elected to the Senate while several potential presidential candidates, including Averill Harriman, were defeated. *Time* put Humphrey on the cover along with Kennedy, Symington, and other leading Democrats, pronouncing him the current leader of an undeclared race for the nomination in 1960.[22] In November, Humphrey embarked on a trip to Europe and Russia, an itinerary designed to keep him in the public eye as one of the nation's foremost statesmen. Though his agenda in Russia focused on cooperation on health issues and the expansion of PL 480, when he stopped over in Geneva to visit the disarmament talks Humphrey made a point of telling Russian officials that he hoped to meet with Khrushchev. On November 27, while Humphrey was in Germany, the

Soviet leader abruptly announced that he was turning over East Berlin to the East German government, unilaterally abrogating the system of shared occupation established by the Allied governments. The Cold War, which had moderated in recent months, had become frigid once again.

Humphrey arrived in Moscow that night. The next day, a Friday, he met with Foreign Minister Andrei Gromyko and Anastas Mikoyan, a reformer who had helped write the "secret speech" of 1956 in which Khrushchev had denounced the crimes of Stalin. Monday morning Humphrey held talks with officials in the agricultural and educational ministries. When he returned to the National Hotel after lunch, a messenger arrived to say that "the first minister" would meet with him at 3:00—half an hour away. No, he could not spend time preparing, nor could he bring an aide with him. Humphrey was whisked to the Kremlin, where, as in a dream, he was escorted down an endless carpeted hallway, then another hallway, and then into an anteroom, until finally, at 3:00 to the minute, he was admitted to the vast office of the first minister. Khrushchev, short, pudgy, and smiling, came out from behind his plain wooden desk with a hand outstretched.[23] There can be no doubt that the meeting was premeditated on the part of the premier, who knew the role that Humphrey had been playing in supporting Eisenhower's tentative moves toward peaceful coexistence, and knew that Humphrey was a leading voice on foreign affairs of the majority party in Congress.

The two men sat across from each other at a long conference table, with a translator—the American-educated Oleg Troyanovsky—sitting at the head between them. At first the conversation was stilted, Humphrey raising his formal agenda of international medical research. Then the two men talked about disarmament. Humphrey wasn't sure what he was allowed to say or do. Finally, he turned to Troyanovsky and asked if the first minister would mind if he took notes. Not at all, said Troyanovsky, handing him a sheaf of blank paper. Humphrey then covered twenty-four pages with notes of both men's remarks. Eager to impress and intimidate his visitor, Khrushchev revealed to Humphrey the details of a "secret" nuclear warhead that could deliver a payload of five megatons by virtue of reducing fissionable material to a tenth of its usual weight. This turned out to be a theme with the Soviet leader, who insisted that his scientists had developed an ICBM with a range so vast—fourteen thousand kilometers—that it could not be tested within the limits of Soviet territory. Humphrey entered into the spirit of Khrushchev's raillery by suggesting that he turn the weapon over to American scientists, so they could test its limits in outer space.

Humphrey began to relax and enjoy himself as he saw that Khrushchev was a man something like himself—he told jokes and long stories and he waved his arms around. He told Humphrey about his impoverished boyhood and cried when he recalled his son's death in World War II. Khrushchev plainly loved gossip, and he boasted to Humphrey about how he had bullied and outwitted his colleagues in the Politburo on a crucial vote over decentralization. He talked about the world leaders he knew. France's Edgar Faure was "not very smart," Britain's Anthony Eden was "smart but weak," President Eisenhower was a fine man but thoroughly unprepared at the recent Geneva disarmament talks, where Secretary Dulles had virtually watched from his shoulder. Khrushchev loathed Dulles, whom he regarded as an unreconstructed Cold Warrior. Humphrey felt that he had to stop the premier there; for all his own difference with Dulles, the secretary, Humphrey said patriotically, and not quite sincerely, was "not a warmonger."

As the hours passed, Humphrey came to understand that Khrushchev was an extraordinary man—witty and wise, a peerless politician, yet withal a committed Communist ideologue. When Humphrey suggested that it was Stalin's bellicosity that had forced the United States to rearm in the late forties, the Soviet leader waved him off—not angrily, but firmly. Rearmament had failed, he said, because the Soviet Union had managed to keep up with the arms race while continuing to raise its people's standard of living. The real goal of American policy, he knew, was "to liquidate the Socialist system!" (Humphrey punctuated most of Khrushchev's remarks with an exclamation point to indicate his expostulatory tone.) The Truman Doctrine had failed; the Eisenhower Doctrine had failed. Why this nuclear buildup? We need no more H-bombs, Khrushchev declared. And we need no more abusive language. Let us have a treaty outlawing such language! There Humphrey could agree.

Humphrey now felt confident enough to raise the most sensitive of all topics—Berlin. Humphrey was extremely conscious of not falling too deeply into the spirit of camaraderie that Khrushchev seemed to be offering; he knew that back home he would have to explain himself both to Eisenhower and to the public. "I hope you understand the seriousness of our purpose," he said. Khrushchev reiterated his demand that Berlin become a unified free city. Now he, too, turned firm, fixing an icy glare on his visitor. "Why do you have 25,000 troops in Berlin?" he asked. "If you don't want to make war, why this thorn? Some of your generals make stupid statements—send in tanks to Berlin. We have tanks too. And rockets." An attack on the German Democratic Republic, Khrushchev concluded, "is war!" Troyanovsky, who would become a leading diplomat, would later write that Khrushchev had argued to the Politburo that the Americans had rejected all his appeals for moderation, and "the obvious spot to apply pressure was West Berlin, the Achilles' heel of the Western powers." Troyanovsky recalled Khrushchev grilling his visitor: "What are your president and secretary of state thinking? What are their counterproposals?"[24]

The two men rallied back and forth, Humphrey asking how Khrushchev proposed to guarantee access to Berlin, and whether the "confederated" Germany that the premier imagined would be allowed to join the North Atlantic Treaty Organization (NATO). And then, almost three hours having passed, Khrushchev suggested—just as LBJ would have done—that he and Humphrey adjourn to the toilet.

Khrushchev kept circling back to Berlin, which he called "a bone in my throat." At some point the Soviet leader walked Humphrey over to a big wall map and showed him the cities at which NATO weapons were targeted, including Moscow. "If you just keep talking about bombing us," he said, "why, by God, we'll bomb you!" Khrushchev asked Humphrey to show him where in America he was from. When he pointed out Minnesota, Khrushchev joked, "I promise you, we shall never bomb it." But Khrushchev was deadly serious: he had probably invited Humphrey to the Kremlin to deliver the message that Berlin was not a matter for compromise. But, he added, "we want no evil to the United States or free Berlin. You must assure the President of this." That, too, was presumably part of the message.

Humphrey began to worry that he was overstaying his welcome, but Troyanovsky told him to stay until Khrushchev indicated otherwise. At 7:00 or so Khrushchev ordered up a meal—first sandwiches, then caviar, then beef and an unidentified fowl. Humphrey later said that Khrushchev drank only mineral water, but in the course of the evening he himself downed both vodka and brandy. Humphrey had the chance to pose the kinds of questions any committed Cold Warrior would like to ask of the Soviet supremo, though he hardly got satisfying answers. Why did you crush the Hungarian uprising? "That was started by American agents," Khrushchev shot back. Besides, didn't you know they held elections of their own? Humphrey asked about religious freedom in Russia. My daughter-in-law is Jewish, said Khrushchev. And antisemitism was forbidden by law.

Khrushchev plainly didn't want the evening to end. He called for Mikoyan, who may have been rousted from bed. The three talked about trade issues until 11:25, at which point Mikoyan announced that he was tired and wanted to go to sleep. If not, Humphrey later reflected, these two master talkers "might have gone on for another eight and a half hours."[25]

That conversation was the most thrilling and the most important event in Humphrey's life since the 1948 Democratic National Convention. (The same apparently cannot be said for Khrushchev, who does not mention the affair in his three-volume memoirs.) Humphrey told reporters how deeply impressed he had been: "This boy was born early and leaves late, believe me." The premier had delivered an amazing impromptu speech against racism. "We really got along just fine," Humphrey said. "I liked him like nobody's business." This was not the line that American statesmen were supposed to take with Soviet leaders, but Humphrey's prudence was no match for his enthusiasm.

Humphrey knew that he was sitting on a political gold mine. In the days after the talk he drew up a list of storylines for his aides to market to the press: "Humphrey Urges Directorate of Free World to Mobilize Economic Resources for Expanding Economic Aid to Developing Areas." (He had talked to Khrushchev about working together on Middle East development.) He could, he suggested, write articles for the *New York Times*, the Herald Tribune Syndicate, the women's magazines, the Minnesota papers. He should sit down with the big columnists and political reporters. He needed to contact a "top-flight Lecture Bureau for High-Paying Lecture Engagements."[26] Humphrey started talking to reporters almost as soon as he woke up from his talkathon and kept doing so as he made his way back home. He made the right-hand column—the pole position—of the *New York Times* front page on December 3—"Khrushchev Firm in Talk with Humphrey." The reporter noted that no American visitor had ever before held so long a conversation with the Soviet premier. *Time* called it "the longest, perhaps the most revealing and certainly the most fascinating audience ever given by a Soviet premier to an American citizen."[27]

Back in Washington, Humphrey held one of the most gratifying press conferences of his life. It had to be moved from his office to the chamber of the House Armed Services Committee in order to accommodate the one-hundred-odd newsmen in attendance. Humphrey tried to deliver a nuanced message to the American public. "I don't think we're going to make any progress with the Soviets for a long time," he said. On the other hand, "They're not interested in war, at least not for the next seven years"—the term of the current economic plan, at the end of which the Russians imagined that they might have caught up with the West as an industrial power. He had concluded that "the policy of threats is barren, sterile and futile." We should instead learn to live with the Soviets, and enhance people-to-people contact in order to satisfy what Humphrey believed was a tremendous hunger to know about Americans and American culture.[28]

Humphrey drew up notes for himself before briefing Dulles and Eisenhower. "Do not seek to embarrass Mr. Dulles!" (Humphrey may have been reminding himself to pass over in silence Khrushchev's expression of contempt for the secretary.) "We need to study Russian literature, art, science and history—urgent!" Neither Dulles nor Eisenhower might have found that mission urgent, but Humphrey had come back from Moscow convinced that Americans needed to understand the wellsprings of Soviet thought and action. When he met with Eisenhower, he talked about what he had sensed behind Khrushchev's bravado. The Soviet leader struck him, he said, as "a man who is insecure, who thinks [Americans] are rich and big and . . . keep picking on him." Khrushchev was, he thought, desperate to be invited for a summit in the United States. (The Soviet leader would have his wish gratified in September 1959.)

Humphrey was booked again on *Meet the Press*, where he sagely observed that war over Berlin could be avoided "if we remain firm." Asked if Khrushchev was trying to scare him with talk of the alleged five-megaton bomb, Humphrey nodded and said, "But I wasn't frightened."[29] This was a Humphrey the public hadn't seen before—calm, resolute, statesmanlike. The venerable *New York Times* columnist Arthur Krock quipped that Americans had witnessed "the launching of the first American presidential campaign from the steps of the Kremlin." The anointing process had, indeed, begun. *Life* put Humphrey on the cover and gave him five pages to recount "My Marathon Talks with Russia's Boss."[30] Russell Baker of the *Times* wrote a long piece both repeating the received wisdom—"The public Humphrey is clattering, strident and bellicose"—and disclosing heretofore unnoticed virtues, including the senator's astonishing fluency on all matters of policy and the deep reservoir of compassion deposited by his personal experience of the Depression.[31] Back in 1956, Humphrey had hoped that serving as Adlai Stevenson's running mate would elevate him in the mind of the broad American public. That hadn't worked, but Nikita Khrushchev had elevated him instead.

13

No Match for Camelot

*"There was no distance about him, no separation,
none of the majesty that must surround a king."*

T HE HUBERT HUMPHREY WHO RETURNED FROM MOSCOW IN
December 1958 was a man in his prime. He was forty-seven
years old; his hair had thinned up front and he had begun to
develop a slight paunch. His chin had taken on the rubbery shape
and texture that fell lamentably short of the square-jawed profile that made a man loom presidential. Though still regarded as a
long-winded liberal idealist, he had long since shed his reputation
as a troublemaker. He was a man deeply shaped by America's political institutions at a time when those institutions were still held in
high regard. The Khrushchev encounter had raised him to the plane
of the statesman. Virtually everything he said about East-West relations, whether it was that more Americans should learn Russian or
that Congress should have its own version of the National Security
Council, made the major newspapers or the evening news.[1] And with
Ike stepping down, and the blunderbuss anti-Communist Richard

Nixon likely to win the Republican nomination, the time for a presidential run might never be more propitious.

Several months earlier, Humphrey had begun taking soundings from Jim Rowe. This redoubtable operator had sent him a memo in October conveying the prediction of one of the many political professionals with whom he regularly spoke: Kennedy, Harriman, and Humphrey would block one another, creating a vacuum that Adlai Stevenson would once again fill. Humphrey thanked Rowe for his "clarity and candor," adding, with painful candor of his own, "I just keep saying to myself and truly believing that I am not really up to all this."[2] That was before Moscow; the adulation in which he had been bathed upon his return had at least temporarily quelled that inner voice.

Rowe was to play a large role in Humphrey's life for the next eighteen months, as well as in years to come. He was the kind of party professional whom the idealists around Humphrey looked on with grave suspicion. A small-town boy from Montana, he had graduated from Harvard Law School, clerked for Justice Oliver Wendell Holmes, and at age twenty-six joined the Roosevelt administration, where he quickly rose to become FDR's administrative assistant. Thereafter Rowe served in the US Navy, helped run the Nuremberg trials, and worked in Truman's budget office. In 1948 he had used his legal skills to help Lyndon Johnson get on the ballot in his run for the Senate, thereby cementing an intimate relationship that would last until LBJ died. He then joined the law firm of Tommy "The Cork" Corcoran, FDR's master fixer. Now a fixer in his own right, Rowe got to know everybody who mattered in the Democratic Party, as well as every important newspaperman and columnist. Rowe assumed that he would work on Lyndon Johnson's run for the presidency in 1960. But in the summer of 1958 Johnson told him that he wasn't running, and urged him to go to work for Humphrey. In fact, Johnson believed that none of the candidates then being touted had the ability to put together a majority of Democratic delegates; he seems to have expected to call in his chits with Senate leaders to win a brokered convention. Johnson's view of politics as a game played by insiders blinded him to the truth that a presidential race was becoming a popularity contest to be waged with, and in, the public.[3]

Rowe doubted Johnson's disavowal; nevertheless, in the first days of January, he wrote Johnson to say that he had agreed to work for Humphrey. Rowe then wrote a long memo to Humphrey outlining a proposed political strategy. Rowe understood that, unlike Truman or Johnson, Humphrey was first an idealist and only second a political professional. He had the insight to recognize that Humphrey's compassion was both the source of his appeal and the obstacle to his ambitions. He introduced his memo with a provocative passage from Lady Macbeth's speech to her hesitant husband: "Yet do I fear thy nature: It is too full of human kindness to catch the nearest way." So much did Rowe fear Humphrey's kind nature that he began his memo by noting that he had asked Joe Rauh if he and his friends at Americans for Democratic Action were going to pressure him to lead a politically ruinous fight against the filibuster in the new session of Congress. "I do not think there is anything to be gained by being the public leader of this parade," Rowe asserted.[4]

Humphrey might have bristled at the suggestion that he was caving in to the liberal purists. A few weeks after the 1958 elections, he and Paul Douglas had sent a letter to the thirteen new Democratic senators stating that "majority rule can only be restored in the Senate by an effective change in Rule 22." They called on the newcomers to back a proposal to end a filibuster by majority vote once fifteen days had passed.[5] Johnson had, inevitably, opposed the effort and had succeeded in imposing his own extremely minimal alternative, restoring the old rule that allowed two-thirds of those present, rather than two-thirds of all the members of the body, to end a filibuster. In May 1959, Humphrey and the liberal group would introduce a bill to restore Title III of the 1957 Civil Rights Act. That, too, failed.

Rowe's point was that whether Humphrey liked it or not, a Democratic candidate who was anathema to the South could not be nominated or elected. Neither, of course, could a southern loyalist win enough support among liberals or the working class to gain victory. Humphrey needed "liberal-labor" support to bear him aloft to the upper ranks of the Democratic candidates. Rowe shrewdly mapped out Humphrey's narrow path to a victory at the convention. Any candidate, he explained, would need to appeal to two of the three major constituencies: liberals, the South, and what Rowe called the "professionals," meaning state and national power brokers. In order to win over this last group, whose sole concern was backing a winner, he must be seen as a "reasonable man," a "man-in-the-middle," as Stevenson had been in 1952 and 1956. In the general election, Rowe added, Republicans would go after two "whipping boys": Walter Reuther and the ADA, which is to say, labor and liberals. Humphrey needed to "shape and modify" his relationship with both. Here was political counsel in the mode of Machiavelli, who described the ideal prince as a good man willing to act badly.

Rowe then explained to Humphrey something the latter would not want to hear: he would have to enter the primaries. Every campaign, he wrote, began with an announcement that the candidate would not contest primaries, which were expensive, exhausting, and degrading—and then ended by doing just that. "This is because the men without enough organization strength," Rowe observed, "learn that they can get publicity if there is no opposition and can 'catch up' if they can beat a front-runner." Kennedy had the organization strength; Humphrey needed to catch up. The trick, Rowe went on, was to enter as few primaries as possible, and only those that he could win. Rowe suggested California and perhaps Pennsylvania. Then he doled out one more dram of bitter medicine. Humphrey should spend an hour a day cultivating the professionals. In New York, for example, he must "pay court" to Tammany boss Carmine DeSapio; in Pennsylvania, to Governor Dave Lawrence, the party boss.

Whatever their disagreements in recent years, both labor leaders and ADA officials regarded Humphrey as the one politician with a real chance at the presidency who was committed body and soul to their own aspirations. Rowe seemed to be trying to force Humphrey to choose between them and him. The activists regarded that as both a moral and a political mistake. On January 25, 1959, Jim Loeb, who had recruited Humphrey for the ADA in 1946, sent him a letter rebutting Rowe's central claims, adding that it also represented Joe

Rauh's views. While a centrist campaign might work against Nixon, Loeb wrote, it would surely fail against the moderate Nelson Rockefeller, who might well win the nomination. What's more, "you cannot change your program without losing face badly." The press "would murder you." And he asked a series of pointed questions. What would become of Rowe if Johnson entered the race? How would liberals react if Rowe became the public face of the Humphrey campaign? What if a fight over the civil rights plank broke out at the convention? Perhaps trying to find common ground, Loeb suggested that, rather than moderate his politics, Humphrey "make an effort to be somewhat less belligerent, less brash, more thoughtful."[6]

Fractious battles for control beset all but the most disciplined presidential campaigns. But this struggle was not, at least not chiefly, a battle of egos; it was a battle for Humphrey's soul. No other figure simultaneously occupied the insider and outsider wings of the Democratic Party—the Johnson wing and the ADA wing. Adlai Stevenson never provoked such a tug-of-war, because he was both less idealistic and less ambitious than Humphrey. John Kennedy would run a far more coherent race because he was less distracted by ideals. Humphrey didn't believe that he had to sacrifice his principles in order to win, but the Academy of Lyndon Johnson had long since taught him that intellectual and moral absolutism was a political dead end. On January 28 he wrote to Rowe to say, "Quite frankly Jim, I need you." At that same moment, however, Rowe was writing to Humphrey what he called a "here's where we get off the train" letter. He had, he said, talked to Loeb and Rauh. He had not fully understood how bitterly they resented Johnson for derailing the liberal agenda. "They have a phobia about Lyndon, as they do about Humphrey's 'expediency.' I, perhaps, have a phobia about the picture of Humphrey as 'the wild-eyed ADA liberal.'" Since at this early stage Humphrey needed the liberals in his corner, he was bowing out.[7]

This produced yet another letter, this one from Rauh, denying that he and Loeb had a phobia about Humphrey's "expediency," because the very few times they had known him to act expediently he had "looked like a man just handed a life sentence." To them, Humphrey was not a wild-eyed ADA liberal but a liberal that Democrats across different factions of the party could see as "the best man to lead in the cold war because he cares deeply about the problems at home and even more because he is the man they trust to stop Communist Russia without war." He and Loeb respected Rowe despite the disagreements and were, Rauh said, looking forward to working with him.[8] The rift between the necessary and the good was healed—for the moment.

Behind the scenes, a Humphrey campaign had begun to take shape. In late March, Rowe convened a group of Humphrey's friends and loyalists, including Max Kampelman and Evron Kirkpatrick, in his office. They incorporated as the Committee on National Issues, a fund-raising mechanism for early efforts. Rowe began firing off memos to the candidate. How could you possibly be wasting your time talking to the Arlington, Virginia, Real Estate Board? (Answer: a friend asked him and he was too "soft-hearted" to say no, which was just what Rowe feared.) Drew Pearson and Averill Harriman wanted to help. "Adlai is your political enemy." You must cultivate him and the people around him. Rowe sent a memo to himself—"not for the files"—memorializing a conversation with Kennedy, who had already analyzed the race in detail. Humphrey would never raise enough money to be competitive, Kennedy coolly explained; only Stevenson or Johnson could beat him.[9]

Humphrey began to book speaking engagements in primary states—California, Oregon, Wisconsin. He wasn't alone: by May, Kennedy was in Wisconsin and Stuart Symington in Maryland; even Johnson was planning his own West Coast visit. None were announced candidates, but the campaign was underway, earlier than ever before. In June, Humphrey met in a suite at the Leamington Hotel in Minneapolis with the people he trusted most personally and politically—Governor Orville Freeman; Gene McCarthy, who had just been elected senator; his aide Herb Waters; Muriel; and other Minnesota political figures. Everyone there knew that Humphrey had already fallen behind Kennedy in early polls, though none of them understood how much hard work the Massachusetts senator had put in over the past several years canvassing party leaders across the country.

Humphrey was the candidate of the old-line liberals: Eleanor Roosevelt said that she had divined in him "the spark of greatness." The ADA crowd had always regarded Kennedy with suspicion. So reluctant was Kennedy to stand up to anti-Communist fervor that he hadn't voted to censure Joe McCarthy. On civil rights Kennedy was no more than lukewarm. In 1957 he had promised the NAACP that he would vote against the jury trial amendment, and then he had switched at the last moment. In his 1958 reelection campaign he had said that the timetable for desegregation "should be purely one of local option."[10] Jackie Robinson, the retired Dodgers great, and the best-known and most widely admired Black man in America, was so disgusted with this timidity that he refused to have his picture taken with Kennedy and ultimately campaigned for Humphrey. Kennedy had taken up the cause of labor, but Humphrey had been fighting for the workingman since the contest over Taft-Hartley. At the end of October, Kennedy, Symington, and Humphrey addressed the annual convention of the United Auto Workers (UAW) in Atlantic City. The first two received polite applause. Then Humphrey delivered a full-throated attack on Eisenhower's labor record, and the three thousand delegates "roared and stamped their approval for twelve minutes," according to a press account.[11] When Walter Reuther of the UAW quizzed Kennedy on his civil rights views, the latter said that he just followed Hubert's lead. Reuther himself had been reliably reported as a Humphrey supporter.[12]

Yet as Kennedy had shifted to the left, and Humphrey to the right, that political difference looked more like a matter of nostalgia. Wayne Morse, a member of the Senate's very small purist wing, told reporters in Minnesota, "I don't know of any candidate who is running on a true liberal program." The problem with Hubert Humphrey, he said, was that he was "always walking out on Hubert Humphrey." He recalled that Humphrey had pressed the freshman Democrats to line up behind Johnson's Rule 22 non-reform proposal when his own effort had failed.[13]

At bottom, Kennedy and Humphrey differed more profoundly in character and temperament than in policy. Kennedy was analytical and detached; what he believed he believed with his mind. In a campaign appearance before a Black audience, he spoke of "the irrationality of racism."[14] What Humphrey believed, on the other hand, he believed with his entire being. The journalist Theodore White quoted him telling an audience that "intellectual liberalism must be buttressed with an understanding of people and a love of them that goes far beyond texts or documents. For if you can't cry a bit in politics, the only thing you'll have is hate." JFK heard that—rightly—as a shot at his own dispassion. It would be included on a list of Humphrey "smears," most of which consisted of perfectly orthodox political criticism.[15]

Kennedy himself saw this distinction with characteristic clarity. In his journals, Arthur Schlesinger recorded a comment that Kennedy had made to him: "Hubert is too hot for the present mood of the people. He gets people too excited, too worked up. What they want today is a more boring, monotonous personality, like me."[16] The second part was, of course, disingenuous: the forty-one-year-old scion was almost absurdly handsome and glamorous, an aristocrat with FDR's gracious manner, a certified war hero, a best-selling author thanks to *Profiles in Courage*, with a beautiful young wife and a perfectly photogenic little daughter. JFK was, moreover, the standard-bearer of "the Kennedys," a juggernaut of well-educated, telegenic brothers, wives, in-laws, and camp followers, all underwritten by the stupendous wealth of Joe Kennedy, a ferocious old man determined to put one of his boys in the White House. Jack didn't need to belong to any of the big political factions; he belonged to the Kennedys.

Though not by nature an envious man, Humphrey was enraged at the crush that the press seemed to have on the Kennedy clan. An Associated Press piece on Kennedy as a kind of modern Marcus Aurelius drove him to fire off a furious memo to his aides: "I would imagine that I've read as much Plato or Aristotle as Kennedy and possibly even more—in fact I had to teach some of it. Nevertheless, the image of Kennedy is one of the cultured, educated man, who is the fighter of the right against evil, good-looking and dynamic." Even more egregious was the swoon over Jackie, who stood silently by her husband's side like a china doll. "The main difference between our campaign and Kennedy's is our wives," Humphrey absurdly fumed.

Maybe Jackie "speaks a few words of French," but Muriel, a mother of four who made her own clothes and kept her own house, "in her very looks and demeanor represents a good wife, a fine mother and a lovely lady."[17] The *Washington Post* even attributed Humphrey's superhuman stamina to the "energy soup"—actually, beef stew—that Muriel kept simmering on the back of the stove when her husband came home late from work. "Three bowls of vitamin soup and half a quart of milk with jello (strawberry or cherry) for dessert makes a meal," confirmed the all-American senator.[18]

The Kennedy juggernaut rumbled onward while the wheels began to wobble on the Humphrey Studebaker. In September, Humphrey formally appointed Rowe as campaign manager—at which point Loeb and Rauh withdrew. They had remained so long as the hierarchy was fluid, but they would not work under Johnson's man. Rauh wrote to Humphrey, "We would be doing you a major disservice if we were to try and stick with any Rowe-directed campaign that, in our view, would be bound to end not only in failure, but in shattering the liberal hopes that today ride on you."[19] The "we" included not just Loeb but three or four other senior ADA figures. Loeb and Rauh would ultimately work with the campaign—they loved Humphrey too much to stay away—but would play far more marginal roles than had once been envisioned. Rowe offered once again to withdraw, and once again Humphrey said he couldn't live without him.

Kennedy had been right about Humphrey's money problem. The September kick-off dinner for the Humphrey for President campaign had managed to raise $30,000, a good sum for an undeclared candidate.[20] But an October fund-raiser in New York yielded a grand total of $2,050 with promises of another $3,500. Larger sums, but still modest, came from Minnesota businessmen, above all Dwayne Andreas, the food-processing magnate, who had traveled with Humphrey to the Middle East (and signed several important deals while there). Robert Barrie, the chief fund-raiser, estimated that the campaign would need $200,000 to $250,000. "The kind of bills we're paying now won't elect a mayor in Elizabeth, New Jersey," he wrote despondently. Humphrey admitted to his friend Eugenie Anderson that he didn't have a dollar to spend on TV or radio. He had, he conceded, failed to project himself on the national scene despite all the articles in *Life* and appearances on *Meet the Press*. He confessed that he no longer had the energy he had had at thirty-eight, when he had joined the Senate; at times he felt exhausted.[21]

The polls went from bad to worse. A Louis Harris sounding in December put Humphrey at 5 percent, with Kennedy leading the pack. Humphrey did not have to be told how long the odds were. He would later say he had estimated his chances of winning the nomination at one out of ten.[22] (Rowe was no more optimistic, though he didn't say so.) Humphrey's prospects became yet more dire in early December, when LBJ invited him down to the ranch. Johnson woke up his visitors at 5:00 a.m. with a giant breakfast courtesy of the Johnson pigs, chickens, honeybees, and so on. Just as Humphrey was tucking in, Johnson said, "Hubert, are you going to do me out of the nomination?" Humphrey paused, perhaps to collect his wits, before saying, "Lyndon, you have all *this*. Let me have the nomination."[23]

Nevertheless, Humphrey was an optimist; the part of him that made a dry-eyed assessment of the odds was not the part that controlled his actions. And who could tell when an open race would come again? Kennedy was to formally announce in early January 1960; Humphrey's team felt that any announcement of his own would feel like an anticlimax if it came afterward. He thus felt compelled to declare his candidacy on December 30, when the nation and much of the press corps were on holiday. In a speech before Washington reporters, he said, "I know from personal experience what it means to be the victim of depression, distress and natural disaster—those unpredictable forces over which so many human beings have no control." He promised to be the voice of "Americans who lack the means, power or the influence to fully control their own destiny." He would fight the Communists, to be sure; but he would also fight "the older and greater enemies of men—disease, hunger, poverty and illiteracy."[24]

But the fraction of Americans who felt powerless before the forces of destiny, who lived in fear of the ancient scourges, had been steadily shrinking since the 1930s, when Humphrey's politics had been formed. Reviewing Humphrey's oration, James Reston of the *Times* noted sardonically, "Old Bob LaFollette and William Jennings Bryan would have loved it." We will learn, Reston wrote, if Americans "still like underdogs and hate 'the interests.'" The *Times* editorial board more generously observed that, though once dismissed, Humphrey was now "listened to, inside the Senate and out, and listened to with increasing seriousness." The editors also noted that Humphrey had himself conceded that he faced "an uphill fight." For once, they said, the senator could not be accused of hyperbole.[25]

JIM ROWE HAD ADVISED HUMPHREY TO ENTICE KENNEDY INTO A primary that Humphrey could win. He appeared to have done just that in Wisconsin, a farm state with progressive cities, and one where he was regarded almost as a third senator. The Kennedy forces, far from wandering unawares into a trap, felt that even a solid showing in Humphrey's neighboring state could prove Kennedy's national appeal. An early poll by Louis Harris showed Kennedy in the lead. In January, Gerald Heaney, a Duluth lawyer and longtime Humphrey supporter who would soon take over the Wisconsin operation, reported that Humphrey looked strong only in the two rural districts bordering Minnesota. Milwaukee, Madison, Eau Claire, and other big cities had become quite prosperous in recent years and were not swayed by Humphrey's new New Deal message. Humphrey himself returned from a swing through the state in February to pronounce his organization a complete mess. He repeated a new favorite phrase: "It's later than you think."[26]

The organization *was* a mess, and not just because Humphrey only had the money to keep two district offices open. Nobody was sure which of his Minnesota friends had the final say. Philleo Nash, Wisconsin's lieutenant governor and Humphrey's most important proxy in the state, later said, "It was a loose affiliation with a lot of people able to make the same decision over again and reverse each other. It was basically a Minnesota Democratic operation"—i.e., a Humphrey operation. The Humphrey people marveled at Kennedy's smooth machine, run by Ken O'Donnell, a political pro, and manned by operatives in each of the state's ten districts. Both sides benefited from squads of volunteers, Humphrey's recruited from the ranks of the Democratic-Farmer-Labor Party and Kennedy's from his network of Ivy League friends and "the Kennedys."[27]

Primary, a 1960 documentary centered on the Wisconsin race (and filmed by future giants D. A. Pennebaker and Albert Maysles), though carefully neutral in tone, offered a vivid sense of the contrast between the two men. In the one-hour film, Humphrey tells a few dozen farmers in a small-town school gym that the swells in Washington and New York don't give a hoot for farm problems. Kennedy addresses a mighty throng in Milwaukee and tells them that the presidency is "the key job." Humphrey, in a fedora, tries to find citizens to take a card with his name on it; the hatless Kennedy, his coiffure immaculate, is mobbed by teenage girls and grown women acting like teenage girls—"I can't wash my hand for a week!" Humphrey pumps a fist and unleashes a torrent of proposals while Kennedy keeps his speeches short and vague. The one wears a furious grin, the other a detached smile.[28]

Humphrey tried to compensate by keeping up his usual Stakhanovite schedule. One stupefied reporter detailed the Humphrey itinerary: arriving at the Lorraine Hotel in Madison at 1:00 a.m., Humphrey woke up at 5:00 and skipped breakfast in order to reach the gates of the Oscar Mayer plant at 5:30, when it was 8 degrees Fahrenheit outside. A campaign aide handed him galoshes, and the old pro hopped on one foot while slipping a galosh on the other, never missing a hand to shake all the while. Once the morning shift had filed in, Humphrey left for another plant, returned at 8:00 a.m. to greet incoming office employees, then made stops in Sun Prairie, Beaver Dam, Columbus, Horicon.[29] Kennedy was also up early and kept at it until late, but he got around the state on his private plane, the *Caroline*. Humphrey bumped around on a chartered bus with a bed in the back. He had Muriel, the all-American wife, telling the people of Wisconsin what a fine man she had married, but Kennedy had Jackie standing glamorously—and silently—by his side.

The Kennedy clan was famously tough. What this entailed, or so Humphrey concluded, was a willingness to play dirty. On February 1, the *Minneapolis Star Tribune* reported that Bobby Kennedy had told campaign workers that Jimmy Hoffa, the Teamster leader widely regarded as a tool of organized crime, had pledged to spend $1 million in Wisconsin to beat Jack. Hoffa was said to be angry that in 1959 Jack had sponsored the Landrum-Griffin Act, which provided for government oversight of union elections. Hoffa was also said, very plausibly, to hold a grudge against Bobby for his role as counsel to Senate labor racketeering hearings. Hoffa had ridiculed Jack before an audience of Wisconsin truckers as "a millionaire playboy brought up by nursemaids." But Bobby had fabricated the million-dollar claim, and then apparently sent FDR Jr., JFK's most trusted proxy, to repeat the allegation in public, insisting that he had heard "ugly rumors" about the source of Humphrey's funds.[30]

Humphrey knew he couldn't beat Kennedy on organization, money, or charm. The only path to victory was convincing voters that he was the real deal and Kennedy a poseur with no fixed principles. In mid-March he began hitting his rival on the issues. Kennedy had ducked the tough votes on Joe McCarthy; a March 11 press release quoted Eleanor Roosevelt writing that she had refused to support Kennedy in the past because the presidency "should not go to someone who knows what courage is and admires it"—as he had demonstrated in *Profiles in Courage*—"but has not quite the independence to have it." Humphrey challenged Kennedy to a debate; but the latter, with the same prudence once shown by Marvin Kline, insisted that their views were so similar that there was nothing to debate. Then Humphrey tried to play the money card. He was the man of the people while his opponent, as he put it punningly, "has the jack." And it was true: Kennedy was able to buy vastly more radio and television time than the Humphrey campaign could afford. In early April the *Madison (WI) Capital Times* estimated that the two had spent as much as $1 million, with Humphrey accounting for at least $200,000—far more than he had expected to spend, though still far less than his opponent.[31]

Kennedy's great liability was not his money or his record, but his religion. Ever since Al Smith had lost badly to Herbert Hoover in 1928, conventional wisdom had it that Americans would not vote for a Catholic for president. But Kennedy had chosen to contest a primary in Humphrey's backyard because Wisconsin was one-third Catholic. What's more, the Wisconsin primary allowed Republicans and

Democrats to vote in one another's primaries, thus enabling Catholic Republicans to vote for Kennedy. A few days before the vote, a one-man group called Square Deal for Humphrey ran an ad in local papers asserting that "five out of six Catholics" supported Kennedy, though many of them were Republicans who would vote for Nixon in the general election. The ad boomeranged, for the press accused Humphrey of playing the religion card, which he had studiously avoided doing. Now it was Humphrey playing dirty and Kennedy the beleaguered victim. The state attorney general later found that the ad had been funded by an official from the Teamster pension fund that Hoffa controlled, thus giving a modicum of credibility to Bobby's allegation. Humphrey would later complain to Eugenie Anderson that he had become, in effect, the anti-Catholic candidate. "It has almost become a sin to vote against Kennedy," he wrote.[32]

On April 5, Kennedy won 57 percent of the vote and carried six of ten districts. Yet many of his supporters had expected to win all ten. (The candidate, ever the realist, had predicted exactly six.) Humphrey won not only the three districts bordering Minnesota but the district surrounding Madison, the state capital. Though the truth was that he had been beaten in his own backyard, Humphrey treated his narrow loss like a vindication. Meeting that night in the Schroeder Hotel in Milwaukee, he asked his advisers—Jim Rowe, Orville Freeman, Max Kampelman, Joe Rauh, Gerry Heaney, and others—if they thought he should go on to West Virginia. He had no money and little organization; everyone was exhausted. Privately, many of them thought Humphrey had lost his chance at the nomination. Labor officials saw that Kennedy had taken Racine, a Lutheran rather than Catholic town, where the head of the local UAW had endorsed Humphrey. If Kennedy had even the Protestant rank and file, the game was over. Nevertheless, these men knew what Humphrey wanted, and every one of them vowed to fight onward.[33]

As a political entity, West Virginia offered Humphrey two great advantages. First, the state was 95 percent Protestant and just about equally anti-Catholic, at least by reputation. In late November,

Humphrey had traveled to the state to meet with Miles Stanley, head of the state AFL-CIO, who had pledged his support and expressed confidence in a Humphrey victory. "He suggested," Humphrey wrote in a memo, "that West Virginia is 1) Protestant and 2) very provincial about it." Second, West Virginia was one of the poorest states in the country, a semifeudal society in the grip of coal barons who paid low taxes and suffered few regulations. And coal was giving way to oil and gas. The hills and hollows were full of towns where the local mine had closed and much of the population survived on relief. All too many people, in Humphrey's phrase, lacked the power to control their own destiny. A local campaign aide wrote, "The terrible economic conditions in West Virginia make most of the people enthusiastically receptive to a Populist-type politics for which Senator Humphrey is brilliantly suited."[34]

Starting even before the Wisconsin primary had finished, Humphrey delivered speeches decrying the apathy of the Eisenhower administration and promising his favorite remedy—a Marshall Plan—for West Virginia. But his rival checked him once again. Whether because he sensed his vulnerability on domestic affairs or because, as his friends later said, this rich and cosseted figure had been genuinely shocked by the poverty he saw as he traveled around the state, Kennedy himself promised a "New Deal" for West Virginia, with many of the same elements Humphrey had proposed. There wasn't much to choose between the two.

West Virginia should have been an inexpensive state in which to campaign, but the opposite was true. With so little money and so few jobs to go around, politics helped pay the bills for thousands of local workers. Humphrey's campaign lawyer, David Ginsburg, laid out the math in a memo to the candidate and his aides. In every precinct, campaigns were expected to hire a captain, a driver, and a few clerical workers, for a total cost of about $90 for each of 2,900 precincts. In each of the state's 55 counties, voters were furnished with "slates" of candidates for every statewide office; most could be counted on to vote the whole slate. The printing and distribution of these documents came to about $1,000.[35] The money was typically paid to the county sheriff, who often sold his services—for the "expenses" involved—to the highest bidder. Humphrey later recalled that when Herb Waters had explained to him that he needed $25,000 to pay for slates with his name on them—which still would have covered only half the state's counties—he had laughed him out of the room. (In his memoirs, Max Kampelman concedes that the campaign was prepared to pay the required toll but just couldn't afford it.) Kennedy paid to get himself slated all over the state. Lawrence O'Brien, a senior campaign aide, later wrote that he had personally given $5,000 in cash to sheriffs in two important counties.[36]

Kennedy had hesitated entering West Virginia until Lou Harris showed him a poll that had him beating Humphrey 60–40. But it turned out that locals hadn't known that Kennedy was Catholic until he had won in Wisconsin. Now Harris showed him running behind. Though few voters knew Humphrey's religion, virtually all knew Kennedy's.[37] Reporters went to town on semiliterate Appalachians who believed Catholics had horns. Joseph Alsop managed to persuade a woman he described as "a grim harridan with a face ravaged by rage, suspicion, pride and deprivation" to open her door a crack to express an opinion of Kennedy. "I wouldn't never want the Pope to be in the White House," she croaked.[38]

Kennedy then rolled the dice with the intuition of a great politician: he would, he decided, not only face the religion issue directly but invite voters to congratulate themselves for their own tolerance. Kennedy began talking about his religion without waiting to be asked. "Is anyone going to tell me," he asked an audience, "that I lost this primary 42 years ago on the day I was born?" The following day, April 20, Kennedy spoke before the American Society of Newspaper Editors in Washington. The only legitimate question about his religion, he said, was "Would you, as President of the United States, be responsive to ecclesiastical pressures or obligations of any kind that might in any way influence or interfere with your conduct" of the presidency? The answer, he said, was no.[39] It was a brilliant act of political jujitsu. Soon those same reporters were finding that Kennedy was getting a warm welcome from Protestant voters eager to show that they weren't the ignorant rednecks whom the reporters had said they were. Humphrey was reduced to complaining about those who "continue to raise the bloody shirt of bigotry against the people of this state."[40]

Humphrey enjoyed what ought to have been a secret advantage. Potential candidates who had been waiting in the wings—chiefly Lyndon Johnson, but also Stuart Symington—understood after Wisconsin that Kennedy was going to take the nomination unless Humphrey blocked him. Johnson dispatched Harry Byrd to his home state to deliver a bizarre qualified endorsement in which Byrd admitted that he wanted the majority leader to be the party nominee but much preferred Humphrey, his nemesis of a decade earlier, to Kennedy. Jim Rowe approached both Johnson and Symington supporters for funds, but came away empty. Johnson didn't want his fingerprints to show; he funneled money to Humphrey through his own network of Texas millionaires. But the funds came too late to do much good; Kennedy was able to accuse his rival of serving as a stalking horse for a "stop-Kennedy" campaign.[41]

In late April, a group of local editors picked Humphrey to win but noted that Kennedy was closing fast thanks to the religion issue. Humphrey felt everything slipping away. In a memo to campaign aides, he unleashed a furious blast that disclosed the crushing pressures of a presidential campaign, at least one that was rapidly losing altitude. Complaining that his schedule was full of local political leaders who couldn't deliver anything, he demanded an outreach to local labor leaders who could set up phone banks, the way they had for him in Minneapolis. "Either we do this one," he added with a swell of fear and self-pity, "or I am washed up and I know it. If I take a licking in West Virginia it is going to hurt me definitely in Minnesota. So I have my political life on the block and I expect people to stand up and do what I ask them with no questions any longer."

And the Kennedys played rough again. A supporter in Minnesota had sent the campaign a copy of Humphrey's draft record. Bobby, Ken O'Donnell, and Mike Feldman, a senior campaign aide, debated how and whether to use what they regarded as explosive material. West Virginians prided themselves on their martial tradition; no state had suffered as many fatalities per capita in World War II. Bobby gave the folder to Freddy Forbes, a local newspaperman who had joined the campaign and served as a minder to FDR Jr., whose father enjoyed godlike status in much of West Virginia. Roosevelt had already demonstrated his willingness to serve as hatchet man in Wisconsin. Kennedy instructed Forbes to let him read and digest the material, but not to use it until he or O'Donnell signaled him to do so. Forbes later claimed that the one time he let his charge out of his sight he blurted out to an NBC crew the allegation that Humphrey had been a draft dodger. "I don't know where he was in World War II," said Roosevelt. The fears that Humphrey had expressed almost twenty years before had finally come back to haunt him.[42]

Humphrey was, for once, completely outraged. After Bobby complained that Humphrey had become the figurehead of a massive "stop Kennedy" movement, the gentlemanly candidate snarled, "I'd suggest brother Bobby examine his own conscience about smears and innuendos; if he has trouble knowing what I mean, I can refresh his memory." Humphrey sent a letter to Hyman Bookbinder, a leading Jewish supporter, saying that he could no longer imagine supporting his rival after such an "unforgivable" tactic that was "undoubtedly sponsored by and cleared by Kennedy." That probably wasn't true. Months later, Roosevelt came to Humphrey's office to apologize. "Bobby asked me to do it," he said lamely.[43]

In the very last days of the campaign, Humphrey finally goaded Kennedy into a televised debate. But even after the FDR incident, Humphrey couldn't bring himself to launch an attack; instead he railed at the Eisenhower administration's indifference to the state's plight. Kennedy, far more attuned to the theatrics of the contest, lavished praise on West Virginians for their courage in war and in the coal mines; he introduced his own welfare proposal by reading a letter from a voter itemizing the pitiful contents of the grocery basket he got on relief. Kennedy escaped with no worse than a draw.[44]

Over the final weeks of the primary, Kennedy ran half-page ads in the state's daily papers and full-page ads in the weeklies. He sent out thousands of pieces of direct mail and maintained a dozen offices across the state. And of course he fielded the brothers and the wives and the in-laws and the Ivy League army. Humphrey was broke. On the Saturday before the election, Herb Waters told Humphrey that the station on which he had booked his final half hour of television time was demanding to be paid in advance. Humphrey finally snapped. "Pay it!" he shouted. Waters and Jim Rowe went silent; both knew there was literally nothing left in the till. Humphrey pulled out his personal checkbook and wrote out a check for $750—money he and Muriel had been saving for their daughter Nancy's wedding the following week.[45] The telethon he paid for turned out to be straight from amateur hour, with unscreened callers telling Humphrey off and mortifying periods of silence between conversations.

As the returns came in on election night, and the numbers looked worse and worse, Humphrey came down from his hotel suite to the ballroom where his supporters were gathered. He stood in the center of the room looking at the big blackboard with the district-level figures; everyone else seemed to shrink back along the walls. Humphrey stood and stared at what he knew was the end of the line for him. The hired banjo player started to cry and Humphrey went over to comfort him. Kennedy had won 61–39, an overwhelming triumph. This time, when Humphrey gathered his advisers in his suite, everyone agreed to throw in the towel. But they disagreed fiercely over the terms on which Humphrey would leave the campaign. The loyalists, such as Joe Rauh and Jim Loeb, who had rejoined the campaign, wanted the candidate to make a gracious concession speech endorsing Kennedy; the stop-Kennedy crowd, Jim Rowe foremost among them, wanted him to hang on to his delegates. The old divisions had never gone away. Humphrey authorized Loeb to write the speech.[46]

Jack had already flown back to Washington, so it was left to Bobby, upon whom Humphrey's family and friends had focused all their bitter resentment, to visit Humphrey in his hotel suite. Rauh watched Bobby advance across the room to the Humphreys; Muriel flinched when he gently kissed her. For a moment, Rauh thought she was going to hit him. Bobby asked Humphrey to come to Kennedy headquarters for a closing of ranks. In the ride over, Muriel kept repeating, "I can't, I can't, I can't." Finally Hubert asked their friend Geri Joseph, also in the car, to take Muriel back to the hotel. No one had ever seen this sturdy woman so undone by rage—or by anything else, for that matter.[47]

Humphrey's view of the race was always colored by a deep feeling of injustice; he felt that he had been abandoned by his labor allies, that he had lost out to the Kennedy money, to gutter tactics, to a fawning press. There was truth in all that; yet Kennedy was a better candidate and ran a better campaign. Orville Freeman later described the Humphrey campaign as "poorly handled, poorly organized and poorly administered." What's more, the wide-eyed innocence and enthusiasm, the pepper-pot energy and crusading zeal, that had endeared Humphrey to the people of Minneapolis and Minnesota ill fitted the America of 1960. Rowe said as much in a consolatory letter: "The simple truth is that the times were out of joint for Hubert Humphrey." Rowe said he had believed in Humphrey because he, too, was a child of the Depression who understood suffering. "There is," he concluded, with what passed for sentimentality in this paragon of harsh realism, "no other way to explain, really, why I was for you because you never had much chance anyway."[48]

Theodore White wrote movingly of Humphrey's unfeigned belief in the ordinary American, the astonishing wealth and diversity of his knowledge, his instinct of compassion in the face of suffering and helplessness. Yet, he wrote, in a eulogy for a competitor who barely made his rival sweat,

> What spoiled the Humphrey campaign—apart from the underlying fact that this country, Democrats and Republicans alike, was unwilling to be evangelized in 1960—was the very simplicity, the clarity, the homely sparkle he could bring to any issue. He could talk on almost any subject under the sun—to farmers, to workers, to university intellectuals. And when he finished there were no mysteries left; nor was he a mystery either. He was someone just like the listeners. There was no distance about him, no separation, none of the majesty that must surround a king.[49]

Humphrey had one final scene to play in the 1960 election. Men close to Kennedy, including labor leaders such as Arthur Goldberg, intimated that he was Kennedy's first choice for vice president. Humphrey told his friends that he had burned his hand on this stove before. His anger over his loss was still fresh. And Muriel would not hear of it—"she'd divorce me if I ran for vice president," he told Drew Pearson. He publicly announced his support for his campaign manager, Orville Freeman, who could also help deliver Minnesota and the Midwest. In June, however, Freeman heard a rumor that Humphrey was telling friends that, in fact, he was still prepared to serve as Kennedy's running mate under certain unspecified conditions. Freeman confronted him, and Humphrey admitted that the story was true, but then, perhaps ashamed of himself, added that he had now decided to stay out and back Freeman. Several days later Kennedy came to Humphrey's office and said that the liberal champion was strong with key constituents where he himself was weak—Jews, labor, farmers. What would you think about the vice presidency? he asked. Humphrey turned him down.[50]

Humphrey's friends still wanted him to keep his hat in the ring, and he continued to equivocate. According to Freeman's contemporaneous notes, the two men had another conversation provoked by Humphrey's ambivalence a few days before the Democratic National Convention in Los Angeles. Once there, Walter Reuther approached Freeman and implored him to pledge the Minnesota caucus, which had not yet declared itself, for Kennedy; Reuther, who seemed to know nothing of Freeman's own hopes, told him that doing so would strengthen Humphrey's shot at the vice presidency. After a caucus meeting July 10 that ran until 3:30 the next morning—the witching hour, it seemed, of all Humphrey conclaves at national conventions—Freeman confronted Humphrey once again; they talked until dawn. The latter, plainly distraught, asked, "What would you do in my place?" Freeman, the ex-Marine, said—or said that he said—"I would never be in your place," because, having made a commitment, "I would have honored it." Humphrey had never been as sure of himself as Freeman was. He was profoundly ambitious but not ruthless. Unlike Lyndon Johnson, he shrank from the thought of trampling his friend in order to reach the prize he sought. Later that morning, Humphrey told Freeman that he had withdrawn his name; he asked the caucus to endorse JFK, with Freeman as running mate.[51]

But the drama still hadn't reached its denouement. Kennedy had arrived in Los Angeles short of the 761 delegates he needed. A week earlier, Lyndon Johnson had finally declared his own candidacy. Lurking at the edge of the convention was Adlai Stevenson, the Democratic Hamlet, neither declaring nor forswearing, but allowing a campaign in his name to go forward. Either could benefit from a deadlocked convention. Sometime the next day Humphrey agreed to support Stevenson, though it's not clear whether he did that to put wind in Stevenson's sails or to block Kennedy in order to help Johnson. Unwilling to come out publicly, Humphrey instead prevailed on Gene McCarthy, who took a dim view of Kennedy, to place Stevenson's name in nomination. Nor, it seems, could Humphrey bring himself to tell Freeman. At a meeting of the leading figures of the Minnesota caucus, held that night in Humphrey's suite, Freeman recalled that Humphrey remained strangely silent while he himself pleaded for an endorsement of Kennedy, without which he had no chance of being chosen. When, later that morning, Humphrey admitted his change of heart, Freeman felt every bit as betrayed as Humphrey had four years earlier. In the end, Kennedy won on the first ballot, and then, of course, chose Johnson as his running mate.

The Minnesota delegation played an outsize role at the convention. Governor Freeman nominated Kennedy while Senator McCarthy delivered a stirring oration on Stevenson's behalf. Hubert Humphrey, the man who more than any other had made the state a pillar of liberalism, remained, for once, in the background. Nevertheless, Humphrey could take satisfaction in the remarkable progressivism of the party's civil rights plank. The draft platform had advocated "equal access for all Americans to all areas of community life," including voting booths, schoolhouses, jobs, housing, and public facilities, and called on southern school districts to begin desegregating by no later than 1963. Kennedy, who regarded platforms with the blithe nonchalance of most professional politicians, looked it over for fifteen minutes and gave his approval. Kennedy's advisers assumed that it would be watered down in committee, but it passed as written.[52] Humphrey called it "the best statement on civil rights ever made by any political party in America."

In November, Humphrey won reelection against another lackluster opponent by a record 235,000 votes. Kennedy, however, beat Nixon by a whisker—his national margin was one half of Humphrey's. Though Kennedy took 70 percent of the Black vote, he also won all but three states in the South. A man already cautious on civil rights would need to tread very carefully.

14

Concert Master
of the Senate

"I'll bargain for you. I'm not so pure."

NINETEEN SIXTY-ONE WAS A WONDERFUL YEAR TO BECOME
president of the United States. America had never been
so prosperous, so self-confident, so eager for renewal and
change. Had history worked out differently, Hubert Humphrey might
have made an excellent president, inspiring the public to demand that
Congress pass the long-delayed agenda of the Fair Deal, and working
with Khrushchev to reduce Cold War tensions and restrain the arms
race. John Kennedy was not nearly so bold a reformer. Early in the
new administration, Walter Lippmann, no left-winger, sneered that
under Kennedy, Washington looked like "the Eisenhower Administration thirty years younger."[1]

But it wasn't Humphrey's nature to dwell on what might have
been. The bitterness of the campaign had simply evaporated. When
he had stood in the arctic winds of the inaugural address and

heard the new president say, "Ask not what your country can do for you, but what you can do for your country," he thought it was right that Kennedy had won and he had lost. He believed that Kennedy "would get America moving again"—with his help.[2] Humphrey's years-long internship in the Lyndon Johnson Academy had prepared him to serve a Democratic president as a legislative leader. And now, wonderfully, Johnson himself was gone, transported up and out to the White House. In December, the vice president elect had called Humphrey to say that he, Kennedy, and Mike Mansfield, who was to succeed Johnson as majority leader, wanted him as majority whip, responsible for rounding up the vote for the White House's agenda. Adlai Stevenson, Jim Rowe, and Humphrey's friend and benefactor Bill Benton advised Humphrey to turn the offer down, lest he be reduced to an administration mouthpiece. But Humphrey *wanted* to be part of the White House team; he wanted, finally, to pass ambitious liberal legislation; he liked the idea of being legislative traffic cop; and it was not in his nature to turn down a request from the White House.

But there was a problem: Johnson still planned to be the leader of the Senate Democrats. He told Mansfield that he hoped to remain chairman of the Senate Democratic Caucus and keep his giant Senate office, known as the Taj Mahal—and Mansfield, incredibly, agreed. In early December, Johnson convened a secret meeting at the Sheraton-Carlton Hotel with Humphrey, Richard Russell, two other senior senators, and Johnson's aide and fixer Bobby Baker to explain how things would work going forward. Humphrey and the others gently tried to tell Johnson that he was proposing an unprecedented violation of the constitutional separation of powers. Perhaps they were too gentle; Johnson left the meeting feeling that he had their approval to effectively run the Senate while serving as vice president. Only on the morning of January 3, 1961, when Johnson formally convened the caucus—he would remain a senator until noon—and oversaw the selection of Mansfield and Humphrey, did the members, one by one, tell the crestfallen Johnson that he was no longer welcome among them. He finally withdrew from the institution he had dominated for years. Hubert Humphrey, as majority whip, now replaced Johnson as the concert master of the Senate orchestra.

In his memoir, Humphrey wrote that as a colleague he had at times resented Senator John F. Kennedy for not pulling his load; as a rival in 1960 he had envied Kennedy for all that came so easily to him. But once Kennedy became president, Humphrey wrote, "I grew to love him for his warmth and wit and compassion." Humphrey felt that he and Kennedy "got along just marvelously." The president honored almost every request he made and saw almost everyone he asked him to see. Humphrey was thrilled to see Camelot from the inside. The least jaded of men, he almost had to pinch himself when every Tuesday at 8:45 he met for breakfast at the White House with congressional leaders and White House political staff to map out strategy.[3]

What's more, in Mike Mansfield Humphrey had a boss who didn't believe in his own job. "A leader can't do much leading," he groused to a reporter. "What magic can change a man's vote?"[4] Humphrey knew what magic: members who wanted to move a bill up the calendar, or absent themselves for a delicate vote, or insert self-serving language in a piece of legislation, streamed into the little third-floor whip's office above the Senate chamber where Humphrey held court. Generally, however, Humphrey could be found out on the floor, exercising the parliamentary mastery he had learned from Johnson or just talking to members. As a longtime aide recalled, "He would spend long, long hours in the Senate on the floor talking to his colleagues, not necessarily about the legislation at hand or what the president wanted or what Humphrey wanted or the administration wanted, but he took a very deep interest in each of his colleagues, in their family life, in the things they themselves wanted on a legislative basis."[5] Johnson had buttonholed his colleagues; Humphrey listened to them.

A whip is a loyal soldier, which is to say that he occupies the opposite end of the spectrum of political action from a "wild-eyed ADA liberal." But Humphrey had long since ingratiated himself with all the party's factions, including the southerners, and may have been the only man in the chamber without an enemy. He rarely slept or took vacations; he was preternaturally enthusiastic; and he was prepared to settle for crumbs. He never had a job for which he felt so perfectly suited. He served as the voice of the Kennedy administration on all the talk shows, he was close to all the big reporters and columnists, and he was friends with everyone in town. And he adjusted so rapidly to his new role that within weeks reporters were marveling at an all-new Humphrey: "His Senate speeches were few and to the point. He seldom talked longer than two or three minutes."[6]

Humphrey would say later that the period from 1961 to 1964 was his happiest time in Washington. In his journals, Arthur Schlesinger records an evening in Humphrey's company in September 1961:

> Dinner w Hubert. Hubert was in marvelous form, overflowing with wit, charm, energy, eloquence and sheer animal vitality. . . . Hubert is really unique: George McGovern, who lives next door to him, told me today that he heard shouts of exultation outside his window this morning, looked down, saw Hubert striding around his lawn and saying, "What a wonderful day," looked further, saw absolutely no audience—what a pure and charming expressing [*sic*] of Humphreyan exuberance![7]

Humphrey was not, in fact, a normal whip. He was a man with an agenda; and he tried to export his agenda to the White House in order to then promote it in the Senate. He succeeded to a truly remarkable degree. Every new term since he had arrived in Washington, his secretary had drawn up a long list of bills that he had previously proposed and stuck them into a black binder. The list only got longer. But, starting in 1961, a growing number of them bore tick marks—"approved" or "signed into law."[8] In June 1960 Humphrey had introduced a bill to establish the Peace Corps, which he envisioned as a highly selective three-year program in which volunteers would first receive extensive grounding in area and language skills and then would be sent out to impoverished areas—first in the United States and then abroad—to apply their skills in agronomy or hydrology. It was an inspired instance of Cold War liberalism, though Humphrey made a point of saying "it would be worth doing even if Marx and Engels never lived."[9] The idea appealed immensely to Kennedy, who in his inaugural address had spoken to "people in the huts and villages of half the globe," promising to "help them help themselves." Kennedy endorsed the Peace Corps concept during the campaign and then created it by executive order on March 1, 1961. The romance and the crusading spirit of the Peace Corps would define Kennedy's New Frontier as much as any other program.

In West Virginia, Kennedy and Humphrey had both proposed an "area redevelopment" bill to target funding to distressed regions. Paul Douglas introduced such a bill early in 1961. His bill would have had funds automatically appropriated from the Treasury budget, but Kennedy agreed to a compromise that would require an annual appropriation. When Douglas balked, Humphrey told him, "I'll bargain for you. I'm not so pure." The bill passed, and Kennedy signed it May 1. Kennedy also shared Humphrey's view that the PL 480 legislation, the Food for Peace program, should be an integral element of foreign aid rather than a sop to farmers. He established a separate White House office to administer the program, and Humphrey helped get his friend and Chevy Chase neighbor George McGovern appointed as the first director. In June 1961, the administration also endorsed the Youth Conservation Corps, a New Deal–style program to find useful employment for young people that Humphrey had been pushing for years. Only with the establishment of the Job Corps in 1964 would Humphrey's dream finally be realized.

One of Humphrey's more inspired, if improbable, ideas was what he christened the Great White Fleet, a peaceful twist on Teddy Roosevelt's bristling column of warships. In May 1960, Humphrey had proposed that the nation refit mothballed naval vessels as floating humanitarian missions that could steam to disaster areas. He told the Senate that he had been inspired by an article written by a naval officer in *Life* magazine. In February 1961, his aide Bill Connell wrote Humphrey a memo suggesting that the ships serve as logistical support for the Peace Corps, which the president was about to establish. The navy had nine demobilized floating machine shops and eleven "floating hotels."[10] Humphrey persuaded the Senate to pass a resolution recommending the creation of a White Fleet; he had dropped the "Great." The idea lingered on until March 1964, when a White House aide wrote Humphrey that he had run his suggestion for an executive order on the White Fleet past a number of agencies, but none of them had expressed any interest.[11]

Humphrey's greatest achievement during this period lay in the field of disarmament, a subject he had made his own almost from his first years in the Senate. In early 1960, when prudence would have dictated a single-minded focus on the primaries, he had given a series of long and learned speeches occasioned by his introduction of a bill to establish a federal Peace Agency as well as a new position of assistant secretary of state for disarmament and atomic energy. United Nations–sponsored talks had been paralyzed for years, but Humphrey argued that inaction threatened world peace. A nuclear arms race was inherently destabilizing, deepened distrust between Washington and Moscow, and tipped power toward the military and away from civilian control. Spending $100 billion a year on weapons designed never to be used was "a clear sign of mental sickness"—language common in the movement to "ban the bomb," but not, at the time, in the US Senate. He proposed that the United Nations be empowered to resolve disputes in a denuclearized world. And he suggested asking Russia to invite China, which did not then have a nuclear capacity, to the ten-nation talks in Geneva. Yet Humphrey was, of course, no peacenik. He insisted that the United States needed to close the gap with the Soviet Union, which spent twice as much as the United States on defense as a fraction of gross national product. Only then, he believed, would the Soviets negotiate in earnest.

Humphrey harped on the subject in the weekly breakfast meetings. In early June, Kennedy asked him to stay afterward and join him for a swim in the White House pool. The pool was heated to 90 degrees to soothe the president's perpetually inflamed back, and Kennedy did his swimming naked. While the two men floated around in the altogether, Humphrey brought up his hobbyhorse, an arms control agency. Kennedy, too, wanted to find a way out of the "mental sickness" of the arms race, though he was deeply suspicious of the doctrine of full disarmament. He had also just returned from his disastrous Vienna summit meeting with Khrushchev, in which he had seemed to assent to the permanent division of Berlin. Kennedy was wary about signaling weakness. Nevertheless, he gave his support for such an agency, conditioned on acceptance from the State and Defense Departments, which proceeded to wage an internecine war over where the office would be located and what it would be called.[12] In late June Humphrey introduced a White House bill to establish a disarmament agency. While anti-Communist hard-liners in Congress opposed the idea, it won public statements of support from Eisenhower and several senior members of his national security team. In September Congress approved the creation of the Arms Control and Disarmament Agency, which would stand alone rather than being part of State or Defense.

An agency, however, was only a means; the goal Humphrey had sought since the mid-fifties was a treaty banning nuclear tests. In a speech before a European and American group in Switzerland in July, he issued an eight-point plan for immediate disarmament that would, controversially, include Red China, and would be overseen by the United Nations. He also proposed a new UN space peace agency.[13] Humphrey's willingness to grant the United Nations authority over the United States on such matters—including through sharing American satellite intelligence with the organization—would continue to set him apart from more hardheaded Democrats, such as Washington's Henry "Scoop" Jackson. Kennedy didn't share Humphrey's faith in the United Nations, but he had spoken favorably of a test ban as early as 1956.[14] He agreed to try to reinvigorate the moribund Geneva negotiations.

The Soviets ended a moratorium on nuclear testing in the fall of 1961, and the Americans resumed testing the following April. Yet Kennedy continued to press for either a limited or a total ban on tests, to be verified both remotely and through onsite inspections. Humphrey was the one member of the Senate who followed technical breakthroughs in remote sensing; he came to understand that the United States was developing the ability to monitor nuclear tests without having to build a vast and intrusive network of outposts. He pounded away, both in public and in the White House, on the idea that a test ban treaty had become truly verifiable; he was far more enthusiastic about the idea than Secretary of State Dean Rusk, who kept issuing gloomy updates from the talks in Geneva.[15] In May 1963, Humphrey and thirty-two other senators sponsored a resolution calling on Washington to pursue a limited test ban even if the Soviets rejected it. Humphrey had persuaded Thomas Dodd, a rabid anti-Communist Democrat from Connecticut, to sign on, giving Kennedy crucial protection on the right. The following week, in a major speech at American University, the president issued a call to lower Cold War tensions, including through a test ban treaty. Khrushchev seemed to accept the idea, offering for the first time to receive American negotiators. In July Kennedy dispatched Averill Harriman, who reached an agreement with the Russians to ban all tests in the atmosphere, in outer space, and underwater.

The treaty was an immense achievement for a president who had spoken so eloquently of world peace and yet had done so much to bring the world to the edge of war. Washington insiders recognized that it was a great achievement for Humphrey as well, the fruit of immense persistence over more than a decade on a subject of very little interest to most voters, or even colleagues. A glowing profile in the *New York Times Magazine* argued that Humphrey deserved more credit for the treaty than anyone else.[16] At the White House ceremony celebrating Senate ratification, Kennedy asked Humphrey to stay behind. "Hubert," he said, "this is your treaty. And it better work."[17]

HUMPHREY TRAVELED WIDELY THROUGHOUT THIS PERIOD. HE VISited West Berlin in the summer of 1961, weeks before one of the most dangerous provocations of the Cold War—the building of the Berlin Wall. Humphrey sent a memo to the president proposing a stepped-up propaganda war designed to remind the people of the Eastern bloc of the Soviets' rhetorical commitment to "freely elected governments of self-determination," language that the White House leaked to a reporter as an example of practical measures that could be taken to counter the Russians' own propaganda measures.[18] Publicly, Humphrey assigned himself the job of explaining Kennedy's policy to the American people, and the press looked to him to do so.[19] Once the Senate adjourned in September, he embarked, along with Muriel, on a frenetic tour of Europe and the Middle East. In Rome he met with

Pope John XXIII and Prime Minister Amintore Fanfani, in London with Harold Macmillan, in Bonn with Chancellor Konrad Adenauer, in Cairo with Gamal Abdel Nasser, in Amman with King Hussein, in Tel Aviv with David Ben-Gurion.[20] This was Humphrey's idea of pure joy.

During this period Humphrey made himself a specialist in Latin America, which the Kennedy administration regarded as the most important site of the contest between Washington and Moscow for the loyalty of the developing world. Kennedy had established the Alliance for Progress as a scaled-down Marshall Plan for the Southern Hemisphere; the administration's argument for foreign aid depended on evidence that the program was succeeding. This was hardly self-evident: very few Latin countries had democratic governments; regimes were overthrown by coups with dizzying frequency; and in almost every country wealth was concentrated in the hands of a few families that typically profited from relations with giant American firms, such as United Fruit. Humphrey, who knew as much about the foreign aid program as virtually anyone else in government, saw this problem very clearly. During a trip to the region in the fall of 1961, he proposed the establishment of a fund, to be backed by regional nations as well as industrialized countries, that would purchase virgin lands from "powerfully entrenched land owners" and distribute it to the landless without having to resort to expropriation. Earlier that year he had harshly criticized the State Department for shying away from politically sensitive measures such as the establishment of farmers' cooperatives, as well as for devoting too large a fraction of aid to the military.[21]

Kennedy's 1963 request for $4.5 billion for his new aid organization, the US Agency for International Development (USAID), ran into heavy weather in the House, which proposed a $1 billion cut. Humphrey now pulled out all the stops in a campaign to preserve the president's priorities. He solicited a letter from Assistant Secretary of State Edwin Martin refuting an article in the *Saturday Evening Post* claiming that Latin American universities were honeycombed with communism. Behind the scenes, he blitzed his colleagues with calls and visits, urging them to spare the Alliance for Progress, scheduled to receive about $700 million, from further cuts. He refused to cosponsor an amendment from Senator Frank Church to cut off military and economic aid to South Vietnam as punishment for Saigon's persecution of Buddhists. "Sometimes," he ruefully wrote to constituents, "we find ourselves forced to tolerate governments whose policies and practices we do not approve of."[22] And he urged patience on his colleagues: "The reform and modification of social and economic traditions that have persisted for two centuries are not going to be accomplished in two years—and probably not in a decade."[23]

Humphrey succeeded in saving the budget for the Alliance for Progress, a proud achievement that he would include in material circulated to the press to advance his vice presidential hopes in 1964. Humphrey was Latin America's most important friend in the Congress. The Alliance for Progress, however, did not turn out to be a Marshall Plan redux. The social and economic traditions to which Humphrey referred, including profoundly unequal land ownership and the impunity of elites, could not be uprooted in two years or a decade, although American aid might have made more of a difference had it been accompanied by the demand for difficult social and economic reforms that Humphrey had proposed. Nor did socialist India achieve the "takeoff" Humphrey expected with the injection of American assistance; that would only come with market reforms thirty years later. Humphrey and other liberal internationalists proved to be too optimistic about America's ability to refashion other countries in its own image.

Humphrey's final trip during this time was a triumphal one—a return to Russia in August 1963 to witness the signing of the historic Test Ban Treaty. Humphrey now felt a special kinship with this country that for so many Americans seemed the incarnation of evil. The Cuban missile crisis had provided a reminder, lest any were needed, of the world-threatening designs of Soviet leadership. But Humphrey no longer thought of Russia in strictly ideological terms. He felt that he understood Khrushchev's insecurities and the yearnings of ordinary Russians. He spent time walking the streets of Moscow, where he found many passersby eager to engage him. In a Senate speech soon afterward, Humphrey recalled that a young man had asked him how much he had paid for his suit, which would have set a Russian back several months of salary. Fifty-nine dollars, replied the thrifty Humphrey, who proudly noted that it had been made by the discount brand Botany Bay. He saw hundreds of people lined up to buy "stockings with elastic bands." But Humphrey had also gone to church and seen people praying with passionate rapture despite the godless doctrine of communism. The system was failing; it could not satisfy either the material or the spiritual hungers of the people.

And then, rather than gloat at the failures of the adversary, Humphrey launched into the kind of panegyric that had moved audiences to tears—and others to cynical disbelief—since he had first begun delivering speeches in Minneapolis twenty years before. Once we acknowledge that true power lies not in the mighty atom, he said, but in "the force of love itself, the force of human understanding, the force of respect for human dignity and the recognition that man is weak, indeed, and that more powerful forces are at work than man himself, and that there is a Supreme Being, then I believe we will inevitably win, not so much for ourselves but for mankind."[24] Perhaps that was speechifying, but it was speechifying from the depths of Hubert Humphrey's being.

To civil rights activists and their advocates in Congress, the election of John F. Kennedy meant that the Democratic Party would finally act on the promise it had made in 1948 to end the second-class citizenship of Black people. They knew that Kennedy himself had been no more than lukewarm on the subject, but at the convention he had accepted the boldest civil rights plank either party had ever published. He had promised Martin Luther King Jr. an activist presidency. In the weeks before the election he had asked Humphrey to chair a meeting of the nation's leading civil rights actors; the conference's report had called on the president to turn the promises of the platform into legislation. And he had asked Representative Emanuel Celler and Senator Joseph Clark to write bills that would do just that.

But Kennedy did not regard those promises as binding; he had made them in order to win the election. Kennedy didn't care about civil rights nearly as much as he did about raising the minimum wage and increasing federal aid to education, issues he had campaigned on heavily. Once it became clear that he would have no chance of navigating such bills through Congress without placating the southerners who controlled the major committees, Kennedy set out on a charm offensive of barons such as Harry F. Byrd.[25] Civil rights became an afterthought; in December 1960 he did not even list it among his domestic priorities for the coming year. On January 3, 1961, when Humphrey and others moved the chair to rule that the Senate was not a continuing body, and thus could change its rules prior to the commencement of new business, Lyndon Johnson, in the chair, ruled that it could not do so. The president remained silent. In May, after Clark and Celler submitted their civil rights bill, White House press secretary Pierre Salinger announced that they did not, in fact, have the support of the White House. "The president does not consider it necessary at this time to enact new civil rights legislation," said Salinger. Kennedy had, in fact, used the powers of the federal government to advance civil rights in ways that the Eisenhower administration had not. He appointed Black individuals to subcabinet positions, to the federal bench, and to diplomatic posts; he instructed the Department of Justice, run by his brother Bobby, to begin actively enforcing the voting provisions of the 1957 and 1960 Civil Rights Acts. In short, Kennedy was prepared to act so long as he would not have to bear a political cost.[26]

Humphrey responded by standing alongside the liberals—but not out in front. He let others introduce bills before he did. He tried to defend the administration from increasingly impatient activists. In August he wrote to Joe Rauh and Sam Beer, the Harvard historian who now headed Americans for Democratic Action, promising that in the next year civil rights legislation would "be given high priority." Mansfield, he said, would seek to use the Rules Committee to change cloture rules.[27] Mansfield did so in September, but the southerners prevented debate and easily turned back an effort to bring the question to a vote. When challenged in public, Humphrey either changed the subject or emphasized the positive. Asked on *Meet the Press* in the first days of 1962 about his chief domestic priority for the coming year, he came up with health care for the elderly and a tax cut. What about civil rights? asked a surprised interviewer. Humphrey pointed out that in March Kennedy had established the President's Committee on Equal Employment Opportunity, a fairly toothless version of the Fair Employment Practices Commission.[28] Humphrey was reprising the role he had assigned himself defending Lyndon Johnson on civil rights in the 1950s.

But the civil rights struggle had already moved beyond official Washington; a younger generation of activists concluded that little would change unless they could dramatize for northerners the real conditions of the Jim Crow South. In May 1961, "Freedom Riders" boarded Greyhound buses to the South in order to test state laws mandating segregation in public facilities and transportation—laws that the Supreme Court had declared unconstitutional the year before. The protesters, Black and white, were savagely beaten once they reached Alabama. Police stood by in Anniston while a mob of Klansmen boarded a bus and attacked riders. Newspapers all over the country— indeed, all over the world—covered the violence in graphic detail. Again and again the pattern played itself out—Black protest, white backlash, dramatic news coverage. Pressure for civil rights legislation mounted.

In November 1962, with the congressional election safely behind him, Kennedy issued a long-promised executive order prohibiting discrimination in public housing. But he remained convinced that a civil rights bill would derail the rest of his agenda, including a tax cut that he cared about a great deal more. He did not include civil rights in a list of twenty-seven agenda items he prepared in late January 1963.[29] Humphrey had remained silent all this while. But he prepared to act at the beginning of the new session of Congress. On January 7 he wrote to Johnson saying that he and colleagues were planning a new battle on Rule 22. The following day he and four other liberals wrote to Kennedy thanking him for his actions on civil rights to date but arguing that failure to enact legislation would harm the party. They also asked for his support on their challenge to the cloture rules.[30] But once the cloture debate began, January 15, Johnson refused, as he had before, to state that the Senate was not a continuing body, and Kennedy did not bestir himself. Absent White House support, the South mounted a filibuster and turned aside several cloture votes. Humphrey won a moral victory when, for the first time, a majority, though well short of two-thirds, voted for cloture—a harbinger of better times to come.

Humphrey's patience was being sorely tested. On January 29, when Senator John Sherman Cooper of Kentucky asked him to cosponsor a bill restoring Part III of the 1957 Civil Rights Act, Humphrey responded, "I do not want to commit myself to any specific piece of civil rights legislation until I have a clearer picture of what the President will be proposing."[31] But would the president be proposing anything? On the 31st, liberal Republicans introduced a package of civil rights bills far more serious than anything Kennedy was prepared to consider. That was a challenge that could not easily be ignored. Bobby Kennedy continued to pressure his brother to offer something. Finally, on February 28, the administration rolled out a very modest bill that would extend the life of the Civil Rights Commission and correct several problems with implementation of the 1960 law authorizing the appointment of federal election referees. Even Republicans derided the legislation as feeble. The Kennedy team was notably half-hearted about its own measure. After a meeting at the White House, Senator Joseph Clark sent a memo to Humphrey memorializing their agreement: once the bill was referred to committee, Humphrey would convene supporters to tell the president that if he would "really fight for these measures," they would "pitch in to the best of [their] ability." But his group would not "make a frontal fight without strong White House pressure."[32]

Humphrey began to raise the volume at the weekly White House breakfast. As he later recalled, "I urged the president to take command, to be the moral leader, and I recall time after time urging that the message go all the way." By this Humphrey meant that Kennedy should submit a civil rights bill with all the major elements—voting rights, school desegregation, access to public accommodations, a fortified Title III.[33] On April 2, when Bobby Kennedy introduced the legislation in Congress, the White House still seemed diffident.

The very next day, however, Martin Luther King Jr., who by now had despaired of Kennedy, agreed to stage a dramatic confrontation in the racial caldron of Birmingham, Alabama, where Bull Connor, the white supremacist who had led the Dixiecrat walkout in 1948, oversaw the police as commissioner of public safety. After several days of skirmishes, Connor's policemen began to set police dogs on peaceful protesters. On April 12 King himself was arrested. (It was then that he composed his "Letter from Birmingham Jail.") In the ensuing weeks, Connor's men used snarling dogs and high-pressure water hoses on Black people, including children and high school students. Klan violence provoked a riot that reduced a portion of the city to ashes. Once again, the violence dominated the nightly newscasts and the pages of the nation's newsweeklies and dailies.[34]

On May 15, Humphrey managed to gather eleven other senators, including centrists who had not joined before, to write Kennedy urging him to introduce a new version of Title III that would allow the attorney general to intervene to protect all rights guaranteed by the Fourteenth Amendment, including the right to peacefully assemble—that is, the right to protest.[35] Two days later, Bobby Kennedy instructed senior aides to begin drafting civil rights legislation, though his brother had not yet agreed to endorse it. On May 20, the president met with his senior aides to consider new legislation. Political advisers favored a new Title III bill, but Bobby Kennedy and other Justice Department officials feared an avalanche of new civil litigation. The president himself, baffled to learn that Blacks couldn't sit next to whites in southern movie theaters, proposed doing something on access to public facilities. Still, nothing happened.[36] Then Alabama governor George Wallace hastened the decision by pledging to defy orders to desegregate the state university, provoking a new round of news stories.

Every Tuesday morning Humphrey told the president and his team that they needed to present meaningful civil rights legislation if they wanted to hold on to Black and liberal voters. The AFL-CIO sent Humphrey a memo saying it could not support the bill without an employment-discrimination provision; Humphrey showed it to the Justice Department team drafting the bill—but to no avail.[37] If you're not willing to call for an FEPC, he told Kennedy, at least put the idea in a speech. On June 11, in a prime-time address carried live over television and radio, Kennedy gave Humphrey and civil rights leaders what they wanted, though not all they wanted. Describing civil rights as "a moral issue" that was "as old as the Scriptures and . . . as clear as the American Constitution," Kennedy laid out a legislative package he planned to introduce that included Title III—though only for school desegregation—and a law mandating equal access to public accommodations. Kennedy declined to include fair-employment legislation, though he did, as Humphrey had asked, allude to it in his speech.

Humphrey had predicted that if the White House didn't act, the streets would—and the streets had. This was something new in postwar American politics. An old decorum, in which the politics of civil rights was conducted by gentlemen in Washington—white and Black, liberal and conservative—was beginning to end. Agitation in the streets made civil rights ineluctable; over time, that ungovernable force would overwhelm conventional politicians, including Humphrey.

On June 19, Mike Mansfield introduced the administration's civil rights legislation and, by prior agreement with Minority Leader Everett Dirksen, referred it to the Judiciary Committee, whose chairman, James Eastland of Mississippi, was as virulent an opponent of civil rights as any representative of the Deep South. The issue was temporarily out of Humphrey's hands, but that very day he took to the floor to discuss the bill. What was striking, then and in the weeks to come, was Humphrey's preoccupation with what wasn't in the bill— economic opportunity. He would, he said, reintroduce his own FEPC legislation. In a speech the following month, he cited a recent Labor Department study showing that, as the economy shifted from farm and blue-collar jobs to office employment, the racial gap in income was likely to grow, owing to a combination of poverty, discrimination, and poor education and training. Humphrey introduced his own Equal Employment Opportunity Act, which required employers to offer equal access not only to jobs but also to training and recruitment efforts.[38] It is remarkable that, at a moment when his colleagues were celebrating the prospect of giving Black people access to buses and train stations, Humphrey was looking far beyond to the more vexing question of economic equality.[39]

On August 28, the Leadership Conference on Civil Rights organized the March on Washington. White House officials, fearing violence, asked the organizers to call it off. Humphrey, however, was gleeful with anticipation. The day before the march he told his colleagues, "There is no threat or intimidation in these people. . . . [T]hey are coming to express their deep convictions that the president's legislation should be enacted promptly." The following morning, he and Gene McCarthy led a Minnesota delegation to the Lincoln Memorial, the site of the gathering. "It truly was America the beautiful," Humphrey later wrote, "with a sea of shining faces parting at one moment to let a smiling group of bib-overalled Minnesota farmers, marching proudly and with immense dignity, move closer to the platform." On that day, said Humphrey, his "spirit soared on the wings of the American dream of social justice for everyone."[40] It was, tellingly, a day of exquisite courtesy when, Humphrey recalled, no one shook their fists. Such days would not last.

The civil rights bill made rapid progress in the House and none at all in the Senate, where Eastland, predictably, kept it bottled up in committee. In early September, New York senators Jacob Javits and Kenneth Keating complained that the administration was frittering away crucial time. Humphrey immediately took to the floor to ask for patience: once the House passed the bill, he promised, the Senate would stay in session all year, if that's what it took, to overcome a filibuster and pass a bill. In fact, he had no assurance on that from the White House. Nevertheless, Kennedy and Johnson were explaining and promoting the legislation in a vast round of White House meetings with Black leaders, with governors and mayors in the South as well as the North, and with labor groups, newspaper editors, and others.

On September 15, in perhaps the most heinous act of racist violence of the civil rights era, Sixteenth Street Baptist Church in Birmingham, the headquarters of the local protest movement, was firebombed, killing four Black girls. Humphrey unleashed a genuine howl of outrage, not only at the perpetrators, but at southern and northern elites, from banks and insurance firms and other big corporations, who had, he said, "at least partly acquiesced in the policies of racial degradation and humiliation," and had "done nothing to raise the educational level or job prospects not only of blacks but of all Americans." It was as if his moral fury had popped the lid on his Midwestern populism. Humphrey seemed to be saying that even civil rights would mean nothing without expanded economic opportunity. "We ought to be wearing ashes and sackcloth," Humphrey lamented. He joined a call for a national day of mourning—which President Kennedy, worried about southern reaction, declined to accept.

On October 29 the House Judiciary Committee reported out the Kennedy civil rights package, plus an FEPC provision to which Bobby Kennedy had given only vague support in backroom negotiations. Richard Russell prepared his troops for the mother of all filibuster fights. President Kennedy predicted that a bill might take eighteen months to work its way through the Senate; his tax cut would have to come first. Given southern resistance and Kennedy's skepticism, the legislation might well have been doomed to the kinds of compromises that had produced crumbs in 1957 and 1960. And then, on November 22, the president was assassinated in Dallas. Humphrey had been at a luncheon at the Chilean embassy. A newsman whispered to him that the president had been shot. Humphrey raced to his car, turned on the radio, and learned that Kennedy would not survive. "I stood by myself for several minutes in the library room," he later wrote in a long memo. "A great wave of emotion spread through my mind and body." Humphrey went to the White House and then, that night, to Andrews Air Force Base to receive the casket bearing the president's body and to welcome the new president, Lyndon Johnson.[41]

15

Breaking the Filibuster—
and the South

---

*"I can recall literally talking to myself,
conditioning myself for the long ordeal."*

WE WILL NEVER KNOW WHETHER PRESIDENT KENNEDY
would have put all his strength behind civil rights legislation, just as we will never know whether he would
have waded neck-deep in Vietnam. What is clear, however, is that
the moment that Hubert Humphrey had been preparing for, and
training himself for, since the day he had arrived in the Senate fifteen years earlier had arrived with Lyndon Johnson's succession to
the presidency. The passage of the 1964 Civil Rights Act would be
the great legislative achievement of Humphrey's life. It would draw
equally on the moral passion and the analytical powers that had
propelled him into politics and on the parliamentary skills that he
had gained as a pragmatist who, until that moment, had had to content himself with half a loaf, or less. Now, finally, Humphrey would

vindicate the promise he had made at the 1948 Democratic National Convention.

What had made this possible was President Johnson's personal commitment. According to Johnson's aide Jack Valenti, soon after assuming office Johnson had called Richard Russell, his former mentor, to the White House and warned him about his commitment to civil rights legislation. "Dick, you've got to get out of my way," Valenti recalled the president saying. "I'm going to run over you. I don't intend to cavil or compromise." Right after New Year's Day, Johnson had asked the chief civil rights lobbyists to come to the White House. He needed them to know that he was far from the defender of the Old South that they imagined him to be. They met for forty minutes. Though legislation had not yet even passed the House, Johnson, preparing for the moment, said, "You tell Mike Mansfield to put that bill on the floor and you tell everyone that it's going to stay there until it passes. I don't care if it stays for four, six or eight months." Johnson overcame their skepticism completely. Joe Rauh told Humphrey's aide John Stewart that he "had never talked to anybody so determined to pass the civil rights bill."[1]

Johnson was committed not only to civil rights but to Humphrey himself. Normally the chairman of the committee to which a bill was referred serves as floor leader for the legislation, managing its path to approval, but James Eastland of Judiciary was hardly going to perform that function. Johnson told Mike Mansfield that he wanted Humphrey as floor leader. There really was no other choice. Only Humphrey had the network of relationships on both sides of the aisle, the energy, the moral commitment, and the substantive knowledge of the legislation to serve as floor leader. It would be the greatest assignment of his life.

Humphrey also understood that he was now auditioning for the vice presidency. Johnson would need a northern liberal; Johnson would insist on a man he could trust. Hubert Humphrey was the obvious candidate. In public, Humphrey was the loyal partner to the new president, whipping through the Kennedy tax-cut bill. In private, he was organizing a vice presidential campaign. In December

Humphrey's most trusted friends, including Evron Kirkpatrick and Joe Rauh, began meeting at Max Kampelman's house in Washington. Humphrey himself talked to Walter Reuther for two hours; the labor leader was said to be "100% committed." He talked to Al Barkan, head of the AFL-CIO body that disbursed campaign funds. Barkan was on the fence. He worried about Bobby Kennedy, an obvious rival.[2] Humphrey asked Marvin Rosenberg, the New York businessman who had helped finance the 1960 campaign, to come down to Washington to help with strategy; Rosenberg found Humphrey closeted with his aide Bill Connell, Kampelman, and Rauh. "All four of us argued against it," Rosenberg later said. "We said he'd lose his freedom. We said Johnson would cut his balls off." Humphrey was unmoved. "I want to become president," he told his friends, "and the only way I can is to become vice president."[3]

In late January 1964, as if by providence, Ted Van Dyk, a twenty-nine-year-old press officer for the European Common Market, walked into Humphrey's office bearing a three-page memo titled, "How Hubert Humphrey Can Become President by First Becoming Vice-President." Humphrey had been Van Dyk's boyhood hero; this ambitious young would-be player wanted a role in elevating Humphrey to the highest office. The memo argued—wrongly, as it turned out—that Johnson was inclined to choose Bobby Kennedy or Sargent Shriver as his running mate; the best way to make him change his mind was to show that Humphrey "would be the best President in the event of tragedy." Van Dyk proposed that Humphrey make an implicit case for himself through big speeches on foreign policy and prominent foreign travel while a small group of operators disseminated speeches, articles, endorsements, and the like. It would be a political campaign targeted at one voter. Bill Connell was so impressed that he hired Van Dyk to work exclusively on the campaign. One of the first targets of the propaganda effort was Jim Rowe, Johnson's confidant and liaison, to whom the Humphrey team sent a daily loose-leaf notebook of favorable material.[4] Humphrey's friends and aides would carry out this quiet campaign while he consumed himself with the civil rights bill.

The Kennedy bill had remained trapped in the Senate Judiciary Committee; in the House, however, the bill not only moved through the committee process but became bolder and broader. On February 10, the House approved HR 7152, as it was labeled, 290–130. Congressmen had added, as Title VII, the all-important employment-discrimination provision that Kennedy had resisted. The other six parts strengthened voting rights in federal elections, outlawed segregation in public facilities, authorized the attorney general to sue to stop discrimination in those facilities and to enforce school desegregation orders, extended the life of the Civil Service Commission, and mandated a cutoff of federal funds where discrimination was found.

Humphrey understood that the great test of his life now lay before him. As he later wrote in a memo recapping the whole experience, "I had to make up my mind as to mental attitude and how I would conduct myself. I can recall literally talking to myself, conditioning myself for the long ordeal." He would not lose his temper no matter how provoked by the forces of Jim Crow. He would not get distracted: Humphrey cleared his schedule so that he could be on the floor for hours each day, and available almost every other waking moment. Johnson, endlessly goading, called Humphrey to say, "You have got this opportunity now, Hubert, but you liberals will never deliver. You don't know the rules of the Senate, and your liberals will be off making speeches when they ought to be present in the Senate." But Humphrey would not repeat this mistake. For years he had watched Richard Russell outflank the liberals; this time he would overcome liberal individualism to infuse a spirit of discipline and teamwork in the ranks. One of Russell's great tricks was to filibuster until the other side drifted off, and then call for a quorum; if the quorum call failed, the session would be adjourned. Humphrey appointed a rotating team of four "captains" to remain on the floor at all times; they would alert their colleagues to assemble the moment a quorum was called. Humphrey appointed another set of captains to master each of the bill's titles and to defend them from southern attack.

But Humphrey understood that, unlike Russell, whose negative goal of blocking legislation depended upon internal discipline,
he needed to marshal the public to put pressure on the fence-sitters.
Humphrey's deep ties to activists, which Johnson had always ridiculed, proved invaluable. He met with religious leaders and labor
leaders to plan a massive lobbying campaign at the national, state, and
local levels. He published a daily newsletter written by staff members
and sometimes legal scholars.[5] Humphrey and his team convened
every morning thirty minutes before the start of the day's session.
Though on Mondays and Thursdays civil rights lobbyists were permitted to join the sessions, they were not going to run the show; staffers thought of those meetings as at least part charade, designed to
keep the advocates on board.[6]

Johnson gave Humphrey one piece of advice, though Humphrey
already knew it perfectly well: "That bill can't pass unless you get Ev
Dirksen." Dirksen was the minority leader of the Senate, a moderate from Illinois who needed to prevail on his fellow Republicans to
defeat a filibuster and pass legislation. "You make up your mind now
that you've got to spend time with Ev Dirksen. You've got to play to
Ev Dirksen. You've got to let him have a piece of the action. He's got
to look good all the time."[7] Dirksen's objection to the legislation was
of a different order from that of the southerners. As a pro-business,
Main Street Republican, he was uncomfortable with the prospect of
government intervention in private-sector decisions. He had opposed
Title II, on access to public facilities, when Kennedy had proposed it
the year before; he objected to the strong enforcement provisions of
Title VII, on employment. If Dirksen could not be moved, then civil
rights advocates would once again have to accept half a loaf—or even
crumbs. But even this might prove impossible, because the Justice
Department officials whom Johnson had deputized to represent the
White House on the legislation had reached an agreement with Representative William McCulloch of Ohio, the leading Republican congressman on civil rights, that the Senate would not be permitted to
weaken the bill. Humphrey would thus have to influence Dirksen to
drop or greatly soften his objections to the legislation.

Johnson, with his genius for the strategic weak spot, knew that Dirksen was a vain man who fancied himself a great statesman; that was how he could be "played." Humphrey thus began to bait what John Stewart would later call "the great man hook."[8] Humphrey was able to draw on the deep well of humility, of deference, that had endeared him to his colleagues. Humphrey's flattery could be as hyperbolic as Johnson's but never felt as calculated; he really did put the other man first. Though it worried, and sometimes disgusted, the civil rights lobbyists who watched his every move, Humphrey visited Dirksen almost daily—in Dirksen's office. And he spoke publicly of Dirksen as the reincarnation of the great Illinois Republican who freed the slaves. Appearing on *Meet the Press* March 8, Humphrey described his colleague as "a man who thinks of his country before he thinks of his party." At the hour of decision, Humphrey added, "he will not be found wanting."[9]

Dirksen was the key; but he could not, by himself, win over the middle-of-the-roaders, and especially not the Democrats among them. An unsigned and undated memo, probably written by Bill Connell in mid-March, concluded that five out of six undecided senators from the Midwest and Rockies had to be persuaded to vote for cloture. This would have included figures such as Roman Hruska of Nebraska and Karl Mundt of South Dakota. Their constituents were rural, small-town folk with little exposure to Black people. They watched *The Lawrence Welk Show* and *The Beverly Hillbillies*. The way to get at such voters was through a direct moral appeal—"the denial of civil rights is evil and unjust"—delivered in a tone of "dignity, straightforwardness and earnestness." Delivered by whom? The author of the unsigned memo wondered if America's talk-show hosts—Johnny Carson, Jack Paar, Steve Allen—would agree to endorse the legislation. Humphrey wrote to President Johnson March 18 forwarding precisely these suggestions.[10]

Humphrey faced excruciating difficulties on all sides. His friends in the civil rights community, who had been sold out time after time, had every reason to fear that they would be sold out again. On February 28 Joe Rauh and Clarence Mitchell Jr., chief lobbyist of the

NAACP, came to the whip's office to plot strategy with Humphrey and Thomas Kuchel, the Republican whip and Humphrey's indispensable partner. Mitchell, who, like Humphrey, essentially would not leave Capitol Hill for the next three-plus months, called for an open campaign of pressure against the fence-sitters, including an order to the Senate sergeant-at-arms to arrest members who failed to appear for a quorum call. Humphrey and Kuchel knew this would backfire. Humphrey implored Rauh and Mitchell to ease off the pressure and refused to put his colleagues in the hoosegow, but also promised that he would not permit the bill to be weakened.[11] The two agreed, uneasily.

Johnson had already decided to ride straight into the teeth of southern opposition by provoking a filibuster and then winning a cloture vote. This was the exact opposite of his approach in 1957, but he understood that since he would never gain southern agreement on an uncompromised bill, confrontation was the only available path. He knew, from painful experience, that Russell would hold all pending business hostage until the faint of heart cried uncle. For that reason, in fact, he had advised Kennedy not to introduce his civil rights package before he won approval of his tax cut.[12] Johnson solved that problem by pushing through the tax cut early in 1964. Humphrey told him that they also had to pass the farm-subsidy bill in order to prevent Midwestern senators from getting restive. Johnson agreed, and Humphrey got the bill through the Senate in early March. The decks were cleared: the Senate, as Johnson had vowed, would do nothing else until the civil rights bill passed.

On March 9, Mike Mansfield introduced HR 7152. Immediately Richard Russell's troops launched into a filibuster to prevent the bill from being debated. Here Humphrey made another strategic decision: he and his lieutenants, rather than waiting for the southerners to run out of steam, would actively argue with them. On the 10th, Humphrey dueled with Senator Stennis over the reach of the Fourteenth Amendment, which Stennis insisted, incredibly, did not apply to local ordinances enforcing segregation. The next day he goaded Allen Ellender of Louisiana into a remarkable confession: "I am frank to admit that in many cases the reason why the voting rights were not encouraged is that the white people in those counties who are in the minority are afraid they would be outvoted." Rightly so, he added: they were "scared to death to have Negroes in public office without qualifications."[13] This was catnip for the national press. So, too, a mid-March debate with Russell on *The Today Show* in which the latter described Title II, on public accommodations, as "a serious invasion of the right of private property." Do you mean, shot back a faux-incredulous Humphrey, that "we permit people to come into public accommodations that are dope addicts . . . so long as they are white," but not "a decent, wholesome citizen" who happens to be Black?[14]

Humphrey was making the case for common decency, just as his memo had proposed. And the southerners were obliging by saying what people said to one another in Selma or Biloxi, but not in Lincoln, Nebraska. The filibuster was holding perfectly well, but Russell began to worry that he was losing in the court of public opinion, which had turned decisively against him in the aftermath of Birmingham and the spreading protests against the denial of voting rights and of access to restaurants and bus terminals. He passed the word to Mansfield that he was prepared to hold a vote to make the civil rights bill the Senate's "pending business." On March 26, the Senate voted 67–15 to do so.

Humphrey took this opportunity to make the affirmative case for the legislation. From March 30 through mid-April, he and his captains explained the bill, title by title. This gave Democrats such as Joseph Clark and Philip Hart, and also Republicans such as Roman Hruska and Gordon Allott of Colorado, a chance to enjoy both the Senate spotlight and the media attention that came with it. Humphrey himself kicked off this public seminar with a three-hour speech introducing the whole bill. He explained the rationale for Title I, which mandated uniform standards for voter registration, by ticking off a list of southern counties where Blacks outnumbered whites, but none—zero—had been allowed to register. In the case of Title II, access to public facilities, he observed that while a popular travel guide for people with pets included many hotels and restaurants where they would be welcome, a guide published for Black motorists showed no place at all in many of those cities where they could dine or stay. Ten years after the *Brown* decision, he noted in regard to Title IV, no Black children were attending school alongside whites in the South. "It is," Humphrey observed, "nothing short of amazing that the American Negro has been so patient"—a sharp reminder to Americans who bristled at "illegal" sit-ins.

Russell began deploying his weapons. On April 4—a Saturday—one of his lieutenants issued a quorum call; only thirty-nine of the needed fifty-one senators answered. Humphrey was furious and publicized the names of the absentees. On the 13th, opening day for the Washington Senators baseball team, and thus an undeclared holiday for Congress, Spessard Holland of Florida called for a quorum—a low blow. Humphrey, at the game, had the announcer page members and sent limousines to pick them up. This time they mustered a majority; never again during the debate would the bill's supporters fail to meet a quorum call. Humphrey also publicized the tactics of the opposition. In early April, as he was preparing to appear on *Face the Nation*, John Stewart reminded him to tell viewers that a group called the Coordinating Committee for Fundamental American Freedoms had already spent $320,000 publicizing the allegedly ruinous consequences of the legislation—and that $50,000 of those funds had been appropriated by the Mississippi state legislature.[15]

All this time Humphrey had been pressing Dirksen to state his concerns about the legislation. Finally Dirksen issued a twenty-one-page memo that laid out objections to Titles II and VII as well as Title IV, on school desegregation; Dirksen did not believe the statute would preclude mandatory school assignment to achieve racial balance even though the language expressly prohibited it. Dirksen began raising his concerns within the Republican caucus. By the time he introduced proposed amendments in the Senate April 16, he had whittled the list down to one change to Title II and eleven to Title VII. Most of them were technical, though Dirksen also wished to rely more on voluntary compliance, and less on federal enforcement powers, than the legislation envisioned. In contemporaneous notes, John Stewart observed that while none of the proposed amendments were fatal, civil rights and labor groups "interpret any particular change in the legislation as some manner of dastardly sellout." Humphrey would have to fend them off.[16]

Events now proceeded on two tracks. Privately, the bill's advocates were working with Dirksen to reach language that would not weaken the bill. Publicly, Russell's men were holding a filibuster and probing for weak spots in the enemy's line. On April 21, Senator Herman Talmadge of Georgia introduced an amendment that would have required a jury trial for any official accused of violating any of the bill's provisions, thus reprising the most controversial element of the 1957 Civil Rights Act. Russell may have thought this would split the advocates. In fact, Dirksen now teamed up with Mansfield, who had himself been courting his Republican counterpart since the 1963 civil rights debate, to offer a compromise that would guarantee a jury trial only if the defendant faced more than thirty days in jail or a fine of more than $300. Russell rejected the measure. He knew that the longer the filibuster continued, the more impatient the moderates would become.

That group included Dirksen himself. He and Mansfield publicly called for a cloture vote on their amendment, even though Humphrey and Kuchel had argued that a failed vote on cloture would force a 1957-style compromise. Indeed, the two men had promised the civil rights leaders that they would ward off premature calls for cloture. At a meeting in Mansfield's office April 28, Humphrey passionately rebutted the argument for an early cloture vote. Mansfield listened mutely; staff members had come to see him as Dirksen's instrument. Humphrey went to the White House to brief Johnson and tell him that victory was in sight if they could hold off the clamor for compromise. The following day Dirksen scheduled his own White House session. The Illinois senator probably hoped to lure Johnson into brokering compromise legislation. But Johnson, having already been reassured by Humphrey, refused.[17] Dirksen saw that he would have to choose between a southern filibuster and a deal with the true believers.

One of the striking features of this whole process was Johnson's remove. Through what must have been a superhuman effort at self-restraint, he had allowed Humphrey to play his role as legislative quarterback. John Stewart recalled, "We were not getting orders from the White House. We were making the decisions about what would happen." The president, he said, was "a shotgun behind the door"—to be brandished at decisive moments, such as the Dirksen visit.[18] Some-times Humphrey found the gun aimed at himself. On April 30, after he was quoted in an article implying that Johnson would, in fact, accept a compromise, the president called. His very first words, delivered in an ominous growl, were, "I don't believe you ought to be quoting me on what I'm going to do on these amendments." Humphrey protested that he had been misquoted. Johnson, barely listening, shot back, "I'm against any amendments, and I'm going to be against them right up until the minute when I sign them." Johnson, that is, did expect to compromise, but he was going to keep bluffing until he had to. And, more important, he was going to keep publicly insisting that he would remain committed to the bill no matter how much longer the South filibustered.[19]

Humphrey was operating from a rare position of strength with Johnson. The president was depending on him to deliver the most important legislative achievement of his life. And Humphrey knew he was playing the role of maestro—the Johnson role—with great flair. In a conversation in mid-May, as Johnson probed for signs that Humphrey was going soft, the latter responded, with an air of brio he didn't always strike before his old leader, "We haven't weakened this bill one damn bit." At the same time, Johnson had what Humphrey wanted—the vice presidency—and Humphrey was acutely conscious of being watched, and judged. Jim Rowe paid regular visits bearing ambiguous messages from Johnson, who was publicly flirting with Gene McCarthy and even Robert McNamara, a Republican. If the civil rights bill failed, Humphrey had good reason to fear that his cause would fail as well. After news of the April 30 call was reported in the press, Johnson called again to deny that he had yelled at his friend Hubert as the newspapers had said. "You just talked when you ought to be listening, that's all." In fact, Johnson said, "I'm trying to build you up." Humphrey giggled nervously as the president indulged in his special brand of sadistic levity. "I'm not about to say that I corrected you; I might say that *you* corrected *me*."[20]

In a meeting May 5, Dirksen suddenly unveiled a new set of proposed amendments. There were seventy in all, divided into three "tiers"—purely technical, semi-technical, and substantive. The activists erupted; Walter Reuther cabled Humphrey and Kuchel to say that labor could not live with the proposed restrictions on Title VII. Humphrey's team, senior staff members, and Justice Department officials began meeting every day to try to see if Dirksen's amendments, or some of them, could be grafted on to the bill without destroying it. It soon became clear that Dirksen didn't want to wreck the legislation but rather to leave his fingerprints on it. The only real sticking point was his insistence on weakening the attorney general's power to enforce Title VII, the fair employment provision.

At a Democrats-only meeting the morning of May 13, Humphrey insisted on drawing a line at Title VII. Dirksen and other Republicans joined at 10:30. Dirksen reiterated his demand for an early cloture vote; Stewart recalled Humphrey saying, "If Dirksen is not willing to go this route then there is really no business to talk to him." But the GOP members had adopted a party line. George Aiken, Republican of Vermont, said flatly, "As of now the bill is dead." Only a victorious cloture vote could revitalize it. Then Dirksen argued for removing the language granting the attorney general enforcement power to an entirely new title. As everything began heading in the wrong direction, Humphrey engaged in some Johnson-level trickery. Senator Clark, by prior design, heatedly accused Dirksen of trying to ram major changes to the legislation down the throats of the advocates in the guise of "technical" amendments. "It's a goddamn sellout!" Clark shouted before storming out of the room. "You see what I have to deal with?" Humphrey said. Soon a new spirit of comity reigned, and Dirksen agreed to forgo a cloture vote and take his proposed amendments back to the GOP caucus.[21]

By May 26, the Justice Department had produced a new seventy-four-page version of the bill incorporating Dirksen's language. Even Joe Rauh conceded that the legislation was none the weaker for the changes. One of the very few substantive alterations was language that required the attorney general to give states and localities the opportunity to comply with the provisions of Titles II and VII before intervening; the Justice Department could initiate a lawsuit only in the face of a "pattern or practice" of discrimination. On June 4 Humphrey took to the floor to explain the terms of the Dirksen-Mansfield-Kuchel-Humphrey amendment to HR 7152. Senator Dirksen, said Humphrey, laying on the flattery with a trowel, "will go down in history as one of the greatest friends of civil rights and one of the chief architects of the Civil Rights Act of 1964."[22]

Dirksen now had the means to win over enough Republicans to defeat the filibuster. On June 1 Mansfield had announced that he would call for cloture on the 9th. Russell understood that the civil rights forces needed more time to get to sixty-seven votes; he called for an immediate vote instead. This forced Humphrey and his captains to engage in a bizarre counter-filibuster in order to give themselves enough time to be sure of winning. The situation grew yet more tense on June 2, when Dirksen fell ill, and Bourke Hickenlooper of Iowa used his absence from the GOP conference to organize a revolt among conservatives. On the floor, Hickenlooper asked for unanimous consent to vote on three amendments prior to the cloture vote; one of them would modestly expand access to jury trials while another would limit the reach of fair-employment law. Hickenlooper had won the support of enough colleagues to make the cloture vote fail if he didn't get his way. Humphrey was in a quandary. If he refused, the whole bill might collapse. If he agreed, and the amendments passed, he would gravely weaken the legislation and lose civil rights and labor support. He told Hickenlooper that he would postpone the cloture vote by one day and hold debate on the amendments June 9. Then he went to work on his colleagues. The amendments were duly debated. Two were voted down while the jury trial amendment succeeded. Hickenlooper and his allies were now prepared to vote for cloture.

The cloture vote looked like it would be agonizingly close. A May 26 tally by the Associated Press found only fifty-six definite votes to end the filibuster. Humphrey activated the lobby of heaven: ministers, priests, and even bishops began to badger their local senators. Johnson promised Carl Hayden, an Arizona Democrat who had never cast a cloture vote in over thirty-seven years in the Senate, that he would deliver a central Arizona water project if Hayden would vote to end the filibuster. By June 9, Humphrey knew he had the votes, but he stayed in the office beyond midnight, calling colleagues and keeping a running tally. He called Johnson to say he had crossed the threshold. "How are you counting Hayden?" Johnson asked. How many Republicans is Dirksen going to deliver? Humphrey stood firm: he had sixty-eight and counting.[23] Humphrey went back to work, calling and tallying. By the time he was done, well past midnight, he had picked up J. Howard Edmondson, an Oklahoma Democrat, as well as two Republicans, Carl Curtis of Nebraska and John Williams of Delaware.

The next morning opened with the conclusion of a sulfuric four-hour diatribe against the bill by Robert Byrd. The former Klansman concluded at 10:51 a.m. At 11:00, the hour appointed for the cloture vote, each side was first given thirty minutes to speak. In a gesture both humble and eloquent, Mike Mansfield read a letter he had received from a twenty-nine-year-old white mother of four who wrote of the sense of shame she felt when she reflected that, had she been born Black, she would have to tell her children that they couldn't go to the store to buy a Coke or an ice cream cone. Richard Russell responded with an eleventh-hour exercise in hyperbole, warning that the passage of the bill would mark the end of free enterprise, federalism, and the separation of powers. Mansfield then yielded two minutes to Humphrey, who wore a red rose in his lapel. Three months of round-the-clock work and infrequent meals had burned away the flab he had put on over the years; he weighed twenty pounds less than he had in March. Ebullient, on the edge of the great legislative triumph of his life, Humphrey quoted the words that Shakespeare put into the mouth of Henry V at Agincourt: "You will be able to tell your children that you were here on this day." Last came Everett Dirksen, still sick from a peptic ulcer. Dirksen quoted, or misquoted, Victor Hugo: "Stronger than all the armies is an idea whose time has come." The time has come, Dirksen added, "for equality in sharing in government, in education and in employment."[24]

Then the question was put: "Is it the sense of the Senate that the debate should be brought to a close?" The clerk read out the roll in almost perfect silence. The newsman Roger Mudd, receiving word from a reporter inside the hall, ticked off each vote for a nationwide audience. Clair Engle of California, dying of a brain tumor, was wheeled into the chamber, where he had not appeared in months. Engle tried, but failed, to raise his arm. Instead he pointed to his eye—and then the clerk called, "Aye!" When John Williams of Delaware cast the sixty-seventh vote, Humphrey threw his arms over his head in triumph. In the end, seventy-one senators voted for cloture—the first time in history the body had ended a filibuster over civil rights by vote.[25]

Russell made one last attempt to weaken the bill by introducing hundreds of amendments. This protracted the process by another week and utterly exhausted Humphrey and his team; but virtually every amendment was defeated. On June 17, with the end in sight, Humphrey was pulled off the floor to receive a phone call from a tearful Muriel: his son Robert, who had gone to the hospital with a lump on his throat, had been diagnosed with cancer and would undergo surgery immediately. Humphrey withdrew to his office. How could he stay when Robert's life was in jeopardy? But how could he leave when this bill, of all bills, was still balanced on a knife edge? Humphrey was sitting alone, despondent, when Rauh and Mitchell barged in full of celebration—until they saw Humphrey. Soon all three were weeping. Humphrey decided to stay; that was the man he had become, for better or worse. Robert's operation would be completely successful, but afterward, Humphrey would always think of how his great victory was mingled with pain.[26]

On June 19, the civil rights bill passed the Senate 73–27. On July 2 the House passed the amended legislation and President Johnson signed it on a live television broadcast. The greatest breakthrough on civil rights since the end of Reconstruction had many fathers: the fearless protesters who had stood up to Bull Connor and his fire hoses and attack dogs; Johnson and Dirksen and congressmen such as William McCulloch; Mitchell and Rauh and Wilkins; churchmen and labor leaders. But it was Hubert Humphrey who had defeated the South. *Congressional Quarterly* ascribed the victory to Humphrey's "masterful, day-in and day-out perseverance," and sharply contrasted his organization, patience, and good humor to Russell's intransigent failure to find compromise when and where it might have been possible.[27] At no point had Humphrey violated his own gentlemanly code. The South had no reason to feel ill-treated; it is, in fact, remarkable to see how often his opponents lavished praise on him even in the midst of bitter disputes. At one point, when Russell Long implored Humphrey to give the other side a chance to talk, John McClellan of Arkansas, an ardent segregationist who had in fact been waiting to speak, blurted out, "I am in favor of his speaking daily, repeatedly, and thereafter, because he is always helpful and always informative, even if we do not agree with him."[28]

Hubert Humphrey, who worried so much about falling short of the high standards set for him by his father, must have known how very proud Hubert Humphrey Sr. would have been.

16

The Johnson
Death March

LYNDON JOHNSON HAD NEVER SAID, BUT HUBERT HUMPHREY still believed, that he could not become vice president unless first he slew the dragon of civil rights. He had done that; but he still had no promises. There is no record that Johnson even thanked him for this extraordinary achievement. Johnson's proxy, Jim Rowe, had been careful to deliver nothing like the promise that Humphrey felt he had received from Adlai Stevenson in 1956. The courtship dance delighted Johnson, who knew how to put other men in his debt. He picked up one candidate after another without ever discarding any of them. As late as July 23, less than a month before the 1964 Democratic National Convention, he shared his list with economist John Kenneth Galbraith: Humphrey, Bobby, Stevenson,

Sargent Shriver, Defense Secretary Robert McNamara, Gene McCarthy.[1] His courtship of this last had been particularly public: in January the president had made a surprise appearance at a McCarthy fund-raiser and brought virtually the entire cabinet with him.

The possibility that the liberal Nelson Rockefeller would win the Republican Party's nomination for president had sent Johnson into an agony of calculation: he needed a liberal, a Midwesterner, a Catholic. But on July 15 the archconservative Barry Goldwater had won the prize. That ended any thought of Bobby Kennedy, a liberal Catholic whom Johnson despised. "I don't need that little runt to win," Johnson told his brother Sam. "I can pick anybody I damn please."[2] Johnson and his aides devised a pretext to painlessly dispose of Bobby. On July 30 the president announced that it would be "inadvisable" for him to "recommend to the convention" a running mate who was a member of his cabinet, or even "any of those who meet regularly with the Cabinet."[3] That implied the existence of a rule or norm unknown until that moment: FDR had added Agriculture Secretary Henry Wallace to the ticket in 1940. But it served Johnson's purpose. In a single stroke he had eliminated not only Kennedy but McNamara and even Stevenson, who as UN ambassador was not a cabinet member.

Later that day, Johnson called Rowe and told him to deliver a message to Humphrey. "Just say that he'd better make up his mind right now whether he's ready to go . . . all the way with me on my platform, on my views, on my policies." Kennedy had sat Johnson down and issued a demand for absolute loyalty; Johnson, an even less forgiving man than his predecessor, would insist on the same pledge. Tell him, Johnson said, "if he don't want to be my wife, he don't have to marry me." Rowe then delivered what must have been a very near replica of this demand for submission. That evening, with Rowe sitting in his office, Humphrey called the president and said, "If your judgment leads you to select me, I can assure you—unqualifiedly, personally, and with all the sincerity in my heart—complete loyalty. . . . And that goes for everything. All the way the way you want it." Johnson said nothing. He wasn't ready to let his old friend stop squirming.[4] He instructed Rowe to conduct an in-person vetting. Rowe later said that after he had asked Humphrey whether he had any skeletons in his closet, including other women, Humphrey finally blew his stack, saying that after twenty years in office his life was an open book. Rowe assured him, somewhat improbably, that Republicans would ask the same questions.[5]

Johnson kept asking people who he should pick, and the answer was almost always the same. In March, George Meany, the immensely powerful head of the AFL-CIO, said he had one and only one candidate: Hubert Humphrey. But Johnson insisted that he needed a Catholic like McCarthy or Shriver. At a meeting of political advisers, Larry O'Brien, the former Kennedy confidant—and a Catholic—said that Kennedy had put the religion issue to rest in West Virginia. "I'm for Hubert Humphrey," O'Brien said. "He deserves it." Johnson heard the same thing from everyone in the room.[6]

On August 1, right after he had made his announcement clearing the decks, Johnson called Walter Reuther, who said that he, too, was a Humphrey man. "Nobody sees him but they like him," Johnson admitted. "He's a laughing fellow, you cannot insult him, he just smiles you out of the room. He's logical as hell, he's eloquent as hell, he's been a poor man and there's where you get a lot of poor people." It was a piercingly accurate summation.

"Pat Brown"—the California governor—was "red hot for Hubert," Reuther reported. What about "the Roosevelt thing"? Johnson asked—the notorious West Virginia allegation.

"He wasn't a draft dodger," Reuther said flatly. But Johnson still wasn't ready to call a halt to the dance. "I want to throw more names into the mix so people don't get mad at Hubert," he said, as if anyone could get mad at the laughing fellow.[7]

But Humphrey did have a problem—civil rights. In May, George Wallace, the governor of Alabama and an avowed segregationist, had entered the Wisconsin primary at the last minute, and won a third of the Democratic vote as well as many Republicans. He had taken 30 percent in Indiana despite well-organized opposition. And he had, shockingly, won the Maryland primary. He had taken Baltimore suburbs that had voted for Kennedy in 1960. "Being a Southerner is no longer geographic," he had said ominously. "It's a philosophy and an attitude."[8] Unrest in the North had unnerved many voters, who had complacently regarded race as a problem of the Jim Crow South. On July 15 a riot began in Harlem after an off-duty policeman shot and killed a Black teenager. The violence lasted five nights and led to hundreds of injuries and arrests as well as extensive property damage.

Humphrey knew he couldn't duck the issue. On July 24 he took to the floor of the Senate. First he made the obvious point: "Civil disorder cannot be tolerated in a civilized society." But then he added that "generations of racial prejudice, discrimination, deprivation and injustice have contributed directly to this tragic situation." The short-term answer was enforcement, but the long-term answer was justice. The Senate, he pointed out, had just passed the Economic Opportunity Act, an early cornerstone of Johnson's War on Poverty, by a vote of two to one. Humphrey predicted that the legislation would ultimately end the slum conditions that had given rise to the riots.[9] That was always his hope; it soon came to seem terribly naïve.

Johnson wasn't worried about Wallace, who by this time had dropped out of the race, but he was worried about Goldwater. In a gesture that seems unimaginable today, Goldwater had visited Johnson in the White House after the riots and promised that he would not exploit the issue for political gain. Nevertheless, he had delivered a violent diatribe against the Civil Rights Act, calling it "the hallmark of the police state and a landmark of the destruction of free society." Goldwater was well positioned to pick up the Wallace vote. On August 3, a White House aide sent Walter Jenkins, Johnson's confidant, a copy of Humphrey's 1948 speech to the Democratic convention. On an attached note he wrote, "Does this give us any trouble?" Jenkins sent the speech to George Reedy, Johnson's press secretary, who responded, "Not in substance, but Humphrey made it in a highly charged atmosphere. I do not know the extend [sic] to which the South has forgiven him."[10] Columnists Rowland Evans and Robert Novak reported that southerners were clamoring for Gene McCarthy, who had never been a civil rights firebrand; they quoted one southern congressman as saying that Humphrey could send the entire South to Goldwater.[11]

Humphrey set in motion a campaign of his own. He called leading southern officeholders to rally support, as he had in 1956 when trying to make the same case to Adlai Stevenson. He sent a memo to Jack Valenti noting that he had been talking to Allen Ellender, Louisiana's ardent defender of Jim Crow. Humphrey reported that Ellender, who had been "helpful" on food stamps and farm price supports, if not on civil rights, had been feeling neglected by the White House. "The more the President sees these Southern senators and lets the Southern newspapers know that they have been in to see the President the better it is going to be for the President." Humphrey was simultaneously displaying his prudence, his pragmatism, and his close ties with the Deep South. The effort was wearing on Humphrey. Johnson's aide Eric Goldman saw him eating lunch in the White House mess in mid-August. "Despite his ebullience," Goldman noticed, "his face was that of a man being drained."[12]

Humphrey was destined to perform the labors of Hercules to win the prize he so desperately sought. In April, civil rights activists in Mississippi had formed the Mississippi Freedom Democratic Party (MFDP). After the regular state party had chosen an all-white delegate slate for the upcoming convention in Atlantic City—Blacks were not permitted to attend, much less seek election—the MFDP convened its own convention August 6. The party elected an integrated slate of sixty-eight delegates and adopted a platform that—unlike that of the regular party—pledged to support the Democratic nominee, condemned white-supremacist organizations, and called for the elimination of poll taxes and literacy tests. The MFDP planned to challenge the seating of the regular delegation at the upcoming convention.

The formation of the MFDP was the culmination of the Freedom Summer, a movement that had brought hundreds of northern volunteers together with seasoned civil rights activists and, crucially, rural Black people who had shown the courage to register to vote, and as a result had faced savage violence. On June 21, three civil rights workers—Mickey Schwerner, James Chaney, and Andrew Goodman—had been murdered in Neshoba County, Mississippi, their car dumped into a swamp. While legislators in Washington were congratulating themselves on passing the Civil Rights Act, the real drama of civil rights was playing out in the Deep South in a stark combination of astonishing bravery and sickening violence. The

MFDP became a cause. In June, John Roche, chairman of Americans for Democratic Action, wrote a letter to the heads of the fifty state parties urging them to send delegates to the Credentials Committee committed to seating the MFDP.[13] Joe Rauh, who understood the ins and outs of party procedure, volunteered to guide the party through the process.

The prospect of a floor fight that could repeat the dramatic split of 1948 drove Johnson almost crazy. On July 23, he told John Connally, the governor of Texas and a Johnson crony, that he thought Bobby had ginned up the whole affair with Martin Luther King to drive the South out of the party and thus improve his own vice presidential prospects. (The president also said that he had heard a rumor that a Texas oilman—a Republican, of course—had been in Harlem "spreading money around" just before the riots.) Hubert, he said, "is doing his best to put an end to it, but he hasn't had much luck."[14]

Johnson began to bear down on his would-be running mate. Early on the morning of August 14 Johnson called Humphrey and began yelling into the phone about "the civil rights crowd" that was going to get Goldwater elected. Already, he said, southern governors were declining his invitation to dinner. And Connally had told him about another ADA letter to southern delegates—"with your name right on the top." Humphrey responded weakly, "I don't have as much influence or control with those people as I would like." Johnson kept raving about how the Negroes would make the South bolt en masse. Humphrey murmured agreement, lamenting, "We're just not dealing with what I call emotionally stable people, Mr. President." Johnson asked him to call with an update that night.

But the president was too worked up, and instead he called Humphrey later that morning. Humphrey reported that he, Kenny O'Donnell, and Dave Lawrence, the Pennsylvania boss who headed the Credentials Committee, had all talked to Joe Rauh. They were working on a compromise to seat members of both delegations. "There's no compromise," Johnson shot back. "There's no justification at all for messing with the Freedom Party of Mississippi." Then Johnson cut to the quick in his brutal, masterful way. "The union members themselves are upset," he told Humphrey. "They think the nigra man is going to get his job. They've gone to every real estate man, they think the nigra man is going to move next door to him." This, of course, from a man who had put his presidency on the line to pass historic civil rights legislation. Humphrey said nothing. That night he called in to say that he had talked again to Rauh and to Roy Wilkins. "It's got to be done through them," he explained. The only way to avoid a ruinous split in the party was to get the civil rights moderates—the old guard—to prevail on the young radicals to stand down. For once, Johnson listened, and agreed. Humphrey had always been Johnson's liaison to the bomb-throwers; now it would be his job to disarm them.[15]

The Democratic convention was supposed to be a coronation for an immensely popular incumbent facing a challenger widely regarded as an extremist, if not a crackpot. The only mystery, held by the president as a precious trump card, was the choice of running mate. Delegates began to converge on Atlantic City, a louche, frowsy seaside resort known to most Americans from the Miss America contest and the game Monopoly—"a strung-out Angkor Wat entwined in salt-water taffy," as Teddy White put it.[16] But the struggle over the MFDP had upset the stagecraft. The rival delegation had driven up from the campus of the historically Black Tougaloo College in Mississippi in a caravan that included the wrecked station wagon of the three slain activists as well as the charred bell from a burned Mississippi church. As if to further raise the stakes, George Wallace had arrived early to urge the platform committee to demand repeal of the Civil Rights Act as "an alien philosophy of government"—just what Goldwater had called it. Johnson saw a looming disaster. "We're going to have one explosion after another at the convention," he warned Humphrey. "It's going to require some personal attention." He read Humphrey passages from FBI wiretaps of Rauh and others—all of whom Humphrey admired or even revered. "The Communists are in this thing deep," Johnson informed him. "King is completely owned and directed by them." Humphrey kept his mouth shut, as he generally did while the president raged. He agreed to keep leaning on the liberals.[17]

The MFDP had one hour—Friday, August 21, at 3:00—to make its case. Joe Rauh had insisted on a room big enough to fit news cameras, spectators, and the MFDP delegation, and LBJ himself had grudgingly told his aides on the ground to provide it. Edwin Newman of NBC News would be broadcasting the hearing live. First Aaron Henry and Ed King, two of the party's leaders, spoke of the abuses Black voters in Mississippi had suffered, and the restorative work the MFDP had done. Then a short, stout woman with a pronounced limp shuffled to the front of the room. This was Fannie Lou Hamer, a sharecropper from Ruleville, Mississippi. Hamer told the committee that after registering to vote she had been fired from her job on a farm and forced to leave her home and family that very night. Black families in Ruleville were then terrorized by a series of shootings and bombings. The following year, she and others were pulled off a bus by a highway patrolman in Winona, Mississippi, and brought to the local jail. She heard terrible screams as the new inmates were beaten. She heard a voice shout, "Can you say 'Yes, Sir,' nigger?" All this Hamer said in a deep, slow, patient voice—the voice of rural Mississippi. The highway patrolman then came for her. "We're going to make you wish you was dead," he told her. A Black prisoner was ordered to beat her with a blackjack, which he did "until he was exhausted." A second prisoner beat her. Then a white man took over the job; another had pulled up her dress. By now many members of the Credentials Committee were openly weeping. "All of this," Hamer concluded, "is on account of we want to register, to become first-class citizens. And if the Freedom Democratic Party is not seated now, I question America."[18]

That eight-minute testimony had something like the electrifying effect of Humphrey's ten-minute speech in 1948. Martin Luther King spoke after Hamer, but all three network news shows opened with Hamer's speech. Americans had heard the orotund cadences of King and other leaders; few had heard the voice of rural Black suffering, dignity, and anger. The MFDP now seemed to have sufficient votes on the Credentials Committee to force a floor vote, which, Johnson was advised, it would almost certainly win. He ordered Dave Lawrence to stall while he set his men in motion. Reuther later reported to Johnson that at 3:00 the next morning he had bludgeoned Rauh into agreeing to the appointment of a subcommittee of the Credentials Committee to work out a compromise.[19] To lead the group, Lawrence appointed Walter Mondale, Humphrey's protégé since the 1948 Senate campaign, and thus a link to Humphrey and to Johnson.

On Monday the 24th Humphrey met in his suite at the dowdy Pageant Motel with the leading delegates as well as virtually the entire leadership of the civil rights community. There wasn't much room, and people sat on the bed, or crowded on couches, or stood. That whole week was hot and steamy, and it's unlikely the Pageant's air conditioning could have cooled off the crowd. Humphrey must have felt the hostility of the delegates, who had sacrificed so much and expected an outcome worthy of their suffering. Into this supremely tense atmosphere he introduced what could only be considered an insulting offer: the MFDP delegation could attend the convention as nonvoting members. In addition, the party regulars would be seated only if they pledged to support the nominee and accept the party's civil rights platform. And starting with the next convention, the Democratic Party would no longer permit segregated delegations.

When Humphrey claimed that the proposed bargain constituted a great step forward for civil rights, Fannie Lou Hamer looked straight at him and said, "Senator Humphrey, I been praying about you and I been thinking about you, and you're a good man. The trouble is, you're afraid to do what you know is right." Hamer began to cry. Then Humphrey, too, started to cry. Some part of him may have felt that she was right. According to an MFDP delegate, Humphrey then said that Johnson wouldn't make him vice president if they held out, in which case he wouldn't be able to push the civil rights agenda from inside the White House. At that point, Hamer said, "Mr. Humphrey, do you mean to tell me that your position is more important than four hundred thousand black people's lives?"[20] The meeting, Mondale later said, was "agony" for Humphrey. That afternoon Humphrey spoke to Walter Jenkins and said, "I used all the heartstrings I had, and I made no headway."[21]

By Tuesday morning, Mondale's subcommittee had agreed that the convention would add two "at-large" seats and award them to the MFDP. Johnson approved the offer and ratcheted up the pressure campaign. Humphrey had been leaning on Rauh for days to persuade the delegates to see reason, at least as he saw it. Reuther told Martin Luther King that if the delegation didn't accept the new deal he could kiss his labor funding goodbye; he informed Rauh that he would get him fired as the UAW lawyer. Rauh would later say, "You had the whole Democratic machine, the President, the whole White House, the whole labor movement, all trying to stop a few Mississippi Negroes and me from making a stink at the Democratic convention."[22] That was not an exaggeration: when Lyndon Johnson didn't want something to happen, he would stop at nothing to prevent it—and neither would his loyal lieutenants.

Rauh urged the delegation to take the deal. The civil rights leadership class—King, Wilkins, Bayard Rustin, all wise in the ways of politics—took his side. That morning, Tuesday the 25th, Humphrey convened yet another meeting in his suite to convey the new offer. Aaron Henry and Ed King would be named at-large delegates. Humphrey seems not to have considered how profoundly condescending it was to impose the choice of delegates—and to insist on the most "presentable" members. (Henry was the state NAACP chairman and King a white minister.) King said he would step aside in favor of a foot soldier; clearly he meant Fannie Lou Hamer. Robert Moses, the deeply inspirational figure who had organized the Freedom Summer and virtually brought the MFDP into being, later wrote that Humphrey had pronounced this impossible: "The President will not allow that illiterate woman to speak from the floor of the convention."[23] Did Hubert Humphrey really say that? It is, at the least, imaginable. Perhaps until that very moment Humphrey had been able to regard impoverished and ill-educated Black people as the passive victims of prejudice—as silent martyrs—rather than as potential peers in the civil rights movement. His idea of a demonstration was the supremely genteel March on Washington, with its wonderful oratory. Hamer, and the raw anger he felt from her, had given him a shock.

The meeting was going badly when suddenly someone opened the door to the bedroom and shouted, "It's over!" Mondale was on TV announcing the compromise, which had been reached over the heads of the delegation. Bob Moses, calm and masterful under even the most trying circumstances, stomped out of the room and slammed the door behind him. The MFDP, now divided between older and more established figures and younger and angrier ones, voted to reject the deal. Hamer, usually extraordinarily slow to anger, told Aaron Henry that she would slit his throat if he tried to force a compromise.[24] On the other side, the Mississippi regulars were not about to accept either the platform or the loyalty oath. The net effect was a walkout by the regulars and a "walk-in" by members of the MFDP, who managed to borrow credentials and then occupy the vacated area, forming a ring around the empty seats.

The far deeper effect was to divide the civil rights movement— to alienate younger and more radical members both from their leadership and from white politicians, including Hubert Humphrey. Moses, though an apostle of integration, vowed that he would never talk to a white man again. John Lewis, the young and fearless head of the Student Nonviolent Coordinating Committee (SNCC), later wrote, "This was the turning point of the civil rights movement. . . . We had played by the rules, done everything we were supposed to do, had played the game exactly as required, had arrived at the doorstep and found the door slammed in our face." The lesson was: "Anyone who trusted the white man . . . was a fool, a Tom."[25] The moderate Lewis would ultimately lose control over SNCC to the radical Stokely Carmichael.

Hubert Humphrey had no idea of the bitter fruits he had sown. If Joe Rauh and Martin Luther King could swallow the compromise, then the civil rights movement, so far as he knew, was satisfied. It is striking, in fact, that neither in Humphrey's memoirs, nor in Walter Mondale's, nor in other accounts by white liberals, is there any recognition of a lingering bitterness. Humphrey didn't know the people who were angry, and the people he knew weren't angry. But those people were losing control of the civil rights movement. If the Civil Rights Act of 1964 had represented the fulfillment of the dream of 1948, the repudiation of the MFDP, a little more than a month after the act's passage, marked the end, or the beginning of the end, of the racial solidarity that had shaped Hubert Humphrey's political career and served as its moral core.

HUMPHREY HAD NOW COMPLETED HIS HERCULEAN TASK; BUT JOHN-son wasn't finished wringing whatever drama he could out of his selection. On Tuesday afternoon, as Humphrey and Reuther were finally putting the MFDP problem to rest, Johnson dispatched Jim Rowe to tell Humphrey that he was the choice. The previous day the president had given the *Washington Star* an off-the-record interview in which he listed all the demands he would make of his running mate. He told Rowe to show Humphrey the piece and once again win an explicit statement of acquiescence. Humphrey, of course, agreed. Rowe added that Humphrey couldn't tell anyone, though after an explosion from the candidate-to-be he agreed to an exception for Muriel. Humphrey was to fly to Washington that night. And then he wasn't: Johnson canceled the flight and told his aides to put McCarthy on the plane with Humphrey the next day in order to keep the reporters guessing. But McCarthy, who felt almost as ill-used as Humphrey had in 1956, understood that he had lost and withdrew from the competition. When Humphrey got to the Atlantic City airport the next day, not McCarthy but Connecticut senator Thomas Dodd, a last-minute stand-in, was there.

Johnson was having his fun, albeit at Humphrey's expense. And not only Humphrey: early Wednesday afternoon, when the temperature in Washington had reached 89 degrees, the president appeared on the South Lawn and beckoned the reporters to follow him as he took a walk. Johnson was walking his beagles; his tie was knotted and his suit jacket buttoned. As he walked, he talked to the reporters nonstop about all the wonderful vice presidential candidates he had been considering. The South Lawn circuit measured about a quarter mile. Johnson took fifteen laps—four miles on what came to be known as the Death March. Sweat-soaked reporters staggered off and camped under trees, gasping for breath. Johnson revealed absolutely nothing. Meanwhile, Humphrey, utterly spent, had slept all the way on the flight, and then slept again in the limo that brought him to the White House. At 4:30 p.m. he was awakened by a knock on the window and told that the president would see him.[26]

Johnson, now dead serious, subjected Humphrey to one last grilling. "I know that you are an active man and very gregarious," the president said, "but this office is going to require that you not be out front, that you not be in the headlines." Johnson made the job sound as unpleasant as possible. "Seldom do a president and a vice president get along," he told Humphrey. "You'll find out that all the people associated with the President will look down on you." The bitterness that Johnson had stored up during three years as vice president was never more than an inch below the surface. Nevertheless, he said, his door would always be open. "I want you to feel that you can confide in me and I can confide in you." Humphrey yet again reassured Johnson, telling him, as he later recalled, "that I was prepared to be loyal, that I would try to confine my activities to consultation and discussion within the administration."[27]

When Humphrey included this exchange in his memoirs, he left out more pungent remarks that he recited the next day to his old friend Tom Hughes, now assistant secretary of state for intelligence and research. Johnson had told him, "I know you, all about you, every damn thing you have done and thought. Never forget that. I'll know where you are, who you're with, what you're up to." The president was presumably tapping his phone. According to Hughes's contemporaneous notes, Johnson went on to praise his running mate and to outline the role he envisioned for him as vice president. "Agriculture, space, disarmament, poverty, labor will be your responsibility, and I will see to it that the departments and agency heads concerned report through you. On foreign policy, I want you to play a big role. You're gonna travel. You're gonna make speeches. You're going to greet heads of state and be very ceremonial."[28] It was, as was so often the case with LBJ, an intensely mixed message.

Johnson then summoned the reporters for a press conference, where he announced that he would be going to Atlantic City that night with Senators Dodd and Humphrey. Then he threw a little party for the press with cocktails and cake; the next day was his birthday. Afterward they all motored out to Andrews Air Force Base. And then, on the tarmac, apparently with no premeditation—but with Johnson, who could ever tell?—he marched Humphrey over to a gaggle of reporters and said, "I want you to meet the next Vice President of the United States."[29]

The rest was bathos—chocolate-covered bananas on the board-walk and balloons dropping in the giant convention hall. Humphrey, being Humphrey, gave a rafter-raising speech with a great refrain. Most Americans, he shouted, supported a tax cut—but *not* Senator Goldwater; most supported the civil rights bill—but *not* Senator Goldwater. Johnson, being Johnson, gave an earnest and clunky speech that was instantly forgotten. The most moving spectacle was Bobby Kennedy introducing a thirty-minute documentary about his fallen brother. Many wept; but soon the hubbub began again. Humphrey's ebullience had been fully restored. An unsigned "Man in the News" piece in the *New York Times*, extremely erudite and sounding suspiciously like Arthur Schlesinger, described Humphrey's "pink cheeks and broad, smiling face" and "winning, beamish-boy expression." Humphrey was pragmatic, fair-minded, all too self-deflating. But "anyone who has ever heard him give an hour to a group of twelve-year-olds on the need for an education will never forget it."[30]

EVEN LYNDON JOHNSON, WHO SAW DISASTER LURKING AROUND every corner, knew that Barry Goldwater was a heaven-sent opponent. The one eruption that he feared, and that he strove mightily to control, was Vietnam, where America had stationed fifteen thousand troops officially designated "advisers" to the South Vietnamese army. Johnson came into office as a committed, unreflective Cold Warrior. Two days after he had been sworn in, he had told Henry Cabot Lodge, the American ambassador in Vietnam, "I am not going to lose Vietnam. I am not going to be the President who saw Southeast Asia go the way China went."[31] But neither could Johnson see how to win. American doctrine from the time of Eisenhower had predicated American assistance on the establishment of a legitimate Vietnamese government, but one set of generals kept upending another. Defense Secretary Robert McNamara came back from a trip in March to report that the government was collapsing and the Vietcong had gained control over the crucial Mekong Delta. The president's old comrade Richard Russell advised him to find a face-saving solution and leave. The State Department's intelligence and research division, headed by Tom

Hughes, issued a stream of reports documenting the weakness of the Saigon regime and the resilience of the Vietcong. Johnson summed up his tormented feelings in a remark to his national security adviser, McGeorge Bundy, in mid-1964: "I don't think it's worth fighting for and I don't think we can get out." The Joint Chiefs wanted to bomb the North; Johnson held them off. Throughout 1964 he instructed his advisers to keep a lid on Vietnam until the election was over.[32]

Humphrey shared Johnson's fears of Communist aggression, but he had been deeply engaged for years in debates over Vietnam, and over the broader question of how to confront nationalist uprisings in the Third World. He had always argued that, whatever role Communists might play, insurgencies gained fuel from the frustrations of the people under corrupt and undemocratic rule. Since the problem in Vietnam was ultimately political rather than military, the United States had to support a regime in Saigon that the people believed in. But no such regime existed; the problem seemed insoluble on Humphrey's own terms. Then he met a man who had not only thought far more deeply about these problems than he had but had actually solved them: Edward Lansdale, a former CIA agent and US Air Force officer now working at the Agency for International Development. Lansdale was known as the man who had saved the Philippines from the Communist-led Huk insurgency. He had shown that what was known as "counterinsurgency theory" could work by combining psychological operations, military force, and political support to Ramon Magsaysay, the charismatic reformer who became the country's leader. In 1955, when he had moved on to Vietnam, Lansdale had written that the only way to fight communism was "by giving the guy in the street or the rice paddy something he could believe in so strongly that he'll defend it with everything he has."[33] Lansdale had, however, failed to work the same magic in years of advising President Ngo Dinh Diem, who had been overthrown at Kennedy's instigation in October 1963.

In June 1964, a USAID official arranged a meeting between Humphrey, Lansdale, and the latter's longtime colleague Rufus Phillips. Lansdale's belief that the war could be won through democracy and social reform, as well as unconventional warfare, offered Humphrey a solution that was deeply congenial to his own thinking. Phillips would later write of Humphrey, "He was the first and last high-level official I ever encountered in the United States government who took the time to listen to a detailed explanation of what Vietnam was about and how it had to be fought." When they talked about how the Vietcong had penetrated villages, Humphrey exclaimed that the Communists in Minnesota had used the same tactics to take over the Farmer-Labor Party. Lansdale came to hold Humphrey in such regard that he later hung a portrait of him in his house in Saigon; he would describe Humphrey as his "patron saint."[34]

Humphrey forwarded a report that Lansdale had written, "Concept for a Victory in Vietnam," to McGeorge Bundy, along with a memo of his own. Lansdale argued that sending further troops or bombing the North would be counterproductive; the Vietcong had already struck such deep roots in the countryside that they would flourish even if wholly cut off from northern support. Instead, Lansdale proposed his characteristic mix of psychological operations, economic reform, and democracy promotion. He suggested that the program be implemented by a "Catalyst Team," a group of experts, presumably to be headed by himself. Bundy sent the documents to an aide, who noted that he and other advisers already agreed with most of the memo.[35]

In August, when Johnson insisted that American forces had been fired on in the Gulf of Tonkin, Humphrey readily joined his Senate colleagues in authorizing the president to use "all necessary measures," including force, to repel Communist aggression. Johnson asked Humphrey to deliver a speech defending his policy, and he did so in Los Angeles on the 17th, a week before the Democratic convention. America's commitment to defending the South Vietnamese from communism, Humphrey observed, went back to the Eisenhower administration. "We must stay in Vietnam," he said, "until the freedom of the South Vietnamese people has been established."[36] Yet Humphrey knew better than to rely on such simple-minded formulas. Once he was nominated, Tom Hughes received permission to become his regular intelligence briefer, and Humphrey learned how desperate the situation in Vietnam had become. But Johnson succeeded in keeping a lid on it until November.

HUMPHREY HAD RENTED A HOUSE NEAR THE OCEAN IN NEW JERSEY for the days after the convention. The whole clan gathered there, including his brother Ralph, his sister Frances, and their children. Humphrey was going to finally give himself a vacation. And then, out of nowhere, Johnson told him to come to the ranch and bring Muriel. First the president and his running mate performed for the press. Johnson kitted Humphrey out in a Texas-sized riding outfit that flowed over his arms and his legs, and then put him on a big, lively horse that the Minnesota senator, a hunter and fisherman rather than a rider, could barely control. Johnson, of course, had been riding all his life. The contrast between the two seemed artfully, and cruelly, contrived. Nicholas Katzenbach, the deputy attorney general, who was also present, later observed that Johnson seemed to be "holding Humphrey up by the ears the way he did with the beagles." Johnson then got down to business. He told Humphrey that he wanted him to campaign down South and "let them see . . . that you don't have any horns." That is, talk about farm prices and government spending and things southern voters care about, but go easy on civil rights. He wanted Humphrey to also show the business community that Democrats didn't have horns—that the party believed you could have Medicare and corporate profits, too.[37]

No Republican could have defeated Lyndon Johnson, John Kennedy's legatee, but in Barry Goldwater the GOP had chosen a conservative zealot. In his 1960 credo, *The Conscience of a Conservative*, Goldwater had described a progressive tax system as "repugnant to my notion of justice." And while not personally a racist, Goldwater viewed civil rights, like taxation, as an imposition on individual liberty. He insisted, like many southerners, that *Brown*, wrongly decided, was not "the law of the land." He had denounced the Civil Rights Act.[38] And in his fervent anti-communism he seemed prepared to go to any lengths—perhaps even the use of tactical nuclear weapons—to defeat the insurgents in Vietnam. The choice of Goldwater thus turned the election into a referendum on the consensual liberalism that had dominated American politics since 1932.

This was a contest that Hubert Humphrey could not have been happier to wage. After months of high tension, he campaigned like a colt frisking across a meadow. He shook every hand and kissed every girl. Everywhere he went he repeated his catchphrase: "Most Americans . . . but *not* Barry Goldwater." But he also eagerly accepted the intellectual challenge of rebutting Goldwaterism—"a philosophy which seeks to license individual selfishness at home, and to isolate America from the family of nations." One reporter noted that while Humphrey changed his stump speech daily, he always came back to elemental questions: "What kind of government do you think the founders intended? . . . What kind of people do we want to be?" He quoted John Adams on "the spirit of public happiness." He posed his own idealism against Goldwater's deep pessimism: "What a blessed people we are—divinely blessed."[39]

Humphrey carried out Johnson's orders faithfully. He reassured businessmen that Democrats would increase growth more than the Republicans ever had. And he plunged into the Deep South. In Moultrie, Georgia—"redneck territory," according to a staff memo— Humphrey talked about his great friends Herman Talmadge and Richard Russell. Then he recalled how FDR had rescued farmers and brought development to the South. Democrats, he said, would protect the constitutional rights of "all our citizens—white and Black—and North and South and East and West—rural and urban— Catholic and Protestant and Jew." In a press conference later that day, he insisted that "the views I state in Georgia are the same views I state in Minnesota."[40]

Johnson won the most smashing victory since FDR beat Alf Landon in 1936. (LBJ took an even higher percentage of the popular vote than Roosevelt had.) Goldwater won only his home state of Arizona and four states in the Deep South—almost a reprise of the Dixiecrat performance in 1948. If liberalism had been on trial, then Americans had roundly endorsed it. Johnson prepared to fully launch the Great Society.

PART 3

White House Ordeal

17

Whatever Became
of You, Hubert?

---

*"A vice president ought to bend himself in every way . . .
to be in tune with, and working with, and cooperating
with, at all times with his President."*

HUBERT HUMPHREY'S FOUR YEARS IN THE WHITE HOUSE ARE remembered as an exercise in humiliation and pathos—and rightly so. Lyndon Johnson belittled and marginalized him as he felt the Kennedy clan had done to him; indeed, far more so. Yet the rational, strategic Johnson recognized that he needed his vice president's help. Johnson planned to pass the most ambitious battery of legislation since FDR's first term—landmark civil rights legislation, anti-poverty programs, health-care reform, and more. Humphrey, he thought, could serve as his unofficial congressional whip. And then there was space, agriculture, labor—the earthly paradise that Johnson had spread before Humphrey the previous August.

In the fall of 1964, Nicholas Katzenbach, whom Johnson was soon to name attorney general, and Burke Marshall, head of the Justice Department's Civil Rights Division, had concluded that the White House needed to coordinate the vast and increasingly ramshackle machinery of civil rights enforcement; both considered it the perfect role for Humphrey, who, as Katzenbach later wrote, "had worked all his life for racial equality, had the confidence of black leaders," and probably would have few other pressing assignments.[1] Johnson didn't like the idea; he did not, Katzenbach concluded, want to share credit with his vice president for what he regarded as his life's great achievement. But he accepted the logic of the case with his usual brute realism. A week after the election, Johnson spoke on the phone with Roger Wilkins, a Black assistant attorney general who served as an informal civil rights adviser. He repeated the idea that Humphrey was the right man to ride herd on civil rights enforcement; as vice president, he would outrank all the cabinet members whose fiefs he might be invading. What's more, Johnson added, "They would think more highly about him than they did about me when I was Vice President."[2] That was sour grapes; but it was also a candid assessment of one of Humphrey's strengths.

After the election, Johnson invited the Humphreys and key aides down to the ranch. On the flight back to Washington, Humphrey revealed to Max Kampelman that Johnson had said something startling: "Lyndon says that he will not run for re-election in 1968 and wants me to prepare for it." Johnson had had a massive heart attack a decade earlier—heart disease ran in the family—and he told Humphrey that if he survived the first term he would have to step down lest a second term kill him. Humphrey swore Kampelman to secrecy, and indeed his aide only disclosed the conversation a quarter century after Humphrey's death.[3] Humphrey knew better than to take Johnson at his word, but the thought that the presidency could be his after only four years must have entered his mind.

Humphrey had a wide ambit during the transition period. He had always had a strong relationship with Secretary of State Dean Rusk, and Rusk told him that he would make anyone up to the level of assistant secretary available to him as a staff member. He agreed that Tom Hughes could continue briefing him after the inauguration. He furnished a State Department office for John Rielly, Humphrey's chief foreign policy aide. Humphrey held long and detailed conversations with both Rusk and Johnson about filling diplomatic postings and State Department positions. He and the president agreed that the department had too many overage fossils and needed young men, especially in the developing world. Nevertheless, Rusk worried that the vice president would invade his turf. He told Hughes that since Humphrey had to preside over the Senate, he wouldn't have the time to play a major role in diplomacy. "The vice president should not become a miniature government," he admonished Hughes. "He should not have a staff."[4]

On December 2, Johnson formally asked Humphrey to deliver a report on the reorganization of the civil rights apparatus by the beginning of the new year. Within a week, John Stewart, Humphrey's chief aide on civil rights, had put together a team, sent out letters to federal agencies asking them to outline their civil rights operations, and scheduled interviews with mid-level officials. Humphrey embarked on a whirlwind series of meetings with Johnson's cabinet as well as with leading figures in civil rights, labor, and business, along with governors, mayors, and even police chiefs. The questions he and his team were posing went far beyond logistical matters. The Civil Rights Act had thrust the federal government deep into the unfamiliar and intrusive work of enforcement. How would those agencies carry out their new mandates? In a December 14 memo, Stewart listed hundreds of issues he was raising at the agency level. In the case of the Department of Health, Education, and Welfare (HEW), he wrote, "How will HEW implement fully the regulations recently issued under Title VI of the Civil Rights Act of 1964," mandating desegregation in schools and hospitals? "How can the factor of civil rights be made a relevant one to operating heads of line agencies?" What about manpower? Funding? How to ensure "prompt and effective response" to issues of discrimination? And so on.[5]

At the center of the effort would be Humphrey himself. At a December 20 meeting that brought Burke Marshall together with Humphrey's senior staffers and personal advisers, including Evron

Kirkpatrick and Max Kampelman, it was agreed that the vice president should preside over a "cabinet-level committee" that would max-
imize his status in the White House and allow him to "do whatever
has to be done."[6] The committee would have no operational role but
would referee jurisdictional disputes among agencies, develop broad
strategies, and perhaps recommend important reforms beyond its
reorganizational remit. Few, if any, of Humphrey's predecessors had
played such a role. But Johnson had made it clear that Humphrey was
to figure significantly in his domestic agenda. On January 13, 1965,
Humphrey wrote a note to himself memorializing a cabinet meeting
in which the president had ordered each officer to take responsibility for legislation in his area, and appointed Humphrey and Larry
O'Brien, his senior political aide, to coordinate the process. The president told congressional leaders, "Hubert is my man on the Hill. I want
you to deal with him."[7]

The idea quickly got around that Hubert Humphrey was going to
be a vice president who actually mattered. In a big *New York Times
Magazine* profile, an almost awestruck David Broder wrote, "It is an
amazing instrument, that Humphrey mind." Broder took LBJ at his
word when he said that he did not want to do to Humphrey what Kennedy had done to him, though he cautioned that the president was
"not interested in subdividing his power and responsibility." Humphrey would be an executor, not a policymaker. *Newsweek* reported
that Johnson was "loading Humphrey down with important work."
Skeptics, noted columnist Kenneth Crawford, were overlooking the
"mutual respect and understanding" of the two men born of long
hours together.[8]

On January 4, right on schedule, Humphrey submitted to Johnson a twenty-nine-page document proposing the creation of a new
body, the President's Council on Equal Opportunity, that would oversee, and make recommendations to reorganize, the vast welter of civil
rights agencies inside the federal government. On February 5 Johnson
issued an executive order establishing the council. Humphrey had
everything he wanted—big responsibilities and a president counting
on him to deliver. Humphrey treated the inauguration like a new wedding day. His dear friend Freddy Gates held the Bible as he was sworn

in. The Doland High School marching band, which had brought along his old baritone horn, serenaded him. Arthur Schlesinger was struck by the sight of the president and vice president at an inaugural ball. Johnson, he wrote, was "grim and self-satisfied" while Humphrey was "illuminated with joy." When he took to the dance floor, his old friend Hubert "was so filled with gaiety and charm and life that everyone else stopped, formed a circle around him and applauded."[9] That was how Hubert Humphrey began his tenure as vice president.

JOHNSON'S WILLINGNESS TO DISCUSS DIPLOMATIC APPOINTMENTS with Humphrey did not extend to the one issue that dominated all others—Vietnam. Soon after the election, William Bundy, McGeorge's brother and the assistant secretary of state for East Asian and Pacific affairs, convened an interagency team to recommend a course of action to the president. Humphrey not only was not included in the group, but did not receive accounts of its deliberations. When the team issued a report at the end of November, John Rielly asked a Rusk aide for a copy. The aide, unsure what to do, asked Rusk; Rusk asked McGeorge Bundy; Bundy asked the president—who gave no answer.[10] Had Humphrey seen the document he would have known that Johnson's team had coalesced around "Option C," the bombing escalation that the Joint Chiefs had been clamoring for. In a meeting on December 1, Johnson accepted the recommendation and agreed that escalation shouldn't be contingent on the formation of a government the Vietnamese people could believe in; it was the bombing that would help prop up the regime by showing that the enemy could be defeated—or so it was hoped.[11]

This was, of course, the exact opposite of the view that Humphrey had imbibed from Lansdale and Phillips; the Bundy team was far more optimistic about the effectiveness of bombing than was Tom Hughes, whose judgment Humphrey trusted. Unlike the men around Johnson, Humphrey saw the war as a political effort that required a legitimate regime; and Saigon was descending into farce. Yet another military coup, on December 20, established a new general as head of state. When, in the last days of the year, Humphrey read that Senator

Frank Church of Idaho had declared that it would be "folly" to escalate, he sent his colleague a letter saying, "You have performed a great service for American foreign policy."[12]

The administration moved inexorably toward making the Vietnam War its own. At the end of January McNamara and McGeorge Bundy urged the president to "use our military power . . . to force a change in Communist policy," as the interagency task force had recommended. Johnson once again agreed that "stable government or no stable government, we'll do what we have to do." In early February he dispatched Bundy to Vietnam. Bundy was at Pleiku, in the Central Highlands, on the morning of February 6, 1965, when guerrillas breached the perimeter of a US Army base and attacked a nearby helicopter base, killing eight Americans and wounding over one hundred others. An enraged Bundy fired off a memo to Johnson calling for "gradual and continuing reprisal" through bombing raids on North Vietnam. American interests and influence were, he asserted, "directly at risk in Vietnam," though he also bluntly conceded that "prospects in Vietnam are grim." The president convened a National Security Council (NSC) meeting and did not notify his vice president, who was then in Minnesota. At the end of the meeting Johnson ordered bombing raids in the North.[13]

Humphrey returned to Washington deeply alarmed about the direction the war was taking. But he also knew he would be treading on very thin ice with the president. A few weeks after the election, John Rielly had sent Humphrey a memo warning him not to expect to exercise much influence in the NSC, of which he would be a statutory member. "To the extent that you participate actively in the discussion," Rielly cautioned, "you run a grave risk of getting into clashes with the president." It would be best, he suggested, to speak to LBJ only before and after meetings. Rielly says that he recognized that Humphrey's views would not line up with Johnson's, and Johnson wouldn't like it.[14]

Johnson convened another meeting of the NSC on the 10th. This would be the first time Vietnam was discussed in Humphrey's presence. Johnson wanted to order another round of strikes. Undersecretary of State George Ball, the lone skeptic of escalation among senior figures, argued for a pause while Soviet premier Alexei Kosygin was in Hanoi. McNamara, Bundy, and CIA director John McCone wanted to go ahead; the defense secretary nominated specific targets. Johnson then asked whether all those present agreed. Humphrey had not yet opened his mouth. "He had vowed to his wife, his staff and his closest friends that he would not speak up on Vietnam at a meeting," Rielly recalls. But now, Humphrey jumped in on Ball's side, saying he had "mixed feelings about whether we should retaliate as Secretary McNamara had recommended."[15] Johnson, who was looking for consensus, not dissent, especially from Humphrey, seethed—inwardly, for the moment.[16]

The following day, Humphrey and Ball spoke, agreeing that they must find a way to focus the president on the dangerous consequences of the escalation. The State Department Bureau of Intelligence and Research—Tom Hughes's fief—had concluded that bombing the North would not raise Saigon's morale, as McNamara and Bundy hoped it would; that Washington would then be forced to send in ground troops; and that such escalation could bring China into the war.[17] Hughes called Humphrey, then hunting quail at the Georgia plantation of his friend Ford Bell, chairman of a chain of Minnesota supermarkets. Humphrey asked Hughes to get on a plane right away in order to deliver a briefing in person. Once he had heard the latest intelligence, Humphrey, who had convinced himself that Johnson could still be persuaded to see the light, asked Hughes to write a memo arguing against escalation. Hughes says that while he did all the drafting, Humphrey insisted that the memo be written as counsel from one politician to another.[18]

"You do not need me to analyze or interpret our information from Vietnam," Humphrey wrote. What he did bring to the president, Humphrey said, was an "ability to relate politics and policies"—which was quite true. Humphrey then observed that "a military attack on North Vietnam, with the attendant risk of Chinese involvement," would jeopardize all the progress Johnson had made and hoped to make in US relations with Russia. It would "shift the administration's emphasis from the Great Society oriented programs to further military outlays." Such a war might lose the support of the American people, who had yet to hear a compelling account of the national interest at stake in this faraway country, and who remembered all too well the failures of the last Asian land war, in Korea. They would ask why America was making sacrifices for "a country which is totally unable to put its own house in order." If the ultimate goal was a negotiated settlement, why not seek it now, before more blood was shed? Barry Goldwater could no longer compel the administration to prove its toughness. There would never be a moment when the president could so well afford to "cut losses."[19]

Humphrey would later feel so proud of this memo that he would include a draft of it in his autobiography. And rightly so: very few documents written at this early stage of the war predicted the consequences of escalation with such eerie prescience. The vice president delivered the report to Johnson's aide Bill Moyers on February 17. Moyers later said that Humphrey had only intended to have the document read by the president's aides, but that he—Moyers—had made the terrible mistake of giving it to Johnson. That is possible but unlikely, since Humphrey very consciously addressed the memo to "you," the president. The effect, however, was cataclysmic. Far from feeling that he was receiving sage counsel from a peer, Johnson regarded the report—like the comments in the NSC meeting—as a violation of the promise to speak up only behind closed doors that he had drawn from Humphrey in blood the year before. "We do not need all these memos," Johnson shouted. "I do not think you should have them around your office."[20]

The president now made it brutally clear to Humphrey that his foreign policy role did not include expressing his own opinion. On that same February 17, the vice president delivered a speech in New York honoring Pope John XXIII's encyclical *Pacem in Terris*. McGeorge Bundy had taken Rielly's draft and reduced it to a string of vacuous platitudes. After the speech, Rielly found himself in an elevator with Humphrey and William Benton, who turned to his dear friend and said, "That was the worst speech you ever gave." That same day, the Senate began a debate on Vietnam that included some of the first serious criticism Johnson had encountered. The president instructed Humphrey to gather the critics, who included Frank Church, George

McGovern, and Gaylord Nelson of Wisconsin, in his office at the Capitol. There they received a stern lecture from McGeorge Bundy. Nelson later recalled that the national security adviser told them that he had read their comments in the *Congressional Record*, and while he certainly did not impugn their sincerity, their remarks might lead people to believe that "the country isn't behind the president." The legislators bristled at the implication that criticism of the war was unpatriotic, which made them, if anything, even less willing to defer to the White House line. Throughout this tense exchange Humphrey sat silently at his desk.[21]

Johnson expressed his fury with Humphrey by moving discussion of Vietnam policy and strategy to Tuesday lunches, where he did not have to invite Humphrey—and didn't. Rielly got wind of the meetings and asked Bill Connell to ask an NSC official if Humphrey was invited. As with Rielly's request for the Vietnam report a few months earlier, White House officials were afraid to give any answer at all. The NSC official asked Bundy, who in turn asked the president—who, Rielly later heard, shouted, "Can't I have a meeting in this town without everyone hearing about it?" The situation was humiliating, for the vice president could neither express his views on Vietnam nor even learn where policy stood, which made it almost impossible for him to talk about the war in public. He thought about sending Bundy a note about the Agency for International Development's operations in Vietnam—a subject he knew a great deal about—but decided that doing so would be "demeaning." Should he transmit ideas to the president's young press secretary, Bill Moyers, to whom Johnson was now turning for information on Vietnam, and who seemed uneasy with the McNamara-Bundy view? In May Humphrey proposed to Rielly that he send a memo on Vietnam to Johnson. Rielly responded with a comment that must have been almost as painful to write as to receive: "I think this will be mis-interpreted as an attempt by someone who has been cut out to get back in."[22] Humphrey was so thoroughly shut out of national security issues that he had no idea that Johnson had ordered troops into the Dominican Republic in April until he started receiving frantic phone calls from his many contacts in Latin America.

Humphrey's humiliation became public July 14, when the *New York Times* published on its front page a picture of Johnson with sixteen of his advisers on Vietnam emerging from a Tuesday lunch. Humphrey wasn't there, though a figure as junior as Carl Rowan, head of the US Information Agency, was. At a press conference the next day, Moyers was asked why Humphrey hadn't been included. "I know of no particular reason," Moyers said. "The President has been conferring with each of his advisors."

"The Vice President has not been in any of them?"

"No."[23]

Humphrey's transgression was wildly out of proportion to Johnson's punishment. Johnson hadn't told him not to send him private reports, while at the NSC he had done nothing more than side with George Ball. Johnson not only accepted but welcomed criticism of his policy when it came from Ball. Indeed, several weeks later, Ball submitted a memo he had written the previous fall directly contradicting Bundy, saying that "losing" Vietnam would not hurt American prestige. By this time Johnson had already loosed the dogs of war; yet he virtually memorized Ball's memo and called a special NSC meeting to discuss it. Some part of Johnson surely believed that Ball was right, and at the very least, he wanted to force McNamara and Bundy to respond. Yet when Humphrey made a far less sweeping argument, Johnson dismissed it contemptuously. "In a choice," he said in a White House meeting, "between Humphrey and General Taylor"—the US ambassador to Vietnam, Maxwell Taylor, a staunch hawk—"I would be disposed towards Taylor."[24]

Ball himself was shocked at the president's treatment of Humphrey, which, he said, "reminded me of the old system of hazing a college freshman."[25] Johnson really wanted Humphrey to serve as a partner in advancing his agenda; but he also wanted, or needed, to dominate and humiliate him. In his memoirs of the administration, Joseph Califano, then a young Defense Department aide, wrote that he had assumed that Johnson would never do to Humphrey what Kennedy had done to him, but within weeks of the inauguration he was hearing from Jack Valenti that any Humphrey requests for help from the Pentagon would have to be cleared through the White

House.[26] That was true. When Humphrey's aides asked for authorization for the vice president to use the JSTARS planes that LBJ himself had used for official travel, they were told that each trip would have to be cleared with a White House military aide. When LBJ, on the Potomac River in the presidential yacht, saw a White House boat nearby and learned that Humphrey had been given it to entertain visiting dignitaries, he issued an order—no more boats for Humphrey. Johnson refused to give high-security clearance to a national security official whom McNamara had detailed to the vice president's office. In June, Johnson's aide Marvin Watson wrote that Bill Connell had asked that a small mess be set aside for Humphrey's use in the Executive Office Building, along with a navy steward and a valet. Johnson checked "No."

Kennedy had utterly disregarded Johnson's advice and expertise, but he hadn't demeaned him in this petty fashion. What's more, Johnson routinely belittled and ridiculed Humphrey to aides and to reporters. Humphrey knew this, and it made him live in fear of the president. It made him compliant; and perhaps that was the ultimate goal of the hazing. Yet Johnson would have said that he had a good reason for his impatience with, and even distrust of, his own vice president: he was convinced that Humphrey suffered from what he called "Minnesota running-water disease." Humphrey, he thought, couldn't be trusted to keep secrets from the press. That was part of the message that he had told Jim Rowe to drill into his prospective running mate. In late July 1964, he had told Rowe, "Hubert leaks everything to the papers, and you've got to sit him down and say, if there's one thing I can't stand it's a confidant of mine that leaks things." And then, a week later, after he became convinced that Humphrey had leaked the substance of secret briefings over the Gulf of Tonkin incident in a television appearance, Johnson conveyed a serious threat to his proxy: "This boy our friend Hubert is just destroyin' himself with his big mouth. He's just got hydrophobia."[27] Once Humphrey became vice president, Johnson regularly complained to Bundy that either Humphrey or his staff was leaking national security briefings.

Johnson's aides came to accept the diagnosis of Minnesota running-water disease. Marvin Watson, technically the president's

"appointments secretary" but functionally one of his spies and operatives, later wrote, "Humphrey trusted reporters. He ceaselessly confided in them. He believed that if he was frank with them, they would
honor his confidences, understand his problems and treat him well
in their stories." Watson recalled that Johnson had dispatched him
"dozens of times" to admonish Humphrey about those undue confidences.[28] It is certainly true that Humphrey was extremely fond of
reporters and was close to leading Washington columnists, such as
Drew Pearson and the Alsop brothers. He didn't think twice about
inviting a reporter to his summer place in Waverly. Andrew Glass, the
head of the *New York Herald Tribune*'s Washington bureau from 1962
to 1964, and then a reporter for the *Washington Post*, says that he used
to stop by Humphrey's office in the Executive Office Building on the
way home from work and, often finding the vice president alone, chat
about policy, or anything else, for twenty minutes or so. That was how
senior political figures worked and socialized with the press in those
palmy days.

But Glass says that Humphrey was not a leaker. "Occasionally he
would tell you something off the record," Glass recalls; "but that was
rare."[29] And Humphrey was almost certainly innocent of leaking
anything about deliberations over the Gulf of Tonkin. In the only
television appearance he made during that time, on *Face the Nation*,
he revealed nothing he could have learned in a White House briefing. But even if Johnson's suspicions had little basis in fact, including
in the surveillance he may have been conducting, his distrust wore
away at Humphrey. The vice president's aides, deeply loyal, watched
in pain as their boss's apparently infinite supply of *élan vital* drained
away. According to Patricia Gray, Humphrey's longtime appointments secretary,

> The vice president would go and meet privately with LBJ about
> Vietnam. Then he would come back and come into the office and
> close his door. He *never* closed his door. If he closed the door,
> you knew that it had been a very difficult meeting. Or I would get
> a call from the president's military guy and he would say, "You
> know that speech in LA the vice president has tonight? We've

had to take the vice president's plane for maintenance, so you're going to have to cancel all of that." That kind of thing happened repeatedly.[30]

One practical consequence of Johnson's pique was his refusal to let Humphrey travel abroad, despite the enticing prospects he had held out the previous August. When Winston Churchill died in February, Johnson himself had the flu. His aide Bill Moyers later said, "He didn't want Humphrey to have the attention that he would have liked to have had at Churchill's funeral."[31] Johnson toyed with the question for days before sending Chief Justice Earl Warren instead—a minor humiliation that Washington insiders took as an early sign of the president's conflicted attitude toward his vice president. Secretary Rusk routinely received requests from ambassadors, including from Chester Bowles in India and Maxwell Taylor in Vietnam, for a vice presidential visit. The answer was always no, and sometimes angrily so.

At times Johnson said that he needed Humphrey on civil rights and domestic legislation, which was true; but the message that he sent was that this longtime member of the Senate Foreign Relations Committee would have no role in foreign affairs. In an April television interview, *New York Times* columnist Tom Wicker asked Humphrey if he planned to go abroad, and Humphrey, working himself up into a lather of loyal submission, responded, "A vice president ought to bend himself in every way to lean over backwards, as we say, to be in tune with, and working with, and cooperating with, at all times with his President." After Humphrey rhapsodized about LBJ's leadership gifts and about the glorious times to come, Wicker asked what, exactly, he hoped to do in order to best contribute to the president's work. Humphrey was ready with a reply: "To give him a sense of my feeling of friendship, of loyalty, of comfort."[32]

Leaning over backward was nothing new for Humphrey, at least in regard to Johnson. But something even worse seemed to be creeping into his manner—the flinch, or cringe, of a creature who expects a beating. In May, Bill Connell, who had the standing with Humphrey to speak brutal truths, wrote a memo to which he attached yet another article in which the latter had fawned on the president and poked fun at himself. He told Humphrey to stop joking about his long-windedness and to resist the impulse to say, as he was wont to do, "I have to try harder; I'm only number two." Stop asking Bill Moyers or Jack Valenti to intercede for you with the president. "The President must never get the idea that you are at the level of his staff." That, after all, would only encourage Johnson to treat Humphrey like staff.[33]

A new view of Humphrey was taking hold: that the poor man was a puppet dancing at the end of Johnson's string. That spring, Tom Lehrer sang a wicked song about Humphrey on the satirical news show *That Was the Week That Was.*

> *Once a fiery liberal spirit*
> *But now when he speaks, he must clear it*
> *Second fiddle's a hard part, I know*
> *When they don't even give you a bow. . . .*
> *Does Lyndon, recalling when he was VP*
> *Say, "I'll do unto you as they did unto me?"*
> *Do you dream about staging a coup?*
> *Hubert, what's happened to you?*[34]

THE ANSWER TO LEHRER'S DROLL QUESTION WAS NOT AS SIMPLE, OR as mortifying, as he and his listeners imagined. Since Johnson still needed Humphrey, the vice president still mattered. In a conversation March 6, Johnson said to Humphrey, "I want to go to the Texas delegation every day. I don't want to be sitting here receiving the ambassador from Ghana. . . . But I can't do it. The Vice President *can.*" Johnson worried that Senate Majority Leader Mansfield and Speaker of the House Carl Albert weren't keeping close tabs on legislation. Humphrey would have to keep close tabs on *them.* "I don't care if it's the Humphrey-Johnson program," the president said (a comment that strained credulity). "This is a dual operation." The whole White House apparatus would be at Humphrey's disposal on legislation. Johnson, who never expressed confidence until victory was in the bag, was worried about education, Medicare, relief for Appalachia, the Voting Rights Act. He was worried about a group of liberals organized by

Congresswoman Edith Green of Oregon. "Have two of them to your home on Sunday," Johnson ordered. "Have two of them to breakfast on Monday, two in the office in the afternoon . . . and their names are going to be written in fire on every schoolhouse in the country."

"Yes, sir."

"Good-bye."[35]

Even as he was being exiled from national-security debates, Humphrey was on Capitol Hill lobbying congressmen and planning strategy with Mansfield and Albert. Johnson kept urging him to hound both cabinet members and congressional leaders to keep legislation moving through the hopper. "It'll make a great president or a great emperor out of you if you'll just be here and do these things," Johnson told him in the tone he sometimes adopted toward Humphrey— flattery that felt more like raillery. "Be here and do these things" may also have been a semi-veiled reference to the ban on foreign travel.[36] During the summer, after Johnson had expressed concern about the reliability of the seventy freshman Democrats, Humphrey reported that he had "met with each and every one" of them at receptions, at his home, or on the Potomac boat cruises that the president would soon ban.

Humphrey's job of legislative quarterback mattered most to Johnson, but by far his most consequential role was in coordinating the vast federal machinery of civil rights compliance as head of the President's Council on Equal Opportunity. The question that Humphrey and his team found themselves having to answer again and again was: How can the government get cities and states, unions and employers, schools and hospitals, to obey the innumerable mandates contained in the Civil Rights Act and other legislation? If they would not act on their own, what form of compulsion was the government prepared to deploy? Even before the council first met on March 2, Hobart Taylor, executive director of the President's Committee on Equal Employment Opportunity, a Kennedy-era body, wrote to Humphrey's aide John Stewart to flag a serious problem: owing to total intransigence from trade unions, virtually no Blacks held skilled positions at the construction site of the massive Cleveland Federal Office Building—a violation of Title IV of the Civil Rights Act. The sheet metal local had 1,225 members, of whom 55 were Black. All apprentice jobs were filled by whites. "I am advised that the Cleveland situation is general around the country," Taylor wrote.[37]

A late April memo to John Stewart from David Filvaroff, chief of staff of the President's Council on Equal Opportunity, captures the remarkable range of the group's agenda. Alabama officials, apparently acting under direct orders from George Wallace, were openly defying orders to hire Blacks to work in local offices of federal agencies; major government agencies, including civil rights bodies, were themselves falling far short of promises to increase hiring of minorities; southern school districts had begun returning questionnaires from the Office of Education falsely claiming that they were completely desegregated; Martin Luther King wanted the federal government to withdraw all funds from Alabama unless voting registration went forward; the Cleveland situation was going nowhere; federal worksites in other big northern cities looked no better.[38]

Humphrey had deeper and longer ties to Black leaders than any other white figure in Washington. His office was the first stop for Martin Luther King, A. Philip Randolph, Roy Wilkins, Whitney Young, and the rest of official Black leadership.[39] From Johnson's point of view, Humphrey was the man to keep a lid on Black anger. In the midst of the crisis in Selma, Alabama, which began in February when state troopers violently confronted peaceful protesters seeking to register to vote, Johnson asked Humphrey to take up the issue in the council. If he was hoping that Humphrey would calm the hot-heads, he would have been disappointed. Humphrey wrote back to report what he had heard: "Confidence of the civil rights movement in the federal government is threatened."[40] Humphrey had gotten the same message from Martin Luther King after a meeting with him March 5. The only action any of the activists proposed was one that Johnson had so far resisted: introduce the Voting Rights Act. Fearing that the measure would be bogged down in a filibuster, Johnson kept vacillating. Only on March 9, after the horrific and widely publicized violence of the march across Selma's Edmund Pettus Bridge, when John Lewis had his skull broken, did he commit to sending a bill to Congress.

The South worried Johnson less than the North. What he and his White House aides feared above all was another hot summer of strikes, demonstrations, and even riots. A briefing paper prepared for a Humphrey meeting with the Building Trades International Presidents noted the widespread expectation of unrest in Cleveland, Newark, New York, Washington, St. Louis, and elsewhere over the lack of summer jobs for Black youth. Johnson put Humphrey in charge of one task force after another that all had the same purpose: stop the riots with jobs for young Black men. The Community Relations Urban Taskforce helped big-city mayors access federal jobs programs. The Special Cabinet Committee on Employment brought together the major federal agencies to find jobs for graduates of federal training programs. There was the Taskforce on Urban Problems and the Youth Opportunity Campaign, which, Humphrey boasted to Johnson, had created 253,000 jobs.

Johnson and Humphrey shared a deep, and, in retrospect, naïve faith in the efficacy of federal action on civil rights. If only, they thought, they could find enough summer jobs for otherwise idle Black teens, they could forestall the predicted urban violence. In fact, everything proved to be harder than they thought. When Humphrey met with the union bosses, he planned to threaten that the federal government would cancel construction contracts or report them to the Department of Justice if their locals failed to comply with civil rights statutes. But when the meeting produced nothing more than a promise by the electricians to hold an open exam for apprentices, the Johnson administration chose not to bring down the hammer, as Humphrey had threatened. In May, David Filvaroff wrote to Humphrey that the exam was not expected to yield any Black apprentices, whose average level of education was too low to pass. Eventually federal authorities agreed instead to work with the NAACP and the Urban League on a jobs training program.

Humphrey chafed at the administration's soft line. In August he wrote to Johnson to tell him about the problem of school district noncompliance: in Louisiana, fifty-one of sixty-seven school districts hadn't even returned the form asking for information about desegregation; Mississippi was almost as bad. Southern schools were not going to accept Black children just because the Civil Rights Act said they had to. Humphrey proposed that the Department of Justice initiate legal proceedings immediately, before the school year began.[41] Johnson declined. The president worried much more than Humphrey did about the political consequences of siding with the civil rights activists.

One of the most stubborn problems was housing. In 1962 President Kennedy had issued an executive order on housing discrimination that had applied only to a tiny fraction of new units; both the NAACP and Johnson's own Committee on Housing were proposing that the order be strengthened so that virtually all new housing be subject to antidiscrimination rules. But doing so would provoke much the same resistance that school desegregation orders had while exposing the entire private building industry to legal liability. In May, Humphrey wrote to the president to say that he "need not belabor the potentially explosive nature" of such a decision. On the other hand, at least three members of the group had threatened to quit absent a sweeping housing order. Humphrey judiciously suggested that they impanel yet another task force to find a way to accomplish the goal without issuing a new executive order.[42] Johnson, no doubt relieved, agreed.

In November, Humphrey invited the Housing Committee to meet with cabinet members. After listening silently for ninety minutes, he told the group that the proposal for an executive order "had been given full consideration," but owing to "grave doubts" about whether it could withstand court challenge, the White House had concluded that it was best to go the legislative route. That, too, would prove "an uphill fight," Humphrey conceded. In a memo to Johnson, he noted that several members wanted to dissolve the committee, which would have been a public relations disaster. He had reminded them that the administration needed the committee to help craft legislation.[43]

Every bill Lyndon Johnson had worried about at the outset of the term passed between March and August 1965—Medicare, the Voting Rights Act, the Appalachian Regional Development Act, the Elementary and Secondary Education Act. It was an astonishing record of achievement. Yet he and Humphrey found that all those laws, and all the task forces and jobs programs, could not forestall riots. The Voting Rights Act, Johnson's greatest achievement in the field after the Civil Rights Act, passed August 6. On August 11, a massive riot broke out in the Watts neighborhood of Los Angeles. Over the course of the next six days, sixteen thousand law enforcement officers battled thousands of people in the streets; thirty-four people died and more than a thousand were injured. What people saw on television were Black mobs trashing their own neighborhood. It felt like a dreadful rebuke to the liberal faith in government programs. The message of Watts seemed to be that the liberal agenda was powerless to drain the force of Black anger.

In the summer of 1965, Hubert Humphrey still mattered. The *New York Times* even ran a long article under a headline meant to rebut the Tom Lehrer song: "Ask Not 'What Became of Hubert Humphrey?'" The author wrote admiringly of the vice president's leadership role on Great Society legislation and on civil rights enforcement; the regular intelligence briefings he received; the high secrets of state to which he was allegedly privy. Humphrey might, it was true, writhe under what appeared to be a travel ban. Asked if the president feared he would upstage him abroad, an indignant Humphrey responded, "That's like Rembrandt worrying about a college art student." In fact, it was a thoroughly plausible suggestion.[44]

Johnson used his aides to convey his increasingly corrosive distrust for Humphrey. Most of these aides were very young; some of them had been starry-eyed devotees of Humphrey only a year before. In April Bill Moyers complained to John Stewart that he had seen a minister on ABC News say that Humphrey had told him and others to keep up the pressure on the White House on civil rights. Moyers had all but worshiped Senator Humphrey, who in 1963 had taken to the floor to demand that the Senate confirm this twenty-nine-year-old as deputy director of the Peace Corps despite his tender years. ("Did not Pitt the Younger, as a rather young man, prove his competence as prime minister of Great Britain?" Humphrey had thundered.[45]) Now he was the president's designated scold. In June, he called Humphrey on the carpet again over a quote in *Life* magazine.

Then the pressure escalated. In late August, Johnson called to read Humphrey a press report of the vice president's schedule. "Why don't you just try keeping this out of the papers?" Johnson said sharply. When Humphrey insisted that he had nothing to do with the account, Johnson flew into a passion. "You look at my record and see which one of us has kept out of the newspapers," he snapped. "I had to tell 'em today not to send over any more task force reports because we had one on the cities and *The Washington Post* published it, by God, before I'd even seen it." The president told Humphrey to fire his press spokesman. He raged on about the vice president's outsize media profile. At last Humphrey said softly, "I agree with that."[46]

Humphrey knew there was something wrong, and not only regarding Vietnam. On August 26—five days before the president yelled at him—Humphrey wrote a plangent memo to Marvin Watson in which he listed a series of recent events that he cautiously described as "inadequate communications on civil rights matters." He had, he said, been startled to hear that the president had appointed a task force to coordinate federal efforts in Watts, since the community relations task force that he headed had been working on the problem for months and was scheduled to convene; the White House had instructed him to cancel the meeting. The vice president had been equally dismayed to learn, through the press, that Johnson had directed HEW secretary John Gardner to notify school districts that had failed to prepare desegregation plans that they faced a cutoff of funds; the assistant secretary of education, Francis Keppel, had just sent out the same directive pursuant to a decision by the President's Council on Equal Opportunity. The White House had recently released a report on compliance with the Civil Rights Act that duplicated work the council was doing.[47] The implication was obvious: the White House was taking over the work of civil rights compliance.

On September 17, Humphrey sent one of his weekly memos informing Johnson of the work of the council. The following day, Johnson met with Nicholas Katzenbach and Joseph Califano, whom he had moved from the Pentagon to become his chief adviser on domestic affairs. Califano later wrote that Johnson said, "I want you and Nick to get together and put out a plan to get the civil rights program out from under the Vice President." Johnson, Califano noted, felt that he needed to make a push for a new raft of civil rights legislation, including a fair-housing bill to replace the Kennedy executive order, and doubted that Humphrey had "the guts, toughness, and ability" to see it through.[48] Did Johnson actually believe that? Given the guts, toughness, and ability Humphrey had shown passing the Civil Rights Act, it's hard to imagine the evidence Johnson had in mind. Johnson's phone conversations from that period contain no sign that he had lost faith in Humphrey's effectiveness.

On September 20, Katzenbach delivered a memo to Johnson asserting that civil rights compliance had "put an almost impossible burden on the Vice-President," who lacked the staff to coordinate functions across the federal government. It's not clear if Katzenbach actually believed this; the real problem, he later wrote, was "Humphrey's desire to always please black leaders without adequate consideration of other constituencies."[49] Katzenbach proposed that much of the responsibility be returned to individual departments under the coordination of the attorney general. Both the President's Committee on Equal Employment Opportunity and the President's Council on Equal Opportunity would be eliminated. There was a perfectly sound bureaucratic argument that Humphrey had originally been tasked with reorganizing the civil rights effort rather than actually coordinating enforcement action, and thus the time had come to restore traditional reporting lines. Johnson could have accomplished that goal without losing Humphrey's valuable counsel or causing him undue pain. He chose a very different path.

Later on the 20th, Lee White, Johnson's special counsel and adviser on civil rights, sent Johnson a memo preparing for a planned meeting with Humphrey. White wrote, "Although there is no written record, it is perfectly obvious that you issued the Executive Order creating the Council with considerable reluctance and indicated to the Vice President that it was to be a temporary body." Katzenbach writes of Johnson's initial reluctance; there is, however, no evidence that the council had been conceived as a temporary stopgap. White suggested that the transition be presented as Humphrey's own idea, thus obscuring the president's central role. "Humphrey," White explained, "can show his 'bigness' by recommending the dissolution of a group that he heads which has performed its assignment and no longer needs to remain in existence."[50]

That part of Johnson that took an almost sadistic pleasure in watching other men grovel before him must have enjoyed the idea of Humphrey publicly taking responsibility for his own humiliating demotion. On September 22 he called Humphrey to the White House. They were joined by Califano; no one else appears to have been present. Humphrey was expecting to talk about the progress of the civil rights agenda. Instead, the president, sitting in his rocker, said to Humphrey, "They say that the best way to strengthen these programs and speed up Negro rights would be to fold up a lot of the responsibilities you've got and put 'em on the Attorney General's shoulders." Humphrey, Califano recounted, turned pale as he understood what he had walked into. "But I don't want to move on it without talking to you and getting your views," Johnson continued. "Do you think it's a good idea to strengthen our civil rights effort this way?" There was only one answer to this question; Humphrey said that he agreed.

Califano said that on the following day Johnson suggested that he have Humphrey sign a memo proposing the change of responsibility. He wanted this token of Humphrey's acquiescence that very day. At 7:00 p.m., Califano went to Humphrey's office, handed him the memo, and asked him to have it typed up on his own stationery and signed. Here Humphrey balked, if barely; he wanted to discuss it first with his staff. But Califano was under orders; he asked Humphrey to give him vice presidential stationery so that he could have the memo typed up and delivered back to Humphrey for signature. At 1:20 the morning of the 24th, Califano and Lee White sent Johnson Humphrey's memo and a draft of the gracious thank-you letter the president would send in response. Johnson woke up with a bright idea: "If the Vice President is so enthusiastic about this reorganization, why doesn't he come over here and announce it himself, instead of my announcing it?"

Perhaps the president wanted to watch his puppet dance; if so, he got his wish. The next day, Bill Moyers and Humphrey presented the decision to reporters. Moyers explained that "the President agreed to implement the recommendation that the Vice President is making," adding that Humphrey would "continue . . . to work very closely as the President's chief advisor in the field of civil rights." Humphrey insisted that the president had given him six months to reorganize civil rights agencies, and that time was now up. A reporter asked, "You no longer have any title save your commission from the President?"

"I'm still the Vice President."

The press at least claimed to buy the imposture. The story in the *Washington Post* the next day began, "Acting on a recommendation from Vice President Humphrey . . ."[51] But no one in the know was fooled. In mid-October the *Times* wrote that Humphrey had signed the memo against his will; the whole affair had been shrouded in such secrecy that key figures had only learned they were to be divested of authority half an hour before the press conference. Two weeks later, Whitney Young, head of the Urban League, wrote in the *Baltimore Afro-American* of the deep concern in the civil rights community that Humphrey would be "unable to exercise his tremendous power of office in the insistence that civil rights decisions be made with minimum delay." Activists knew that Humphrey was more willing to defend their interests than either the White House or the Justice Department. Young added—as if it were necessary—that the decision had "downgraded Humphrey politically."[52]

Despite all the petty slights, Humphrey had begun his tenure as quite possibly the most important vice president in history. Eight months later, he was every bit the forlorn appendage that Tom Lehrer had made him out to be.

18

Vietnam Warrior

---

*"I fought those bastards then and I'm going
to fight them now."*

ALTHOUGH HUMPHREY HAD BEEN EXCLUDED FROM MEAN-
ingful deliberations over foreign policy only a month into
his tenure, President Johnson still had a role for him, the
role he had foreseen from the moment the two men got to know
one another: ambassador to the bomb-throwers. That was why he
had asked Humphrey to convene the doves to hear a lecture from
McGeorge Bundy in February 1965. The rising tide of criticism over
the war in the ensuing months had sent him into fits of rage. "I am
not going to have anything to do with the liberals," Johnson snarled
to his speechwriter Richard Goodwin that summer. "They all just
follow the Communist line—liberals, intellectuals, Communists."[1]
Johnson wouldn't talk to them, but Humphrey could.

Humphrey delivered more than two hundred speeches in 1965
alone; many of them were at college campuses where opposition to the
war was growing. The more he was challenged, the more combative

he became. In mid-May, while addressing a crowd at the University of Pittsburgh, a student asked the vice president how, "as a liberal," he could "explain the utterly ghastly, barbarous American attacks in North Vietnam." According to a newspaper account, "Mr. Humphrey reddened, his teeth clenched, his eyes flashed, and he pointed a finger at the student and shouted, 'I'm going to let you have it good.'" Humphrey then delivered a minutely detailed history of Communist infiltration in Southeast Asia. "What's been going on?" he asked. "Systematic burning of villages, systematic slaughter of the mayors of villages, systematic destruction of hamlets, systematic destruction of hospitals." Humphrey worked himself up into a furious passion. "We will not give up," he cried. "We will not be defeated. We are the powerful nation. . . . We're not going to weaken if it takes ten years. We've got what it takes to win this fight if we'll win it."[2] The students cheered; in the spring of 1965 most students still supported the war and the larger Cold War effort.

Humphrey was still steamed that night when he addressed the Jefferson Day Dinner at the Penn-Sheraton Hotel in Pittsburgh. "Don't you forget," he admonished his listeners, "that there is no difference between the Nazis and the Communists. . . . If we weary and tire, the Communists won't weary and tire. They are hard and they are dedicated. They seek division in our ranks and confusion. If we fail now, the free world is gone." Humphrey had believed that in 1947 when the enemy was the Communist Party of the United States, and he believed it in 1965 when the chief threat came from Red China. At the same time, he recognized that Vietnam was a nationalist struggle that could not be reduced to a chess game between black and white pieces; but that more nuanced understanding might not play well with the White House, which was listening closely.

Indeed, Johnson angrily rebuked Humphrey for saying in a speech that "the United States must be prepared for a long, costly, ugly war." That was precisely what Johnson most feared, and thus refused to say in public. He had begun sending in ground troops in April, and the American war effort escalated rapidly. In late July, the president delivered a message to Congress announcing that he was sending another 40,000 soldiers in order to bring troop strength to 180,000 by the end of the year. Humphrey concluded that he had to undertake an escalation of his own. He left a message for Johnson with his secretary: "I have a roomful of senators here in the Capitol, and we thought that the [statement] was tremendous. I personally was inspired and moved, and I couldn't be happier if they had Christmas every day and every dream I wanted came true."[3]

Humphrey never flinched from his job of justifying the war to its critics. In November he entertained Prime Minister Tage Erlander of Sweden at the Greenbrier spa in West Virginia. No country had been more critical of the war, and Humphrey spent much of the time trying to persuade this old social democratic friend of the merits of administration policy—as he afterward told Johnson. On December 2, Humphrey sent Johnson a memo describing a meeting he had held with Dr. Benjamin Spock and other leaders of the March on Washington. He had instructed them, he said, to dissociate themselves from the anti-American left, to criticize Hanoi and Peking as well as Washington, to bring their criticisms to him and to other "responsible officers of government" rather than "just parading and holding public demonstrations." The Johnson administration, he had insisted, was "wholeheartedly dedicated to the cause of peace."[4]

The private Humphrey remained deeply skeptical of the war effort. Tom Hughes continued to deliver briefings and took extensive notes after meeting Humphrey at home for ninety minutes December 19. "HHH thought we should try to break off some non-Communist elements in VC," Hughes wrote, "had to negot with VC." At present, he went on, "our required outcome is impossible; so not enough room for bargaining." He described Johnson as "a master politician being boxed in." Johnson was "using his power to get us further in in VN, not to get us out." As he traveled around the country he sensed "a great unease" over the war. "Pall over everything." We were, he said, "sacrificing all of our other policies, foreign and domestic," to "a tiny little place of enormously disproportionate interest."[5] That was precisely what Humphrey had predicted in the memo he and Hughes had prepared for Johnson.

By virtue of keeping all such seditious thoughts to himself, Humphrey had begun to work his way back into the president's good graces. In early December Johnson told Bundy that he no longer needed to edit Humphrey's speeches on Vietnam. And on December 19 the White House announced that the vice president would be going to Southeast Asia to attend the inauguration of President Ferdinand Marcos of the Philippines. (That was probably why Humphrey had requested a briefing from Hughes that day.) Several days later, Japan, Taiwan, and South Korea, key Asian allies, were added to the itinerary. This offered a tremendous political opportunity for the vice president. Earlier that month a Gallup poll had found that only 23 percent of Americans wanted to see Humphrey as president while 58 percent didn't. Staff members believed that he needed to take a more prominent role in national security matters in order to show that he was "Presidential material." Now that opportunity had arrived.[6]

On December 27, Humphrey left for Honolulu with Muriel; their eighteen-year-old son, Douglas; and Jack Valenti, whom Johnson had sent along to watch and report. The vice president was seen as a wounded figure, and not just because of the dismal poll numbers. A "new and rather colorless Humphrey," as one newspaper account put it, seemed to have lost the luster of the ebullient senator of 1964. He spoke too often and too thoughtlessly, reported another; his remarks were typically "thin and platitudinous."[7] Bobby Kennedy, now representing New York in the Senate, had just made a whirlwind tour of Latin America; the White House was thought to have dispatched Humphrey in the hopes of taking some of the shine off this potential rival in 1968. Johnson also had a more immediate goal: he had decided on a "peace offensive" to persuade the Vietcong—and his domestic critics—that Washington really did want to negotiate, and Humphrey was to strengthen his hand by winning commitments of support from Vietnam's neighbors.

The whirlwind trip took Humphrey through four countries in four days. In the Philippines he sweated his way through the outdoor presidential inauguration and visited wounded GIs. More importantly, he persuaded President Marcos to send a battalion of combat engineers to Vietnam. He won a similar commitment in South Korea. The vice president made no missteps; in Seoul he said he was "more optimistic" than ever about Vietnam now that he had gauged the commitment of America's allies.[8] And he sent a stream of encouraging memos back to Johnson. Marcos, he said, "is a man of great courage—firm, tough and mature." (Only years later would Marcos and his wife Imelda come to be seen as kleptocrats.) Chiang Kai-shek, the dictatorial president of Taiwan, had assured him that Hanoi was merely "a puppet regime"; the real enemy was Communist China. President Park Chung Hee of South Korea worried that the peace offensive could lead to abandonment of an ally. Anti-Communist Asia, in short, wanted more, not less, American engagement in Vietnam.[9]

The trip received scant coverage in the press and could not have done much to raise Humphrey's standing with the public. But it helped him with the constituency he cared about most, the president. Valenti had reported nothing but good news. Upon his return, Humphrey briefed the National Security Council on his trip, which Johnson publicly declared a success. And when Indian prime minister Lal Bahadur Shastri died the following week, Johnson, after initially bridling, agreed to send Humphrey as the head of a delegation that included Secretary of State Dean Rusk. The high point of the trip was a series of meetings, formal and informal, with Soviet premier Alexei Kosygin. He was, Humphrey concluded, no Khrushchev, but rather "one of those hard-to-talk-to Russians, reasonable about being unreasonable, going through those insulting comments but never personal, very proper." By now an old hand at sizing up world leaders, Humphrey was nonetheless struck by Kosygin's self-possession: "His hands, I noticed, were never weak and sweaty."[10]

Kosygin hadn't given an inch on Vietnam. Johnson's peace offensive had failed; he feared that he was pouring ever more men into a bottomless pit. In early February 1966 Senator William Fulbright, chairman of the Senate Foreign Relations Committee, would be convening hearings on Vietnam that would train a spotlight on the war's failings. Johnson had to find a way to accentuate the positive. In a speech at Johns Hopkins University in April 1965, he had spoken of Vietnam as if it were Appalachia before the New Deal. With

American help, he had declared, "the vast Mekong River can provide food and water and power on a scale to dwarf even our own TVA."[11] This was also Humphrey's dream; it was what made the Vietnam War distinctively "liberal." Now Johnson revived that vision, though more out of political calculation than actual conviction. The White House announced that on February 4—the date, not coincidentally, of the opening of the Fulbright hearings—the president would attend a conference in Honolulu with Vietnam's leaders to focus on social, economic, and political reform. He told Humphrey, cryptically, to keep his bags packed for another trip to Asia.

The Honolulu conference was a minutely scripted affair. Field Marshal Nguyen Cao Ky, Vietnam's prime minister, was a pistol-packing soldier who had expressed his admiration for Adolf Hitler. William Bundy described Ky and Nguyen Van Thieu, the head of state, as "absolutely the bottom of the barrel." Nevertheless, in an address written by American advisers, Ky promised a "social revolution" that would allow all Vietnamese to live with "respect and dignity." The Americans vowed to rededicate themselves to that goal. The two governments issued the Honolulu Declaration, in which the government of South Vietnam pledged to "eradicate social injustice" and "build true democracy." Some administration officials took these professions at face value. Secretary of Agriculture Orville Freeman, who was to work with the Vietnamese on rural development, recorded in his diary how deeply impressed he had been by both Thieu and Ky; he regarded his Vietnamese interlocutors as young, sincere, and eager to learn. Others took a far more jaundiced view. Robert McNamara had already privately concluded that Vietnam was a hopeless cause from which one could expect nothing better than "withdrawal with honor." In Honolulu he gave an off-the-record interview in which he described the Rolling Thunder campaign as a failure and conceded that "no amount of bombing can end the war."[12]

Humphrey was the most eloquent and committed spokesman for the liberal vision; that probably accounted for his attraction to Edward Lansdale's doctrine of counterinsurgency. Now, threatened on the left, Johnson ordered his liberal wingman into the fray. On

February 6 a Johnson aide reached John Rielly at 11:30 at night to tell
him that Humphrey had to be in Los Angeles at noon the next day
so that the president could brief him in person on developments in
Honolulu. He would then leave for Vietnam and half a dozen other
countries. At that moment Humphrey was flying back to Washington
from a speech in Chicago. Rielly frantically dictated a memo to his
wife, who typed it up, and raced to Humphrey's home at 1:30 a.m. The
vice president had just arrived; the two men spent the next hour planning a two-week trip of the highest national security importance for
which they had not made the slightest preparation. Neither even had
his shots. Johnson could, of course, have briefed Humphrey over the
phone or waited until he had returned to Washington.

Humphrey reached Los Angeles later that morning, boarded
Air Force One to confer with Johnson, returned to his own plane,
and took off for Honolulu with a high-level retinue meant to signal
the importance the president placed on the trip: McGeorge Bundy;
Averill Harriman; Orville Freeman; the ambassador to Vietnam,
Henry Cabot Lodge Jr.; and, of course, Jack Valenti. When he landed
in Hawaii on the 8th, Humphrey donned a lei and pronounced the
Honolulu Declaration "one of the greatest documents of our history."
His mission in Vietnam, Humphrey explained, would be to show-
case "the social revolution towards rapid human progress" now taking place there.[13] Humphrey left for Vietnam with his White House
colleagues, Lansdale, staff members Bill Connell and John Rielly, and
Thieu and Ky, who were getting a lift back home. The latter terrified
the Americans by ostentatiously twirling his pistols mid-flight before
restoring them to his side holsters.

On the 10th Humphrey landed at the giant Tan Son Nhut Air Base
outside Saigon. Tanks, artillery pieces, and fighter jets stretched off
in neat lines in every direction. Helicopters whirled overhead to provide security for the high-level visitors. The alleged social revolution
lay elsewhere; here were the colossal logistics of war. Humphrey's
initial message alluded to both of those struggles. "One," he said, "is
on the battlefield. The other is against poverty, illiteracy, and disease.
Both are being won." Humphrey immediately set off to the countryside to bear witness to that second war, visiting a model village called

New Prosperity and plunging into a dismal Saigon slum where young people—"Peace Corps–types," said the traveling press—were working to improve social and economic conditions. This was the sort of setting in which Humphrey shone. He taught children to say "hello," walked up to dumbstruck peasants, delivered impromptu speeches. Marshal Ky, the democratic apprentice, followed in the vice president's wake and was soon observed rolling up his own sleeves and addressing remarks to startled farmers.[14]

Humphrey sent a stream of upbeat cables to the president. The first reported that Vietnam's leaders "have returned from Honolulu buoyed up and with renewed vigor and determination to follow through on the program reforms discussed in Hawaii." More important, Valenti sent a cable to Johnson that day saying that Humphrey "has been tireless and good-humored and has made an excellent impression," including on reporters. He had focused relentlessly on "the war to defeat social misery." The traveling press, still largely pro-war, unlike many of those based in Saigon, made much of Humphrey's bottomless energy and enthusiasm and his love of children, and for that matter everyone else. "The Vice President," as one reporter put it, "is a people-to-people program all by himself."[15]

Humphrey went on to Thailand and Laos, where he vowed that America would not tire. He heard much the same message as he had during his December trip: the Thais worried about a domestic fifth column, which might overrun the country should America allow the Communists to win in Vietnam; the Laotians supported the American bombing campaign in the North because it kept the Vietcong out of Laos. From Vientiane he wrote to Johnson, "China wants war, not peace." His views hardened as he met one Southeast Asian leader after another who begged Washington to stay the course. "Here in Southeast Asia," he said, "they are not talking about nuance, they are talking about survival." Tom Wicker of the *New York Times*, traveling with Humphrey and no doubt privately talking to him, reported that Humphrey had "become convinced that the Asian problem was broader than the struggle in Vietnam and that it resulted from a Communist Chinese intention to expand its influence over all Southeast Asia and into the Indian subcontinent."[16]

The trip ultimately took Humphrey not only to the three Southeast Asian countries but to India, Pakistan, Australia, New Zealand, and South Korea—all within ten days. By the end, he had no more patience for nuance than did his hosts. In Wellington he was asked about Bobby Kennedy's proposal, widely supported among skeptics of the war effort, to include the National Liberation Front (NLF), the political arm of the Vietcong, in a coalition government. That, Humphrey shot back, "would be like putting the fox in the chicken coop." That crack made the headlines, though he said something else that may have been a more useful clue to his thinking. Popular Front governments, he said, "have been either paralyzed or taken over by the Communists working from within." Bobby Kennedy had been a yet more fierce anti-Communist when young than Humphrey had been, but he saw Vietnam in a very different light. Humphrey still thought about Minneapolis, and the CIO. "I fought those bastards then and I'm going to fight them now," he told reporters.[17]

After a very late dinner in Canberra, Humphrey and the aides on the trip began talking through the report they would write up for President Johnson. This discussion laid bare the drastically different views among them. According to Rielly, Valenti said, "If we don't stop 'em in Saigon, they'll be in San Francisco." When Humphrey repeated that domino-theory chestnut, James Thomson, a China expert with the NSC who saw the war as a nationalist rather than an ideological struggle, disagreed, producing what Rielly recalls as a "very, very heated exchange" with Humphrey. All of them were exhausted, and Averill Harriman ordered everyone to get some sleep. The next day Humphrey would be speaking to the Australian parliament; Rielly and Thomson had written the speech. Humphrey put the speech aside and instead launched into a fervent refutation of Thomson's dovish view. Vietnam, he said, was not a civil war but "the projection of a massive international communist doctrine at work—wars of national liberation being tested in the test tube of Vietnam."[18] That was the Hubert Humphrey that Lyndon Johnson wanted to hear, but not one that other liberals recognized.

The trip had been a terrific success, at least by Humphrey's reckoning. Valenti had given him high marks. So had the far more discriminating Averill Harriman, who wrote to Johnson that Humphrey's "whole-hearted reassurance of US determination was well-received everywhere and, I feel, needed." He added that the vice president had counteracted the negative effect of the Fulbright hearings. Robert J. Donovan, the Washington bureau chief of the *Los Angeles Times*, who had followed Humphrey on the trip, wrote that "there is no one—not the President, not the Secretary of State, not the Secretary of Defense nor any Senator nor columnist nor publicist—who is stating the case for American intervention with anything resembling the persuasiveness of the Vice President." A more skeptical assessment came from Tom Wicker, already doubting the merits of that case; Wicker gave Humphrey an A+ as a goodwill ambassador and a C as a "cheerleader in South Vietnam."[19]

For the past year LBJ had been squelching Humphrey's long-running affair with the Washington press. Now, however, the president put him on parade. Humphrey had no sooner landed at Andrews Air Force Base on February 23 than a helicopter whisked him to the South Lawn of the White House, hovering overhead for ten minutes so that the landing would coincide with the 5:30 p.m. news shows. Johnson, accompanied by Rusk and Bundy, greeted the returned pilgrim and wrapped him in a bear hug, congratulating him on his "mission for peace." Humphrey was not then permitted to speak; instead he released a statement proclaiming that "the tide of battle in Vietnam has turned in our favor."[20]

The following morning Johnson had Humphrey brief White House officials and leaders of both parties on his trip. Then he spoke to two hundred members of the six House and Senate committees that had jurisdiction over foreign and military affairs. The atmosphere was extremely cordial, but John Rielly was struck by the fact that the only Democratic senators who openly praised Humphrey were John Stennis and Strom Thurmond. "I could not help but think about the political distance he had come in so short a time," Rielly later reflected. Wayne Morse, one of the leading critics of the war, had much the same impression. "I never expected my Vice President to make this plea for war that he is making," Morse told reporters.[21]

Humphrey then addressed a giant press conference. The vice president reported that the Honolulu Declaration, with its pledge of reform, had "had a tremendous impact on every one of the countries that we visited." Asian leaders, he went on, now understood that they could only defeat communism by giving their own people "hope and promise and the reality of achievement"—precisely what Humphrey himself had been saying for years. Asked about his "chicken coop" metaphor, which had gained wide circulation as a proof of his conversion to Cold War hard-liner, Humphrey stated explicitly that any sign of American willingness to include Communists in a South Vietnamese government would "weaken the resolve of the Vietnamese."[22] He did not, of course, repeat his idea of December that Washington should negotiate with non-Communist VC sympathizers.

Humphrey's staffers, as well as outside officials, had been churning through drafts of the report he was to submit to Johnson almost from the time their plane had landed. Jack Valenti had said, "The president wants optimism," and he and Bill Connell, the in-house hawk, had written a highly optimistic account. Rielly and Ted Van Dyk had written a far more sober version. Tom Hughes read a draft on February 28; he found it "simple, naïve," and with "no skepticism of any kind." When he told Rielly that it was no good, the latter said, "You should have seen the earlier drafts." That night, Hughes met with the staff and the vice president. Humphrey embarked on a fifteen-minute monologue "on how out there communism was not an 'academic, intellectual exercise.'" Men were "fighting and dying." Humphrey recalled—rather admiringly, Hughes thought—what Ky had said to his own restive students: "You demonstrate and I'll shoot you." Humphrey ridiculed the dovish left at home in a way that Hughes found strikingly anti-intellectual. "The only protestors on Vietnam," he said, "are those beatniks with beards that never take baths."[23]

On March 3 Humphrey delivered a forty-four-page document to the White House. He summed up the contents in a brief memo to Johnson: "The tide of battle . . . had begun to turn for the better"; regional leaders now recognized that they must deliver reform; the American effort in Asia must rival the one in Europe; "We need Asian solutions to Asian problems." The next day Valenti told the president that Dean Rusk wanted the report to be suppressed. Nobody wanted to hear about Humphrey's Marshall Plan for Southeast Asia. Why not just have Humphrey send a note telling Johnson that he had already briefed him on his views? The report, which State Department and White House officials had labored over for two weeks, finally appeared as a bland seven-page statement that contained none of Humphrey's boldest recommendations for reform. That, Rielly sadly concluded, "confirmed the futility of the whole exercise." What it confirmed above all was that Johnson wanted cheerleading from his vice president, not advice.[24]

Humphrey was, of course, prepared to serve as cheerleader. Though the White House would not allow him to address the Fulbright hearings, he did spend three and a half hours defending the administration's position in closed session. Afterward he reported to Johnson that when it came to Vietnam, Fulbright "talks about it and thinks about it so much that he's lost his sense of judgment." Senators Albert Gore (senior) and Joseph Clark were, Humphrey thought, even worse. They all insisted that "we're not going the extra mile for peace and the Vietcong is just a nice little outfit." Johnson listened silently save to ask if Fulbright enjoyed the respect of his colleagues. "Two or three," said Humphrey.[25]

All the big news shows wanted to book the vice president; and for once he was permitted to oblige. On *Meet the Press* Humphrey asserted that "the rate of casualties among the enemy is running five to one over that of the allies"; that encouraging things were happening in rural development; that the rate of defections among the Vietcong was rising. President Johnson was prepared to negotiate, but the Communists spurned his every offer. Why were world leaders pressing Washington instead of Hanoi? Watching Humphrey deliver the administration's message on one of the shows, Arthur Schlesinger was struck by "a new and different Humphrey." His old friend was "hard-faced," he thought, "and uncharacteristically coarse in his language." Perhaps, Schlesinger thought, he was overcompensating for his own doubts.[26]

That may well have been true; after all, Johnson's ferocity felt like a device to keep his own terrible fears at bay. A more obvious explanation, and one that came to be taken for granted in Washington, was that Humphrey would do anything to return to Johnson's good graces; if this was the price, he would pay it. But the vice president lacked the dark gift of cynicism; he could not have spoken as he had were he not genuinely convinced of the rightness of his views. Like many Cold War liberals, Humphrey had long held mutually incompatible views of the developing world. On the one hand, he saw Chinese communism as an existential threat. A decade earlier, he had said, "Losing Southeast Asia is unthinkable. It cannot happen." Yet Humphrey also looked around the world and saw people unwilling to put up with immemorial suffering and mistreatment. He understood localized struggles in both ideological and nationalist terms. And then, like Bundy in Pleiku, he had seen "men fighting and dying." He had met with the leaders in the region and found them united in their fear of Chinese expansionism. Visceral experience filled whatever gaps were left in logic.

Yet it's hard to believe that, had he remained a senator, Humphrey would have allied himself with the hawks rather than the doves; he would have recognized the reality of the situation. But he hadn't. Tom Hughes, who deeply admired Humphrey yet was terribly dismayed by his new hard-line views, wrote a note to himself when he came home after meeting with the vice president and his staff. "HHH accommodates to his environment so instantly," he wrote, that he had been able to give a perfect speech in India and a perfect speech in Australia—"but you wouldn't know the same man delivered them." He had internalized the views of American allies in Southeast Asia, and of the generals and diplomats in Vietnam, and, Hughes reflected, of the "Philistine environment" of the White House. Now, Hughes wrote sardonically, "he almost sounds as if he is aiming for the Birchers." At the bottom of his note Hughes wrote: "The enhawkment of HHH."

HUMPHREY DID NOT WANT TO CHOOSE BETWEEN LYNDON JOHNSON and his old friends on the left; but when he had to, he chose without hesitation. Soon after he had become vice president, Humphrey and his neighbor George McGovern had gone to Sunday services at Chevy

Chase Methodist and then come back together to Humphrey's home. McGovern, who had himself made a futile bid to persuade Johnson of the dangers of escalation, now said he understood that Humphrey would have to support the president on Vietnam, but added that he hoped he could do so without "personally identifying himself" with the war policy. And Humphrey had flared up, saying vehemently that "he believed in the policy—that we had to stop the Communists or they would take all of Asia." Thereafter the two men avoided the subject at home, and a once close friendship became uneasy.[27]

Most doves were not so genteel. In the fall of 1965, Don Edwards, chairman of Americans for Democratic Action, had told the ADA's national board that American foreign policy had become "sick." LBJ, he said, was "apparently committed to an aggressive continuation of the bipartisan foreign policy followed by our country for twenty years, which is the avid pursuit of the Cold War." Edwards was still ahead of his board, which opposed unilateral withdrawal and worried about rising Chinese influence in Southeast Asia. But the military stalemate, and the rising count of both American and Vietnamese casualties, turned the organization increasingly against the war. In April 1966, when Humphrey wrote to Schlesinger asking for help with his upcoming keynote address to the ADA national convention, the latter responded that the two differed so fundamentally on the war that he could not furnish remarks that the vice president would accept. Humphrey's insistence that the Vietcong was the spearhead of a monolithic Communist force was, the historian declared, "nonsense."[28]

In his speech, Humphrey tried to take account of Schlesinger's critique; the NLF, he conceded, was not merely a pawn of Peking, but neither did it represent a majority of the Vietnamese people. Nevertheless, totalitarianism was on the march in Asia. "Saigon is as close to this ballroom tonight as London was in 1940," Humphrey portentously declared. If it was wrong to intervene in Vietnam, then it had been wrong to intervene in Greece in 1947 (where the United States had not, in fact, sent troops). But it wasn't wrong, for containment would work against China as it had then against Russia. Humphrey was wasting his breath: earlier that day, the ADA had approved a resolution stating, "We reject the unthinking application in Asia of our containment policy in Europe, or the false analogy of Munich." In fact, the resolution said, "the United States has only a marginal interest in Vietnam, or at most a self-created interest." That statement constituted a definitive parting of the ways with one of the ADA's founding giants.[29]

Humphrey dug in further. Two days after he spoke to the ADA he addressed executives of the Associated Press, mocking those who characterized the struggle as a "civil war" as well as those who suggested that the United States was no more likely to defeat the Vietnamese Communists than the French had been. The very next day the intelligentsia fired back: a group of twenty-four leading intellectuals, among them John Hersey, Edmund Wilson, Alfred Kazin, Anaïs Nin, and Muriel Rukeyser, met with Humphrey to present him with a petition calling on the Johnson administration to immediately end the bombing of North Vietnam and hold elections that would include the NLF. Few of these writers had ever admired Johnson, but many of them had regarded Humphrey as a thinker and an idealist; in their embittered disappointment they were far gentler on the president than on the vice president, whom they accused of hypocrisy, cynicism, and indulgence in the "Hemingway syndrome of runaway masculinity"—certainly the first time Humphrey had been accused of chestiness.[30]

Perhaps the most piercing judgment came from James Reston, doyen of the *Times*, who recognized, unlike the disillusioned poets and essayists, that Humphrey was sincerely persuaded of the merits of the war. "Like many others who have gone to Vietnam," Reston concluded, "he got caught up in the spirit of battle." Reston's tone was almost elegiac, for, like virtually all the other senior newsmen of the era, he regarded Humphrey as one of Washington's finest figures. "This was the mind that was more creative than almost any other in the Senate in the fifties," he wrote, "but it is scattered now in an endless tangle of little chores, ceremonial greeting and repetitive political arguments." Tom Lehrer's droll ditty had now come once again to define the vice president. Reston's article bore the headline, "Alas, poor Hubert!"[31]

Humphrey had left behind the family he loved for a new one that did not really love him at all. He was welcomed back in the White House. He began once again sending memos to Johnson with advice on Vietnam, much of it probably transferred from Lansdale and Phillips: forge closer ties with the Buddhist opposition, initiate a "massive" program of land reform. In mid-April Tom Wicker reported that Humphrey had been invited to join the Tuesday lunches where Vietnam strategy was hammered out. Wicker wryly reported that the vice president had finally found "a place at the White House table, just above the salt."[32]

19

Hubert Meets
the Sixties

---

*"I was raising Cain with the system
before you were born!"*

IN HIS FIRST SIX MONTHS AS LYNDON JOHNSON'S VICE PRESIDENT,
Hubert Humphrey had wielded more real power than almost any
of his predecessors ever had—and then suffered a public mortifi-
cation such as few vice presidents ever had. By the spring of 1966, he
appeared once again to be in his mercurial boss's good graces, but he
no longer held a position of authority in the White House. Joe Califano and Nicholas Katzenbach oversaw civil rights, and on matters
of foreign policy Humphrey could do little more than lob memos at
a distracted president. During the UN General Assembly meetings
in September, a desperate Humphrey offered to meet with "some
of the delegations and foreign ministers of the smaller countries"
who might not have been able to gain an audience with senior State
Department officials. He was a man who could not bear a vacuum.

His aide John Stewart recalled that Humphrey "threw himself enthusiastically into second-level administration assignments," such as the Council on Oceanography or the President's Council on Physical Fitness and Sports. "I'm sure it hurt him deeply," said Stewart, "but he was not a complainer."[1]

In 1966, as in 1965, Humphrey delivered more than two hundred speeches. He often ventured to college campuses to talk about the war. These were still early days in the protest movement, and Humphrey was typically met with fifty or sixty placard-bearing students who would walk out when he began speaking—the bearded "beatniks" he had ridiculed to Tom Hughes. At the Michigan State University commencement, the signs read, "Hubert Humphrey, Master of War," and the protesters delivered the new chant: "Hey, hey, LBJ, how many kids did you kill today?" Humphrey mostly took the demonstrations in stride, but at times he recoiled at being included in the hated Establishment. "I was raising Cain with the system before you were born!" he told the critics in Lansing. They must have been amused at that vintage expression.[2]

While Humphrey may have remained a Cain-raising Midwestern populist in his own mind, the protesters weren't wrong to regard him as a pillar of the Establishment. LBJ had ordered him to reassure the business community that the White House was on their side. Humphrey dutifully told the US Chamber of Commerce and the National Association of Manufacturers that the Great Society depended on the engine of the private sector. When the vice president addressed a group of forty-seven corporate moguls assembled by Roger Blough, chairman of U.S. Steel, he "wowed 'em," according to one guest, leading the columnists Rowland Evans and Robert Novak to marvel at the distance the vice president had traveled since his time as head of Americans for Democratic Action. Humphrey himself acknowledged in an interview with *Fortune* magazine that he had changed: "When life has been good to you, you become more tolerant."[3]

Life *had* been good to Humphrey. He had come to know virtually every powerful man in America and every important head of state. He was a friend of Frank Sinatra and stayed at his place in Palm

Springs. He no longer dressed in double knits and Regal shoes. The house in Waverly now included a heated swimming pool and a sauna, and he reached it by government helicopter. Finally, in early 1967, he had moved out of Coquelin Terrace to an elegant apartment in southeast Washington paid for by the US government. (The Naval Observatory had not yet been converted to the official residence of the vice president.) At a moment when the world had come to seem divided between a small cadre of older white men who held power and everyone else, there was no ambiguity about where Humphrey belonged.

It wasn't only the Vietnam War that had turned ugly for the White House. Though Humphrey much preferred talking about civil rights and the War on Poverty, he could no longer count on the moral simplicities of 1948. The Johnson administration had delivered almost everything that activists had once dreamed of—civil rights and voting rights, job training, urban development, "community action," expanded access to welfare, and new spending on schools. Yet America's racial climate had grown steadily more tense. The sense of common purpose that had filled Humphrey with joy during the March on Washington had become the stuff of nostalgia. The seeds of bitterness sown during the confrontation over the Mississippi Freedom Democratic Party in Atlantic City had now sprouted in ways that Humphrey could scarcely have imagined. Younger leaders such as James Forman of the Student Nonviolent Coordinating Committee had lost patience with white politicians. In the midst of the protests at Selma in March 1965, Forman had whipped up a crowd by shouting, "If we can't sit at the table of democracy we'll knock the fucking legs off."[4] In June, Stokely Carmichael, the confrontational radical who had succeeded John Lewis as head of SNCC, for the first time publicly called for "black power," in effect allying SNCC with anti-integrationists such as the late Malcolm X. In October 1966, Bobby Seale and Huey Newton founded the Black Panther Party in Oakland, California.

Humphrey had spent the past two decades identifying himself with the struggle of Black people. He tried to meet the new anger with a deeper sense of compassion. On June 1, 1966, the White House convened 2,500 civil rights and community activists, politicians, businessmen, and labor leaders for a two-day conference titled "To Fulfill

These Rights"—a very conscious echo of the title of the path-breaking Truman report, "To Secure These Rights." President Johnson, Thurgood Marshall, A. Philip Randolph, and others addressed the throng. In his own speech, Humphrey coined a new word, "slumism," to describe the all-pervasive atmosphere of the ghettos in which so many Black people lived. He may have been thinking of Daniel Patrick Moynihan's 1965 Labor Department study, *The Negro Family: The Case for National Action*, for, like Moynihan, who described a "tangle of pathology" in the Black poor, Humphrey spoke of "the burden of dependency and despair" that ghetto dwellers bore. This did not, however, lead him to criticize welfare or propose greater self-reliance as others had done in the wake of the Moynihan report. The vice president called for a renewed effort to reduce poverty and unemployment by federal, state, and local governments, churches and community groups, and business and labor. He condemned those who "see in the struggle for freedom and equality a license for irresponsibility and violence," but equally, and perhaps more forcefully, those who responded to isolated incidents with "heavy-handed indiscriminate retaliation against the many."[5]

The twin notes of identification with the downtrodden and rejection of extremism and Black nationalism continued to vie with one another in Humphrey's speeches. He emphasized the first to white audiences and the second to Black ones, which is to say that he did not pander to either. At an address to the NAACP National Convention in July, Humphrey expounded at great length about what he called "the dogma of our oppressors": that "a person's skin color determines a person's worthiness or unworthiness." Two weeks later, at a meeting of the National Association of Counties, Humphrey declared, "You can't tell people you have a nice place to sleep and swimming pools in the rich part of town . . . and nothing in the poor part of town. That's all over." If he lived in those conditions, Humphrey said, "I could lead a mighty good revolt."[6]

For all that he now consorted with the likes of Frank Sinatra, when he spoke of social justice Humphrey remained the inspiring figure, the romantic and the visionary, that he had always been. When he met in his office with a group of teenage beneficiaries of the administration's Upward Bound program, Humphrey threw away his speech and instead told them about his son Robert, who had just married a young woman who had been born poor but earned enough money to put herself through school and become a teacher, and about the president, who had been forced to leave school and then found his way back. Education—that was the ticket to the American Dream. He told the kids that whenever they were in Washington they should call him and tell whoever picked up the phone, "I'm one of Mr. Humphrey's Upward Bound boys or girls." He'd be there for them. *New York Times* reporter Nan Robertson reflected, "Few men in Washington, including President Johnson, can evoke that dream better and with more passionate sincerity, particularly for the young, than the Vice President out of the South Dakota Plains."[7]

LBJ didn't really like campaigning, and he certainly didn't like campaigning when his own name wasn't on the ballot, as would be the case in the congressional elections that November. Humphrey, of course, loved campaigning, for himself or anyone else. That fall, Johnson was happy to have Humphrey as the party's face in the hustings. Between mid-September and the November 8 election, the vice president campaigned almost daily, visiting twenty-five states, many more than once. A reporter following him across the Midwest noticed how happy he seemed to be to leave Vietnam aside and just talk to local voters. Barely waiting for his introduction to be finished, Humphrey, he wrote, "names the town, the county, the river, kids the local business leader about his business, gets all the intricate local titles right. Within five minutes he seems more at home than most of his audience." He recited the Pledge of Allegiance, with apt historical footnotes. He made fun of himself, telling his audience that the eagle on his seal "has his wings down, like he's not taking off for any place, like he's coming in for a crash landing."[8] The voters ate it up, like they always had.

But the Democrats crash landed. The party lost forty-seven seats in the House and three in the Senate, though it retained a majority in both. The stalemate in the war didn't help, but that drove very few Democrats to the other party. What plainly did hurt was the new issue of "law and order," code for rising crime and racial conflict. Even as

America finally granted Black people the rights they had been so long denied, the dramatic increase in crime and violence seemed to render a terrible verdict on the liberal project. Watts in 1965 was followed by Chicago and Cleveland in 1966. Between 1960 and 1966 the crime rate grew 60 percent, though the population increased only 10 percent; Blacks committed a disproportionate share of crime, especially violent crime (and were disproportionately the victims of both). Both the welfare rate and the rate of out-of-wedlock births among Blacks rose rapidly.

The political effects were devastating. In the middle of 1965, half of Americans thought the president was pursuing civil rights to the right degree or not fast enough; by the fall of 1966, that number had fallen to 39 percent. By the following summer, it would drop to 24 percent. Republicans discovered a new language. "How long," asked moderate Republican congressman Gerald Ford that September, "are we going to abdicate law and order—the backbone of any civilization—in favor of a soft social theory that the man who heaves a brick through your window or tosses a firebomb into your car is simply the misunderstood and underprivileged product of a broken home?" White working-class voters in the North, the core of the modern Democratic Party, were prepared to listen. Humphrey's friend and mentor Paul Douglas lost to Republican Charles Percy in his Senate race when white ethnics in South Chicago, who had long voted monolithically Democratic, abandoned him en masse. A new "silent majority" had begun to form.[9]

HUMPHREY'S FEALTY ON VIETNAM HAD RESTORED HIM, AS TOM Wicker had put it, to a place at the White House table, albeit an inferior one. He now attended National Security Council meetings at which Vietnam was discussed and sent advice on the war to the president—privately, in memos. (Humphrey had told Tom Hughes that while Johnson responded to his memos, conversations accomplished nothing, "because the President wants to do all the talking in them."[10]) But the terrible complex that Johnson's brutality had fostered in Humphrey, the flinch before the blow and the elaborate gratitude at the pat, was too deep-seated to change. A few months after returning from Southeast Asia, Humphrey recorded in a note to himself that the president was now receiving him for occasional long visits, typically in the bedroom where Johnson had retired for an afternoon nap. Sometimes LBJ invited him and Muriel for a movie and dinner. "On my birthday," Humphrey happily added, "the president gave me a watch, a razor, and three wonderful photos." The pictures were presumably of Johnson himself. At the August wedding of Johnson's daughter Luci, the president winked at Humphrey as he walked down the aisle with his daughter on his arm. (Even the *New York Times* noted that the only nod the president bestowed was on his number two.) It was "like two cymbals coming together in this clash," Humphrey later said. "He looked at me and right away I said to Muriel, 'I'm back in good standing with the man.'"[11]

That was true, in a limited sense. Humphrey's loyalty and effectiveness had stilled the endless chatter that LBJ would dump him in favor of Bobby Kennedy, who was now making a name for himself as an antiwar senator. "The melancholy days are ending for Vice President Hubert H. Humphrey," wrote columnist William White, on whom Johnson had long relied for strategic leaks.[12] But the almost sadistic satisfaction Johnson derived from belittling his vice president had not abated. In May 1967, Humphrey asked Tom Hughes, who had arrived to give him a briefing on Vietnam, to take a walk with him in Rock Creek Park. Both Humphrey and his staff were convinced that the FBI had bugged their office and possibly Humphrey's home, and Humphrey needed to get outside and even out of earshot of the Secret Service in order to tell Hughes of the most recent indignity. The Humphreys had invited the president and his wife Lady Bird to their swanky new apartment in a high-rise overlooking the Potomac. While the women were in the kitchen, Johnson stretched out on the sofa, scratching himself, and said, "Hubert, I hear you make the best speeches in explaining our country's effort in Vietnam. . . . I don't know what we'd do without you. Now Hubert, I'd like to hear one of those speeches. I'd like to hear what you say." Humphrey realized that the president was literally telling him to declaim, like a child asked to stand up on a chair and recite the Gettysburg Address. He tried to beg off, but LBJ wouldn't hear of it. So the vice president of the United States got to his feet and began reciting a speech in his living room to an audience of one. Or none, because Johnson then left the couch for the bathroom. "Keep talkin'," he said.[13] Humphrey could hardly miss the note of derision. Perhaps LBJ hated to keep reading about how the vice president was better at explaining his policies than he himself was.

By early 1967, defending the war to any audience left of center had become almost impossible, even for Humphrey. The problem was most acute on elite college campuses, where neither the president nor his most senior national security officials dared venture. Humphrey was still prepared to enter the lion's den. In February he addressed a student panel at Stanford University. The event was a dialogue of the deaf. Humphrey opened with some feeble jokes about the "Now Generation," which *Time* had voted "Man of the Year." His own nominee, Humphrey said, was Snoopy. Then he pivoted to solemn avowal. "I'm with you," Humphrey declared. "I want to be where the action is." The students blitzed him with questions about the growing national disenchantment with the war. Humphrey responded seriously and thoughtfully, as he always did, but he also made a claim that invariably enraged his critics. "The message of our division," he said, "is projected into Hanoi to give them false hopes." The students, that is, were giving aid and comfort to the enemy. They did not take it well. As Humphrey left Memorial Auditorium and climbed into his car, three hundred students rushed at him. Secret Service men and sheriff's deputies shielded the vice president from a screaming mob that pounded on the windows and sides of the car as it sped away.[14] The era of quiet walkouts and symbolic sit-downs was over.

That jeering crowd was a small foretaste. Sometime in the previous two to three years, the sixties had given way to "the Sixties"—the era of confrontation and rage, of radical repudiation of social and political institutions, of disdain for "bourgeois" values, of utopian dreams and revolutionary plans. It was the great misfortune of Hubert Humphrey's life that he reached the heights of political power in the midst of that tumult. More than any other of the major politicians of his day, Humphrey had dedicated his life to the pursuit of justice through politics. But the kids he was debating did not share Humphrey's faith in liberal reform or even his understanding of what politics was.

To young people growing up in the late fifties and early sixties the anti-communism that shaped the outlook of the Cold War liberals seemed like an almost laughable bugaboo, a cheap trick designed to scare off critics of capitalism. The 1962 manifesto of Students for a Democratic Society (SDS), known as the Port Huron Statement, argued that containment had proved "more effective in deterring the growth of democracy than communism."[15] The New Left, as it came to be known, regarded the Soviets as more hapless than dangerous, and thrilled to the liberatory language of Fidel Castro, Che Guevara, and Frantz Fanon. By the spring of 1965—at the same time that SNCC was expelling white liberals, and James Forman was issuing threats in Selma—the antiwar movement was turning against not just the effort in Vietnam but the very fact of American power. In April, at the first major antiwar protest in Washington, Paul Potter, head of SDS, made the shocking declaration that Communist forces in Vietnam and student protesters were "united" in their common struggle against "a system that frustrates these movements." Far from being Chinese pawns, the Vietcong were comrades in the battle against capitalist oppression.[16]

By early 1967 the administration, and Humphrey, had lost not just radicalized college students and poets but the liberal elites who had cheered their rise to power. In April, Humphrey asked Joe Rauh to assemble senior ADA figures at Rauh's Washington home for dinner and a talk about Vietnam. Arthur Schlesinger came, as well as John Kenneth Galbraith; James Wechsler—who had begun denouncing Humphrey in the *New York Post*; syndicated columnist Clayton Fritchey; and Rauh himself. These were not romantic idealists but hardheaded pragmatists. Schlesinger recorded in his diary that when the vice president was asked what vital US interests were at stake in Vietnam, "he lapsed into Ruskese and talked about 'militant, aggressive Chinese communism.'" The Asian leaders he had met, he said, were terrified of Chinese expansionism. This was absolutely true, but no longer convincing to these men of the center-left. Humphrey confessed that he, too, thought the White House should declare a unilateral halt to bombing in the North, but said that the president's advisers disagreed—and LBJ didn't listen to him. Many of these figures had been friends of Humphrey's for twenty years, and afterward they felt something like pity for the old firebrand. "Most of us," Rauh later said, "were struck by the sense that he was increasingly conscious of the dead end into which his own political life might be headed as a result of the war." Several weeks after the dinner, the ADA board voted to support any Democratic candidate who would bring the war to an end.[17]

By the summer of 1967, Vietnam had become, as Jack Valenti later put it, "a fungus, slowly spreading its suffocating crust over the great plans of the president, both here and overseas." American troop strength had passed three hundred thousand, then four hundred thousand, but the endless "search-and-destroy" missions and the ever-rising "body counts" of Vietcong soldiers did nothing to break the spirit of Communist forces. Meanwhile, American battle deaths would double that year, from five thousand to ten thousand. The gap between the president's relentless optimism and bellicosity and the truth that Americans saw on television every night began to destroy Johnson's presidency. By the fall, polls found Americans evenly divided between those who regarded Vietnam as a "mistake" and those who still supported the war.[18]

Vietnam was both a central fact and a symbol of the collapse of the confident, incremental liberalism of the postwar era. At home, the nation was burning; riots broke out in 150 cities in the summer of 1967. On July 13, a crowd in Newark, enraged by news that white policemen had beaten a Black cab driver, began to set fires, smash storefronts, and loot the stores. New Jersey governor Richard Hughes sent state troopers and then the National Guard to back up the local police. That only increased the body count: twenty-six people died during four days of violence. Riots in Detroit the following week reduced much of the central city to ashes. President Johnson, who wanted to have as little as possible to do with the riots, nevertheless felt compelled to send in units of the US Army's 82nd and 101st Airborne Divisions. The body count there reached forty-three. The "Long Hot Summer," which was to engulf New York, Milwaukee, and

Chicago as well as some southern cities, including Birmingham, displaced Vietnam on the front pages of the nation's newspapers and the top-of-the-network broadcasts.

Humphrey was powerless to affect policy in Vietnam, but he felt called upon to act as the riots jeopardized the work of a lifetime. He called Governor Hughes, an old friend, from a White House plane, and then sent a memo to Johnson saying that "tanks, half-tracks, large field pieces rumbling down city streets give the appearance of a major military contest." He suggested both that Black policemen replace the largely segregated National Guard and that officers receive riot-control rather than military equipment. This was wise advice; but after the Associated Press reported, wrongly, that Humphrey had promised Hughes he would send US marshals, Johnson blew his stack. Joe Califano later wrote that the president called him and commenced a tirade: "I've been good to Humphrey, haven't I? Why do you think he's doing this to me?"[19] Humphrey had to show Johnson the transcript of the call to calm him down.

The riots demonstrated the hopeless mismatch between federal programs of any kind and the infectious spirit of inner-city violence. Newark had received more anti-poverty funding per capita than any other major city. In Detroit, the auto-manufacturing economy had kept Black unemployment low and income and home-ownership rates high. Humphrey confessed to that city's mayor, James Cavanaugh, "If it can happen here, it can happen anywhere." That seemed all too true, yet Humphrey would not accept that the government was helpless to address the underlying problems that had provoked the violence. In late July he delivered a rafter-raising address to a conference sponsored by the National League of Cities, indicting Congress for cuts in appropriations and a "go slow, take-it-easy attitude" toward the administration's proposed spending on urban problems. The columnist Marquis Childs described Humphrey as "a one-man riot abatement squad," squeezing out every last summer job from existing programs or imploring the National Education Association to keep schools open year-round—knowing all the while "how marginal these efforts are."[20]

Riot abatement had, in fact, been part of Humphrey's portfolio, and that summer Johnson appointed him to yet another interagency task force, this one designed to review federal legislation for the cities. The group met three times; Humphrey reported to the president their despairing conclusion that the riots implied "widespread rejection of our social system and not simply dissatisfaction with conditions." Nevertheless, the group recommended a massive new jobs program. That was Humphrey's natural inclination; he had delivered a speech in Detroit a week after the riots in which he had declared that the federal government must spend "whatever it takes" to rebuild the nation's cities—i.e., an urban Marshall Plan. When he came back to Washington, Johnson had ordered him to the White House and barked, "Hubert, what makes you think you can go around announcing programs like that?"[21]

Johnson had a point. Vietnam had finally begun to force a choice between guns and butter, and the president was not about to silence the guns. In that year's budget, the White House cut funding for the War on Poverty from $2.5 billion to $1.6 billion—a modest figure in a $157 billion budget. Califano told the vice president to forget about his jobs program and disband the task force with as little notice as possible. In fact, for all the heroic rhetoric and the epic legislation and the dazzling array of new agencies, Johnson's War on Poverty never devoted large sums of money to the direct creation of jobs. Job training and "community action" were privileged over direct infusions of funds. Humphrey began to wonder if that was a mistake. In one memo in late 1966 he told aides that "instead of constantly harping on the phrase civil rights, we ought to talk about jobs, education, housing." But civil rights didn't cost money, and those things did.

IF THE FOLK SONG THAT EXPRESSED THE MOOD OF 1964 HAD BEEN "We Shall Overcome," the tune of mid-1967 was "The Big Muddy," Pete Seeger's baleful allegory on Vietnam, with its celebrated refrain, "We're neck deep in the Big Muddy, and the big fool says to push on." It wasn't just the war; liberals increasingly felt that Lyndon Johnson was plunging the country into a swamp. A new question presented itself: Could someone stop him? That desperate hope brought together two figures who had been close to Humphrey and now broke with him: Allard Lowenstein and Gene McCarthy. Lowenstein was a kind of Humphrey alter ego, born almost a full generation later, in 1925. A brilliant Jewish kid from Newark, Lowenstein threw himself into politics and political causes; as president of the National Student Association in 1950 he had been an ardent anti-Communist and civil rights activist. He had, almost inevitably, gravitated toward Humphrey, working as a foreign policy aide in 1959 and then as a speechwriter in 1964. He had worked with SNCC in Mississippi, and inside the organization had defended the Atlantic City compromise. But Lowenstein remained tied to the student movement; in late 1966 he had brought a group of thirty-nine student body presidents to meet with Dean Rusk. When a student had asked what would happen if the United States dropped a nuclear bomb on Vietnam, the secretary of state had taken a long drag on his cigarette and said, "Well, someone's going to get hurt." That confirmed their growing belief that the United States government was being run by a bunch of heartless warmongers.[22]

Lowenstein continued to think of himself as a liberal; he became a bridge between the activists and the Democratic Party. After meeting with Humphrey and William Bundy he concluded that the war would simply grind on absent drastic action. In the summer of 1967, he teamed up with Curtis Gans, a young official of the ADA, to search for a candidate who would run against Johnson. They hoped to use the organization almost as Humphrey had used it in 1947 to break the Communist hold on the Democratic-Farmer-Labor Party; Lowenstein became ADA vice president in a vote that illustrated growing divisions between old-line liberals and the New Left. Lowenstein and Gans then went looking for a challenger to Johnson. At first they approached Bobby Kennedy, who declined. Then they spoke to George McGovern, who said that with his own reelection coming up the next year he couldn't afford to wage a symbolic campaign. McGovern went through the *Congressional Directory* and found that almost all the other doves were in the same boat. He found two who weren't: Lee

Metcalf of Montana and Gene McCarthy. Why don't you try one of them? McGovern said. Lowenstein approached McCarthy.[23]

Gene McCarthy's career had been intertwined with Humphrey's without either becoming an intimate of the other. The one ran cool where the other ran hot. A Catholic who had prepared for the priesthood as a Benedictine novice, McCarthy had a taste for speculative thinking, a perpetual sense of irony, that kept him at a remove from the furious debates into which Humphrey flung himself. The early hero of his political life had been Adlai Stevenson, whose name he had placed in nomination—thanks to a push from Humphrey—in a famous speech at the 1960 convention. His oratory was slow, sonorous, even-keeled, elegant, and very often witty. His politics were moderate; the fact that his name raised few alarms in the South had helped recommend him as a potential running mate in 1964. But McCarthy did not share Johnson's fervent anti-communism, and he had begun to turn against Johnson when the president sent the Marines into the Dominican Republic in April 1965. He called for an investigation of the CIA's role there and elsewhere. He questioned American arms sales abroad. In early 1967, McCarthy openly broke with the White House, speaking out against the Vietnam War at college campuses across the country. For the first time in a century, he said, the American people had begun "to question seriously the rightness of our involvement in a war"—a war that was, he believed, "morally unjustifiable."[24] Here, in the quasi-theological question of just war, McCarthy had found his voice, and his passion. By the time Allard Lowenstein came to his office in early October, McCarthy had seen an opening for a national campaign to stir opposition to the war; a Harris poll showed that only 31 percent of Americans supported the war. Three weeks later he told his closest allies that he was in.

At this very moment, Humphrey was intensifying his assault on the war's critics. On October 21, one hundred thousand people had gathered at the Lincoln Memorial to protest the war while another thirty-five thousand had marched on the Pentagon in a serio-comic effort, fueled by folk songs, to gain access to the war machine. Humphrey felt called on to respond. In an address to a business organization, the National Defense Executive Reserve, two days after the march, Humphrey repeated the arguments that he had made dozens of times—an expansionist China menaced all of Southeast Asia, and the United States was called once again to defend freedom from tyranny. "I have not forgotten the lessons of the Thirties," the vice president said. Then he turned to the protesters. "I feel sorry for the honest dissident," he said, "because of the ridiculous, abusive actions of some who say they do it in the name of dissent." But Humphrey also had a harsh question for the "honest dissident." Each critic, he said, must ask himself "whether his dissent will add to, or subtract from, intelligent and well-reasoned discussion of this issue." The Communists had driven out the French because the government in Paris "was divided and weak." That was their only hope for victory today.[25] Humphrey was saying, as he had to the Stanford students, that the war would be won or lost inside America, and that Gene McCarthy and his followers had taken the side of the enemy.

Humphrey now sounded no different from Johnson; and the president once again rewarded him for his conspicuous loyalty with a trip to Vietnam. In a September election, Vietnam's military rulers, President Thieu and Vice President Ky, gained a new democratic legitimacy by winning the posts they had seized by force. The White House regarded the election as a possible turning point for the country, though all such moments had proved illusory in the past. On the 27th, Johnson dispatched Humphrey to the inauguration in Saigon. He dispensed with the pageantry that had accompanied the vice president's previous trip. Humphrey would be accompanied not by the most senior national security officials, but by William Randolph Hearst Jr., chairman of the family company, and James Suffridge, president of the Retail Clerks International Association, a friendly union. Humphrey was going not to oversee the process of reform but to celebrate it.

He did so with a vengeance. Once in Saigon, after delivering a stirring toast to Thieu and Ky about the enduring contest between totalitarianism and democracy, Humphrey gathered the entire staff of the US embassy, as well as Ambassador Henry Cabot Lodge and General William Westmoreland, for a stem-winding address. He invoked the 1930s and the global struggle against "subversion and aggression" and the nuclear threat. He vowed that America would stay, and build, and protect. Having thrown away his prepared speech, he concluded with an Athenian peroration: "I believe, when the histories are written, Vietnam will be marked as the time and the place where men finally learned the lessons of the past." A *Newsweek* reporter wrote that Humphrey spoke "with the barely controlled frenzy of a football coach at halftime of an uphill game."[26]

Humphrey *knew* it was an uphill game. From his regular briefings with Tom Hughes, he understood how little the bombing had accomplished. He knew that Secretary of Defense McNamara had given up on the war and was planning to resign. On the flight to Saigon, Marine colonel Herb Beckington, his former Pentagon attaché and now a civil affairs officer in Vietnam, delivered a briefing that focused on widespread government corruption, popular support for the Vietcong, and the failure of Westmoreland's "search-and-destroy" missions. The Vietnamese director of cadre training in the provincial capital of Vung Tau told the vice president that "most district and province officials" were corrupt. In Saigon, the vice president bluntly informed Thieu that America would wind down the effort if the government didn't undertake serious reforms. Thieu listened, a cigarette smoldering in its holder. He flicked away a bit of ash and said, "No, you will be here a long time." Humphrey had gotten nowhere.[27]

Ted Van Dyk and John Rielly, who had accompanied Humphrey on the trip, prepared a memo for him to send to Johnson disclosing what he had learned. And Humphrey, who knew what the president wanted to hear, refused to send it. The report he sent to Johnson instead began by claiming that "the extraordinary performance of U.S. and Free World forces, together with the increasing efficiency of the forces of South Vietnam," had checked the military effort of the North, and had thus enabled the civilian campaign "to secure the confidence and support of the people of South Vietnam for their newly elected government." Humphrey conceded that the Vietcong remained entrenched in large parts of the countryside, and disclosed, if gently, the concerns about corruption; but he emphasized the commitment of the Vietnamese leadership to the work of "redevelopment and reconstruction." Strikingly, he stated that he had "come to agree with those who believe that our constant repetition of pleas to negotiate with the North Vietnamese strengthen their conviction that the U.S. government is weakening under the pressure of public opinion." That was everything the president could have asked for.[28]

Though utterly exhausted after an eleven-day trip that had also included Malaysia and Indonesia, Humphrey returned to the ritual fanfare: helicopter straight from the plane to the White House lawn; reception from the president and the cabinet; meeting with congressional leaders; press conference. Then, once again, he was sent out to deliver those Vietnam speeches that the president had loved so much that he had demanded a private recital. This time Humphrey bypassed the nation's campuses, where he was no longer welcome, in favor of the Grocery Manufacturers of America and the Farmers Union and the Young Democrats National Convention. In December Humphrey spent two hours defending the war in front of a thousand members of his own party, the Minnesota DFL. He handled the most hostile questions with aplomb; afterward, the Central Committee overwhelmingly adopted a resolution declaring "strong and unequivocal support" for a Johnson-Humphrey ticket in 1968.[29] Humphrey still enjoyed the profound admiration of millions of mainstream Democrats, including those at home.

Though Johnson had lost the nation's elites, the American people had not given up on the war. Many of those who opposed Johnson's Vietnam policy believed he had been too soft: one poll from late 1967 found that while 44 percent favored withdrawal, 55 percent preferred more escalation. A near majority of women favored withdrawal; a similar fraction of men wanted military victory even at the risk of war with China.[30] A deeply divided public yearned for news of battlefield victories. Then came word of shocking failure. On January 31, 1968, Americans watching the nightly news saw images of dead bodies, American as well as Vietnamese, on the grounds of the supposedly impregnable US embassy in Saigon. The North had begun the Tet Offensive, which targeted major Vietnamese cities and American military compounds. American and Vietnamese troops would ultimately roll back Communist forces, which would suffer terrible losses. But the onslaught had devastated Vietnamese morale and shocked Americans. The revered newscaster Walter Cronkite returned from a visit to Vietnam in late February to declare the war a bloody stalemate. In mid-January, Gene McCarthy's improvised campaign in the New Hampshire primary had limped along with a few dozen Ivy League volunteers; after Tet, hundreds of students, then thousands, joined the crusade.[31]

Humphrey wrote in a memo to senior allies in Minnesota that Tet had "totally failed" and actually increased support for the Thieu regime.[32] That was the White House line. But Humphrey later wrote that Tet changed the discussion inside the White House. He and others argued for a bombing halt. At one of his tête-à-têtes in the White House bedroom, Johnson said that he had decided to halt the bombing above the 19th parallel, which would spare Hanoi and Haiphong. "What you should do is stop it all," Humphrey said he rejoined—all the bombing in the North. But Johnson refused.[33]

As Tet delivered a dreadful verdict on Vietnam, so did the report of the National Advisory Commission on Civil Disorders—the Kerner Commission—argue that Johnson's domestic policy had failed in its greatest goal. The report, released February 29 over Johnson's objections, concluded that "little basic change in the conditions underlying the outbreak of disorder has taken place. Actions to ameliorate Negro grievances have been limited and sporadic; with but few exceptions, they have not significantly reduced tensions." Race relations were moving backward; the authors concluded, in their most resonant phrase, that "our nation is moving towards two societies, one black, one white—separate and unequal." The Great Society had barely scraped the surface; new programs in education, housing, and welfare would "require unprecedented levels of funding and performance."[34] The report was an instant sensation: a paperback version of the 462-page study sold two million copies. The president refused to address the findings at all; Humphrey, though very much in favor of the call for a Marshall Plan–like commitment to racial justice, complained that the report's insistence that white racism was to blame for Black poverty and despair came "dangerously close to a doctrine of group guilt."[35]

On March 12, McCarthy shocked the political pros around Johnson by winning 42 percent of the vote in the New Hampshire primary to LBJ's 49. Three days later, Bobby Kennedy, now convinced of the president's vulnerability, announced that he, too, was running. Humphrey, however, still felt supremely confident of Johnson's chances. On March 31 he and Muriel were scheduled to fly to Mexico City for a ceremonial signing of a nonproliferation treaty. That morning, while he was packing—a meticulous packer, Humphrey could not allow anyone else, including his navy aide, to help him—the president called to say that he and his daughter Luci and son-in-law Patrick Nugent were going to drop by on their way back from church. This was very unusual; presidential visits were always arranged by the White House. LBJ took Humphrey aside and showed him a draft of a major speech he was to give that night on Vietnam. Then he showed him another version in which, to Humphrey's amazement, he would announce that he would not run for reelection. When Humphrey implored the president not to give that speech, Johnson, close to tears, spoke of the terrible anguish he felt over the war, and over the divisions in the nation that he was powerless to heal. "As much as I've tried to do for the Negro," he lamented, "even they're against me." Only, he thought, by bringing the war to a conclusion could he salve the nation's wounds.[36]

Johnson had told Humphrey in 1964 that he did not expect to seek reelection. The thought had preyed on the president's mind more and more as he came to feel trapped by the war. In November 1967 he had told Lady Bird and Texas governor John Connally that he didn't want to run. But he hadn't told his aides. He had asked for a similar statement to be included in his 1968 State of the Union address, but he hadn't used it.[37] But Johnson was haunted by death, and by political death. The war had aged him terribly; Humphrey had seen the anguish Johnson felt at ordering "my boys" into the Vietnamese jungle. Now, as Humphrey and Muriel sat in the library of the ambassador's residence in Mexico City, they heard Johnson promise to stop the bombing above the 19th parallel, praise President Thieu's commitment to root out corruption, commit another thirteen thousand troops and another $4.5 billion to the fight. And then they heard him state that in "a house divided," as America's now was, he needed to remove himself from partisan divisions, and so "I shall not seek, and will not accept, the nomination of my party for another term as your president."

The Humphreys and their hosts sat for a moment in stunned silence. Then Muriel excused herself to go to the bathroom, where, stoic though she was, she wept. Her husband understood that the dream of a lifetime now glimmered before him. But in the spring of 1968, that golden opportunity looked very much like a poisoned chalice.

20

The Apocalypse

*"Chicago was a catastrophe. . . . I just felt like
we had been in a shipwreck."*

O NE DAY IN EARLY APRIL 1968, WHILE HE WAS STILL DEBAT-
ing with himself over whether he should seize the opportunity presented by Johnson's shocking announcement to
run for president, Humphrey confessed to his aide Ted Van Dyk, "I
have this feeling in the back of my hands." That was an expression
Humphrey sometimes used to describe his intuitions. "Bad things
are going to keep happening. If I run, I'll be engulfed by them."[1] Bad
things—unspeakable things—would, in fact, engulf Humphrey, and
the nation, in the ensuing months. First Martin Luther King Jr. would
be assassinated, and then Bobby Kennedy. The Democratic National
Convention in Chicago would descend into mayhem and madness;
Humphrey would gain the bitterest of victories. In the general election Humphrey would be ground to a paste between the millstones
of the right and the left. He would lose to Richard Nixon, who would,
a few years hence, become a hated figure for liberals. The loss was not

merely personal, for Nixon's victory would usher in an almost uninterrupted generation of Republican rule. Nineteen sixty-eight was the year the liberal consensus came to an end.

That night in Mexico City, Humphrey's emotions were in turmoil. The prize he had sought was within his grasp, but he had done nothing to prepare for a campaign. Two other Democratic candidates had already entered the race. Once the guests had left, Humphrey convened the staffers who had accompanied him as well as Muriel, their son Skip, and Edgar Berman, his personal physician and an increasingly intimate friend. They urged him to announce right away that he would run, but Humphrey told them to calm down and give him a chance to reflect and to test his standing with political leaders. When he returned to Washington the following day he held another meeting with key aides and friends, including Bill Connell and Max Kampelman. They told him that a flood of calls and cables had come in from longtime allies and party leaders urging him to run. George Meany called to say that within an hour of the speech both Bobby Kennedy and Gene McCarthy had asked him for his support. He had declined; Humphrey was his man, and he, too, wanted Humphrey to announce right away. Jim Rowe and Jim Farley, the old warhorses, urged Humphrey to announce. But the vice president still demurred. In a note to himself April 2, he wrote, "Quite frankly, I'm not sure I have the stomach for it, knowing the ruthless methods that are employed by both Kennedy and Nixon."[2]

That evening Humphrey went to New York to attend an annual dinner of corporate moguls given at the Waldorf Astoria by Gardner Cowles, owner of a major media conglomerate (including the *Minneapolis Star Tribune*). After the dinner, Dwayne Andreas asked Humphrey to come up to his Waldorf apartment to meet with a select group of supporters that included Henry Ford II and Sidney Weinberg, CEO of Goldman Sachs. They were all prepared to help fund a campaign. Humphrey was still taking the position that he had not yet decided whether to run, but no one close to him had any doubts. The press coverage was positive, and early pledges of delegates put the noncandidate close to McCarthy.

Humphrey's plans were brutally interrupted on April 4, when he learned, while speaking at a congressional fund-raising dinner, that Martin Luther King had been killed. In a spontaneous explosion of rage, riots broke out in Washington, Chicago, Baltimore, and a hundred other cities. Fifty thousand federal troops and National Guardsmen were deployed across the country. The nation's capital became an armed camp, with soldiers manning machine guns on the western steps of the Capitol Building and patrolling the White House grounds while shops were looted and burned to the ground. Pleas for calm from civil rights leaders, and from Humphrey, had no effect on the rioters and arsonists. America seemed to be convulsed with violence and revolutionary extremism.

Humphrey had to keep moving forward. On the 6th he asked Larry O'Brien, who had left the Johnson White House to become postmaster general, to run the campaign; but O'Brien had already committed himself to Kennedy.[3] Humphrey then turned to Walter Mondale, the thirty-nine-year-old senator from Minnesota who had cut his teeth in the Young Democratic-Farmer-Labor Party. Mondale suggested that he serve as cochair with Senator Fred Harris of Oklahoma, another young progressive. Humphrey, who felt that he needed their youth and liberal credentials to counteract his age and centrism, agreed. The following week, Dwayne Andreas invited Humphrey, Mondale, Harris, and several others to stay on his yacht moored outside the Anglers Club in Key Largo. On the way down, Mondale said to Harris, "I've been working for Humphrey since I was eighteen years old. We're going to have to make clear what our position will be."

In Florida, Mondale asked Humphrey whether he wanted the two senators to serve as figureheads. "No, I intend for you to run the campaign," Humphrey said. "You say that, but you'll wind up with two or three campaigns," Mondale rejoined. Humphrey swore he wouldn't. The three men, along with Andreas, Max Kampelman, and a few others, roughed out plans for policy papers, polling, advance work, fund-raising, and press relations and began laying out a state-by-state strategy. It was agreed that Humphrey would not enter the primaries: the filing deadline had already passed for some crucial contests, and in any case Humphrey would pile up delegates in an inside game. The effect of the decision, however, was that while McCarthy and Kennedy went to the people, Humphrey would win by holding private meetings with party kingmakers. No amount of window dressing could disguise the fact that Humphrey was the insider—the candidate of George Meany and Jim Rowe—against the insurgents.[4]

On April 27, Humphrey finally announced his candidacy before two thousand supporters in the ballroom of the Shoreham Hotel in Washington. For once he stuck to the script, delivering a short speech—only twenty minutes—in which he talked about his humble background, his decades of public service, his maturity, responsibility, and readiness to lead. The crowd was shouting and clapping, and Humphrey, carried away, added a spontaneous peroration. "Here we are," he cried, "the way politics ought to be in America, the politics of happiness, the politics of purpose, the politics of joy. And that's the way it's going to be, too, all the way, from here on out."[5]

Bobby Kennedy responded to that effusion of Humphreyan ebullience with a self-righteous sucker punch: "If you see a small black child starving to death in the Mississippi Delta, as I have, it is not the politics of joy."[6] Humphrey's own joy was sincere; but the times were out of joint. Perhaps a more serious sign of danger came the next day when Humphrey was featured on *Meet the Press*. In the absence of any sign of support for his candidacy from the president, Humphrey cautiously declined to even say whether he would like such a sign. Asked about his role in formulating policy on Vietnam, Humphrey said, in another exquisitely tailored statement, "I've had the opportunity to participate in the discussions that have led to decision-making." He defended Johnson's policy and lambasted Bobby Kennedy, who had said that the United States was intervening in the internal affairs of Southeast Asian nations. Asked to respond to Chicago mayor Richard Daley's blustering assertion that he would order cops to "shoot to kill" rioters, the vice president praised Daley's commitment to helping Chicago's poor before conceding that perhaps he "overspoke himself." Humphrey insisted to James Reston that "I am my own man," but since he could do nothing to prove it without breaking with the administration, which he would not do, he seemed frightened of his own shadow.[7]

Humphrey was the victim of two immense changes. First, the emotional and intellectual energy of the Democratic Party—though not its actual political center—had shifted well to the left, leaving Humphrey looking like a cautious moderate at a moment when voters clamored for decisive change. Second, after spending four years dancing to Johnson's tune, Humphrey now looked like a man driven by ambition rather than passion. The true believers who had once regarded Humphrey as the most effective idealist in politics, figures such as Joe Rauh and Jim Loeb, had defected to McCarthy and Kennedy. The sense that time had passed him by was not only ideological; Humphrey's *practice* of politics felt archaic. In October 1966 Ted Van Dyk had given Humphrey a memo from Frederick Dutton, a prominent California liberal who had spent time with the vice president on a swing along the West Coast. "The projection (not just 'image') of genuine human qualities," Dutton wrote, "not legislation or other government programs and policies, seems to me now to be the cutting edge of what is emerging as influential and persuasive." Yet Johnson and Humphrey, he noted, were clinging to an older style of "working primarily in governmental rather than directly 'human models of action.'" Humphrey thought enough of Dutton's critique that he distributed it to other staff members.[8] Dutton was struggling to describe what came to be known, often vaporously, as "the new politics," a politics of personal authenticity, of skepticism in the face of official optimism and bombast.

Gene McCarthy had mastered the ironic edge of the new politics; Bobby Kennedy seemed to incarnate its tragic dimension. Humphrey wasn't ironic or tragic; he was stuck with his archaic politics of joy. Sometimes he would present what he regarded as an innovative program—promoting volunteer activity in the inner city—as his version of "the new politics."[9] It wasn't going to work: Humphrey was a man who called his wife "Mother"; she called him "Daddy." The habits of small-town America in 1930 made him a figure of ridicule in 1968. The novelist and political essayist Norman Mailer pictured him not so much as a pharmacist as a pharmaceutical—"an emollifacient, a fifty-gallon drum of lanolin." The McCarthy campaign had the bright idea of bringing Tom Lehrer back to the stage to lampoon the happy warrior. Lehrer was a Bobby supporter, but he agreed to write a new song about Humphrey and perform it at McCarthy fund-raisers. In one of the more wickedly ingenious verses, Lehrer crooned, "For three lonely years he's been pinned in / And spent them out-Lyndoning Lyndon. / So pardon us please if we gawk / At a parrot who's also a hawk."[10] That summed up the sophisticated view of Humphrey—ludicrous, but also dangerous.

The campaign itself looked more like a wounded duck. Mondale's prediction had been all too accurate: since Humphrey lacked the ability to say no to the hundreds of people who regarded themselves as close friends, he needed to appoint a single person with that power; but he hadn't. Orville Freeman could have been the dictator Humphrey needed, but the candidate asked him instead to work with Mondale and Harris at what was known as United Democrats for Humphrey (UDH). They, in turn, worked with, and sometimes answered to, Citizens for Humphrey, a separate organization manned by Kampelman, Rowe, and other cronies, most of them more conservative than the UDH crowd. And both groups more or less coordinated with Humphrey's longtime aides, who made their own claims to control. Kampelman disliked Mondale and tried to get him ousted; in the end, it was Kampelman who was frozen out. Ted Van Dyk vied with Bill Connell for control; he sent Humphrey a memo telling him how to organize the campaign. Connell sent a furious memo of his own complaining to Humphrey that Mondale and Harris were bringing in mediocrities and demanded that the candidate clarify that Connell was answerable only to him, and not to the cochairs. Humphrey had to lay down the law to his most trusted aide. "The chairmen are Mondale and Harris and I don't want them to be bypassed," he wrote. "And I don't want to be bothered about this one more time by anybody."[11]

The Humphrey campaign was a jerry-built machine but a machine nevertheless. Immense advantages accrued to Humphrey's status as the candidate of the party establishment. Humphrey won all of Maryland's 49 delegates when the state delegation voted to adopt the "unit rule" awarding all votes to the candidate with the majority. On April 23 Gene McCarthy carried over three-quarters of the vote in

Pennsylvania's nonbinding primary; none of the other candidates had entered. But when the party bosses convened a month later to distribute the delegate seats at their disposal, Humphrey got 52 and McCarthy just 1. And since most of the unbound delegates went with Humphrey, McCarthy received only 25 of the state's 160 delegates.

Humphrey didn't just have the delegates; he had the votes of the great middle of the party that didn't want to hand Vietnam to the National Liberation Front and recoiled at campus protest and urban violence. An early Harris poll showed Humphrey with 38 percent of the vote, Kennedy with 27, and McCarthy with 25. The two left-of-center candidates were struggling for supremacy in the primaries, with Kennedy taking Indiana but McCarthy shocking him in Oregon. The conventional wisdom had it that Humphrey would reach the convention in Chicago with a strong plurality of delegates and sew up the rest once there. And then, in the early hours of June 5, just after he had won a narrow victory in the California primary, Bobby Kennedy was shot in the Ambassador Hotel in Los Angeles. Humphrey, awakened from sleep, ordered a military plane to bring the family neurosurgeon from Massachusetts to California; but it was too late to help.

Kennedy's murder did not provoke riots. Nor can it be said that it robbed young people of their sense of hope, for it was McCarthy, not Kennedy, who was the candidate of the young. But his assassination was devastating for a generation of Americans that had grown up with the Kennedys, that regarded the family with something of the deference and awe that belongs to myth. People waited in a line twenty-five blocks long—"a cross-section of everybody," Russell Baker wrote in the *New York Times*—to view his body in St. Patrick's Cathedral. To a generation of liberals that had moved left with the war and with racial conflict, Bobby appeared to be the peacemaker America needed. His death felt like a blow to those hopes. Humphrey, who had overcome the bitterness he had felt toward Bobby during the 1960 campaign and recognized his extraordinary charisma, felt this immediately. "What I think the Kennedy assassination did," he reflected later, "was to sour the whole public, and particularly the Democratic Party, on the election and on the political process. . . .

It was like a mental breakdown for the American political community."[12] Humphrey believed that, if he had defeated Kennedy for the nomination, the latter would have given his unstinting support; now he would be seeming to don a mantle that belonged to the martyred man.

McCarthy and Humphrey spoke immediately after Kennedy's death and agreed to call a temporary halt to the campaign. McCarthy apologized for some of the harsh things he had said about Humphrey, blaming them on errant speechwriters. In fact, he went on, aides had complained that he had removed anti-Humphrey material from speeches. Humphrey apparently believed this hokum, for he made the reciprocal statement that anyone who approached the McCarthy camp with the suggestion that the latter call off his campaign in order to become Humphrey's running mate did not speak for him. "We are both men of ability," he solemnly declared.[13]

The two men had never had a straightforward or even reciprocal relationship. Humphrey regarded McCarthy as a protégé whom he had helped usher into politics through Americans for Democratic Action in Minnesota; the younger man had been swept into Congress in 1948 on Humphrey's coattails, and Humphrey and Orville Freeman had then paid off McCarthy's campaign debts. McCarthy bridled at the label, later claiming that on election night Humphrey had no idea who he was. Humphrey continued to play the role of patron, endorsing McCarthy against his dear friend Eugenie Anderson in their 1958 Senate campaign and suggesting that McCarthy place Adlai Stevenson's name in nomination in 1960. McCarthy chafed at his dependence and became openly resentful after Johnson chose Humphrey over himself in 1964. "He had always been jealous of Humphrey," one biographer later wrote. "Now jealousy became contempt, as he mocked his subservience to Johnson, his cheerful garrulousness, and even his intellect." (The same author also observed, however, that "McCarthy was much less rude about Humphrey than he was about most of his other colleagues.") Humphrey was thus deluding himself about his rival. While he publicly stated that he would endorse McCarthy were he the nominee, McCarthy pointedly refused to return the favor—then, and later.[14]

A week after Kennedy's death, a full-page ad in the *New York Times* featured a letter from Ted Sorensen, who had been very close to both Jack and Bobby. Sorensen said that he—and, presumably, the other knights of Camelot—was no longer committed to a candidate but to an "ideal." In order to fulfill that ideal, a Democratic candidate would need to "break with the errors of the past" on foreign policy, and halt violence and crime not through "repression" but through gun control, law enforcement reforms, and urban redevelopment.[15] Humphrey tried very hard to fulfill that role when he returned to the campaign trail with a speech to the National Press Club on June 20. Saying nothing about Vietnam, he spoke of the need for what he called an Agenda for Civil Order and an Agenda for Social Justice. Under the first heading he called for stronger anti-riot laws and a stepped-up campaign against drug trafficking. Under the second, he committed himself to much more far-reaching federal spending than the president had. He endorsed the findings of the Kerner Commission as well as the goals of the Poor People's Campaign, a movement begun by Martin Luther King soon before his death that called for the recognition of a right to food, to a decent job, and to good education.[16] It could not be said that Humphrey was indifferent to the plight of starving children in the Mississippi Delta.

Humphrey had to walk a much more delicate line on Vietnam. He told the *Times* editorial board that he favored an immediate cease-fire and believed that the Vietcong were now prepared to negotiate. His position on the war was thus essentially the same as Bobby Kennedy's. Since Humphrey also claimed to have the same position as the president, this implied, absurdly, that Kennedy had mistakenly regarded himself as a critic of an administration whose views he actually shared. James Reston, buying none of this, remarked that Humphrey seemed extremely uncomfortable with his own Vietnam position. Reston noted that the children of many of Humphrey's friends and advisers agreed with McCarthy. (That may well have been so, but Skip Humphrey, then twenty-six, says that neither he nor any of his three siblings broke with their father over the war.[17]) Asked on *Face the Nation* on June 30 whether he agreed that the United States should never again be involved in a land war in Asia—a staple of McCarthy's rhetoric—Humphrey responded that no one seeking to be president "ought to be making premature commitments about what might happen." Asked directly on *Issues and Answers* a week later whether he opposed escalation of the war, he rejoined that it was the president who was de-escalating by ending bombing below the 20th parallel, whereas the Vietcong were escalating.[18]

Humphrey was trying to edge ever so slightly away from the president without provoking his wrath, which seemed next to impossible—in part because Johnson didn't actually seem to want him to win. In early April, Califano had asked the president if he would mind if Irwin Miller, a prominent Republican supporter of LBJ, chaired the presidential campaign of Republican New York governor Nelson Rockefeller. Go ahead, said LBJ. Johnson offered a very different response three weeks later when several cabinet members asked Califano to tell Johnson that they wanted to attend Humphrey's announcement. Tell them, the president said, "Stay out of the race or get out of the government." Johnson routinely ridiculed Humphrey to visitors as soft on Vietnam and hopelessly undisciplined. Fred Harris said, "At least three times Johnson had me down to the White House in the morning while he was still in his pajamas, in his bedroom. And he wanted to rail against Hubert to me. 'If Hubert were a woman he'd be pregnant all the time.' 'He cannot say no to these red hots.' 'He's got diarrhea of the mouth.'" This, of course, to Humphrey's own campaign manager. Utterly mortified, Harris never said a word about these visits to Humphrey himself.[19]

Humphrey was trapped between a vengeful president and a profoundly disillusioned party elite. Walter Lippmann, the Nestor of the liberal pundits, had now turned sharply against the war and denounced Humphrey as all but indistinguishable from the likely Republican nominee, Richard Nixon. Even Humphrey's old friends in the ADA now treated him as a hapless Johnson puppet. In early July, Arthur Schlesinger rebuffed a request for support from a senior campaign aide, David Ginsburg, writing that "if we are to have a stupid and reactionary foreign policy, it should be carried out by a Republican administration, not a Democratic administration." Humphrey, according to Schlesinger, kept quoting General Westmoreland and

Earle Wheeler as authorities on the war. As president, the historian wrote with the unkindest cut of all, Humphrey wouldn't have the guts to overrule them. Deeply stung, Humphrey wrote back with a long point-by-point rebuttal. "Don't overrate yourself, Arthur," he said in a bitter conclusion. "No one's trying to blackmail you or anyone else into coming over to support my candidacy." Schlesinger was not going to let Humphrey get in the last word. "If you do not understand and will not recognize that some of your old friends might oppose your candidacy on grounds of principle," he rejoined, "then you have lost your own sense of reality and are in deep trouble."[20]

Humphrey was shipping water both to his right and his left. A July 14 Gallup poll showed that support for George Wallace had shot up from 9 to 16 percent since April. A Harris poll the following week showed that while Humphrey would eke out a 2-point victory over Richard Nixon, the all-but-certain GOP candidate, McCarthy would beat him by 8. The politics of joy were running on empty. Bill Connell recorded the details of a tantrum that Humphrey threw at a meeting of campaign staff earlier that month. The advance work was lousy, the candidate complained; no one was challenging the protesters; events were thinly attended; money was coming in too slowly; the press was circling. "I don't like these reports of HHH's aides saying we are all so depressed," Humphrey moaned. The following day, sure enough, the *New York Times* reported that Humphrey was stirring so little enthusiasm that "even the protests against him are uninspired." The campaign continued to drift without clear leadership.[21]

In mid-July an anonymous aide wrote a memo, "The Campaign Task Ahead," listing work that was not being organized: bird-dogging the platform and credentials committees, coordinating television appearances, counting delegates, staving off the mounting attacks from George Wallace. At that same moment, Orville Freeman wrote in his diary that he had just received a call from "a very unhappy, frenetic, despondent Vice President." Humphrey begged his old friend to take over the campaign. Freeman suggested he ask Larry O'Brien instead. No, Humphrey said, I want you. A week later, just as Freeman was preparing to talk to Johnson about taking a leave from the cabinet, Humphrey said he had decided to go with O'Brien.[22]

Humphrey had teams of top-flight policy analysts grinding out papers on every possible topic. The Vietnam team included such eminent figures as Samuel Huntington and Edwin Reischauer of Harvard as well as Zbigniew Brzezinski, then a rising star at Columbia, all middle-of-the-road or center-left figures who shared the candidate's own impulses. By mid-July they had produced a report whose almost agonizingly contorted wording perfectly met Humphrey's needs. After referring to encouraging reports of diminished shelling and infiltration from the North, the report went on, "If these trends should continue, they might at some point approximate the reciprocal action that our Government has called for on previous occasions." Should that prove to be the case—but only then—Humphrey would advocate "an immediate halt in the bombing of North Vietnam." Once both sides had withdrawn military forces, an election would be held, for which, Humphrey would say, "I am prepared to accept the free decision of the South Vietnamese."[23]

Humphrey called Harris and Mondale, both more dovish than he, off the floor of the Senate to read them the key paragraphs. "Mondale and I said, 'Don't change a word,'" Harris recalls. "We got to the door and Mondale turns back and says, 'Hubert, are you going to have to clear this with the president?' Hubert says, 'No, I don't have to clear it. It's not an official statement as vice president. But I owe him the courtesy of it.'" Humphrey knew that Johnson had laid down explicit forms of "reciprocal action" for the Communists: respect the Demilitarized Zone (DMZ), stop shelling southern cities, and permit Saigon to join the United States at peace talks. What's more, he had been warned: on the 17th, the day of a Rowland Evans and Robert Novak column saying that Humphrey's advisers felt that he had to break with Johnson on the war, Charlie Murphy, Johnson's special counsel and confidant, wrote to Humphrey to admonish him that "an open break with Johnson on Vietnam would make it impossible for you to win the election." Nevertheless, Humphrey believed, or hoped, that his fuzzy alternate language would satisfy LBJ.[24]

On the evening of July 25th, Humphrey went to the White House to show the report to Johnson. Ted Van Dyk advised the task force members to stay with him in the office for whatever edits were needed.

Hours passed, and everyone drifted away save Van Dyk. Humphrey finally returned, utterly dejected. Going straight to the bathroom, he began energetically washing his hands, an old habit that was a Humphrey response to anxiety. When he emerged, he very reluctantly admitted to Van Dyk that he had failed utterly. Any relaxation of conditions, Johnson had threatened, would endanger American troops, including his son-in-law Chuck Robb. "I would have their blood on my hands," as Humphrey later recalled Johnson saying. "He would denounce me publicly for 'playing politics with peace.'" Texas governor John Connally would see to it that Humphrey would get none of the four hundred delegates he controlled. Humphrey seemed shattered.

A younger Hubert Humphrey, burning with the hard flame of moral certainty, had been as eager as Quixote to unsheathe his sword. But this Humphrey was not only wiser and more temperate, more habituated to compromise, but had also been beaten down after four years as Johnson's valet. He was not the man he had been not only in 1948 but in 1964. Van Dyk recalled him saying, very uncharacteristically, "I've eaten so much of Johnson's shit in this job that I've grown to like the taste of it."[25]

The very next day, Johnson had a much more pleasant conversation with Richard Nixon, whom he invited to the White House for a full-dress briefing with Dean Rusk and National Security Adviser Walt Rostow. Johnson outlined his three conditions, which Nixon accepted. The men agreed that the war was not lost. Nixon then told the press that the president had been "candid" and "forthright." In the coming months, the Republican nominee would take the position that he would say nothing, and propose nothing, that would undermine the president's negotiating position, thus offering a principled pretext for his cynical decision to advance no proposition about the war that might attract criticism. Johnson felt the contrast between the two sides and knew which he preferred. "The GOP," he said to aides, "may be of more help to us than any of the Democrats in the last few months."[26] Nixon had given Johnson good reason to believe that Republicans would be likelier than Democrats to hold the line on

Vietnam, and thus to allow him to achieve peace on what he regarded as honorable terms.

Humphrey flew to Los Angeles immediately after the blood-letting with LBJ. Things got no better. On July 26, an angry Black crowd at an Elks hall near Watts, the scene of the 1965 riot, forced Humphrey off the platform and, a reporter wrote, "so alarmed Humphrey and his security guards that they fled the hall and raced to the security of the luxurious Century Plaza Hotel"—which was soon surrounded by five thousand antiwar protesters who competed to come up with mocking references to Humphrey's initials. Among the favorites were "Hitler, Hubert, Hirohito," and "Help Hubert Hibernate." Humphrey was now protected everywhere he went by a phalanx of local policemen and Secret Service men, separated from the crowds that had always given him strength.[27]

Humphrey was nailed to the cross of Johnson's Vietnam policy. On August 9, immediately after the Republican National Convention had concluded, Johnson summoned both major-party candidates to the ranch for another briefing. Nixon and his running mate, Spiro Agnew, came first, on August 10. This time Johnson had brought Cyrus Vance, the deputy to chief negotiator Averill Harriman at the Paris peace talks, to brief the GOP team on the latest developments; Rusk was present once again. Humphrey came the following day, armed with yet another—and even less objectionable—draft from the Vietnam task force. This one proposed a bombing halt "if North Vietnam was willing to offer an appropriate act of reciprocity." Humphrey later stated that while Johnson largely accepted the new language, he asked Humphrey to shelve the statement, cryptically promising that there were "situations afoot" that "would not only clarify but advance the peace negotiations."[28]

Humphrey later wrote that Johnson's optimism lifted his spirits with the hope that the peace logjam might soon be broken. Ted Van Dyk, who met Humphrey and Bill Connell on a flight from Texas to the Midwest, recalled that in fact Humphrey was grim and tight-lipped, and said nothing about the president's forecast. Van Dyk believed that Humphrey had tried to put the best face on another failure. In any case, the promised breakthrough did not materialize; on August 17 Johnson called to say that Hanoi had gone back on the offensive and there was no longer any cause for hope for progress in the peace talks. Humphrey understood that the war would continue to hang over him like a black cloud. A Gallup poll published August 21, on the eve of the Democratic convention, showed Nixon leading Humphrey 45–29, with Wallace not so far back at 16.

In early August, Larry O'Brien, a moderate dove but a devout Kennedy loyalist, had agreed to run the campaign through the convention after Humphrey promised that he would break with Johnson on the war. O'Brien had begun convening planning meetings. Strikingly, the agenda never included discussion of the violent disruptions then being planned by antiwar demonstrators and fringe groups. These were hardly a secret. On June 29, Rennie Davis, field director of the National Mobilization Committee to End the War, had promised "massive confrontations" in Chicago. The Yippies, anarchists rather than ideologues, had applied for a permit near the convention center to hold events of their own. Even the newest of new politics would have been helpless before this potent blend of Mao Tse-tung and Dada; but the Humphrey campaign was way out of its depth. Humphrey suggested to Larry Hayes, press officer for United Democrats for Humphrey, that the campaign bring youthful celebrities in sports, science, and entertainment to Chicago to celebrate a "Young Americans Day." A campaign aide advised Hayes to organize "several busloads of attractive, clean-cut young ladies in H-line dresses" who could be sent as "flying squads" to counter scruffy demonstrators. As the convention approached, and the dimensions of the protests became clearer, Robert McCandless, a senior campaign aide, received a memo suggesting that Humphrey win credit for averting bloodshed—or at least trying to do so—by meeting with, and listening to, the leaders of the National Mobilization Committee. Routed to O'Brien, the memo came back with a note: "Larry looked at this and said to skip it."[29]

The new campaign manager had what felt like much more important things to worry about: not only the usual logistical business of hotel rooms, phones, speech schedules, delegate counts, credentials fights, media management, and the like, but also preventing the giant rifts in the party from wrecking the traditional show of harmony. This meant, above all, achieving some kind of entente with McCarthy, who had fallen into a deep state of self-absorption after Bobby Kennedy's death and never fully emerged. On August 10, a disillusioned George McGovern announced his own candidacy for the nomination in order to focus attention on the antiwar cause. Yet McCarthy remained the pied piper of the left, drawing overflow crowds in Fenway Park and Madison Square Garden in the weeks leading up to the convention. The contrast with Humphrey's often listless gatherings was impossible to miss. Humphrey invited his former Minnesota colleague to join him for breakfast at his apartment in Washington the week before the convention met. Humphrey later said that he repeated his vow to support McCarthy should the latter win the nomination and hoped that McCarthy would do the same. He would, he added, support a dovish plank if the convention adopted it. McCarthy, in turn, said that he would not be able to immediately offer his support absent a Vietnam plank he agreed with—a virtual impossibility—but that "if I gave him a couple of weeks for a turn-around, he could do it." McCarthy, Humphrey said, promised an endorsement by mid-September. Humphrey again chose to believe him.[30]

Vietnam was the key to party unity; the platform was the place where the debate would be joined. On August 1, a group of aides to McCarthy and McGovern, former aides to Bobby Kennedy, and the dovish senators Claiborne Pell and Wayne Morse met in Washington to coordinate efforts to shape the Vietnam plank. Many submitted draft versions of their own to the platform committee, but the differences among them were minor; all wanted an immediate halt to the bombing and favored a coalition government that could include the NLF. Humphrey's campaign was deeply divided on how far to move to meet the critics. Doug Bennett, the campaign aide responsible for drafting the Vietnam plank, was a hawk. On August 16 he laid out talking points for the campaign: "HHH demands quid pro quo from the North, albeit a very modest one, whereas the others demand it from the South only. This is a very weak negotiating position. The demand for 'no more Vietnams' implies an unacceptable criticism of the Johnson Administration, and thus of Humphrey. We should feel grateful to the President for committing to the Paris peace talks."[31]

The platform head, Congressman Hale Boggs of Louisiana, had been appointed with Johnson's approval and was a Johnson loyalist. He had stacked the platform committee with like-minded men. From the outset, therefore, it had been clear that the official Vietnam plank would not deviate far from Johnson's policies; Humphrey's goal was to find language that the doves could live with in order to persuade them not to present a minority plank to the convention. That was not, of course, Johnson's goal. The president, by now conducting a kind of subterranean dalliance with the Republican nominee, called Nixon on August 18 with talking points, drawn up by Rusk, that the latter could use to attack the doves and Humphrey, should he join them. Rusk had sardonically proposed that the critics come right out and say, "You should stop bombing men and arms moving southwards across the DMZ to kill US and allied forces." Johnson liked that one. "You can take this down if you want to," he told Nixon, who did just that.[32]

The platform committee began meeting the week before the convention opened, first in Washington and then in Chicago. Support for the antiwar side all but collapsed on August 20 when the Soviets sent tanks into Czechoslovakia to crush a nascent democratic movement. McCarthy did not help his own cause when he dismissed the invasion as "not a major crisis" requiring the late-night National Security Council meeting that LBJ had convened. The invasion forced the doves to moderate their demands. On the 23rd, the group approved language calling for "an unconditional end to all bombing of North Vietnam" while continuing to support the American campaign in the South, and an effort to "encourage" the Saigon government to negotiate with the NLF. The group's designated envoy, Congressman John J. Gilligan of Ohio, then huddled in a room at the Statler Hilton in Chicago with David Ginsburg, the counsel to the Humphrey campaign. After closely scrutinizing the document, Ginsburg proclaimed, "There's not ten cents of difference between this and the Vice President's policy." An excited Ginsburg called Humphrey, who took the text down word for word. Humphrey in turn read the proposed plank to Dean Rusk, who suggested minor edits and then said the magic words: "We can live with it, Hubert." Walt Rostow signed off on it as well. Humphrey hoped that he had finally laid Vietnam to rest.[33]

THE HUMPHREY CAMPAIGN HAD MISREAD NOT ONLY THE PROTESTers who planned to converge on Chicago but the mayor who planned to confront them. Rennie Davis of the Mobilization had rightly calculated that Mayor Daley would meet peaceful marches with violence. Daley was not the kind of mayor Hubert Humphrey had once been. He was a short, jowly, cigar-chewing, and often splenetic man who looked like a Thomas Nast caricature of a machine politician. After thirteen years in office, Daley ran Chicago like a giant fief, adroitly exploiting his national Democratic connections to rain money on the city and cement his own authority. Liberal in many respects, an early supporter of Bobby Kennedy, Daley nevertheless harbored the autocrat's rage at challenges to his authority. He had vowed to shoot violent rioters. And he prepared Chicago for the convention as if it were Saigon bracing for a Vietcong attack. The mayor put the city's twelve-thousand-man police force on twelve-hour shifts and mobilized six thousand National Guardsmen and six thousand more army troops, equipped with flamethrowers and bazookas. He established a one-mile security cordon around the International Amphitheater, where the convention would be held, with chain-link fences topped by triple strands of barbed wire. He sealed manhole covers to prevent bombings.[34] Daley was brute American power personified—a radical's dream adversary.

In fact, fear of bloodshed had drastically reduced the ranks of protesters; no more than three to four thousand came to Chicago, not the hundred thousand that organizers had once bragged of. But many were prepared for confrontation. Tom Hayden, head of Students for a Democratic Society, had concluded that appeals to conscience would never end the war, just as the Black Panthers and the advocates of Black Power had concluded that America would never voluntarily end racial abuse. The goal of action was polarization—"to arouse the sleeping dogs of the Right," as Hayden told a colleague. At the same time, Abbie Hoffman, spokesman and mascot for the Yippies, dreamed up and talked up a series of "actions" just ridiculous enough to throw Mayor Daley and his cops into a panic: spike the water supply with LSD, release greased pigs in the street, send 230 "hyper-potent" Yips to seduce the wives and daughters of clean-living delegates. The sixties, and its backlash, would be enacted live and in color on the streets of Chicago.[35]

The convention would open Monday evening, August 26. Johnson had already dispatched a series of lieutenants, including Marvin Watson and John Criswell, treasurer of the Democratic National Committee, to ensure that he, not Humphrey, controlled the proceedings. Larry O'Brien soon learned that any request for telephones or hotel rooms had to be routed through them. The president's own motives were opaque. He had, in fact, begun to have second thoughts about his principled decision to withdraw from the race. Johnson had dispatched John Connally to sound out southern governors; the answer, Connally said, was "no way." Joseph Califano thought that Johnson wanted to be drafted, bathe in the acclaim, and then nobly spurn the request.[36]

If Johnson couldn't be renominated, he could at least ensure that the convention would reaffirm his presidency. The only real issue was, of course, Vietnam. Johnson may not yet have known about the modified peace plank that Humphrey had accepted and that his own senior officials had cleared. On Saturday night, Humphrey had asked Fred Harris and David Ginsburg, already in Chicago, to make sure that Hale Boggs and John Connally would allow the platform committee to adopt that language. Boggs, who must have known that trouble was coming, said to Harris, "Do you look me in the eye and say that's what Hubert wants?" It was, said Harris. In that case, Boggs said, he would recommend it to the White House. Connally said, "I can't support it, but I won't fight it."[37]

Humphrey was hoping to simultaneously appease the president and end the deadlock with the war's critics. On a Sunday morning appearance on *Meet the Press*, Humphrey flatly asserted that the platform would not demand unconditional withdrawal, and that he would not give Hanoi reason to believe that they would get a better deal from him than from Johnson. But when asked, "Who is the candidate for those who dissent from Vietnam policies?" he responded, bizarrely, "I am." By this time, unbeknownst to Humphrey, the president had sent a plane to bring Boggs, his loyal lieutenant, to the ranch to show him the proposed Vietnam plank. Rusk and Rostow hadn't seen a problem with it, but Johnson did.[38]

Johnson had yet another operative in Chicago, Charlie Murphy. On Sunday evening Murphy convened a meeting with Boggs, now back in Chicago, and senior Humphrey aides, including Ginsburg. The White House put through a call from Johnson's ranch to Boggs's hotel room; an aide, Tom Johnson, went over each line while the president spoke, with increasing vehemence, in the background. There was one insoluble disagreement. The draft said, "Stop the bombing. The action and its timing shall take into account the security of our troops and the likelihood of a response from Hanoi." That had been a huge concession from the doves. But the president insisted that the language be changed so that the bombing would be halted only "when" those conditions were met. Who would decide if Hanoi had complied? He would, of course. The doves would never accept that.[39]

That evening, Gene McCarthy arrived at Midway Airport in Chicago along with the poet Robert Lowell, the novelist William Styron, the journalist Shana Alexander, and three European correspondents; he was greeted by an exultant crowd of perhaps five thousand supporters. The Prince Hamlet of the Democratic Party then retired to his hotel suite. Hubert Humphrey and his team arrived at the military side of O'Hare—"like thieves in the night," recalled Edgar Berman.[40] They were greeted by a bagpipe band, several dozen girls whom Mayor Daley had sent, and a hundred or so reporters. Silent, for once, before cameras and mikes, Humphrey went straight to a meeting with the Illinois delegation, firmly under the control of Mayor Daley. He then went to his suite in the Conrad Hilton, by that time a wild scrum filled with aides, reporters, local delegates, celebrities, and assorted hangers-on.

David Ginsburg seized the vice president, drew him into a quiet bedroom, and showed him the language that LBJ had refused to endorse. Humphrey must have felt dizzy; the rug was being pulled out from under him again. Nevertheless, he insisted on keeping the disputed phrase. Monday morning Ginsburg resumed his negotiations, getting nowhere. Johnson told Marvin Watson that he would not accept the plank without the "when" clause; Watson then told the vice president. Humphrey was outraged; he called Johnson and told him that Rusk and Rostow had cleared the language. Johnson, unimpressed, said, "This plank just undercuts our whole policy and by God, the Democratic party ought not to be doing that to me and you ought not to be doing it." Humphrey was still prepared to keep the plank and risk the president's wrath until Hale Boggs said that he would not present anything Johnson couldn't accept. Humphrey admitted defeat; Boggs presented the plank to the platform committee, which approved it in fifteen minutes. That night the convention opened, its great rift fully exposed. Humphrey had made his reputation with his brave stand on the great platform battle of 1948; twenty years later, with the Democrats even more bitterly divided than they had been then, he stood with the party against the activists.[41]

While the routine business of a political convention began to get underway inside the International Amphitheater, Chicago was teetering on the brink of a collapse. Thanks to a telephone strike, much of the city had no phone service. Inside the Conrad Hilton, the convention headquarters, the only way to get a phone call was through the hotel switchboard, which quickly became overwhelmed. So, too, were the elevators and the laundry service—even as waitresses in skimpy Gay Nineties skirts and décolletage kept delegates lubricated in the Haymarket Lounge on the ground floor. Security guards posted at the entrances to the amphitheater rigidly enforced protocols that required a special card for admission—though Norman Mailer, covering the event, reported that a Diners Club card worked just as well. Some delegates, unable to navigate the system, got into shouting matches with the poker-faced guards and were hauled off in the backs of paddy wagons. The *Washington Post*'s David Broder described the convention as "theater of the absurd" with a sharp tang of Kafkaesque futility.[42]

But it was on the streets where the real theater took place. At midnight on Sunday, five hundred policemen swinging nightsticks drove a thousand or so people out of Lincoln Park to enforce an 11:00 p.m. curfew. Reporters were astonished by the violence of the episode. "The attack began with a police car smashing a barricade," according to a news account. "The kids threw whatever they had the foresight to arm themselves with, rocks and bottles mostly. . . . Next, the cops burst out of the woods in selective pursuit of news photographers. . . . They'd taken off their badges, their name plates, even the unit patches on their shoulders to become a mob of identical, unidentifiable club swingers."[43] The following night the cops again fought protesters, and protesters again rained down bricks and paving stones on police cars.

Tuesday, August 27, was Lyndon Johnson's sixtieth birthday. The convention had been scheduled for the very end of August, almost a month after the GOP convention in Miami, in order to deliver what had at one time seemed to be the best of all birthday gifts for the incumbent. Johnson had toyed with joining the delegates when he still dreamed of becoming the nominee, but had then decided against it, becoming the first sitting president in memory to skip his party's convention. Instead, in the most discordant possible note of the politics of joy, the delegates opened the second day of the event by rising to sing "Happy Birthday" to LBJ. The real business of the convention continued to be conducted off the floor. A sub-rosa campaign to nominate the thirty-six-year-old Teddy Kennedy had begun several weeks earlier when McCarthy had acknowledged that he could not win the nomination. Daley was known to be in Teddy's corner; a delegate had opened a Teddy for President office in his hotel room. Kennedy had made it clear through proxies that while he might accept a draft, he would not offer himself. The Teddy boomlet ended Tuesday afternoon after extensive conversations between Kennedy allies, McCarthy aides, and ultimately McCarthy himself. Kennedy had finally ruled himself out, even though McCarthy had, according to some reports, offered to step aside before the first ballot. Humphrey now had an unobstructed path to the nomination; through proxies, he would offer to make Kennedy his running mate, which the latter would firmly reject.

That morning the candidates held the closest thing to a debate among themselves. The California delegation had asked Humphrey, McCarthy, and McGovern to address them, and all three agreed to do so. McCarthy began by saying the kind of thing that endeared him to his followers and convinced mainstream Democrats that he was not fit for office. McGovern had accused him of holding a "passive" view of the presidency—a kind of do-no-harm posture—and McCarthy agreed, saying, "I think a little passivity in that office is all right, a kind of balance." The subject of the moment was, of course, Vietnam. Humphrey was asked, "In what ways, if at all, do you disagree with President Johnson's position with reference to Vietnam?" Humphrey responded with his usual dodge: "The President of the United States is not a candidate." Then he recited Doug Bennett's talking points: three prior presidents had made commitments to Vietnam, Johnson had responded to escalation by the North, unconditional withdrawal would be catastrophic. McGovern, a gentleman, refused to condemn Humphrey personally even as he made mincemeat of his argument. McCarthy, genuinely passive, didn't deign to respond to Humphrey at all. The delegation gave McGovern a standing ovation. The era when Humphrey had been the favorite son of coastal elites was long gone.[44]

The debate over the minority Vietnam plank began at midnight on Tuesday. Delegates from New York, California, and Wisconsin—the doves—tried to shout down speakers who defended the majority plank; the hall descended into pandemonium. Daley, crimson with fury, turned to Carl Albert, presiding, and made a slashing gesture across his throat. Albert then slammed down his gavel and brought the proceedings to a close. The debate resumed Wednesday morning. The Humphrey forces had placed a "fact sheet" on each seat in the hall denouncing the peace plank—the one that Humphrey had personally endorsed—as "emotional, unreasoning, inflexible, unworkable—and a threat to any rational U.S. policy in Southeast Asia." A three-hour debate now proceeded calmly; the delegates rejected the plank

1,567–1,041. New York delegates staged a march led by the folk singer Theodore Bikel, singing "We Shall Overcome," amplified through a portable loudspeaker, drowning out the patriotic tunes being belted out by Lou Breese and His Orchestra, the convention band. Hundreds of other doves joined the parade. Humphrey had won—but this time, unlike in 1948, against the liberals. At that moment, the possibility of a united front linking the Humphrey and the McGovern-McCarthy forces came to an end. Some liberals, including George McGovern, believed that at that moment the 1968 election was lost.[45]

Political conventions played to one of Humphrey's strengths—he needed less sleep than most men. Tuesday night he had been awake through much of the night working through lists of potential running mates and planning his acceptance speech. Wednesday morning he breakfasted with Daley and then had a second breakfast with Governor John McKeithen of Louisiana, an important southern ally. He met with the delegation from Connecticut, and then the delegation from Washington State. He had lunch with Jackie Robinson and Elgin Baylor, the Los Angeles Lakers superstar. He went back up to his suite, 2525A, which was jammed at almost all hours with the usual crowd. The Vietnam debate was showing on all the televisions. Then, just after 7:00 p.m., the unmistakable acrid smell of tear gas began to permeate the suite. People all over the Conrad Hilton went to their windows and saw a phalanx of policemen below moving in on a crowd gathered in Grant Park across the street.

Beginning the night before, eight to ten thousand protesters had gathered in the park, shouting to the delegates in the hotel to blink their lights to show sympathy with the cause. (Lights on the fifteenth and twenty-third floors, where the McCarthy team was quartered, went on and off.) That afternoon the police had waded through the protesters swinging their billy clubs, but the crowd had re-formed in their wake. The police had hemmed in the protesters by blocking bridges out of the park. At a few minutes before eight, with neither warning nor provocation, a phalanx of policemen poured into the park from Balbo Drive just north of the Hilton, firing rounds of tear gas. "The kids screamed and were beaten to the ground by cops who had completely lost their cool," one newsman wrote. "Some tried to surrender by putting their hands on their head. As they were marched to vans to be arrested, they were rapped in the genitals by the cops' swinging billies. . . . Some of the demonstrators were thrown against a window of the hotel and pushed through it." Other accounts said a demonstrator had smashed the window in order to escape. Soon policemen were bloodying protesters as well as newsmen in front of the waitresses of the Haymarket. Shoes, purses, and torn clothes were scattered for two blocks in all directions. Bleeding kids streamed into the Hilton, where they were bandaged by McCarthy aides.[46]

At this point, outside and inside converged. As Mayor Carl Stokes of Cleveland put Humphrey's name in nomination at 9:55 p.m., the television networks cut away to footage of Daley's myrmidons assaulting kids. The video lasted seventeen minutes—an interminable period during which eighty-nine million Americans saw the mayhem in the streets rather than the ritual self-congratulation in the convention hall. Soon after the footage ended, Senator Abe Ribicoff of Connecticut stood up to nominate George McGovern. With a President McGovern, he said, "we wouldn't have Gestapo tactics on the streets of Chicago." The cameras immediately cut to Daley, who jumped up, shook his fist, and mouthed an expletive. "How hard it is to accept the truth," said Ribicoff.[47] Humphrey later insisted that he had been too busy to see the pitched battle with the cops, though those with him then, including Fred Harris, say that everyone felt the tear gas come through the air-conditioning vents. Humphrey seemed ebullient, as always; the moment he had long awaited was only minutes away. When the balloting began at 11:20, he sat before the TV with pad and pencil, toting up the delegate count. But well before Pennsylvania put him over the top, Humphrey excused himself; Edgar Berman later wrote that he found him in the adjacent bedroom, weeping. Later he would admit the awful truth: "Chicago was a catastrophe. . . . I just felt like we had been in a shipwreck."[48]

Johnson started calling Humphrey to discuss running mates at 2:30 a.m., soon after the balloting was done. The premise of this and subsequent conversations was that, as Marvin Watson bluntly informed him, Humphrey had to choose someone satisfactory to Johnson.[49] The president had no shortage of ideas. "Everybody knows that you're kind of a peacenik at heart," he said on that middle-of-the-night call. He suggested hawks, such as Henry "Scoop" Jackson of Washington. Humphrey needed someone strong. "You're weak on the war thing that Franklin Roosevelt Jr. gave us," Johnson said, alluding to the ancient draft-dodging allegations that he knew to be baseless. "I think you're weak because of your age and the Kennedys are just cutting you and gutting you." Weak—that was just about the lowest term of abuse in the Johnson lexicon. It was as if LBJ had to undermine the implied position of strength Humphrey had just gained as the Democratic nominee. Johnson warmed to his topic. What about Terry Sanford of North Carolina? Or Daniel Inouye of Hawaii, who had lost an arm in combat. "They talk about war," Johnson snorted. "He'll just stand there with his sleeve."

Later that morning, Johnson called again; then Humphrey called him. Humphrey said he had spoken to George Meany, Dick Daley, Jim Farley, and Jim Rowe—all the old pros. Johnson, who now seemed to have all the time in the world, recalled all the jobs he had given Humphrey—cities, civil rights, housing, youth, Vietnam—"every damn thing." Humphrey bit his tongue. Now, said Johnson, he was just trying to help his vice president, not "influence" him as the others were. But don't give it to the Kennedys, he said—no matter how much they want it. Find a loyalist, as he had.[50]

Humphrey was considering a number of progressives, including Sanford and Fred Harris, his own campaign cochairman, who might bring back the alienated McCarthyites. But a man who wants to make a bold choice doesn't limit his consulting to George Meany and Jim Rowe and Lyndon Johnson. Humphrey wanted someone safe and reliable, someone he trusted. He didn't need to send proxies to administer loyalty tests; that wasn't Humphrey's way. But he agonized over the decision, which *was* his way. Instead of making an announcement at noon, as he had told the press he would, Humphrey walked downstairs to Fred Harris's suite and asked him to come up the back stairs to one of the spare bedrooms in his own suite a floor above. Humphrey had decided on Senator Edmund Muskie of Maine, who was tall, taciturn, dignified, and Catholic, as he wasn't, and had stood with him on Vietnam, and so was acceptable to Johnson. But he confided to Edgar

Berman that he had learned that Muskie's daughter was pregnant but unmarried. Some advisers considered that disqualifying; others didn't. Humphrey ducked into the Harris bedroom for another opinion; Harris loyally told Humphrey that the pregnancy wouldn't matter. An hour or two later, Humphrey came back and said, with tears in his eyes, "Fred, I'm going to choose the older man." Then—memories differ—Humphrey either asked Harris to nominate Muskie, or Harris volunteered to do so.[51]

Nothing remained but to give the acceptance speech. Humphrey's old Minnesota friends—Max Kampelman, Evron Kirkpatrick, Herb McCloskey—had concluded that the only way Humphrey could convince the American people that he was his own man was to use his acceptance speech to make a shocking announcement—he was resigning as vice president. No sitting vice president had ever stepped down. They wrote the speech, full of flattery for the president, and worked out an elaborate plan in which Humphrey would notify the press corps before handing the speech to Johnson so that he could not turn back no matter what Johnson said. They told a few others who were close to Humphrey—Averill Harriman, Orville Freeman, John Rielly, Tom Hughes—and all of them approved. Then they told Larry O'Brien, who brought the proposal to Humphrey on the morning of the 28th. To no one's surprise, Humphrey refused. "It would look like a gimmick," he told O'Brien. "It would seem strange. And it would enrage the President." Whether out of loyalty or fear or risk aversion, Humphrey would not do it.[52]

Practically everyone in Humphrey's circle had submitted a draft of an acceptance speech—David Ginsburg, Jack Valenti, John Stewart, and even Bill Moyers, now a newspaper publisher. Ted Van Dyk had taken a shot at a version produced by Labor Secretary W. Willard Wirtz. Humphrey told Van Dyk that he didn't like any of them. At that point, according to Berman, Humphrey ordered two secretaries to come in and dictated a new speech over the next two hours. Humphrey always said in the aftermath of the event that the speech had been almost entirely his own. Van Dyk, however, says that he did most of the new drafting, largely marking up an existing text. The speech bore the traces of collective composition. Humphrey discovered as he was being driven to the convention center that Van Dyk had removed a prayer from St. Francis that he found "hokey and inappropriate." Humphrey, furious, ordered it put back.[53]

Humphrey took the rostrum at 10:30 p.m. He began by speaking, slowly and gravely, of his sorrow at "the troubles and the violence which have erupted regrettably and tragically in the streets of this great city." Violence could not "be condoned whatever the source." Was he condemning the violence of the cops or the kids or both? Danger lay in both directions; thus the need for ambiguity. Then Humphrey added the prayer that Van Dyk had found too corny. For that very reason, of course, it was echt Humphrey: "Where there is hate, let me sow love / Where there is injury, pardon"—and on through doubt, despair, and darkness. Humphrey was trying to find the words to bind up wounds without taking sides. But who, on either side, wished to join him?

Now, in the portentous tremolo he adopted at moments of high drama, Humphrey began unspooling the sonorous phrases he had polished over a career in politics. Lou Breese and His Orchestra earned their keep by punctuating each fine sentiment with a flourish of trumpets or percussion. "Majority rule has prevailed but minority rights have been preserved"—"Braat!" "We have nothing to fear but fear itself"—keyboard thunder. "I say, 'Thank you, Mr. President'"—and the band launched into a sprinting rendition of "Happy Days Are Here Again." The whole thing was so utterly tone-deaf, so close to self-parody, that Van Dyk, watching from his hotel room, got himself connected to Breese and told him to knock it off, claiming to be the official who would yank his Musicians' Union card if Humphrey got elected. The band went silent, and Humphrey closed by promising to bring peace in Vietnam, "peace and justice in our cities," and "unity in our country." The gentlemanly George McGovern joined him at the podium, though McCarthy, sulking in his tent, remained out of sight—a visual reminder of a wounded party.[54]

At some other moment—1960, for example—the speech might have inspired Democratic foot soldiers across the country. But on air and in the papers the next day, the bloodshed got equal billing with the pledges on Vietnam and the cities. Humphrey made things worse, at least with party activists, by shedding his careful neutrality on "the troubles" in Chicago. "Goodness me," he told Roger Mudd of CBS. "Anybody that sees this sort of thing is sick at heart, and I was. But I think the blame ought to be put where it belongs. I think we ought to stop pretending that Mayor Daley did anything wrong. . . . I know what caused these demonstrations. They were planned, premeditated by certain people in this country that feel all they have to do is riot and they'll get their way." And the obscenity—"You'd put anybody in jail for that kind of talk."[55]

Humphrey had proved not just to the kids in Grant Park but to the McCarthy devotees and the older men and women who had gathered around Bobby Kennedy that he was on the wrong side—the side of LBJ and George Meany and Richard Daley. He emerged from Chicago terribly wounded. Yet so did the idealists on the left. "The whole world is watching," the demonstrators had chanted with the self-centered hyperbole of the young and self-righteous. Chicago was supposed to be the Birmingham of the antiwar movement, shocking viewers out of their complacency about the war; but a Harris poll found that two-thirds of Americans endorsed Daley's use of force. Todd Gitlin, the former head of SDS, later reflected that "our giddiness kept us from reckoning with the majority of 'the whole world' that, watching, loathed us." Chicago was a calamity not just for the Democratic Party and its nominee, but for the left, which appeared to have been devoured by its own extremists. In his memoir of the era, Richard Goodwin, a senior figure in the Kennedy and then the McCarthy camp, writes that the sixties, understood as a movement for justice at home and abroad, came to an end in Chicago.[56]

21

The End

---

*"There has been almost too much pain,
too much shock, too much violence, too much
uncertainty for our people to sustain."*

I N THE MIDST OF THE MADNESS OF CHICAGO, IT WAS ALL TOO easy to believe that the upcoming election would pit Hubert Humphrey against Lyndon Johnson in an Oedipal struggle to destroy the terrifying father figure. In fact, Humphrey was running against Richard Nixon and George Wallace—and doing no better than he was against Johnson. Polls taken immediately after the convention showed that Humphrey had gained only a 4-point "bump," narrowing Nixon's lead to a still very formidable 12 points. Wallace gained altitude every week, so that by the end of September he had the support of 21 percent of respondents—7 points behind Humphrey. Bitterly though he had disappointed the left, the space that mattered in the election was to Humphrey's right.

Richard Nixon was not then the despised figure he would become in the aftermath of Watergate. Though grayer heads remembered all too well the way he had Red-baited his way to victory over Helen Gahagan Douglas in the 1950 California Senate race, the left hated LBJ much more vehemently than it did Nixon. Though he had given a great deal of thought to foreign policy, Nixon was, according to a biographer, indifferent on the domestic policy issues that Humphrey cared about so much—"save crime, where his indignation was very great."[1] He had won a narrow first-ballot victory over the progressive Nelson Rockefeller and over Ronald Reagan at the thoroughly placid Republican convention in Miami. Fully aware that the Democratic Party was coming apart, Nixon had run a nothing-ventured, nothing-lost campaign, vowing to end the Vietnam War without explaining how—the so-called "secret plan." He had shored up his right flank by gaining the support of Strom Thurmond, the Dixiecrat-turned-Republican, and by choosing Maryland governor Spiro Agnew as his running mate. Nixon left it to Agnew to exploit anger over law and order.

George Wallace had scrambled the election, but to whose benefit no one could say for sure. Having seen his path as a Democrat blocked in 1964, Wallace now ran as an independent. He used an appearance on *Meet the Press* in May 1967 to offer an unmistakable hint of his candidacy and to present a new face to the American people. He was not, he explained, a segregationist—much less a racist—but a states' rights man who wanted each state to decide for itself how the races should relate. He was running as a tribune of the forgotten people—"this man in the textile mill, this man in the steel mill, this barber, the beautician, the policeman on the beat . . . the mass of people that are going to support a change in the domestic scene in this country." Wallace cast himself in the tradition of the southern populists—men such as Huey Long—whom he genuinely admired; the change he promised, however, was not economic justice for the working class but law and order, an end to "permissiveness," and the preservation of the racial order. That last part was usually, but not always, offered sotto voce. When speaking in the South, he was prepared to say that he welcomed the support of the Ku Klux Klan.[2]

An overtly racial campaign might have made Wallace a hero in the Deep South, but he became a national candidate because he spoke openly to the growing fears over riots, protests, and campus demonstrations. The Kerner Commission may have blamed urban violence on the "root causes" of poverty and racial isolation, but many Americans, in the North as well as the South, regarded it as a symptom—the worst, but hardly the only—of a liberal culture of permissiveness. Wallace made deep inroads among men in the steel mills and the textile mills. One poll found that 90 percent of the members of the UAW locals in Illinois supported him, even as another found that 88 percent of the union's leadership supported Humphrey. Indeed, Humphrey passed up the Labor Day Parade in Detroit, the traditional Democratic campaign kickoff event, because he was advised that the route would be lined with workingmen sporting Wallace buttons.[3]

In the immediate aftermath of the convention, the Humphrey campaign looked dead in the water. There was no plan for the general election. In the run-up to Chicago, Mondale and Harris had been sidelined by O'Brien and had returned to their senatorial lives; neither would play an important role henceforth. Humphrey pleaded with O'Brien to continue as campaign manager after the convention, offering to make him chairman of the Democratic National Committee to ensure him a role should Nixon win. O'Brien only agreed on August 30, the last day of the convention. He later confessed that he felt Humphrey was imploring him to take on "a hopeless task," and that he finally agreed only because he felt a responsibility to the party—and because of the DNC position.[4]

O'Brien and two aides arrived in Waverly on Labor Day, worked all night and the following morning, and then presented Humphrey, Orville Freeman, campaign treasurer Robert Short, and others with very little more than travel plans for the coming weeks and an ad blitz for the final weeks. Even that posed a problem, since the campaign was more than $500,000 in debt from the convention and had only about $200,000 in cash on hand. At a moment when he desperately needed to make up the gap with Nixon and shrink Wallace's support, Humphrey could not afford to buy time on radio or television. "How could you raise money?" Humphrey would later explain. "Any time you picked up a magazine it would say that I was going to suffer the most disastrous defeat of any candidate in the history of the Democratic party." He may have been thinking of a Stewart Alsop column in *Newsweek* that described his coronation in Chicago as "more like an execution."[5]

In fact, the campaign had only seemed to hit bottom in Chicago. Rowland Evans and Robert Novak summarized Humphrey's first week back on the campaign trail as "perhaps the most calamitous week ever experienced by a Presidential nominee." The week began with an hour-long interview on *Issues and Answers* in which the candidate was relentlessly grilled on two subjects: Are you your own man? Are you prepared to call for an unconditional bombing halt in Vietnam? (Answers: yes and no.) While Nixon pursued a leisurely schedule, Humphrey tore across the country like a tornado: Philadelphia, Denver, Los Angeles, Houston, New Orleans, Flint, Wilmington, Sea Girt (in New Jersey), Pittsburgh. The reporters who traveled with him were struck by the sparsity of the crowds, the ubiquity of the hecklers, the unwillingness of senior politicians to be seen in the candidate's company, the poor advance work that left Humphrey wandering the streets of Pittsburgh looking for voters to talk to.[6]

Vietnam continued to haunt Humphrey. Nixon was barely challenged when he insisted, repeatedly and without offering any details, that once elected he would "end the war on an honorable basis." Humphrey had to measure out, in inches, his distance from Johnson. In Philadelphia he predicted that troops would begin coming home by later that year or early 1969. The following day in Denver he said he could have supported the minority plank on Vietnam since it was so similar to his own. In Houston he brandished a copy of the local paper with an article about troops returning stateside; mortifyingly, Humphrey then had to admit that he hadn't actually read the piece, which was describing a routine rotation. He had, however, incited the president, who delivered a previously unscheduled speech to the American Legion convention in New Orleans. "We yearn for the day when our men will come home," Johnson said. "But no man can predict when that day will come." Despite calls for a bombing halt—including by "some of our friends at home"—the United States would "continue to bomb the panhandle of Vietnam." Humphrey responded to this very public rebuke by his own president by reversing his position on the minority plank.[7]

The backing and forthing, the *New York Times* reported, "had created an impression of bumbling and indecision." Humphrey seemed to be trapped in a no-man's-land, separating himself from the president just enough to bring down his wrath but not nearly enough to appease the hecklers. At a rally outside Filene's department store in Boston, Humphrey was joined by Teddy Kennedy, who bravely said that he had "no hesitancy" in supporting the vice president at a time when political leaders far less liberal than he would not even share the same stage with him. But even Teddy could not serve as a heat shield: five hundred or so protesters shouted "Dump the Hump!" and "Shame!" and even "Sieg heil!" so loudly that the speakers had to be cranked up just to make Humphrey audible. The rattled candidate vented his wrath. "Your actions are going to disgust the American people," he shouted over the din. Humphrey was somehow soldiering on, but the apparent futility of it all was taking a toll even on his ebullient spirit. Edgar Berman came in to Humphrey's hotel room one morning and found him sitting up on the edge of his bed. "You know," Humphrey said wearily, "the toughest part of the day is right now—just getting out of bed to face the music."[8]

The press was obsessed with Vietnam, but the shocking success of the Wallace candidacy had shown Humphrey's advisers that anger over crime and disorder was far deeper and more widespread than they had realized. A Gallup poll found that 81 percent of respondents agreed that "law and order has broken down in this country." Black people were disproportionately victimized by crime; yet many white Americans saw Blacks as the cause of crime. The riots had led to a drastic polarization of opinion. Gerald Hursh, Humphrey's pollster, cited surveys showing that 70 percent of whites believed that riots were being "organized by groups hating whites." (Only 7 percent of Black respondents agreed.) Eighty-two percent of whites now said they were opposed even to nonviolent civil rights demonstrations; three-quarters of white respondents believed that Blacks were now treated the same as whites and thus had no need for protest. From the point of view of the electoral calculus, mollifying the left on Vietnam mattered far less than mollifying the right on law and order.[9]

Humphrey's urban task force had spent the summer debating the issue. On September 17 the campaign published the "Task Force Report on Order and Justice." That was a very conscious reframing, for Humphrey wished to condemn the chaos and anarchy of the riots and violent demonstrations but, like the Kerner Commission, also wished to treat rising crime rates as a symptom of broader social failure. The report called for gun control, reforms to court administration, and increased spending on police equipment and training as well as on youth and on the "root causes" of crime—inner-city poverty, unemployment, schools, and housing. Nixon and Wallace both blamed rising crime on Supreme Court decisions bolstering the rights of criminal defendants, and most Americans agreed. The report explicitly rebutted this view: "The hysterical cry that murderers can now roam the streets with impunity as a result of Supreme Court decisions constitutes a dangerous kind of fraud and deception."[10]

Liberal editorialists welcomed the report as a triumph of sanity in an increasingly heated debate, but some of Humphrey's advisers regarded it as a suicide pact. At the very first meeting of O'Brien's senior campaign team on September 16, Jim Rowe said, "All the boys in the white hats are for gun control. All the votes are the other way." Two days later, Rowe repeated his argument; as for order and justice, he said, "We're going too far on the justice emphasis." Ted Van Dyk agreed: "Our biggest problem on this issue is that Hubert Humphrey projects as 'a nice guy' who doesn't fit this issue." Max Kampelman observed that voters were well to the right of Humphrey on the issue, but Blacks were to the left. Yet it was just this fact that made the issue insoluble inside the Humphrey campaign. Louis Martin, a Johnson adviser who was one of Humphrey's leading Black supporters, said that Congressman Adam Clayton Powell Jr. of New York had objected to the racial framing of the issue and proposed that Humphrey focus on organized crime rather than street crime. Organized crime was, of course, a nonproblem so far as the public was concerned, but Martin didn't have to remind anyone that the Mafia was white. David Ginsburg seconded that view: "We must separate law and order from race." No conclusion was reached.[11]

Richard Scammon, the political scientist and pollster, used to remind campaign aides that most American voters were un-poor, un-black, and un-liberal. That was who they had to win over. Humphrey himself didn't need reminding; he had spent much of his life out campaigning, talking to ordinary American men and women. He had a better feel for them than he did for alienated young people. In mid-September he sent a memo to Orville Freeman that he copied to Larry O'Brien. "One thing has become very clear as I have traveled about," he wrote. "The blue-collar worker, the lower-income white feels that the government has no interest in him. . . . The emphasis here in Washington is on the black. It is on Harlem. It is on the ghetto. Every time we continue to pound that emphasis, the blue-collar worker reacts negatively. It isn't that he's against the black or the poor. In fact, he would like to help. But he just feels that everybody in government has forgotten him. Yet he pays taxes and his kids fight the war."[12] Humphrey was groping toward a way out of a choice that felt to him both impossible and false, a choice between telling white voters to sacrifice themselves for Blacks or spurning Black voters in order to cater to angry whites. He was imagining a different and more inclusive Great Society.

Law and order may have been the most salient issue, but it was the war that filled the streets with protesters, that turned Humphrey into a "fascist" for the young and a puppet who was also a hawk for mainstream liberals. On the 18th, O'Brien went around the room and asked each participant what they, personally, thought was right. Robert McCandless, a dove, said that Humphrey should resign and break with the president. Bill Connell, a hawk, said that polling showed that most voters opposed an unconditional bombing halt, as did he. "The best way to do it," Connell insisted, "is with law and order." O'Brien said, "I would develop a program for troop withdrawal, based on being President January 20." Van Dyk said Humphrey should stick with the majority plank. John Hoving, another senior aide, said the opposite. Finally, a weary Connell asked if "we can get off Vietnam to something positive." The group was every bit as divided on Vietnam as they were on law and order and, on both, every bit as divided as the American people.[13]

Humphrey was in Washington that day, and he met with Johnson. According to his handwritten notes, Johnson said, "I do not think proper for VP or ex VP or ex President"—a reference to Nixon and Eisenhower—"to play Commander in Chief." "Troop movements very delicate things." "1½ million cables each year from State." "3 hours a day President reads cables." In short, Johnson knew more than Humphrey, and Humphrey was not to second-guess him on Vietnam. Johnson even told Humphrey how he was to handle the issue: "When I become President I'll spend every hour finding peace." That was the pressure Humphrey was operating under.[14]

The one thing all of Humphrey's advisers agreed on was that he had to make his own position clear—whatever it was. The Vietnam task force began to produce new speech drafts. A version on September 23 proposed a mutual and simultaneous troop withdrawal followed by an immediate cease-fire. In a small but significant shift, Humphrey was to urge Saigon to accept "dissident South Vietnamese elements" in the National Liberation Front and Vietcong into a new government. Humphrey tried to roll out the new plan in a television interview in Columbus, Ohio, that day, but so twisted himself in knots that only the most discerning viewer would have noticed: "But I do think," he said, "and I can predict myself, that it will be possible some time in the future, to be able to have a systematic reduction in American forces in South Vietnam when and if the army of Vietnam improves its combat effectiveness." Humphrey sought to give an impression of decisiveness to this muddle by asserting that while he believed that this was also the president's position, if not, "so be it."[15]

Nothing Humphrey had done since Chicago had altered the dynamics of the race. Quite the contrary: a Harris poll September 26 showed Nixon lengthening his lead to 15 points, with Wallace trailing Humphrey by 7 points. The vice president's frantic schedule was dictated in part by the imperative to raise money from big donors, yet he barely had the funds to print campaign buttons, much less run TV ads. McCarthy had refused to give the endorsement Humphrey felt had been promised. Even when Humphrey drew big crowds, as he had begun to do, the hecklers managed to take over. At the Seattle Center Arena on September 29, the demonstrators jeered Humphrey's warm-up act, the comedian Bill Dana, a Hungarian Jew who pretended to be a Bolivian named José Jiménez. Humphrey took the stage to cries of "Fascist!" Humphrey first told them to let him speak, then decided to let them speak—through a bullhorn—then reminded the protesters, as if he were Emily Post, that "the mark of ladies and gentlemen is good manners"—and finally told them to "knock it off" and "shut up." On a signal, dozens of demonstrators in the balcony began chanting "Dump the Hump!" They were violently dragged from their seats by Secret Service men and federal agents. By this time the rally had fizzled out.[16]

Humphrey had to make a break on Vietnam; there was simply no other way of changing the narrative. In mid-September, O'Brien had bluntly said, "Let's face it, Mr. Vice President, as of now, we've lost. It's on every newsman's lips. It's on everybody's lips. You're not your own man. Unless you change direction on this Vietnam thing, and become your own man, you're finished." Humphrey hadn't argued the point. He persuaded George Ball, his onetime ally, to step down as UN ambassador in order to join the campaign and oversee the drafting of a new statement on Vietnam. O'Brien and Humphrey agreed to spend a precious $100,000 to buy thirty minutes of television time to air the new position on September 30; that would be the campaign's make-or-break moment.[17]

The first circulating draft of the speech was a version of the August task force report that Humphrey had shown to Johnson. Both Ball and O'Brien considered it hopelessly feeble. Joining Humphrey in Seattle, Ball wrote his own version with William Welsh, a Humphrey aide. Fred Harris arrived from California and began working with Welsh and Connell. Nicholas Katzenbach, who had moved to the State Department, had written another draft, which Humphrey had liked. There were drafts from Moyers, Valenti, and Douglass Cater, another former Johnson aide who had moved to the Humphrey campaign. It was, in short, the usual chaos in which Humphrey asked for help from everyone and imposed no discipline on the process. On the morning of the 29th, the campaign staff went out for a cruise in Elliott Bay outside of Seattle. Ted Van Dyk found Humphrey wielding his electric razor in the bathroom of his Seattle hotel. "I don't want to see the drafts," Humphrey snapped; he told Van Dyk to just go ahead and write something based on the August statement that LBJ had rejected. Humphrey then went to work on Van Dyk's version. Meanwhile, O'Brien arrived from Washington. After Humphrey's ill-fated speech at the Seattle Center Arena, the campaign left for Salt Lake City, where he was to tape the televised address.[18]

The debate resumed in a new venue. Jim Rowe, DNC chairman John Bailey, and Bill Connell argued for hewing close to Johnson's position; Harris and O'Brien argued for a clean break. The conditions Humphrey would stipulate as sufficient to halt the bombing were the pivotal issue. Van Dyk's latest draft was regarded as "unconditional." Ball, who had flown to New York to tape *Face the Nation*, met with a messenger whom he had dispatched to Paris to ask Averill Harriman, Johnson's chief negotiator, what language he could live with. Harriman had said that an offer of a bombing halt seen as unconditional would undercut Washington's negotiating position. Humphrey desperately needed Harriman's support; the debate dragged on and on. Humphrey ultimately agreed to a phrase that had originated with the Katzenbach draft: in weighing the risks of a bombing halt, he would place key importance on evidence—"direct or indirect, by deed or word"—that the Communists would respect the Demilitarized Zone between North and South. That was still much too conditional for Harris and O'Brien, though Humphrey was now reducing Johnson's three conditions to one. Finally, at 4:30 in the morning, the candidate and his staff, utterly exhausted, went to bed.[19]

The indefatigable Humphrey woke up three hours later to have breakfast with Utah Democrats and then deliver a speech at the Mormon Tabernacle. He then returned to his hotel, where Van Dyk and Welsh had attached still more conditions to the bombing halt, adding that "before taking action" he would insist on seeing the word or deed. Humphrey felt that he had to give the president advance warning of the speech, but he couldn't let Johnson once again bully him into silence. He waited until moments before his taped speech would go on the air at 7:30 p.m. Fred Harris recalls standing in a studio with Humphrey to watch the telecast when the latter hurried into a corner to make the call. Humphrey later wrote that he told Johnson what he planned to say, and Johnson responded, "I gather you're not asking for my advice." Humphrey comes out well in the exchange. In fact, when Humphrey read the key passage, Johnson immediately reminded him that the administration had three conditions, not one, and tried to argue him out of his view. Humphrey did then stand his ground, and the conversation ended. He knew he had not mollified the beast of 1600 Pennsylvania Avenue. Harris says the vice president returned "shaken."[20]

The trappings of the speech were almost as important as the words. Humphrey was introduced not as vice president but as the Democratic candidate for president. The vice presidential seal had been removed from his lectern. He had heeded those who told him to speak as "his own man." Nevertheless, Humphrey began with his usual elaborate praise of Johnson's courageous search for peace. A stronger South Vietnam and a stronger Southeast Asia, he said, made peace more possible than ever—another tribute to the president. "We must always think of the protection of our troops," Humphrey said. But here began his micro-pivot. While Johnson had made the safety of American troops one of his preconditions for a bombing halt, Humphrey described the bombing halt itself as "the best protection for our troops." Then he proffered his "word or deed" threshold. He would, he said, "take the risk" that the South Vietnamese military would continue to improve as Saigon promised that it would rather than wait for it to do so. That being so, Humphrey said, the "de-Americanization of the war"—that is, the gradual withdrawal of troops—could begin "next year," not later this year as he had said a month earlier.[21]

Reporters who had followed the issue minutely, and who had been hoping for something dramatic, described the speech as an anticlimax. "If Humphrey moved out from Johnson last night," the *New York Times* wrote, "it was only by about a foot." The *Washington Post* noted that nothing in the speech was new save the bombing threshold. Yet newsmen also conveyed the post-speech spin by an unidentified aide—George Ball. "The speech was not cleared with the White House." The operative meaning of the phrase "direct or indirect" was "almost anything." Respecting the DMZ was only "an example" of a reassuring step the Vietcong could make. The letter of the speech, in short, was LBJ-compliant, but the spirit was the break with the White House the critics had been demanding.[22]

The speech was "purposely ambiguous," as the *Christian Science Monitor* put it; each auditor could interpret it according to his wishes. Teddy Kennedy, who had already endorsed Humphrey with the proviso that they disagreed on the war, concluded that Humphrey had healed that breach. "I applaud the courage of your statement," he wrote in a cable that fell upon the Humphrey campaign like the first drops of rain after a long drought. Gene McCarthy, who had returned from a vacation in the south of France and, presumably as a hoot, had become a sportswriter for *Life* magazine, said, "I'd like to help Hubert, but all those kids who believed in me would consider it a sellout." Richard Nixon professed himself bewildered. Had Humphrey decided to break with Johnson and "pull the rug from under" the Paris peace talks, Nixon asked—or hadn't he?[23]

Lyndon Johnson had been expecting the worst. In mid-September he had shouted at Orville Freeman that Humphrey was a "coward" who was surrendering to the doves. "A lot of the language was four-letter words," Freeman wrote in his journal. Johnson and Nixon had agreed that Hubert couldn't be trusted on Vietnam. Unbeknownst to Humphrey, Johnson and Nixon had talked about the speech even before he had discussed it with the president. Shortly after 6:00 that evening, a UPI report had published the key passage of the speech, and Nixon had seized the opportunity to call Johnson. He was wondering, he said with consummate disingenuousness, if the White House had changed its position. No, Johnson said, the three conditions remain. The president then took the extraordinary step of reading Nixon a secret cable from General Creighton Abrams stating that a bombing halt would allow the North to "initiate a large-scale invasion of South Vietnam with minimum warning time." Nixon piously observed that Humphrey's speech "will be interpreted, as I'm sure you know, as a dramatic move away from the Administration." He, of course, would not "move in that direction."[24]

Johnson told Senator Everett Dirksen that he would have his National Security Council staff analyze the speech to see whether or not Humphrey was deviating from the White House peace plan; he promised to use Dirksen as "the transmission belt" for White House talking points on the speech for Republican candidates, of course including Nixon. Johnson's aide Charlie Murphy reported back on the overall air of confusion over Humphrey's red lines, but concluded that the bombing passage was "more unconditional than conditional." That's where Johnson himself landed. His young aide Tom Johnson, who sat in on the Tuesday national security meeting October 1, says that LBJ regarded the speech as "treasonous almost."[25]

The person most affected by Humphrey's speech was probably Humphrey himself. "I feel good inside for the first time," he admitted. Humphrey was someone who *had* to feel good inside himself; whenever he hadn't, as in the doldrums of the mid-1930s, he had suffered physically. In recent weeks he had been tired and irritable; his stomach hurt. Now, suddenly, he was himself again. Larry O'Brien saw the effect right away. "He felt good about it," he told the reporter Teddy White; "He was his own man." Disaffected Democrats had been so yearning for Humphrey to become worthy of their enthusiasm that even his tiny sign of independence was enough to loosen the floodgates of support. The campaign, which had been running on empty, took in $250,000 right after the speech—mostly in small donations—and $1 million over the ensuing ten days. The center-left began to come around. On October 3 ten House Democrats announced that they were shifting from McCarthy to Humphrey. Two days later, Americans for Democratic Action voted seventy-one to sixteen to issue a belated endorsement. In Jacksonville, Florida, new supporters waved a sign that read, "If You Meant It, We're with You." On October 9 Humphrey even got a friendly greeting from a group of college students in Boston. "I was glad to see they had smiles for a change," said the deeply relieved candidate. The students said that Humphrey had tears in his eyes.[26]

The liberals were almost bound to come home; they always voted, and they couldn't bring themselves to vote for Nixon. But there weren't nearly enough of them to put Humphrey over the top; he needed to bring back the working-class Democrats who had defected to Nixon and Wallace. Here Humphrey finally reaped what he had long sowed. At a meeting of the general board of the AFL-CIO

September 19, George Meany had approved "an unprecedented mobilization of union resources" for Humphrey, the one national political figure who had always championed their cause. The labor confederation remained an immensely powerful force, for at least one-third of workers in each of the Midwestern states that Humphrey hoped to win—Pennsylvania, Ohio, Illinois, Michigan—belonged to a union. The AFL-CIO's entire organizing staff of one hundred would be released to work for the Humphrey campaign; an even larger number of officials from locals would do so as well. COPE—the Committee of Political Education, the union's political arm—would print and distribute more than fifty million pieces of literature. The union would undertake the kind of voter-registration drive that ought to have been the business of the Democratic National Committee; but LBJ had starved the committee of funds and allowed it to atrophy. The AFL-CIO would ultimately open voter-registration units in thirty-one Black communities and add a staggering 4.5 million voters to the rolls.[27]

The situation in early October was desperate. On October 6, the *New York Times* reported that Nixon was leading in thirty-four states with 380 electoral votes, Wallace in six states with 64 votes, and Humphrey in only four states with 28 votes. A Gallup poll showed that three times as many Democrats as Republicans were turning to Wallace, who was winning the South and draining off Humphrey support elsewhere. The former Alabama governor had learned to couch his appeal in language acceptable to northern voters. "I don't talk about race or segregation any more," he explained to reporters on his campaign plane in September. "We're talking about law and order, and local control of schools, and things like that." In early October Humphrey began stripping off that camouflage. Wallace, he said, was "the apostle of hate and racism." His running mate, a former US Air Force general, Curtis LeMay, "said he would bomb Vietnam back to the Stone Age." Humphrey continued to hammer away at Wallace while unions flooded their members with literature telling them that Alabama was a low-wage, right-to-work, anti-union, high-crime state.[28]

The appeal to conscience, and to pocketbook, could only take Humphrey so far. He needed to address voters' fears; his report on "Order and Justice," with its strong focus on the latter, hadn't done the trick. A Gallup poll of union members found that 80 percent thought the police couldn't do their job because "their hands [were] tied" by politicians and the courts. On September 30, Evron Kirkpatrick spoke to the thrice-weekly meeting of campaign strategists. "Law and order is the biggest issue across the country," he said—and with all major subgroups. "More Negroes than whites," Kirkpatrick went on, favored "federal action" on crime prevention. The comforting idea that "order" was for the hard hats and "justice" for the white hats was a liberal illusion. Max Kampelman had sent a memo to O'Brien suggesting that the next time Humphrey faced hecklers he should say, "I call upon the law enforcement officers to enforce the law so that the rights of the majority to hear and participate may be protected." This idea provoked a remarkable conversation in which Jim Rowe proposed that a "labor team"—presumably of roughnecks—be stationed near demonstrators while Louis Martin proposed a program of covert infiltration. (There is no evidence the campaign did either.)[29]

O'Brien and Humphrey had agreed to spend another $100,000 for a half-hour speech on law and order October 12. This address had none of the eleventh-hour drama of the Salt Lake City speech. Promising to deliver "straight talk" to the American people, Humphrey spoke openly of the fear that white Americans had of Blacks—and Blacks of whites. He condemned extremists and promised to crack down on urban violence. He promised federal action—but not the kind that would "untie" the hands of police, which, in any case, arose from court decisions and local law enforcement. Humphrey repeated the proposals his task force had made, promising once again to uproot the "poverty, despair, [and] alienation" that "all of us" knew served as "the breeding grounds of crime." Humphrey could not bring himself to pander, even with the election in the balance. His address broke no new ground and received almost no press coverage. Within a few days the press was reporting that he had abandoned law and order to

Wallace and Nixon, and was back to talking about social justice and expanded Great Society programs.[30]

Humphrey was bleeding votes to Nixon as well as to Wallace, but Nixon had run a studiously bland and almost attack-proof campaign. For lack of better, Humphrey seized on that very fact, challenging Nixon to debate him as he had once debated Kennedy, and lampooning his rival for substituting vague promises for Humphreyesque ten-point plans. Nixon was "the Shadow," "fearless Fosdick," "Richard the Chicken Hearted." But Nixon was far too disciplined to be goaded into a debate, which he understood would play to Humphrey's strengths. On October 12 the Nixon campaign said there would be no debates even if Humphrey paid for them, as he had offered to do. So Humphrey held a televised panel discussion with two empty lecterns. On the show he tried out a new metaphor, saying that America needed a pilot who knew how to navigate storm systems. "Wallace," he said, "is the kind of pilot who says, 'hit the thunderhead.'" Nixon would say, "Maybe we ought not to take off." He himself, however—and here, having apparently not come up with a pithy self-definition while his fertile mind was devising mockery for his rivals, Humphrey got tangled up in radars and evasive maneuvers and whatnot. "It's not for the faint-hearted," he concluded.[31]

What Humphrey really needed was Lyndon Johnson, who still had great appeal to centrist Democrats. On October 8 Larry O'Brien sent a desperate plea to the president, imploring him to publicly stand up to "the Nixon attacks on your record." O'Brien proposed an extensive speaking tour; he never heard back. In fact, one day earlier, when Richard Daley had asked Johnson if he would campaign for Humphrey, the president had growled, "Every day they're talking about how they've broken with the Administration." Maybe, he conceded, he would criticize Wallace and Nixon without speaking up for his vice president. Johnson did, however, agree to tape a short speech endorsing Humphrey to be broadcast on NBC October 10. He contrasted Nixon's "record of reaction and recession" to Humphrey's "forward-looking leadership." But he held out no hope for an imminent breakthrough in Vietnam. If the North refused to meet what Johnson called "the minimal requirements of fairness," then American forces would have to retain "a strong position on the battlefield."[32]

Humphrey felt that he needed to meet with the president at the White House as an implicit statement of support. Johnson agreed to meet Humphrey October 19 before he left for Camp David, after Humphrey had finished an appearance at a shopping mall in suburban Maryland. The candidate was caught in a downpour and raced back to his apartment to change into dry clothes. By the time he reached the White House he was a minute, or, in another version, twelve minutes, late for a meeting that is variously said to have been scheduled for noon, 1:00, or 2:00. All accounts agree, though, that Humphrey arrived at the basement entrance to the West Wing, went inside—and found his way blocked by presidential aide Jim Jones. The president, said Jones, had decided to leave. Humphrey could see and hear LBJ in the Oval Office. He was so enraged that for once he let his feelings show. "Tell Johnson he can cram that goddamn appointment up his ass!," he shouted, loud enough for Johnson to hear. That was a cheap thrill for Humphrey and his aides, but it did nothing to improve the situation.[33]

Nevertheless, by mid-October Humphrey was exulting in his underdog status. "Do you remember back in 1948," he shouted to a crowd of ten thousand packed into a square in downtown Kansas City, "when Harry Truman whistle-stopped across America telling it like it was?" He would beat the odds by going to the people, just as Truman had. Humphrey was hearing the cheers; almost as good, he was getting heckled from the right instead of the left. When he heard jeers from Wallace supporters at the Avco Lycoming plant in Stratford, Connecticut, Humphrey pointed into the crowd and said, "Let me tell the young man with the white face down there it isn't a black man that's going to take your job, it's a Republican Administration." The crowds were still often sparse or even apathetic, but Humphrey himself was so incandescent with hope and faith that even battle-hardened reporters and columnists, most of them longtime members of the Hubert fan club, caught the spirit. "It is hard," wrote the columnist Joseph Kraft on the 24th, "not to feel a thrill of excitement for Hubert Humphrey, a truly decent man who all his life has been fighting and not quite beating the odds that make it so rare for a nice guy to finish first." The narrative began to shift; Humphrey was "surging."[34]

The professionals felt it, too; politicians who had shunned Humphrey before were eager to join him now. When the campaign plane landed in Waco, Texas, October 22, reporters were astounded to see Governor John Connally and Senator Ralph Yarborough, leaders of the right-wing and left-wing factions of the state party, men who were not on speaking terms, standing shoulder to shoulder to greet Humphrey. At Love Field in Dallas later that day, an army jeep pulled up on the tarmac next to Humphrey's plane and out popped Lady Bird to deliver both an endorsement and a hug. On the 26th, Gallup reported that Nixon was at 44 percent, Humphrey at 36, and Wallace at 15, a 5-point shift from Wallace to Humphrey over the previous week. A *Daily News* poll had Humphrey trailing by only 2 points in New York, a state that he had to win but that Nixon had considered in the bag a few weeks earlier. That same day, the president hit the campaign trail for the first time, campaigning for Humphrey in West Virginia and Kentucky. Johnson defended his record and managed to mention the presidential candidate in passing.[35]

The sledgehammer attack on Wallace as a racist had taken its toll. In September, 53 percent of respondents to a Harris poll had said that, as president, Wallace "would handle law-and-order the way it ought to be handled." That percentage had fallen to 21. Gerald Hursh reported that Humphrey was narrowing the gap with Nixon among the eight million undecided voters. Humphrey needed to raise his standing on the left as well as the right. A McCarthy endorsement and a breakthrough in the Paris talks would help the turnout among liberals in Illinois, New Jersey, California, and other tightly contested states. McCarthy continued to treat his endorsement as a pearl of too rare a price to be surrendered absent dramatic concessions. Finally, on October 29, a week before the election, McCarthy released a statement noting that while "most Americans are quite capable of making their own decisions about the Presidency," he was prepared to tell those who might be looking to him for guidance that he would be voting for Humphrey—despite the fact that the nominee's position on Vietnam and political reform "falls far short of what I think it should be." This "endorsement" was so preposterously grudging that two days later McCarthy felt compelled to issue a clarification: "Do everything you can . . . to make Hubert Humphrey president."[36]

Vietnam was the only remaining variable. A breakthrough *was* imminent. The North had reduced incursions into the DMZ as well as attacks on major cities in the South, satisfying Johnson's preconditions. On October 15 Johnson instructed Harriman to offer the Communists an immediate bombing halt should they agree to Saigon's presence at the peace talks. This time they did. On October 26, Le Duc Tho, the Communists' chief negotiator, finally informed Harriman that the North would agree to the White House terms, with a mutual bombing halt to be declared October 30 and talks to begin November 6. But as the North made concessions, President Thieu began digging in his heels. He told Ambassador Ellsworth Bunker that he would only sit with the NLF if the group was incorporated into the northern delegation, a condition he knew Hanoi would not accept. He urged Washington to continue the bombing. On the 28th, Thieu agreed to sit with, though not recognize, the NLF. But when Dean Rusk called Thieu at dawn on the 29th, the latter mysteriously said he could not prepare a delegation in time for the proposed talks; they would have to be delayed. The following day Thieu flatly refused to hold talks before the American election.[37]

Thieu had always feared the popularity of the NLF; in a fair electoral fight, he might lose. He also recognized America's exhaustion with the war, and he worried that Johnson would sacrifice him in order to win the lasting legacy of a peacemaker. But why had he suddenly reversed himself and dug in his heels? The week before, Thieu had received a cable from Bui Diem, his ambassador in Washington, saying, "Many Republican friends have contacted me and encouraged us to stand firm. They were alarmed by press reports that you had already softened your position." In a cable several days later, Ambassador Diem attributed these sentiments directly to "the Nixon entourage." Diem told Thieu that if he would only hold out long enough to deny the Democrats a peace deal, Nixon would win the election and offer the South better terms than either Johnson or Humphrey would.

"The longer the present situation continues," Diem wrote on October 27, "the more we are favored."[38]

Diem's contact inside the campaign was Anna Chennault, the glamorous Chinese-born widow of Air Force general Claire Chennault. Anna Chennault had become a leading figure in the pro-Taiwan China Lobby and a major Republican fund-raiser. In July, she had introduced Diem to Nixon and his campaign manager, John Mitchell. Nixon had told the emissary to rely on Chennault henceforward "as the only contact between myself and your government." After the Nixon campaign had learned of Johnson's determination to convene peace talks, Mitchell had called Chennault; Thieu, he said, must refuse to go to Paris. Chennault had then relayed this message to Diem, who had in turn conveyed it to the Vietnamese leader. Because the CIA and the National Security Agency had bugged Thieu's phone, and the CIA and FBI had wiretaps on Diem's calls, the White House knew by late October that information was passing from the Nixon campaign to Saigon. By October 30 Johnson had learned that Chennault was the go-between, and he had to decide whether to go ahead with the peace talks without Saigon. He delayed a planned announcement for the 30th, but then on the following evening delivered a televised address announcing the bombing halt and the beginning of talks November 7, the day after the election. South Vietnam, he said carefully, would be "free to participate."[39]

Before he went on the air, Johnson spoke once again to the three candidates, informing them of the terms to which Hanoi had agreed. He asked them to say nothing in public. Johnson then lodged two complaints. First he objected to those who said that "we would stop the bombing without . . . obtaining anything in return." That, of course, was Humphrey. Only then did the president reveal something of what he knew: "Some of the Old China lobbyists, they're going around implying to some of the embassies and some of the others that they might get a better deal out of somebody that was not involved with this." Johnson then called Humphrey back and told him more of what he knew, though not everything. He blamed the "China Lobby crowd" for Thieu's intransigence. LBJ said he wasn't sure whether Nixon was personally involved, but he knew that "some of the people supporting him" had been talking to Saigon. He did not disclose Chennault's name.[40]

Nixon was now on notice that he was being watched. Anna Chennault began to complain to friends that she was no longer able to get through to Mitchell, and Mitchell put it out that he was reading the riot act to staffers, demanding to know if they had been in contact with "any embassies." They had not, he found. Very serious reporters would later repeat this malarkey to prove that neither Nixon nor his chief lieutenants had been involved with the back channel to Saigon. Johnson, however, had no doubt about the campaign's complicity and said so to friends, including Everett Dirksen and Richard Russell. On November 1 he called Jim Rowe to say that Nixon was working through Chennault to upend the Paris peace talks. Rowe, as Johnson would have assumed, immediately told Humphrey, who also heard Chennault's name from William Bundy, who had become a source inside the Johnson administration.[41]

Johnson now began an urgent debate with aides over whether he should reveal or leak the information, perhaps destroying Nixon's candidacy. He was now enraged at Nixon. But he did not want to be seen as manipulating the outcome of an election; he feared provoking a public firestorm, and he did not wish to reveal that America was spying on its own allies. Johnson decided to say nothing. His aide Tom Johnson, who felt sure the revelation would swing the election to Humphrey, was horrified. "I will go to my grave not understanding why he didn't authorize one of us to leak it or to go public," Johnson says. Secretary of Defense Clark Clifford, who had little doubt that the president would have found a way to leak the news had his own political future been at stake, felt he had glimpsed the reason for his silence. He later wrote—in pointed italics—that at the time he asked himself, *"In his heart of hearts, does Lyndon Johnson really want Hubert Humphrey to win?"*[42]

Humphrey was now in an exalted state. The president's cease-fire announcement had filled his sails. On the flight from Newark to the Midwest the night of the 31st, he was singing in the aisles and cracking jokes with reporters. He was flying to Chicago, scene of his Golgotha. A number of aides had urged him not to go, but Humphrey had insisted. In the event, big crowds had lined the streets while Mayor Daley cooperated by keeping out of the way of photos. Humphrey's hands had become so scarred from shaking hands with people and being roughed up by their rings that his physician Edgar Berman had to keep applying salve and bandages. A new poll had him only 3 points back in Illinois. Humphrey flew on to Youngstown, Ohio, and then back to New York for big rallies in Suffolk County and Manhattan. As he did so he talked to friends, including Max Kampelman; Larry O'Brien and other senior aides; and his own longtime staffers—Norman Sherman and Ted Van Dyk—about how he should handle the Chennault revelations. Virtually all of them implored him to expose the Nixon campaign. Sherman offered to protect the candidate by leaking the news himself and taking the fall; Humphrey would fire him in outrage. But it all felt wrong to Humphrey. He couldn't believe that Nixon himself would stoop so low; a rogue staffer, he thought, must have carried out the plot. "Nixon may win and I can't leave a president with the label of treason," he told Sherman. What's more, the public might turn on him if he was seen to be using classified information to discredit his opponent. And he was winning. Why sully the victory?[43]

Humphrey had finally found an attack on Nixon that felt right. "The one overwhelming issue," he said in Newark, "is, Who do you trust with the most powerful position on earth? You can trust me, you can't trust Nixon." In fact, people didn't trust "Tricky Dick." So when he asked who they trusted, the crowds roared, "Humphrey!" In the frenzied blur of the final days—Humphrey would address thirty-one events between October 28 and November 2—he resorted to the phrase again and again. Humphrey and the crowds were feeding off each other. He told them he felt a "miracle" coming on. To Norman Sherman he said he had that feeling on the back of his hands. Everyone on the plane had that feeling. Max Frankel, covering Humphrey for the *New York Times*, says he warned his editors against taking his own assessment at face value, since the mood of optimism had become hopelessly infectious.[44]

On November 3 Humphrey flew into Houston for a giant rally in the Astrodome with Johnson, who had agreed to appear alongside him. Edgar Berman writes that on the flight down Humphrey grew freshly agitated as he read news of Thieu's refusal to send a delegation to the peace talks. "I could lose the election on this," he told the doctor. Maybe he should have George Ball tell Diem that if he didn't cooperate he'd "blow this thing sky-high." He would talk to Johnson about it, he said. Humphrey did ride with the president to the Astrodome, but if they talked about Nixon and Chennault, neither did anything about it. Still, a thrilling moment awaited Humphrey in the giant domed baseball stadium. The two men entered together and walked the entire circumference of the field, basking in the cheers of almost fifty thousand people. The crowd was rapturous. "It was," Humphrey later wrote, "Babe Ruth, Joe DiMaggio, Mickey Mantle, taking the cheers of the crowd."[45]

This would be Humphrey's last speech before the election; he spoke with great sobriety and, remarkably for that occasion, real sadness. "There has been almost too much pain, too much shock, too much violence," he said. "Too much uncertainty for our people to sustain." Modern life, he went on, was forcing us to ask whether man can truly live free, whether from repression, "the tyranny of the machine," or "the fear of his fellow man." Yet, he said, "I have believed that within the sharecropper, the son of the immigrant, the grandson of the slave lay such human potential that America has only to call it forth to see its full realization." Those were the words, and the sentiments, with which Humphrey wished to leave the long and agonizing campaign.[46]

On November 4 he and his campaign staff flew to Los Angeles for a final rally and telethon. Rowe had told Van Dyk that all efforts to move Thieu had failed; the peace talks would not be held. When Van Dyk conveyed the news to Humphrey, he exploded again. He instructed Van Dyk to draw up and circulate a statement to the press: "As President, I would sever all relations with the South Vietnamese and leave them on their own." Van Dyk, knowing that the candidate had reached the end of his tether, did no such thing. Instead, a calmer Humphrey released a statement saying the United States would hold the talks with or without the South. In Los Angeles, Humphrey got the final polls: Gallup had Nixon up by 2 points, but Harris had it the other way around. Euphoria was spreading among the giddier staff members. Bill Connell, who had been walking on air since the Astrodome event, was confidently telling reporters that Humphrey would win four hundred electoral votes. The crowds on the streets of Los Angeles were twice as big as they had been a week and a half earlier. The telethon was manned by Humphrey's Hollywood stars: Paul Newman, Vincent Price, Eva Gabor, Danny Thomas. Humphrey was so utterly exhausted that Muriel couldn't wake him up in time for the event; Van Dyk had to roust him from bed and drag him to the studio. Once seated, however, he and Muskie made a perfect, comfortable tag team—a foretaste of an equable White House.[47]

The campaign plane took off for Minnesota at 2:00 a.m. While the campaign set up shop in the Leamington Hotel in Minneapolis, Humphrey, Muriel, Berman, and a few others drove out to Waverly. That morning, watched by one hundred newsmen, Humphrey voted in the little clapboard Marysville Township Hall, filling out his ballot by pencil and dropping it into a box. The sheer weight of the moment almost overwhelmed him. "I had a feeling," he said later, "that it was more or less life and death. I sort of stood in silence and I guess I made a little prayer—ecumenical, nonpartisan prayer—that my efforts would be successful." For all his public bravado, Humphrey was far too experienced and too realistic to believe his own press clippings.[48]

Humphrey returned home and went back to sleep. That afternoon, as he drove to get a suit pressed, and paced around the house, and went off with his family to dinner at Dwayne Andreas's nearby lakefront home, Humphrey found himself—or so he would later write—thinking about why Johnson had shot him down repeatedly over Vietnam, and how he'd managed to get out; about who he would put in his cabinet; about how Ed Muskie was doing; about whether he "should have blown the whistle on Anna Chennault and Nixon." He thought of how proud his father would have been—and how helpful. At 11:00 p.m. Humphrey and his family arrived at the Leamington. He felt oddly numb as he entered to a big ovation; he didn't know whether the greatest triumph of his life, or a career-ending failure, lay before him. Humphrey retired to his fourteenth-floor suite and asked Dr. Berman for a tranquilizer to calm his stomach and nerves.[49]

By midnight, the deadline for most daily papers, David Broder was reporting in the *Washington Post* that the election was looking very much like the nail-biter of 1960. In the South Nixon was doing better, and Wallace worse, than expected; Humphrey held a slight overall lead in electoral votes. Most of the big states—California, Texas, Illinois, Ohio, New Jersey—hung in the balance. Humphrey's optimistic aides still had him winning an outright majority. But over the next few hours Nixon began winning bellwether precincts in New Jersey. He took California. At 2:00 a.m. Humphrey went downstairs to speak to the crowd gathered in the Hall of States. "We're full of optimism," he yelled—but he no longer was. He went back upstairs and slept for a few hours. Up at dawn, he had breakfast and went through the returns. Now it was truly over. He had lost Ohio, New Jersey, and Missouri; Illinois was all but gone. At 11:00 he went downstairs again to deliver his concession speech. "This is the worst moment of my life," he later wrote. "We could have won it. We should have won it."[50]

But was that so? Though Humphrey only trailed Nixon by 500,000 votes, the electoral count was 301 to 191, with 46 for Wallace. In *The Real Majority*, published the following year, Humphrey's pollster Richard Scammon and political scientist Benjamin Wattenberg concluded that Humphrey's momentum was not great enough to have carried him to victory had the campaign lasted another week. And the problem didn't lie principally on the left. Humphrey carried all the big states of the liberal Northeast save New Jersey, as well as his home state of Minnesota, progressive Washington, heavily Black Michigan, diehard Democratic West Virginia, and Lyndon Johnson's Texas. He lost the South to Wallace and the border states to Nixon. He lost heavily blue-collar, Catholic Pennsylvania, Ohio, and Illinois. He suffered a serious erosion from 1960—not to mention 1964—among men, among whites, among the non-college-educated. As the pollster and political theorist Kevin Phillips would later show, the 1968 election marked a drastic geographical reversal in which the South passed out of the hands of the Democratic Party while the economic and cultural elites of the Northeast shifted from Republican to Democratic.[51] Humphrey took a remarkable 85 percent of the Black vote. While the Democrats still held a major advantage among Catholic voters, the party increasingly depended on Blacks and white liberals.

If Humphrey somehow *had* won, Nixon would have had every reason to believe that George Wallace had cost him the victory. Thanks in part to the immense effort by the big unions, Wallace barely registered in the states where Humphrey was most popular. Elsewhere, he and Nixon split the vote. Nixon surely would have carried the Deep South states that Wallace took as well as Texas and possibly Michigan. Wallace supporters, Phillips concluded, were Nixon voters waiting to be cultivated—as, in fact, they would be in 1972. The immense psychodrama of Vietnam had devastated Humphrey personally and sapped the spirit of his campaign. But he had lost the election because America had shifted to the right after a long era of Democratic rule.

PART 4

Rebirth

22

Down, but Never Out

"It's a resurrection! . . . I'll win in a walk."

O N NOVEMBER 6, HUBERT HUMPHREY FOUND HIMSELF FOR
the first time in decades with nothing to do. Though he
would remain vice president until January 20, 1969, he no
longer had any real responsibilities. He took his family to Caneel Bay
in the Virgin Islands, a favorite vacation spot. Back in Minneapolis,
he got a call from President Johnson, who said that Nixon wanted
to make his defeated rival the ambassador to the United Nations.
The president-elect was hoping to build bridges to the Democrats by
appointing several hawks, including Humphrey and Scoop Jackson,
to national security positions. According to a later account, Humphrey met with Nixon at the Opa Locka Airport in Florida. Nixon
added several remarkable sweeteners to the UN offer: Humphrey
would be free to pursue his political ambitions, would have the right
to vet other Democrat appointments, and would have direct control
over some unspecified number of jobs. Humphrey's views of foreign
policy appeared to be compatible with Nixon's. Taken by surprise,
Humphrey briefly considered the offer, but he ultimately declined, in

part because he recognized that he would have to surrender his titular control of the Democratic Party. But if Nixon was hoping to strategically flatter his defeated rival, he had succeeded.[1]

For several weeks, the usually ebullient Humphrey allowed himself to mope. He went over and over what he could have done or should have done. Unlike his angry staff members, he was inclined to blame himself. He said to his aides. "I'm sorry I let you down." He said the same thing to Johnson. Though in fact he had almost pulled off a miraculous victory, Humphrey felt like a failure. At the stroke of midnight on December 31, he went into his bathroom and flushed the toilet, a theatrical gesture lost on no one. On January 21, he and his remaining staff members were moved out of the big suite in the Executive Office Building as well as his Capitol Hill hideaway and into several rooms in an office building on 17th Street. His giant collection of framed pictures, official citations, and gifts from abroad, as well as his personal documents, filled the corners and the hallways.[2]

Humphrey abhorred a vacuum; he needed work. He also needed money, for his vice presidential pension came to only $17,000. His friends came through for him in very short order. DeWitt Wallace of *Reader's Digest* paid a $30,000 stipend for Humphrey to teach at Macalester College, as he had done a quarter of a century earlier. Humphrey's great patron William Benton, owner of Encyclopedia Britannica, put him on the board and invented some duties for him; that would pay $75,000 a year. Humphrey supplemented this income with paid speeches, which he often delivered two or three times a week, at his standard rate of $2,500. He wrote a weekly newspaper column. Later in the year he got a $70,000 advance on a memoir. In 1969 Humphrey would earn the staggering sum of $200,000. He had the time and the money to go out to dinner and the theater; he traveled to Europe and to Russia and stayed in the best hotels when he did so.[3]

Humphrey regarded himself as a thinker, but the era when he read books and pondered larger meanings was long behind him. His first class at Macalester, which he invited the press to attend, offered a *tour d'horizon* of the Humphrey domestic agenda: extend the Model Cities program to all municipalities, establish a parallel Model States program, break down the barriers between inner city and suburb.

Humphrey praised Nixon for putting Daniel Patrick Moynihan at the head of a new Urban Affairs Council. Many of the students recoiled at hearing warmed-over speeches from a figure they regarded as a Vietnam apologist; some were impertinent enough to make that clear in classroom questions and remarks. His old friend Geri Joseph said, "I think he had to swallow his pride every morning with his coffee, because that's how insulting some of the kids were." Humphrey had been traumatized by his campus encounters in 1968; it would take a few months before he was comfortable with the students before him.[4]

Humphrey was still recognized as the head of the Democratic Party. He installed Fred Harris as head of the Democratic National Committee once Larry O'Brien stepped down—a consolation prize for losing the running-mate sweepstakes. He still employed several of his key aides; they talked about how to position Humphrey for 1972 and debated ideas for newspaper columns or magazine pieces that would help redefine him. Maybe, Humphrey wrote to Bill Connell, he should write a piece for *Reader's Digest* titled "The True Story of the Democratic Convention" or, more charmingly, "It Wasn't All Bad." John Stewart should work something up about the real demographics of American poverty, more rural than urban, more white than Black. Stewart briefed him on positive developments in Vietnam that might bring Ho Chi Minh to the peace table.[5]

Humphrey yearned to get back in the game, but his path was blocked. He was considered a shoo-in for governor of Minnesota, but it wasn't a job he wanted. Walter Mondale and Gene McCarthy occupied the Senate seats. At the national level, Teddy Kennedy held a commanding lead among potential candidates for 1972. A poll in May found Teddy 1 point behind the popular Nixon, and Humphrey 19 points behind. Then Humphrey's prospects changed in a single terrible moment. Sometime around midnight on July 18, 1969, Kennedy drove off a bridge on Chappaquiddick Island off Martha's Vineyard and then abandoned the car in which his passenger, twenty-eight-year-old Mary Jo Kopechne, was trapped. This was yet another tragedy for the Kennedy clan, and Humphrey, then traveling in Russia, treated it with all due solemnity. But he knew, and everyone around him knew, that a path to the Democratic nomination had just opened up. As if that weren't enough, McCarthy announced that he would not stand for reelection in 1970. Humphrey danced a jig. "It's a resurrection!," he shouted. "I'm high as a kite. I'm on the run. I'll win in a walk."[6]

Bill Connell summed up Humphrey's bright new prospects in a long memo to his boss. He had gone from an afterthought in 1972 to one of the two top Democratic candidates, along with Ed Muskie. Everyone in Washington agreed that Humphrey should run, though he should play it cool, as befits a front-runner. He should, on the other hand, go "hell for leather" on the 1970 Senate campaign while also working to reelect key senators. Connell, the in-house conservative, warned Humphrey that in beginning to assemble an agenda for 1972, he should resist the temptation to move left in order to capture "the old RFK-McCarthy followers." He should instead identify himself with "strict law enforcement." He should stop trying to play up his youth; Americans wanted gray hair in their president. Continue to be gracious and supportive to Nixon. Don't court the minorities; you already have them. Here was an early effort to sketch out a post-1960s, perhaps even a post-liberal, politics for the Democratic Party. Humphrey would never embrace it wholeheartedly.[7]

Humphrey now began very consciously addressing himself to the national scene. Fred Harris had returned the favor Humphrey had done him by forming a Democratic Policy Council to build an agenda for 1972 and naming Humphrey as its head. From the time the council first met in November 1969, Humphrey urged the members to think ambitiously about crafting forward-looking proposals for legislation on all the main issues likely to dominate the next presidential contest: the environment, arms control, taxes, unemployment, and the like. In an interview he laid out the path for a Democratic victory in 1972: make the GOP the party of inflation and the Democrats the party of tax cuts and economic growth; blame rising crime on Nixon. Humphrey gave these new themes an airing in a speech to the AFL-CIO national convention, accusing Nixon of allowing inflation and unemployment to rise while reducing spending on domestic needs. He tried out a new rhetorical trope: "They have remembered their friends in the banks and the financial institutions"—and in the corporate boardrooms, and in the South—"and forgotten the rest of us," above all the poor and Blacks.[8]

Humphrey was conspicuously silent on Vietnam. He supported Nixon on the war, both because he held the patriotic belief that the nation only has one commander-in-chief at a time and because he believed that Nixon, like himself, was searching for an honorable path out of Vietnam. He had met with the president in February, emerging to tell reporters, "There's no use downgrading the man; he's done well so far." On *Meet the Press* he described the president's foreign policy as "sane, sensible and responsible." Nixon had seemed to vindicate Humphrey's view in his first major address on Vietnam, May 14, when he had proposed a phased, mutual withdrawal of combat troops over the course of the year. "The time is approaching," the president forecast, when the United States could begin reducing troop strength regardless of negotiations over the long-term outcome.[9]

When the North, predictably, rejected Nixon's terms, discussions ground to a halt, and American soldiers continued to fight and die. In the fall, Senate doves, increasingly frustrated, presented resolutions demanding unilateral withdrawal, in some cases with a specified end date. For Humphrey, that was going too far. In early October he wrote to Nixon to say he would publicly endorse Nixon's approach to the war so long as he pursued a "systematic withdrawal" of troops. Humphrey may have felt he could influence Nixon by offering the olive branch of bipartisanship. If so, he was naïve. Both the president and National Security Adviser Henry Kissinger believed that the Communists would respond only to a superior show of force; they had discussed, though not formally endorsed, a major increase in bombing and ground combat called Duck Hook.[10]

Antiwar activists had planned massive protests across the country on October 15. Nixon, who intended to very publicly ignore the Moratorium, as the nationwide protest was known, recognized that a Humphrey endorsement could provide much-needed political cover. He invited Humphrey to visit him at the White House October 10. In a phone call with Kissinger that day, the president said, "The Humphrey move is very important, very useful to us." Humphrey had breakfast with Kissinger, whom he had once said would serve as secretary of state in a Humphrey administration, and then met with Nixon. Afterward he told reporters that he agreed with Nixon's strategy, which he described as withdrawing even while convincing Hanoi that sufficient troops would remain to make victory impossible. In a comment that startled even Kissinger, Humphrey said, "I believe that no man in the country is more desirous of bringing about an acceptable and workable settlement in Vietnam than the President of the United States." What he of course did not say was that this supposedly honorable statesman was the same man who had secretly conspired with Saigon to obstruct peace talks in order to guarantee his own victory.[11]

Humphrey's actual message to Nixon was tougher than he let on in public. In a note memorializing the conversation the following day, he wrote that he told the president, "I had come to realize since being out of office that the depth of bitterness was much more than I had previously realized." He advised Nixon to go on television after the Moratorium to say that he had heard the protests and to vow that he would quicken the pace of withdrawal. In a memo to Kissinger, he observed that, while a hasty withdrawal would be dangerous, worse still was "the risk and danger of hanging on and hoping for something better." But he kept that advice private. Whatever adroit political positioning for 1972 Humphrey may have felt he was adopting, his chief motivation was plainly just what he said it was—helping the president to end the war on the best possible terms.[12]

Humphrey issued a statement simultaneously endorsing the Moratorium, because it constituted a "peaceful and responsible" form of protest, and calling on Americans to support the president so long as he pursued a "prudent but systematic and accelerated withdrawal," which Humphrey asserted he was then doing. *The New Republic* treated the statement as proof of Humphrey's ludicrous desire to please all sides. And in a low point in Humphrey's relations with his former allies, Americans for Democratic Action declared itself "shocked and saddened" by his acquiescence to Nixon's formula. "We condemn his stand," the group wrote. Undaunted, Humphrey told students at the University of Minnesota in Duluth that an immediate withdrawal would leave 25,000 American troops "to be trapped and massacred in another Dienbienphu." On October 15, the day of the

Moratorium, which drew 250,000 people to Washington and 100,000 to New York, Humphrey held a special class on the war—to which, of course, the national press was invited. Humphrey tempered his praise of Nixon, saying, "I told him that there is a sickness in this country as a result of the war—that we must get out of it." But he still argued that the president was pursuing peace.[13]

Nixon responded to the growing clamor by delivering another major address on the war November 3. Kissinger called Humphrey in advance to say he hoped the latter would "feel that his recommendation that we say words of compassion for the young people has been taken into account." It's hard to imagine what Kissinger had in mind; Nixon said he would be violating his oath of office if he allowed policy "to be dictated by the minority" mounting demonstrations in the street. Nixon reiterated his refusal to order even a partial withdrawal absent reciprocal measures from the North, adding the condition that Saigon must improve its capacity to take over the burden of fighting. He was not pursuing anything like a "systematic and accelerated" withdrawal; nor had he intended to on October 10. Humphrey told reporters that Nixon shouldn't have given both the North and the South "veto power" over the withdrawal decision. But to his old friend Stewart Alsop, he insisted that Nixon "not only intends to withdraw our forces faster than anyone thinks, he is compelling the South Vietnamese to accept responsibility for their own defense—*and I want to help him.*"[14]

By early 1970, the happy warrior was back on the warpath. He used a February meeting of the Democratic Policy Council to condemn the Nixon administration for ignoring the concerns of the poor and called for "further redistributions of our wealth." Black people, he said, had every reason to feel "sold out" by Nixon. He returned to the old issue of disarmament, calling for an immediate halt to the testing and deployment of MIRV missile systems (the acronym for Multiple Independent Reentry Vehicles), overall cuts in defense spending, and improved relations with both Moscow and Peking. He began to break with Nixon on Vietnam when news of the secret bombing of Cambodia broke in May, regarding it as a reckless widening of the war. He applied more urgent adjectives to his rhetoric on Vietnam, calling for an "immediate ceasefire" and a "continuous and accelerated" with-drawal. On June 13, Humphrey announced his candidacy for the Senate, though that felt almost like an afterthought. He admitted, "I would be less than candid if I said that I would turn away" from the nomination for president "if it came my way."[15]

A sleeker, smoother Humphrey now presented himself to the public. He had exchanged the old Botany Bay outfits for tailored suits from Fioravanti, dyed his hair a brown tint that reminded some reporters of cordovan, and shed some of his excess avoirdupois. As befitted a member of the Establishment, Humphrey now faced a challenge from the left, in the form of primary opponent Earl Craig, a thirty-one-year-old Black instructor in Afro-American Studies at the University of Minnesota. Humphrey found it vexing—"ironic," he wrote to Eugenie Anderson—to be challenged on his civil rights record by a Black rival. A radical Pillsbury heir was funding Craig, he told Anderson, and "the left-wing money" would be "directed to destroying me." In fact, Craig was a soft-spoken gentleman who posed no real threat. Humphrey barely bothered to campaign, dispatching his rival in the mid-September primary by a margin of four to one.[16]

In the general election Humphrey faced Clark MacGregor, a five-term congressman who had risked his House seat on the assump-tion that he would be facing Gene McCarthy. With Dwayne Andreas's helicopter at his disposal, Humphrey was able to cover even more ground than usual in his sixteen-hour campaign days. He had the money for television broadcasts of his half-hour "Humphrey Open Forums" with carefully vetted local citizens. He agreed to hold a series of debates with MacGregor, but the latter couldn't make a dent in the Humphrey juggernaut. The old warhorse took 60 percent of the vote and carried Wendell Anderson, a young gubernatorial candidate, into office on his coattails.[17]

The senatorial campaign had offered Humphrey a chance to don not only a new suit and hair color but also a new and tempered understanding of liberalism. In late June he forwarded to aides a let-ter he had received from Zbigniew Brzezinski offering an analysis of the national mood with which Humphrey said he agreed. Hum-phrey's former foreign policy adviser argued that the nation's elites had suffered a "loss of confidence" that had, in turn, licensed the alienation of the young. Humphrey needed to offer "reassurance" about America's resilience and prospects to middle-class Americans and "direction" to youth. Humphrey must have already been thinking along these lines, because earlier in the month he had delivered a commencement speech at Hamline University in St. Paul titled "A New Bill of Rights and Responsibilities in the Twentieth Century." The "rights" included elements more common in the constitutions of European social democracies than in America's more individualistic culture—a right to peace, to justice, to a "wholesome environment," to a meaningful role in society and access to the political process. But these would come with corresponding responsibilities, also a departure from liberal individualism—to engage in public service, to support the rule of law, to "respect and defend the rights of others." Humphrey was offering an implicit bargain to the young: you have a right to expect more from society, but in return you must respect society's rules.[18]

Humphrey was now working closely with Dick Scammon, his old friend from Minnesota, and Scammon's coauthor Ben Wattenberg, whom he had hired as a speechwriter. In *The Real Majority*, published in 1970, the two had urged Democrats to separate the traditional issue of government spending, which working-class and middle-class voters continued to support, from "the Social Issue," above all law and order, where they had turned conservative. In 1968 Humphrey had tried to follow that advice, but he had not been able to bring himself to say "law and order" without adding the all-important word "justice." Now he was a convert. In his acceptance speech before the Democratic-Farmer-Labor Party convention in June, Humphrey, remarkably, defended the participants in New York's "hardhat riot" the month before—construction workers who had attacked demonstrators protesting the killings of four students at Kent State University. They were, Humphrey said, angry at flag burning, as any patriotic American might be. And it was wrong to think they were defending the war. Their motto was "U.S.A. all the way," not "Bomb Hanoi." (Humphrey conveniently neglected their other, more notorious chant: "America, love it or leave it.") Democrats, Humphrey said with his usual fondness for the symmetrical formulation, must find a path between the students' "excess of passion" and the Nixon administration's "lack of compassion."[19]

Humphrey delivered the most important speech of the campaign not in Minnesota but in St. Louis, at the annual meeting of the American Bar Association August 11. The title, a provocation straight from *The Real Majority*, was "Liberalism and 'Law and Order': Must There Be a Conflict?" The answer, of course, was no, if only because, for Humphrey, no good could ever be in permanent conflict with another good. Humphrey repeated the claim that blue-collar workers were not conservatives and could be cultivated if liberals would show that "they know what is bugging them and that they condemn crime, violence and extreme social turbulence." Humphrey offered a new formulation of the "law and order and justice" problem. In order to make the case that "root causes," such as poverty and urban blight, contributed to the crime rate, liberals must first gain credibility with working-class voters by showing they shared their concerns about disorder and did not regard it as a symptom of racism. Students, said Humphrey, clamored to be "heard"; but who heard the workingman, who felt that his values were under attack? It is not too much to say that Democrats have been circling around this problem without finding a solution for the half century since Humphrey gave that speech.

Two years after his humiliating defeat, Hubert Humphrey was back in business.

23

He's Got Runitis

"A man who would rather be President than right."

ONLY TWO MEN IN AMERICAN HISTORY HAVE SERVED IN Congress *after* serving in the White House—John Quincy Adams and Hubert Humphrey.[1] Most men have had enough of politics by then. But Humphrey, like Adams, could never get enough, and—unlike Adams—hadn't yet been president, and still burned to be. On January 21, 1971, when Humphrey was sworn in as senator by Vice President Spiro Agnew, his former colleagues rose in a spontaneous round of applause for a colleague as if raised from the dead. Once Humphrey had returned to his seat, one senator after another came over to pump his hand and squeeze his shoulder. That night, 750 of Humphrey's closest friends, including Defense Secretary Clark Clifford, Senator Edmund Muskie, and Larry O'Brien, threw him a party at the Shoreham Hotel.[2]

Hierarchically, it was true, Humphrey was just another freshman senator; he was relegated to the Government Operations and Agriculture Committees rather than Foreign Relations and Appropriations, which he had requested. But this freshman had an outsized megaphone. He was titular head of the Democratic Party and the chairman of the Democratic Policy Council. The latter position soon afforded Humphrey a chance to mitigate his gravest White House sin. At a meeting in mid-March, the council endorsed the McGovern-Hatfield amendment calling for the complete withdrawal of combat troops by the end of the year. Humphrey smacked his forehead and cried, "My God, it finally happened"—as if all the while he had been demanding such a measure. Humphrey delivered a short oration of his own, using the opportunity to lambaste Nixon on his domestic record as well as on Vietnam.[3]

At the same time Humphrey found himself facing an issue, and a dilemma, that was quite new to him—further funding for the supersonic transport (SST), a futuristic boondoggle upon which the Johnson and Nixon administrations had already lavished $1.3 billion. As chairman of the Space Council under Johnson, Humphrey had endorsed the project. But now pollution was an issue; and the highly polluting SST was the chief target of the budding environmental movement. Minnesota's senior senator and Humphrey's former protégé Walter Mondale, a new-generation politician, resolutely opposed the deal. Organized labor was strongly behind the SST, a source of high-paying union jobs; Humphrey was therefore widely expected to support the program and thus cast a crucial vote in an evenly divided chamber. But he didn't; he voted against it—and with his vote, the tide shifted and the SST went tail-up. Humphrey appeared to be sending a message that he was prepared to endanger his relations with old allies in order to embrace new causes. The message was received. One anonymous colleague was quoted as saying that the vote "restored a great deal of credibility to Hubert Humphrey."[4]

No longer the bumptious youth of 1949, Humphrey waited until March 25 to give his maiden speech, on disarmament, a passion of long standing. In an address every bit as extensive and analytical as in days of yore, he called for a moratorium on the deployment of the antiballistic missile and for a mutual freeze with the Soviets on the deployment of all nuclear weapons. No effort to achieve stability would succeed, Humphrey said, "if it does not measure fairly the other side's perceptions and fears." Disarmament was thus a political problem that could never be solved by technicians (such as surrounded Nixon). The following week, *Washington Post* columnist Stephen Rosenfeld wrote almost reverently of Humphrey's "comprehensive and profound understanding of the issues." Rosenfeld celebrated the arrival, finally, of "a strong leader, a counter-president," who could make the case for arms control both in the Senate and for the general public.[5]

Had Humphrey been content to remain a senator, he might have soon towered over his colleagues as Johnson once had, though for quite different reasons. After watching the overage freshman for a few months, James Reston observed wryly, "Humphrey is more serious, more amusing and more effective than all of the old boys and the new boys put together, and this is creating problems for the Democratic Party." Even the liberals, Reston noted, "are embarrassed by his bounce and zeal." At a time when the party was trying to pivot to a new generation, Humphrey kept stealing the show. Reflecting an increasingly common line of thought, Reston said that the leading undeclared presidential candidates, including Edmund Muskie and Teddy Kennedy, might cancel one another out and leave room for Humphrey to return as nominee.[6]

Humphrey was all too happy to fan those embers. On May 27, his sixtieth birthday, he invited a select group of reporters to breakfast at the National Press Club. The birthday boy was expansive about his prospects. "I'm licking my chops," he said, thinking about taking on Nixon. That night his friends threw him a party at the Mayflower Hotel. It was, by Humphrey standards, a very exclusive affair—one hundred guests, mostly major donors rather than the activist friends of former years. The fat cats included Walter Shorenstein, Arthur Krim, and Eugene Wyman from Los Angeles; Dwayne Andreas from Minneapolis; and S. Harrison "Sonny" Dogole, who ran a major detective agency in Philadelphia and would become a key fund-raiser for Humphrey. In the ensuing days, Bill Connell and Max Kampelman talked up Humphrey's prospects all over town. Humphrey himself entertained the columnists Rowland Evans and Robert Novak,

James Reston and David Broder, the town fixtures like himself, by forecasting which primaries he would enter, who he would overtake when, and how he would forge a path to the nomination.[7]

But the past kept seizing Humphrey by the collar. On June 13, the *New York Times* published the first of a series of excerpts from the report of the Vietnam Study Task Force, soon to become known as the Pentagon Papers. Among many other things, the documents strongly implied that President Johnson had decided to escalate the war in the early fall of 1964 and then lied to the American people about his intentions until the bombing of the North began in early 1965. If that were so, it was reasonable to assume that the people closest to him, including Vice President Humphrey, had also concealed the truth. He hadn't; but this was a case where the truth seemed implausible. Humphrey pronounced himself "surprised and shocked." The papers, he said carefully, described "decisions of an Administration of which I was a part. Whether I disagreed with some of them history will have to tell." To Broder, of the *Washington Post*, he said, desperately, "I am not a liar." Neither, he insisted, was Johnson, who in 1964 still thought that Asian boys could fight an Asian war. But he would not tell Broder what he had actually said to the president. "I'm not going to try to make myself look good at his expense," said Humphrey, in a display of loyalty that had never been remotely reciprocal.[8]

It was a bad moment. Humphrey's hometown paper, the *Star Tribune*, took him to task; Gene McCarthy wrote that as vice president Humphrey had evidently had "a constituency of one"—Lyndon Johnson. But Humphrey's friends rallied publicly to his side. Ted Van Dyk, who regarded Humphrey as a spent force and was leaving his office to join the campaign of Senator George McGovern, nevertheless emphatically told Broder what Humphrey himself would not—that Humphrey had been systematically excluded from the councils of war, that he had consistently argued to curb the bombing and the search-and-destroy missions, that he had been "almost physically nauseated" by the tales of corruption he had heard on his second trip to Vietnam. (That may have amounted to embroidery on Van Dyk's part.) "Humphrey never lied to the American people," Van Dyk insisted. John Roche, the former head of Americans for Democratic Action, who said he had had a hand in all of Humphrey's Vietnam speeches, wrote an editorial explaining that Humphrey had never believed that the bombing would work. Humphrey did one thing for himself: finally, after six years, he leaked the memo that he and Tom Hughes had written in February 1965; it was published in the *Baltimore Sun*. The entire episode confirmed that Humphrey was an honorable man while reminding people how hapless he had been in the White House—and, of course, how duplicitous was LBJ's conduct of the war.[9]

Vietnam was the quagmire from which Humphrey needed to extricate himself; the issue for 1972, he felt, would be spending and the economy. He used his opening remarks before another meeting of the Democratic Policy Council, in May, to assail Nixon for presiding over low growth and increasing inflation and unemployment. What really exercised Humphrey, however, were the administration's cutbacks in domestic spending. The council called for a full federal takeover of welfare programs, a family assistance plan guaranteeing a minimum income of $4,000 a year, an increase in the minimum wage, and a hike in the estate and gift taxes. The following week Humphrey indicated just what he had in mind by introducing the National Domestic Development Bank Act, which would raise funds by issuing bonds and then make strategic investments in local infrastructure, including health centers, sewage plants, school facilities, day care centers, and the like. This European-style social democracy constituted the other side of Dick Scammon and Ben Wattenberg's policy ledger.[10]

In his public speeches Humphrey returned to the framing device of a "new bill of rights," having lopped off the onerous part about responsibilities, which he may have intended only for transgressive young people. To the AFL-CIO and the NAACP, and before the Commonwealth Club of San Francisco, where FDR had delivered his famous 1932 speech outlining a "new economic bill of rights," Humphrey delineated the rights to which the citizen of 1971 was entitled. They had now grown to comprise twelve in all, including the rights to privacy, to safe neighborhoods, and to recreation. The ever-expanding list felt like an invitation to an ever-expanding government role, for all that Americans appeared to have voted for a reprieve from the visionary activism of the Great Society. Yet Humphrey's belief in the benevolent state was undimmed. Those Great Society programs, he said, "were only beginnings pointing the way towards more adequate and comprehensive efforts by the public and private sectors." Comprehensiveness was, in fact, the point: all Americans would benefit from a new New Deal, as they had not from the War on Poverty. As Humphrey told the NAACP's national convention, "The battle for civil rights for the balance of the century is the struggle to guarantee every American certain basic minimum services, benefits and facilities."[11]

Two days later, on July 6, Humphrey convened his kitchen cabinet in Washington—Connell, Kampelman, Dogole, Norman Sherman, and Jack Chestnut, who had run his Senate campaign. In a meeting that, like so many Humphrey meetings, lasted until 3:00 a.m., it was agreed that Humphrey would mount another run, though he would stay out of the early primaries in order to let his rivals beat one another up. This time he would have an effective organization. Humphrey had learned all too well that he needed one undisputed figure on top, and he gave the job to Chestnut, a thirty-nine-year-old lawyer who was universally described as cool, methodical, and meticulous—the human antidote to the rumbustious candidate. The *Minneapolis Star Tribune* described him, not quite tongue in cheek, as Humphrey's "first campaign manager," since all the others had found themselves competing with old friends, Senate aides, and people Humphrey had met the day before.[12]

In September Humphrey let it be known that he was taking "a stronger look" at the race. In mid-October Chestnut presided over a meeting of money men who had collectively pledged $500,000, with more to come. Humphrey's fall speaking schedule accelerated, sending him back and forth across battleground states: California, Texas, Pennsylvania, New York, California, Pennsylvania, New Jersey, Wisconsin, Ohio, California, New York, California, Florida, Texas, Wisconsin, California. He focused his attention on the core Humphrey audience: labor, Blacks, Jews, the elderly. He spoke on college campuses—but not the radical ones. In August he had trailed

Muskie by 10 points; by October, according to a memo from Bill Connell, Teddy Kennedy—a noncandidate—was at 25, Muskie at 19, and Humphrey at 18. None of the potential candidates on the left— McCarthy, McGovern, Fred Harris, New York mayor John Lindsay— registered above 5 or 6. The same was true of the candidates on the right, including Senator Henry Jackson and Congressman Wilbur Mills of Arkansas. The bulk of the party was in the center, with Humphrey.[13]

By late fall Humphrey had concluded that the nomination would not fall in his lap if he waited until the late primaries in New York and California; he would have to present himself on an equal footing with his rivals. In December Chestnut opened a Washington office that startled reporters long accustomed to the genial Humphrey chaos—not a bumper sticker in sight, or the usual crowd of loose-lipped aides. America was about to meet "the new Humphrey." This Humphrey had longer hair, which was dyed, and gold-framed glasses. He wore double-knit suits with wide lapels and flared pants. His ties were snazzy. He still talked fast, though he had learned to stop. But nobody fell for the makeover—not even his old friends. A reporter found a great many uneasy guests at the $1,000-a-couple dinner in Miami Beach at which Humphrey unofficially announced his run. "He's got runitis," one complained. "Nobody's going to tell him he couldn't make it."[14]

ON JANUARY 10 HUMPHREY MADE HIS CAMPAIGN ANNOUNCEMENT IN Philadelphia, the scene of his heroic stand for justice in 1948 and the largest city of a heavily unionized state whose primary he knew he had to win. From there Humphrey headed to Florida, the first state whose primary he planned to contest. Within a few days, the New York Times was reporting that Humphrey was conducting a "dawn-to-midnight" campaign like a newcomer introducing himself to the voters; in fact, Humphrey didn't know any other way of campaigning. And, as always, he promised new programs for his traditional constituents— more Social Security for the elderly, a "basic right" to kosher food and Sabbath observance for Jews, more spending on day care, food stamps, and free school lunches for Blacks. On domestic policy, Humphrey was very much running on the new New Deal platform that the Democratic Policy Council had been advancing: national health insurance, state-subsidized jobs for the young and the unemployed, a doubling of the federal expenditures on education, a complete federal takeover of welfare costs.[15] His big-state liberalism felt not so much avant-garde as nostalgic.

Humphrey's goal in Florida was to best Muskie, his chief rival among Democratic moderates. The clear favorite to win the state, however, was George Wallace, now running as a Democrat. The George Wallace of 1972 had an issue even more potent than law and order—busing. In 1971 the US Supreme Court had ruled that the federal government could require municipalities to use busing in order to desegregate school systems. In mid-January 1972, with candidates just beginning to campaign across Florida, the Federal District Court in Richmond ordered the city and its surrounding suburbs to draw up a school desegregation plan that would bus children from the largely white suburbs to the almost all-Black urban schools and send Black children to the suburbs—one of the first "metropolitan plans." White families in Richmond and cities throughout the South had fled to the suburbs as the Black population of the cities had increased in the 1950s and 1960s; now their children would be ordered onto buses to be taken away from their neighborhood schools and sent into inner-city ones.

Busing was liberalism's gift to George Wallace. "This thing they've come up with of busing little children to school is the most asinine, atrocious, callous thing I've ever heard of in the whole history of the United States," he declared. Wallace helpfully described the experts who "came up" with busing as "sociologists, anthropologists and zoologists." On February 15 the Florida legislature raised the issue to a fever pitch by adding to the primary election a referendum on a constitutional amendment to outlaw compulsory busing. While Humphrey and the others addressed modest rallies, Wallace drew monster crowds—6,000 in Jacksonville, 3,500 in liberal Miami Beach, 5,000 in Lake City in the panhandle, Florida's own Deep South, who waited two hours in ninety-degree heat to attend his rally. And he wasn't just addressing the faithful: busing angered racial moderates almost as much as segregationists. A poll the previous September had found that only 15 percent of whites and 45 percent of Blacks approved of court-ordered busing.[16]

Humphrey was counting on the Black vote, which was estimated to make up about a third of his likely support in Florida. He had the backing of old-line figures such as Roy Wilkins as well as younger leaders, including Julian Bond, the Georgia state legislator and head of the Southern Poverty Law Center. In mid-January Humphrey had returned to Washington to deliver a speech in defense of the Equal Employment Opportunity Act, which would give the Equal Employment Opportunity Commission, established as part of the Civil Rights Act, the power to issue cease and desist orders in cases of alleged job discrimination, and thus act against systematic discrimination. The government, said Humphrey, must take "affirmative measures" to stop pervasive discrimination in the workplace as well as in schools.[17]

But what were the limits of such "affirmative measures"? In his Johns Hopkins speech in 1965, President Johnson had said that formal equality was not enough; the federal government had to remedy the cumulative disadvantages created by generations of mistreatment. That meant forcing unions to stop discriminating against Black workers and going to court if need be. Did it also mean busing Black and white students across city lines to counteract the de facto segregation of Black city and white suburb? That was the logic of the Great Society. Yet the Democrats had suffered a terrible backlash after having asked far less of white voters than the courts were doing now. And the experiment was being carried out on people's children. Politically, it was suicide for anyone, including Humphrey, who had to win the votes of nonprogressive whites. On February 29, Senator Abraham Ribicoff sponsored a bill that would have authorized $1 billion to help localities carry out metropolitan busing plans. Muskie, McGovern, Kennedy, and Mondale, among others, voted for it; Humphrey joined the majority in defeating the measure.[18]

Humphrey no longer had any illusions about the political costs of drastic remedies to racial discrimination. He told a Florida audience, "I'm not for taking a child from a good school and busing him into a bad school just to solve some kind of philosophical attitudes that I have." No one, of course, was proposing busing to vindicate an abstract proposition; there was no other way to overcome segregated residential patterns. Humphrey said he favored open-housing laws to integrate neighborhoods—though he rarely said so in the South. He was more open about his preference for "freedom-of-choice" plans that allowed students to attend schools beyond their own neighborhoods. In reality, that meant one-way busing for Black students to attend largely white schools. When a reporter on *Meet the Press* said as much, Humphrey bridled, insisting improbably that many white students would like to attend excellent schools in Black neighborhoods. In mid-March Humphrey endorsed Nixon's call for a temporary halt to all mandatory busing. Only when his civil rights allies accused him of betrayal did he abruptly reverse himself, saying he hadn't read "the fine print" of the president's announcement.[19]

Humphrey felt that, on race and crime, he needed to be slightly to the right of Muskie in the center lane; at times, however, he seemed to be drafting in Wallace's lane. A radio ad in Florida promised, astonishingly, that a President Humphrey would "stop the flow of tax dollars to welfare chiselers." And that wasn't all: this redoubtable champion of foreign aid vowed that he would "put your tax dollars to work here at home before giving handouts around the world." When confronted with the ad Humphrey immediately withdrew it, calling it "a most unfortunate statement." But a man who had called himself "emancipated" seemed in fact to be shackled to his own ambitions. A *New York Times* editorial observed that Humphrey's repositioning implied "a man who would rather be President than right." Stewart Alsop, a confirmed centrist, like most of the members of the permanent establishment, even quoted the gonzo journalist Hunter S. Thompson to the effect that Humphrey "was a swine in '68, and he's a swine now. He should be put in a goddamn bottle and sent out with the Japanese Current." Of course he, Stewart Alsop, said he thought no such thing. What he thought was that nothing remained of the old, liberal Hubert Humphrey save the brown—now dyed—hair.[20]

Humphrey's rightward turn damaged his standing with civil rights leaders. Carl Stokes, who had placed Humphrey's name in nomination in 1968, accused him of trying to "out-Wallace Wallace." In an anguished memo, Ofield Dukes, a newspaper publisher and Humphrey's leading Black aide, complained that Humphrey had turned against busing at a time when Blacks had come to regard it as the single most important civil rights issue. "He keeps reminding audiences of all he has done in the past," Dukes wrote to Max Kampelman, "but what matters is what he is doing now." If Humphrey had sold a piece of his soul, he had barely gotten a mess of pottage in return: on March 15 he finished second with 18.6 percent of the vote while Wallace took 42 percent, winning every county and running remarkably well in heavily Jewish districts and liberal Dade County as well as the poor white districts in the northern panhandle. The anti-busing referendum carried 74 to 26.[21]

Nevertheless, Humphrey declared a tactical victory, since he had finished ahead of Muskie, McGovern, and Lindsay. "In his first primary," as an aide put it in a fine piece of spin-doctoring, "Humphrey proved his leading role in the moderate-liberal consensus of the Democratic Party." Humphrey moved on to Wisconsin, where busing would be a nonissue. There he worked the factory gates at dawn, just as he had in 1960. A whole new generation of political reporters now had a chance to goggle at the man's fathomless gusto. "Some may be tired of Hubert Humphrey," as one of them archly observed, "but Hubert Humphrey is not tired of anyone or anything." If the old Humphrey had been too hot for 1960, as Jack Kennedy had said, the new one was almost charmingly incandescent in an age of cynicism and irony. "Humphrey addresses a Jewish audience as though it was his mother," wrote Peter Jenkins, the amused correspondent for *The Manchester Guardian*. "The space program wasn't just trips to the moon, the space program was disarmament, weather control, it was saving lives, it had brought a new system of communication which was making worldwide education possible," and so on. When Jenkins gently asked Humphrey if he wasn't perhaps a bit too nice to be president, the candidate thrust out his jaw and said, "Goddammit, what this country needs is a nice man as President of the United States."[22]

Wisconsin had almost crippled Humphrey in 1960 when it went for the centrist Kennedy; now, far more progressive than it had been then, the state shunned Humphrey for McGovern, who won the primary with 30 percent of the vote. Worse still, Wallace edged Humphrey 22 to 21. A Harris poll found that Americans agreed by 46 to 31 that Humphrey "belongs more to the past than the future of American politics." Humphrey's campaign seemed to have run aground once again. But the candidate himself declared another tactical victory, for Muskie only won 10 percent of the vote, and soon after dropped out of the race. With the center lane to himself, Humphrey advanced to the big Midwestern primaries in Pennsylvania, Ohio, Michigan, and Indiana.[23]

Humphrey may have felt that he now needed to shore up his bona fides on the left, because a few days after Wisconsin he issued a remarkable apology in the midst of a Senate debate on Vietnam. The time had come, he said, to end American involvement in the war as quickly as possible. "I heard every argument that has been said here today," Humphrey remarked. "I hear we ought not to seek a cease-fire because it was not the right time. Let me tell you, Mr. President, I heard it often, and I believed it. And quite frankly, in retrospect, what I heard did not make much sense, and in retrospect what I believed did not make much sense." He wanted to say, he went on, "I am sorry that I did not come to that point of view sooner." No doubt Humphrey was hoping to blunt George McGovern's appeal, but no one could gainsay the sincerity of that painful admission.[24]

Humphrey kept his campaign alive by winning in the more conservative or heavily unionized states of Ohio, Pennsylvania, West Virginia, and Indiana. But in Michigan, the biggest of the Midwestern prizes, he ran into the brick wall of busing. District Court Judge Stephen Roth had just ordered a metropolitan busing plan similar to the one in Richmond. Evans and Novak reported in early May that Wallace was making huge inroads into Humphrey's working-class support, owing to anger over busing and spending on programs benefiting Blacks. At an event in Macomb County, whose schools would be blended with inner-city Detroit's, according to Judge Roth's plan, a woman attending a Humphrey rally stood up to explain that while she had voted for the senator in 1968, now she and her friends would cast their ballots for whoever was "anti-busing." Humphrey repeated his opposition to sending children to inferior schools. Such was the atmosphere in Michigan that even the faultlessly progressive George McGovern conceded that the Virginia judge perhaps "went too far."[25]

On May 15 George Wallace was shot and paralyzed in an assassination attempt. The following day, nevertheless, he won in Maryland and took 50 percent of the Michigan vote; McGovern placed second with 26 percent, and Humphrey garnered a dismal 17 percent. Wallace won half the votes of UAW workers and their families—a core Humphrey constituency. Humphrey came in third in the three southeastern blue-collar counties, including Macomb, that he had carried in 1968. The Democratic pollster Stan Greenberg would later use the shifting vote in Macomb to illustrate the rise of the "Reagan Democrats," who had switched to the Republican Party despite the party's hostility to unions. What Scammon and Wattenberg had called "the Social Issue" outweighed economic self-interest; it would continue doing so in the decades to come. The Democratic Party had now delaminated into a Wallace right, a McGovern left, and an increasingly narrow Humphrey center.

Though McGovern led Humphrey 900 delegates to 760, Humphrey could vault into the lead by taking the June 6 primary in California, whose 271 delegates would be allotted on a winner-take-all basis despite new party rules requiring a proportional award. Contesting California was a hugely expensive enterprise, but the finance gap between the two candidates was far greater than the electoral gap. McGovern entered California with $2 million; what's more, his army of 10,000 volunteers, as energized as McCarthy's youth crusade had been by the prospect of transformative change, staffed 283 storefront offices across the state. Humphrey, by contrast, was tapped out. He had had to devote precious campaign time to fund-raising and had little to show for it. Eugene Wyman had managed to scrape up $400,000 to contest the primary—until he received a call from Washington headquarters saying that the campaign was $1 million in debt. Wyman later wrote that he was told to wire $16,000 right away to keep the phones from being shut off. He wrote a $900 check to keep the campaign plane in the air. Ultimately he sent $250,000 of his precious cache to make up overdrafts. The Humphrey campaign would have to run on fumes. Dan Spiegel, a Senate aide conscripted for the campaign, recalls banging out position papers from a "fleabag motel."[26]

Humphrey faced another problem, and in some ways a more painful one. George McGovern had been his closest friend in the Senate. They had lived next door to each other for twelve years. Younger by eleven years, representing the state of Humphrey's birth, McGovern had always treated the older man with the deference due a mentor. Both their children and their wives were close friends. McGovern was precisely the kind of figure Humphrey most admired—a good man and true, deeply courteous, intellectually serious, uncorrupted by power. Bobby Kennedy had called him "the most decent man in the U.S. Senate." Now that Humphrey had him in his sights, what kind of ammunition could he bring himself to fire? Humphrey publicly answered that question in his California kickoff speech May 18: "I pledge to conduct a campaign based on the issues," he announced— "not personalities." He proceeded to lay out the substantive differences between them on defense spending, the space program, welfare. Humphrey would stay in the center lane and try to depict McGovern as a man of the left. He suggested, as he always did when he was behind, a series of debates. McGovern had no good reason to agree; but he did, because he was George McGovern.[27]

As in Florida, Humphrey seemed prepared to authorize proxies to take the low road. Los Angeles mayor Sam Yorty described McGovern as the mirror image of Barry Goldwater, an unyielding ideologue of the left. Mailings sent out to Los Angeles suburbanites described McGovern as "an ultraliberal" who favored "total busing." Evans and Novak, who had virtually turned their syndicated column into a running account of the travails of the Humphrey campaign, alleged that it was the ubiquitous Dr. Edgar Berman who had convinced Humphrey to put in the shiv. "The good doctor's talent for loony advice," they wrote, "has been known to Democratic insiders for a long time."[28]

By May 28, the date of the first of three scheduled debates, polls showed McGovern up by 15 points. Unable to mount a media campaign, Humphrey saw the debates as his only chance to reverse the momentum. The first debate, aired as part of CBS's *Face the Nation* series, featured the two men sitting next to one another. Both began with anodyne opening statements. Then, in response to a softball question about California's role in his prospects, Humphrey pivoted to launch a withering attack on his rival, who had adopted a slogan designed to point up the difference between himself and Humphrey on Vietnam: "Right from the Start." In fact, he said, McGovern had often been wrong from the start. "We were both wrong on Vietnam," he said. And McGovern was wrong today on Israel, on unemployment compensation, labor law, tax cuts, welfare, the defense budget. Gary Hart, later a senator from Colorado and a presidential candidate, but then McGovern's campaign manager, said, "I was watching McGovern's face when Humphrey was going on like this and almost literally his jaw dropped. He couldn't believe it. It was like seeing one of your closest friends become someone else." McGovern's eldest daughter, Terry, who as a little girl had worshiped Humphrey, and whom Humphrey had dubbed "the queen of Coquelin Terrace," was in tears afterward, asking if her father had managed to say anything to "Uncle Hubert."[29]

More detached observers were no less shocked. The columnist Mary McGrory wrote that "The Mr. Nice Guy of American politics" had turned into "a snarling tiger." She joked that Humphrey was "more psyched up than a Washington Redskin when he took the field." Declining to descend to his rival's level, McGovern responded evenly, "I heard him state on many a platform that George McGovern was the only Senator who was right on Vietnam, all those years when he and others were wrong, and I am somewhat amazed to enter the final days of this campaign—I realize the pressures we are under—and have the Senator say that our records are parallel." No one, by contrast, had been more enthusiastic for the war in those days than Humphrey himself, as McGovern pointed out. All that was true; no one knew better than Humphrey that McGovern had opposed the war since Johnson's escalation in early 1965. Ambition, perhaps the one passion that Humphrey could never control, had reduced him to violating his own promise to keep to the high road and misrepresenting the record of a man whom he had long admired.[30]

McGovern later wrote that while he understood "the desperation that was in Hubert's mind," and thus forgave him the wild haymakers he threw, "being slashed and blasted by one of the most experienced, best-known figures in American politics" had proved deeply damaging to his campaign. Whatever the reason, McGovern's ultimate margin of victory over Humphrey in California was only 5 points. But he also took primaries in New Jersey, New Mexico, and South Dakota. Two weeks later McGovern all but swept New York. He now had a clear path to the nomination.[31]

Humphrey wasn't quite through; he joined other losing candidates in filing a petition asking the Democratic National Convention's Credentials Committee to overturn California's winner-take-all rule—even though the party's Commission on Delegate Selection had already approved the system. A proportional award would prevent McGovern from winning on a first ballot, thus giving Humphrey a chance to triumph in a brokered convention. Humphrey would have howled with righteous fury if a rival had tried to snatch victory from him on such a pretext; but since he considered McGovern the stalking horse for progressive elements out of tune with the average voter, Humphrey had what he felt was a non-selfish reason for throwing a spanner in the works. In a statement to the platform committee, he warned of a Republican landslide if "the Democratic Party falls into the hands of any narrow ideological elite" that "neglects the day-to-day concerns of the many." In an interview on *Face the Nation* he acknowledged that he was referring to the progressives around McGovern who wanted to put the legalization of marijuana or gay marriage in the party platform, thus driving away blue-collar voters.[32] Half a century later, Democrats continue to be torn between the pocketbook interests that appeal to middle-class and working-class voters and identity issues that matter most to a small but zealous band of progressives.

How low would Humphrey go to preserve a shred of a chance at victory? Though he had earlier ruled out George Wallace as a possible running mate, in mid-June he told *Time* that he would consider anyone, including Wallace, who would abide by the Democratic platform.

That sounded like a patently insincere effort to appease followers of the now wheelchair-bound candidate, but there is some evidence that Humphrey had been secretly soliciting Wallace's favor. Several years later, Jimmy Faulkner, an Alabama politician and Wallace friend, would state that in late April he had been approached by John Amos, a southern Humphrey supporter and principal founder of the company that became Aflac insurance. Amos said he had been authorized to say that, in return for Wallace's support, Humphrey would be prepared to "consider such things as letting Wallace suggest the Vice President . . . or help nominate Cabinet members." Several weeks later, after the victories in Michigan and Maryland, Faulkner said, Amos told him that Humphrey was "willing to take George Wallace on the ticket on crutches, in a wheelchair, or any way."

This second claim seems absurd, both because Humphrey would have gagged at the prospect and because his own followers would have abandoned him en masse. Norman Sherman, Humphrey's former aide, who assisted Humphrey with his autobiography, confirms that Amos had the candidate's ear, but says he finds the alleged scenario unimaginable. What is not so implausible, though, is that an increasingly desperate Humphrey would have sought to explore terms under which he could inherit Wallace's delegates in order to prevent a first-ballot McGovern victory at the convention, as he then sought to do through the California challenge.[33]

At the Democratic convention in Miami Beach, the Credentials Committee upheld the challenge to the California rules, but the full convention voted to keep winner-takes-all. On July 11, Humphrey issued a statement of withdrawal; McGovern then won on the first ballot. In a retrospective account, James Reston, the unofficial bearer of the scales of justice in American politics, traced Humphrey's candidacy back to the humiliation of Chicago, and thus to his yearning for redemption. This effort, which Reston regarded as misbegotten, constituted Humphrey's "last tragic effort to recoup his losses." Instead he had come to the end of the line; and not just the man but the "old guard" whom he had come to represent, the big-city bosses and the labor leaders.[34]

Four months later, McGovern lost the most lopsided contest in history—520 electoral votes to 17. Nixon became the first Republican president to win the Catholic vote and the blue-collar vote. Whatever damage Humphrey had done in May and June hardly explained so complete a repudiation. The truth was that the FDR coalition that had begun to unravel in 1968 had now collapsed altogether; the centrist liberalism that had been the mainstay of Humphrey's political life had lost its purchase on the average American voter.

24

Elder Statesman

"Are you ready to speak up for the people?
Are you ready once again to be the sort of
party that we're supposed to be?"

WHEN CONGRESS RECONVENED IN JANUARY 1973, HUBERT Humphrey was no longer the leader of the Democratic Party, titular or otherwise. He had been defeated for the nomination by a younger and more popular man. Humphrey was now a party elder, though one without a single senior position in the Senate. Yet in the vacuum created by demoralizing defeat, Humphrey exerted a remarkable gravitational pull. He used his position on the Joint Economic Committee (JEC) to highlight the economic failures of the Nixon administration. He introduced the Fiscal and Budgetary Reform Act to bring more congressional oversight to the budget process, as well as legislation to end underground nuclear tests, to reform the Post Office, and to let the elderly and the handicapped fly at reduced rates. The press began to take notice. Under the headline "Humphrey Slips into Elder Statesman's Robes," Godfrey Sperling, the longtime senior correspondent of the *Christian Science Monitor*, wrote that Humphrey was somehow looking younger despite having let his hair grow gray again. "His words," said Sperling, "are being given special attention." Alongside the front-page articles about Humphrey's broadsides against the White House, there appeared a whole spate of pieces announcing that the old man, who after all was still only sixty-one, had "recharged his batteries."[1]

On April 11, Humphrey addressed the Democratic Party's Charter Commission, whose mission was party renewal. It was the kind of breakfast meeting to which the Washington bureaus of the big papers felt they had to assign a reporter just in case someone said something interesting. The meeting was predictably somnolent—until Humphrey got up to speak and, as a reporter wrote the next day, "caught fire." First he rebuked his own party for a moralism so averse to compromise that it regarded winning elections as "almost immoral," and reminded them of FDR's spirit of pragmatism. Then, channeling that ancient hero, Humphrey unleashed a furious assault on a Nixon White House trying to lie its way out of the spreading Watergate scandal. It was governing "by fiat," he said; the administration was imagining that deep social problems could be solved by the free market. "There is some poor little crippled child out there," Humphrey cried, "some poor little mentally retarded boy or girl. And we're told that if we help them we will unbalance the budget and cause inflation. I think the Democratic Party ought to give a great mirror as a gift to the White House and the executive branch of government and let them take a look in it and see their own dirty faces and find out what's going on in this country." Now the party solons as well as the NAACP chieftains were clapping and shouting over their bacon and eggs. "Well, are you ready to go to work?" Humphrey wound up as if he were goading a crowd of campaign volunteers. "Are you ready to speak up for the people? Are you ready once again to be the sort of party that we're supposed to be?" Hubert Humphrey wasn't tired of anyone or anything.[2]

Humphrey was the living link between the party's past and its future. When LBJ died on January 22, 1973, it was Humphrey who served as eulogist-in-chief. In a speech in the Senate, he recalled how

Johnson had once consoled a lonely freshman. That friendship, he said, had never flagged, despite reports of "some problems" between the two in the White House. "When I happened to be getting public criticism on a matter," Humphrey told his colleagues, "I could be sure of getting sympathy from the President." That was how the vice presidency lived in Humphrey's rosy memory. Yet a month earlier, when he had been invited to speak at a civil rights symposium at the new LBJ School of Public Affairs in Austin, Humphrey had declined to indulge in nostalgia. Instead he had chastised liberal intellectuals—no doubt including many in the audience—who had, he alleged, indulged in "an emotional binge about a cruel and lasting war" rather than tackling the nation's domestic ills. And he confronted the progressive wing of the civil rights movement itself. Since the Democrats could never muster a political majority from Blacks and other marginalized groups, Humphrey argued, "we must create a climate of identity of interest between the needs, the hopes and fears of the minorities and the needs and hopes and fears of the majority." Humphrey said bluntly that party reforms that had guaranteed spots to Blacks, women, and young people had harmed the party in the eyes of the white middle class. A new civil rights movement had to focus on providing education, jobs, housing, and health care to *all* Americans, not just to the disadvantaged. Only then would Democrats find the mass constituency they sought. This was to be the great theme of Humphrey's last years in office.[3]

Humphrey had hired a new generation of aides, and they discovered the mingled joys and terrors of working for the man. Dan Spiegel had arrived in 1971 to work on foreign affairs. One of his jobs was to answer all the mail on the subject. "Humphrey would prowl around the office late at night after we left and open our drawers and look at the letters," Spiegel recalls. "And then he would write nasty notes: 'Dan, the people have written letters and we haven't responded.'" Spiegel would be greeted the next morning not only with the late-night billet-doux but with a stack of messages Humphrey had dictated overnight, which had been typed up on onion-skin paper. But what Spiegel most remembers from that time was how Humphrey fought to preserve funding for foreign aid at a time when even liberals had come to regard it as a tool of American neocolonialism. On October, 6, 1973, the first night of the Yom Kippur War between Israel and Egypt, Humphrey was on the Senate floor with Spiegel. "We drafted an amendment on a yellow pad to provide Israel with $2.2 billion in military aide," Spiegel recalls. "And it passed."[4]

Humphrey seemed eternally young; but an elder statesman must deal with encroaching mortality. In 1967 he had been found to have a disease of the urinary bladder, and ever since had endured a very painful cystoscopy every six months to check for signs of bladder cancer. A test in the fall of 1973 found evidence of cell growth that could be cancerous. Edgar Berman showed the results to eleven cancer specialists; nine of them concluded that Humphrey did not have cancer. Nevertheless, it was agreed that he would get radiation therapy but not chemotherapy. For six weeks in November and December Humphrey received five minutes of radiation every day at 8:00 a.m. and then went straight to the Senate. He began to experience terrible side effects; a man who had barely been sick since having pneumonia at age eleven found himself doubled over with kidney spasms. In the first days of 1974, his legs and feet swelled alarmingly; he was admitted to Bethesda Hospital and spent two weeks there receiving intravenous treatment. For the next few months Humphrey took Demerol, codeine, and aspirin to keep the pain at bay, though nothing really worked. He barely slept more than a few hours a night. Finally, in April, the siege lifted and he was able to return to his usual schedule. Even more important, the tumors were gone.[5]

Humphrey's suffering during this time was psychological as well as physical. He had always looked up to the incorruptibles of the Senate, men like Paul Douglas and Herbert Lehman, and regarded himself as one of them. But in the aftermath of Watergate, politicians and their acts were being scrutinized as they had not been before, and Humphrey fell afoul of new standards on campaign finance. The Federal Election Campaign Act, which had come into force in April 1972, required campaigns to disclose the identity of all donors contributing over $100 to a campaign; it also prohibited the use of "straw donors" to disguise the actual source of gifts. Individuals and organizations that feared disclosure tried to evade the rules by making

off-the-books donations, often in cash. But the impaneling of the
Senate Watergate Committee in February 1973, and the appointment
three months later of special prosecutor Archibald Cox, ensured that
such immemorial dirty tricks would now be picked out in a harsh
spotlight. That light was often trained on Nixon's Committee to
Reelect the President, with its wonderful acronym "CREEP," but it
fell on Humphrey as well.

In many of the cases that came to light, neither Humphrey nor his
campaign had been aware of malfeasance on the part of donors. In
June 1973, the New York investment banker John Loeb was charged
with giving $48,000 to eight employees and instructing them to give
$6,000 each to the Humphrey campaign—in May 1972, a month
after the straw donor rule had come into effect. (Loeb pleaded guilty
to three of the eight acts and was fined $3,000.) Much more serious
allegations were lodged against Dwayne Andreas, Humphrey's great
friend and most important donor, though, once again, Humphrey
himself had no knowledge of the affair. In October, Watergate special prosecutor Cox charged Andreas with making $100,000 in illegal
contributions (under earlier law) to Humphrey's 1968 campaign. (A
judge would later find Andreas not guilty of the charge.) More hurtful
to Humphrey, Maurice Stans, Nixon's campaign finance chairman,
told the Senate Watergate Committee that in the spring of 1972, when
Humphrey was still the leading candidate for the Democratic nomination, Andreas had given the Nixon campaign $25,000 in cash in
order to hide the gift from his friend. Stans had then deposited the
funds in the account of Watergate burglar Bernard Barker, who had
used the money to fund the break-in. Andreas was not quite as loyal
to Humphrey as Humphrey had been to him.[6]

A staff report by the Watergate committee in June 1974 noted
that Humphrey's campaign manager, Jack Chestnut, had destroyed
records of campaign contributions made before the new law came
into effect. Both Chestnut and other Humphrey aides refused to testify under oath. The committee was thus unable to measure the full
extent to which the campaign had sought to circumvent the new law
before it came into effect. The report concluded, however, that in January and February 1972 Humphrey himself had donated $89,000 in

stock and $23,000 from a blind trust managed by Andreas to his own campaign. That did not violate the law at the time, but Humphrey had not included the funds in a list he had released of early donations. Nor had he included $276,000 that Andreas, his daughter, and a friend had transferred to the campaign. Humphrey declined to meet with the committee.[7]

The allegations painted a picture of desperation in the 1972 campaign, and that picture was accurate. The campaign had burned through the funds that Humphrey's longtime network of donors had given in late 1971 and early 1972. After the Florida primary, with contests coming up in big and expensive Midwestern states, the treasury was so empty that Humphrey had interrupted his campaign to fly to Minneapolis with Sonny Dogole, his chief fund-raiser, for a meeting with key backers. There Humphrey and his staffers had begged for $5,000 or $10,000 loans, promising to pay them off with the proceeds of an upcoming fund-raiser (which they hadn't, in fact, been able to do). By May 1972, they had run out of money once again, forcing Eugene Wyman to bail out the campaign with funds reserved for the California primary. Jack Chestnut thus may have had good reason to destroy the fund-raising records from the spring of 1972.[8]

Chestnut himself fell beneath the Watergate scythe after he was found to have solicited $12,000 in illegal contributions from Associated Milk Producers, Inc., or AMPI, a giant dairy cooperative. Through its political action committee, known as C-TAPE, (Committee for Thorough Agricultural Political Education), the cooperative had always been a major donor to both parties, both in the Midwest and nationally. As a corporation—even though it was in fact a network of dairy farmers—AMPI was banned from making contributions under the 1907 Tillman Act, which prohibited corporate contributions to federal election campaigns. But the organization's executives had come to draw on corporate funds in order to circumvent reporting requirements. An audit conducted by the Watergate committee found that in the 1968 presidential campaign AMPI had given Humphrey $96,000 to pay for a campaign aide, various campaign expenses, and the reimbursement of individual donations. (Humphrey stated that he had had no way of knowing that the funds had come from AMPI rather than C-TAPE.) In January 1974, two AMPI officials, Donald Parr and Keifer Howard, pleaded guilty to funneling $22,000 in corporate contributions to Humphrey's 1968 campaign. In July, Parr and Harold Nelson, former general manager of AMPI, admitted making over $500,000 in illegal contributions to a range of candidates in 1968, 1970, and 1972.[9]

Humphrey aides had an unusually cozy relationship with AMPI. Both Bill Connell and Ted Van Dyk had worked as consultants for the firm after Humphrey left office. Chestnut had done legal work for AMPI. Barry Nova, an advertising executive, told the Senate committee that in 1970, when he was working for Humphrey's Senate campaign, Chestnut had instructed him to send $12,000 in bills to AMPI, which would then reimburse him. In 1970, before the straw donor law, this would have been legal, if shady, save for the fact that AMPI then paid Nova's firm through its corporate account. AMPI officials had already admitted doing so. Background documentation showed that Chestnut was aware of the subterfuge. He was indicted in December 1974 and convicted the following year. He served four months in prison, an unusually harsh punishment for violating the Tillman Act. It was a serious blow to Humphrey, who felt great loyalty to Chestnut and believed that his campaign manager had been unjustly treated for AMPI's own misdeeds.[10]

One very bizarre allegation, involving the 1968 rather than the 1972 campaign, appeared to directly implicate Humphrey. In 1973, the eccentric billionaire Howard Hughes was sued for libel by a former executive named Robert Maheu, who, Hughes had said, "stole me blind." Maheu set out to prove that he had, in fact, distributed almost all the half million dollars in cash that Hughes had given him for clandestine political contributions. (Even Hughes's lawyer testified that Maheu had doled out $389,000 of the $475,000 Hughes furnished.) One of the recipients was Hubert Humphrey, who, Hughes had believed, not unreasonably, would take his side against the Atomic Energy Commission, which was planning to carry out nuclear tests on land Hughes owned in the Nevada desert. Hughes had given a $50,000 check to the campaign in the spring of 1968. Maheu gave a deposition in which he stated that on July 27, 1968, he had handed another $50,000 in cash to Humphrey in an attaché case. He explained that he had waited in a room at the Century Plaza Hotel in Los Angeles for a prearranged signal from a Humphrey aide, who knew that he planned to give Humphrey money. (This was the day after the incident in which an angry Black crowd had forced Humphrey to flee an event in Watts.) The aide, whose name he could not recall, told him that Humphrey's hotel suite was too crowded for a safe handoff and instructed him instead to come outside to Humphrey's limo, which would take the candidate to the airport. "I went outside, entered the limo, shook hands with Mr. Humphrey," Maheu testified. "There was a driver in front of the car, several people in the back seat of the car. I left the attaché case on the floor and, pursuant to instructions from Mr. Hughes, did not request a receipt and left."[11]

The Humphrey aide in question would have been Lloyd Hand, who knew Maheu, though Hand does not remember the call. Hand does recall—and testified at the trial—that Maheu had entered the car with an attaché case. Maheu, he said, sat on a jump seat, reached into the attaché case, and pulled out, not a stack of hundreds, but a memo on the planned tests, which he gave to Humphrey. Maheu then left the car, depositing the attaché case below the jump seat. Hand says it never crossed his mind that $50,000 was inside. However, Ted Van Dyk, who was also present, took it for granted that Maheu was offering an under-the-table donation. Van Dyk recalls that he placed the case in the trunk. When they reached Washington, Van Dyk says that he gave it to Humphrey's personal assistant, David Gartner, who in turn placed it in the trunk of Humphrey's own car. And then it vanished. Van Dyk recalls getting calls about the missing case soon after from Bill Connell and campaign treasurer Bob Short, and, later, from Humphrey himself. If Van Dyk's memory is right, Maheu had tried to ensure that Humphrey received the money and that he knew where it came from.[12]

In 1968, campaigns still ran on wads of cash, winks and nods, implicit quid pro quos. But Hubert Humphrey had never conducted himself as just another old pro marinated in the ancient juices—that is, as Lyndon Johnson. That, however, was just the impression that the Maheu story, and all the other stories, gave. Humphrey was humiliated by the torrent of revelations. "There's no way you can live this thing down," he said. Fund-raising was not a problem for rich men like the Kennedys, or for pro-business Republicans like Nixon; for others it was a curse. In an interview with the *New York Times*, Humphrey launched into a blistering and self-lacerating monologue on the subject. "I've had to break off a campaign and fly through the night," he said, no doubt thinking of that desperate moment in March 1972, "and you come in and you just have to grovel around in the dirt. And you see people there—a lot of them you don't want to see . . . and out of the twenty-five who have gathered, four will contribute. And most likely one of them is in trouble, and is somebody you shouldn't have had a contribution from." Fund-raising, Humphrey said, "is the most disgusting, demeaning, disenchanting, debilitating experience of a politician's life."[13]

HUMPHREY'S LIFE-LONG FAITH IN AMERICA'S CAPACITY, AND CALL-ing, to shape a more just world had not been dimmed by Vietnam, for all that he increasingly regarded the war as a terrible mistake from which the nation must rapidly extricate itself. Humphrey wanted to return to the Senate Foreign Relations Committee, even as low man on the totem pole, so that he could work on the issues he cared about most. The East-West struggle that had shaped his generation had increasingly given way to so-called "North-South" issues that pitted the industrialized nations against the Third World—above all, questions of economic development. Once Humphrey regained a seat on Foreign Relations, he was assigned the chairmanship of the Africa subcommittee, a post for which there was zero competition. Humphrey, though, declined to treat Africa as a backwater; he instructed Dan Spiegel to call the School of Advanced International Studies at Johns Hopkins University and tell them to send over the smartest graduate student they had working on African affairs.[14]

Humphrey soon found a campaign worthy of his efforts. In 1965, Rhodesia (the future Zimbabwe) had declared independence from Great Britain and established a South Africa–style white suprema-cist regime under Prime Minister Ian Smith. The United Nations had responded with comprehensive sanctions, which the Johnson administration had endorsed and applied. Southerners, however, sympathized with the Rhodesians, and in 1971 Harry Byrd had introduced and passed a bill that exempted chrome, a key Rhodesian export, from the sanctions, on the pretext that the United States had become too dependent on chrome from the Soviet Union. Gale McGee, a liberal Democrat from Wyoming, was then head of the Africa subcommittee and introduced a measure to overturn the Byrd amendment, but he could not overcome a southern-led filibuster.

In May 1973, Humphrey reintroduced McGee's bill, S. 1868. "Many developing nations," Humphrey said, "question whether the United States has really given up white supremacy. They want proof that we are serious about replacing colonialism with real self-determination." He had said much the same thing a decade earlier, but now the stakes had changed. The United States needed to regain the sympathies of developing nations not to defeat communism but to collectively solve global problems such as overpopulation, food scarcity, and disease.[15]

Inside the Senate, the political alignment over Rhodesia was eerily familiar. Marianne Albertson (later Spiegel), the graduate student Humphrey had hired, describes Humphrey's fight over the chrome sanctions as "almost a replay of the civil rights struggle," with southerners sustaining a filibuster with the help of conservative Republicans while liberals flailed helplessly. Humphrey, says Spiegel, threw himself into what appeared to be a hopeless contest. Working with activist organizations, he put together an outside lobbying campaign, as he had in 1964, enlisting Black celebrities, including Ruby Dee and Ossie Davis; African ambassadors; and, crucially, the steelworkers union. Members were outraged at the central role of the steel industry in defending the Byrd amendment, which had lowered the price of chrome, a key ingredient of stainless steel. Internally, Humphrey worked on Republican moderates who had voted against cloture. Spiegel was struck by the difference between the new generation of liberals, who only consorted with one another and with the activists, and Humphrey, who spent much of his time on the floor with Southern Democrats and Republicans.[16]

Humphrey had a secret weapon in his tug-of-war with Byrd—National Security Adviser Henry Kissinger. The two had known each other since the 1960s; Kissinger had given the impression that he was a Humphrey man in 1968 even as he was ingratiating himself with the Nixon campaign. Humphrey had said that Kissinger would have been his top candidate for secretary of state had he won. He was more drawn to Kissinger's worldly realism than to the deep skepticism of American power of the Democrats' antiwar wing; what's more, he regarded Kissinger as a friend and was perhaps a bit in awe of him. The two men met for lunch or breakfast as often as their schedules allowed. Over the phone, Humphrey addressed Kissinger as "my friend," and the secretary of state lavished praise on the senator as a great American. Staffers for the two met monthly to discuss the agenda of the Senate Foreign Relations Committee. Once Humphrey gave Kissinger advice intended for the Republican president who had defeated him. "May I tell him you said that?" Kissinger asked. Of course, Humphrey rejoined; "I'm a Democrat, but I'm not only a Democrat." As a citizen, he said, he wanted Nixon to succeed.[17]

In early September, the two men talked about Rhodesia. Humphrey had invited the US ambassador to the United Nations, John Scali, to the Hill to discuss the administration's position on the sanctions, which had been no better than equivocal. He had told Scali that if the White House "played the same games" as it had the year before, he'd be furious, and Kissinger could no longer count on his cooperation on other issues. Scali had dutifully reported this to Kissinger. When he called Humphrey, Kissinger put in the needle: Was his gentlemanly friend even capable of anger? Just watch, Humphrey had needled back. Kissinger promised that he would testify in favor of repeal. He did so, as Humphrey made a point of saying when he finally attempted a cloture vote December 11. That one failed 59–35. Two days later the vote was 62–33, with two Republicans having crossed to Humphrey's side. Finally, on December 18, cloture carried 63–26, and S. 1868 passed 54–37. Humphrey had accomplished what Gale McGee could not. The *Times* attributed much of the victory to Humphrey and to the pressure he had put on Kissinger.[18]

Victory was still far off. The companion bill had died in the House. The following year Humphrey asked Kissinger to make more phone calls on Rhodesia, and Kissinger said he would call whomever Humphrey recommended. But repeal failed again. Only in March 1977, under President Jimmy Carter, did Congress finally overturn the Byrd amendment. Marianne Spiegel had stopped working for Humphrey two years earlier, but she got a call from her former boss. "Are you going to the signing at the White House?" he asked. Spiegel said she hadn't been invited. Humphrey said he wanted Carter to know who deserved credit for the victory. "I want to take you down and introduce you to the president," Humphrey told her. And to her immense gratitude, he did.

For most of its members, and especially for chairman J. William Fulbright, the Senate Foreign Relations Committee served as a check on presidential power in foreign affairs. Though Humphrey cared very much about that role, he also, and always, wanted to *do* things—to legislate. This inevitably led him back to foreign aid, one of the great preoccupations of his earlier Senate career. Liberal disillusionment with the tools of American statecraft had made foreign aid an even more thankless issue than it had been before. No one even bothered to draw up new legislation; each year the foreign aid budget passed as an amendment to the 1961 Foreign Assistance Act. Now the impetus for foreign assistance came chiefly from the Nixon administration, which wielded it as a reward for allies and an incentive for Israel and the Arab countries to end the fighting in the Middle East.

Humphrey stepped into this vacuum. In sponsoring the 1973 foreign aid bill, he insisted that the goal of assistance should be not simply to promote economic growth through big infrastructure projects, such as dams and highways, but—as development experts believed—to help people escape poverty. The bill he piloted through Congress in October 1973 authorized $600 million for each of the next two years for agriculture, rural development, and nutrition; population planning and health; and education and overall economic development. Humphrey rewrote PL 480, the bill he had written years before, to similarly address rural development. And he spoke out on the devastating famine in the Sahel region, forcing the Nixon administration to provide humanitarian assistance. At the same time, he was ensuring that Congress would deliver critical military aid to Israel.[19]

Humphrey served as a balance wheel between Kissinger and liberals in Congress. In early 1974, the secretary of state called hoping to overcome Humphrey's resistance to development loans for Vietnam. Kissinger asked if a White House push for aid to Vietnam would make Humphrey "jump ship on foreign aid." Henry, said Humphrey, "I am not a petulant young man about stuff like that." At other times Kissinger would ask Humphrey to safeguard military assistance to Egypt or Saudi Arabia. Humphrey would protect Kissinger's diplomatic goals while imploring his colleagues to direct the remaining funds to the neediest. In March 1975, Humphrey introduced an amendment to add $100 million to the food assistance bill. Senator Daniel Inouye of Hawaii questioned whether impoverished Third World countries, such as Pakistan, had the expertise to benefit from high-yielding seeds and the like. Humphrey took him and his fellow skeptics to school. "I am interested in the study of soil chemistry," he noted. "I am interested in the experiments in herbicides and pesticides that will take care of plant diseases and infestations in these tropical areas and these arid areas." His colleagues might not know, for example, that "the Mexican wheat has increased the yield of a wheat that has a higher protein that can be planted in many areas of the world, for example in Pakistan." Humphrey's amendment carried, 61–31.[20]

In early 1975 Humphrey persuaded Fulbright to establish a new subcommittee on foreign aid that Humphrey would chair, giving him a perch from which to drive the reforms he sought—just as he had with the disarmament subcommittee years before. That November he introduced the first attempt in years to replace the 1961 act with new legislation, modeled on the bill he had passed in 1973. Humphrey made a point of saying that aid proponents now recognized that assistance would not end poverty or "make the world safe for democracy." Perhaps it couldn't even buy friends. Nevertheless, he said, "we believe that our generosity and compassion may in the long run result in a more just and stable world order." It would be hard to say, in retrospect, that that was true; foreign assistance would never produce the outcomes its most passionate advocates envisioned. Yet Humphrey's insistence on poverty eradication—on helping those who most needed help—left a lasting mark on the American aid program.[21]

Humphrey and Kissinger could talk to one another easily because both regarded themselves as patriots who considered America the preeminent force for good in the world. Yet Humphrey did not accept Kissinger's morally neutral great-power statecraft; he had spent twenty-five years arguing that America must hold itself to the highest standards of conduct both at home and abroad in order to preserve its capacity for leadership. Nothing had endangered that standing so much as Vietnam. By the summer of 1974, Humphrey had turned decisively against the war and favored a swift American withdrawal. In March 1975, he appeared on *Face the Nation* to argue against the administration's request for $222 million in military aid to Cambodia, whose crumbling regime Humphrey regarded as a lost cause. The White House got wind of Humphrey's plans—probably through Kissinger—and placed a call to Humphrey in his office soon before he was to go on the air. When Dan Spiegel told him that President Ford was calling, Humphrey said, "I don't want to talk to the president. You tell the White House that I'm unavailable."[22]

Humphrey hated to confront a friend; his telephone conversations with Kissinger betray none of his feelings about either Vietnam or Watergate. Yet in 1976, when Kissinger offered American support to General Augusto Pinochet, who had led a coup against Chile's elected leader, Salvador Allende, Humphrey could no longer hold his peace. He wrote a letter to Kissinger saying that the Pinochet regime was founded on "torture, imprisonment and murder," and calling for a complete break of diplomatic relations. Humphrey was through with justifying American support for right-wing dictators in the name of fighting communism. But a few weeks later he was calling Kissinger to arrange lunch.[23]

25

Last Things

"He will have a larger place in history than many
of those who defeated him along the way."

AS THE COLD WAR CONTEST THAT HAD SHAPED HUMPHREY'S worldview had begun to slip away, so, too, had the preoccupation with civil rights at home. Black people had won the rights so long denied them, yet that victory had done little to improve daily life. Black family income, adjusted for inflation, had not budged since the Voting Rights Act passed in 1965. Black labor force participation, which had been 85 percent when the Supreme Court decided *Brown v. Board of Education* in 1954, had slipped to 67 percent by 1972, as factory jobs left the cities where most Blacks lived or disappeared altogether. Scholars began to recognize that such "structural" forces in the economy had at least as much to do with persistent Black poverty as discrimination did. Hubert Humphrey had been making this case since he had returned to the Senate. He did not want to talk about busing, which made him deeply uneasy. He did not want to talk about "welfare rights," because he thought welfare sapped initiative. He feared that affirmative action programs would turn whites against Blacks. He no longer spoke of "fair employment"; his new watchword was "full employment," for whites and Blacks, old and young. "We must shift the battlefield for equal opportunity in America from the courts to the marketplace," he told attendees at the Congressional Breakfast for Full Employment in early 1975.[1]

Humphrey was a politician, and the impulse behind this new doctrine was profoundly political. "He felt some guilt about losing in '68 and '72—about the splitting up of the party," recalls Tim Barnicle, who joined Humphrey's staff in the fall of 1972. "He wanted to do something that could bring back the labor unions, the minority community, and the liberals in one fell swoop." The idea of "economic justice" could restore the New Deal coalition sundered by civil rights. Humphrey continued to hammer away at Nixon's free-market ethos and his cuts to social welfare programs (still, to be sure, extremely generous by historical standards). He advocated major increases in spending on school lunches, and on prenatal and pediatric care. In a speech to the Democratic Governors Conference in April 1974, he reiterated his call for an American version of European social democracy: national health insurance, guaranteed public employment, the federalization of the welfare program, and tax cuts for the working class. He proposed eliminating tax preferences for the rich and for oil companies in order to raise the revenue needed to pay for this major expansion of government activism. These were the colors he wanted to nail to the Democratic mast.[2]

The issue that Humphrey ultimately focused his energies on was full employment. The right to a decent job had been central to FDR's "economic bill of rights" and to Humphrey's own updated version of it. In August 1974 he introduced the Equal Opportunity and Full Employment Act, which called for guaranteed public employment for all Americans unable to find a job in the private market. All working Americans would have access to "useful and rewarding work, at a fair rate of compensation." A Black congressman from California, Gus Hawkins, later introduced a companion version in the House, and the bill became known as "Humphrey-Hawkins." Civil rights groups and progressive churches endorsed the bill and formed the core of a lobbying group known as the Full Employment Action Council. But even the big unions worried about the bill's inflationary effects. Indeed, many economists, including liberal ones, regarded the idea of guaranteed employment as wildly inflationary. At a time of Republican budget-cutting, the bill, like Humphrey's larger agenda, had no chance of making it through Congress. Yet the crisis to which the bill was addressed was all too real. By early 1975, the unemployment rate had reached 7.1 percent. The Urban League put the real unemployment rate for Blacks, including those who had given up looking for work, at 25.8 percent. The Black teenage unemployment rate was a shocking 38 percent. A Black economic calamity thus seemed to be linked to a wider pattern of unemployment and underemployment.[3]

Tim Barnicle says that Humphrey's goal, at this early stage, was to provoke a conversation rather than to pass a bill. In January 1975 Humphrey became chairman of the Joint Economic Committee, allowing him to stage that conversation in the splashiest possible way. President Ford had authorized an ill-fated public relations campaign around the slogan "Whip Inflation Now." Humphrey would make the counter case that the real national scourge was unemployment. He had his own economics faculty in the form of the JEC's twelve staff economists. Humphrey began to convene meetings of the JEC on the first Friday of every month, when the administration would release the new unemployment figure; it was Barnicle's job to make sure Humphrey's comments made it into one of the lead paragraphs that the *Washington Post* would almost invariably run on its front page. In the fall Humphrey took the JEC to Boston, Chicago, New York, Atlanta, and elsewhere to dramatize the real-world consequences of those unemployment figures. The hearings he convened in New York came days after President Ford had ruled out federal help for the city as it teetered on the edge of bankruptcy, provoking a famous *New York Daily News* headline, "Ford to New York: Drop Dead." Humphrey was able to bring together Governor Hugh Carey, Mayor Abe Beame, Senator Jacob Javits, and former treasury secretary Douglas Dillon as well as union leaders, economists, civil rights leaders, and even several bona fide socialists. All of them agreed that bankruptcy would lead to economic catastrophe for New York and for the nation. The *New York Times* carried two articles on the hearings, one on the front page.[4]

Hubert Humphrey was rediscovered—again. This remarkable return to the center of the national conversation was a tribute not only to Humphrey's almost animal persistence but also to his willingness to rethink his own premises in light of new information and his gift for finding ways to publicize his views and turn them into legislation. In late April he received a rapturous welcome at, of all places, the Yale campus. America had withdrawn from Vietnam, and Saigon was about to fall; the kids had either forgiven him or were too young to hate him. In an article in late July that must have astounded readers of the lefter-than-thou *Village Voice*, political reporters Alex Cockburn and James Ridgeway reported that "in all likelihood Hubert Humphrey will be the next president of the United States"—suggesting that this once despised puppet of a despised president had earned the job through adroit positioning and real dedication to the nation's welfare. "At last he may have found his hour," wrote Cockburn and Ridgeway. He was "a man for all seasons at a time of economic crisis, an old New Deal liberal at last rid of the trappings of the war criminal."[5]

The *Voice* reporters had learned something new and telling: George McGovern had begun talking up a Humphrey-McGovern ticket for 1976. Earlier that summer, four wise young men of Democratic politics, including pollster Patrick Caddell and consultant Robert Shrum, had met with McGovern to tell him of a conclusion they had reached: a liberal could beat Gerald Ford, but that liberal shouldn't be George McGovern, whom the public saw more as the conscience of the party than its standard-bearer. Only Hubert Humphrey had broad enough support to defeat Ford. Humphrey's great vulnerability was Vietnam; McGovern could immunize him by agreeing to run with him. "It would have been something quite new," says Shrum, "to have former rivals get together, run together, and seem to unite the two sides of the party." A normal politician would never have agreed to serve as the running mate of the man he had defeated for the nomination in the previous election; but George McGovern was not a normal politician. He saw the logic of the argument, and agreed. In late August he met with Humphrey at the latter's Senate office. Humphrey, who may have recalled his late-campaign assault on McGovern with embarrassment, began to tear up as he realized that McGovern was willing to bury old grievances for a common cause. But he was not prepared to make a commitment.[6]

It wasn't just Caddell and Shrum who thought Humphrey's moment had come at last. A spate of what-about-Hubert? articles began to appear in the middle of 1975. Tom Wicker reported in the *Times* that Humphrey was "looking good, feeling healthy, and turning down more invitations to speak, he says, than most Senators receive." With the passions of Vietnam cooled and no convincing challenger to Ford appearing, Wicker noted, party professionals were beginning to wonder if they should turn again to "their oldest hand and most experienced campaigner." Jules Witcover reported in the *Washington Post* that tourists were stopping Humphrey in the halls of the Senate to say, "Why don't you run for President again?" In November a complete stranger organized a write-in campaign for New Hampshire, which Humphrey disavowed—though without saying he would repudiate delegates should he get them. Congressman Paul Simon of Illinois began to put together an unauthorized draft-Humphrey committee. Despite, or perhaps because of, his unwillingness to enter the race, Humphrey was outpolling everyone who had entered. A widely publicized December 13 Gallup poll put him at 30 percent, George Wallace at 20, and Scoop Jackson, Senator Birch Bayh of Indiana, and Representative Mo Udall of Arizona far off in the gloaming. That, in turn, produced a fresh spate of articles.[7]

To all such blandishments Humphrey offered the same response: Why would I? "Look at my beautiful home in Minnesota!" he blared to one reporter. "Look at the job I've got. I'm a respected United States Senator. And that's not bad. I've been Vice President of the United States. I came within a hair of being President. The Prime Ministers call me on this telephone as often as the head of a trade union in Minnesota does. They know me. I can go to the Soviet Union; I can go to Germany, France, China. So why should I scramble? If it happens, it happens. And if it doesn't, the country will get along." Gratifyingly,

Humphrey found himself in the opposite situation from 1972: others wanted him to run, but he demurred.[8]

Humphrey's ambitions hadn't died; the answer he had finally given to George McGovern, whom he had invited to Waverly, was that he just couldn't decide. His real fantasy was that he could win without running, accepting the nomination at a deadlocked convention. But he knew that such things didn't happen in the second half of the twentieth century. Humphrey may have been, as he claimed, enjoying life in the Senate too much to sacrifice it on a long shot; he was up for reelection in 1976. But he also felt the terrible burden of fund-raising. Several people he regarded as dear friends had been convicted of or pled guilty to crimes in connection with his past campaigns. And he had not paid off past debts. In 1974 he had been sued by the firm that had provided travel services to his 1972 campaign. He was being dunned by the company that had insured the campaign. The Triple H Committee, established to retire $825,000 in debts to individual donors, was desperately trying to persuade benefactors to accept four cents on the dollar; most, but not all, ultimately would. The idea of running this gauntlet again must have made Humphrey ill.[9]

In late 1975 and early 1976, when Jimmy Carter, then governor of Georgia, was still regarded as a long shot, the only Democrat with broad popularity other than Humphrey was George Wallace. Humphrey's political aides began raising the question of how to deal with him. In August, before Humphrey had reached a decision about the race, *Time* had reported that Humphrey was prepared to let Wallace participate in shaping the Democratic platform and drawing up a Humphrey cabinet. This is, strikingly, the same offer Humphrey is said to have made in 1972. In late October 1975, Bill Connell wrote a memo speculating about the effect of a Humphrey-Wallace ticket. Polling showed that many Democrats would switch to Ford. As a third-party candidate, on the other hand, Wallace would draw votes from the president. Several weeks later, Mike Berman, another political aide, wrote to Humphrey in reference to a memo from "Martin"— the identity is unclear—weighing the benefits of an understanding between the two. "There is no way to argue that Humphrey and Wallace don't represent an interesting combination of the left and the right," Berman observed. Nevertheless, he had "serious reservations" about such a ticket. Members of Humphrey's inner circle were prepared to consider the possibility of teaming up with Wallace; perhaps they had also been considering that four years earlier.[10]

Declining to run allowed Humphrey to present his attacks on the Ford administration as principled statesmanship. In February 1976 he convened a hearing of the JEC in Washington on the state of the national economy. Because it was Humphrey, both Alan Greenspan, head of the Council of Economic Advisers, and Treasury Secretary William Simon agreed to testify. Humphrey asked both if they were satisfied with a 7.8 percent unemployment rate. "Isn't it perfectly obvious," he jabbed, "that without stimulus from the federal government in a jobs bill it's going to stay at 7 percent or above for the rest of the year?" In March Humphrey introduced a modified version of his full employment program designed to bring organized labor into the coalition. The new bill eliminated proposed price controls as well as the enforceable right to a job, added a European-style planning body—something Humphrey had long proposed—and set an unemployment target of 3 percent, to be achieved in three years. Despite what Humphrey regarded as major concessions, he was able to attract only six senators and ten congressmen as cosponsors. The new crop of Democrats coming to Congress did not share Humphrey's view of the state as an unmixed blessing.[11]

Humphrey was unrepentant. He did not really dispute the economic argument; he found it morally repellent. He addressed those who professed alarm over inflation. "I wish they would take a walk with me through some of our cities," he said. "I'd show them something alarming. Like the fact that the richest nation on this planet is willing to sacrifice the suffering of millions of Americans to some notion of 'price stability.' . . . Like the fact that in this land of hot-lather-shaving machines and electric can openers, there are millions of Americans who have never seen the inside of a decent school or a doctor's office." Nor could Humphrey accept the diminished horizons of a new and more modest Democratic politics. On April 1 he joined Carter, Jackson, and Udall in addressing the National Conference of Democratic Mayors—even though they were candidates and he wasn't. In the usual pattern, each got polite applause, and then Humphrey brought the crowd to its feet. "Why is it," Humphrey thundered, "that we can rebuild the cities of Germany, and of Italy, and of England, but we can't rebuild the cities of America?" Instead of Nixon and Ford's feeble "New Federalism," Humphrey said, we need a "New Partnership" between the federal government and the cities in order to deliver an urban Marshall Plan.[12]

A voter could have been excused for thinking that Humphrey was, in fact, running for president. His speaking schedule took him through key primary states, including New Jersey and Pennsylvania. He collected unsolicited endorsements. In early April, Congressman Paul Simon revived the idea of a Humphrey draft—even though Simon was a centrist Democrat and a cosponsor of a proposed constitutional amendment prohibiting deficits. George McGovern said he couldn't "think of anybody better" to lead the Democratic Party. A survey of primary delegates found Humphrey to be the most popular among them, though they were all pledged to other candidates. Humphrey himself was helping the Udall campaign in Wisconsin in order to suppress the vote for Carter, who had surged to an early lead by winning the Iowa caucus and the New Hampshire primary. In Pennsylvania, Humphrey encouraged labor leaders to go with Jackson for the same reason. They were all, of course, Humphrey men. At the state labor convention in Pittsburgh, Humphrey was serenaded as he walked down the center aisle. Delegates unfurled a forty-foot banner saying, "Pennsylvania for Humphrey." The noncandidate was drawing such crowds that Jackson had to beg him to cancel a planned appearance in Buffalo at the same time as his own.[13]

In mid-April, Humphrey was dead even with Carter. He was telling reporters that he had the best chance in the party to defeat Ford; Carter, a southerner with no history in progressive causes, was too far to the right to mobilize the party base. Humphrey had begun to waver on entering the primaries. If Jackson could head off Carter in the Pennsylvania primary April 27, Humphrey would have two days to decide whether to enter the June 8 New Jersey primary. The draft-Humphrey movement was ready for him; Bob Short, his 1972 campaign treasurer, was eager to hit the phones. And then Carter won handily in

Pennsylvania, defeating Jackson 35–26, with Udall, Wallace, and others trailing behind. Short, who had planned a fund-raising breakfast the following morning, canceled it after a visit to Humphrey, who said he wasn't running. Paul Simon held off on a letter he planned to send to ten or twenty thousand local party leaders after Humphrey said he wouldn't lend his support.[14]

But Humphrey was still torn; he was now sixty-five, and he understood that the chance would never come again. On the night of the 29th he brought his friends and advisers to a suite at the Shoreham Hotel. The old guard was there, including Kampelman and Connell; so was Walter Mondale and his administrative assistant Richard Moe, a Humphrey friend, as well as leading New Jersey Democrats. Virtually everyone wanted Humphrey to run. The feeling in the room, as Moe recalls, was "You gotta do it. The party needs you, the country needs you. If you don't do it, we're going to Hell." Nothing could have been sweeter for this battered warrior. But Humphrey didn't tip his hand. All night he jumped up from the sofa to call another governor, another state party head. At 1:00 a.m., he told everyone to go home. Moe felt sure that Humphrey was going to announce his candidacy the next day. Edgar Berman was so certain that he instructed John Y. Brown, the future governor of Kentucky, who was to run the campaign, to buy a ticket to Washington. A news conference was scheduled for the Senate Caucus Room the following morning.[15]

By the time Humphrey woke up, the euphoria had faded. He made a new round of calls starting at 6:30. He sat down with his family; Muriel and three of their four children wanted him to run. Everyone wanted him to run. But, as he would later explain to James Reston, he didn't believe that he could stop Carter; and if he won the nomination and lost the election, he would have lost his Senate seat, and thus ended his hopes of becoming majority leader after Senator Mansfield stepped down, as he planned to do. The press conference was postponed as Humphrey dithered. Finally he went to his office and began calling the other candidates to say that he wasn't running. At 11:30 a.m. Humphrey finally appeared in the jam-packed caucus room. Many of the reporters had known Humphrey for twenty years or longer, and they were certain almost to a man that he would run;

that's what he was biologically programmed to do. And then—with tears in his eyes, of course—Humphrey told them, "I shall not seek it. I shall not search for it. I shall not scramble for it. But I am around." That was the last echo of a vanished hope.[16]

Humphrey still had one important job to do. Mondale knew that with Humphrey out of the race, Carter might well turn to him as a running mate—a Midwestern liberal to balance a southern moderate. In May, he and Moe went to have lunch with Humphrey in an empty Senate Dining Room. Mondale explained all the reasons why he feared the offer—until Humphrey cut him off. "Don't go there," Humphrey said. "Being vice president was the best thing that ever happened to me, regardless of how I was treated. You can get more done there in a day than you can up here in a year." You can get more done—that was what mattered, not how Humphrey had been treated. From that moment, says Moe, Mondale began taking the idea of serving as Carter's running mate seriously.[17]

In late September, Humphrey called Dr. Berman to say, "I'm really peeing blood." This time doctors found unmistakable evidence of cancer in Humphrey's bladder. Surgeons at Memorial Sloan Kettering removed his bladder along with an inch-long tumor. Henceforward he would wear a bag outside his body, underneath his suit, to void his urine. Ebullient as ever, Humphrey worked the crowd on his hospital floor and encouraged visitors, including Henry Kissinger, to do the same. Doctors declared Humphrey cancer free, but later tests found that his cancer had moved into the lymph nodes. This time the only possible course of treatment was chemotherapy, which left Humphrey sick, weak, and fatigued.[18]

THE LAST OFFICE FOR WHICH HUBERT HUMPHREY YEARNED WAS majority leader—the seat from which Lyndon Johnson had once pulled all the strings. Humphrey's cancer, and the debilitating treatment that followed, left him unable to campaign for the position and probably unable to fulfill its duties. In any case, Robert Byrd of West Virginia had been lining up commitments. Nevertheless, from his hospital bed Humphrey persuaded Teddy Kennedy and other friends to round up support for him. This futile endeavor conveyed precisely the impression of desperate hunger for office that Humphrey had avoided by standing aside in the primaries. Why, James Reston asked, was Humphrey putting himself through this wringer? He answered his own question: "Why do fish swim?" To those of Humphrey's friends who feared that the job would kill him, Reston offered a different metaphor: "Hubert Humphrey is like a plane that takes off and soars only at high speed. Work and responsibility are what keep him at his best cruising altitude." After Humphrey withdrew in the face of certain defeat, grateful colleagues awarded him a new and superfluous post, deputy president pro tem, which carried a $7,450 bonus, a chauffeured limo, and formal access to White House leadership meetings. It was like a shiny toy for a disappointed child.[19]

Humphrey returned to cruising speed with a rapidity that would have been startling for anyone save himself. He was thin and drawn, the chemo had left him bald, and in February his right leg swelled up from a tumor mass; but Dr. Berman told him to keep his leg up at committee meetings. The hair began to grow back, now white and curly, and then Humphrey's energy returned. The White House scheduled the weekly leadership breakfasts around Humphrey's chemo sessions. Carter and his Georgia circle had regarded Humphrey as a New Deal relic; but they were amazed to find that he was a dedicated team player who was prepared to fight for White House bills. One aide was quoted as saying, "I think Humphrey is a great man, and I never would have said that before I came here." Humphrey established a completely unexpected rapport with a president who had called him a "loser" during the campaign. They "had an extraordinarily close relationship," says Stuart Eizenstat, the former Humphrey aide, who had become head of domestic policy in the White House. "Carter saw him as a spokesman to the liberals in the Senate." Once again Humphrey was serving as the moderate's ambassador to the bomb-throwers.[20]

Humphrey was filling the Senate hopper, if not quite with the frenzy of olden days. He championed the cause of child nutrition; McGovern took the issue to the Agriculture Committee, ultimately leading to new standards for school lunches and welfare programs. He prodded the White House to supply more funding for youth unemployment. He got into a terrific row over busing with fresh-man senator Joe Biden, who had cosponsored a bill to preclude the Department of Health, Education, and Welfare from ordering school desegregation. Humphrey said the bill sent a message that the United States was no longer committed to desegregation; Biden rejoined that his real target was executive overreach. Humphrey said the bill would prevent the use of busing even in the service of voluntary solutions; Biden insisted that it would not. By this time busing had lost much of the modest political constituency it once had; the bill passed.[21]

Busing was the fight Humphrey didn't want; employment was the fight he did, and he kept up the pressure on Humphrey-Hawkins. Eizenstat, who headed the White House team negotiating with Humphrey and his aides, says the administration was torn between the "intensive economic pressure" of rising inflation, which Carter had vowed to bring down, and equally intensive political pressure to prove to the party's left that Carter actually cared about the poor and was prepared to act on their behalf. Humphrey had made his full employment measure the litmus test of compassion. It was, from Carter's point of view, a bad idea that he could not afford to resist. Humphrey was in fact prepared to jettison additional parts of the legislation, which he had included to attract the support of the Black leadership; according to Jerry Jasinowski, his chief economic aide and later the head of the Chamber of Commerce—and thus no flam-ing liberal—Humphrey was always focused on the unemployment target, which he wanted to keep as close to 3 percent as possible. That number was too low for Carter.[22]

In August 1977, Humphrey called Dr. Berman from Waverly to say he had stomach cramps. Berman ordered him to go to the hospital right away. Surgeons at the University of Minnesota Hospital oper-ated to remove an intestinal blockage and found that Humphrey's cancer had spread to his pelvic area. On August 18, the chief surgeon, perhaps unaccustomed to briefing the press, declared Humphrey's condition to be "terminal." The senator would remain in Minnesota to undergo another round of chemotherapy. Henceforward all discus-sion of Humphrey would be elegiac; he had begun disappearing into the past.[23]

On October 23, at the tail end of a domestic trip, President Carter stopped in Minneapolis in order to bring Humphrey to Washington on Air Force One—a privilege that Johnson had never extended him. Carter then brought Humphrey to Camp David, where he had also never been. The president and former vice president spent two days talking about foreign and domestic politics, though these two pious Christians must surely have spoken of life and death. The one thing Carter could not bring himself to do was capitulate on Humphrey-Hawkins. The bill had to pass, for now its great author was dying. But the negotiations continued at the White House. On November 15, Carter endorsed a severely reduced version of the bill. The unemployment target was now 4 percent by 1983. The White House had insisted on including language allowing the president to miss the target in order to ensure "reasonable price stability" as well as adequate capital formation by private markets. The mandatory jobs programs and all other forms of required spending had been shorn. Yet the new law would not be merely hortatory. In his annual economic message to Congress, the president would have to identify policies designed to reduce unemployment. Most important, the Federal Reserve, whose central mandate had always been reining in inflation, would have to treat reducing unemployment as an equal goal. That dual mandate now defines the Fed's institutional culture. For that reason, says Eizenstat, Humphrey-Hawkins "has turned out to have a really lasting impact."[24]

That final legislative achievement constituted the fulfillment of four decades of work and thought. Humphrey had recognized early on that civil rights alone would not address entrenched poverty among Black Americans; he had championed economic programs meant to address historical mistreatment. Yet civil rights and the Great Society had torn apart the country without achieving anything like economic equality. In the final chapter of his life, Humphrey had sought a new framework that would apply nonracial solutions to the economic struggles of both Black and white citizens. This debate, between race-specific and broad national economic policies, continues to both animate and divide today's thinkers on the left. Humphrey was also ahead of his time in arguing for full employment, in refusing to accept the zero-sum relationship between inflation and employment, and in asking Americans to see one another not simply as consumers eager to buy the next electric can opener but as workers and as citizens whose lives had to be founded on dignified and secure labor. That is where progressives are today; Humphrey got there half a century ago.

HUBERT HUMPHREY WAS NOW A HUSK OF HIMSELF, HIS CHEEKS HOLlow and his broad chin sharply protruding from a face strikingly narrow. He walked slowly and tired quickly. The time of acting and speaking was over. Humphrey had become something else, a living symbol of all that seemed most worth cherishing about the nation's political life. He had done Washington the favor of dying slowly and publicly, so that he could be duly celebrated. President Carter named the headquarters of the Department of Health, Education, and Welfare after Humphrey—the first time such an honor had been conferred on a living person. On December 2, more than two thousand people gathered at the Washington Hilton on the pretext of raising funds for a new Hubert Humphrey Institute of Public Affairs at the University of Minnesota. Carter and Mondale were there, as were much of Carter's cabinet and the Supreme Court, Henry Kissinger and Frank Sinatra, Liz Taylor, Angie Dickinson, and Helen Reddy. The *New York Times*, abandoning all critical distance, described it as "a night of unabashed and unphony sentimentality."[25]

The older generation of columnists, who had listened to all Humphrey's stories and laughed at all his jokes, who knew his foibles as well as they knew their own, who hoped that he would be president but never thought he would—these men and women now found that they were losing a great friend who seemed to have been with them forever. They could now write openly, unashamedly, of the man's nobility. Under the headline "Hubert Humphrey—He Never Learned How to Be Mean," Mary McGrory described a gaunt Humphrey at the Hilton lavishing praise on everyone who had ever defeated him, from John Kennedy to Jimmy Carter to Robert Byrd. "Humphrey might have been mean if he had the time," she wrote. "But he was always too busy pushing his thesis that 'every American deserves a chance.'" In a similar vein, David Broder described Humphrey's stoicism and good humor in the face of one loss after another and concluded that he would "have a larger place in history than many of those who defeated him along the way."[26]

On December 22, Walter Mondale accompanied Humphrey back to Minneapolis. Humphrey had been given a WATS line, and he immediately began to make phone calls. He would claim to be wishing his friend a Merry Christmas or a Happy New Year, but everyone knew it was goodbye. He called Richard Nixon and astonished the disgraced ex-president by asking him to come to his funeral. He called Stu Eizenstat and told his former aide how much he had grown in his role with President Carter. Eizenstat could barely speak; he stammered, "You're my hero. You're my role model." Humphrey lingered on for several more weeks. He slipped into a coma and died the evening of January 13, 1978.[27]

The following day Humphrey's body was flown to Washington to lie in state in the Capitol Rotunda, and then flown back to Minnesota, where again his casket was placed on view at the statehouse in St. Paul. Over the course of several hours, some twenty or thirty thousand people, many of them sobbing, filed past. The funeral service was held at the House of Hope Presbyterian Church in Minneapolis. Sixty-five of the one hundred members of the Senate had flown from Washington to attend. A week before his death, Humphrey had said that he wanted a funeral "in the style of a celebration," with no eulogies. President Carter and Vice President Mondale each delivered what sounded very much like a eulogy, but no one seemed to mind. Isaac Stern and Eugene Istomin, both longtime friends of the late senator, played a Brahms sonata. Robert Merrill asked the crowd to join him and the House of Hope Choir in "America the Beautiful," a song whose very title succinctly summed up Humphrey's own feelings about the nation he had served. After the service, a crowd of several thousand walked in the bitter cold to a knoll in the nearby Lakewood Cemetery, where Humphrey was buried.[28]

Seven months earlier, Humphrey had conducted one of his innumerable still-going-strong interviews with the *Washington Post*'s Haynes Johnson. He proudly recited his schedule for the day: two congressional leadership meetings, another with Carter in the White House, lunch with National Security Adviser Zbigniew Brzezinski, two Senate committee meetings, a spell on the floor leading an administration bill, interviews, a speech, and then a private dinner. He knew the end was near; he was reconciled to never reaching the presidency or even becoming majority leader. "But," he said, "what I do want is to be known in the history books . . . as an effective man in government: that I was a decent man, that I knew my job, that I knew how to get things done and that I did important things in government."[29] He did that.

Acknowledgments

A biographer is indebted to archivists. Jenny McElroy and Chris True were my indispensable guides during the long months I spent navigating the Humphrey archives at the Minnesota Historical Society. I also received valuable assistance from Liza Talbot and Jenna de Graffenried at the LBJ Presidential Library in Austin; Sally Jenkins at the Wisconsin Historical Society; and Curtis Loesch, who is not an archivist but who sent me to all the right people and places in Huron, South Dakota. Catherine Dunn used her South Dakota contacts to help set me up in both Doland and Huron.

Many of the dozens of friends and former aides of Humphrey with whom I spoke were in their nineties. Two remarkable figures died not long after I met with them: John Stewart, Humphrey's chief aide on civil rights in the 1960s, and Tom Hughes, a fellow Minnesotan who had known Humphrey since 1944 and who, as a senior State Department official, served as an intelligence briefer and confidant to Vice President Humphrey. I feel fortunate to have been able to speak to both.

I owe special thanks to Kara Barker, my Minnesota research assistant, who tunneled into the archives when I wasn't able to be there.

Many people read portions of the manuscript—or even all of it—and offered valuable suggestions: my son Alex, my friends Dick Tofel and Lenny Groopman, and the members of my writers group: Matt Connelly, James Goodman, David Greenberg, Nicole Hemmer, James Ledbetter, Michael Massing, Natalia Petrzela, Claire Potter, and Clay Risen.

I am indebted, as always, to my agent, Andrew Wylie, and to Lara Heimert, the publisher of Basic Books. My editor, Brandon Proia, treated me, and my manuscript, with the combination of tact, generosity, and firmness for which writers yearn. My copyeditor, Katherine Streckfus, saved me from errors not only of language but of fact.

I would be remiss if I did not thank the front office staff of the St. Paul Hotel, which took care of me with Minnesotan solicitude.

Notes

Abbreviations

Boston Globe (*BG*)
Christian Science Monitor (*CSM*)
Humphrey Papers (HP)
    Autobiography Files (AF)
    Interim Files (IF)
    Mayor's Office Files (MOF)
    Mayor's Political Files (MPF)
    Personal and Family Papers (PFP)
    Personal Files (PF)
    Senate Legislative Correspondence (SLC)
    Senate Miscellaneous and Personal Files (SMPF)
    Senate Political Files (SPF)
    Speech Files (SF)
    Vice Presidential Files (VP)
      Administrative Office Files (AOF)
      Civil and Human Rights Files (CHRF)
LBJ Library
    General Files (Gen)
    White House Famous Names (WHFN)
    White House Central Files (WHCF)
Los Angeles Times (*LAT*)
Mick Caouette Production Materials (MCPM)
Minneapolis Star Tribune (*MST*)
New York Times (*NYT*)
The New Republic (*TNR*)
Wall Street Journal (*WSJ*)
Washington Post (*WP*)

Introduction

1. *NYT*, 8/30/68.

2. HP, SF, 6/12/66; Hubert H. Humphrey, edited and with an afterword by Norman Sherman, *The Education of a Public Man: My Life and Politics* (Minneapolis: University of Minnesota Press, 1991), 297.

3. James Traub, *What Was Liberalism? The Past, Present, and Promise of a Noble Idea* (New York: Basic Books, 2019), 121–126, 88–89.

4. Bill Moyers interview, MCPM.

5. Charles L. Garrettson III, *Hubert H. Humphrey: The Politics of Joy* (New Brunswick, NJ: Transaction Publishers, 1993), 222.

6. HP, SF, 11/3/68 (emphasis in original).

7. Humphrey, *Education of a Public Man*, 77; HP, SF, 7/14/48; Robert Mann, *The Walls of Jericho: Lyndon Johnson, Hubert Humphrey, Richard Russell, and the Struggle for Civil Rights* (San Diego: Harcourt Brace, 1996), 19.

Chapter 1. Home

1. Many details of early Doland come from a centennial volume privately printed in 1982, as well as from *Spink County Area History* (Dallas: Curtis Media, 1989).

2. Julian Hartt interview, MCPM.

3. HP, SF, 6/13/76.

4. HP, SF, 6/1/64.

5. Eric Sevareid, *Not So Wild a Dream* (New York: Alfred A. Knopf, 1958), 6–7.

6. HP, SF, 6/1/64.

7. Because of his fair skin, writes Winthrop Griffith (*Humphrey: A Candid Biography* [New York: William Morrow, 1965], 35). But Carl Solberg writes that the boy's skin "was not especially pink," and attributes the nickname to his mother's belief that as a baby "he looked so nice dressed in pink" (*Hubert Humphrey: A Biography* [New York: W. W. Norton, 1984], 35).

8. HP, AF, Box 2.

9. *Huron Plainsman*, 1/15/78.

10. Julian Hartt, "Hubert Humphrey and the Pieties of the Prairie," *Dialog* 23 (Summer 1984): 174–182; Hartt interview, MCPM.

11. HP, PF, Box 148.B.10.10F.

12. HP, AF, interview with Norman Sherman.

13. *Doland Times-Record*, 10/2/52, in HP, Additional Files: Miscellaneous Senatorial, Vice Presidential, Political, Personal, and Other Files, Box 148.A.2.1.

14. HP, PF, Boxes 148.B.10.10F and 148.A.19.3B.

15. Solberg, *Hubert Humphrey*, 29–33.

16. HP, Additional Files: Miscellaneous, etc., 148.A.2.1B.

17. Samuel Freedman, *Into the Bright Sunshine: The Young Hubert Humphrey and the Fight for Civil Rights* (New York: Oxford University Press, 2023), 8.

18. Charles L. Garrettson III, "Home of the Politics of Joy," *South Dakota History* 20 (Fall 1990): 165–184; Solberg, *Hubert Humphrey*, 41.

19. *WP*, 3/14/65.

20. Hartt interview, MCPM.

21. Ibid.; Hartt, "Hubert Humphrey and the Pieties of the Prairie."

22. Garrettson, "Home of the Politics of Joy."

23. Charles L. Garrettson III, *Hubert H. Humphrey: The Politics of Joy* (New Brunswick, NJ: Transaction Publishers, 1993), 19–37.

24. Arthur Naftalin interview, MCPM.

25. Timothy N. Thurber, *The Politics of Equality: Hubert H. Humphrey and the African-American Freedom Struggle* (New York: Columbia University Press, 1999), 15.

26. Hubert H. Humphrey, edited and with an afterword by Norman Sherman, *The Education of a Public Man: My Life and Politics* (Minneapolis: University of Minnesota Press, 1991), 15; HP, SF, 6/1/64.

27. Humphrey, *Education of a Public Man*, 15.

28. Humphrey's lyricism extended to recollected lists of the pharmacy's products. HP, Additional Files: Miscellaneous, etc., Box 148.A.2.1B.

29. Freedman, *Into the Bright Sunshine*, 31.

30. HP, PF, Box 148.A.19.2F.

31. Frances Humphrey Howard interview, MCPM.

32. Humphrey, *Education of a Public Man*, 8–9.

33. Albert Eisele, *Almost to the Presidency: A Biography of Two American Politicians* (Blue Earth, MN: The Piper Company, 1972), 16.

34. Michael Kazin, *A Godly Hero: The Life of William Jennings Bryan* (New York: Alfred A. Knopf, 2006), 72.

35. William Jennings Bryan, "Cross of Gold" speech, July 9, 1896, available at History Matters, http://historymatters.gmu.edu/d/5354.

36. *Atlantic Monthly*, 10/66.

37. Humphrey, *Education of a Public Man*, 8.

38. Charles Hyneman interview, HP, PF, 148.B.9.10F.

39. Solberg, *Hubert Humphrey*, 89.

40. See Norman K. Risjord, *Dakota: The Story of the Northern Plains* (Lincoln: University of Nebraska Press, 2013), and Herbert Schell, *The History of South Dakota* (Lincoln: University of Nebraska Press, 1968).

41. Woodrow Wilson, *The New Freedom: A Call for the Emancipation of the Generous Energies of a People* (Leipzig: Bernard Tauchnitz, 1913), 22, 89.

42. HP, SF, 6/1/64.

43. Harvey Wollman and Tip Miles, personal interviews.

44. *Atlantic Monthly*, 10/66.

Chapter 2. Loss

1. Hubert H. Humphrey, edited and with an afterword by Norman Sherman, *The Education of a Public Man: My Life and Politics* (Minneapolis: University of Minnesota Press, 1991), 24.

2. HP, PF, Box 148.B.10.15B.

3. Humphrey, *Education of a Public Man*, 15.

4. Julian Hartt interview, MCPM.

5. Samuel Freedman, *Into the Bright Sunshine: The Young Hubert Humphrey and the Fight for Civil Rights* (New York: Oxford University Press, 2023), 18. Freedman uncovered the relevant real estate records in the Spink County courthouse.

6. Norman K. Risjord, *Dakota: The Story of the Northern Plains* (Lincoln: University of Nebraska Press, 2013), 221–222; Herbert Schell, *The History of South Dakota* (Lincoln: University of Nebraska Press, 1968), 283.

7. HP, Additional Files: Miscellaneous Senatorial, Vice Presidential, Political, Personal, and Other Files, Box 148.A.2.1B.

8. HP, PF, Box 148.B.10.15B.

9. Humphrey, *Education of a Public Man*, 23.

10. HP, PF, Box 148.B.10.15B.

11. Paula M. Nelson, *The Prairie Winnows Out Its Own: The West River Country of South Dakota in the Years of Depression and Dust* (Iowa City: University of Iowa Press, 1996).

12. Humphrey, *Education of a Public Man*, 28.

13. Carl Solberg, *Hubert Humphrey: A Biography* (New York: W. W. Norton, 1984), 49.

14. HP, PF, Box 148.B.10.15B.

15. Solberg, *Hubert Humphrey*, 50.

16. HP, PF, Boxes 148.B.10.16F and 145.C.10.3B (emphasis in original).

17. Humphrey, *Education of a Public Man*, 27.

18. John L. Shover, "The Farm Holiday Movement in Nebraska," in *Americans View Their Dust Bowl Experience*, ed. John R. Wunder, Frances W. Kaye, and Vernon Carstensen (Niwot: University Press of Colorado, 1999).

19. *Evening Huronite*, 11/13/33.

20. *Time*, 2/1/60.

21. HP, SF, 5/24/68.

22. R. Alton Lee, *A New Deal for South Dakota: Drought, Depression, and Relief, 1920–1941* (Pierre: South Dakota Society Historical Press, 2016).

23. Harvey Woolman and Don Mendel, personal interviews.

24. *Evening Huronite*, 11/8/33–12/23/33.

25. *Time*, 1/17/49.

26. HP, PF, Boxes 148.B.10.11B and 148.B.10.15B.

27. Humphrey, *Education of a Public Man*, 32.

28. Solberg, *Hubert Humphrey*, 52.

29. Edgar Berman, *Hubert: The Triumph and Tragedy of the Humphrey I Knew* (New York: G. P. Putnam's Sons, 1979), 47.

30. Humphrey, *Education of a Public Man*, 35.

31. *MST*, no date, in HP, Additional Files: Miscellaneous, etc., 150.A.1.6F.

Chapter 3. Books

1. University of Minnesota Archives, Box 26.

2. *A Short History of the Department of Political Science*, in ibid., Box 82.

3. Oskar Lange, Benjamin Lippincott, and F. M. Taylor, *On the Economic Theory of Socialism* (Minneapolis: University of Minnesota Press, 1938).

4. Freeman bio, undated, in HP, MPF, Box 150.A.8.3B.

5. HP, AF, Box 1.

6. Carl Solberg, *Hubert Humphrey: A Biography* (New York: W. W. Norton, 1984), 69.

7. Hubert Humphrey Papers, LSU Archives, Folder 1.

8. Hubert H. Humphrey, edited and with an afterword by Norman Sherman, *The Education of a Public Man: My Life and Politics* (Minneapolis: University of Minnesota Press, 1991), 42.

9. T. Harry Williams, *Huey Long* (New York: Alfred A. Knopf, 1970).

10. Humphrey, *Education of a Public Man*, 41.

11. Jerry Purvis Sanson, *Louisiana During World War II: Politics and Society, 1939–45* (Baton Rouge: Louisiana State University Press, 2020), 13–15.

12. Hubert Humphrey, "The Political Philosophy of the New Deal" (master's thesis, Louisiana State University, 1940), xxxix.

13. Ibid., 9–10.

14. Louis Hacker, *American Problems of Today* (New York: F. S. Crofts and Company, 1938), 204.

15. Humphrey, "Political Philosophy," 14.

16. Harold L. Ickes, *The New Democracy* (New York: W. W. Norton, 1934).

17. Walter Lippmann, *The Good Society* (Boston: Little Brown, 1943), 51.

18. James Traub, *What Was Liberalism? The Past, Present, and Promise of a Noble Idea* (New York: Basic Books, 2019), 90–91.

19. Humphrey, "Political Philosophy," 89.

Chapter 4. Fusion

1. Charles Hyneman interview, HP, AF, 148.B9.10F.

2. *Daily Plainsman*, 2/14/40.

3. Hubert H. Humphrey, edited and with an afterword by Norman Sherman, *The Education of a Public Man: My Life and Politics* (Minneapolis: University of Minnesota Press, 1991), 45.

4. Herbert McCloskey interview, MCPM.

5. *St. Cloud Times*, 9/1/42.

6. HP, PF, 148.B.9.9B; HP, SF, Speech Fragments, circa 1941–1945.

7. HP, PF, 148.B.10.10F.

8. Jane Freeman interview, MCPM; Arthur Naftalin interview, MCPM.

9. Naftalin interview, MCPM.

10. Charles Hyneman Oral History, 11/17/79, Louis B. Nunn Center for Oral History, University of Kentucky. Herb McCloskey described an almost identical experience in an interview with Humphrey biographer Carl Solberg for *Hubert Humphrey: A Biography* (New York: W. W. Norton, 1984), 91.

11. Winthrop Griffith, *Humphrey: A Candid Biography* (New York: William Morrow, 1965), 141–142 (emphasis in original).

12. HP, SF, 4/27/43, 5/1/43, and 5/7/43.

13. HP, PF, Box 148.B.9.9B.

14. *Minneapolis Morning Tribune*, 5/26/43.

15. McCloskey interview, MCPM. Humphrey tells the story in *Education of a Public Man* but tellingly leaves out the part about the house.

16. See Millard Gieske, *Minnesota Farmer-Laborism: The Third-Party Alternative* (Bloomington: University of Minnesota Press, 1979).

17. Humphrey, *Education of a Public Man*, 22–23.

18. HP, PF, Box 148.B.9.9B; HP, SF, 4/14/44.

19. *MST*, 4/16/44.

20. HP, PF, Boxes 148.A.19.5B and 148.B.9.9B.

21. Ibid., Box 148.B.9.9B.

22. HP, SF, 7/23/44.

23. Tom Hughes, personal interview.

Chapter 5. Mayor

1. Hubert H. Humphrey, edited and with an afterword by Norman Sherman, *The Education of a Public Man: My Life and Politics* (Minneapolis: University of Minnesota Press, 1991), 56–57.

2. Geri Joseph interview, MCPM.

3. HP, MOF, Box 24.

4. Ibid., Box 22.

5. HP, SF, undated.

6. HP, MOF, Box 22.

7. Carl Solberg, *Hubert Humphrey: A Biography* (New York: W. W. Norton, 1984), 103.

8. HP, MOF, Box 19.

9. *MST*, 7/22/45.

10. HP, MOF, Box 19.

11. *TNR*, 10/18/48.

12. Max Kampelman, *Entering New Worlds: The Memoirs of a Private Man in Public Life* (New York: Harper Collins, 1991), 63.

13. HP, SF, 7/2/45.

14. Eric Nathanson, *Minneapolis in the Twentieth Century: The Growth of an American City* (Minneapolis: Minnesota Historical Society, 2010), 95.

15. Timothy N. Thurber, *The Politics of Equality: Hubert H. Humphrey and the African-American Freedom Struggle* (New York: Columbia University Press, 1999), 23.

16. Ibid., 26.

17. Samuel Freedman, *Into the Bright Sunshine: The Young Hubert Humphrey and the Fight for Civil Rights* (New York: Oxford University Press, 2023), 239–240.

18. HP, AF, Box 1; Cecil Newman interview, in HP, PF, 148.B9.10F.

19. HP, MOF, Box 17.

20. Gunnar Myrdal, with the assistance of Richard Sterner and Arnold M. Rose, *An American Dilemma: The Negro Problem and American Democracy* (New York: Harper and Brothers, 1944), 375.

21. Ibid., 110.

22. Uncle Harry gave Humphrey a copy of *American Dilemma*; Humphrey's thank-you note, dated 12/1/48, implies that he had not read it before. HP, PFP, Box 148.B.10.11B; HP, SF, 7/30/47.

23. Thurber, *Politics of Equality*, 45.

24. Freedman, *Into the Bright Sunshine*, 277.

25. *Baltimore Afro-American*, 8/7/48.

26. HP, MOF, Box 15.

27. Jennifer Delton, *Making Minnesota Liberal: Civil Rights and the Transformation of the Democratic Party* (Minneapolis: University of Minnesota Press, 2002), 104–106; HP, MOF, Box 15.

28. Dave Kramer, "The Dunne Boys of Minneapolis," *Harper's Magazine*, 3/42, 388–398.

29. HP, MOF, Box 12.

30. Arnold A. Offner, *Hubert Humphrey: The Conscience of the Country* (New Haven, CT: Yale University Press, 2018), 35–36.

31. Joseph interview, MCPM.

32. *MST*, 5/13/47.

33. HP, MOF, Box 14.

34. *The Nation*, 10/30/48.

35. *TNR*, 10/18/48.

36. HP, PF, Box 148.B.10.11B.

Chapter 6. Fighting the Commies

1. Hubert H. Humphrey, edited and with an afterword by Norman Sherman, *The Education of a Public Man: My Life and Politics* (Minneapolis: University of Minnesota Press, 1991), 71; Carl Solberg, *Hubert Humphrey: A Biography* (New York: W. W. Norton, 1984), 113.

2. Thomas Devine, *Henry Wallace's 1948 Presidential Campaign and the Future of Postwar Liberalism* (Chapel Hill: University of North Carolina Press, 2013), 7–8.

3. *TNR*, 5/13/46.

4. Transcript of interview by Norman Sherman in HP, AF, Box 2.

5. Humphrey, *Education of a Public Man*, 58.

6. *MST*, 2/14/44.

7. John C. Culver and John Hyde, *American Dreamer: The Life and Times of Henry A. Wallace* (New York: W. W. Norton, 2000), 297.

8. Solberg, *Hubert Humphrey*, 98.

9. Culver and Hyde, *American Dreamer*, 422.

10. HP, MPF, Box 27.

11. *MST*, 10/31/46; HP, AF, Box 2.

12. *Politics*, May–June 1947.

13. HP, MPF, Box 27.

14. Papers of Americans for Democratic Action, Wisconsin State Historical Association, Part 1, Box 9 ("ADA Papers" hereafter).

15. Ibid.

16. Ibid.

17. Devine, *Henry Wallace's 1948 Presidential Campaign*, 28.

18. Albert Eisele, *Almost to the Presidency: A Biography of Two American Politicians* (Blue Earth, MN: Piper Company, 1972), 62–63.

19. HP, MPF, Box 27; Jennifer Delton, *Making Minnesota Liberal: Civil Rights and the Transformation of the Democratic Party* (Minneapolis: University of Minnesota Press, 2002), 121.

20. Orville Freeman Papers, Gale Family Library, St. Paul, Box 1.

21. ADA Papers, Part 7, Box 79.

22. Harry S. Truman, "The Truman Doctrine," March 12, 1947, available at American Rhetoric, www.americanrhetoric.com/speeches/harrystrumantruman doctrine.html.

23. Ibid.

24. ADA Papers, Part 2, Box 65.

25. Culver and Hyde, *American Dreamer*, 437.

26. HP, MPF, Box 26.

27. Ibid., Box 27.

28. Walter Mondale, *The Good Fight: A Life in Liberal Politics* (New York: Scribner's, 2010), 12.

29. Solberg, *Hubert Humphrey*, 115–118.

30. Winthrop Griffith, *Humphrey: A Candid Biography* (New York: William Morrow, 1965), 148.

31. HP, MPF, Box 25.

32. Ibid., Box 26.

33. Ibid., Box 27.

34. Solberg, *Hubert Humphrey*, 119.

35. ADA Papers, Part 1, Box 74; HP, MPF, Box 28.

36. Devine, *Henry Wallace's 1948 Presidential Campaign*, 56.

37. HP, MPF, Box 28.

38. Ibid., Boxes 27 and 28.

39. Ibid., Boxes 24 and 27.

40. HP, SF, 4/23/48.

41. ADA Papers, Part 2, Box 53.

42. Ibid., Part 6, Box 20 (emphasis in original).

43. *MST*, 5/1/48.

44. ADA Papers, Part 6, Box 1.

45. *MST*, 6/14/48.

Chapter 7. The Bright Sunshine of Human Rights

1. HP, MF, Box 28.

2. ADA Papers, Part 5, Box 7.

3. See William Leuchtenburg, *The White House Looks South: Franklin D. Roosevelt, Harry S. Truman, Lyndon B. Johnson* (Baton Rouge: Louisiana State University Press, 2005).

4. See John Frederick Martin: *Civil Rights and the Crisis of Liberalism* (Boulder: Westview Press, 1979).

5. *Herald Tribune*, 2/15/48, in ADA Papers, Part 2, Box 29.

6. Leuchtenburg, *The White House Looks South*, 177–180; Timothy N. Thurber, *The Politics of Equality: Hubert H. Humphrey and the African-American Freedom Struggle* (New York: Columbia University Press, 1999), 53.

7. ADA Papers, Part 2, Box 29.

8. Ibid.

9. HP, MPF, Boxes 24 and 28.

10. Ibid., Box 26.

11. *Spokane Spokesman-Review*, 7/10/48.

12. *WP*, 7/9/48.

13. Winthrop Griffith, *Humphrey: A Candid Biography* (New York: William Morrow, 1965), 152.

14. HP, MPF, Box 26.

15. *Bristol (TN) Herald-Courier*, 7/14/48.

16. Robert Mann, *The Walls of Jericho: Lyndon Johnson, Hubert Humphrey, Richard Russell and the Struggle for Civil Rights* (New York: Harcourt Brace, 1996), 4.

17. HP, PFP, Box 148.B.10.11B.

18. Hubert H. Humphrey, edited and with an afterword by Norman Sherman, *The Education of a Public Man: My Life and Politics* (Minneapolis: University of Minnesota Press, 1991), 77.

19. Carl Solberg, *Hubert Humphrey: A Biography* (New York: W. W. Norton, 1984), 16.

20. Humphrey, *Education of a Public Man*, 77.

21. Ibid., 16–17. The *Philadelphia Inquirer* reported on July 15 that the big-city bosses had concluded that the Wallace candidacy would "wreck their political organizations" unless blunted by a strong civil rights plank.

22. Mann, *Walls of Jericho*, 5.

23. *Democracy at Work: Being the Official Report of the Democratic National Convention* (Philadelphia: Local Democratic Political Committee of Pennsylvania, 1948), 178–180.

24. The original typescript is in HP, Reserve Materials, Reserve 20.

25. HP, SF, 7/14/48.

26. Mann, *Walls of Jericho*, 19.

27. Thurber, *Politics of Equality*, 62.

28. See, for example, "South's 'Revolt' Defied in Vote on Civil Rights," *Philadelphia Inquirer*, 7/15/48, 1.

29. *MST*, 7/18/48.

Chapter 8. A Harsh Welcome to America's No. 1 Liberal

1. Carl Solberg, *Hubert Humphrey: A Biography* (New York: W. W. Norton, 1984), 126.

2. ADA Papers, Part 7, Box 79.

3. Solberg, *Hubert Humphrey*, 128.

4. *MST*, 10/1/48 and 10/11/48; HP, MPF, Box 26.

5. HP, SF, 10/5/48.

6. *MST*, 10/14/48.

7. Ibid., 10/19/48 and 10/20/48.

8. Rufus Jarman, "The Senate's Gabbiest Freshman," *Saturday Evening Post*, 10/1/49.

9. HP, PF, Box 148.A.9.5B.

10. "The Education of a Senator," *Time*, 1/17/49.

11. Hubert H. Humphrey, edited and with an afterword by Norman Sherman, *The Education of a Public Man: My Life and Politics* (Minneapolis: University of Minnesota Press, 1991), 87.

12. *NYT*, 1/14/49.

13. Max Kampelman interview, MCPM; Humphrey, *Education of a Public Man*, 85.

14. Solberg, *Hubert Humphrey*, 135–136.

15. Humphrey, *Education of a Public Man*, 87–88.

16. HP, AF, Box 8.

17. HP, PFP, Box 148.B.10.11B; *Congressional Record*, vol. 95, 3/2/49, 1713–1716.

18. Paul H. Douglas, *In the Fullness of Time: The Memoirs of Paul H. Douglas* (New York: Harcourt Brace Jovanovich, 1972), 216.

19. Robert Mann, *The Walls of Jericho: Lyndon Johnson, Hubert Humphrey, Richard Russell and the Struggle for Civil Rights* (New York: Harcourt Brace, 1996), 80.

20. *Meet the Press*, 2/20/49.

21. *NYT*, 2/22/49.

22. Mann, *Walls of Jericho*, 84.

23. Jennifer Delton, *Making Minnesota Liberal: Civil Rights and the Transformation of the Democratic Party* (Minneapolis: University of Minnesota Press, 2002), 66.

24. William S. White, *Citadel: The Story of the U.S. Senate* (New York: Harper and Brothers, 1957), 60.

25. HP, SF, 3/2/49.

26. Ibid., 2/1/49.

27. *Congressional Record*, vol. 95, 3/15/49, 2462ff.

28. White, *Citadel*, 67.

29. Letter from Dr. Luther Terry to Muriel Humphrey, 6/17/49, in HP, Additional Files: Miscellaneous Senatorial, Vice Presidential, Political, Personal, and Other Files, 148.A.2.1B; Solberg, *Hubert Humphrey*, 147–149.

30. Max Kampelman Papers, Gale Family Library, St. Paul, Box 44.

31. *Congressional Record*, vol. 96, 8/29/49, 12449.

32. Ibid., 2/24/50, 2328–2329.

33. *WP*, 3/21/50.

Chapter 9. Cold War Liberal

1. *Congressional Record*, vol. 95, 4/7/49, 4041–4049.

2. James T. Patterson, *Grand Expectations: The United States, 1945–1974* (New York: Oxford University Press, 1998), 140.

3. "'Enemies from Within': Senator Joseph R. McCarthy's Accusations of Disloyalty," with the transcript of his speech in Wheeling on February 9, 1950, available at History Matters, https://historymatters.gmu.edu/d/6456; Joseph McCarthy, "'Enemies from Within' Speech Delivered in Wheeling, West Virginia (1950)," available at University of Texas at Austin, Thomas Jefferson Center for the Study of Core Texts and Ideas, https://minio.la.utexas.edu/webeditor-files/coretexts/pdf/195020mccarthy 20enemies.pdf.

4. Patterson, *Grand Expectations*, 161.

5. Arnold A. Offner, *Hubert Humphrey: The Conscience of the Country* (New Haven, CT: Yale University Press, 2018), 77.

6. *Congressional Record*, vol. 96, 2/12/50, 1220.

7. David Oshinsky, *A Conspiracy So Immense: The World of Joe McCarthy* (New York: Free Press, 1983), 197–199.

8. *Congressional Record*, vol. 96, 9/1/50, 14457–14490.

9. Offner, *Hubert Humphrey*, 78.

10. *Newsweek*, 10/2/50.

11. Max Kampelman, *The Communist Party vs. the CIO: A Study in Power Politics* (New York: Frederick Praeger, 1957), vii–viii.

12. *U.S. News & World Report*, 12/28/51.

13. As noted earlier, Humphrey had begun speaking of a "vital center" in 1947. It is not clear if Schlesinger took it from Humphrey or the other way around—or if both found it in a common source.

14. Arthur Schlesinger Jr., *The Vital Center* (Boston: Houghton Mifflin, 1962), xxiii–xxix, 37, 153.

15. *Congressional Record*, vol. 95, 3/7/49, 703.

16. Ibid., vol. 96, 5/16–17/50, 7101ff.

17. Ibid., 6/25/50, 7018–7026.

18. HP, Senate General Correspondence, Box 3.

19. HP, Senate Miscellaneous and Personal Files, Box 88.

20. Mary L. Dudziak, *Cold War Civil Rights: Race and the Image of American Democracy* (Princeton, NJ: Princeton University Press, 2000), 82, 88.

21. Offner, *Hubert Humphrey*, 81.

22. *Congressional Record*, vol. 96, 7/11/50, 9914.

23. Ibid., vol. 98, 4/24/52, 4378.

24. See Robert Packenham, *Liberal America and the Third World: Political Development Ideas in Foreign Aid and Social Science* (Princeton, NJ: Princeton University Press, 2015).

25. *NYT*, 9/14/50.

26. *Congressional Record*, vol. 97, 5/15/51, 5306.

27. ADA Papers, Part 2, Box 65.

28. *WP*, 10/16/50.

29. *NYT*, 4/23/51.

30. Albert Eisele, *Almost to the Presidency: A Biography of Two American Politicians* (Blue Earth, MN: Piper Company, 1972), 95.

31. HP, AF, Box 8.

32. William S. White, *Citadel: The Story of the U.S. Senate* (New York: Harper and Brothers, 1957), 92.

33. Carl Solberg, *Hubert Humphrey: A Biography* (New York: W. W. Norton, 1984), 146.

34. Hubert H. Humphrey, edited and with an afterword by Norman Sherman, *The Education of a Public Man: My Life and Politics* (Minneapolis: University of Minnesota Press, 1991), 106.

35. *Congressional Record*, vol. 97, 9/20/51, 11705ff.

36. Max Kampelman, *Vital Speeches of the Day* 69, no. 17 (1/15/2003).

37. Roger Biles, *Crusading Liberal: Paul H. Douglas of Illinois* (DeKalb: Northern Illinois University Press, 2002), 41; Paul H. Douglas, *In the Fullness of Time: The Memoirs of Paul H. Douglas* (New York: Harcourt Brace Jovanovich, 1972).

38. HP, AF, Box 8.

39. *WP*, 9/22/51.

Chapter 10. Lyndon Johnson and the Instruments of Power

1. Max Kampelman interview, MCPM.

2. *BG*, 5/16/52.

3. Timothy N. Thurber, *The Politics of Equality: Hubert H. Humphrey and the African-American Freedom Struggle* (New York: Columbia University Press, 1999), 80.

4. *Atlanta Daily World*, 7/12/52.

5. *NYT*, 7/21/52.

6. Steven M. Gillon, *Politics and Vision: The ADA and American Liberalism, 1947–1985* (New York: Oxford University Press, 1987), 87.

7. *MST*, 7/24/52.

8. *Philadelphia Inquirer*, 7/25/52; *MST*, 7/25/52.

9. *NYT*, 7/26/52 and 7/27/52.

10. *BG*, 7/25/52.

11. *NYT*, 7/27/52.

12. James T. Patterson, *Grand Expectations: The United States, 1945–1974* (New York: Oxford University Press, 1998), 199.

13. George E. Reedy, *The U.S. Senate: Paralysis or a Search for Consensus?* (New York: Crown, 1986), 34.

14. Robert A. Caro, *The Years of Lyndon Johnson*, Book 3, *Master of the Senate* (New York: Alfred A. Knopf, 2002), 450.

15. Hubert Humphrey, Oral History I, 8/17/71, LBJ Library, Austin, Texas.

16. WHFN, LBJ Library, Box 3.

17. Hubert H. Humphrey, edited and with an afterword by Norman Sherman, *The Education of a Public Man: My Life and Politics* (Minneapolis: University of Minnesota Press, 1991), 116–118; Hubert Humphrey, Oral History III, 6/21/77, LBJ Library; Kampelman interview, MCPM.

18. Caro, *Master of the Senate*, 494.

19. Humphrey and Johnson, though separated by a thousand miles, both grew up along the 98th meridian, the eastern edge of the prairie, where tall grasses gave

pioneers an illusion of prosperity. In fact, wheat could not flourish there with the agricultural practices of the time.

20. See Robert A. Caro, *The Years of Lyndon Johnson*, Book 1, *The Path to Power* (New York: Vintage, 1982).

21. Recordings and Transcripts of Telephone Conversations and Meetings ("Phone logs" hereafter), LBJ Library, 11/16/64 (emphasis in original).

22. Robert Mann, *The Walls of Jericho: Lyndon Johnson, Hubert Humphrey, Richard Russell and the Struggle for Civil Rights* (New York: Harcourt Brace, 1996), 138–139.

23. HP, SLC, Box 92.

24. Gillon, *Politics and Vision*, 94.

25. Stephen E. Ambrose and Douglas G. Brinkley, *Rise to Globalism: American Foreign Policy Since 1938* (New York: Penguin, 2011), 128.

26. *Congressional Record*, vol. 99, 4/17/53, 3248.

27. HP, SF, 5/23/53.

28. *Congressional Record*, vol. 99, 6/18/53, 6767; 6/22/53, 6690; 6/23/53, 7049; 7/21/53, 9261.

29. Ambrose and Brinkley, *Rise to Globalism*, 132.

30. HP, SF, 11/19/53.

31. *Congressional Record*, vol. 100, 4/19/54, 5289.

32. HP, SLC, Box 710, undated floor speech.

33. Ibid., Box 109.

34. Ibid., Box 104.

35. Merle Miller, *Lyndon: An Oral Biography* (New York: G. P. Putnam's Sons, 1980), 170–172; Robert Dallek, *Lone Star Rising: Lyndon Johnson and His Times, 1908–1960* (New York: Oxford University Press, 1991), 453.

36. HP, SLC, Box 710, floor speech 5/10/54.

37. *Congressional Record*, vol. 100, 8/12/53, 14208.

38. *WP*, 8/20/54.

39. HP, SLC, Box 104.

40. ADA Papers, Part 5, Box 16.

41. Gillon, *Politics and Vision*, 108.

42. Hubert Humphrey, Oral Histories, Columbia University, 1958 and 1977.

43. HP, PFP, 148.B.10.11B.

44. *WP*, 10/15/54.

45. *MST*, 11/7/54.

Chapter 11. A Man with Southern Connections

1. HP, Additional Files: Miscellaneous Senatorial, Vice Presidential, Political, Personal, and Other Files, 144.A.7.4F.

2. Paul H. Douglas, *In the Fullness of Time: The Memoirs of Paul H. Douglas* (New York: Harcourt Brace Jovanovich, 1972), 280.

3. WHFN, LBJ Library, Box 3.

4. Ibid.

5. *Congressional Record*, vol. 101, 6/7/55, 7759.

6. *TNR*, 11/14/55; Douglas, *In the Fullness of Time*, 231.

7. William S. White, *Citadel: The Story of the U.S. Senate* (New York: Harper and Brothers, 1957), 115–116.

8. Hubert Humphrey, Oral History, 8/17/71, LBJ Library.

9. Cited in *MST*, 8/18/55.

10. *Time*, 11/22/54.

11. Personal interview with Tom Hughes.

12. HP, SPF, Box 6.

13. Dwayne Andreas interview, MCPM.

14. Merle Miller, *Lyndon: An Oral Biography* (New York: G. P. Putnam's Sons, 1980), 176.

15. Carl Solberg, *Hubert Humphrey: A Biography* (New York: W. W. Norton, 1984), 168.

16. Hubert Humphrey, Oral History, 8/17/71, LBJ Library.

17. Solberg, *Hubert Humphrey*, 171.

18. HP, SPF, Box 18.

19. Arthur M. Schlesinger Jr., *Journals, 1952–2000* (New York: Penguin, 2007), 10/16/55.

20. HP, SPF, Box 19.

21. Mark DePue (interviewer), "Interview with Newton Minow," May 31, 2017, available at Abraham Lincoln Presidential Library and Museum, https://president lincoln.illinois.gov/Resources/8ebef278-d028-4fe5-af99-8a1eee3c686d/download.

22. HP, SPF, Box 20.

23. Ibid., Box 19.

24. Ibid.

25. Kampelman Papers, Box 45.

26. Max Kampelman, *Entering New Worlds: The Memoirs of a Private Man in Public Life* (New York: Harper Collins, 1991), 132; Humphrey, Oral History, 12/14/64, Kennedy Library.

27. Humphrey, letter to Eugene McCarthy, 7/23/56, Waters memo to Kampelman, 7/23/56, and Kampelman letter to Percy Villa, editor of the *Las Vegas Sun*, 7/30/56, in HP, SPF, Box 18.

28. Tom Hughes, personal diary, 3/1/56.

29. *NYT*, 8/13/56.

30. "1956 Democratic Party Platform," August 13, 1956, American Presidency Project, UC Santa Barbara, www.presidency.ucsb.edu/documents/1956-democratic -party-platform.

31. Tom Hughes, personal papers, 8/16/56.

32. Hubert Humphrey, Oral History, 12/14/64, Kennedy Library.

33. Solberg, *Hubert Humphrey*, 176.

34. Newton Minow, personal interview.

35. WHFN, LBJ Library, Box 3 (emphasis in original).

36. *WP*, 6/28/66.

37. Solberg, *Hubert Humphrey*, 197–198.

38. Skip Humphrey, personal interview.

39. HP, PF, 148.A.10.4F and 148.A.19.6F.

40. Solberg, *Hubert Humphrey*, 184, 232–233.

41. John Bartlow Martin, *The Deep South Says Never* (New York: Ballantine Books, 1957).

42. Solberg, *Hubert Humphrey*, 178.

43. "Congress Approves Civil Rights Act of 1957," *Congressional Quarterly Almanac 1957.*

44. *Congressional Record*, vol. 103, 7/17/57, 11979.

45. Ibid., 7/31/57, 13116.

46. Roy Wilkins, *Standing Fast: The Autobiography of Roy Wilkins* (New York: Viking, 1982), 246.

47. *Newsweek*, 8/19/57.

48. Robert A. Caro, *The Years of Lyndon Johnson*, Book 3, *Master of the Senate* (New York: Alfred A. Knopf, 2002), 1003.

Chapter 12. Caviar with Khrushchev

1. "How Dulles Averted War," *Life*, 1/16/56.

2. *NYT*, 1/13/56; Tom Hughes, personal diary, 1/12/56.

3. HP, SF, 2/16/57.

4. HP, SLC, Box 710.

5. HP, SMPF, Box 89.

6. HP, SPF, Box 6.

7. Arnold A. Offner, *Hubert Humphrey: The Conscience of the Country* (New Haven, CT: Yale University Press, 2018), 136–137.

8. HP, Senate Trip Files, Box 2.

9. *WP*, 5/21/57.

10. HP, SF, 2/22/50.

11. HP, SLC, Box 710.

12. See Lawrence S. Kaplan, *Harold Stassen: Eisenhower, the Cold War, and the Pursuit of Nuclear Disarmament* (Lexington: University Press of Kentucky, 2018).

13. *Congressional Record*, vol. 105, 2/4/58, 1607.

14. *NYT*, 2/6/58.

15. *Congressional Record*, vol. 104, 4/1/58, 5895.

16. *WP*, 3/12/58.

17. *Meet the Press*, 6/1/58.

18. HP, SPF, Boxes 25 and 45.

19. *TNR*, 4/28/58.

20. *NYT*, 3/10/58 and 8/23/58.

21. *Congressional Record*, vol. 105, 6/4/58, 10102.

22. "The Men Who," *Time*, 11/24/58.

23. Hubert H. Humphrey, edited and with an afterword by Norman Sherman, *The Education of a Public Man: My Life and Politics* (Minneapolis: University of Minnesota Press, 1991), 142–148.

476 | Notes for Chapter 12

24. Oleg Troyanovsky, "The Making of Soviet Foreign Policy," in *Nikita Khrushchev*, ed. William Taubman, Sergei Khrushchev, and Abbott Gleason (New Haven, CT: Yale University Press, 2008), 218–219.

25. The chief source for this conversation is Humphrey's contemporaneous notes, as well as the transcript of an extensive press conference he gave several days later. HP, Senate Trip Files, Box 2.

26. Ibid.

27. "Eight and a Half Hours in the Kremlin," *Time*, 12/15/58.

28. HP, SF, 12/8/58.

29. *Meet the Press*, 12/14/58.

30. *Life*, 1/12/59.

31. *NYT*, 1/11/59.

Chapter 13. No Match for Camelot

1. *WP*, 2/3/59 and 5/4/59.

2. HP, SPF, Box 45.

3. Or perhaps, as Robert Caro suggests, he had fallen prey to his morbid fear of failure. Robert A. Caro, *The Years of Lyndon Johnson*, Book 4, *The Passage of Power* (New York: Vintage, 2012), 17.

4. HP, SPF, Box 45.

5. *WP*, 11/18/58.

6. HP, SPF, Box 45.

7. Ibid.

8. Ibid.

9. Ibid.

10. Nick Bryant, *The Bystander: John F. Kennedy and the Struggle for Black Equality* (New York: Basic Books, 2006), 87.

11. *Time*, 10/26/59.

12. Kevin Boyle, *The UAW and the Heyday of American Liberalism, 1945–1968* (Ithaca, NY: Cornell University Press, 1995), 141; *WP*, 3/13/59.

13. *MST*, 12/20/59.

14. Bryant, *Bystander*, 102.

15. Theodore White, *The Making of the President 1960* (New York: Atheneum, 1965), 89; JFK Campaign 1960 Files, JFK Library, 0989 014.

16. Arthur M. Schlesinger Jr., *Journals, 1952–2000* (New York: Penguin, 2007), 1/2/60.

17. HP, SPF, Box 45.

18. *WP*, 6/11/59.

19. Ibid.

20. *MST*, 9/19/59.

21. HP, SPF, Boxes 35 and 39.

22. White, *The Making of the President 1960*, 32.

23. Albert Eisele, *Almost to the Presidency: A Biography of Two American Politicians* (Blue Earth, MN: Piper Company, 1972), 141 (emphasis in original).

24. HP, SF, 12/30/59.

25. *NYT*, 12/31/59.

26. Myron Feldman, Oral History, 5/13/66, JFK Library; HP, SPF, Box 37.

27. Feldman Oral History; Philleo Nash, Oral History, 1/28/66, JFK Library.

28. *Primary*, produced by Robert Drew, cinematography by Richard Leacock, D. A. Pennebaker, Albert Maysles, and Terence Macartney-Filgate (1960, Time Life Television).

29. *Madison (WI) Capital Times*, 3/21/59.

30. *MST*, 2/1/60; *Madison (WI) Capital Times*, 3/18/60.

31. *Madison (WI) Capital Times*, 4/1/60.

32. Carl Solberg, *Hubert Humphrey: A Biography* (New York: W. W. Norton, 1984), 207; HP, SPF, Box 37.

33. Joe Rauh, Oral History, 12/23/65, and Andrew Biemiller, Oral History, 3/11/65, JFK Library.

34. HP, SPF, Box 35.

35. Ibid.

36. HP, AF, 148.B.10.1B; Max Kampelman, *Entering New Worlds: The Memoirs of a Private Man in Public Life* (New York: Harper Collins, 1991), 155; Lawrence F. O'Brien, *No Final Victories: A Life in Politics from JFK to Watergate* (Garden City, NY: Doubleday, 1974).

37. *Charleston Gazette*, 4/14/60.

38. HP, SPF, Box 36.

39. "Remarks of Senator John F. Kennedy at American Society of Newspaper Editors, Washington, D.C., April 21, 1960: 'The Religion Issue in American Politics,'" JFK Library, www.jfklibrary.org/archives/other-resources/john-f-kennedy-speeches/american-society-of-newspaper-editors-19600421.

40. HP, SPF, Box 36.

41. Jim Rowe, Oral History, 5/10/64, JFK Library; Caro, *Passage of Power*, 85.

42. Feldman Oral History; Fred Forbes, Oral History, 3/4/66, JFK Library.

43. Albert Eisele, *Almost to the Presidency*, 147; Hyman Bookbinder, Oral History, 7/22/64, JFK Library.

44. Kennedy-Humphrey Debate, 1960 West Virginia Primary, accession number 16RNC:187, available on YouTube, posted by JFK Library at www.youtube.com/watch?v=oFk7dgS8V18.

45. Solberg, *Hubert Humphrey*, 211; White, *The Making of the President 1960*, 110.

46. Rauh, Oral History, 12/23/65, and Jim Loeb, Oral History, 11/12/67, JFK Library.

47. Merle Miller, *Lyndon: An Oral Biography* (New York: G. P. Putnam's Sons, 1980); Rauh Oral History; Geri Joseph interview, MCPM.

48. Orville Freeman, Oral History, 7/22/64, JFK Library; HP, SPF, Box 45.

49. White, *The Making of the President 1960*, 87–88.

50. Eisele, *Almost to the Presidency*, 152; Freeman Diary, Freeman Papers.

51. Freeman Diary.

52. Bryant, *Bystander*, 143–143; Thomas Hughes, Oral History, 7/7/99, Library of Congress, https://tile.loc.gov/storage-services/service/mss/mfdip/2011/2011hug02/2011hug02.pdf.

Chapter 14. Concert Master of the Senate

1. Steven M. Gillon, *Politics and Vision: The ADA and American Liberalism, 1947–1985* (New York: Oxford University Press, 1987), 139.

2. Hubert H. Humphrey, edited and with an afterword by Norman Sherman, *The Education of a Public Man: My Life and Politics* (Minneapolis: University of Minnesota Press, 1991), 180.

3. The meetings may have mattered less to the clannish Kennedy team than to the invited guests. According to Theodore Sorensen, the breakfasts "usually served as little more than a means of maintaining rapport, *esprit de corps* and open channels of communication." *Kennedy* (New York: Harper and Row, 1965), 355.

4. *NYT*, 7/10/61.

5. Robert Mann, *The Walls of Jericho: Lyndon Johnson, Hubert Humphrey, Richard Russell and the Struggle for Civil Rights* (New York: Harcourt Brace, 1996), 296.

6. *WP*, 2/12/61.

7. Arthur M. Schlesinger Jr., *Journals, 1952–2000* (New York: Penguin, 2007), 9/22/61.

8. Winthrop Griffith, *Humphrey: A Candid Biography* (New York: William Morrow, 1965), 258–259.

9. *Congressional Record*, vol. 106, 6/15/60, 14194.

10. William Connell Papers, Gale Family Library, St. Paul, Box 1.

11. WHCF, LBJ Library, Box 467.

12. Humphrey, *Education of a Public Man*, 185–186.

13. *WP*, 7/9/61.

14. Of the Kennedy biographers who knew him best, Arthur Schlesinger takes this conviction at face value, while Theodore Sorensen suggests that at the time Kennedy was chiefly interested in the "propaganda" value of a treaty. Arthur M. Schlesinger Jr., *A Thousand Days: John F. Kennedy in the White House* (Boston: Houghton Mifflin, 1965), 453; Sorensen, *Kennedy*, 518.

15. *LAT*, 3/12/63.

16. *New York Times Magazine*, "Hubert Comes On Strong," 8/25/63.

17. Griffith, *Humphrey*, 266.

18. *BG*, 8/1/61.

19. See, for example, the long article that the *Washington Post* invited Humphrey to write on the Berlin crisis, "Long View of Crisis Gives Odds on West," 8/6/61.

20. HP, Senate Trip Files, Box 5.

21. *WP*, 11/12/61; *BG*, 6/19/61.

22. HP, SLC, Box 432.

23. Ibid., Box 426.

24. *Congressional Record*, vol. 108, 8/8/63, 13997.

25. Tom Wicker, *JFK and LBJ: The Influence of Personality upon Politics* (New York: William Morrow, 1968), 87–88.

26. Nick Bryant, *The Bystander: John F. Kennedy and the Struggle for Black Equality* (New York: Basic Books, 2006), 190, 236; Mann, *Walls of Jericho*, 301.

27. ADA Papers, Box 5/10.

28. *Meet the Press*, 1/5/62.

29. Bryant, *Bystander*, 365ff.

30. HP, SLC, Box 220.

31. Ibid.

32. Ibid., Box 710. See also Robert Dallek, *An Unfinished Life: John F. Kennedy, 1917–1963* (Boston: Little Brown, 2003), 589–592.

33. Humphrey memo on the Civil Rights Act of 1964, in *The Civil Rights Act of 1964: The Passage of the Law That Ended Racial Segregation*, ed. Robert D. Loevy (Albany: State University of New York Press, 1997).

34. Taylor Branch, *Pillar of Fire: America in the King Years, 1963–65* (New York: Simon and Schuster, 1998), 77–78; Bryant, *Bystander*, 387–423.

35. HP, SLC, Box 220.

36. Taylor Branch, *Parting the Waters: America in the King Years, 1954–63* (New York: Simon and Schuster, 1988), 808.

37. John Stewart, unpublished PhD diss., in Loevy, *The Civil Rights Act of 1964*.

38. *Congressional Record*, vol. 109, 6/19/63, 11165, and 7/24/63, 13242.

39. Timothy N. Thurber, *The Politics of Equality: Hubert H. Humphrey and the African-American Freedom Struggle* (New York: Columbia University Press, 1999), 120.

40. Humphrey, *Education of a Public Man*, 201–202; Mann, *Walls of Jericho*, 328.

41. Humphrey, *Education of a Public Man*, 191; Humphrey, Oral History, 1977, Columbia University; Carl Solberg, *Hubert Humphrey: A Biography* (New York: W. W. Norton, 1984), 239–240.

Chapter 15. Breaking the Filibuster—and the South

1. Robert Dallek, *Flawed Giant: Lyndon Johnson and His Times, 1961–1973* (New York: Oxford University Press, 1999), 112; Roy Wilkins, *Standing Fast: The Autobiography of Roy Wilkins* (New York: Viking, 1982), 299–300; Connell Papers, Box 1.

2. HP, SMPF, Box 715.

3. Carl Solberg, *Hubert Humphrey: A Biography* (New York: W. W. Norton, 1984), 240.

4. Connell Papers, Box 1; Ted Van Dyk, *Heroes, Hacks, and Fools: Memoirs from the Political Inside* (Seattle: University of Washington Press, 2007), 29.

5. Humphrey memo on the Civil Rights Act of 1964, in *The Civil Rights Act of 1964: The Passage of the Law That Ended Racial Segregation*, ed. Robert D. Loevy (Albany: State University of New York Press, 1997).

6. John Stewart, personal interview.

7. Humphrey, Oral History III, 6/21/77, LBJ Library.

8. HP, Senate Research Files, Box 625.

9. *Meet the Press*, 3/8/64.

10. HP, SLC, Box 710.

11. John Stewart, unpublished PhD diss., in Loevy, *The Civil Rights Act of 1964*.

12. Robert A. Caro, *The Years of Lyndon Johnson*, Book 3, *Master of the Senate* (New York: Alfred A. Knopf, 2002), 258.

13. *Congressional Record*, vol. 110, 3/10/64, 4815, and 3/11/64, 4999.

14. *The Today Show*, 3/19/64.

15. HP, SLC, Box 710.

16. Ibid.

17. Stewart notes, in Loevy, *The Civil Rights Act of 1964*; Robert Mann, *The Walls of Jericho: Lyndon Johnson, Hubert Humphrey, Richard Russell and the Struggle for Civil Rights* (New York: Harcourt Brace, 1996), 417.

18. Stewart, personal interview.

19. Phone logs, LBJ Library, 4/30/64.

20. Ibid., 5/13/64 and 5/2/64 (emphasis in original).

21. Mann, *Walls of Jericho*, 419; Stewart notes, in HP, SLC, Box 710.

22. *Congressional Record*, vol. 110, 6/4/64, 12702.

23. Phone logs, LBJ Library, 6/9/64.

24. *Congressional Record*, vol. 110, 6/10/64, 13307.

25. Hubert H. Humphrey, edited and with an afterword by Norman Sherman, *The Education of a Public Man: My Life and Politics* (Minneapolis: University of Minnesota Press, 1991), 210; Mann, *Walls of Jericho*, 426.

26. Humphrey, *Education of a Public Man*, 211–212.

27. *Congressional Quarterly*, 6/19/64.

28. *Congressional Record*, vol. 110, 3/12/64, 5042.

Chapter 16. The Johnson Death March

1. Arthur M. Schlesinger Jr., *Journals, 1952–2000* (New York: Penguin, 2007), 7/23/64.

2. Robert Dallek, *Flawed Giant: Lyndon Johnson and His Times, 1961–1973* (New York: Oxford University Press, 1999), 139.

3. Eric F. Goldman, *The Tragedy of Lyndon Johnson* (New York: Alfred A. Knopf, 1969), 199.

4. Phone logs, LBJ Library, 7/30/64.

5. Hubert H. Humphrey, edited and with an afterword by Norman Sherman, *The Education of a Public Man: My Life and Politics* (Minneapolis: University of Minnesota Press, 1991), 222; Carl Solberg, *Hubert Humphrey: A Biography* (New York: W. W. Norton, 1984), 244.

6. Robert Mann, *The Walls of Jericho: Lyndon Johnson, Hubert Humphrey, Richard Russell, and the Struggle for Civil Rights* (San Diego: Harcourt Brace, 1996), 437.

7. Phone logs, LBJ Library, 8/1/64.

8. Gary Donaldson, *Liberalism's Last Hurrah: The Presidential Campaign of 1964* (Armonk, NY: M. E. Sharpe, 2003), 155.

9. *Congressional Record*, vol. 110, 7/24/64, 16957.

10. Donaldson, *Liberalism's Last Hurrah*, 207; WHFN, LBJ Library, Box 3.

11. *WP*, 8/6/64.

12. Goldman, *The Tragedy of Lyndon Johnson*, 202.

13. ADA Papers, M97-135, Box 28.

14. Michael Beschloss, *Taking Charge: The Johnson White House Tapes, 1963–1964* (New York: Simon and Schuster, 1997).

15. Phone logs, LBJ Library, 8/14/64.

16. Theodore White, *The Making of the President 1964* (New York: Atheneum, 1965), 276.

17. Phone logs, LBJ Library, 8/20/64.

18. Kate Clifford Larson, *Walk with Me: A Biography of Fannie Lou Hamer* (New York: Oxford University Press, 2021), 171–175.

19. Phone logs, LBJ Library, 8/24/64.

20. Robert P. Moses and Charles E. Cobb, *Radical Equations: Organizing Math Literacy in America's Schools* (Boston: Beacon Press, 2001); Larson, *Walk with Me*, 181; Taylor Branch, *Pillar of Fire: America in the King Years, 1963–65* (New York, Simon and Schuster, 1998), 465.

21. Walter Mondale, *The Good Fight: A Life in Liberal Politics* (New York: Scribner's, 2010), 27; Phone logs, LBJ Library, 8/24/64.

22. Donaldson, *Liberalism's Last Hurrah*, 220–221.

23. Moses and Cobb, *Radical Equations*, 83; Branch, *Pillar of Fire*, 470.

24. Larson, *Walk with Me*, 182.

25. John Lewis, *Walking with the Wind: A Memoir of the Movement* (New York: Simon and Schuster, 1998), 282.

26. Goldman, *The Tragedy of Lyndon Johnson*; White, *The Making of the President 1964*, 283.

27. Humphrey, *Education of a Public Man*, 224.

28. Tom Hughes, personal papers.

29. This story is told most fully in White, *The Making of the President 1964*, 282–293; Goldman, *The Tragedy of Lyndon Johnson*, 210–212; and Humphrey, *Education of a Public Man*, 221–226.

30. *NYT*, 8/27/64.

31. Cited in Tom Wicker, *JFK and LBJ: The Influence of Personality upon Politics* (New York: William Morrow, 1968), 205.

32. David Halberstam, *The Best and the Brightest* (New York: Ballantine Books, 1992), 352–353; Dallek, *Flawed Giant*, 144–145.

33. Max Boot, *The Road Not Taken: Edward Lansdale and the Tragedy in Vietnam* (New York: Liveright, 2019), 281.

34. Rufus Phillips, *Why Vietnam Matters: An Eyewitness Account of Lessons Not Learned* (Annapolis, MD: Naval Institute Press, 2008), 231; Charles L. Garrettson III, *Hubert H. Humphrey: The Politics of Joy* (New Brunswick, NJ: Transaction Publishers, 1993), 177.

35. HP, VP, Foreign Affairs Files, Box 917; Boot, *The Road Not Taken*, 437; WHFN, LBJ Library, Box 195; Phillips, *Why Vietnam Matters*, 239.

36. HP, SF, 8/17/64.

37. Nicholas Katzenbach, *Some of It Was Fun: Working with RFK and LBJ* (New York: W. W. Norton, 2008); Solberg, *Hubert Humphrey*, 258–259.

38. Robert Alan Goldberg, *Barry Goldwater* (New Haven, CT: Yale University Press, 1995), 49; Barry Goldwater, *The Conscience of a Conservative* (Princeton, NJ: Princeton University Press, 2007), 30, 56.

39. HP, SF, 10/5/64; *NYT*, 9/30/64.

40. HP, SF, 9/27, 10/27.

Chapter 17. Whatever Became of You, Hubert?

1. Nicholas Katzenbach, *Some of It Was Fun: Working with RFK and LBJ* (New York: W. W. Norton, 2008), 152.

2. Phone logs, LBJ Library, 11/12/64.

3. Max Kampelman, *Vital Speeches of the Day* 69, no. 127 (6/15/2003).

4. Tom Hughes and John Rielly, personal interviews; Tom Hughes, personal papers.

5. HP, VP, CHRF, Boxes 821 and 825.

6. Ibid., Box 825.

7. HP, VP, AOF, Box 763; *Newsweek*, 3/15/65.

8. "The Triple H Brand on the Presidency," *NYT*, 12/6/64; *Newsweek*, 1/11/65.

9. Arnold A. Offner, *Hubert Humphrey: The Conscience of the Country* (New Haven, CT: Yale University Press, 2018), 217; Arthur M. Schlesinger Jr., *Journals, 1952–2000* (New York: Penguin, 2007), 235–236.

10. Hughes, personal papers, 12/28/64.

11. Fredrik Logevall, *Choosing War: The Lost Chance for Peace and the Escalation of War in Vietnam* (Berkeley: University of California Press, 1999), 268; Stanley Karnow, *Vietnam: A History* (New York: Viking, 1983), 378.

12. Logevall, *Choosing War*, 287.

13. *Foreign Relations of the United States, 1964–1968* (*FRUS* hereafter), vol. 2, *Vietnam, January–June 1965*, Memorandum 84, 2/7/65; Logevall, *Choosing War*, 318.

14. Rielly, personal interview.

15. *FRUS*, Memorandums 97 and 98, 2/10/65.

16. Vice President Joe Biden would occupy the identical position in 2009 when he told President Barack Obama in a series of NSC meetings that the generals' proposed civilian-military strategy in Afghanistan wouldn't work. Obama, his ego entirely under control, welcomed the advice.

17. *FRUS*, Memorandum 90, 2/8/65, and Memorandum 102, 2/10/65; Tom Hughes, Oral History, 7/7/99, Library of Congress, https://tile.loc.gov/storage-services/service/mss/mfdip/2011/2011hug02/2011hug02.pdf.

18. Hughes, personal interview.

19. *FRUS*, Memorandum 134, 2/17/65.

20. Charles L. Garrettson III, *Hubert H. Humphrey: The Politics of Joy* (New Brunswick, NJ: Transaction Publishers, 1993), 181; Robert Dallek, *Flawed Giant: Lyndon Johnson and His Times, 1961–1973* (New York: Oxford University Press, 1999), 253.

21. Rielly, personal interview; Albert Eisele, *Almost to the Presidency: A Biography of Two American Politicians* (Blue Earth, MN: Piper Company, 1972), 234–235.

22. HP, VP, Foreign Affairs Files, Box 917; VP, AOF, Box 763.

23. *NYT*, 7/27/65.

24. Dallek, *Flawed Giant*, 253.

25. Ibid.; Eisele, *Almost to the Presidency*, 234.

26. Joseph A. Califano Jr., *The Triumph and Tragedy of Lyndon Johnson: The White House Years* (College Station: Texas A&M Press, 2000), 64.

27. Phone logs, LBJ Library, 7/29/64 and 8/6/64.

28. W. Marvin Watson, with Sherwin Markman, *Chief of Staff: Lyndon Johnson and His Presidency* (New York: St. Martin's Press, 2004), 129.

29. Andrew Glass, personal interview.

30. Patricia Gray, personal interview.

31. Bill Moyers interview, MCPM.

32. *At Issue*, 4/65.

33. Connell Papers, Box 1.

34. Lyrics appear at Genius, https://genius.com/Tom-lehrer-whatever-became -of-hubert-lyrics.

35. Phone logs, LBJ Library, 3/6/65 (emphasis in original).

36. HP, VP, AOF, Box 764; National Security Files, LBJ Library, Box 4; Phone logs, LBJ Library, 5/4/65.

37. HP, VP, CHRF, Box 823.

38. Ibid.

39. Ofield Dukes interview, MCPM.

40. Connell Papers, Box 1.

41. HP, VP, CHRF, Box 824.

42. Ibid., Box 823; *WP*, 5/14/65.

43. HP, Additional Files: Miscellaneous Senatorial, Vice Presidential, Political, Personal, and Other Files, 148.A.4.7B.

44. *NYT*, 7/25/65; *WP*, 6/16/65.

45. Moyers interview, MCPM.

46. Connell Papers, Box 1; Phone logs, LBJ Library, 6/21/65 and 8/31/65.

47. WHCF, EX HU 2, LBJ Library.

48. Califano, *Triumph and Tragedy*. The ensuing account comes from pp. 65–69.

49. Katzenbach, *Some of It Was Fun*, 153.

50. WHCF, EX HU 2, LBJ Library.

51. *NYT*, 9/25/65; *WP*, 9/25/65.

52. *NYT*, 10/17/65; HP, VP, CHRF, Box 828.

Chapter 18. Vietnam Warrior

1. Robert Dallek, *Flawed Giant: Lyndon Johnson and His Times, 1961–1973* (New York: Oxford University Press, 1999), 281.

2. *Pittsburgh Press*, 5/14/65; HP, SF, 5/13/65.

3. Phone logs, LBJ Library, 7/28/65; Carl Solberg, *Hubert Humphrey: A Biography* (New York: W. W. Norton, 1984), 282.

4. WHCF, EX FG 782, LBJ Library, Box 4.

5. Tom Hughes, personal papers.

6. Connell Papers, Box 2.

7. *Kingsport (TN) Times*, 12/27/65; *NYT*, 12/27/65.

8. *NYT*, 1/2/66.

9. National Security Files, LBJ Library, Box 25.

10. Solberg, *Hubert Humphrey*, 285.

11. Lyndon B. Johnson, "Address at Johns Hopkins University: 'Peace Without Conquest,'" April 7, 1965, available at American Presidency Project, University of California, Santa Barbara, www.presidency.ucsb.edu/documents/address-johns -hopkins-university-peace-without-conquest.

12. Stanley Karnow, *Vietnam: A History* (New York: Viking, 1983), 444; Robert McNamara, *In Retrospect: The Tragedy and Lessons of Vietnam* (New York: Times Books, 1995), 187, 245, 498; Lyndon B. Johnson, *Lyndon B. Johnson: 1965: Containing the Public Messages, Speeches, and Statements of the President*, vol. 1, Public Papers of the President of the United States (Washington, DC: Office of the Federal Register, National Archives and Records Service, 1966), 153–155; Freeman Diary, Freeman Papers, Box 15; Dallek, *Flawed Giant*, 343.

13. *Honolulu Bulletin*, 2/9/66; *LAT*, 2/10/66.

14. *BG*, 2/12/66; *LAT*, 2/12/66; *NYT*, 2/12/66.

15. National Security Files, LBJ Library, Box 25; *LAT*, 2/15/66.

16. National Security Files, LBJ Library, Box 25; *NYT*, 2/16/66 and 2/21/66.

17. *NYT*, 2/21/66; Arnold A. Offner, *Hubert Humphrey: The Conscience of the Country* (New Haven, CT: Yale University Press, 2018), 237.

18. John Rielly, personal interview; HP, SF, 2/19/66.

19. WHCF, Meetings/Conferences, LBJ Library, Box 3; *LAT*, 2/23/66; *NYT*, 2/27/66.

20. *NYT*, 2/24/66.

21. HP, AF, Box 8; *NYT*, 2/25/66.

22. Vice Presidential Trips, LBJ Library, Box 40.

23. Tom Hughes, personal interview and personal notes.

24. HP, VP, AOF, Box 768; HP, AF, Box 8; WHFN, LBJ Library, Box 4.

25. Phone logs, LBJ Library, 3/2/66.

26. *Meet the Press*, 3/13/66; Arthur M. Schlesinger Jr., *Journals, 1952–2000* (New York: Penguin, 2007), 3/11/66.

27. George McGovern, *Grassroots: The Autobiography of George McGovern* (New York: Random House, 1977), 105.

28. ADA Papers, M97-135, Boxes 17 and 36; Arthur Schlesinger Jr., *The Letters of Arthur Schlesinger Jr.* (New York: Random House, 2013), 3/23/66, 4/1/66, and 4/11/66.

29. HP, SF, 4/23/66; *Newsweek*, 5/9/66; *WP*, 4/24/66.

30. *NYT*, 4/26/66 and 4/27/66.

31. Ibid., 4/29/66.

32. Ibid., 4/17/66.

Chapter 19. Hubert Meets the Sixties

1. HP, Additional Files: Miscellaneous Senatorial, Vice Presidential, Political, Personal, and Other Files, 144.A.4.7B; John Stewart, personal interview.

2. *Battle Creek (MI) Enquirer*, 6/13/66; HP, SF, 6/12/66.

3. *WP*, 6/6/65; Carl Solberg, *Hubert Humphrey: A Biography* (New York: W. W. Norton, 1984), 280.

4. Steven M. Gillon, *Politics and Vision: The ADA and American Liberalism, 1947–1985* (New York: Oxford University Press, 1987), 174.

5. HP, SF, 6/1/66; James Traub, *What Was Liberalism? The Past, Present, and Promise of a Noble Idea* (New York: Basic Books, 2019), 163.

6. HP, SF, 7/7/66 and 7/19/66.

7. *NYT*, 9/17/66.

8. Ibid., 9/25/66.

9. Thomas Edsall and Mary Byrd Edsall, *Chain Reaction: The Impact of Race, Riots and Taxes on American Politics* (New York: W. W. Norton, 1991), 49–60.

10. Tom Hughes, personal papers, 12/14/65.

11. Solberg, *Hubert Humphrey*, 296; *NYT*, 8/7/66.

12. *WP*, 4/20/67.

13. Solberg, *Hubert Humphrey*, 302; Tom Hughes, personal interview.

14. HP, SF, 2/20/67; *Oakland Tribune*, 2/21/67.

15. Traub, *What Was Liberalism?*, 156–157; Todd Gitlin, *The Sixties: Years of Hope, Days of Rage* (New York: Bantam Books, 1993), 108.

16. Gitlin, *The Sixties*, 184.

17. Arthur M. Schlesinger Jr., *Journals, 1952–2000* (New York: Penguin, 2007), 4/18/67; Albert Eisele, *Almost to the Presidency: A Biography of Two American Politicians* (Blue Earth, MN: Piper Company, 1972), 253; Gillon, *Politics and Vision*, 197.

18. Stanley Karnow, *Vietnam: A History* (New York: Viking, 1983), 479, 488.

19. Joseph A. Califano Jr., *The Triumph and Tragedy of Lyndon Johnson: The White House Years* (College Station: Texas A&M Press, 2000), 210.

20. *WP*, 8/01/67 and 8/18/67.

21. Timothy N. Thurber, *The Politics of Equality: Hubert H. Humphrey and the African-American Freedom Struggle* (New York: Columbia University Press, 1999), 193–194.

22. William H. Chafe, *Never Stop Running: Allard Lowenstein and the Struggle to Save American Liberalism* (New York: Basic Books, 1993), 252.

23. Ibid., 271–272; George McGovern, *Grassroots: The Autobiography of George McGovern* (New York: Random House, 1977), 111.

24. Eisele, *Almost to the Presidency*, 259–272.

25. HP, SF, 10/23/67.

26. Ibid., 10/29/66 and 10/31/66; *Newsweek*, 11/13/66.

27. Hubert H. Humphrey, edited and with an afterword by Norman Sherman, *The Education of a Public Man: My Life and Politics* (Minneapolis: University of Minnesota Press, 1991), 260; Ted Van Dyk, *Heroes, Hacks, and Fools: Memoirs from the Political Inside* (Seattle: University of Washington Press, 2007), 55; memo from Colonel D. S. N. Karrick Jr., HP, 1968, 150.F.18.10F; Arnold A. Offner, *Hubert Humphrey: The Conscience of the Country* (New Haven, CT: Yale University Press, 2018), 263.

28. HP, 1968, 150.F.18.10F.

29. HP, SF, 12/9/67; *MST*, 12/10/67.

30. Karnow, *Vietnam*, 546; HP, 1968, 150.F.18.10F.

31. Eisele, *Almost to the Presidency*, 295.

32. Connell Papers, Box 3.

33. Humphrey, *Education of a Public Man*, 266.

34. *Report of the National Advisory Commission on Civil Disorders* (Washington, DC: Government Printing Office, 1968).

35. Thurber, *Politics of Equality*, 197.

36. Berman Journal, Edgar Berman Papers, Gale Family Library, St. Paul, Box 2.

37. Robert Dallek, *Lyndon B. Johnson: Portrait of a President* (Oxford: Oxford University Press, 2004), 329–330.

Chapter 20. The Apocalypse

1. Ted Van Dyk, personal interview; Ted Van Dyk, *Heroes, Hacks, and Fools: Memoirs from the Political Inside* (Seattle: University of Washington Press, 2007), 66.

2. HP, Additional Files: Miscellaneous Senatorial, Vice Presidential, Political, Personal, and Other Files, 148.A.4.7B; Berman Journal, Berman Papers, 4/2/68.

3. Berman Journal, 4/6/68.

4. Ibid., 4/14/68; Fred Harris, personal interview.

5. HP, SF, 4/27/68.

6. Michael Cohen, *American Maelstrom: The 1968 Election and the Politics of Division* (New York: Oxford University Press, 2016), 145.

7. *Meet the Press*, 4/28/68.

8. Connell Papers, Box 7.

9. HP, VP, AOF, Box 774.

10. Norman Mailer, *Miami and the Siege of Chicago* (New York: Random House, 2016), 223; personal email communication with Tom Lehrer.

11. Freeman Diary, Freeman Papers; HP, Additional Files: Miscellaneous, etc., 144.A.1.7B.

12. Lewis Chester, Godfrey Hodgson, and Bruce Page, *An American Melodrama: The Presidential Campaign of 1968* (New York: Viking, 1969), 359; Albert Eisele, *Almost to the Presidency: A Biography of Two American Politicians* (Blue Earth, MN: Piper Company, 1972), 332–333.

13. Humphrey, memo to himself, 6/7/68, in Connell Papers, Box 3; HP, Additional Files: Miscellaneous, etc., 148.A.4.7B.

14. Dominic Sandbrook, *Eugene McCarthy: The Rise and Fall of Postwar American Liberalism* (New York: Alfred A. Knopf, 2004), 50, 115–116, 204.

15. *NYT*, 6/13/68.

16. HP, SF, 6/20/68.

17. *NYT*, 6/23/68 and 6/24/68; Skip Humphrey, personal interview.

18. HP, SF, 6/30/68 and 7/7/68.

19. Joseph A. Califano Jr., *The Triumph and Tragedy of Lyndon Johnson: The White House Years* (College Station: Texas A&M Press, 2000), 289, 292; Harris, personal interview.

20. *BG*, 7/7/68; Arthur Schlesinger Jr., *The Letters of Arthur Schlesinger Jr.* (New York: Random House, 2013), 7/9/68, 7/13/68, and 7/24/68.

21. Connell Papers, Box 3.

22. *NYT*, 7/4/68; HP, 1968, Box 150.F.18.5B; Freeman Diary, Freeman Papers, Box 15.

23. Huntington note to Humphrey, 9/17/75, in HP: Additional Files: Miscellaneous, etc., 148.A.4.8F.

24. Harris, personal interview; HP, Additional Files: Miscellaneous, etc., 148.A.4.7B.

25. Van Dyk, *Heroes, Hacks, and Fools*, 74; Ted Van Dyk and John Rielly, personal interviews.

26. Ken Hughes, *Chasing Shadows: The Nixon Tapes, the Chennault Affair, and the Origins of Watergate* (Charlottesville: University of Virginia Press, 2014), 11–14.

27. *WP*, 7/31/68 and 7/28/68; *New York Times Magazine*, 8/25/68.

28. Hubert H. Humphrey, edited and with an afterword by Norman Sherman, *The Education of a Public Man: My Life and Politics* (Minneapolis: University of Minnesota Press, 1991); Hughes, *Chasing Shadows*, 17.

29. *NYT*, 6/30/68; HP, 1968, Box 150.G.5.5B.

30. Eisele, *Almost to the Presidency*, 343.

31. Chester et al., *American Melodrama*, 527; HP, 1968, Box 150.G.5.2F.

32. Hughes, *Chasing Shadows*, 17–18.

33. Chester et al., *American Melodrama*, 533–534; Humphrey, *Education of a Public Man*, 291.

34. See Chester et al., *American Melodrama*, 503–512, and Theodore White, *The Making of the President 1968* (New York: Atheneum, 1969), 261.

35. Todd Gitlin, *The Sixties: Years of Hope, Days of Rage* (New York: Bantam Books, 1993), 289; Chester et al., *American Melodrama*, 519–520.

36. Califano, *Triumph and Tragedy*, 320.

37. Harris, personal interview.

38. *Meet the Press*, 8/25/68.

39. Chester et al., *American Melodrama*, 524–537.

40. White, *The Making of the President 1968*, 269; Edgar Berman, *Hubert: The Triumph and Tragedy of the Humphrey I Knew* (New York: G. P. Putnam's Sons, 1979), 184.

41. Humphrey, *Education of a Public Man*, 292–293; Chester et al., *American Melodrama*, 536.

42. Gitlin, *The Sixties*, 333; Norman Mailer, *Miami and the Siege of Chicago* (New York: Random House, 2016), 116; *WP*, 8/25/68.

43. In Mailer, *Miami and the Siege of Chicago*, 154.

44. *NYT*, 8/28/68.

45. Ibid., 8/29/68; Chester et al., *American Melodrama*, 579; George McGovern, *Grassroots: The Autobiography of George McGovern* (New York: Random House, 1977), 125.

46. Chester et al., *American Melodrama*, 582–593; Gitlin, *The Sixties*, 333; *NYT*, 8/29/68.

47. Carl Solberg, *Hubert Humphrey: A Biography* (New York: W. W. Norton, 1984), 365; *Chicago Tribune*, 8/29/68.

48. Chester et al., *American Melodrama*, 584; White, *The Making of the President 1968*, 303.

49. W. Marvin Watson, with Sherwin Markman, *Chief of Staff: Lyndon Johnson and His Presidency* (New York: St. Martin's Press, 2004), 301.

50. Phone logs, LBJ Library, 8/29/68.

51. Harris, personal interview; Solberg, *Hubert Humphrey*, 367.

52. Solberg, *Hubert Humphrey*, 361–362.

53. Berman, *Hubert: The Triumph and Tragedy*, 190; Van Dyk, personal interview.

54. Humphrey acceptance speech, available at "1968 Hubert Humphrey Democratic Convention Acceptance Speech," YouTube, www.youtube.com/watch?v =FsOg0wv8Q-M.

55. Solberg, *Hubert Humphrey*, 370.

56. Richard M. Scammon and Ben J. Wattenberg, *The Real Majority: An Extraordinary Examination of the American Electorate* (New York: Coward-McCann, 1970), 162; Gitlin, *The Sixties*, 335; Richard Goodwin, *Remembering America: A Voice from the Sixties* (Boston: Little, Brown, 1988), 15.

Chapter 21. The End

1. Stephen E. Ambrose, *Nixon: The Triumph of a Politician, 1962–1972* (New York: Simon and Schuster, 1989), 172.

2. Stephan Lesher, *George Wallace: American Populist* (Cambridge, MA: Perseus, 1994), 389–390; *NYT*, 9/30/67.

3. Lesher, *George Wallace*, 401, 412; *NYT*, 9/24/68; Arnold A. Offner, *Hubert Humphrey: The Conscience of the Country* (New Haven, CT: Yale University Press, 2018), 307.

4. Albert Eisele, *Almost to the Presidency: A Biography of Two American Politicians* (Blue Earth, MN: Piper Company, 1972), 366.

5. Ibid., 368; HP, AF, Box 1; *Newsweek*, 9/9/68.

6. *WP*, 9/18/68; *Issues and Answers*, 9/8/68; *NYT*, 9/11/68 and 9/12/68; *CSM*, 9/13/68; *WP*, 9/15/68 and 9/17/68.

7. Ambrose, *Nixon*, 190; *CSM*, 9/13/68; *WP*, 9/15/68 and 9/18/68.

8. *NYT*, 9/9/68, 9/12/68, and 9/20/68.

9. Thomas Edsall and Mary Byrd Edsall, *Chain Reaction: The Impact of Race, Riots and Taxes on American Politics* (New York: W. W. Norton, 1991), 72; HP, 1968, Box 150.G.5.7B.

10. *WP*, 9/18/68.

11. *WP*, 9/18/68; HP, 1968, Box 150.G.5.4F.

12. Richard M. Scammon and Ben J. Wattenberg, *The Real Majority: An Extraordinary Examination of the American Electorate* (New York: Coward-McCann, 1970), 21; HP, 1968, Box 148.B.15.8F.

13. HP, 1968, 150.G.5.4F.

14. HP, Additional Files: Miscellaneous Senatorial, Vice Presidential, Political, Personal, and Other Files, 148.A.4.7B.

15. HP, 1968.

16. *Toronto Globe and Mail*, 9/30/68.

17. Berman Journal, Edgar Berman Papers; *CSM*, 10/2/68.

18. Carl Solberg, *Hubert Humphrey: A Biography* (New York: W. W. Norton, 1984), 380–382; Lewis Chester, Godfrey Hodgson, and Bruce Page, *An American Melodrama: The Presidential Campaign of 1968* (New York: Viking, 1969), 646.

19. Berman Journal; Solberg, *Hubert Humphrey*, 382–385.

20. Phone logs, LBJ Library, 9/30/68; Ken Hughes, *Chasing Shadows: The Nixon Tapes, the Chennault Affair, and the Origins of Watergate* (Charlottesville: University of Virginia Press, 2014), 22–23; Hubert H. Humphrey, edited and with an afterword by Norman Sherman, *The Education of a Public Man: My Life and Politics* (Minneapolis: University of Minnesota Press, 1991), 403; Fred Harris, personal interview.

21. *NYT*, 10/1/68.

22. *NYT*, 10/2/68; *WP*, 10/1/68.

23. *CSM*, 10/1/68 and 10/3/68; *BG*, 10/1/68; *Chicago Tribune*, 10/2/68.

24. Freeman Diary, Freeman Papers; Phone logs, LBJ Library, 9/30/68.

25. GEN FG 440, LBJ Library, Box 349; Hughes, *Chasing Shadows*, 23; Tom Johnson, personal interview.

26. *NYT*, 10/4/68 and 10/6/68; Theodore White, *The Making of the President 1968* (New York: Atheneum, 1969), 355; *BG*, 10/10/68 and 10/13/68.

27. *WSJ*, 9/19/68; Quoctrung Bui, "50 Years of Shrinking Union Membership," NPR, 2/23/2015, www.npr.org/sections/money/2015/02/23/385843576/50-years-of-shrinking-union-membership-in-one-map; Solberg, *Hubert Humphrey*, 389.

28. *NYT*, 10/6/68, 10/5/68, and 10/4/68; HP, 1968, 150.G.5.7B; Chester et al., *American Melodrama*, 668.

29. *NYT*, 10/9/68 and 10/8/68; HP, 1968, 150.G.5.4F.

30. HP, SF, 10/12/68; *NYT*, 10/16/68.

31. *BG*, 10/12/68; HP, SF, 10/20/68.

32. HP, 1968, 150.G.5.4F; Phone logs, LBJ Library, 10/7/68; *NYT*, 10/11/68.

33. Berman Journal; Ted Van Dyk, *Heroes, Hacks, and Fools: Memoirs from the Political Inside* (Seattle: University of Washington Press, 2007), and personal interview; Solberg, *Hubert Humphrey*, 392.

34. HP, SF, 10/15/68; *NYT*, 10/19/68; *WP*, 10/24/68.

35. *WP*, 10/22/68, 10/24/68, and 10/27/68; *NYT*, 10/27/68.

36. White, *The Making of the President 1968*, 364; John Rielly, personal interview; *NYT*, 10/30/68; *BG*, 11/1/68.

37. A. J. Langguth, *Our Vietnam: The War, 1954–1975* (New York: Simon and Schuster, 2000), 523–525; Hughes, *Chasing Shadows*, 23.

38. Langguth, *Our Vietnam*, 524–525; Hughes, *Chasing Shadows*, 37.

39. Ambrose, *Nixon*, 208; *NYT*, 11/1/68; Langguth, *Our Vietnam*, 526.

40. Phone logs, LBJ Library, 10/31/68.

41. Chester et al., *American Melodrama*, 733–734; Hughes, *Chasing Shadows*, 44; Robert Dallek, *Lyndon B. Johnson: Portrait of a President* (Oxford: Oxford University Press, 2004), 586. Both Chester and Theodore White take the Mitchell account at face value.

42. Offner, *Hubert Humphrey*, 324–327; Tom Johnson, personal interview; Clark Clifford, *Counsel to the President: A Memoir* (New York: Random House, 1991), 580–581. In judging Johnson's behavior, it is worth recalling that in 2016 Barack Obama chose not to publicly disclose what he knew of Russian interference in the election in order to avoid being seen as intervening on behalf of Hillary Clinton.

43. *BG*, 11/1/68; Berman Journal; personal interviews with Norman Sherman, Ted Van Dyk, and Stuart Eizenstat. The question of Nixon's personal complicity is now regarded as settled. In *Richard Nixon: The Life* (New York: Doubleday, 2017), John A. Farrell cited notes by Nixon aide John Ehrlichman stating that Nixon had authorized "throwing a monkey wrench" into Johnson's peace plan.

44. *WP*, 11/1/68; *BG*, 11/3/68; Norman Sherman, personal interview; Max Frankel, personal interview.

45. Berman Journal; Humphrey, *Education of a Public Man*, 304.

46. HP, SF, 11/3/68.

47. Van Dyk, personal interview; Berman Journal; *WP*, 11/5/68; Van Dyk, *Heroes, Hacks, and Fools*, 93; Bill Connell, interview, MCPM.

48. Berman Journal; Solberg, *Hubert Humphrey*, 403.

49. Humphrey, *Education of a Public Man*, xviii–xix; Berman Journal.

50. *WP*, 11/6/68; Solberg, *Hubert Humphrey*, 405–406; Humphrey, *Education of a Public Man*, xxii.

51. Scammon and Wattenberg, *The Real Majority*; Kevin Phillips, *The Emerging Republican Majority* (New Rochelle, NY: Arlington House, 1969).

Chapter 22. Down, but Never Out

1. Phone logs, LBJ Library, 11/21/68, 11/22/68, and 11/23/68; *NYT*, 3/2/69.

2. Phone logs, LBJ Library, 11/6/68; *New York Times Magazine*, 3/30/69.

3. *New York Times Magazine*, 3/30/69; Carl Solberg, *Hubert Humphrey: A Biography* (New York: W. W. Norton, 1984), 412–413.

4. *NYT*, 3/30/69; Albert Eisele, *Almost to the Presidency: A Biography of Two American Politicians* (Blue Earth, MN: Piper Company, 1972), 423.

5. *NYT*, 2/21/69.

6. Edgar Berman, *Hubert: The Triumph and Tragedy of the Humphrey I Knew* (New York: G. P. Putnam's Sons, 1979), 247.

7. HP, IF, 148.A.12.4F.

8. HP, IF, 150.J.19.4F; *U.S. News and World Report*, 2/23/70; HP, SF, 10/6/69.

9. *Meet the Press*, 4/21/69; HP, IF, 148.A.12.2F; *NYT*, 5/15/69.

10. *NYT*, 10/9/69; Henry Kissinger, *The White House Years* (Boston: Little, Brown, 1979); Robert Dallek, *Nixon and Kissinger: Partners in Power* (New York: Harper Collins, 2007), 158–160.

11. Henry Kissinger Telephone Conversations of 1969–77, Digital National Security Archive, DNSA Collection, 10/10/69; *NYT*, 10/11/69.

12. HP, Additional Files: Miscellaneous Senatorial, Vice Presidential, Political, Personal, and Other Files, Box 148.A.1.7B.

13. HP, SF, 10/13/69; *TNR*, 10/25/69; *MST*, 10/14/69; *CSM*, 10/15/69; *NYT*, 10/16/69.

14. Kissinger Telephone Conversations, 11/3/69; *NYT*, 11/4/69; *LAT*, 11/23/69; *Newsweek*, 12/15/69 (emphasis in original).

15. *NYT*, 2/10/70, 2/26/70, and 6/13/70; HP, SF, 2/16/70 and 5/8/70.

16. Solberg, *Hubert Humphrey*, 418–419; HP, IF, 150.J.19.4F.

17. HP, IF, 150.J.19.3B and 150.J.19, 4F; Arnold A. Offner, *Hubert Humphrey: The Conscience of the Country* (New Haven, CT: Yale University Press, 2018), 343–345.

18. HP, IF, 148.A.12.4F; HP, SF, 6/7/70.

19. Richard M. Scammon and Ben J. Wattenberg, *The Real Majority: An Extraordinary Examination of the American Electorate* (New York: Coward-McCann, 1970), 167; HP, SF, 6/27/60.

Chapter 23. He's Got Runitis

1. Andrew Johnson, who spent seventeen days in the Senate before dying, is only a technical member of this elite club.

2. *MST*, 1/22/71; Albert Eisele, *Almost to the Presidency: A Biography of Two American Politicians* (Blue Earth, MN: Piper Company, 1972), 432–433; Carl Solberg, *Hubert Humphrey: A Biography* (New York: W. W. Norton, 1984), 423–424.

3. *MST*, 3/25/71 and 3/28/71.

4. *WP*, 3/28/71; *MST*, 3/21/71 and 3/28/71.

5. *WP*, 4/2/71.

6. *NYT*, 5/2/71.

7. *WP*, 5/28/71 and 6/3/71; *NYT*, 6/6/71.

8. *NYT*, 6/13/71; *MST*, 6/17/71; *WP*, 6/17/71.

9. *WP*, 6/18/71 and 7/14/71; *TNR*, 7/10/71; *Baltimore Sun*, 6/25/71.

10. *NYT*, 5/14/71; HP, SF, 5/13/71; *Congressional Record*, vol. 117, 5/26/71, 17062.

11. HP, SF, 5/17/71 and 7/5/71.

12. Eisele, *Almost to the Presidency*, 438; *MST*, 11/28/71.

13. *WP*, 8/15/71, 9/21/71, and 10/6/71; *NYT*, 9/24/71; HP, SF; HP, IF, 148.A.12.4F.

14. *NYT*, 12/28/71; *WP*, 1/11/72.

15. *NYT*, 1/11/72 and 1/15/72; HP, SF, 3/10/72, 3/7/72, and 3/10/72; HP, Additional Files: Miscellaneous Senatorial, Vice Presidential, Political, Personal, and Other Files, 1972, 150.K.8.1B.

16. Stephan Lesher, *George Wallace: American Populist* (Cambridge, MA: Perseus, 1994), 471–473; Theodore White, *The Making of the President 1972* (New York: Atheneum, 1973); Timothy N. Thurber, *The Politics of Equality: Hubert H. Humphrey and the African-American Freedom Struggle* (New York: Columbia University Press, 1999), 227.

17. *Time*, 12/4/91; *Congressional Record*, vol. 117, 1/20/72, 589.

18. *NYT*, 2/15/72 and 2/24/72.

19. Ibid., 2/21/72 and 3/21/72; *Meet the Press*, 3/12/72.

20. *MST*, 3/26/72; *NYT*, 3/26/72; *WP*, 3/24/72.

21. HP, Additional Files: Miscellaneous, etc., 1972, 150.K.8.3B.

22. HP, Additional Files: Miscellaneous, etc., 1972, 147.D.9.6F; White, *The Making of the President 1972*; *NYT*, 4/4/72; *Manchester Guardian*, 5/28/72.

23. *WSJ*, 3/28/72.

24. *Congressional Record*, vol. 118, 4/7/72, 11785.

25. *WP*, 5/8/72 and 5/15/72; *NYT*, 5/16/72.

26. White, *The Making of the President 1972*, 121–124; Solberg, *Hubert Humphrey*, 433; Dan Spiegel, personal interview.

27. Thomas J. Knock, *The Rise of a Prairie Statesman: The Life and Times of George McGovern* (Princeton, NJ: Princeton University Press, 2016), 177–179; HP, SF, 5/18/72.

28. *NYT*, 5/21/72; *WP*, 6/3/72.

29. HP, SF, 5/28/72; Gary Hart, personal interview; Knock, *Rise of a Prairie Statesman*, 148; Arnold A. Offner, *Hubert Humphrey: The Conscience of the Country* (New Haven, CT: Yale University Press, 2018), 358.

30. *Newsday*, 5/31/72.

31. George McGovern, *Grassroots: The Autobiography of George McGovern* (New York: Random House, 1977), 185.

32. *NYT*, 6/25/72; HP, SF, 6/25/72.

33. Lesher, *George Wallace*, 486–488; Sherman, email exchange.

34. HP, SF, 7/11/72; *NYT*, 7/12/72.

Chapter 24. Elder Statesman

1. *Baltimore Sun*, 2/15/73; *CSM*, 3/17/73; *Chicago Tribune*, 4/12/73 and 5/11/73; *WP*, 4/14/73.

2. HP, SF, 4/11/73.

3. HP, SF, 12/11/73.

4. Dan Spiegel, personal interview.

5. Edgar Berman, *Hubert: The Triumph and Tragedy of the Humphrey I Knew* (New York: G. P. Putnam's Sons, 1979), 273; "Hubert Humphrey's Gallant Fight Against Cancer," *Ladies Home Journal*, 11/74.

6. *NYT*, 6/8/73; *MST*, 8/25/72, 2/4/73, and 6/13/73; *LAT*, 7/12/74.

7. *Hartford Courant*, 6/27/74 and 6/28/74.

8. Letter from Percy Ross to David Gartner, 4/14/76, in HP, Additional Files: Miscellaneous Senatorial, Vice Presidential, Political, Personal, and Other Files, 148.A.5.3B.

9. *NYT*, 1/11/74; *WP*, 3/27/74.

10. *WP*, 8/3/74 and 12/24/74; Jack Chestnut pardon application to President Gerald Ford, 11/7/76, in HP, Additional Files: Miscellaneous, etc., 148.A.5.3B.

11. Transcript of Senate Select Committee interview with Maheu, and Maheu testimony in *Maheu v. Hughes Tool Company*, in HP, Additional Files: Miscellaneous, etc., 148.A.5.5B; *LAT*, 12/16/73; *NYT*, 4/3/74.

12. Transcript of Senate Select Committee interview with Maheu; Lloyd Hand, personal interview; Ted Van Dyk, email communication.

13. Carl Solberg, *Hubert Humphrey: A Biography* (New York: W. W. Norton, 1984), 445; *NYT*, 10/13/74.

14. Dan Spiegel, personal interview.

15. *Congressional Record*, vol. 119, 5/22/73, 16396, and 11/20/73, 37787.

16. Marianne Spiegel, personal interview.

17. *NYT*, 3/12/73; Dan Spiegel, personal interview; Kissinger telephone transcripts, Digital National Security Archive, DNSA Collection, 10/6/69, 5/17/71, 9/18/72, 11/2/72, and 9/5/73. Kissinger did not record his conversations but rather had them surreptitiously monitored by secretaries taking shorthand, according to Dan Spiegel, who learned of the system as special assistant to Cyrus Vance, who replaced Kissinger as secretary of state under Jimmy Carter.

18. Kissinger transcripts, 9/5/73; *Congressional Quarterly Almanac*, vol. 29 (Washington, DC: Congressional Quarterly News Features, 1973); *NYT*, 12/19/73.

19. S. 2335: Foreign Assistance Act, 1973–1974, available at Congress.gov, www .congress.gov/bill/93rd-congress/senate-bill/2335; *Congressional Record*, vol. 119, 10/2/73, 32536, and 10/18/73, 34630.

20. Kissinger transcripts, 3/23/74, 3/17/76, and 8/24/76; *Congressional Record*, vol. 119, 3/19/75, 7442.

21. *Congressional Record*, vol. 119, 10/2/73, 32536, and 10/18/73, 34630; *Congressional Record*, vol. 121, 11/3/75, 34725.

22. Kissinger transcripts, 10/10/75; *Face the Nation*, 3/9/75; Dan Spiegel, personal interview.

23. HP, Staff's Office Memoranda Files, 1969–78, Box 148.A.12.2F.

Chapter 25. Last Things

1. Timothy N. Thurber, *The Politics of Equality: Hubert H. Humphrey and the African-American Freedom Struggle* (New York: Columbia University Press, 1999), 234; HP, SF, 1/15/75.

2. Tim Barnicle, personal interview; *Congressional Record*, vol. 119, 9/13/73, 29601; *Congressional Record*, vol. 120, 3/1/74, 5019, and 4/23/74, 11310.

3. *Congressional Record*, vol. 120, 8/22/74, 29875; Barnicle, personal interview.

4. Barnicle, personal interview; US Congress, Joint Economic Committee, "Impact of New York City's Economic Crisis on the National Economy," 11/10/75.

5. *NYT*, 4/27/75; *Village Voice*, 7/28/75.

6. George McGovern, *Grassroots: The Autobiography of George McGovern* (New York: Random House, 1977), 261; Robert Shrum, personal interview.

7. *NYT*, 6/24/75 and 10/16/75; *WP*, 10/13/75 and 11/3/75; *NYT*, 11/27/75, 12/11/75, 12/28/75, and 1/3/76; *MST*, 12/14/75 and 12/25/75; *LAT*, 12/15/75; *WSJ*, 12/24/75; *CSM*, 9/2/75.

8. *New York Times Magazine*, 4/4/76.

9. McGovern, *Grassroots*, 262; HP, Additional Files: Staff Members: David Gartner, Boxes 148.A.5.3B and 148.A.5.5B.

10. *Time*, 8/18/75; HP, David Gartner, Box 148.A.5.5B.

11. *WP*, 2/18/76; Thurber, *Politics of Equality*, 238.

12. Thurber, *Politics of Equality*, 240; HP, SF, 4/1/76; *Congressional Record*, vol. 122, 4/14/76, 11016.

13. *NYT*, 3/31/75, 4/9/75, 4/10/75, 4/11/75, 4/14/75, and 4/23/75.

14. *MST*, 4/15/75, 4/22/75, 4/23/75, and 4/28/75.

15. *Chicago Tribune*, 4/29/75; *Newsday*, 4/30/75; Richard Moe, personal interview.

16. *Time*, 5/10/75; *NYT*, 4/30/75 and 5/2/75; *Newsday*, 4/30/75.

17. Moe, personal interview.

18. Edgar Berman, *Hubert: The Triumph and Tragedy of the Humphrey I Knew* (New York: G. P. Putnam's Sons, 1979), 278; Carl Solberg, *Hubert Humphrey: A Biography* (New York: W. W. Norton, 1984), 453–454.

19. *NYT*, 1/2/77 and 1/6/77.

20. Berman, *Hubert: The Triumph and Tragedy*, 282; *BG*, 7/12/77.

21. Barnicle, personal interview; *Congressional Record*, vol. 121, 4/20/77, 11401, and 6/28/77, 21259.

22. Stuart Eizenstat, personal interview; Jerry Jasinowski, personal interview.

23. Berman, *Hubert: The Triumph and Tragedy*, 282; *NYT*, 8/19/77.

24. *NYT*, 10/23/77 and 11/15/77; Eizenstat, personal interview.

25. *NYT*, 12/3/77.

26. *BG*, 12/5/75; *WP*, 1/18/78.

27. Solberg, *Hubert Humphrey*, 455; Eizenstat, personal interview.

28. *MST*, 1/17/78; *BG*, 1/16/78.

29. *WP*, 6/23/77.

Index

Photo Credit: Elizabeth Easton

James Traub has spent the past forty years as a journalist for America's leading publications, including the *New Yorker* and the *New York Times Magazine*. He now teaches foreign policy and intellectual history at New York University Abu Dhabi and is a columnist and contributor at *Foreign Policy*. He is the author of eight previous books on foreign and domestic affairs. He lives in New York City.